Cottage Lake Soliloquy

by
John E. Shephard, Jr.

Order this book online at www.trafford.com
or email orders@trafford.com

Most Trafford titles are also available at major online book retailers.

Printed in Victoria, BC, Canada.

ISBN: 978-1-4269-1706-6 (sc)

Library of Congress Control Number: 2009935503

*Our mission is to efficiently provide the world's finest, most comprehensive book publishing
service, enabling every author to experience success. To find out how to publish your book,
your way, and have it available worldwide, visit us online at www.trafford.com*

Trafford rev. 10/14/2010

 www.trafford.com

North America & international
toll-free: 1 888 232 4444 (USA & Canada)
phone: 250 383 6864 ♦ fax: 812 355 4082

To Beth,
earth princess,
whose heart blesses the world

"Awakening begins when a man realizes he is going nowhere and does not know where to go," (Gurdieff)

Chapter 1

"I am a solitary man. Unless a writer is capable of solitude he should leave books alone and go into the theatre." (John Steinbeck)

THE TWILIGHT SHADOWS OF the tall evergreens shimmered boldly across Cottage Lake like huge feathered spears pointing eastward. On the western horizon the scarlet-edged flickering of golden sunlight licked the fading pink sky good-bye and sank flaming behind the silhouetted forest. Random crow calls and blue jay cries rang from the cathedral of towering pine trees and were briefly submerged in the whining roar of a small silver aircraft droning northward overhead. Sunday evening, mid-September, the soft glow of northwest Indian summer lingering lazily, awaiting autumn's inevitable arrival.

Nestled amidst the lakeside cabins and houses was a cedar-shake cottage perched on a knoll above the western shoreline that curved in and around it. Being the closest house to the water, it offered its occupants a panoramic view from the north to the south end of the lake. Houses away a dog barked intermittently and the delightful screams of children on a diving board carried over the water from the far eastern shore. Inside the master bedroom at a small roll top desk in the corner, Jay could hear their laughing squeals and hollers on a light breeze through an open window laced with creamy-colored curtains barely swaying like windblown wheat near the wine glass at his elbow. He'd just finished reading a book on the Romantics, his favorite literary figures; Coleridge, Byron, Shelley and Keats.

Gazing out over the tops of the sweeping twin willow trees down by the lake, he took the last sip of his wine and watched the water flow unhurriedly left to right, back into its source, Bear Creek, finally forging through a crowded mesh of lily pads before meandering away again somewhere downstream. For fourteen years he had spent countless quiet moments enjoying the lakeside spectacle of each season passing from his intimate bedroom perspective, and summer was always his favorite time. In the early evening warmth it felt like the perfect occasion to write reflectively in his journal. He withdrew a tan leather-covered notebook from the middle panel of the desk, unsnapped the strap and opened it to a blank page, unsheathed the attached black sharp felt pen and began to write.

9/15 The summer sun still holds at bay the impending shadow of fall this year but my personal circumstances are clearly darkening. After fourteen years of a successful practice the new revisions in the health care industry are making it increasingly harder to for me to continue earning a living as a psychotherapist.

He paused for a moment to ponder the best way to state his predicament. Two recent events had shaped his thinking with respect to the current downturn in his practice. Until a half year ago he had been the only mental health professional in Forestville. Since moving there in 1980, upon completion of his Master's degree in California, he had sown and grown his business well. Forestville Counseling Service had given him a career that he loved, plus a good income. Coincident with the radically new developments in health care to lower the burgeoning costs of treatment had been the arrival of a second practitioner in the spring, a female clinical psychologist from New York, Marianne, who had leased office space next to him in the same building. He had welcomed her presence agreeably enough, knowing that increasing competition was inevitable in their continuously fast-growing community.

In the course of ensuing conversations between them she had cautioned him that the proliferation of managed care networks would soon be problematic for any therapist without a doctorate. Before deciding to be in private practice she had worked in a large medical clinic in Manhattan where she had made extensive contacts in the health care field. She assured him that well-placed confidants in the industry had advised her that managed care companies were intending to weed out counselors without doctoral degrees in order to restrict the field to professionals with the most advanced training. This was to minimize the length of time for patients in treatment so as to lower its overall costs. She had encouraged him to enter a Ph.D. program to ensure his continued success in the field.

While appreciating her collegial interest in his welfare, her advice for the most part was not particularly well-received. He really did not want to pursue another degree. He had tired long ago of listening to the teachings of psychology professors. His practice had been great for long past a decade and he thought his level of competency was sufficiently good enough to continue serving his clients well. On the heels of her well-intentioned advice however had come the calls and letters from multiple managed care firms. He could continue to be a mental health care provider in the various insurance company networks as long as he agreed to the new procedures governing treatment. Those new restrictions piqued the spirit of pride and independence that had originally motivated him to be self-employed. As he hated being told what to do by anyone, he had ultimately refused their solicitations to join. He didn't even respond to their calls or letters, trusting Marianne for the facts of the matter. But being on his own for the last six months, no longer subsidized by clients' health insurance, had resulted in a steady decline in income and he had recently applied to a Ph.D. program in a reluctant attempt to restore his fortunes.

In the meantime the newly emerging third parties, managed care agencies, created to lower and monitor health care costs for the insurance companies, were stringently enforcing their new stipulations on health care practitioners. The number of counseling sessions per year covered by insurance was being reduced as well as the amount of money paid per session. On top of that, practitioners were being required to furnish treatment plans, progress reports, and session notations to justify the work they were doing with patients. These were to be scrutinized by the agencies to see if the work was justifiable in terms of the newly established criteria. As the lessening of costs was solely intended to serve corporate profits instead of health care patients, their welfare was not a prime consideration. They would have to make do. Overall, in effect, any health care professional who wished to continue to be reimbursed by insurance must be willing to do more work for less pay. Though counselors without a Ph.D. were not excluded, as Marianne indicated would happen in time, those with one were being compensated at a higher rate of pay. He sighed for a moment as a wave of aversion washed over him with the thought of it all, and then began writing again.

Since refusing to join the new "mangled care" networks, as I like to call them, I'm getting fewer new clients. Most people want a therapist their insurance will cover. I keep getting new clients who can't afford insurance but they also can't afford to pay me much in cash. It may have been a mistake to refuse to join the networks but I just don't want the hassle of the new regimentation – more rules, more paperwork, lower fees, less income. Worst of all I simply do not want bureaucrats peering over my shoulder to judge the work I am doing by their monetary scale. I've been counseling for too many years to start explaining and justifying my ways to some "managing" corporate interest. The healing art of psychotherapy is coming under greater control of the insurance lobby with the blessing of the state, and those of us unwilling to comply are becoming the exception. At forty-two, I'm too young to retire and couldn't afford it if I wanted to, which of course I don't. I've half-heartedly applied to some Ph.D. programs but have not yet been notified of acceptance. I'm not sure that I would accept them if I am. At this point, the only things I do know for certain are that I want to succeed in life on my own terms somehow and I need to start making some more money soon."

He stopped for a second, as the breeze caressed his cheeks, while his mind spun lightly, like an unchecked roulette wheel, flitting through various financial possibilities.

"I'd like to write a book, or make a CD, perhaps combining music and psychology together in a therapeutic modality. But at best these are probably long-term solutions and right now

I need a short-term one. In the past, if a serious problem arose, I could always call Saul, my reliable psychic, for a session and some guidance, but he's almost impossible to reach anymore since moving away. I try to stay positive but am growing more anxious and tense underneath. In my attempts at meditation I feel no connection and sometimes end up feeling worse for having tried. If God is attempting to communicate with me I wish to hell he'd speak up. As far as paying the bills goes, it's really the income from Bea's work that's been increasingly carrying us; much like mine did until this last year. I appreciate her success but feel guilty about not carrying my equal share of the load. Also as she's so busy in her office now or traveling the globe there's less time for us as a couple or a family and I miss the time we used to have together. There's always the possibility that I could join her company.

He paused at the thought of his wife and lowered his pen absently, hand on his thigh, as he envisioned her countenance in his mind's eye. Bea, his sweet and lovely woman; such a soft and earthy creature whose dimpled ready smile and heart-felt presence was a boon to all others as a spring flower to honey bees. Graced by a wholesome Taurean charm and sensuality, her gray-green eyes sparkled with gaiety while her cheerful speech sang soft and pleasant to the ear. He imagined her standing au naturale in their bedroom; her white sturdy breasts, such firm ripened pears, her pretty face, short blonde hair and pert nose; her petite well-shaped feet and perfectly tapered legs curving deliciously upward into herself, past the farther reaches of his fertile imagination. He found her beautiful...*mmmmmm... my yummy one...*

A quiver of warmth arose in his gut, pulsating through his heart and groin simultaneously. He loved loving her and being loved by her, though it was difficult to be a good sweetheart recently with her being so busy and as rotten as he'd felt about his declining practice. With all their ups and downs she was still his balance wheel, his anchor, his companion and his confidant; the true love of his life. She had made it clear recently, through subtle suggestions, that she would welcome his help in running her company. That would likely give them more time together, or at least more space, in sharing her downstairs office. He had resisted her muted entreaties so far, partially due to his disinterest in business. His leanings were more towards the arts and professions. But really he simply wanted to make it on his own terms in the work that he felt himself destined to do. That thought pulled him back to the open pages of his journal. He reread his entry and began writing again.

"If I were to do that, it would be quite a transition. Having spent over twenty years primarily in psychology, I'm ill-trained for and uninterested in much of anything else. Music, my other passion, offers solace when I play, but I'm too preoccupied with worries to do much with it these days. I alternate most nights between keyboards and guitar, but primarily I'm just playing old tunes. Sometimes I fiddle with the four-track recorder, playing or singing, laying down some tracks, but haven't been inspired to write any new songs lately. I rarely pick up the flute now at all. I had hoped this year to complete a CD and send it out to prospective record

companies before Christmas. Without some new material there's no way do that. Something's got to happen soon. Something's got to give.

He stopped writing and reread it, wondering where he was going. Had he said too much or perhaps not enough? Deciding it covered his basic points of self-reference adequately at the moment, however dismal, he leaned back in his chair to survey the lake. It was gradually darkening with the lengthening shadows fading into the water, which seemed suited to his mood as he mulled over what he'd written...*too late for a swim and nothing more to say... are these words really useful*...Over the years he'd often recommended journals, at least to certain clients, but now found himself wondering, as he felt an abiding pressure to take some kind of action soon, if such writings were valuable in any way at all.

By recording his entries he had hoped to chart the furthering of his progress in life; making a mark, making a difference, making the world a better place, and most of all somehow making sense of God's will. Yet in all those desires he was feeling frustrated, blocked, deprived, and stuck, while still being sustained by an intermittent mishmash of hard work, good luck, blind faith, and his wife, in varying degrees. With a mild but final sense of subdued satisfaction in having noted the current status of his life, unsatisfying as it was, he sheathed the pen and shut the book with a thump. As he snapped tight the button of its thick leather strap, the shrill eruption of his telephone on the desk pierced the air. He grabbed it just as the first ring subsided and spoke gently into the receiver.

"Hello."

"Jay, this is Barry."

"Yes, Barry. How are you?"

"I'm busted!"

Chapter 2

"Good Heavens, man! Haven't you any righteous indignation?"
*"Oh doctor, years ago my mother used to say to me, 'Oh Elwood' – she always called
me Elwood – 'in this life you must be oh so smart or oh so pleasant.' For years I was
smart. I recommend pleasant. You can quote me." (Elwood P Dowd, Harvey)*

THE CEDAR-SHAKE COTTAGE SAT roughly twenty feet above the lake and fifty feet back from
the water's edge. A second story sunroom made of cedar-trimmed glass panels, wall to
wall and floor to ceiling, held a corner of the dwelling, facing eastward across the water.
Three yards outside the corner where the glass walls met, slightly down the hillside towards
the shoreline, rose an ancient sturdy cedar tree whose lofty limbs provided mid-day shade.
Inside the glass sunroom a black open-air woodstove squatted on an adjacent corner square
of pink-chafed bricks surrounded by a plush sea of forest green carpet. Next to a glass-
topped rattan coffee table, in a cushy rattan chair, under a skylight, curled Bea, like a blonde
kitty, reading a book about primitive peoples.

With rapt attentiveness she absorbed both her reading and the pleasant twilight
atmosphere. The wind chimes clanged lightly in random merriment outdoors, as the current
slipped by the lily pads and slapped at the clay embankment below. Weekend reading
was a pleasant respite to the hectic goings-on during the busy workweek in her embattled
basement business office. Once Monday dawned it was off to the races all week long, and
sometimes the weekend too, especially in the summer.

It had been a frantic summer for her business, but hard work had paid off and things had gone well. Now she had a relatively few slow weeks of down time before flying off to Europe for her big marketing conference in Vienna. It was a chance to meet more student-exchange agents of different nationalities and expand the frontiers of her company like never before. She finished a chapter and paused a moment to listen to the wind-bells make their spontaneous music. Their sounds reminded her of the name of Jay's recently disbanded band, Terra Mystique. His flute would go well with them. The thought of him gave her a subtle stab of discomfort...*ahhh...such a sweetie, but Jesus such a pain in the ass...if only my husband's affairs would blossom as beautifully as my own...just like they used to... life would be so simple and secure, with some room for a little extravagance...wish he'd work with me...i could surely use him...or else just get a second job somewhere...so talented and underemployed and so unhappy lately...with all his energy and imagination he could do almost anything...funny how a man who has helped so many others now seems stopped short of fulfilling his own life...*

The phone rang loudly from the kitchen one time, disturbing her momentary musings. She assumed he'd picked it up in the bedroom and began reading her novel again, half-listening for his call. Something in the pages was beckoning her; something in the story was alluring. She had read widely for years about women in early natural settings, like American Indians, frontier women and those of prehistoric times. She felt an easy kinship with the spirit of primitive peoples, especially their holy men and women, or shamans, and often quietly displayed her own healing powers in the simplicity of her solutions to complex problems at work. While her honesty and humility had always lent her strength of character, with the rise of her company, she had also grown more assured as of late. She bore the presence of a self-made woman, with a friendly confidence and quiet dignity felt by nearly everyone she dealt with. Sometimes her husband teasingly called her "Shamamama" in admiration for her invisible magic as a healing influence with others. Her intelligent and friendly common sense approach to matters had a way of bringing out the best in people, often causing even the worst of situations to improve.

Hearing no call from the bedroom she became entranced in reading while the tranquil tinkling of the wind chimes scattered about the adjacent sun deck and through the sliding door screen a few feet from her chair. As she nestled more cozily into the thick beige pillow of the rattan seat her eyes widened with increased interest to the erotic twists and turns of events in her tale of our ancestors...*hmmmm...when he wants her he just takes her...*She felt a mixed appreciation for the rigors of prehistoric courtship. Though liking her men bearded and sexy, she wasn't so sure about the subjugation. After the scene came to a fitting climax she set the book on the lush green rug and lit a small presto log in the black Swedish fireplace. Sitting back in the cushion, she felt the warm air counter the impending chill of night and watched contentedly the little fire burn brighter as the day's luster slowly disappeared.

Chapter 3

"You can see me tonight with an illegal smile,
It don't cost very much but it lasts a long while,
Won't you please tell the judge I didn't kill anyone,
I was just trying to have me some fun." (John Prine, Illegal Smile)

"WHAT?"

"I just got busted last night! Four cops came into my house, searched my garage, and found ten plants growing."

"You're kidding!"

"I wish. For real, Jay."

"I never realized you were growing plants."

Barry, who lived further east in the woodsy hills, had alluded to the pleasures of homegrown marijuana five years back at his wedding reception when he slipped Jay a free bud. But Jay, who had performed the ceremony, didn't know where he had gotten it and thought it best at the time not to ask. About a year later, and only that one time, he had called Barry to see if he knew where he could get some. Barry had said that he would take care of it and later sold Jay a very small quantity without referring to where and how he'd obtained it.

"It's crazy, Jay," he moaned. "I don't know what to do. They cut up the sail on my boat. Those guys were assholes. They thought they were so cool. Ten little pot plants. Big deal!"

"Ah man, that's tough. Sorry to hear it." Barry, or "Bear" to his buddies, a popular and respected young supervisor at a local industrial plant, had two small children, a pretty wife, and a great many friends. Before marriage or children he and his lady had seen Jay for couples counseling, which eventually led to the altar, or halter as Barry liked to joke.

"I'm scared. Someone turned me in and said I was a dealer. I don't know what to do."

"Are you?" He knew there were rumors about the remote parts of the county – phantom pot farmers, vast hidden fields.

"Well, not exactly. I've sold it to various friends over the years but never large quantities and never to anyone I didn't know. It's mostly just been for my own use." He paused. "Listen," his voice lowered, "I think this is part of a bigger crackdown in this area to find dealers. They're goin' after anybody and using them to get others. I've told them I'm not involved with anyone but they don't believe me." He snorted in derision. "These jerks actually said they'll go easy on me if I give them some names."

"What did you say?"

"I said I didn't know anybody that had anything to do with anything, and that I was just minding my own business."

"We'll that's that," offered Jay. "What else can you say?"

"Yeah," his voice rose indignant with frustration, "but they don't believe me." He paused, then added apologetically, "I'm afraid that you're in it too."

"How do you mean?"

"Well, I kept a little black book of everyone I sold to. It has their telephone numbers."

"Yeah, so?"

"They took that book and your name's in it. They think it's my contacts."

"Oh, great."...*whoops...don't upset him more...*

"I'm sorry, Jay. I shouldn't have had you in there. We only did it once."

"It's okay. It's not your fault. I'm sorry for you. Besides, what's the harm in that? I haven't done anything but that one time, and that was years ago."

"I know that Jay, but these guys don't, and they probably won't believe it. You don't know what they're like. I haven't done much more than help out some friends but the cops acted like I was the Mafia. So if you've got anything around…" He let the insinuation hang in the air.

"Thanks for the tip, but I gave that up awhile back. Sounds like someone you turned on turned on you. Any idea who?"

"No," he said seriously, sounding, hurt, and resigned. " I really don't."

"Probably someone in trouble," guessed Jay.

"Yep. No doubt." His voice rose in anger at the thought of betrayal. "Some jerk."

"So," asked Jay, "what are you going to do?"

"I don't know. Probably get a lawyer. They all want two thousand bucks up front and I don't have it," he muttered bleakly. He groaned in exasperation. "What would you do?"

Jay paused, took a long deep breath, then stated calmly, "Call a psychic I know."

"Really!" exclaimed Barry, in bewilderment and disbelief. "What's he charge?"

"$50 an hour."

"That's not bad," he paused to clear his throat. "But I need to save my money for a lawyer."

"That's okay Bear. I'll try to reach him and ask about you. I'll pay for it. I'd like to talk with him anyway."

"Thanks, Jay! Thanks a lot."

"Sure. I'll call you back after I connect with him. It may take a few days to get an appointment. He's pretty busy, but he might give some preference to an emergency situation."

"That's okay, Jay." Barry sounded lighter, his spirits lifting slightly from the shell shocking humiliation and helplessness he'd been feeling.

"Do you need help paying for a lawyer?"

"God, would you do that?" he blurted out in surprise. Before Jay responded Barry spoke again. "Thanks alot, but I think my father's going to loan me money for that, or part of it." He sighed. "You're a good man, and a good friend to me, and I appreciate it."

"Glad to be able to help, Barry. Why don't you check out some lawyers and I'll get back with you as soon as I can."

"Alright. Thanks a million, Jay," he said with genuine gratitude. "Good-bye now."

"Good-bye Barry. Don't worry too much, this too shall pass," said Jay, hoping it sounded reassuring. He placed the telephone in its cradle on the desk and spun his chair around ninety degrees to his left to gather through the window a broad perspective of the soothing lakeside landscape, while contemplating the significance of Barry's bad news. He sat perfectly still, staring instead at the screen, for almost a full second until the dread began to spread.... *damn*...His mind began racing like a carousel jammed in fast forward and anxiety flooded his upper body like a sinking sub taking on water...*last thing i need in my life right now is being hassled by some cops who think i'm part of a big drug operation*...He'd seen from enough clients involved with the legal system, how anyone under investigation by the government was normally treated as a number or puppet, with some duly constituted authority, like a judge or a faceless bureaucrat, self-righteously pulling the strings....*but i haven't done anything...much...still, they may not believe me...you knew him...you were his therapist... you performed his wedding...you were in his little black book...did you buy something from him...*

Three swirling thoughts surfaced from the blender of his brain. The first was to immediately call Saul, his spiritual mentor, to see if he could talk now or set a short appointment for later, soon. Though no longer taking individual appointments since moving to Hawaii to found a spiritual retreat, he might not likely turn away anyone in need, except when immersed in meditation all day Sunday, which unfortunately was today. He could call and leave a message but he didn't know the time there and wished not to place a call to him that might disrupt his sleep...*better call tomorrow...*

Another notion, tugging at his mind like a weighted fishline, led him outside to the vegetable garden in his large front yard. Leaning over the tomatoes he stooped to grasp and uproot several healthy hemp plants from the shelter of their hidden cornstalk sanctuary... *sorry guys...its you or me...*

The last thought took him back inside and downstairs to the wine cellar for a taste to shave the sharp edge off Barry's distasteful tale. With a bottle in one hand and a wine glass in the other he walked out into the smaller backyard area between the house and lake. Pouring half a glass of ruby-colored Rhone he sauntered down the grassy path to the water's edge, absorbing the evening chill as he savored each sip. Searching the sky for planets and constellations, he stood motionless in the stillness, while the purple sky grew darker. He turned his attention to the moon as it rose, round as a pearl, spreading like lamplight over the lake. Atop the silhouetted trees it shone through the drifting chimney smoke from a half-lit house on the far bank, suspended in space like a luminous eyeball, curiously observing him with silent detachment.

Chapter 4

*"Let me live in my house by the side of the road
and be a friend to man." (Sam Walter Foss)*

IN THE EARLY MORNING silence of a cool misty Monday, Cottage Lake glistened in the hazy dawn as sunbeams broke into an ecstatic dance upon the water. At a gentler tempo, Bea padded down the stairs in her furry beige slippers while sipping strong creamy coffee and coming gradually to her business senses. She entered her office, approached her paper-cluttered desk, and set her steaming mug down on it....*no faxes...no phone calls... great...* Through the picture window behind her desk, she surveyed the lakeside splendor with a deep appreciation for both its never-ending beauty and her office view of it. She was positioned directly underneath the sunroom, where the hillside sloped and curved around the huge cedar outside anchoring the land a few yards from her desk. Thumbing through work papers until finding the right one, she brought it closer to her eyes and scrutinized it carefully. It was her checklist of things to do in preparation for her upcoming conference in Vienna and subsequent trip to Toronto.

Forgetting her coffee, she turned and walked into the adjoining office room, sat down at the computer and brought up the work she'd left unfinished late Friday. She was crafting a letter to a New York business colleague who, like herself, ran a company offering Homestays with Host Families for foreign students. She was confirming his sponsorship of her company to attend the Viennese gathering, as she was not yet a member of the sponsoring group.

Teeming with excitement and curiosity, she relished the prospect of extending her networks with different countries, nationalities, agents, programs, and unknown possibilities. Through three and a half years of finding homes for students her company had steadily grown at a modest pace, this year being the best, and this was her best marketing opportunity ever. It was her first chance to parley with the big guns of the industry, and someone other than the Japanese. As associates they were just fine, in many ways excellent, but she didn't like having all her eggs in one country's basket.

Having cut herself loose from an important Japanese partner last year, she felt it crucial to her survival that she broaden and expand. It had seemed a dangerous risk to break off their arrangement but he was growing intolerably more abusive, arrogant, and paranoid about their partnership. She sighed while remembering the tortuous turmoil his vitriolic morning faxes would bring to each day's beginning. Jay became angry when hearing about them but she forbid him to interfere for fear of jeopardizing her maniacal meal ticket. Recalling his mistaken notions and violent accusations of betrayal in business dealings, she wondered how she had tolerated him as long as she had. She hadn't seen nor heard from him in six months….*i almost forgot just how bad he was*…Her curiosity piqued, she paused before starting on the letter again and turned her attention instead to the closet beside her with past records filed in boxes on the floor...*where are those faxes anyway*...Pulling out a cardboard box, she sorted through old faxes...*ah, there they are...let's see...here's a great one*...She read to herself from the middle of a tattered fading fax a section so typical of his ranting; a numbered list of her many failings.

3. Receipt of money. Don't be silly. I wired it 2 weeks ago. Why you still call it a deposit. Not a deposit!! Foolishly you seem still unaware why I am furious. First you must admit you lied. Your fax is full of stupidness. Look into the OXFORD DICTIONARY. I don't trust WEBSTER, as this has many spellig errors.

Bea had to smile as she recalled the inane madness of his tirades….*spellig errors*…The saving grace of this difficult period was the humor they found in his constant misspellings and misuses of grammar. Towards the end he reminded her of a cartoon caricature she had seen once of Hitler jumping up and down on a miniature world, throwing a loud tantrum until someone tossed him a baby bottle. She felt grateful she had found the wherewithal to cut him off. No one had ever treated her that way or sent such hateful and cruel messages. She had joked darkly about making a book of his faxes and marketing them as a work entitled "Fax You". She and Jay had especially reveled in the last words she ever wrote him, 'Check your OXFORD', as she corrected one of his misspelled words. She knew that would arouse his ire to no end. Breaking off with him had been the most riskiest and rewarding step taken in her young business career. More than ever before she felt free now to pursue endlessly diverse options, especially in Vienna. She hoped he wouldn't be there.

She stuffed the paper back in its file and, smelling the pungent French Roast as a reminder, sauntered into the main office to retrieve her coffee. As she swallowed a warm sip the fax machine by her desk whirred and hummed a transmission in from Toronto. It was Perry, the Area Coordinator, who was to meet with her soon after her jaunt to Europe. He expressed enthusiasm toward meeting her and assured her that all back receipts would be accounted for. She was tentatively pleased to see that the troublesome chapter in Toronto might finally be ending well after all. She hoped, with some concern, that next year would not be a repeat performance...*where was all the money going...why had his program drawn so many complaints...*You could screw up once with Japan, a truism of the industry, but not twice, and her upcoming visit with him was to ensure exactly that very understanding.

As with all of her employees, Bea wanted to trust that he was honest. It would be so much easier that way. To fire him and then hire and train new people took a great deal of time and money, and experience was the best teacher if you made it past the first season. Both Jay and Candy, her office secretary, distrusted Perry. Especially Candy, with her attitude toward men, felt compelled to proclaim her doubts and suspicions. Fighting down a wave of worry, she took a deep breath and stared out at the sun-speckled lake where the haze had lifted. The gleaming blue waters evoked serenity, and peace crept over her as slow and certain as quicksand as she shifted her gaze to the hanging bird feeder in the cedar colossus just outside her window.

A young gray and brown-flecked sparrow darted back and forth from the feeder to the tree's rough-barked trunk, unable to stay balanced on the feeder's edge while eating. She laughed at its dainty rapid jump-steps from the birdseed to the tree and back again ...*she never gives up...*

Returning her focus indoors, her eyes fell upon a note the size of a business card, in her elegant cursive writing, encased in plastic and dangling on a gold chain from her green and gold desk lamp. "Remember," it said, "as long as you are making the effort, God will never let you down." Heaving a sweet sigh of relief, she turned and strode gracefully back to her computer, sat down and resumed typing, lost again in the rhythm and flow of her work; making friends of strangers, and homes of houses. She felt it best to trust him one more time. If she was wrong, well, she didn't want to think about that now, but in a vague way, she knew, if need be, somehow God would help her through it.

Chapter 5

"Mid pleasures and palaces though we may roam,
Be it ever so humble, there's no place like home." (John Howard Payne)

THE BUS LURCHED LEFT then swayed slightly right as it slowly rounded another tortuous turn through the hilly Mexican countryside. At two hours past midnight its passengers slept fitfully to the weary bumps and grinds of the roughshod road that wound like a narrow ribbon on the moonlit forest floor. The thick tousled curls of the fair-haired youth near the back of the bus fell on a sun-tanned face lost in a slumber deeper than his fellow uneasy riders. He alone slept the sleep of an innocent abroad; a young man on holiday, free of cares and at ease in the hospitable arms of a laid-back land whose language he spoke, culture he embraced, and people he loved. Feeling a growing sensation of appetite, he was dreaming of food, luxurious Mexican food, which seemed to slide about incessantly, inaccessibly, atop a shifting dining table.

Creaking and chugging out of the curve, the tired old bus screeched and jolted to a halt as a half-dozen bright lights appeared in its path from seemingly out of nowhere in the dark. While the paralyzed driver stared ahead in shock, an unshaven hombre with a menacing scowl emerged from the roadside shadows and pressed his sawed-off shotgun to the glass door, demanding entrance. Six surly banditos, bedraggled and fearsome, burst inside brandishing firearms. When they saw the blond gringo their eyes brightened at the prospect of untold riches. Brushing by the other passengers, the swarthy lead gunman approached him, making muzzle-threatening motions.

"Dinero cabrón!" he fiercely insisted, lifting the shotgun barrel to the red-bearded face of the handsome golden boy. The young Americano, roughly shaken from sleep, flushed inwardly with panic as he strove to maintain composure. He noticed with a blend of detached curiosity and repugnance the dirty brown tobacco-stained nails on and about his inquisitor's trigger finger. Although fond of Mexicans in general he'd always disdained poor habits of personal hygiene in particular, without respect to nationality.

"No tengo dinero. Solamente cheques!" he exclaimed diplomatically, as though hating to disappoint the chap. To demonstrate his sincerity, he unzipped his Eddie Bauer backpack to reveal the meager contents of a lad of simple tastes, a camper traveling lightly, of possible yuppie parentage through no fault of his own, who quite clearly now embraced a non-materialistic lifestyle, especially at this moment, not unlike, and actually in sympathy with his third world neighbors and Latino brothers. Pointing to the travelers checks, he hoped his gesture conveyed this sentiment. The lead bandito frowned.

Faced with this predicament, they took his sleeping bag and hiking boots, both brand new, and then swiftly, mercilessly, robbed the other passengers of any noticeable valuables, making resourceful use of his bag in the process. As he watched quietly, the very training that had made him a young karate master helped him stay calm at a time unwise to fight. Yet the muscles in his brawny frame stayed tense a long time well after the last desperado, like a snake slithering warily back into his hole, had shuffled backward off the bus into the oblivion of night.

The bus rambled on, its load the lighter, but its cargo slightly worse for wear, having been awakened from their dreams to a nightmare. The barefoot Americano smelled the odor of fear from his sweat-soaked T-shirt, as he lay on the narrow seat feeling alone and saddened, yet relieved, and so exhausted. Though his heart's disappointment was stronger than his stomach's hunger, in sleep the pangs eventually won out, and rocked by the rough but regular shifts of his cramped bed quarters, he soon dreamt again of food on platters; a fantasy fiesta, Mexican manna, sliding around a table, just beyond reach, then suddenly steadied, yet not served…by a hand…with tobacco-stained fingernails.

Chapter 6

"All for love and the world's well lost." (William Shakespeare)

D EEP IN SLUMBER AS the morning sun rose above his bed Jay moved through the mist of his unconscious, drawn like a kite string through his depths, a twisted trail of yearning, on the scent of love. It was a recurring dream since early adolescence though always occurring in varied scenarios and always ending with a nameless, faceless female presence; Girlness, the promise of youthful womanhood, the pure heart of the sweet goddess of true love. As a youngster once he had dreamed of an Indian princess. She seemed to emerge through some vague association from the wooded fields behind his house in rural Cheyenne, where as a child he had explored with curious wonder the fields and flowers, the trees and birds, the rocks and insects. Her countenance was clear as she stared into his eyes the last moments of slumber. He awoke in the morning light from that first dream with a reverberating echo of the sacred seed of sweetness deeply implanted, infused in his heart; a state he could never quite return back to in sleep and a feeling he could never quite capture when awake.

Yet it stayed with him always as a haunting possibility of what life could offer at its limitless best; romance. Romance with an infinite depth so very sweet that nothing else in life could ever even come close to it. He might go for years without repeating the dream and then it would happen, out of the blue, unbidden, unexpected, unheralded, and unmatched in its bliss. No longer a princess of Indian ancestry nor anyone of any particular identity; just a beautiful young woman whose essence matched his own, whose love was as full, who knew nothing more exquisitely felt or sensed or so purely desired as to embrace him in the light of her ineffable sweetness; gladly oblivious to whatever worlds may endlessly surround them.

Though rare, whenever he did have this dream, perhaps at most once every few years, he would awaken shortly thereafter thronging with the sweetest of feelings in his heart that absorbed his whole body. It set fire to his consciousness like nothing else could, but the fleeting embers of love were easily extinguished and slipped through his mind's grasp like ashes through his fingers. As he grew older, learned about the mind, learned about himself, learned about love and life, he came to regard himself as overly sensitive and dangerously romantic. He thought his early love life relations as being filled with unrealistic emotional expectations. His saw his forays into drugs during the sixties an outgrowth of such unchecked romanticism. And he regarded his ventures into music as he matured a healthy sublimation of those deep-seated intimations.

Still, every once in a great while, it would happen. Just when he wasn't looking, just when he was preoccupied with some facet of his existence, just when he thought his identity was secure and he knew what was really real in reality, it crept in again; an unbearably sweet and effervescent surprise.

This one was no different in content than the others. The form was as faceless, the atmosphere as amorphous. In his mind's eye he saw the figure drifting purposely towards him, moving through the mist, coming closer and closer, her heart melting into his, his into hers, meeting at last in an everlasting kiss that beautifully exploded into utterly everything just before evaporating ever so gently into a universe of absolute nothingness – poof! And then he awoke, saturated in sweetness, that most rare of memorable desirable moments, contentedly numb to any other sensation. He slid his hand slowly across the silk sheet, extending his fingertips to touch the sweet sleepy softness of Bea and felt her blind absence like a hole in his heart.

Chapter 7

"A woman's work is never done." (*Anonymous*)

SUNLIGHT PIERCED THE SLOWLY twisting crystal prism hanging in the downstairs window, scattering broken rainbow bits randomly about the office like a windstorm of stained glass shadows on the walls. At her desk by the picture window sat Bea, deeply engrossed in proofing her letter, oblivious to the surrounding light show. She reread it twice, and then printed it out with an air of satisfaction. It was crucial to her that she attend the Viennese gathering and her energies at work the last month had been almost exclusively focused on that happening. This letter was the last detail. As it printed she stood up to get more coffee and the swirling patches of bright colors caught her eye for the first time. She paused momentarily to watch the dancing fragments decorate the room in phantom twinkle lights before turning to go upstairs to the kitchen.

Stepping softly on the beige carpet in her furry tan slippers, she felt the peaceful charm of the first morning hours. She glided across the oak hardwood floor to the coffee pot and eyed the microwave clock glowing 6:36 in red neon digits. After pouring the steaming brew into her "World's Greatest Mom" mug, she added a dash of half-and-half to reach the right creamy brown luster. While cupping it with both hands to ward off the lingering chill, she turned to take in the lakeside grandeur of late summer's early morning glory.

The stillness in her house was in sharp contrast to the happy clamor of the outside bird calls, sounding like little forest flutes, chirping and twittering in the wind. The two weeping willows on the embankment blew gently in the breeze, waving yellow-tinged leaves gaily to the stoic evergreens. Sipping the hot coffee, she reveled in the moment, savoring the feel and fragrance of her drink and especially the iridescent splash of sunlight on the lake like a spilled bottle of golden watercolors. Year after year the beauty of her backyard vista never failed to move her.

On such a beautiful day she would have liked to go horseback riding on her trusty steed, Cheyenne, an Appaloosa pony. But this summer it had been too busy to enjoy him and she sometimes wondered if having him was worth the expense of boarding and vet bills. Still, he had been a surprise Valentine Day present from her extravagant but loving husband, who knew it was the fulfillment of a childhood dream. To own him had been a blessing and an incomparable joy; her getaway to nature, her gateway to peace and quiet.

She sighed contentedly after a moment's indulgence in her reverie and then headed through the living room to the hallway connecting both bedrooms so she could take a quick peek on her boys. In the bedroom at the far end of the hall her youngest son, Phil, lay sprawled out face down, slumbering heavily in young teen innocence under a faded blue quilt. His well-used blankie, an old-time favorite, had seen better days but still had the right stuffing. He was her youngest darling, her baby, and the very sight of him in the purity of early morning's sleep brought a smile to her face. No mother loved a son more.

She felt the warmth pulsate in her heart as she gazed lovingly upon him. With a soft sigh of contentment she turned to look in the master bedroom at the near end of the hall. There slept her husband under a thick dark green comforter, tucked in a semi-fetal position on his side, large pillow wrapped around his head facing away from her...*my two boys*...She smiled slightly, momentarily feeling the love for her family in her entire being, as though the air itself was giving her a warm hug. As she turned to head back to her downstairs office, she mused to herself....*wonder how the third one's doing...*

Stepping lightly down the stairs she entered the supply room for an envelop for her letter when one of the two phones on her desk clanged through the quiet like a fire bell. She noticed with curiosity it was the home phone as she snatched it up quickly to avoid another ring that might interrupt her sleeping ones above.

"Hello."

"Hi Mom," said a faraway but familiar and slightly forlorn voice. "I'm okay," he assured her, sounding somewhat tentative.

"Jess! Where are you?"

"Mexico."

"What's wrong?"

"I'm coming home."

"What?"

"I got robbed."

"What? Oh no! Are you okay?"

"Yeah, I'm okay. I mean I'm tired and I'm broke but I'm okay overall."

"What happened?"

"Well, basically some bandits hijacked the bus and robbed everyone at gunpoint last night."

"Oh my God!"

"Yeah, it was scary then but now I'm pissed and there's nothing I can do about it." He sounded more dispirited than angry. "They took everything; boots, pack, money – the little that I had. Luckily I've got travelers checks."

"Oh God."

"One guy even held a gun to my head."

"Oh no. I can't believe it. Are you sure you're alright?"

"Yeah, I'm okay, really," he reassured her in a voice gaining strength.

"What are you going to do now?"

"I'm flying up to Lou's house in San Diego later today." Lou was his former college buddy who had been drafted into pro football by the San Diego Chargers last year after graduation; an instant millionaire. "I just don't want to be here anymore."

"Do you have enough money?"

"No, but Lou is paying for it."

"Wow! What a friend."

"Really."

She paused for a moment, absorbing the shock of it all, then asked, "How long will you stay there?"

"Just a few days, I guess. I may go see Grandma and Grandpa," he trailed off. "I don't know."

"How are you getting home from there?"

"Lou is paying for that too."

"You're kidding! What a good friend!"

"Well, you're right, he is a good friend, and the Chargers have made him a rich one too." He paused to clear his throat. "Maybe I can make it up to him someday, but right now he is happy to do it."

"Are you sure you really want to leave there? Maybe you could salvage the rest of your time there somehow."

"Nah, I'll come back someday but right now I just wanna' get outa' here and back to the states."

She paused, struggling with whether to encourage him to stay or support his return. It was easiest to concur. "You know best," she offered. "Do what feels right."

"This feels the best," he said resolutely. "I just wanted you to know what's happening. I'll call you when I get to San Diego. I can't talk much longer now 'cause I'm on a pay phone and runnin' out of change. I need to get to the airport 'cause we're leavin' soon." He reminded her of a tired trail horse heading straight for the barn after a long day's ride. Time to regroup. She sensed his tension and reaffirmed her support.

"Okay. Call us when you get there. Alright?"

"I will. I gotta' go now. I love you, Mom. Don't worry."

"I love you too, honey. Please be careful. Go catch your plane."

"Okay Mom. G'bye."

"Goodbye sweetheart."

Bea felt dazed as she hung up the phone and sat down in her plush executive chair to contemplate the call...*shit...how could he say don't worry...Jesus...grandpa was right... mexico was dangerous*...She winced as she recalled his angry words to her upon hearing that Jess was going deep into Mexico..."What kind of a mother are you?" The words had stung. "The best kind!" she had wanted to retort. "Maybe your son wouldn't have grown up so damn rebellious if you'd given him more freedom when he was younger" was what she'd wanted to say. She was much too wise to do so however and had instead merely stated "I can't stop him." Grandpa may have been right that Mexico was too dangerous but she was right that Jess would have to decide that for himself.

Even now though shaken she felt mixed about his plans. On one hand she wanted him free of any danger but on the other she hated to see him cut short his dream vacation. He had fantasized and later planned his excursion in great detail for many years. It was the perfect culmination of desire and effort after getting his degree in Spanish and before entering the work force as a teacher. She felt pulled in both directions. Wasn't it better to get right back on the horse when you were thrown off? Of course that was easier said than done and this was a near brush with death. It was probably best to take some time to recover. He'd be back. Mexico was in his blood too much to give it up just now, if ever. She started to feel better as she sifted through it all. She took a deep breath and settled on the thought that emerged as she exhaled. The only thing that really mattered was that he was alive and well for now. The rest could be sorted out later.

Almost as if to confirm her conclusion the gray fax machine began to whir, signaling a noisy change of subjects. It chugged slowly like the little train that could and churned out a fuzzy document from a foreign country marked "Urgent". The sponsoring body of her European Conference needed information about her hotel accommodations as soon as possible. She felt a pang of immediacy to respond to their questions. This was an event she couldn't afford to miss. She was looking for the data she needed when the business phone rang out. While letting the first few rings go unanswered she found the necessary information and stuck it into the fax machine. On the fifth ring she grabbed the phone deftly and said in a cheerful voice, "Homestay Connections. This is Bea. May I help you?", as she punched in the fax number to Vienna.

While descending into the routine of activity she heard the muffled bustling above of her husband and son upstairs as they prepared to depart for work and school respectively.

They were finally up and about. She wanted to see them before they left, share a little of the morning, and most of all tell them about Jess. She knew they were on fast-forward to get out of the house since they always slept until the last minute. They might even scamper away without saying goodbye, which she hated. Her phone conversation was winding down when the second line cried aloud for an answer. She toyed with the thought of letting it ring into the machine but felt guilty as though it were irresponsible. No secretary for another two hours. She finished the first call and answered the second, hoping to deal with the caller as quickly as possible and break upstairs to see the boys.

"Homestay Connections. This is Bea. May I help you?"

While listening to the caller she heard again the stirrings overhead in the kitchen. They had both complained about having so little of her time in the summer, and she felt torn between her work and familial needs. Though she loved her family much more than her work, she also knew they depended upon it now. Running her own company had been hard on all of them, especially her, and she hoped that her husband would assume part of it soon. Till then it fell on her.

"That sounds good," she was saying. "I'll get back to you by the end of the day." As she was winding down her conversation, the first line rang again. "*rrriiinnnggg*" The thought of letting it go loomed large….*i'll never get upstairs*…"Yes, thanks. I'm sorry but I need to get the other line. Okay. Bye." She hung up the phone and eyed the blinking light signaling the next call. "*rrriiinnnggg*" She wrestled with answering it or running upstairs instead. The prism colors danced wildly on the walls, adding further to her sense of distraction. Footsteps thumped about hurriedly above. "*rrriiinnnggg*"

Chapter 8

"A therapist does not heal. He lets healing be. The Holy Spirit is the only Therapist. He will tell you exactly what to do to help anyone he sends to you for help, and will speak to him through you if you do not interfere." (A Course in Miracles)

J AY WHEELED HIS ANTIQUE chocolate colored four-door Mercedes onto the asphalt parking lot, easing into a space behind the office near the back door to the stairway inside. He unlocked the door with a brisk twist of his key and bounded up the stairs taking two at a time in an even faster rate than his customary energetic pace. With a half-hour yet till his first appointment, there was time to call Saul, his trusted soothsayer, for a spiritual perspective on Barry's situation as well as his own. He hoped to talk with him now.

While mounting the stairs, he felt distracted by the memory of the brief exchange he'd had with Phil on the way to school that morning during a break on the radio between the songs.

"Mom's working so much we hardly ever see her anymore," Phil had complained.

"I know," he replied, with a slight wince, stalling for the right words to come so he could make it somehow better....*when in doubt, active listening*..."You really feeling sad, like you miss her?" he asked casually but with interest.

Phil arched his eyebrows and almost frowned in serious reflection. "No, not really," he said with a trace of irritation. "I just noticed she's gone alot." He punched the radio to a different station, seemingly engrossed in the task....*yep, i thought so... and feel neglected too*..."Well she's really busy," Jay offered lamely, knowing it didn't help much.

"That's what I mean. We hardly ever see her, in the morning or night. She's always working," he declared, his tone intensifying with resentment.

"Well, at least, thanks to her work, we'll join her in Vienna later and get to see Italy too." Phil shrugged and said nothing, then hit another radio button.

As the car wound around the curving country road, it approached the last turn at the base of the grassy hill, which led to the private school campus at the top. Dew glistened lightly like a film of green satin mist spray-painted on the earth everywhere evenly. In moments the freshly whitewashed school buildings would emerge through a thicket of hilltop trees...*better cut to the bottom line*...

"You know it doesn't mean she doesn't love you," said Jay earnestly. "She's working so hard in part because she does love you, so we can afford things, like this pricey school, for example. If my business were better she wouldn't have to work so much. And that's gonna' change."

"When?"

"Soon. I'm working on it. We're doing our best." He felt an edge of guilt arise and fell silent.

"I know. It just seems funny. It's weird. It wasn't like this before. I don't like it." Phil looked out the window at the school.

"It'll change soon. Really." He tried to sound convincing. They pulled into the bumpy dirt lot, nuzzling through a scattered horde of well-kept cars and clean-scrubbed students, fashionably attired in grubbies and grunge wear and strapped into burgeoning canvas book bags. Phil leaned forward to grab the door handle, shooting Jay a sideways glance. "That's good," he nodded, with a raise of his left eyebrow and a tightening of his lips, indicating the discussion was over as he gathered his bulging backpack in his left arm. He opened the door, bounced out as though spring-loaded, calling "See ya, Dad!" while sending it closed with a sure-felt slam, and turning to join a rising tide of teenagers, was lost in the vast sea of bobbing adolescent heads, all in one long smooth coordinated movement.

Jay slipped on the top step of the stairway, then regained his balance by grabbing the rail and snapped out of his thoughts as he hoisted himself to the landing with a hop. He threw open the upstairs hall door with a whip of his hand as he whisked through it and strode the six steps down the hall to his suite. It occupied the corner space in the back of the building, overlooking the stylish parked cars of the real estate agents in the well-furnished offices beneath him. He preferred the isolation from bordering neighbors, especially since the walls were not insular enough to muffle the sounds of a loud client. The nearby stairway also gave clients a discrete exit should they prefer to avoid the front entrance lobby at the far end of the hall.

Unlocking his office door, he shut it with a sweep behind him while walking on and tossed his briefcase on the rattan couch as he moved to his large oak desk. As he lifted the telephone receiver in his right hand he rolled his brown leather executive chair around to his left, so it faced south through two tall picture windows. He sat down, propping back with his feet on the windowsill, and transferred the phone to his left shoulder where he pinned it with his head. While holding it there he pulled a small blue address book off his desk and thumbed through the soft worn pages for Saul's new number.

They hadn't spoken since Saul left for Hawaii over a year ago. Last summer's newsletter from the Inner Mission Foundation had stated quite clearly that he was no longer available for private consultations. Instead he now devoted his energies entirely, with his wife, to the establishment of a spiritual retreat in the islands….*must be tough… someone's gotta' do it… ah, here it is…*

He started to punch in the digits when he realized he still had no idea of the time difference. He might be calling at a terrible hour. He aborted the call and dialed instead for the operator for assistance. While the phone rang he gazed though the glass, nonchalantly noting Mr. Rainier in the distance. It's craggy white peak towered calmly under a cloudless field of turquoise, imparting a stoic sense of mysterious beauty, as though it sequestered a lost secret city, like Shangri-la, residing deep within its rock walls.

"Information. What city please?'

"Uhhhh, Hawaii," he said, bringing his gaze down to the floor.

"What listing please?"

"Actually I just want the time there."

"It's 6:30 am there now, sir."

He thanked her and hung up, then glanced at the wall clock. It was just past 8:30, giving him nearly a half hour before his first client. If he called Saul right after the session, 8 am in Hawaii, someone might be in the office then to take his call. He paused for a moment, and then decided to check his answer service.

"No calls, sir," assured the switchboard girl. He rolled his chair around to the files and pulled out the one on his client, the "flower lady", as he had dubbed her. Sliding down the back of his cushy high-backed seat, he glanced at his first entry on her. As usual he had merely noted her name, date of birth, contact information and a general diagnosis. He had learned when a grad student as an intern to a psychologist that the less said the better in written notations to minimize the chances of his words being used one way or another in acrimonious court cases like nasty divorces. The doctor had advised him the less time spent in court the better. He thought legal proceedings pretended to be concerned with truth, justice and fairness but were really simply one side trying to attack the other. Jay had taken his advice to heart and made session notations as scant as possible.

Bearing that in mind as he basked in the sun, he mentally reviewed the case of the woman he would see next. He had first met with her seven weeks ago. She was an attractive young single mother in her late twenties, small, trim, with sharp features, who ran the florist shop a half-mile from the lake. As was often the case her psychological stresses were linked to her finances. Raising a seven-year-old boy on her tight income was not easy, though she was friendly with a perky nature and a "can do" attitude. She was mainly concerned with her son's behavior at school. He was acting out angrily, which was "not really like him". She bemoaned the fact that he had never had a father, as the man disappeared before he was born. She had wondered if Jay could help him as a counselor and father figure. He'd agreed to accept payment in houseplants; since there was actually no other way she could afford it.

At their first meeting they had discussed at length her son's history, temperament, and current situation. It was agreed that the boy, Jason, should come in for an appointment, which he did the following week. He was small, with his mother's build and features, shy, yet a trusting boy who opened up easily in therapy. He seemed glad for the opportunity to talk to someone, especially a man. He had no idea why his outbursts in school had occurred but he noted his teacher was "alot like his mom", being "nice, but pretty strict".

They'd had several sessions since then, with the son alone, the mother alone and one with them both together. The boy's behavior had improved in school and in turn the mother's spirits had brightened. A recent occurrence had brightened them further, turning premature worry lines into a smile on her face. A former boyfriend, a high-school sweetheart, was now living in the area, and had looked her up through mutual friends. In a few short weeks their former closeness turned into courtship, and a whirlwind romance was quickly blooming like a rosebud unfurling in time-lapse photography.

They had wanted Jay's blessing on their fast-rising relationship and had come in together to see him last week. It was clear they were in love, or infatuation at least, and very intent on making up for lost time. The boyfriend, Darin, was sure he had located the lost love of his dreams and had given up drinking, out of pure happiness, to underscore his joy. He too was small but wiry, athletic looking, and darkly handsome, with wavy black hair. He had an enthusiastic manner and an engaging grin. His confident optimism stemmed in part from possessing a black belt in karate, by which he had garnered many trophies for his skill in national competitions. Jay wasn't certain which made him more nervous, the knowledge of Darin's lethal skills or the intense gleam in his dark eyes.

He straightened up in the chair and reached for his pen, a gold and slender piece of smooth tapered metal, given him as a graduation gift by the psychologist he'd served as an intern. He knew it was silly, but it made him feel distinguished when he held it in his hand, as though he could render weighty observations with it. He liked to imagine it imparted to him something of the style he'd admired in his mentor. He liked stylish things, or at least his own taste in them, and thought of his office and his automobile as the only two places he could really have it his way. Swiveling the chair around again to the windows he tilted back, enjoying the warmth of the sunlight. He scanned the dates of their previous sessions and reflected on their progress and current situation.

Much had happened in a short time. There has been progress with Jason, whose hostile behavior at school seemed to have originated through unconscious anger at his mom for raising him without a dad. Though he consciously seemed not to hold her at blame, they were there with no father, and he didn't know why. He sensed that his mother felt guilty about the issue in her tone and manner whenever speaking of it. He had sensed this more acutely as he grew older and saw other boys identifying with their dads. He had reached a point developmentally where he needed to express his own feelings about it. He wouldn't talk about it to his mom, sensing her distress and discomfort, so he acted it out in school in the presence of a teacher reminiscent of his mother. Fortunately he had bonded easily with Jay as a father figure and was able and willing to share his troubled thoughts. Since then both mother and son had been growing happier and the sudden rise of Darin had increased that momentum. He now had the possibility of a real dad in his life. With Jason and his mom becoming near ecstatic Jay wondered if things were moving too fast. It was as though an accumulation of everyone's needs were being finally met in a landslide of love. The adults, especially Darin, seemed almost obsessed. Jay knew he was to see her alone in session today, possibly for the last time.

Without moving his body from the oven-baked warmth of the sun, he twisted his head to the right as far as possible and caught the impassive face of the clock. Hearing its persistent tick for the first time since arriving, he saw that the minutes had marched up to the appointed hour. Swiveling back to his files, he closed the folder without making additional notes, slipped it into the cabinet and turned the key in the lock.

As he walked down the long hall of thick beige carpet toward the roomy and comfortably furnished lobby, he was aware of the subtle bounce in his step. It was a rhythmic pulsation, almost as though dancing to a light minuet. He realized again how much he loved doing this and reflected on it....*nothing better in the world to get your mind off your troubles than listening to somebody else's...and nothing feels better than helping someone...*Each session was a challenge and he always felt optimistic. Crises were opportunities. If you couldn't save a marriage you could still save an individual, maybe even more than one. The simple secret he had found, in the course of his duties, was that if people really wanted to be helped in some way, no matter what their circumstances were, he could help them. There were many secrets of the trade, but that one was the first. He entered the golden oak spaciousness of the lobby and turned with a smile to the only person sitting there.

"Good morning," he said with genuine cheer, and looked down at a face smiling back up at him with blue eyes clearly brighter than usual, over a potted red dahlia in her lap. She had shown a good-natured friendliness from the beginning but far surpassed that now with her old flame rekindled. As if to mirror her mood, he grinned and with a sweeping gesture of his arm, motioned towards the hall, almost as if inviting her to dance.

"Good morning to you," she replied on rising, handing him the flowers.

"Thank you," he responded, while turning aside. As he ushered her along the hallway and into the office he realized she was feeling even perkier than usual. Watching her settle into the chunky rattan chair reminded him how clients always returned to the same seat they had selected on their first visit; their original anchor in the choppy seas of inner exploration. He looked at her curiously, sensing her buoyancy, then opened as he so often did with familiar clients.

"Well, what's happening?" He eyed her intently and leaned back in his chair.

"Well, everything," her tone was unusually playful.

"Like what for example?" he smiled, anticipating.

"Like we're getting married!" she exclaimed delightedly, searching his face for any hidden response.

"Oh my God," he said, startled, trying to sound neutral. He crossed his legs. "That's... fantastic," he spoke slowly, choosing the word carefully as to invoke both its meanings. It may seem great to her, but it felt unreal to him, and "fantastic" put it most tactfully without making any judgments.

"When?" he added.

"Next month, we think."

"Wow. What's Jason say?"

"He doesn't know about it yet," her voice lowered in seriousness, "but we're going to talk to him one night this week."

"You and Darin both?" He leaned forward with interest.

"Yes," she said, taking his interest as concern. "Do you think that's alright?"

His eyes twinkled with a flash of humor. "What? Getting married or talking to him about it?" She laughed, tossing her head back gently, then tilted it sideways like an inquisitive puppy, and said emphatically, "Both."

He sat still, silent, formulating his thoughts, recovering from the slight shock of the unexpected news. Despite his hunches, and they were often strong, he believed you had to trust that people knew best how to lead their own lives. If they made mistakes then those were to be learned from. His task was to help them find their own inner guidance.

"What do you think about it? Getting married, that is." As he tossed it back to her, he watched her squirm into a more comfortable position, under the weight of the question. She pursed her lips in hesitation, her eyes clouding in faraway thought.

"I really don't know," she said slowly, scanning his face for clues. "I have a million thoughts about it, most of them good."

"Okay," he responded, wanting to go deeper, "and we can explore every one of them, but first then I wonder, what are you feeling about it?"

"Well, most of the time I feel great about it. It's only when I start thinking that I get a little nervous. But Darin's excited enough for both of us and waves my fears off in a second." She smiled again and shook her head side to side with eyes wide in mock amazement. "And Jason just loves him. He's just like a dad to him, teaching him karate and everything. It could really be so wonderful for both of us." Her plaintive tone was touching.

He remembered the earlier conversation with his own young son that morning. Missing a parent was bad enough but imagine the ache of a boy for a father missing since birth. Not to mention the mom's pain. It was easy to sympathize fully with both of them.

"It's been a long hard road for you two, hasn't it?"

"Well," she spoke guardedly, not wanting pity, "it's been long and hard enough." She stared at the floor; taking in the deep blue tapestry as though arranging her thoughts in its design. Then she met his eyes, and said evenly, "I think it's time for a change."

While the sun continued its patient ascent over Mt. Rainier, their conversation grew to a slow crescendo, ranging far and wide with the issues of the moment, and fading only as the minutes met the next hour. Keeping his skepticism to himself, Jay probed every nook and cranny of her thought and emotion on the impending marriage, hoping to arouse at least a little caution. While she seemed at ease with critical questions, her faith remained unshaken in the viability of the romance. She agreed with his suggestion that her son and fiancé attend the next session with her. "We'll go over everything together," he assured her while opening the door. "Until then, remember, as I said awhile ago, you know better than anyone if this is right for you. Take time to pay attention to the still small voice within."

"All right," she said, seeming relieved. As she strolled down the hall, she turned and yelled "thanks." The specter of her relief and gratitude gave him the happiness he often felt after a session, but by the time he'd closed the door his mind was focused on the thought of calling Saul. He was so difficult to reach now, not like before. And if it was true he no longer held private sessions, then perhaps he couldn't reach him at all.

Standing by the sunlit window with his phone in hand, Jay felt a sense of urgency and thought of what to say exactly. His poor friend Barry needed help and maybe he did too, possibly now in more ways than one. He feared the chances were that he'd simply reach a volunteer on Saul's staff. He wondered how best to couch his message if that were the case. Moreover he assumed he would likely just get an answer machine. The heat of sunshine on his cheeks matched his burning need to find help as he thought through precisely what words to leave. He wanted to convey that he did need urgent help without being verbose or sounding like an emergency. Composing his thoughts, he punched the numbers on the phone in rapid precision and held it to his ear, feeling dread and hope in equal portions... *please someone be there*...It was answered, surprisingly, on the very first ring.

"Hello," said a pleasant and resonant voice, as sweet and relaxed as a tropical flower opening in greeting to sunrise on the island.

"Saul?"

Chapter 9

"I am in stirrups all day, yea, and sleep in my spurs."
(Samuel Taylor Coleridge, in a letter)

THE LAKE AT HIGH noon held the overhead sun quivering in its middle like a white brilliant diamond set boldly in the navel of wild Mother Nature wiggling a belly dance to a birdsong sonata. Since early morning Bea had tirelessly tended a nonstop onslaught of crying telephones plus a flurry of faxes and was intending next to answer the call of her stomach when done with her present conversation. "Okay, sounds good," she nodded intently, barely hearing the sudden shrieks of the cockatiel upstairs.

"tweet-tweet-tweet-tweet!"

'Dog-bird', they called him, with amusement and a little pride. His shrill screeches were an automatic early warning system that went on red alert without fail at the approach of friend, family member, or anyone else to the property as they entered the driveway. From his caged perch by the grand piano he surveyed the yard from street to house as fiercely territorial as a German Shepard at a junkyard.

"tweet-tweet-tweet-tweet!"

"Okay, okay, sounds good. I'll get back with you ASAP. Thanks, bye." She squinted at her black lacquered Japanese clock, glossy with hand-painted orange markings. At 12:15 the bird's alarm calls could mean that Jay was home for lunch. She'd hoped that he was so she could tell him about Jess. It also could mean that Candy, her secretary, was coming back from a long break. *"rrriiinnnggg"…oh shit…*

"tweet-tweet-tweet-tweet!"

"Homestay Connections. This is Bea. May I help you?"…*i could really use candy…*Almost as if on cue her secretary, Candy, came bustling into the room, later than usual due to a dental appointment. Seeing Bea was on the phone, a common sight during the workday, she swung around to her own desk and sat down to a stack of papers. As she shuffled through a series of student applications from Japan, she saw that Bea was motioning to her and about to hand her the telephone.

"So let me give you to Candy, my secretary," she was saying, "and she will go over the details of it all with you." She looked at Candy. "It's about the excursion schedule for next spring." With that she handed the phone off to her subordinate and returned to the task she was doing before it rang. She was grateful for the level of good service that Candy gave her and enjoyed the ease of their interactions in the office. The woman seemed to be capable of anticipating her every need and her skills on the computer had proven invaluable. With such devotion and sensitivity to her boss, Bea wondered why she seemed to have such trouble with men. She had been a single mom for half a dozen years and now had two teenagers, a boy and girl, to get through high school. Lately, Bea had noticed, Candy seemed to have developed a crush on Randy, their reliable handyman, who performed many jobs around the property. He was a likeable, kind-hearted soul in his thirties who had survived a tough divorce after his brother had slept with his wife. Bea couldn't tell if he felt anything for Candy. He seemed mostly oblivious to her long looks, flitting eyebrows and solicitous smiles whenever he appeared in the office to discuss some project he was working on. Maybe she would grow on him.

He had come awhile back to Jay for counseling, a broken-hearted mess of a man, and had ultimately offered to pay off his bill with carpentry and related services. Since there was much to be done both with landscaping their yard and remodeling their home, he had stayed on long past the six months he had been in therapy. During that period he had often stayed on for dinner as well. He had been at the house for nearly a year now, virtually on a daily basis, making repairs on roofing, plumbing, electrical and the like, plus building new structures such as car ports, decks and trellises. His talent for carpentry and endless odd jobs drew fond appreciation from Bea and Jay. He'd eventually established himself in a new home, a near empty apartment, as part of the final phase in his healing, but his time at their house had served everyone well. He'd become friends with Jess and Phil and in many ways seemed almost like another family member. Bea understood why Candy found him attractive and hoped that if they ever became an item neither of them would end up being hurt again.

"rrriiinnnggg"

The insistent clamor of the telephone on her desk jarred Bea from her musings and as Candy was still on the other line she answered it herself.

"Homestay Connections. This is Bea. May I help you?"…*sure be glad when jay gets here…*

Chapter 10

"When the student is ready, the teacher will appear." (A Course in Miracles)

As HE TURNED OUT of town onto the main country road, Jay accelerated swiftly then opened the sunroof to bask in the warm midday breeze. He often came home on his lunch hour, which was anytime his variable schedule allotted, and in summer sat down by the lake for some rays. Occasionally in summer he took an afternoon swim but usually he exercised by jogging after work. The ten minute commute between his office and house was a scenic one, with the road home bordered by scattered evergreens, blackberry fields, horse pastures, and various orchards clad in fading yellow leaves. While cruising home now, Jay was oblivious to the pastoral scenes beside him. Lost instead in rumination he was still absorbed in the two phone conversations he'd just had, replaying them in his mind.

"Saul," his jaw had dropped, "is that you?"

"Well, well, well," came the happy response, in an ancient and familiar tone that felt reassuring, like coming home after a long weary journey to a warm stone hearth. "And how are you?"

The melodious calm in Saul's friendly voice sent smooth sensations of delight through the airwaves like ripples of silent laughter, bringing back memories of previous talks they'd shared. Saul had a natural gift, furthered through meditation, for receiving spiritual guidance. He simply asked, listened and heard a spiritual entity named Rex, who eventually told him to share his gift with others by having individual sessions with them. These became known as Conversations with Rex and within a few struggling years Saul had become somewhat famous and successful simply by being true to himself through honoring this process. Monthly newsletters, comprised of taped talks of individuals with Rex, were mailed to a grateful and growing following.

Though he sought no worldly recognition, his picture had even ironically graced the cover of Parade magazine one Sunday in an article on psychics. Through it all Saul had remained a simple man, his spirit of humility and humor constant, though he had a trying time raising a family and running a business while living by the grace and guidance of God. Saul asserted that everyone had a spiritual guide available to them and that he was merely listening to his. Over the last decade Jay had benefited from many conversations with Rex, ranging from spiritual and psychological matters to relationships, all kinds of predictions, and even the locations of lost objects. Time had proven Rex true much more often than not, and he was the last word whenever Jay sought advice, which wasn't often.

"I'm fine!" he'd exclaimed, delighted and surprised. "Except for a few concerns." He paused, then added, "Actually, one major one, but I can't believe you answered the phone." He suddenly felt very lucky. "I thought you weren't talking to anybody."

"Well," said Saul, gently jesting, amused by the touching yet cosmic simplicity of it all, "every once in awhile someone gets through." Jay's hopes jumped with his heart.

"You mean I can talk with you awhile?"

"Yes."

The word rang softly, open and true, a resolute affirmation, so resounding with promise that relief spread instantly throughout Jay's body and the room, which had warmed as the sun grew taller, seemed cooler and elevated; an oasis with a view. "Thanks," he said with heartfelt sincerity.

"You're most welcome," came the gracious reply in a resonant voice.

"I'm just concerned about one issue."

"Yes?" His patient tone was inviting.

"A friend of mine just got busted for growing and selling pot. He's worried about it and also afraid I might be pulled into it since I'm in his address book, which they confiscated."

"Oh, I see. Listen, I'm still not doing private sessions. I'm sorry, but I'm devoting all my time to the start-up of our center here."

"Oh."...*oh no!*...

"There is, however, a man in Seattle, whom I got to know, and feel completely comfortable with."

"Yes?"...*Goddamnit*...

"His name's Leroy and I can give you his number."

"I appreciate it," Jay declined disappointedly, "but I don't think anyone's as good as you are." As he said that he felt the faintest touch of reconsideration.

"Well thank you, but I can tell you that if I were in a place where I didn't feel I could relax enough to hear my guidance, to hear Rex, that I would have no hesitation to call him and ask to hear his guidance." His tone was so buoyantly matter-of-fact, so positive and plain, that Jay felt a wisp of inspiration and a willingness to trust him that softened the hard edge of his disappointment.

"Really?"

"Yes."

"I appreciate your recommendation but frankly I've talked to various psychics and channels over the years and none of them are as good as you. I don't know if I could call someone else...mmm...what's his name again?"

The Mercedes slowed down just enough for a sharp turn to the right off the main road onto an asphalt dead-end lane bordering the west side of the lake. The long narrow yards of lakefront houses lined the left side of the avenue as Jay cruised along, savoring what sunlight could stream through the old pine trees and the conversation he'd last had. His recollection was in vivid detail and he smiled to himself while remembering it.

"Hello, this is Leroy," said a voice in a higher pitch than Saul's. It seemed relaxed and intense at the same time.

"Hi Leroy, I got your name from Saul. This is Jay."

"Yes, what's up?" The words came with a crisp sincerity that seemed to imply there was no time to lose and no need for formalities. Since Jay himself often spoke this way to new clients, he knew the directness simply meant that help was being offered at this moment and he responded openly, glad to have been asked. They could cover the niceties of fee and payment later.

"Mmmm, I'm having a problem right now and I need some advice."

"Okay, what is it?" His intonation was curious, slightly nasal, almost a drawl, like the actor Jimmy Stewart.

"A friend of mine got busted for growing pot and I'm afraid I might get entangled in it some way."

"How?"

"Well, I really don't know since I haven't done anything. But I guess the cops are treating this guy as a major drug dealer. He was very frightened when we spoke. He was selling to alot of his friends, and my name was in his address book since I was his therapist."

"So what?"

"Well, ultimately nothing I suppose, I hope, but once, years ago I bought a small amount from him. Moreover, he said they treated him like dirt, gave him a hard time, and if they start an investigation and bust some of his friends, well, I'm just scared they'll come after me as well, and I just don't want the hassle. I have enough already. Personally it could be highly inconvenient – I don't trust government agents at all – and professionally it could be embarrassing if they show up at my office or something."

"That's not likely to happen." The definite tone felt reassuring to Jay and he wondered, as Seattle called itself the Emerald City, if he'd come upon their wizard. He wanted to confirm how unlikely, exactly.

"It's not?"

"No," said Leroy, with a tone of finality that sounded like a door closing shut on a dungeon. "Do you have any grass?"

"Uhhh, no…*not on me anyway*…I basically gave that up. I am a child of the sixties, right out of Southern California – the hub of it all – but now I usually just drink wine or beer when I want to relax or socialize with friends. Actually if anything I may be too fond of the grape."

Leroy chuckled; sounding indulgent at the disclosure. He then spoke in a firm clear manner.

"Look, the larger meaning here for you is to give it all up entirely." He stopped momentarily as though to let that sink in, then continued, in a deliberate but understanding tone.

"You don't want to be hassled by this and it's not necessary that you be. The only reason people smoke pot or drink is to relax from their tensions. You'd rather be living in a world where you didn't feel the tensions in the first place, and for you, that's the significance of this event."

The words rang as true as the bang of a gong in a silent Buddhist monastery. As he relaxed, his attention shifted from himself to concern for Barry.

"What about my friend? Can you tell me what will happen to him?"

"He needs to get a lawyer, and then he'll be okay. It's a wake-up call for him. It's a wake-cup call for both of you."

"A wake-up call to what?"

"It's a call from God for you to awaken to his presence within you, which is really what you want."

A feeling of gratitude swept through Jay like a cool breeze on a hot summer day at the beach and he said in a voice resigned to the truth, "You're right, that is exactly what I want."

"I know," said Leroy teasingly. He sounded pleased with himself, or them both, and somehow simply the beauty of it all. Saul (or was it Rex?) had been right once again. He felt compelled to be completely open.

"Uh, actually I do have a little bit of grass at home…just for rare occasions mostly."

"It's time for you to move beyond that."

"I think you're probably right." It was quiet for a few moments. "I'd like to talk to you more," said Jay, "but I'm at work and have my next appointment in a few minutes."

"Okay," he replied, unperturbed at the shift.

"Mmmm...how about if I call you at ten tomorrow morning?"

"That's fine."

"Okay, I'll call you then. Thanks and good-bye."

"Good-bye."

Chapter 11

"Well," he said with his flashing smile when he opened the door – that smile is like the bursting of a flame. It leaps from his eyes and lifts his forehead and plays like summer lightning all about his head and even his body – "I have a little more done on the 'Prologue of the Earth Gods'."
(Mary Haskell's journal, describing her lifelong lover, Kahlil Gibran)

WHEN THE COCKATIEL CRIED out another sally of alarm shrieks Bea finished with her last call and left answering the phones to Candy. As she bounced upstairs from the basement office she saw Jay approaching on the long S-curved pathway of aged red bricks carefully laid by Randy; a yard wide walkway meticulously set in sand through the middle of their lawn several months ago. A long cloud of dust, about fifty yards, was settling behind him on the stretch of gravel driveway that ran from the carport straight back to the sun-dappled street. She felt at once so pleased to see him, relieved at the overdue break in her work and glad for a bite to eat at last, that the piercing clamor of the cockatiel seemed to fill the room more with joy-crazed celebration than hysterical alarm. Bobbing around a bend at the top of the stairway, she sailed by the counter and veered toward the kitchen like a sloop speeding homeward, cutting through the sea on a rising tide of hunger waves.

Strolling along the curving walkway, Jay stepped with a light spring across the tightly knit bricks, listening incidentally to the bang and clatter of two rooftop workers on the new house next door who were bantering good-naturedly about something of interest, unaware of how distinctly their voices carried in the lakefront stillness. At a momentary pause in the hammering din, just as Jay walked under the ivy-covered lattice where the path met the patio, one carpenter's voice sang out to the other, in a cavalier tone of joshing incredulity.

"Does she know you're married?"

Jay stopped in his tracks to hear the reply, but it was lost in the noise of nails loudly whacked into wood and the inquiry simply echoed in his ears like an announcement that had been made on a police megaphone...*Jesus, what a line*...

In five quick words a huge talk had unfolded, speaking volumes dramatically between the lines, implying romance and betrayal in one little question, and revealing something of the character of the workers in the process. Jay started toward the front door, reflecting somewhat seriously on the implications of what he'd just overheard. In a few measured strides he'd become philosophical, live and let live was his natural bent ...*poor bastard doesn't know what he's getting into...maybe i'll see him in therapy someday...or his wife...* and it darted from his mind like a rabbit down a hole as he pulled the cedar-framed screen door aside.

Pushing the front door open, he stepped into the living room and eyeballed the lake. It was ablaze with the surrounding reflection of near autumn; orange-yellow tints. He heard Bea in the kitchen shut the refrigerator door and he yelled in jest, mimicking the accent of Ricky Ricardo from *I Love Lucy* calling to his wife, "Honey, I'm home!"

"Oh good!" came the rejoinder. "Come in and have some lunch with me." He met her smiling eyes with a grin of his own as he gave her a hug. They enjoyed being self-employed, though it was sometimes a struggle, and felt blessed in their condition even through the worst periods. At least they lived without bosses and on their own schedule.

Against a backdrop of two large lemon-leaved willows, superimposed on the shimmering lake, they plunged into food preparation and conversation with relish, moving about the kitchen as sprightly as two elves making Santa a snack.

"How about we eat on the dock?" asked Jay, wanting to get as much sun as possible before the death knell of dark fall days fell with finality. Bea brightened visibly at the prospect of a sunny lakeside lunch and radiated agreement with a childlike grin and nod. Minutes later they were strolling down the zigzag grassy footpath to the lake, carrying small baskets full of ripe green pears, thick blue-veined Gorgonzola cheese, and an oval loaf of peasant bread. Their loads seemed as light as summer balloons in their hands and they floated together to a bench on the dock underneath the speckled twin willows like the graceful landing of a wide-winged heron. Smearing a glob of blue-veined cheese on a torn chunk of sourdough Jay handed it to Bea and cleared his throat. As he made one for himself, he prepared to share his morning news. Before he could speak though Bea looked at him intently, indicating something serious was on her mind.

"I heard from Jess today."

"Really?"

"Yep, early this morning while you were still sleeping."

She bit into her sandwich with satisfaction and watched him react to her announcement.

"Why didn't you tell us this morning?"

"I couldn't get out of the office before you left," she said with a trace of mock exasperation. "The phone kept ringing."

He nodded knowingly and wiped a smudge of cheese from his lips, then searched her face for more clues. A lone seagull swept in low seeking fish or a bread crust and cried out its disappointment as it winged sharply back to the center of the lake, still on the lookout for a watery mouthful. Baby blue forget-me-nots fading with the Indian summer dotted the shoreline on stringy stems like scattered granules of hand-painted candy. His curiosity was rising.

"How is he?"

The concern in her eyes was tempered by her wry smile and she spoke in an ironic tone that conveyed more then the words.

"Well, he's fine *now*," she replied, with an emphasis on the last word that kept him quiet and listening for more.

"Here's what happened," she added, and shared with him all that she had learned of Jess's third-world predicament and unexpected change of plans. Occasional trout, nipping at insects, shattered the mirrored plane of the lake into ever-widening concentric circles that disappeared and reappeared while Jay listened intently. A squadron of riotous ducks honking in calamitous unison veered upward to the south, curving like an arrow lost in flight. Separate tufts of puffy cotton clouds raced above the far side of the lake in slow motion, and one seemed to catch on the sun, momentarily darkening the area as Bea finished her story.

"So he's not sure when he's coming home?" Jay spoke at last.

"No, but he'll call us when he decides."

"Wow, what a tale. Sounds like he was in real danger," said Jay, feeling slightly astonished though relieved overall.

"I'm sure he was," Bea shook her head, "and somehow he survived. Thank God he's okay."

"Really," said Jay in a definite tone. Like anything that troubled him personally he didn't feel much like talking about it at the time. Clearing his throat, he brushed some breadcrumbs off his navy-blue sweater vest as he stood up, glaring at the sun. He turned to her, smiling; a bit of bravado.

"So you think he's okay?"

"I do." She seemed firm but concerned. "I just wish he could have somehow managed to stay anyway. I hate to see him give it up because it meant so much to him."

"I know, I know. But he can always do it again."

"Oh no," she laughed. "It's too dangerous. Grandpa was right."

He smiled and looked down at the ground turning lighter as the sun slipped loose from the cloud's hazy clutches, and then said flatly, "I'd better get back to the office. I've got a client at one." The minutes of lunch, tasty morsels of time, had been consumed so quickly there were none left for seconds. Feeling the press of her work mounting also, Bea stood up, stretching her arms wide to the sky, then said with a toss of blonde curls on her forehead, "I've got to get back to the dungeon myself." She grinned at her self-imposed exile. "Shall we go? I'll put everything away. You'd better get going."

Jay turned wordlessly and they both wandered casually back towards the house, up the crisscrossing path that was bordered by chunky black boulders and lined with fading red rhododendrons standing in lacy pink heather groundcover. Dangling a basket aimlessly he was lost in thoughts of his son, Barry and his next client, all of whom had had a troubling time. He had really wanted to tell her about Saul and Leroy, but now only had time for just a summary at best. He started to speak when she reached for his hand without breaking stride, but she gripped it so tightly and swung it so freely to her own steady gait that he chose to stay quiet, feeling their bond, and only said "Bye" when their hands parted and waved.

Bea entered the kitchen and watched him walk down the path to the carport as she washed her hands in the sink. She picked up a dish towel from the hand rack on the stove and wiped her hands dry....*well, that was fun...now back to the battle...*

Chapter 12

"I have been in this strangely damp city for more than a week. I cannot work no matter how hard I try. I cannot even think." (Kahlil Gibran, in a letter to Mary Haskell.)

WHILE CRUISING BACK TO the office with the sun-roof open wide, Jay found himself anticipating his next appointment, a fellow colleague, another therapist he'd known for years, who had called last week in near desperation for help with his marriage.

"I've got a big problem," he'd started out shakily. " I had sex with a client."

"Uh-oh," Jay intoned...*holy shit...*

"Well, an ex-client," he added hastily, "and not intercourse, just oral sex."

"Ahhhh."...*oh sure...not sex...like clinton...*"Are you still seeing her personally or professionally?"

"No." He was emphatic. "She left for a new job in a different city months ago."

"What's the problem exactly, Will?"

"She wrote me a note, to make along story short, and Colette found it," his voice trailed off weakly, "and you can imagine the rest." He'd rather not.

"Oh, man," Jay groaned, "and what'd you do?"

"I told her truth," he said plaintively, "and she's pretty upset."

"I can imagine."....*to put it mildly...*

"So anyway, I'd like for us to see you next week on Monday. I may move out to a hotel for this weekend. I don't know yet. Can we set up a meeting for Monday?"

He sounded scared and disoriented, like a worried lost lamb who'd wandered far from his flock, and nothing like the confident Dr. Ringer that Jay had come to know. They had met at a training seminar on Grief at a hotel in Seattle and became fast friends as they found they shared much in common. Both favored a humanistic approach to counseling with a spiritual dimension for those clients open to it and their personalities simply seemed to click as well. Later on, when Bea had finally despaired of Jay's dour disposition and constant complaints about the rainy northwest they had seen him briefly in marriage counseling, which had proven helpful. Since then the men had managed to get out to lunch together every few months. Jay wanted to help him not only as a client and as a colleague, but also as a friend, for whom he would have liked to return a favor.

"Of course," was his prompt assurance, meant to give what meager comfort it could. "How about Monday at one?"

"That's perfect. I've got an appointment then but I'll reschedule it. Thanks, thanks alot," he sighed in relief.

"Call me on the weekend if you need to talk – either one of you. You've got my home number. Anything else you want to say now?" Jay listened as Will cleared his throat a moment.

"No. I want to wait until Colette is with me there in your office." His resolve on this point appeared to give him a sense of direction, or at least of being grounded. "She knows what happened. I've told her I'm sorry and that I was crazy. I made a big mistake. I got carried away." He stopped again, as though searching for words, then said in resignation, "We just need some help."

"You've got it," asserted Jay with certainty, wondering apprehensively what Colette would have to say.

He didn't see Will's blue Volvo station wagon when entering the lot, but it was not yet one o'clock and he figured they would likely prefer not arriving early to avoid sitting long in the lobby. It could be challenging for a therapist to assume the role of client. He'd done it in college, regarding his first marriage and at other times as well with his superiors in school. Most of his teachers had been private practitioners who believed self-analysis was essential to the work. Dashing up the steps he strode into his office, reflecting on the upcoming meeting with his friend.

He knew it could be a humiliating moment when one crossed that invisible line from saint to sinner; wise man to fool. Though he also knew, intellectually at least, that such an attitude was utterly wrong. You had to be able to practice what you preached and realize that everyone needed help sometimes. Taken in the right way it was merely another learning experience, humiliating only to one's ego, where unfortunately he knew most people, like himself, hung out quite often. Hopefully Will could set his aside.

He stood in the office in front of the windows, facing the early afternoon sun, while surveying the valley below. It was dotted with lemon-lime and orange-red trees amongst dark evergreens, from the small mall across the parking lot past the fertile farmlands to the far foot of Mt. Rainier, the great white pyramid. Closing his eyes and leaning forward to the glass so his forehead pressed against it, he drew a long sigh in the sweet brief respite of feeling the warmth from the pane when the bell from the church a few blocks away rang out one o'clock. He knew for whom it tolled.

He stepped down the hall with a sense of foreboding. When you cared for clients personally it became a little harder to keep it all clinical, professional, and objective. All in all he was ripe for the session however and felt a stab of disappointment when finding the lobby as deserted as a ghost town. A call to the answer service revealed the cancellation had come during lunchtime. Puzzled, Jay rang Will's office and he answered the phone.

"Hey, I just got your cancellation," he said, hoping to conceal his feelings with neutrality, the preferred camouflage of counselors everywhere.

"I'm sorry," he replied, with appropriate anguish, "but things went better this weekend than expected and then I got a call for an urgent appointment and one was the only time that I could see them. It's a couple in distress I've been seeing for awhile and they really need a session. Frankly, also I could use the money. Can we set it up for another time?"

"Sure, if you want," Jay spoke diplomatically. He knew it was hard for Will to seek help and had also learned through the years never to pressure anyone to come into counseling, no matter what he thought. If they didn't come in under their own steam, it wouldn't go anywhere that was worth getting to. The term "mandatory counseling" had always struck him as an oxymoron. "What's Colette want?"

"She says it's on me to make the appointment and she's right," he declared, lowering his voice with a twinge of guilt, "and I'd like to call you back later on that. My clients are due any minute now and I'm not sure what Colette's schedule is this week." It sounded reasonable enough but Jay knew from experience that when first appointments were put off they generally were very rarely ever made again.

"Whatever you want to do, man," he feigned nonchalance and tried to counter his feelings with the thought that it actually wasn't his decision to make. He knew enough to know that he didn't really know what was right for them, no matter how much he might want to help.

"Thanks," said Will, sounding sincerely grateful. "I'll call you in a day or two."

"Great."….*sure*…"Till then."

He plopped the phone in its cradle and sat down at the desk, wondering if he would hear from him again. Will had a touch of introversion and could easily clam up on personal matters. He might well opt to try to heal this rift in the inner sanctum of their private relationship.…*oh well, i'm here if he needs me*…

Given an unexpected hour of free time, his thoughts turned back to the fascinating chat he'd had with Leroy and the chain of events proceeding it, starting with Barry's frantic call. Remembering that reminded him that he wanted to call Barry back. Before doing that he wanted to be sure that he had the fullest information possible and decided instead to call Leroy first.

"Hello."

"Hi Leroy, this is Jay again," he began, hoping he wasn't imposing.

"Yes, what's up?" He seemed friendly enough.

"I was just about to call my friend Barry and tell him you said things would work out and I thought I better ask if there is anything else specifically I should tell him. He's pretty worried."

"Look," he said in a careful voice, "the sense I'm getting is that he doesn't have to worry. He is safe here." He paused as though receiving data and added, "He's going to need a lawyer though."

"Okay, he's considering that."

"Then he should be able to get off with minimal damages."

"Really?" Jay felt incredulous but it was music to his ears.

"Yes," he affirmed with casual certainty. "I see that."

This felt almost too good to be true. The calm assurances of safety made him feel free and he wanted to extend the liberation to Barry.

"Okay then," he offered, "I think I'll suggest that he call you."...*wonder if he will...*

"Okay," said Leroy with calm confidence. Something in his tone caused Jay to imagine a squirrel in a tree with treasure-trove of acorns. "That's fine."

"Do you do this a lot?" asked Jay. His curiosity was bursting like a microwave bag of fresh hot popcorn.

"Sure," he replied with feeling. "I mean, I make my living at it." He chuckled in self-satisfaction quietly.

"I used to talk with Saul periodically ever since the early eighties," Jay offered.

"Oh? What about?"

"Oh, just about anything of interest to me that I wanted guidance or predictions on; my goals and problems, my clients' problems, my wife's and children's situations, coping with life, the bouts of depression or anger I would have."

"I see."

"But mostly – though I was too often preoccupied with other concerns to focus on it – what I was interested in and really still am is the experience of enlightenment or living with the guidance of God."

"That's great!" Leroy seemed to hum with power line intensity. "That's what I do, as often as possible, and I work with alot of therapists."

"So you're a teacher of teachers?" said Jay in jest, happy to hear this bit of information.

"Yes, at the moment." He seemed to be enjoying his work. "Tell me some more about yourself."

Jay hesitated, breathed a thoughtful sigh, and then spoke his mind to make it perfectly clear. "Well, I started this journey, this search to know God directly, most consciously in the sixties, when many other people my age were also. Before that I had good solid conservative religious training and then a rebellious period of being an agnostic in high school, and then a humanistic liberal in college, like a lot of know-it-all kids that age. Then about the time I finished my Master's degree, I discovered *A Course in Miracles*, which I'm sure you know is purportedly written by Jesus through a psychic channel, and I underwent something comparable to a religious conversion because the spiritual nature of life was so clearly and compellingly spelled out in that book."

"Right." They were in tune.

"So," Jay continued, "I started meditating daily and feeling pretty good, even enthusiastic about life, and significant things happened, almost like magic, like moving here from California right after graduation. I'd lived there since first grade. And anyway, we moved to a house on a lake, which seemed like a dream come true, and I started my own practice, as the first therapist in town, all in the same year, and professionally things just kept getting better and better for a long, long time."

"Yeah?" queried Leroy, sounding interested. "You mentioned bouts of depression and anger."

"Yeah. I couldn't stand the winters, or actually just the constant darkness and the rain. I'd get depressed during those times," he laughed, "which seemed to be most of the year. And it all just seemed to wear on me."

Leroy chuckled and intoned, "Mm-hm."

"Actually, it was more of a culture shock on several levels. Having lived in the sun virtually all my life, in a place where the culture was essentially defined by it, I didn't realize how much I had loved it and identified with it, until I got here. I had taken it for granted. I had no idea people lived or would ever even actually choose to live in a place where the sun shined so little. We saw the house here on a gorgeous day in August and bought it immediately. I had just assumed the sun shined here much more than it does. I would have thought anyone was nuts to live in a place that stayed this dark. I used to wake up every day in California with the feeling that anything was possible, because it all seemed so endlessly bright and warm; endless summer, endless possibilities. The irony was, it was so good there that it was getting bad. I mean, it was getting way too overcrowded because so many folks were moving there, which was one reason why I wanted to leave, along with the smog and the idea of greener pastures and breaking away to somewhere new and different, just to establish myself in my own right."

"I see."

"And I thought I would eventually get a Ph.D. But to make matters worse, I had also misjudged the college scene badly. I just assumed, like California, that there would be a number of colleges here with progressive curriculums in psychology – the sort of thing we had fought for and won on campuses in the sixties – and there wasn't. The only state school, the only affordable school within driving distance, was the UW, which just sucked. Their curriculum was primarily research or clinical with a behavioral thrust, which was the very crap we had managed to advance beyond in California with the whole Humanistic/Holistic movement in the seventies. And the UW, since they were the only game in town, actually thought they were hot – I had several conversations with them on the telephone – almost haughty," his voice grew in indignation, "and to me they were just a joke, a throwback to the fifties, useless to the mainstream of clients in therapy, totally ignorant of all the new inroads we had made. So I was surprised, disappointed and frustrated both with the weather and the academic scene."

"Ahhhh," Leroy affirmed.

"I'm sorry," Jay relented, "I know I'm getting off the track a little, but I had no respect for that place at all, that is, their Psych Department. And actually, all this might have all changed by now. It was over a decade ago in the early eighties. But this whole area then just seemed backwards to me compared to California; narrow freeways, no vegetarian restaurants, no counselor licensing. And lastly, I wouldn't ever go to that school anyway because I really do not like to be in Seattle. Though it seems no worse and even actually a little nicer than most big cities, overall they're all just cesspools to me. I like the country."

"Hmmmm."

"So anyway, to sum it all up, life got unexpectedly harder and complicated. I felt trapped, but too proud to turn around and go back. Besides, I didn't think it was good for my sons to be moved around and also, especially since I had achieved some success, I felt a strong desire to see just what I could do without a Ph.D. and with God instead. I had been so moved by the Course and so put off by the school, that I was both optimistic and determined that somehow I could fly in the face of academic and professional tradition and make it anyway, on my own terms. And for a long time, I did. I was immensely successful; saw alot of people, made alot of money, and built a good life with my wife for our family. I was generally pleased with myself in so far as my work went. I absolutely loved living on the lake in the woods – and still do – which is virtually impossible to do in Southern California."

"So what happened?"

"Well, overall I still became progressively unhappy with the constant rain, and my reaction to that had to do with my own nature, which is sort of emotional, very emotional I guess, and it takes good and bad forms; romantic, artistic, and sensitive sometimes, but then other times temperamental, moody, and touchy."

"That's a mouthful," joked Leroy.

"Right, and a handful, especially for my wife," joked Jay in return. "And when you've had and done as much therapy as I have, you know yourself pretty well, but it's still no guarantee you'll be happy or sane."

"What do you mean exactly?"

"Well, mainly that I still find it hard to control my emotions, especially my temper, and I'm pretty opinionated, so the two can be a challenge. But anyway, as I was saying, I never really stopped missing the sun and though my work was good – somehow I was able to compartmentalize it – I had strong negative reactions about the region. I always hated the cold, dark, wet. The Great Northwet, I call it, and Seattle – the Emerald City – what a joke. It just seemed like a dark, crowded, messy old city to me – no offense – filled with uptight city people, mostly liberals, and a lot of PC types, meaning Political Correctness. I know they're well-meaning. I was once one myself, intensely so – liberal, that is, not PC. That's just stupid totalitarian crap. How shallow to control free speech and think you're making a better world. A better world for fascist socialists maybe. When I was a liberal it included freedom of expression. Anyway, so year after year I still felt pretty negative about the area.

"I tried to adapt and took up skiing for a few years but eventually felt that just like cocaine the going up wasn't worth the coming down. And basically I just couldn't get into typical northwest activities; hiking, biking, cycling, kayaking. Actually those things are fine and looking back now I can see I really just hated the weather, and still do. I don't like being out in the cold, dark, wet. I'd rather lie in the sun and go swimming, which at least the lake affords in the summer. Matter of fact, in the summer, this place, the northwest, has California, and perhaps the whole world, beat – hands down – and that's pretty much what I live for here. But then we get the nine months of winter, so….And then the house, though we have beautified it alot, has been one long constant project, and it's so old. I mean, I grew up in a much younger house and it felt in a way like going backwards. There's only one bathroom, for Christ's sake... Am I talking too much?"

"No, I'm interested," said Leroy thoughtfully. "Please go on."

"Well, it's really been the lake that has been the saving grace. It has such a strong spiritual and aesthetic presence, an overwhelming sense of beauty and peace, that I can't ever imagine living anywhere else that wasn't on water – certainly not in the northwest. It has replaced the sun in terms of the power of nature to touch or move me. But when you leave the house it doesn't follow you around like the sun did in California. Anyway, I gradually stopped meditating – got too busy – caught up in my work and in the late eighties with a band I had – which was an absolute blessing for about four years until we broke up – but that's another story. And I gradually became estranged from my wife – psychologically, not physically – who didn't like being around me when I was angry or depressed, which was alot of the time. I didn't blame her.

"And I started drinking alot of wine, expensive wine, and smoking pot again, like I had in college. So we had a period of being distant from each other that was actually somewhat unbearable to both of us, because we really love each other deeply, but I was hard to tolerate. So we went to marriage counseling for a bit, and then, after we got things better between us – the last several years have been a lot better anyway – the emergence of managed care this year has started to impact my practice very badly. So now my income's trailing off, and it was really good for such a long time." He paused to collect his thoughts. "Anyway, in effect, to make a long story short, in a gradual way, I lost touch with God, and now, fourteen years later, things are really getting terribly messed up."

"How so?"

"Well, in many little ways, you could say, most of which I just touched on – I drink, I smoke, my band broke up, I still miss the sun – but primarily the big one is my practice and income."

"Ah. And what's exactly the problem there?"

"Well, the whole field of psychotherapy is predominantly funded by insurance payments. And in this last year, as so-called managed care has taken over the health care industry – mangled care I call it – many therapists are making far less money than they used to. I used to charge $100 an hour, for example, and get paid for 20-30 hours a week. I made alot of money working virtually part-time at something I loved. And hopefully helped a lot of people. Now I can make $45 an hour, if I want insurance payments through managed care companies, which I don't, since that's the rate they'll pay a Master's level therapist. So I've ended up with less clients and of course less money."

"Why is that?" His voice rose a notch in interest.

"That's my own fault," Jay admitted without guilt or remorse, "because aside from the lower fee to work with these companies, now they require a tremendous amount of paperwork, documentation, notes, files, etc., and the constant pressure of their standards, their approval, their procedures, all of which are based on how much money they can save. You have to justify minimal treatment now for clients with extensive problems." He stopped, feeling his outrage grow, then snickered, "It's crazy...anyway, I decided I'm not going to do this their way no matter what. So then I refused to join the new insurance networks and thus I'm getting far less clients than before, since most folks have insurance and prefer to use it if they want counseling."

"I see."

"You see, I'm more of an artist than a scientist or businessman by nature and I really haven't an interest in trying to make a science or a business out of what I regard as the art of psychotherapy. So I've come to a crossroads."

"What's that?"

"I need to figure out how to make enough money to live on, while doing something more meaningful than just making money. If I'm not going to be rich doing therapy anymore then I want to be rich doing something idealistic; something that's making the world a better place. And if it's not therapy, I don't know what it is. But I do know, most of all, that I really want to live with a sense of spiritual guidance, more than I've had in a very long time, so I'll know I'm doing the right thing all the way; fulfilling my God-given purpose on earth." Jay stopped and heaved a deep breath of a sigh.

"You don't really want to be rich."

"I don't?"

"You want to be secure."

Jay hesitated while evaluating the assertion. "Actually, that's true," he concurred. "That feels right. But either way, can you help me with this?" he asked plaintively. "I mean, I try to meditate and hear or feel God's guidance, but I think I'm just too deeply agitated to do it right anymore. Saul said that if he couldn't hear his guidance, he would call you."

"Yes." His tone was as calm as the sea at low tide. "I can help with that."

"Great." Jay felt suddenly relieved and as light as a buoy, bobbing, floating in that ocean. "Then I'll call you tomorrow at ten. Thanks."

"You're welcome."

After hanging up, Jay sat in his chair, feeling pleased with the fortuitous turn of events... *one thing leads to another*...He called Barry to pass on the good news and suggested he consider calling Leroy himself, which he said he would. Aware that he had another half-hour until his next client, Jay spun around in his chair slowly circling in thought, wondering what to do with his time.

Squinting, he scanned his desk in the sun's glare and pulled a pile of notes close to scrutinize a new project; an article for the paper. It was not an article exactly, but more an advertisement in the form of a column in the hope of attracting clients. It was to be written on issues commonly addressed in counseling with information and advice, as well as his office phone number should further consultation be desired. His desire was to write a series of brief essays, enough to eventually constitute a book, on solutions to various problems of individuals, couples and families. This was his first essay in a prospective collection of twelve, one for each passing month, in a tentative work as of yet untitled, with the theme of maintaining psychological well-being throughout the months or seasons of the year. It was a way, or a forum, for the presentation of his ideas to the public, or at least his community, and he took it very seriously while enjoying it too. Withdrawing his prescription herringbone sunglasses from the pocket of his tan silk shirt, he put them on to subdue the glare. He picked up the top sheet and read the words he had written so far through a second paragraph.

As life is a ceaseless movement of unpredictable happenings, we are undergoing various changes all the time. The rhythm of life being cyclical, we experience significant changes or transitions as beginnings, ups, downs, and endings. This pattern is clearly reflected in the course of a day, the lifespan of an organism, and the turn of the seasons. The seasons especially, each with their own felt meaning, pass through us as we pass through them and we are seasoned each year by greater growth experiences.

While each year's illustrious or lackluster summer slips away, fall brings the feel of turning inward again, reaping and storing for the long Northwest winter. In every community, children and adults alike enter another industrious period of learning and working. With vacations over, families reorient themselves to a new and busier schedule. Children particularly, since they are not in control, may feel unsettled by fall transitions as they refocus their lives.

Jay set down the paper, put his elbows on the desk, and dropped his chin in his cupped hands, warming his cheeks. What did he really want to say about fall? What was the overall meaning of autumn and its relevance to human beings? As he sat in the stillness, awaiting inspiration, his memory retraced to its most recent imprint of families with children struggling to survive. The flower lady flashed in his mind, bringing a painful twinge of sympathy for her and every single mother he'd ever encountered. He thought single parents had the hardest task to handle. He wanted to acknowledge their suffering, which he knew well, because, like most practices, women made up the bulk of clientele. And generally single mothers, not to mention single fathers – that rarest of parents, probably suffered more deeply than any of them, given their constant and overwhelming concerns. He reached for his pen, started to write, and watched, while the words seemed to effortlessly flow in a stream of blue ink through the thin tapered shaft as the emerging ideas of his bubbling mind, with the meaning unfolding more clearly as he wrote.

Single parents and mothers, especially working ones, often find their lives strongly impacted by the revision of family activities. They bear the brunt of new adjustments necessary to accommodate everyone's differing needs. The transition these changes entail is best made with all members of a family coming together in a renewed spirit of cooperative reorganization. Though the seasons endlessly come and go, recycling life into death and back again, we are always left with ourselves. In our adaptation to seasonal variations, we can learn that it is not so much what happens to us, but our reaction to it and our handling of it that counts. Whether changing by choice or by circumstance, we are always free to accept or resist the inevitable transitions life brings. They are most gracefully made in the calm realization that it is time to let go, move on, and start anew, while remaining connected to the continuous flow of life and ourselves.

He stopped, feeling satisfied with his message, spun around to the window and read the whole piece. His allotted space was small and they charged him per line so he had to be cogent, delivering alot with an economy of words. This was the best he could do at being folksy in tone, which his wife had suggested. For her it came naturally. He preferred to discuss psychological issues in psychological terms as with communication, anger, loss or parenting, but the thought of linking the movement of life with the processes of mind did have some appeal. He'd give it a shot and see what kind of response if any it brought back. Perhaps he'd be flooded with calls from single parents, seeking appointments that they could barely afford.

Chapter 13

"If you don't understand how a woman could both love her sister dearly and want to wring her neck at the same time, then you were probably an only child."
(Linda Sunshine)

A s THE LATE AFTERNOON sun, rolling westward on its arc, shed its golden grace on Bea, she labored under it intensively, oblivious to it's presence. She was 'multi-tasking' as she called it, going from fax to phone to computer and back again, working situations into solutions, with scant time for basking in the glow of tiny triumphs. After lunch she'd returned to a mountain of messages and a disgruntled look from her secretary, Candy, upon entering the office.

"You're not going to like this," she warned in her characteristically smug and saccharine manner. A certain holier-than thou tone had emerged over the years, growing markedly after her husband had left her to pursue a promising career as a drug dealer, leaving her with two young children to raise. Her attempts to run a dance school in town in the evenings had thus far proven unprofitable and she was grateful for her secretarial job to pay the bills. She waved some papers at Bea and raised an eyebrow.

"These receipts from Perry just do not add up." Her 'I told you so' tone was unmistakable to Bea, who appreciated the concern but thought perhaps she also overdid it. The fearful thought that the woman might this time be right started to send her stomach lurching, an unfortunate but common condition that had been contracted during the summer. She reached for the Tums, a trusty desktop staple, and popped a couple of colored wafers in her mouth then turned to Candy with an air of steadied calm.

"What's wrong?" she asked, concerned but unruffled, hoping to handle this reasonably.

"Well, two things." She looked at Bea sternly. "Most of his receipts are just handwritten ones and secondly they don't account for all the money he's spent." Bea frowned and held out her hand for the papers.

"Let me see," she murmured, adjusting her glasses. She scanned the receipts and looked up.

"You're right, they're mostly handwritten," she conceded, then added in tone too non-judgmental for Candy, "but he told us he had more receipts and was still looking for them last week."

"He's been saying that for a month," she asserted suspiciously and added sarcastically in a higher pitched tone, "just where are they?" That probing query was met with silence.

Candy's skepticism gave Bea the advantage of a devil's advocate, but she often tempered it with her own skepticism when men were involved as it was evident to her that Candy hated them. She knew Perry's actions seemed somewhat suspicious but she hoped in due course to work things out with him; her usual approach to people problems. Candy's accusations of embezzlement appeared as of yet premature and overblown.

Last week she had felt the cutting edge of Candy's observations, delivered in a singsong manner while she typed, as though she were merely talking to herself aloud, flimsily masking her self-righteous disapproval.

"He's found himself a sugar mama," she affected in a southern drawl, hoping to soften her sharp point with humor.

Since Bea was typing on the other computer, enmeshed in undoing a snarl in Boston, their intermittent conversation about Perry had been sketchy, gossipy, speculative and inconclusive, at least to Bea, and she'd felt no compunction to dignify such a remark with a response. Still it stuck in her craw. She knew it was intended as help from a supportive, if opinionated, subordinate and fellow female, but she also realized he might not be embezzling, and even if he were, which just seemed unthinkable (he taught Sunday school for God's sake!), she was no sugar mama. He had merely betrayed her trust.

Bea came from good stock, solid Midwestern, and both of her parents had made a profound impression upon her character, stamping it indelibly with the values of honor, hard work, optimism, and fair dealings with others. They had run their own family business, a hardware and interior design store, in a small Ohio town where their prosperity and prestige were well earned and respected. She had made these same values the cornerstone of her work and had a difficult time not seeing the best in people. She liked being this way, and even if Candy thought she was a chump, she too like everyone loved Bea's generous spirit. It was worth it to Bea to risk being fooled.

On the other hand, just as deeply, she hated being lied to, as her father had before her, and if it were true that Perry was cheating, as sad and uncomfortable as that might be, she knew ultimately that she must confront him. She found that notion noxious though. It ran against the grain of her characteristic way of dealing graciously with people and gave rise to thoughts of Tums.

Bea studied the receipts, a mix of formal stubs and messy scribbles on torn scraps of paper, and after a moment handed them back, saying with a touch of objective restraint, "These can be settled when I'm back there next month."

"I certainly hope so," said Candy emphatically, feeling the need to get the last word in while sensing she'd best curb her tongue. She was saved from that formidable task by the ring of the telephone, her first line of duty being to answer it, and she did so while still feeling the tension around Perry.

"Homestay Connections. This is Candy. May I help you?" she intoned sweetly, in her professional nasal best. She guarded the gate to the boss like a bulldog with an officious smile and a suspicious ear. "May I tell her who's calling please?" was often the next question, crucial in granting admission to an audience with busy Shamamama. "And may I say what it's regarding?" was usually next if they got past the last one. "Faye who?" she queried, unmoved by an apparently inconsequential answer.

"Ohhh," she said, shifting from formal to friendly, "her sister!" and extended the phone to Bea with an awkward grin and a shrug of embarrassment. "I should have known. She sounds just like you."

Bea took the phone, turned away towards the window, and exclaimed in a tone of joyful surprise, "Faye, is that you? My goodness, how are you?"

"Fine," came the jaunty reply, in a voice as familiar to Bea as life itself. "How are you?"

"I'm doing okay, just busy, busy, busy, finishing up the details of last summer season and attending to a number of other things." A call from Faye was a rare occurrence, coming typically late at night after a gala civic affair had ended and she was too buzzed from socializing with Pittsburgh's elite to go to bed yet. As pleased as Bea was to hear from her now, she felt too pressed for time to suppress her curiosity for the sake of pure conversational decorum.

"Why'd you call?" she laughingly asked, hoping not to seem rude or too brash by impatiently leaning on sisterly graces.

"To talk to you, dummy!" Faye retorted in kind, feigning grouchiness, a manner of teasing bequeathed to his daughters by their impish father, dear old Gabe. Bea giggled in recognition of the humorous intent and said half-apologetically, "I'm sorry, but I'm up to my ears in work and have been all summer."

"I know, or I figured anyway," said Faye empathetically, "and actually I called you about your work, in a way. I heard you're going to Vienna."

"That's right. Who told you?"

"Polly, of course. Who else talks to both of us?"

"Oh yeah. Lucky her," Bea quipped with a chuckle, while Faye sniggered back. They shared a common secret: it was good to have sisters.

"What's the purpose of your going to Vienna exactly? Polly said it was basically to get more business."

"That's it. I'm going to a conference, actually a big convention, and I'll have a chance to meet and make new contacts in this field."

"Good for you. I understand you'll be going to Toronto too."

"Yep."

"Well, I wondered if you would arrange your trip to stop in Pittsburgh for awhile."

"Oh, gosh. I don't know. You mean just a quick visit?"

"Well, actually I was wondering if both you and Polly would come out for a longer stay for awhile. Maybe a week. I've been thinking it's time we had a reunion."

"A reunion?"

"Yeah, a reunion."

"Why?"

"Because we're sisters. Because we're family."

"Yeah, I know, of course, but why now?"

"I don't know. Maybe it's old age. But I went to a high school reunion this summer and saw Ohio for the first time in a while, and visited with dad, and saw some old friends, and it just made me realize how we've drifted apart, and so I thought why not just have our own reunion. You could both stay here and we'll catch up on each other and pay dad a visit too. What do you think? Polly liked the idea."

"Oh God, I don't know," Bea started to object. It was just like Faye to suggest something like this, wringing extra pleasures from a business trip, making festive plans for a great getaway, wanting to have fun with some friends or loved ones, and preferably at a time and place conducive to her. Despite her self-centeredness, ruthless at times, she had a genuine feel for people, especially the "right" ones, and her ardent investment in them over time had been paid back handsomely in social dividends. Her whirlwind lifestyle, a mix of avid globe-trotting and selective social climbing, had moved Jay to christen her "Auntie Mame" many years ago.

"I'd love to come visit but I just don't think I could work it out this time," Bea said regretfully. "I really feel I've got so much to do. I've already bought tickets and it'd cost me to change them."

"Oh," said Faye, sounding disappointed. "I see." She paused for a moment. "Look, I really think this is important. I don't think dad has a lot of time left." That remark hit Bea like a brick to her stomach, different than a Tums anxiety call.

"Why do you say that? Is something wrong?"

"No, not really. Not at the moment anyway. He's just getting old. You never know how long he'll last."

"Well," said Bea, feeling more serious. "I just don't know." She reflected on the thought of rearranging her schedule. She would love to see her Father, but would preferred to have allowed for it well in advance. Also she faintly wondered if her sister had insinuated that his days were dwindling just to satisfy her own ends. She wouldn't put it past her. Yet whether or not the means were manipulative, a reunion itself was not a bad thing. She just hadn't considered it and was reluctant to make a snap judgment now. "We're all getting older," she added flippantly. She wanted to recapture the lighter mood of their talk, but knew well from past experience that when Faye had her mind set on something she wanted it was difficult to sway her away from it.

"Well, will you at least think about it?" Faye implored " I'll check back with you." A pause followed that comment as Bea contemplated the entire scenario.

"Is that a threat or a promise?" she said with a little laugh.

"Oh please. It's both. Okay? How's that? I really want to do this. I think we'd all love it. Anyway, just think about it. It'd be good for us to see each other. And dad."

"Okay," said Bea, willing to table it for now. "I'll see."

"Thanks. Gosh, you're stubborn."

"It seems that one of us is," she said, amused by the charge.

"So" Faye started, warming to other subjects. "How's Jay? Still Mr. Energy?"

"Oh yeah. He's pretty much the same as always; energetic and a little ornery," she laughed, then added, "though actually he's probably feeling worse than usual. His practice has been down quite a bit this year."

"Why's that?" After a touchy and turbulent beginning Faye and Jay had grown closer in mutual affection through the years.

Bea cleared her throat as the other line rang, wondering if she wanted to get into this now. She watched as Candy, still sorting fretfully through Perry's receipts, answered the call, and waited for an indication if it was for her.

"Just a second, Faye, I'm sorry; I'm expecting an important call from Japan." She cupped her hand over the phone and looked inquiringly at Candy without waiting for a reply. "Who is it?" she implored. "Toshi?"

Candy waved her off, shook her head no, and turned away to handle the caller by herself.

"I'm back, sorry, there's a big problem going on I'm trying to fix, and I need to talk with someone in Japan. I've been waiting since yesterday for the call and now it's morning there."

"Okay, I see. Can you tell me briefly what's happening with Jay?"

She decided to give her a quick summation, feeling a slight tension in anticipation that the next call could suddenly end their talk.

"He's not seeing as many clients because the mental health field, is changing over to a new system called managed care and he doesn't want to deal with all the new regulations."

"What regulations?"

"Oh, I guess it comes down to submitting more paperwork, in a word, to the managed care companies who are trying to lower the health care costs for the insurance industry."

"Oh."

"Also, companies are cutting their costs by lowering the fees they pay to therapists, and therapists like Jay, with a Master degree, are getting significantly less than Ph.D.'s."

"Oh."

"Also he heard that the industry eventually wants to eliminate everyone but Ph.D.'s so he's feeling some pressure to go back to school, and he really doesn't want to do that."

"No?"

"No, he says he's had enough of psych profs and would have a hard time pretending to care anymore what they have to say."

"That sounds like him," ventured Faye with a laugh. "Well, it's probably hard to go back to school after being in practice as long as he has."

"Yep," confirmed Bea, "that's just what he said."

"Well, then," said Faye, in her usual fashion, unwilling to accept a negative outcome for any problem that piqued her interest, "what's plan B?" Her optimism was contagious and Bea appreciated the attitude. She relaxed a bit more.

"Well, we're really not sure yet, but if he can't make good money again until or unless he gets a Ph.D., then I'm hoping he'll consider working here with me." She thought she saw Candy flinch noticeably at the mention of a male possibly invading her workspace; virgin territory. She wondered if she'd imagined it.

"Have you grown that much?"

"Oh yeah, especially in this last year. There's plenty of work for both of us to do."

"How does he feel about that?" Faye wondered.

"Mixed, at best, I think. He'd rather be working on music when not counseling, but that doesn't pay, and he knows I'm overloaded, along with our budget, so I think he might be willing to do it anyway. We'll see. I want to discuss it with him. Just waiting for the moment when the timing seems right."

"What could he do?"

Candy hung up from her call and turned her attention to a stack of papers so quietly that Bea suspected that she was intently listening. Eavesdropping was practically unavoidable given their office space, if one were so inclined. She endeavored to give a short answer to Faye.

"Oh, lots of things. But I think we might tap into a market for foreign college students. My programs now are just for high-school groups. "

"Oh, I bet he could do that."

"I have no doubt that he could, if he'd mind his manners. I just wonder if he would. He has a flair for business, but his heart isn't in it." She thought Candy's shoulders scrunched up a notch toward her neck in tension. "You remember he had his headhunting company in California while he was in college. Though he made a lot of money he didn't really like the business and was glad to sell it to his friend when he graduated and we moved here."

"Yeah, I remember. Hmmm," she pondered. Feeling her curiosity satisfied at the moment, she changed the subject again. "So how's Polly doing?"

"I don't know," spoofed Bea. "You tell me. You talked to her last."

"That was over a week ago!" squawked Faye. "And you only live a half hour from her house. I can't believe you guys never see each other."

"Yeah, well, we're both pretty busy. At least I am." She sighed and added, "We talk sometimes"....*that's a whole other story*..."But to answer your question, my impression is she's not making enough money waitressing and so she's thinking about going back to school. I think her marriage to Wade is going well."

"Yeah, he's great guy."

"Yeah, and they'd like to start thinking about having a family. So maybe someday she'll be a busy working mommy, just like us."

"She wants a kid?"

"I think so. I think she's thinking about it. Didn't she tell you?"

"No. We didn't talk for that long. She had to go to work. I just asked about the reunion and she said it sounded good."

"I see."

"She'd better get a better paying job before she has a kid. I told her majoring in American Studies was stupid." Faye could be merciless in speaking her mind.

"Yeah, well, it was her choice. I think it's fine really. It will qualify her for a Masters program and that's all – *"rrriiinnnggg"* – I'm sorry, just a second."

As the phone rang suddenly out again, Bea winced at the reminder of pending matters abroad. She felt like Cinderella at the ball near midnight. With the steady eyes of a hawk she scoured Candy's face for clues to the caller's identity or purpose. On seeing it could be handled without her, she returned her attention to Faye, intent on covering more ground quickly before the next and possibly final interruption.

"Anyway, I think she'll work it out okay." She paused. "And how are you doing anyway?" she probed.

"Not too bad, I'd say," Faye replied.

"What's that supposed to mean? You usually say 'great'."

"Oh, I'm still great," declared Faye, her voice rising. "I was born that way."

"That's more like the sister I know."

"I just don't seem to the have the get up and go that I used to. That's all."

"Well, that happens to everyone. It's called getting older."

"Right," said Faye, sensing an opening. "And that's why I think we should have a reunion."

Just as she started to respond to that remark Bea saw Randy approaching the sliding glass door. "Just a second," she said to Faye. "My handyman's here." She looked up at the man as he entered the room.

"Sorry to interrupt your work," he started, "but Jay's not here, and I don't know if he wanted me to take a look at the dryer – I understand you're having problems – or finish with the gutters while the weather's still good." He took off his cap and held it in his hands while speaking in a voice that was kind and respectful; traits that had endeared him to every member of the family. Bea noticed that Candy seemed captivated by his presence. She'd set her pen down to look up at him, smiling sweetly and fluttering her eyelids with interest.

"Why don't you just finish up first with the gutters? The dryer can wait a day."

"Very good," he said pleasantly, then, noticing Candy's attendant gaze, looked over to her before turning to leave. "Good morning," he offered with a smile and a nod.

"Good morning," she replied, widening her eyes and broadening her smile. She uncrossed and crossed her legs reflexively. "How are you?"

"Fine," he assured her. "And you?"

"Oh, fine." She sat motionless while observing him intently. "Busy," she added, as an absentminded afterthought. Their eyes locked in mutual interest for a moment. "Say by the way, if you don't mind," she inquired tentatively, "do you think you might be able to take a look at some things at my house sometime?"

"Oh sure," Randy answered. "I don't see why not. What sorts of things?"

"Oh, just some odds and ends. Maybe I could call you about it later?"

"Oh, you bet," he assured her. "That's fine. Do you want my number?"

"I'll get it from Bea," she offered softly, still looking trancelike.

"Well," said Randy, smiling slightly while returning her gaze, "that'll be fine." He looked back to Bea as he cleared his throat. "Guess I better get to work." He nodded at both women, put on his cap, then turned and went out the sliding glass door. Bea watched Candy watch him as he trudged out of sight.

"Hey, you still there?" asked Faye.

"Yeah, I'm sorry. Had to answer a question. Now what were you saying?"

"That we're getting older. That it's high time for a reunion."

"Oh yeah. Okay. Well, I'll give it some thought. When's the last time you saw dad?"

"A few months ago. Remember? I told you – my high school reunion."

"Oh yeah. And how'd he seem? You thought he looked bad?"

"Oh, not really. I'm just not sure how good of care he's getting. He seems to be getting along okay. I just know he's just going to get gradually worse." Their father, Gabe, was a solitary widower going several years back. His beloved wife, the angelic Grace, had proven as irreplaceable in his heart as she had been in their old hometown.

"Is his memory okay?"

"It's about the same. Maybe a little worse."

Lately they had feared that he was showing signs of Alzheimer's, as he'd seemed more forgetful, according to his caretaker, on approaching his ninetieth year. He was a strong, short and stocky gentleman, white-haired, mischievous, with a saintly bearing, and a watery twinkle in his knowing blue eyes. He had a ready smile, that spread slowly over his kindly broad face, weathered and wrinkled by many long memories, ear to ear, like a desert sunrise. He still lived in the same aging house in Ohio where the girls had grown up.

"The woman who takes care of him is only there for a few hours a day."

"Good help's hard to find," asserted Bea sympathetically. The long distance care of their father was a concern for all of them. Faye was primarily in charge of it given her proximity to him from Pittsburgh, but she had a busy life too and Bea often worried how well their father was getting by as he was getting on.

"It's not so much that. She is good help, but she's found she has cancer."

"Oh my, and she's not really that old."

"No, I know. She's about my age." Faye sighed. "And I guess she'll be starting chemotherapy pretty soon, so we'll probably have to find somebody else. At the moment the neighbor is taking up the slack."

"Phyllis?"

"Yeah."

"I see," said Bea, feeling sobered by the news. "At least she's good."

"Yeah, but she's old. Anyway I'm going down there next weekend to check on the situation and see if I can find someone to replace her. I'll call you after that."

"Okay, please do," she said emphatically. "Chemotherapy huh? That's what killed mom," she noted with disdain, referring to the cruel irony that a modern medical healing method had hastened not halted Grace's tragic demise.

"I know," acknowledged Faye demurely.

"Well, anyway," continued Bea, "let me know if we need to do something different for dad. Do you think we'll have to move him to a home?"

"Oh no, I doubt it. Not yet, anyway." Bea thought she heard a heaviness creep into Faye's voice. It wasn't the most pleasant of subjects.

"Are you sure you're okay?"

"Oh, I'm fine. I told you. I'm just tired. Busy weekend last week. And talking about cancer and old age isn't exactly upbeat." She paused, then chortled, "At least I feel better than dad's caretaker."

"That's not funny, smarty pants. You sure?"

"Would I lie to you?"

"Probably."

"Ha-ha. That's not funny either. Look," she stated in a tone of finality, "I'm tired and getting older but I'm actually just fine. We're all getting older, and as I've already said, that's just another reason for a reunion. Right?"

Bea hesitated a second, and then asked in earnest, "If I can't arrange to see you back there – and I may not – would you like to come out here for a visit? Both your sisters are here."

"Hmmmm, that's a thought. Let's see." She paused to check the filled pages of her day timer. "No, it looks like I should probably have to be here the rest of the year."

"Since when did that stop you from running off somewhere?" cracked Bea, amused at the implausibility of Faye staying put in one place for long.

"Not funny, again," Faye laughed, drawing the words out in her East Coast accent. "No, but really, this time it's serious. We've got the election coming up this November and I'll be helping to prepare for it." Faye worked as a cabinet head in the office of the mayor of Pittsburgh. She had formerly worked many years for a slick magazine in Washington, DC and was used to traveling in political circles.

Bea herself had little use for politics. It seemed too removed and too abstract to affect her life more than peripherally at most. She was aware though of current issues and events, willing to share her opinions if asked, and appreciative of the fact that Faye's employment was contingent upon her boss's re-election.

"Do you think you'll win?"

"Oh yeah," she said confidently. "But I still should be here. He's a democrat in a democrat town. Besides he's done an okay job and we'll get some support from Clinton being president."

"You mean he's going to campaign for you?"

"No, no, no. I just mean with a democrat in the white house and the economy good, people will tend to vote for the incumbent. At least democrats in a democrat town will."

"I see." Bea felt slightly dubious about Clinton being an asset. She'd heard enough about him from Jay and other people to know that many held him in very low estimation. Jay detested Clinton, with the same consuming passion that he held for all his likes and dislikes, and had scant tolerance for disagreement on the subject. She never bothered to seek out his political opinions, as they were often expressed quite freely. "Jay thinks it's funny the media likes to say he has a favorable rating of fifty percent since it means half the people must rate him unfavorably."

"Jay doesn't like him?"

"That's putting it mildly. He says the best thing that he's ever done was to lose the democrat majority in congress and that's because so many people can't stand him, despite the media saying he's popular."

"Well, that's true about losing congress. It is the first time in about forty years, but I don't know if it's because they can't stand him. In any case, he's still popular enough here among democrats to be an asset in this election and that's all I care about."

"I understand," assented Bea, as she felt herself losing interest in the subject. She noticed through the window for the first time of the day how the water was sparkling like gold on the lake. "Well, good luck," she wished, letting it slide. "And how's your love life?"

"It's okay," she announced, sounding slightly defensive. After two divorces Faye had been single for a number of years."

"Are you dating anyone?"

"Oh, there's one guy I am seeing quite a bit of lately."

"rrriiinnnggg"

"Just a second, Faye, I'm sorry." She stared at Candy who motioned with a wave of her hand that she could handle the call. It felt so unusual to be having a long and enjoyable conversation with someone utterly unrelated to business, and especially with Faye, who seemed more open than she could recall. She leaned back in her chair.

"What's his name?"

"David."

"Do you like him a lot?"

"I'm not sure yet. We need more time together."

"I see. Do you see much of each other?"

"We've had dates, been to parties and gone to various functions together. We're starting to plan some weekend getaways."

"That sounds nice. Where are you going?"

"Oh, just short trips; upstate New York and then later maybe the Carolina coast."

"Sounds fun to me," quipped Bea, feigning envy. "I like short jaunts. My trips are long, like the ones coming up."

"Hey, I know why you're going to Vienna," Faye said, "but why are you going to Toronto?"

"Ohhhh," Bea moaned, drew a deep breath and sighed while reflecting...*where to start*... "Well," she began, "to make a long story short," then slightly lowered her voice, "I need to go there and see what's going on, and how to improve the operation." She hoped her tone low enough to avoid Candy's ear, as she seemed to be finishing up her last phone call. She knew any mention of Perry at all would find Candy hard pressed to keep her mouth shut and she'd heard enough secretarial clamor for today.

"What's the problem?" piped Faye, always ready with unsolicited advice. She believed that her talents in managing problems were generally unrivaled by most other mortals. Bea's own assessment of Faye's management skills predated adulthood, stemming from memories of a domineering big sister. She weighed her response, wary of trying to account for an as of yet unaccountable situation, especially in range of Candy's radar while expecting an imminent call from Japan. Still, she was curious what Faye might have to say.

"Probably the best way to put it is this. I don't know if funds have been misappropriated or simply mishandled." She wasn't sure if imagining it but the office seemed to grow quieter as her voice did. "Either way," she went on, "I need to get to the bottom of it. It's all disorganized, with complaining students, clients, and families."

"Hmmm." Faye's analytical mind was whirring; brainy ball bearings in a fast wheel of fortune. Her acute feel for people ran second only to her acumen with finances. "What are the families complaining about?"

"Mostly that they're not getting paid."

"Ohhhh." She sounded very serious. "What does your Area Director say?"

"Well," she laughed, stretching for humor, "he's either got alot of reasons or alot of excuses."

"I see." She hesitated, then sprung the key question, "do you trust him?" This time Bea felt the heaviness on her end.

"Well...I thought I did...I just..." she faltered, "I just don't know what to believe right now."

"I see," said Faye knowingly, "well, why don't you -" *"rrriiinnnggg"*. Her words were drowned out in part by the telephone, which seemed all the louder as the room had become quieter, plus Bea had stopped listening to catch Candy's response.

"I'm sorry, Faye, let me see if that's Japan."

One look at Candy seemed to confirm her hunch. Her wide eyes were bulging with customary drama, a look usually saved for very important calls, and her tone of voice was higher than usual.

"Just a minute, please." She stared at Bea, looking aghast. "It's him!" she exclaimed, cupping her hand over the phone as she brought it to her chest. Bea gave her a nod and then raised a finger to signal that she would be there in a second.

"Toshi?" she asked, raising her eyebrows in anticipation of an affirmative response. She felt a quick start of anxiety and relief.

"No!" Candy shook her head and tightened her grip on the phone in her palm. She whispered wide-eyed in alarm, "Perry!"

Chapter 14

"If you do not hear the Voice for God you are not listening quietly enough."
(A Course in Miracles)

After dinner that night Bea and Jay went off for an evening walk to soak up the remaining rays of the day and to burn off some pesto tortellini calories. They recounted casually the day's events, exchanging anecdotes and concerns to the twittering of twilight birds above and as they entered the well-worn trail to the woods, passing the crooked "no trespassing" sign posted at the end of their dead end street, Jay's voice dropped lower as he looked at her seriously.

"Bea," he began, "I called Saul the other day for some advice."

"Really?" she asked in surprise. "On what?"

"Well, initially I called him about an ex-client of mine who was just busted for growing pot."

"Oh, wow," she uttered in wonder. "Anyone I know?"

"No, though I think I mentioned him to you before. He's a young guy about thirty, from Duvall and I helped him through a marriage crisis a long time ago. He liked me alot and when he got remarried, which was to the same gal, I performed the ceremony, that outdoor one at Snoqualmie Falls. Remember?"

"Oh yeah."

"Well, we always got along well and he would call me every once in a while for some brief advice and occasionally come in for a session. He really wanted his second marriage to work and was conscientious about keeping it finely tuned."

Being a minister in the Universal Life Church, an organization that had legally though controversially propagated a number of ministers in the sixties through mere dispensation of a mailed certificate, had allowed Jay to conduct the wedding rites, usually highly personalized ones, for a number of clients over the years. Bea eventually obtained one also and had occasionally conducted ceremonies herself.

"So is he in big trouble?" she queried, ducking under an extended pine bough as the forest path became increasingly dense.

"Aw, he'll be okay, I think, but the funny thing is I didn't talk long with Saul since he's no longer granting private conversations." He knew she knew this and paused to step gingerly over the large trunk of a fallen cedar, then extended his hand to her in assistance as she mounted the tree behind him.

"But he referred me to a guy in Seattle," he continued, "who does the same thing – watch your step – as Saul did and he spoke very highly of him so I called him and we had a good talk for a short while." She jumped off the log, landing squarely on both feet and smiled impishly like a kid, her white teeth gleaming in the darkening woods.

"What's he like?" she asked, as they resumed walking.

"Oh, his take on life is purely spiritual, just like Saul's, and in listening to him I realized how much I've gotten away from being that way."

Bea looked at him steadily and nodded, saying nothing. She pulled her brown sweater more snugly around her neck as a chill crept in and the birds became quieter. Their calls were being sung out farther apart, signaling their weary readiness for the night. They stopped walking momentarily and stood on the path listening to the silence pierced by fading bird notes and the periodic rumble of distant rigs barely audible from the highway a half mile away. They both looked around the scraggly mishmash of small and large evergreens, tenacious shrubbery, scrawny speckled-leaf trees, and the gray old-growth trunks, beheaded long ago by loggers and left to sprout huckleberry bushes like sprightly red flowers on rotten-stump tombstones. He turned to face her.

"I've decided to talk with him awhile on a regular basis, maybe weekly, to see if he can help me reach a more enlightened state of mind." He smiled self-consciously at the last few words, thinking they seemed odd in a world where such a thing was rarely mentioned, though he knew that Bea knew the subject well enough through her studies, past conversations with Rex, and her own time in meditation. "Just listening to him seemed to put me in a better place. I felt more..." he hesitated, searching for words, then nodded, "peaceful." He looked in her eyes, which met his in kind and saw her interest. "I'm calling him again next week for a half hour session." He tilted his head sideways and scanned her face for a reaction. "I think you might enjoy talking with him too," he added.

"I might," she offered innocently, "I always enjoyed talking with Saul."

Almost as though to a silent signal, except that it seemed entirely natural, they both turned towards the direction from which they had come and began a slow walk back, while the evening gloom gathered around them and the first stars hovered in the ever-dimming dusk. He put his hands in his jean pockets and she slipped her arm in his. They felt relaxed from the walk in the woods, as the haunting beauty of nature always restored them, and yet tonight, stimulated from the talk, they were also vibrant in remembrance of the spiritual nature of life; an awareness they shared which drew them closer. He felt encouraged by her easy understanding of his idea and wondered if he should share his concerns about the police....*she's on overload already...why give her worry... better not for now...*

"You could ask about your work," he suggested, "like Vienna, or Toronto, or whatever's on your mind, just like with Saul and Rex."

She didn't answer back, a mannerism to which he had become accustomed, and he knew she was likely absorbing it all in her quiet, unassuming style. Wordlessly they trod the forest trail until it opened to the road's end where the streetlight beamed a welcoming glow. They strode along light-footed; almost sauntering in silence, arm in arm, hearing occasional bullfrogs croak and the intermittent barking of neighborhood dogs, both seemingly lamenting the increasing nocturnal cold that heralded the end of summer nearing with each passing night.

Jay thought about the recent days he'd had, running the gauntlet from paranoia to promise, and felt an urgency to make the promise come true. If it were truly possible, he hoped, he'd find a way to reach or be reached by God, and in the meantime, he thought, a glass of cabernet would do nicely, as soon as he got home. As they turned down the long gravel driveway, crushing rocks underfoot, he looked up at the moon, a smiling thumbnail over the lake, and announced aloud, as though to reassure himself, "I'll call him first thing in the morning."

Chapter 15

"I wanted only to live in accord with the promptings which came from my true self. Why was that so very difficult?" (Demian, Hermann Hesse)

"Hello, this is Leroy." The voice on the other end of the phone was welcoming. "Hello Leroy, this is Jay."

"Hi Jay, how ya' doing?" He was at ease, inviting trust and relaxation.

"I'm not sure," he intoned, then quipped, "I was hoping you could tell me," and chuckled.

"I'll do my best," Leroy laughed softly. "I assume you have some questions to ask me." He asked in a tone that was matter-of-fact, "Do you want a tape? They're five dollars."

"Sure," affirmed Jay, "listening to a taped session afterward can be helpful." He knew this from his earlier work with Saul, with whom he had compiled dozens of tapes, many of which were listened to repeatedly, often with additional insights each time. The state of mind was so elevated, the information offered so deep at times, it was usually impossible to absorb it all in one session. Too much was easily forgotten otherwise.

"Okay, just a second while I put one in." The distinct sound of plastic snapping neatly into metal popped aloud. "And we're all set. Now we're taping."

Jay cleared his throat nervously, wondering how best to start as he stared out the windows of his office, past the speckled young maples to the rugged frosty white dome in the distance. Then he plunged in, like diving from a high cliff, and simply said what came naturally, like an animal instinctively swimming for the first time.

"Okay, well I'm just wondering in a general way what I should be doing with my life now, if anything, and to generate income, I suppose, is the main thought. Ah, and I'm not sure at what point to formulate the question, or how specifically, but basically I'm in counseling, private practice, and I just sort of sit and wait for things to get better, and sometimes they seem like they're going to and then they seem to break down, and it's been great in the past, but since I don't take insurance anymore and just function mostly on a cash basis, it's been alot less."

Jay paused, wondering if he were making sense and how many lines could Leroy read between. "But I'm also interested in some form of artistic expression, music or perhaps writing," he continued, "perhaps combining music with psychology. And my wife would probably like for me to help her with her business. And...well I'm just wondering about the appropriateness of all my activities, because it's hard to trust my own centering feelings," Jay broke into light laughter, amused at the obvious, "or I wouldn't be calling you."

Leroy cleared his throat and spoke, in a soft piercing voice, casual yet impassioned, simple and elegant, that transmitted caring to the listener along with a subtle sense of urgency toward impending resolution.

"Well look," he began, "I can't say what you should be doing except to say what you don't feel enough of right now is an experience of being supported. You don't feel support. You feel, umm, that you are required to be self-supporting in some way...and it's the nature of life, in its true form and true experience to be totally supportive.

"And it allows you to yield into that support so that you then don't have to bear the burden of anything. Quite literally you are to be propped up.....and move with that feeling of support, which allows you to be graceful because you can't make awkward moves then."

He paused, as though to let that sink in and then went on. "Loss of balance, awkwardness, are moments when support appears to have vanished. Falling down, losing your balance...all these things, are simply occurring in a dream where support has vanished." Leroy stopped, then summarized his point. "Okay, so you need to do that. You need to feel supported. You can't have it be easier until you get this. You can't have it change until you get this." Jay listened, spellbound, as he elaborated.

"Looking for a way to rectify circumstance or to feel better without feeling supported will get you nothing. You need to have a foundation upon which these new activities can take place in a way that is entirely fulfilling without them being seen as ways of meeting needs. You have to give up the idea of need, and in giving up the idea and feeling of need, you need to feel support." He chuckled. "That's the last need. You need to feel support." He paused as though finished, while Jay said nothing, his mind fairly reeling to comprehend it all...*could it really be that simple...*

Leroy's voice lowered with finality. "And that's a practice. You have to do it everyday. If you feel support you feel safe, and it will allow you to feel unpressured and at ease. So that's what you have to do.

"Any of the things that you want to do are fine, and you can do them right now. But you're not going to feel and see the forward movement until you allow yourself to have this experience that I'm speaking of." He sounded conclusive.

"Well," said Jay, trying to relate, "okay, well, I feel like I partially try to do that or play with it, and also, on a physical level, it feels like a sense of release to give into, that's hard to experience or even describe, but my wife has been fantastically successful financially lately while I've just wallowed around here in this mediocrity, and it's been nice..."

"It's humiliating though," interrupted Leroy.

"In one sense, and in another sense, it feels like I'm being supported that way now and it's odd to give over to it, and yet in a way it's kind of like...just flow with the river. So I don't know what to make of all that, but I do feel like I need to be contributing more, on some level, and she thinks so too, more than I am anyway and – "

"Oh please," Leroy laughed.

"Yeah?" said Jay in wonderment.

"Oh please," he repeated, in a teasing nasal sarcasm. "As though there were some harm here. As though she were supporting you. Hah! As though she were doing anything other than experiencing her own support; capital S support. She's not supporting herself.

"You see," he clarified, "this is the error in thinking; that she is somehow supporting herself and you're not, and she's having to carry your burden for you. She's at the moment, at a point where she's allowing herself to experience some greater support than she has, but she had better get clear as to the fundamental dynamic here because otherwise that support will wane, and go into something else, you see. She had better not be unconscious of what's really going on in her life lest it pass." His certitude seemed almost a veiled warning.

"Yes," said Jay, feeling a bit defensive of Bea. "Well, I think she's less egotistical than I am in certain ways. So, I think she has more humility about it."

"Well, she may," conceded Leroy, "but the point is, it's a good opportunity to recognize exactly what's going on, not three-dimensionally, but understand that the feeling of support has to be there regardless of what the circumstances look like. But if you can disengage from circumstance and feel supported right where you are....things will change." He emphasized the last three words in a persuasive tone of solid conviction and care.

Jay felt moved to respond, in a mixture of relief, gratitude, and wonder. "Alright....that's great....thanks."

"You're welcome," said Leroy, sounding pleased with himself, and breaking into gentle laughter.

Jay felt good. Leroy had been like Saul; spiritual, kind, sensible, accurate, confident. He wondered what else he could glean from his powers. Could he speak to his desire to do something artistic?

"Ahhh," he started, "do you have any sense about my writing, fiction or non-fiction?"

"I can see that," said Leroy confidently, "I can see that happening. I can see not being able to feel the inspiration right now to do it. There's a desire to do it but there's also a kind of blockage here, and what you have to do again, why you don't feel the inspiration to do it, why you feel stuck, is because you don't feel supported."

This made perfect sense to Jay. He felt understood and curious for more, while becoming more at ease, just listening.

"There's that word," stressed Leroy poignantly. "It's not about money, it's about freedom of movement. If you could move freely in any direction according to your desire without the fear of falling, losing your balance, what would you do?

"You see?" he paused. "So by practicing the feeling and feeling the relief that it brings, you then feel the problem is going in a new direction. If you know you have support, you aren't afraid of making a mistake. What you are afraid of right now is something that would constitute a mistake, and something that would be a loss of balance, that then you would have to struggle to get yourself out of."

"Yeah," said Jay, with begrudging acknowledgement.

"Okay," continued Leroy without missing a beat. "That's not grace, that's the world, right here. And by turning into the feeling of support and ease, you have complete forgiveness."

As he paused, Jay wondered if he was searching his thoughts or listening to a source within, or if they were one and the same process.

"I mean it's like a Mercedes going over a bump at high speed: it doesn't feel bad. It doesn't blame the bump. The car is perfectly able to do it gracefully. It rebounds from whatever the ground offers and maintains its equilibrium."

Jay interrupted, questioning to clarify. "Grace comes from feeling supported?"

"That's right," confirmed Leroy, "because if you didn't lose the support, you couldn't make a movement or gesture that took you beyond your limit to execute that. So you have to have this in order to fulfill what you want.

"You see, you're at the point of limitation now where there's no way you can struggle or strive to overcome them. You're ready to learn this. Somehow you have authorized it. It's the answer to your deepest desire to know the truth. Other limits you've managed to get through, through effort, but not this one. Because the perception that there are limits is the problem. And if you are struggling, you are always going to maintain the perception that there are limits. You're keeping, like a dog chasing his tail, you're keeping it going." He stopped for a moment as Jay waited for more.

"So this has to be done entirely differently," he continued. "You have to feel support all the time and then the idea of limits does not occur to you. Because limits are only the moment when support seems to be interrupted. And this leaves you being very connected, in that your desire feels more connected to reality than it would feel if you were being a limited personality. In that case the desire feels like it's something personal and private that you have to struggle to achieve.

"But when you are feeling totally supported, your desire actually feels like the movement of life and you just simply lend yourself to it. You express that movement and desire is fulfilled without there being a question of limits at all."

No one spoke for several long moments.

"I find your words transformational," uttered Jay slowly, feeling more peaceful.

"What?"

Jay spoke a little louder. "It's transformational to listen to you."

"Oh."

"I can experience," explained Jay, "or partially experience, support as we speak."

"Yes, oh absolutely," Leroy affirmed. "It's fast. You see, my only job is to save time for people who are already getting this themselves.

"You know," he continued, "it's interesting. Therapists have been taught that they're supposed to let their clients sort of find their own answers, as if that were the thing to do. And all the therapists I speak with are abandoning that, and what they are doing instead is feeling their own connection and just saying it like it is, and their clients get it right away.

"You see"...he concluded pleasantly, sounding richly content, "it saves time...because everyone is connected.

"Now this," Leroy clarified, "is not a therapist who thinks they know everything, spouting opinions. They're coming from their own sense of being connected...and everybody relates to that."

"Well..." joked Jay in a slight drawl, "we'd better keep talking for awhile." Leroy chuckled as Jay continued. "Thanks. It feels good." He paused. "A new dawn in the fall."

"Yeah," returned Leroy, "so there's nothing here that's out of order, but you need to feel support every moment of your life."

"I'm ready for something different," said Jay with resolve. "I'm tired of fear."

"Okay," said Leroy, as if unlocking a riddle, "any time you feel fear, and this is important, and this is in the Course." Jay knew he alluded to *A Course in Miracles*. "You are never upset for the reason you think you are. And it means essentially that the bad feelings you have are not meaningful. They aren't connected to your circumstances, though your ego says in fact that they are. And if you are able to disconnect the feeling from the circumstances, you then can ask the Holy Spirit to absolve you of any responsibility here – take the feeling from you – and it will be taken right away."

"Give up your emotional attachment to it?" asked Jay, trying to understand his exact meaning. It seemed so simple as to be silly to ask the Holy Spirit to just take the feelings away....*how the hell could that work...*

"Right," rejoined Leroy, "it's very easy, as long as you realize it doesn't mean anything. It doesn't truly connect to the circumstance. It's just that you are viewing the situation through the lens of your ego; the state of mind that thinks or imagines itself to be separate from God, and that's what really feels bad.

"People throughout history have prayed to God for relief from their problems but have done so from their ego. They haven't separated their feeling about the problem, their negative emotions, from the circumstances. And God cannot answer at the level of the problem, because the basic problem is the ego perspective of the situation, which is false by definition. God can only answer at the level of the solution, which is the state of mind that knows it is one with God. So you separate the feelings from the circumstance, and ask for it all to be absolved. You then feel better and things look different."

In struggling again to fully comprehend Leroy's meaning, Jay translated what he thought was meant into his own words.

"You mean stop creating the problem by not focusing on the circumstances?"

"Right."

"So its like first, you realize you are supported by God. Second, in doing that you start to depersonalize or shift from a negative or fearful state into a more peaceful one. And then third, you ask God or the Holy Spirit to take the negative feelings from you, which allows you to shift more substantially into peace. And then last, you have a different perspective on the situation or you will know what to do or you will feel trusting and patient that a solution is underway?"

"Exactly. And it's the same thing Jesus meant when he said, 'Seek ye first the kingdom' which means go to that place of communion. Then everything else is 'added unto you'. In other words, the foundation of peace, stability, safety, and support has to be firmly established. Then everything else is available. So you have to have a life that resonates peace and joy right where you are before anything can change."

"You can achieve that easier," Jay queried, "through practicing feeling supported?" He wanted to be certain he understood this.

"Yes, and in fact when you are trying or allowing yourself to feel centered, you need to ask for support in staying centered too, because otherwise you become responsible for being centered. You see?"

"I've been asking for help. That's what led me to call you," he offered, feeling a little defensive.

Leroy went on as though he hadn't heard him. "So your whole life has to be an experience of being propped up."

"I appreciate your use of the word 'support'. I've heard it used in alot of ways, like the whole world's a mutual support system."…*what am I trying to say?*…"I feel good." …*that was it…*

"Because I'm using it to mean like a bodily experience," explained Leroy. A long pause followed as Jay mulled over it all.

Finally he sighed, "It would probably be useful for me to talk with you every Friday." He felt like a boulder embedded in a hillside, soaking up Southern California sun; grounded, immovable, too happy to budge. "I have a ten o'clock client," he murmured absently, "and I can't see my clock." His next appointment seemed a world away.

"It's ten till ten."

"Oh good, let me ask a few more questions."

"Sure."

"What about music? I'd like to have another band, or at least keep writing music and making tapes with my synthesizer and recording equipment. What about those desires?"

"I can only say to stay with the desire, and stay with it as though it were the leading edge of the fulfillment rather than just an experience of longing. I mean, if you want to give a meaning to 'desire', it is the meaning that it's going to happen.

"Not that 'Oh God I'd love that to happen but it can't'. Desire is like the locomotive of the train and the fulfillment is the caboose. It's how you know what's going to be coming, because you have that feeling of attraction. Desire means 'of the father'. The word 'de' is 'of" in French and 'sire' means 'father'. So these feelings are begotten by the Father. They're not personal wants.

"People are confused here. Wanting, longing, and yearning are desires that have been experienced in the ego state with the extra burden of pressure; a sense of separation from God creates pressure. But when you are centered, when you are unpressured and feel desire then you have what Rex calls 'infinite patience'. To be patient means to be with your desire in an unpressured way."

Jay though of a line he had read in the Course. "Infinite patience brings immediate results?" he offered.

"Right."

"Hmmmm."

It was clear to Jay that Leroy's take on life was strictly spiritual, which was the only way to be if you were truly psychic. It brought to the surface and released any doubts submerged in his mind about the spiritual nature of human life.

"You see, life is always beginning. It never is ending. It's never getting past the beginning. Life is never getting past the beginning. So when you start feeling things moving a little bit in your life, don't try to take it any further. That feeling of being on the verge, of just getting started, is exactly where you are intended to be."

Jay was reminded of an unfinished song he had written on the guitar called "On the Verge" about feeling good without knowing why, which seemed reminiscent of what Leroy was meaning.

"It's when human beings take it beyond that point that they get into trouble, they get into grief, and aging and sickness and death and drama and so on. There's no drama at that point of initiation. There's just newness."

"Discovery?"

"Yeah."

Pausing to consider all he had heard, Jay uttered a barely discernible "Whew," then snickered and added with gentle humor, "Well, that's good to know." He laughed louder and said, "You're just full of good things for me, aren't you?"

"Oh, endlessly so," Leroy broke into laugher with Jay joining in. "Right."

"And I thought," said Jay, erupting with a sense of the ridiculous, "that I had everything nailed down," cracking himself up with these last words. It felt good to be hearing truths again that were grounded in spirituality. It was so easy to get lost in the work-a-day, media-spun, hype-extraordinaire, pain-filled world. "Oh goodness." He felt refreshed. "Yeah, this is great. Like the sunlight. It puts me right out of a question framework of mind, and I find I just enjoy listening to you as though I were listening to a fountain or something."

Leroy laughed in relaxed delight, his voice reverberating like a cascading stream bouncing fancifully off smooth shiny stones.

"What else have you?"

Chapter 16

"I have been inordinately lucky all of my life but the greatest luck of all has been Elizabeth. She has turned me into a moral man but not a prig, she is a wildly exciting lover-mistress, she is shy and witty, she is nobody's fool, she is a brilliant actress, she is beautiful beyond the dreams of pornography, she can be arrogant and willful, she is clement and loving...she is Sunday's child, she can tolerate my impossibilities and my drunkenness, she is an ache in the stomach when I am away from her, and she loves me! And I'll love her till I die."
(Richard Burton on Elizabeth Taylor)

THE SUNDAY MORNING AFTER Bea left for Vienna was noticeably colder and grayer than the prior ones and Jay knew that autumn had finally wrestled time from summer's warm grasp. Dampness hung in the air like a wet bed sheet, clinging to the leaden leaves and smothering the grass in a heavy curtain of dew. Across the lake the pale sun hung low on the hills and burned behind the dense mist like a dying ember buried in ashes. As he slipped into the hot tub, watching the steamy vapors rise against the willows on the bank, he felt keenly the gaping hole of her absence and, to a lesser degree, his own simple aloneness. Though he found some respite in the thought that he and Phil would soon be joining her in a week, nevertheless he was missing her now. Succumbing to the heat, he sunk down until all but his face was covered and looked up at the overhead limbs of the great cedar, hanging protectively above the spa....*wonder what she's doing right now...*

Although he couldn't imagine, as the possibilities were too vast, he knew she was probably very excited and taking it all in, in her quietly observant way. "I'm a people-watcher," she had once told him and he had seen that she was indeed, in a subtle unobtrusive manner that rendered her almost invisible to those she observed, in the most formal or informal of situations. It was a method that confounded him and one that he could never quite hope to emulate. Some unfathomable combination of her directness and humility gave her the ability to study or spy upon others, or even stare at them openly, without their seemingly noticing or caring, or at least feeling threatened, and all the while drawing perceptive conclusions about them. He was sure she was having an eye-opening time in time in Vienna, that fabled old queen of grand European capitals, not to mention the numerous nationalities and sleek cosmopolitan types swarming about her luxurious hotel.

With a slight smile above the water he recalled the moment he had introduced her to Leroy, his newly found psychic, just before her departure. She had been anxious about the trip. Could she hold her own with all those seasoned, sophisticated world travelers of the business? And he had wanted to allay her fears. "Talk to him," he had said. "What do you have to lose?" He knew from experience that whatever Leroy said to her would be positive and helpful, however little or much. She had taken the phone with a little pixie grin on her face, curious to speak with him for the first time and wondering what lay in store for her. By the end of their chat she had been so pleased, it had warmed Jay's heart to see her confidence grow and when she had handed him the phone for his turn he had felt doubly grateful to Leroy for the help. Sinking another inch deeper in the tub Jay sighed in relaxation, and searched his mind, recalling the taped conversation that they'd had then.

"Thanks for sharing with Bea."

"My pleasure."

"Well," Jay started, feeling pressed for time, as Leroy charged by the hour, "my circumstances and issues are basically still the same. I've listened to our tapes over the last few weeks and I enjoy them but nothing much has happened yet in my life."

"It will. You see, the bottom line is that there is always the momentum of life. There is always that going on. At the level of specific individuality there are two things that go on: one is success, that sense of striding through life, and the other is suspense, when the stride isn't going on and something else is happening. Movement or success has been suspended.

"Now this experience of suspense is horrifying to the ego, and what you have to learn, more than anything, is how to be at peace in suspense while the movement of success – that experience of hitting the mark time and time again – is gone. And what happens in suspense, you see, is that there's always a shifting of direction and the old movement of success that was relatively satisfying cannot bring about anything that is being desired.

"Now let's say, for example, that you are desiring a new house and there's nothing in your life, even though it is successful, that would allow that to be, based upon what is going on in the movement. Then once that desire becomes embedded or anchored within you, there will be a cessation of the movement of success and there will be suspense. Now, people will interpret this in a lot of different ways; 'Oh my God, my life's falling apart, nothing's happening, this is a failure', and so on. But if you are able to abide with that without any discomfort, what happens is you will be aimed then in a new direction, when you finally resume the movement again of striding – of being successful – and then that will allow some new good into your life, like a new house, that was not available on the old track. Do you see how this works?"

"I think so," offered Jay tentatively, realizing he'd never thought of it that way.

"It's like if you're going to the store and you suddenly realize you need to go to the bank to get money and the bank is at the other end of the street. You have to turn around and so that forward movement to the store has been suspended.

"Now, because it's occurring in a vaster realm of experience – the overall momentum of life – that time of suspension is not yours to determine. You are not responsible for the length of it. It takes as long as it takes.

"So, if you learn to be comfortable while in suspension, while this big shift is going on, then you will be more firmly placed on the path that allows for remarkable fulfillment without there having been any effort to get there."

"You mean," Jay asked, "periods of inactivity are to be experienced as periods of relative activity, even though they don't seem so?"

"Yes. You have to understand that periods of inactivity are part of the movement of fulfillment, and that being suspended from your old path simply means that you are being placed on a new path, and you can be in these periods of suspense with curiosity but not with apprehension. You see, the ego is in fear, if it's not feeling that movement of success, that it's going to get caught, that something bad will happen, like it has to keep busy in order to stay alive. But being in suspense peacefully requires you give up the ego, so that when these periods of suspense come along and you struggle with them, as you are doing now, what you need to do instead is understand that you are perfectly safe, you're perfectly supported…but that you do have to allow yourself to be in that place comfortably.

"And then the movement starts up whenever it does again, but never during the time of suspension are you depleted of anything but ego. Your worldly goods, anything that you need to have, are not taken from you, just ego…and ultimately, when you're awake, these periods of being in suspense are seen as wonderful moments. There is no apprehension at all in them."

"Hmmm…" Jay had intoned, letting it sink in.… *could it truly be this way or was it too good to be true…*

Lost in the memory, he relaxed a little too much and the searing chlorine waters seeped into his nose, unpleasantly cleansing his nostrils and throat, while bringing him back to the reality at hand. With a snort he sat up, clearing his passage, and noticed the sun had gained height and brightness, piercing the mist with a velvet tangerine glow. He rubbed his eyes gently and laid his head back on the tub sill, then reached over and punched in the button for the turbo-jets. As the bubbles spurted out in explosive unison against his back, he collapsed his upper body against the tub side, stretched his feet diagonally across to the other seat, and released what residual tension was left in his muscles....*ahhhh...what a feeling...what a place...how did i ever find this paradise...*

Gazing at the steam curling lazily off the swirling water, he felt such pleasure and gratitude that he momentarily lost touch with the acute sense of missing Bea and his thoughts floated back, as freely as the rising vapors, like a balloon let go, to the time, fourteen years ago, that bore the answer to his question.....*we were on a search for the new world... visiting friends who had moved here from california...lightheartedly curious to see if we too might do so ourselves...i had only one insistent desire, stated many times – it must be on water...it was a golden august day like southern cal never saw and the blue skies beckoned truly over forests breathing green birdsong...a friend of a friend knew a realtor who knew and we were set to begin seeking for our little piece of eden...just before leaving i spontaneously said i must use the bathroom...locking the door behind me i sat on the closed lid of the toilet seat to pray... where do you want me, God, where do you want me...i asked as sincerely as my soul could muster and feeling i had communicated my desire to be divinely guided, left to be led into the mystery of the day...we visited three properties...none of them moving, none of them right... and i can see them all now though i don't know where they are...then suddenly, inexplicably we were lost...lost...down a dead-end street...and the realtor didn't know... but there, on the right, as we made our way back, was a house for sale that we had missed going by...and the realtor thought maybe cottage lake was on the far side of it...let's take a look...walking in blissful ignorance up the long narrow drive...nearing the faded avocado green cottage... the realtor exclaimed in jubilation "that's cottage lake"... circling the house like hawks on a hunt we scampered up steps and pounced on the lakeside deck, turning to feast our eyes on aquamarine splendor...glistening patterns of tall pine trees and puffy clouds were perfectly reflected...dazzling our senses with unbeknown delight and untold possibilities...our bright eyes locked in suspended animation...questioning, wondering, feeling, knowing..."let's buy it" i said, without a second thought..."alright" she smiled back...and the future was born...and the message was never forgotten by us both...the realtor became lost while God was showing us the way...*

The memory reminded him of the security he had felt then, when it seemed his life kept falling into place, no matter whatever demands arose. It had truly felt as though God was with him. How had he lost the thread? Could he get it back?

Chapter 17

"Because God's sons have everything, they cannot compete." (A Course in Miracles)

CRUISING ABOVE THE MOONLIT field of quilted clouds, Bea awoke slowly to the same muffled vibrating roar of the aircraft that had put her to sleep hours ago. She yawned, extending her arms into the aisle and stretched her body over the three hard-cushioned seats serving as her cramped makeshift bed. Then she leaned to the window, slid up the blind and slowly took in the endless blanket of white dimpled mist floating eerily below and stretching beyond. As her mind fluttered back into full consciousness, she pulled back to her seat and a tingle of excitement arose in her chest....*oh my God, it's really happening...wonder how long till we land*...She felt nervous but excited, like a schoolgirl on her first date, and was anticipating, with a touch of apprehension, something grand and glorious ahead. Such optimism was a basic part of her make-up, and had served her well not only in business but life in general.

In high school, in Ohio, where she'd been ardent in activities, she had also been awarded a well-deserved Most Popular Student designation by election of her peers. She liked people, found them interesting, men and women equally, and they found it easy to return the sentiment. If this conference was to be a party, as Leroy had suggested, then so be it, because she could party with the best of them, as long as, that is, they didn't stay up too late. Leroy had made it sound like this was going to be more of a social event than a business one, but she knew the most enjoyable way to conduct business was when mixing it with pleasure, and she was game for both. Here was her chance, her biggest chance yet, to expand her company in the international arena, and her desire for growth, which had always been restrained, was piqued and fomenting, like a shaken bottle of soda, fizzling under its cap.

TING! "We are about to begin our approach to Vienna," came the Captain's sharp announcement over the crackling loudspeakers. The shock of the declaration at such deafening volume cut into her thoughts like an unseen bolt of lightning, sending a wave of heightened realization through her.... *almost there!*..."Please return to your seat if you have not already done so." Bea struggled to a sitting position, shaking off the residue of sleepiness like a wet dog shaking dry, and fumbled around for her seat-belt. Snapping the buckle locked across her waist, she sat back, adjusting to the stiff contours of the chair, and felt restful, slightly dazed, but attentive and poised. Her thoughts returned to her conversation with Leroy – hopefully prophetic – about the event.

"Good morning," she said, pleasantly.

"I understand you're flying to Europe today," Leroy sprightly spoke.

"I am," came the happy rejoinder.

"How wonderful."

"I know. I'm excited. I'm going to a business conference...and maybe would just ask if there is any thing I should know...or watch out for...or..."

Leroy jumped in, "Look, have it be easy. Don't anticipate there being any difficulty... umm...have it be unpredictable but eminently successful. Go there as though this were going to be a delightful surprise that didn't require any strategy or skill on your part...that didn't require any particular effort on your part except to be fully present with the experience and to trust how you respond to what's going on as being part of the fabric of the event."

"Great advice."

"And so it'll be fun," continued Leroy, "and it'll be like...it's like...the image is like a champagne cork going off...there's a kind of a sense of explosion about it and it's fun...a fun kind of popping...and it'll be different than what people are anticipating. It'll have some real thrust and energy...and people will abandon...umm...kind of, the littleness of their own lives for a bit."

"Hmmm," Bea chuckled, "uhmm...I'm going to room with a friend who's a competitor and I'm wondering if it's alright to trust her."

"No, of course not," said Leroy emphatically, as Bea laughed aloud with surprise.

"Of course not?" she repeated incredulously, amused.

"That's not necessary," said Leroy flatly. "It means that you get to play the game as though you were playing cards. You could play poker with a friend. Do you show your hand?"

"Very good," mused Bea, her voice softening with appreciation.

"You see, of course you don't trust her. It has nothing to do with you as a friend. Do you see what I'm saying?"

"Yeah, I just have trouble separating the two."

"Umm…wish her well. I mean, look, there has to be some sense that there's enough to go around anyway…that everybody gets exactly what they desire and need anyway. The ego's suggestion that it's not enough to succeed – all others must fail – doesn't have to be a part of it. You can have exactly what you desire and it may be that it does not impose any limit on anyone else's fulfillment. That's what I'm talking about when I say this can be done in a way which is startlingly satisfying."

"Yes, yes, I understand," said Bea. "Are there any particular countries I should pay attention to while there?"

"Ummm…I'm getting strong on Spain, a very vivid sense…ummm…there's a lot to be open to.…I don't see anything not to look at. It'll all be out on the table like a buffet, and you can't load everything on your plate, but you'll get what you want."

She had hoped he was right and felt that he was. To her such a high-minded outlook was always right, sooner or later, but was so easily forgotten in the apparent need for secrecy and aggressiveness in the competitive climate of business. She was glad Jay was talking with him, so reminiscent of Saul, and so good to be reminded again of the spiritual nature of life, despite all the appearances and thoughts to the contrary. Closing her eyes she took a deep breath and felt almost smug at her soon-to-be good fortune.…*what could be bad…*In quick response her mind spun back, like an automatic rolodex whirring away, and clicked into place, stopping smoothly at Toronto.…*ugh… almost forgot…troubles with perry…*

There it was, once again, that nettling nub of anxiety, threatening to break into a full-blown attack. To hire and fire or to trust and retrain; that was the question. Was it nobler in the mind to suffer the risk of disaster at the hands of a once-trusted employee? She wished she had discussed the matter with Leroy. Though she was plugging along in her own fashion, heeding the advice of her own inner counsel, it would have been helpful to hear his spiritual perspective above the din of everyone else's opinion. She knew what everyone else thought about it.

TING! "We are landing in Vienna in approximately five minutes," blared the speakers. "Please make sure your seatbelt is fastened, your seat is up all the way up, and your tray table returned to its normal position. Thank you."

Startled, she opened her eyes blinkingly and laughed for a second out loud, as she often did when surprised.…*vienna!…*No thought of Toronto nor anywhere else could subsume the rising tide of joyful expectancy that immediately bubbled to the surface of her consciousness and flooded her entire being.…*oh well…that's then and this is now…*and she let Toronto go in an inescapable fit of glee, like a playful puppy chasing a bouncing ball, oblivious to everything but the moment. Glancing at the watch she'd forgotten she was wearing, as it had only been donned for this special occasion, she noticed with satisfaction that the flight was on schedule and translated the hour into the time at her house.…*hmm…sunday morning back home…wonder what jay's doing right now…*

Chapter 18

"I cannot manage more than two hours a day without calling on Friend Marsala for help. He deludes me into thinking things are really not so bleak as they appear to me when sober." (Sigmund Freud, in letter to a colleague)

AFTER BOARDING THE PLANE, Jay slid the carry-on bag under the seat in front of him. It was a tight squeeze given that it was over-stuffed with snacks, books, games, and tapes to divert from the monotony of the long flight to Vienna. Turning to see that Phil was comfortable, he watched him squirm his legs up onto the cushion, slip some headphones over his ears, and begin bobbing to and fro to the beguiling beat of the music from the cassette player in his hand...*he knows just what to do...why wait until you're bored*...It pleased him to see Phil turn to the music so easily and was amused that he knew exactly what he liked – the Beach Boys! Such an innocent choice, and with so much trash on the airwaves now, especially rap and heavy metal crap, he was more than glad to load up on as many tapes as possible of this merry band of harmonious surfers. He could barely hear the song, but it was catchy and made slightly more audible by Phil singing along under his breath...*let's go surfin' now, everybody's learning how, c'mon' a surfari with me, boom-boom-boom*...

Listening to the upbeat tune brought back a tumult of teenage memories and he drifted unknowingly into nostalgia remembering the strains of "Little Surfer Girl" as the aircraft rumbled down the runway and soared away....*early summer '64...school not quite out yet...newport...with christine on the beach... transistor radio...little surfer...late in the evening…little one…waves crashing in the background…make my heart come all undone… kissing and touching…do you love me…big terrycloth beach towel…do you, surfer girl…soft crunchy sand…surfer girl…still day-glow warm…my little surfer girl…she kissed like love…i have seen you…his first french kisses…on the shore…ahhh the catholic all-girls' school … standing by the ocean's roar…thank you st. mary…do you love me…hormones pulsating all day…do you, surfer girl…waiting for the weekend and a boy…surfer girl…you're arousing my passions, she had teasingly said as he gently stroked her neck between his thumb and forefinger…my little surfer girl…*

"I'm hungry," piped up a thin voice beside him, jolting him back from his reverie while quickening his sense of paternal care. "What do we have to eat?"

"How 'bout some chips?" Jay offered amiably, as he reached down to the floor and tugged them free from the bag.

"Okay," nodded Phil. "Is there anything to drink?"

They waylaid a stewardess who seemed only too happy to comply with his request. Children, Jay observed, often merited special attention on an airplane. He wondered if it was because they touched the inner child of the crew members serving them amid the awesome and wondrous spectacle of hurtling miles above the earth in a huge metal hulk in which all of the adults were seemingly indifferent. Or perhaps it was simply that they were nice little kids.

"We'll be serving beverages soon," she explained, while handing him a coke, "but you can have this now, sweetie."

In a moment's time Phil was again firmly ensconced in listening and moving to the undulating rhythms, aided now by caffeine and sugar, of the west coast teen kings in Brian Wilson's music land, being true to his school, letting his colors fly. Seeing the coast was clear, for at least a little while, Jay reluctantly ordered a beer. His reluctance stemmed from the troublesome fact that it was, first, in a can, an odious affront to his sense of refinement and purity – he was absolutely certain it maligned the taste – and secondly, that it was a commercial-brand domestic lager, neither an import nor a micro-brew. He disdained substandard beers and avoided them like taxes. To assuage his taste buds and make the best of things, he lifted some lime slices from a passing steward's tray to mellow his ale in a plastic cup. He downed it quickly.…*oh what the hell…it's a long ride…*and ordered another. Then he adjusted his seat back to relax.

"Dad?"

"Yes?"

"I have to go to the bathroom now."

"Okay, do you know where it is?"

"Yeah, I saw on the way in." He started to move.

"Wait. Better leave your tape here. It's a small space in there."

"Oh, yeah."

Phil squeezed his slender frame through the opening and was off down the aisle, checking out the other passengers with shy and serious wide-eyed glances as he passed by each row. Just as Jay started to stretch out he was back again, looking perplexed.

"The line's too long."

"Can you wait?" wondered Jay, pensively rubbing his short reddish beard.

"Yeah," he assented, and squeezed back into the row, stepping on Jay's foot.

"Oops, sorry, Dad."

"That's okay." He could see it was shaping up to be a long and restless trip.

Climbing into his seat, Phil resumed his former activity, entranced in the melody and the throbbing surf beat. In shifting positions to regain a comfortable spot, Jay was accidentally elbowed and while moving to accommodate his restive young son, he overheard once again the recurrent strains of the spirited surfers, singing about something in sunny Mexico, and was immediately reminded of the whereabouts of his oldest one.

He thankfully knew that he was now alive and well in sunny San Diego, as they had received a welcomed call on their answer machine one night while out to dinner. Jess had forgotten unfortunately to leave the return number, but no matter, he was safe and sound, back in the arms of America. Pulling off the pop-top of his second beer he wondered what the budding traveler, twenty-four years old, would be doing next. He was a new grad with no job yet on the horizon. To Jay the fact that he had majored in Spanish seemed to limit his job prospects somewhat, but the boy was undeterred and optimistic. He was also optimistic about his college girlfriend, to whom he was devoted, but Jay wasn't sure she was the right one for him.

She was sweet and sensitive, for what that was worth, and would probably cross the street to avoid stepping on an insect. But they had begun dating with Jess on the rebound from a previous girlfriend who has proven untrustworthy. It had been an eye-opening heart-breaking affair for a sincere lad who was incapable of such duplicity himself. Jay knew enough from years of marriage counseling how a rebound romance could make for a rocky new foundation.

Furthermore he wondered if she was robustly spirited enough for the young man. He was a true gentle giant but suffused with intensity, boundless energy, and a high-powered wanderlust that fueled his imagination. He was no desk-jockey, not a stationary creature, being always on the move even as a young child. It seemed to Jay that foretold much about his preferences and destiny in choosing a career and a mate. He sighed philosophically....*ah well...time will tell...not my decision*...and took a reflective sip from his cup of the insipid brine that passed for a beer. Breathing deeply, he stretched his neck side-to-side, relaxed again into the tough love of his seat, and listened to a faint but familiar melody. It was a tiny but unmistakable echo of the past, emanating dimly from the seat next to him; a meandering chorus floating by on sweet waves of sound from Phil's youthful lips....*I wish they all could be California, I wish they all could be California, I wish they all could be California girls...*

Chapter 19

"And happily I have arrived at the last
Unto the wished haven of my bliss." (William Shakespeare)

A T THE AIRPORT IN Vienna, outside Customs, an erstwhile California girl was waiting impatiently in anticipation for her Seattle boys. She was happy and chomping at the bit for their arrival. Sitting in a black leather seat near the door Bea's wait was made easier by her exultant state of mind over the past week's events. Leroy had been right – the conference was a party, a champagne party – and nothing like she had ever seen before. The gala international flavor of it all had been overwhelming in European excesses, from an indoor bungee jump station above a huge pool to an elegant ballroom dining and dance fest right out of Louis XIV's court. At night, in lively parties throughout the hotel, business contacts and deals were made between different countrymen, eager to advance and profit from the growing student exchange market.

Even late into the early morning, long after Bea and most others had called it a night, a few chain-smoking scotch-drinking agents were still knotted together by enterprising schemes, building their empires, networking their dreams. Bea felt uncomfortable around such agents, or "sharks" as she called them, hard-nosed polished businessmen from Europe, Asia, or the States. They were more in it for the money than the student, she thought, and tough negotiators, untrustworthy or both. But while the conference had opened her eyes to the competition of bigger firms, it had strengthened her resolve to stay small all the more, and she had managed there to connect with several excellent business prospects.

The dapper old gentleman from Spain, crippled but warmly charming, with a shiny gnarled cane and a younger female companion to assist him, seemed promising for future projects. A Frenchman, less warm, but also quite charming, had reviewed her prices and seemed sincerely interested in working together. There were other possibilities as well and as soon as she returned to the office she expected to be up to her eyeballs churning price quotes out for different programs in different countries, just as she had hoped. Yes, Leroy had been right; it was indeed a party and there was indeed enough business for all. Only one little thing that he hadn't mentioned, quite probably because she hadn't either: Kazuo.

She had known he might be there but had hoped that he wouldn't. Looking back on it now that seemed foolish and naïve, a form of denial. Of course he would be there. Everyone else in the business was there, trying to network as much as they could. It happened the third day, in the lunch buffet line, where she had sensed someone, dark hair in a dark suit, was staring at her from across the room. As it wasn't uncommon for a blonde woman to be noticed at a gathering of mostly men, she hadn't thought the stare unusual and ignored it while perusing the fare as her appetite grew with each passing dish. Holding a platter of pasta salad she made her way to the nearest seat, carefully weaving amongst fellow diners. A few steps from the chair while still feeling the sense of someone's eyes locked upon her, she casually returned the look to her left, about fifty feet away, and was so shocked by the hateful glare in his eyes that she stepped away to the right and bumped the back of a sitting man's head with her plate, leaving bits of clotted cream sauce, barely noticeable, on his close-cropped black hair.

She apologized profusely, feeling shaken and embarrassed and walked on quickly to the closest chair facing away from Kazuo. She ate with her back to him, neck hairs twittering on edge the entire time, and wondering nervously if he would approach her. Although he did not, and she did not see him again that week, she was aware of his haunting presence each day and night. Perhaps he had left the show before it ended that week, for on the fifth day an unsigned note had been left in her conference mailbox, reading "You will be sorry".

It gave her the shivers now to think of it, but she shook it off, refusing to indulge in it further. He could threaten all he wanted – he was scary – but they were finished and she was off to greener pastures – she hoped. No matter what he did he couldn't stop her now – she hoped. In truth, except for that little incident, the whole conference had been a great success and now she just wanted to play with her boys....*so where the heck are they...*

As they trudged through the Customs line, awaiting release, Jay lifted Phil up in his arms and their droopy eyes sought Bea's shining face through the window, over the heads of the other stooped and straggling passengers. Everyone was tired and tousled, and half-asleep on their feet.

"Hello, boys!" she beamed, as they emerged through the door. "Welcome to Vienna." Flushed with enthusiasm, her smile was an inviting welcome and they both hugged her heartily at the same time, as she embraced one in each arm.

"Hi mom."

"Hi sweetie. Was the flight okay?"

"Hello sweetheart," said Jay in a tired voice.

"Sure," said Phil, who had slept most the way under his father's watchful eye. Jay paused a moment.

"Well, it was long, honey," he smiled at her weakly, hoping that he looked better than he felt, "but it was okay, and I'm glad to be here now."

As they lumbered off in the direction of the car, shouldering their bags, lugging their suitcases, Bea understood the disorientation of her flight-weary family, having felt it herself a week previously, and was quiet to allow them time to find their bearings. Though exhausted and depleted, they were curious and excited, plus ravenously hungry. As they peered about the terminal through half-closed eyelids, Jay was summoning an appetite for a moveable feast of fine continental cuisine; fettuccini Alfredo, quiche Lorraine, or any epicurean delight the chef felt moved to prepare. Just some magnificent morsels, perhaps truffles for example, though chanterelles would do, to pacify the pallet, satiate the stomach and soothe the soul, before he passed out on their European bed in their Viennese room. Oh, and of course, it went without saying, a lovely wine, definitely a Bordeaux or other fine old red, ruby rose petal soft aromatic, a silken splash in the glass, a wet stream on the tongue, aged tannins and the like, oaky, smoky, languorously leading to a very deep sleep. A quick unloading of the bags in the room and – voila! – off to see the wine steward and maitre'd. He flopped down in the front passenger seat of the rented Peugeot, slumped slightly against the door and nurtured his tired body with the succulent promises of his mind's imagined meal, fine dining in the Old World.

"I'm starving," whined Phil. "Do they have a McDonald's?"

Chapter 20

"Can you imagine what it means to have no cares, no worries, no anxieties, but merely to be perfectly calm and quiet all the time?" (A Course in Miracles)

OUTSIDE THE OFFICE WINDOW a stiff autumn breeze raked the second story glass with scrawny bare branches, scratching like fingernails, as though they wanted in. Standing with his arms crossed Jay surveyed the wind-whipped landscape, watching the leaves fly about like wayward gusts of brown butterflies. He was listening intently to a taped recording of his last talk with Leroy, whom he was starting to speak with one hour a week.

"When are you going to Europe?"

"Sunday."

"Oh, wonderful."

"I was just going to ask you if there is anything I should be aware of about that?"

"Ha, ha, ha, mmmm, don't take your life with you. Leave it all here."

"Oh good."

"Go enjoy yourself. Vacations are always a time for renewal and so that will be the best focus for you to have there…but I see it will be a nice trip, and you'll come back with a real new focus it seems, a real sense of shift."

"Oh, that's good. Sometimes I feel like I'm shifting a little more. It feels like shifting into nothing but feeling good."

"Well, but that is the most important thing. That has to be the basis in which everything else unfolds. We've talked about being at peace while in suspense, and there is a word for that, and the word is luxury."

"Hmmmm."

"The consciousness of luxury is always both suspenseful and peaceful. It's suspenseful in that it is not grounded in a place. It has no relative grounding and yet it's not filled with apprehension. It's filled with peace, and it is luxury, and it is the foundation for experiences and activities that identify luxury in your life. So if you can stay in that place while things don't appear to be going on, but be at peace with it, you'll find that when things do move they move in an effortless and thriving way.

"Interestingly, this is why people take drugs: to experience peace and suspense at the same time. It's called getting high. Getting high is the experience of luxury. Ironically all sorts of people, who have yachts and Mercedes and huge bank accounts and mansions, take drugs…because the stuff doesn't provide the experience of luxury…but neither do the drugs ultimately."

"Right."

"And so it is something that happens by recognizing the opportunity that presents itself right now to be at peace right where you are. You can imagine yourself sort of suspended and floating around and that if anything is required you barely have to reach out for it and it's floating by on a tray…and you can just pick it off…take it…and that's how you have to stay."

"Living off the lay of the land?"

"Yes, that is the lay of the land, and what this does, what makes this easy, and what will make doing this easier, is if you understand that luxury is always the absence of the experience of time."

"Hmm."

"There is no time in luxury, and so when you find yourself in reaction to something, being apprehended, it's usually time that's apprehended you. So if you're in that place of peace and suspense then suddenly you're not there, some consideration of time has been injected into the situation and when you recognize that, you can then let it go. You can dismiss it or have it taken from you and go back to that place again.

"So you'll have a lot of – ha, ha, here I use the word time – to practice this while you are in Europe."

"Timelessness?"

"Timelessness. There will be a lot of opportunity to practice not being pressured and not having to force clarity and have answers to questions that the mind keeps making up."

"Hmmmm…that sounds good."

"Yes."

"So you think that if I increase my focus on this way of being – which frankly I find hard to do right now – that I will have a sense of rejuvenation, and that my fortunes will be better?"

"It's inevitable actually. You will find yourself more and more unwilling to move from this bliss, this peace, this luxury, and everything will look like a manifestation of luxury. There will not be any sense of exclusion around any particular possibility that may occur to you as desirable. And what I'm saying to you is, that if you were in this place of bliss, of suspense, of peace, and there was a clear desire for something to be experienced and it was typically beyond your means, being where you are in that place would allow it to unfold nevertheless. There would be no need to consider the constraints of the world. It can happen, and the timing and sequence of steps would be perfectly formed by the Infinite so it would seem ultimately to make some sort of sense to the human mind, but it would be beyond the human mind to engineer it. Do you see what I'm saying?"

"Sort of."

"What I'm getting at is when you are in that place, you feel your desires, they will happen. And there's no requirement for you to know how that's going to be."

"Hmm…okay."

"So you need to see yourself as being supported, and being safe in this place. You've got all the sustenance that you need. Forever. You never have to do another thing to be provided for. That is your provision forever, right there, and this is going to take all the struggle out of your bread winning, because the bread will just be a gift."

"Well, that sounds good. That fits in with my fondest dreams.;"

"Uh-huh. With the emphasis on fond, not dream. It won't seem like a dream when you are actually experiencing this place."

"Hmm…uhhh…okay…look…I'm probably going to have an interview to try to get into this Ph.D. program when I return, if they call me, and I have some apprehension around that, and I wondered if you have any feeling for my prospects of gaining entrance to the school and getting a Ph.D. and all of that tying into my need to make money. I don't want to have to wait that long to make money."

"Going for a Ph.D. program to make money is not worth doing. If there is no greater motivation or intent beyond that then it is not worth doing, and it won't happen either. I can already tell you there is enough movement, enough integrity, enough clarity in your Being to steer you away from attempting to establish yourself in some extraneous or superfluous way at this point.

"Now, I'm not going to entirely douse this. I am going to suggest that you reflect on the other aspects of this desire or intent and see if there is anything there that feels meaningful beyond it being a means to more income. I'll tell you something: even if you managed to get yourself into it and there wasn't a lot of desire for it – it would simply seem to be a practical step – then the curriculum itself might turn you off. You might see it as a little antiquated and you would perhaps wonder why more and more you were investing time and energy into this particular endeavor.

"So what I want you to do is to have no particular apprehension or concern around it. If you feel energy to apply and move forward with this then certainly do so and if it becomes something that you are experiencing because it is easy to experience and seemed to be happening with great ease, then fine, that'll be how you know it's the thing to do; if it is absolutely without struggle. But if it's something that's just like climbing a wall, take that to be significant that now is not an appropriate time to pursue this. You see, it is far more important for you to engage in the consciousness of luxury as I expressed it to you, so that you can start having more right now, without going through some process that ultimately is simply to justify having more."

"Hmmm."

"If you go to Europe and practice this – practice it every day – feeling just suspended and at peace, and recognizing the peace of it, you're going to find things coming to you anyway. And you won't feel that you have to move from this place, this position of being suspended, to look for the new challenge. You'll be able to live without having to have challenges constantly, because, after all, the greatest challenge anyone is going to experience is being right where you are right now, in that place of being suspended, and indeed learning to be at peace with it. There is no greater challenge than that, and once that is mastered, everything else is perfectly easy."

"Well...that sounds good."

"Yes...I'm not trying to discourage you from this Ph.D. program. I just want to make it not particularly consequential."

"Yeah...I don't feel discouraged."

"Good. It's not my M.O. to discourage, ha ha ha."

"No. I think I got the point."

A good place to stop thought Jay, as the clock neared his counseling appointment. These talks were helpful to hear again and now it was time for him to help others. He punched out the cassette and rummaged through his mind at the line-up of clients awaiting him. Today he was especially intrigued about meeting a man whose wife he'd met last week. She was a highly charged and changeable mixture of fragile sadness and touchy anger, desperate to save what felt like a sinking marriage. Her husband was a successful Jewish businessman, originally from upstate New York. He was an independent sales rep, always on the go, who was out of town more often than not, and when he was home showed more interest in their two little girls than in his wife, according to her and much to her consternation.

Jay listened to her story, observing her ventilate up and down the emotional scale, similar to the tortured wind blowing outside. She was a big raw-boned young woman, with a hurting no-nonsense look in her eye, a suburban horse owner, pretty and tough, a former farm girl turned well-off soccer mom, who felt like an abandoned single parent. Though seemingly intelligent, she was not college educated, and, half-complaining half-bragging, described her husband as brainy and a fast-talker.

"Howie will run rings around you!" she had warned, in response to Jay's request to meet with him. "He'll have an answer for everything. He's so smart he reads Moby Dick backwards."

"Okay," Jay had replied. He felt confident but curious. "We'll see."

Upon meeting Howie in the lobby, Jay was struck by the difference between him and his wife. Though equally tall, his stature was slight and less menacing, with none of the woman's muscular roughness. While she had worn expensive dirty cowgirl boots, he had on an expensive clean gray pin striped suit. He had a detached though friendly, almost intellectual manner, his smile revealing an impish sense of humor on a round face with a broad forehead with black thinning hair. As they settled into the session it became apparent to Jay that any trust would take awhile to develop. He didn't want to be there at all and resented his wife's pressure to come. Though Howie was verbal, it was in his defense.

He was working hard to support his family and didn't have time for meetings like this. He wasn't really the problem anyway. It was Sharon, his wife. She was just too demanding. He was willing to talk now, begrudgingly, but he handled his stress with meditation, being a disciple of the Maharishi Mahesh Yogi and wished his mate would learn to do the same. Perhaps it would help to talk just this once but he didn't really think they needed counseling. She just needed to lighten up. It was a cold hard jungle out there in the business world. She wasn't working, had two horses, some acreage and both kids enrolled in private schools. How about some appreciation?

Jay listened intently as he normally did to the man's plaintive tale, knowing there were always two sides to the pain and that he must see both to help them as a couple. When he started probing deeper with questions on the past and present, Howie's answers seemed reasonable and invariably witty, implying there wasn't much there to take seriously. Jay took such messages as a bright red flag, and as the hour progressed, the quips and complaints felt increasingly like a playful game of hide and seek.

His wife had spent her session alternately ranting and whimpering about her husband's faults, and now, though he had presumably come at her bidding, he too seemed focused on only her shortcomings. Although his viewpoint was a valid one too, if he kept on this way, the session would end without getting much beneath the surface; not uncommon with highly verbal new clients. They could waste the session talking away, trying to burn off anxiety or stave off depression, chattering right past the silent peace that they sought. It was even worse in a situation like this where the client really didn't want to be there in the first place. Jay let him finish his anecdote….*better be direct…*

"So then Sharon says, 'if you're getting a new car, I want a new barn'. And that," whined Howie in exaggerated exasperation, "is what it's always like with her." He grinned, shrugged, held his palms out, and shook his head, acting like the butt of his own Jewish joke. "I can't win."

Jay nodded, half-smiled, cleared his throat, paused for timing and then spoke in a slightly more serious tone, hoping to convey, that after hearing so much, he'd reached a point where it was time for a significant comment, like it or not.

"Your wife is afraid you're not very committed to the relationship." Howie jerked upright like a puppet on a string. His high-pitched voice rose in protest.

"I'm so committed I'd kill for us!"...*bingo...that got his attention...*

"That may be true, but if so, I wonder why she doesn't see that."

"I'm busting my balls for us to make it," his tone escalated with fierce indignation, "while she spends money like it's going out of style. And she doesn't even – she doesn't even contribute one solitary cent." He stopped briefly, glancing about as if for a soapbox, then stammered on excitedly in his shrill New York accent, sitting up higher. "When I'm home," he was outraged now, "when I'm home, I am so exhausted that all I want to do is rest. But noooo. She's got a million projects to do, resents my time with the kids, and wants to have sex all the time."

"All the time?" Jay's eyebrows lifted.

"Yes! All the time. Every night. If not – there's hell to pay."

"Some men would kill for your situation," teased Jay.

"I know," he admitted, appreciating the humor, "but instead they'd die of heat exhaustion, because she's always in heat! She's driving me crazy!"

He slumped back in the cushioned chair, temporarily spent, feeling partly better for getting it out and partly worse for bringing it up. He looked at Jay with greater openness and fear at the same time. Jay leaned back, met his look, and nodded with acknowledgement at his predicament. He rubbed his bearded chin thoughtfully. Feeling empowered by their growing rapport, he wanted to ask the one thing that had increasingly gnawed at his awareness throughout the hour.

"Are you gay?"

"What?"

"Are you gay?"

He looked incredulous, then mildly flustered, as the trace of a guilty smile formed the corners of his thin lips. He looked down, then outside the window and back again, his eyes darting back and forth like a trapped creature. No way out.

"Yeah," he said, lowering his voice. "I think I am." He clasped his hands in his lap, interlocking the fingers as if in prayer, and leaned forward imploringly, his curious eyes widening, wretched, seeking hope.

"Can you help me?"

"I don't know," Jay spoke softly and carefully, "but I'll try." He paused, then went on, very gently in tone, "Perhaps you are bisexual."

"Uhhh, maybe."

"You sound hesitant. You don't think so?"

" I just don't know."

"What does your wife know of this?"

"Absolutely nothing."

"Do you want to stay married?"

"Yes."

"Look, we are almost out of time today. This is hugely complex. You need individual therapy and marriage counseling. You don't have to see me for either or both, but I recommend you see someone soon, and of course your wife urgently wants marriage counseling now. What do you want to do?"

"Sharon will kill me if I don't at least try counseling with her so let's definitely do that." His whole manner had softened to one of cooperation.

"Sooner or later, if you can't resolve this in your self, you'll have to level with her," said Jay. "It's not fair to either of you."

"Yeah, well, I don't even want to imagine what would happen if I did that," groaned Howie. "I want to see you alone for awhile and do the counseling with Sharon. Maybe we can get somewhere on both fronts," he laughed nervously, sweating the pressure in anticipation.

Jay sized him up reflectively, so many thoughts swirling.

"Are you having a homosexual relationship with anyone now?"

"Not exactly," squirmed Howie.

"What's that mean?"

"Uhh…occasionally on trips I have these out of town encounters"…*oh Jesus the plot thickens*…

"I see. How often?"

"Uhh…well, every so often."

"And how long has this been going on?"

"Uhh…the feelings or the actions?"

"Both."

"A long time."

"Okay, I see. We better get into it all next session, when we really have the time. How about same time next week?"

"I'm outa' town next week."

Jay cocked his eyebrow in mild suspicion. "Really?" he asked. "And will you have one of your encounters then?"

"Uhh…I don't know. I'm gonna' try not to," said Howie tentatively, "but"… his voice became more authoritative with its faintly nasal east coast twang…"I'll see ya' in two weeks." He pulled out his little black book from inside his suit coat and made a notation in it. "Trust me."

Chapter 21

"Do a thing, and if it is right the money will come in." (*Jiddu Krishnamurti*)

THE LATE AFTERNOON CLOUDS, blowing slowly over the lake, gradually evolved into early evening rain. A windswept net of watery dots on the surface rose up to meet the showering drops like goose bumps rippling over soft skin in a breeze. As the gathering gray grew darker outside, Bea switched on her desk lamp and continued writing a fax to Toronto. She was informing Perry of the points to be discussed in their upcoming meeting there. He had not yet returned her call from yesterday and was frequently hard to reach, being busy with his church and family activities. At last she hoped to settle unaccounted-for expenses, put it all behind them, and use what was learned for a better season next year. Perhaps it had been a mistake to grant him check-writing privileges on the account, but as she had said to Candy more often than she had cared to, if you couldn't trust a Sunday school teacher who could you trust? Candy's opinion of men was so low as to be useless and made Bea wonder if the embittered secretary would ever find another mate or even get along with any man who worked with them. At present her crush on Randy the handyman was relatively new and untested by time. Bea let those thoughts pass and returned to her own issues.

Ever since Vienna she had felt more confident and expansive in her work. She wanted to solve the lingering problems in Canada and move on to new ideas, plans and actions. At the conference she had seen a brochure from an East Coast company, offering Christmas Homestays with American families to foreign students who would otherwise be spending their holidays alone in cold college dorms devoid of yuletide spirit. It had impressed her as a great way to start working with college students. Her instincts sensed a winning opportunity – why not do the same thing on the West Coast – and having no time herself for such a venture, she knew exactly the right person to tap for the job – her husband – if only he'd give it a chance.

It was a perfect fit for him, as far as her business went. He could run the whole operation himself as a branch of her company, truly making it their company while functioning, as he liked it, independently as his own boss. He could still keep counseling, perhaps a few days a week, or work the hours in flexibly somehow. He would be dealing with universities, those hallowed institutions that he hailed as cultural isles in the dead sea of society and in which he had spent nearly a decade of his life. He could converse with humanistic-minded academics rather than the businessmen with whom he felt nothing in common and never have to leave home to do it. The back room in their bottom floor where they kept supplies and the copier was large enough for him to have his very own office. Because winter break was fast approaching for colleges, the time to start for this season was now and she had decided to unveil her proposal tonight.

If he were willing to try it, she could leave for Toronto relieved and hopeful about harnessing his energies productively to their fortunes and then deal with Perry all the better for it. More importantly she could even look past that sticky task to a promising one beyond it: her reunion with her sisters. She had decided to go. Possibly this time, with their mother gone for good and perhaps their father going soon, they could talk more honestly and listen more openly than they had in awhile. They might gradually undo the tight knots that had strained their bonds for so long, like their mother's gentle brushing of their hair as little girls had separated tangles into smooth flowing strands.

Sitting now at her computer she could hear the cockatiel upstairs suddenly screeching his head off, which meant someone was coming up the driveway. At this hour it was likely Jay home from the office. She wanted to go upstairs and say hello but winced at the thought of leaving her work. She didn't want to miss a return call from Canada. He would probably feel too rushed to come down. At this time of day she knew his routine well; a thirty-minute jog, a quick shower, a Corona with lime, then off to get Phil at school and directly to soccer practice. Hours later she would finally see them both over dinner, that precious and fleeting time without which these days they would rarely meet together in the same room as a family. She knew each of them would wind down their own paths afterward: Phil into his bedroom doing homework to music, phone calls, door closed; Jay brooding in the den at his keyboards, playing or recording, huddled in his headphones with a glass of wine or a pipe, door closed, and she to her office, down in the dungeon, plugging away at never-ending work.

"*rrriiinnnggg*" Her thoughts were interrupted by the home phone, a white cellular, on the far right corner of her overcrowded desk. "Hello," she said, welcoming a break from the day's business calls. "Oh, hello. How's my little seester?" she asked teasingly. "Good…Oh yes, I just bought my tickets. How about you?…Good. Then we're all set."

"*rrriiinnnggg*" The black business phone rang out like a jailbreak. "Can you hold a minute? I'm the only one here and expecting a call….Thanks." Bea set the white phone on her desk and raised the black one to her ear, feeling her anticipation rise with it.

"Homestay Connections. This is Bea. May I help you?…Oh Perry, I was hoping it was you. Thanks for returning my call. I'm on the other line. Just a second and I'll be right back." She punched the hold button and picked up the white phone with her right hand while holding the black one in her left and placed it to her ear. "Sorry, I gotta' go. It's an important call…Of course you're important too…No, I do want to talk with you, but I really need to take this other call right now. It's from Toronto and about the problems I've been having there…Okay…Okay…Yep…Yep…Right…Well, we can discuss that in Pittsburgh…Okay…Okay…Uh, I don't want to get into that right now…Okay…We'll see…I said we'll see…Okay…Sorry. Good-bye."

She placed the home phone quickly back on the receiver, feeling relieved but also unfinished…*jeez*…There were complicated family matters, like the care of their father and the handling of his finances, which were pressing for resolution but they would just have to wait until they could sit down as a threesome. At least they would finally have a chance to do that soon. She punched the hold button on the business line. "Hi, Perry, thanks for holding…I'm fine, and you…Uh-huh…Uh-huh…Uh-huh…Sounds like it's a very busy time for you…Uh-huh…" As she listened to the lengthy convoluted response she could feel herself warming up like a radiator in which her patience was draining like a leak. It was nice to be friendly but right now she didn't really want to hear all the details of how hectic his life was. A simple "I'm busy" would have sufficed. She just needed a few specific questions answered. Groping through some papers she found the small Tums bottle, her daily panacea, and chomped down three colored wafers while continuing to listen. "Uh-huh. Well, listen, I just called because we were going over the receipts here for your expenses and they still don't add up…You do…Oh, that's great…Why didn't you mail them with the rest? Ohhhh…So how long till they're organized?…What else do you have to do?…Well, I'd like to see them when I'm there, so…Good…Yes, but a lot of them are just handwritten receipts and rounded off. I really need the actual receipts if you have them…I see…Okay… Uh-huh…Oh you do?…Bible class?…Okay, well then, I guess you need to run…Thanks for calling back so soon this time…Yes, see you soon…Okay…Goodbye."

She hung up the phone wondering what to make of his predicament…*guess i'll see when i'm…- "rrriiinnnggg"*

Chapter 22

"I dislike everybody." (Lee Harvey Oswald, age 13, to his court-appointed psychiatrist)

THE LIGHT RAIN SPRINKLING on the windshield of the Mercedes as it wove its way slowly and deliberately through thick freeway traffic was not wet enough to move Jay to use his wipers. Lost in deep thought, on mental cruise control, he was hardly aware that it was raining at all. Heading home from a trip to the music store and the pawnshop, he felt as deflated as though rolling downhill on four flat tires. On leaving the office after meeting with Howie, it had started to bother him, as his mind revisited his own pressing problems, that poverty, that is, his own lack of income, was forcing him to sell fifty used CDs from his highly prized collection. Despite that irritation, he had assumed that selling them to the Yuppie's Pawn Shoppe would bring a measure of relief to his imperiled bank account and worried mind. But the money gained was less than expected and the attitude of the young clerk was insufferably condescending....*damn kid...*

Though all the CDs were playable and unscratched, the store would only offer top dollar for unopened ones and Jay had only one like that: the professional sampler put out by a small music company that included one of his band's songs that he himself had composed. It had been a peak experience, the crowning glory of his musical endeavors, and the only CD in the world with his mark upon it. The group had hoped, as did all artists on the sampler, to be noticed by one of the larger record labels, but nothing had ever come of it. The record company had given him five copies of the CD, making one for each band member and two for him, and now he was parting with one of those two in the most mercenary manner. The store didn't know him nor his music nor care and while he would willingly part with it for some bucks he knew they would sell it without ever having heard it to someone else who hadn't ever either. No one cared that it was his special souvenir, his consolation prize, his lonely mark of distinction, and it was the last one of the bunch that he had reluctantly handed over to an indifferent clerk with thick bifocals, who having long ago grown tired and unimpressed with the remnants of ruined and aging yuppies, stacked it wearily with the other discs on the dusty counter beside him and prepared to write out a check.

At the last instant as the clerk was about to tear it from the book, Jay said, "I'll take that one back." He reached over and plucked it from the stack without waiting for a response or to have it returned. His action was impulsive but his tone resolute. The tall thin twenty-something looked down through the wire frames resting on his long nose and glared at him with annoyance, resentment and disgust. It was bad enough that Jay had bottomed out in public, hauling in his trifles for a skimpy attempt at redemption, but did he have to wreak havoc on the lives of busy innocents by being so damned uncertain about it all? The clerk changed the check amount, tersely initialing it, and without a word slid it across the counter with his fingertips barely touching the edge, as though to emphasize, it clearly seemed to Jay, a self-protective distance in disdain for the taint of his newly acquired status; another untouchable, a fallen Brahmin, and worse yet in the eyes of material-minded minions like this bespectacled boy, probably an unemployed and unemployable one....*dumb punk... what's he know...*

When Jay left there for the music store to sell back his flute – his practice flute not his best one (but still a treasured possession which he was loathe to lose) – he was burning with anger and despair over his losses and meager gains. Those feelings deepened further when he handed over his silver magic play piece for another slip of paper. Like the coins given Judas, he bitterly reflected, a paltry sum for self-betrayal. They gave him a hundred dollars for the very same instrument they had sold him for four hundred a few years earlier and he realized then, through tightly clenched teeth, as he silently railed at the unfairness of it all, why the teen-age children of the family-owned shop were always so stylishly outfitted in finery and fancy sports cars...*stinking rip-offs...*

As he pulled onto the freeway, oblivious to both the traffic and the rain as mere shapes and shadows, he was lost in an inescapable whirlpool; an ominous sinkhole of debt and depression. He wondered how much deeper he could go and if it would possibly ever get any better. He hadn't told anyone he was doing this today and felt very alone in his assessment of his predicament. Had he finally hit bottom or was it just a new low? His preoccupation with earning money was preempting all other subjects in his phone talks with Leroy. Shortly after returning from Europe he had begun to struggle again with the ongoing decline in his practice as he continued each week to turn away potential clients with the news that he was no longer accepting insurance. They didn't give a damn that he didn't want to deal with the new-fangled restrictions and extra paperwork imposed by managed care. They'd paid for their insurance and they wanted to use it, even if he had been highly recommended by someone. It seemed now impossible to function only on a cash basis. It had been at best a romantic notion, at worst perhaps a ludicrous delusion. Only stubborn pride and his weekly chats with Leroy were keeping him afloat and sadly adrift in a sea of misery.

Through conversing with Leroy, in the past few months, despite his fears and protracted circumstances, Jay had found peace, though quite sporadically, in the idea of letting go and trusting God for support. During their conversations or at least by the end of one, he usually felt good. But in between their talks, he quickly fell prey to doubt, especially in the face of mounting bills and Bea's concerns, and so he listened to the tapes Leroy sent him whenever possible – jogging, driving, alone in his office – to clarify and reinforce what he wished he could believe. If only his life was going like he wanted, it would be so easy to accept all that Leroy said. Here his life was going to hell in a handbag and all Leroy kept saying in effect was "Don't just do something, sit there". It drove him nuts yet somehow kept him sane. He only knew he felt good when they talked or he listened to the tapes, no matter how fruitless and frustrating things seemed. Fumbling through the glove compartment he pulled out the latest one, recorded soon after his return to America, and slipped it in the deck as the sea of cars surrounding him crept along like migrant turtles.

"Hello, Jay. What's going on?"

"Well, I've been listening to the tapes and focusing on the word 'luxury', and wanting to sustain a sense of existing in luxury all the time."

"Um-hm. Well, you will. That's your birthright. That's where you're going. That's where this journey is really ending. So, in a sense, it's in the process of ending right now, as you realize that you *are* in luxury. That's the real dynamic here, that the search is coming to an end, and when it comes to an end this is what it feels like."

"Hmmm."

"So you can not worry about sustaining it because you will discover that it is your very nature that is being revealed to you, and that there is no apprehension of loss any longer which would cause you to entertain the notion that you'd have to sustain it, because you are learning to not feel loss right now as a foundation of being able to experience this bliss, this luxury, all the time. So what would cause you to be concerned at having to sustain it won't cross your mind. Ever."

"Hmmm. What would cross my mind?"

"Oh, whatever you feel moved to do. Building a house, driving a car, eating, playing, making music, counseling people. You see, you're not going to have those moments of doubt and isolation that occur right now that cause you to question the absoluteness of your support. So what happens is you are entering an experience of absolute reality, unsullied by thinking. Now instead of thinking, there's going to be knowing, there's going to be reflection, there's going to be discovery, there's going to be revelation. So the process of movement, the process of unfoldment, continues, but thinking, which is something that goes on only in a private portion of consciousness, won't occur because your consciousness is going to be experienced as infinite, open and universal, and yet as you specifically."

"Okay. So if I go with the feeling of luxury right now, it will follow that my life will continue to be luxurious?"

"Very much so, only what's going to happen is that you are going to understand – and this is the appropriate moment to begin to show you this – how the process of fulfillment occurs.

"Say, for example, you see an apple and you recognize that it is beautiful and there is some desire to eat it and you savor the flavor and the sweetness and the juiciness of it and then it is down in your stomach. It's at that point that really the apple is assimilated and becomes part of you, and it is important to understand that the real purpose of the apple is not to be seen as beautiful or to be tasted and thought to be wonderful, but the fact that it becomes assimilated. And what you are going to be seeing is that desire, and this will help you with your clients as well, has to be felt and has to be digested to the point where you recognize what the purpose, meaning and intent of the desire is, and once it's brought to that point it can be assimilated.

"Now say, for example, you saw a beautiful car, a Mercedes Benz, and you really felt something for it and you decided you wanted it. To digest that particular desire is to recognize you want quality, freedom of movement, style, comfort, integrity of construction, so you take the desire and begin to experience what it is at its essential level. And when you do that, and are also at peace, it can be assimilated.

"To assimilate something means that there is a similarity between you and something else, and once the similarity has been revealed, then it can begin to be embodied, and that's how manifestation occurs. That's how desires are fulfilled. They are digested and assimilated so ultimately you might not end up with that Mercedes that you thought was so attractive but maybe you will have a Jaguar or a BMW, or a Mercedes, but it will be that the essence, the foundation of that desire was brought into manifestation because you could agree with it. You could assimilate it. You were experiencing no lack around it. So anything you desire – this is your assignment – from that place of luxury, from peace, that place of feeling no conflict, recognize what you desire and try to feel what the essential intent really is there. Then be with that intent and you will find it will assimilate automatically and begin to unfold itself in some absolutely appropriate way for you. You have already experienced this, but what I'm encouraging is that you experience it in a more conscious intentional way, so that you know it works, so you know your support is always there, so you can see that it is yours for the asking.

"So every desire you have, reflect on what the essence of it is, and be willing to agree with it to set it in motion. It is your job to do that. That's how you participate in creation, by agreeing to the fulfillment you have of these desires in an essential way."

"Hm. Okay… I'll practice it."

"Yes. It'll make all the difference in the world."

"That's what I'm looking for…It's a little hard to believe…but it seems perfectly sensible too…worth engaging…I don't have anything better to do."

"Good. You don't have anything better to do. I can tell you that. You'll find that when you're able to reach an agreement about what is essentially valuable and meaningful in your desire, and see it from a point of view of no resistance, it's just the nature of reality for it to assimilate. It's just like when you eat the apple. It's the nature of things for your body to assimilate. It does not remain an apple. It becomes you."

"Okay. I want to get this right. So, to use your example, eating it is a form of implementing the desire?"

"Right. Eating it is just a part of agreeing with the desire. It's a willingness to agree with that."

"Hm. But the true meaning is essentially the nutritional experience?"

"Three-dimensionally, that's true. But we're talking about the fourth dimension, the spiritual dimension, which encompasses all others. Ultimately it's just an experience of communion. But in order for there to be communion there has to be a breaking down of all appearances of separation."

"So the initial impulse starts with the perception that the apple is beautiful."

"How pretty it is, yes, and then to savor what it is like, to savor the form and the content of it, and then once you get beyond that you get to the real purpose or value or meaning of it, which is to enrich."

"Hm. This is helping me to think differently about some of my desires and goals."

"Right. There are no goals. There are just desires, because a goal is circumscribed. It's a narrow area and if you don't get it through the goal you don't get what you want. You don't get to have your fulfillment. What I'm talking about doesn't have any failure at all involved with it. All the opportunity to fail has been deleted from the movement or the approach here."

"Just trust my desires?"

"You have a desire. Let's pick a desire here."

"I have a desire to do something with music."

"Okay, which of course I knew you were going to say. Ahhh…the fact is that you love to listen to the music that you make."

"That's true."

"You love to hear music. You love to hear your own music. You see, that's more the essence of it."

"I'm making it for myself."

"You're making it for yourself because you love to make it, because it's moving through you."

"That's true. I do absolutely love it and do feel that I'm making it for myself."

"That's the essence of that desire there."

"I see."

"So by being willing to see that and to agree with it, you set it in motion, the assimilation. Then it can be embodied."

"That helps, thanks."

"So you take the desire to the point where you digest it – to the point where it can be assimilated – which means that you come to the understanding of the intent, which can then be allowed or justified right where you are."

"I enjoy the making and listening of music."

"Right. You enjoy the making and listening of music…and that's sufficient unto the moment. There's no obstacle to that. Then what happens is that all of the concerns about the possibility of 'making it' are over-ridden and the assimilation begins. The problem is that people interpret their desires through the lens of the ego and get attached to the form."

"Hmm. You mean then, for example, that the pressure I put on myself to somehow make it big as a musician or song writer is really a distortion of my basic desire to enjoy making music?"

"Exactly."

"Hmmm. I'm wondering if I can trust the desire to see more people and get into the essence of the feeling of that."

"Oh, you love to talk to people. You love to listen to them."

"Yeah, that's true."

"You love to moderate for them. By that I mean find their point of balance and ease for them. So if everyone who comes to you is off balance and your job basically is to have them experience balance, that's pretty easy, and that's easy to allow. You can do that without any kind of responsibility because it's natural. If what you do for someone is absolutely natural then you don't have to exert anything, you don't have to take care of things, you don't have to be in charge. You just have to be centered and balanced. So everybody who comes to you is coming to experience balance, and clarity, and that's all you need to desire here. That's the essence of that, and if you like doing that, and just stay with that feeling, then more people will come to you.

"So don't let your desire to help and serve and moderate be conflicted with or sullied by fear of not having enough income. And of course, if you're in that place of luxury you will tend not to have that kind of thinking. You will tend not to be concerned with money and having to do it that way."

"So my recourse is to allow myself to feel good, understanding somehow that what God is, is moving through everything in such a way as to meet my needs and I somehow acquiesce and facilitate the process by allowing myself to feel the impulse of my desires."

"That's right. And you agree with it."

"You know, if I try to do that with my goal of getting into a Ph.D. program, I really can't imagine working through one anymore. Yet Rex once told me it was essential, years ago."

"Well, that was then. Just pay attention now and go with the movement. Don't think about it as difficult. Don't be having concepts about it that block you from your good here. Look, everything is about learning to have your absolute good without having to have any advantage in the process of its unfolding."

"Advantage. You mean the Ph.D.?"

"The world in which you live is governed by the idea that in order to have one's good, one has to secure an advantage first. In other words, one has to leave square one. In order to have it you can't have anything in square one. Nice guys finish last. What you're learning is quite the contrary: that you can't do anything but square one."

"You leave your vantage point for an advantage."

"That's it. That's exactly it. And so having a vantage point is not the same thing as being disadvantaged. You have to stay at that point, at the doorway, and if you try to get an advantage, you'll fail. And of course people call up wanting advantages. They think that I will give them one, and I don't because it's not necessary. That's the whole point. Ultimately in the world everyone will be at their vantage point and there will be total abundance. There will also no ego because you can't have ego from this place."

"Hmm...so just relax because things are actually okay and will continue to be?"

"Things will always be promising."

"Well, I'm still feeling unease over the suspended periods as opposed to the successful periods. And I don't know how long it's going to last."

"No, you don't. But it will start and stop again in a different direction, and there's nothing there for you to fear. If you enjoy yourself while you are in suspense you are getting a lot of growth, a lot of value, out of it."

"It seems like I've been in suspense for the last year or so."

"Well, that's fine, because that's what was necessary for you to wake up, for you to basically have the recognition that your life was out of control and that it never could be in control."

*...boy, that's the truth...*He punched out the tape at turning left into the driveway and rolled to the far end of it to pull under the carport. Sprinting down the walkway through the drizzle into the house, he was halfway into his jogging clothes when his beeper began buzzing in his black leather pouch. He shut it off and called the answering service. Would it be a crisis, a cancellation or a new client?

"Good afternoon. Ann's Answer Service."

"Hi, this is Jay. I just got beeped. What's up?"

"Yes sir, a Detective Clark just called for you."

"A detective?"...*oh shit...*

"Yes sir."

"Did he say what it was about?"

"Yes, regarding one of your clients, a Barry Thomas. He would like a call back. Would you like his number?"

The tawny flame of a slender white candle in the center of a round glass dining table cast golden reflections onto the three walls of glass that bordered the sunroom overlooking the dark lake. The lit wick melted into the background of the moonlight glistening upon the water as a broad rippling current eased through mid-lake in the shadows. In a corner the squatting open-mouthed fireplace flickered orange-yellow flames, reflected in the full-length windows, while a sprightly string of twinkle lights bordered the entire ceiling. It was a picture of warmth and enchantment; a perfect room in a candlelit crystal palace, seemingly surrounded by a silvery moat, with soft piano music tinkling in the background. It was a glimmering glass space alight with gold, a huge prism on fire, and probably, thought Jay, one of the most beautiful wine and dine settings in the northwest. As such it had always been a popular place over the years for many dinner parties with their friends.

Jay felt very far from a party mood this evening, but he enjoyed, no matter what, making each supper special, unless dining alone, and that included lights, music, candles and a fire, especially with the advent of autumn's nightly chill. It was a welcome Friday night, with another week spent, and his young son was staying overnight at a friend's house. He carefully poured the crimson claret into two wide-rimmed long-stemmed wine glasses gleaming in the glow and set the bottle down by the crystal appetizer platter where steamy portabella mushrooms lay moist and shimmering like wet lily pads in a shadowy mist.

"Jay," said Bea, looking at him across the table, "I have an idea I want to talk to you about."

"Hm," said Jay, with mild distraction, as he lifted the glass to his nose to inhale that fragrant perfume of the fruit of the vine that promised sweet relief from the day's trials and torments in a mellow oblivion.

"I really want you to work with me in my company," she said in her typical forthright manner. It was a cheerful confidence and graceful candor borne over the years of her integrity and idealism. "And I have just the perfect job for you. It entails working with colleges, and finding homes for their foreign students during school breaks, like at Christmas and possibly Easter."

Jay's eyes widened with interest and he shifted his gaze to her, holding his glass suspended in mid-air. "Really?" He spoke now with greater curiosity.

"Yep. I got the idea in Vienna when I saw another company was doing it on the East Coast. I think you could make a lot of money."

"Hmmm." He chuckled darkly, shook his head in disbelief, and then brought the glass down slowly to rest on the table as a shy smile slyly began to crease his lips. He met her eyes, aglow with dancing candlelight. "When would I start?"

"How about tomorrow?"

Chapter 23

"Fear and love are the only emotions of which you are capable." (A Course in Miracles)

IT WAS SHORTLY AFTER nightfall when the plane began its descent toward the dark Toronto airport and the wide curving arc of its approach to the landing strip allowed Bea to see the city skyline towering above a crazy quilt network of lights extending far in all directions. The flight had been long and she had found a few hours of intermittent sleep between chapters in her book, but for the last half-hour she'd been wide awake, not reading, but mulling over her main concerns in the current state of her work and relationships. Though she had left home hoping to focus on Perry, while being filled with anticipation about it, she had been unable to ignore a nagging sense of apprehension over leaving Jay and Candy to run the office without her. Jay had seemingly adapted to the business easily enough and was busy on the phone contacting colleges, advancing the program as she had hoped. Candy however, in subtle ways, seemed distant and self-contained ever since Jay had begun to work there, though he was only there three days a week.

While she had always been unpredictably moody, the normally talkative secretary was more subdued and withdrawn than usual, which to some degree was a blessing, but also felt strange. So much so that it added a feeling of uneasiness for Bea that made the office operations less smooth and harmonious. She didn't want the distraction of having to think about how Candy might be uncomfortable just because there was a man in her midst. She also knew Jay's temper needed little provocation to explode if he sensed any hostility from a man-hater. She understood well his perspective on it all. Candy had her problems but so did he and she could check them at the door as far as he was concerned because it was his house and also his business. He wasn't really her boss, but she was his secretary now, in so far as she took his calls and typed his papers, and she could like it or lump it as long as she didn't make it any more difficult by having a bad attitude.

As the plane touched down and taxied across the runway she felt the eerie impact of entering another country – she was now a foreigner – and she let go her office worries with a philosophical sigh...*oh well...nothing i can do about it now*...as she surveyed her Canadian surroundings and thought of her imminent meeting tomorrow morning. With Perry at least the mission was clear. She would either fire him or retrain him, depending on what he had to show for himself. If only she could find such black and white resolution with the other problematic people that plagued her thoughts. Her sisters especially were weighing heavily on her mind and heart, as their impending reunion loomed larger in the distance. It wasn't that she didn't want to see them; on the contrary, it was simply that she hadn't enough time to devote to a gathering so important as this one was to her. She wanted to sort out the complex of thoughts and feelings she had around each sister. Personally she would have preferred waiting until early next year, a time not that far off, when her schedule would finally permit a real break. But she had been outvoted, two to one, and with the prevailing undertow of sentiment – it *had* been so long – the idea seemed to gain momentum on its own. Now since she was going, she would try to make the best of it, but wondered what really was on Faye's mind. Was there another agenda behind a friendly family get-together.... *why now...*

She still had bitter memories of herself as a child in the harsh hands of her haughty elder sister; painful remembrances of humiliation and fear. Faye, an ambitious bright star in youth, had been royalty early on in her own mind, playing the imperious red queen to Bea's unassuming Alice, while being raised in the wooded wonderland of their hillside home in a sleepy Ohio town. She recalled certain times, not frequent but memorable, of being bullied, called names, addressed in contemptuous tones, and even physically manhandled on occasion and yet, to her amazement, her older sister seemingly recalled nothing remotely of the sort.

To hear her tell it, she'd been a upright model of sisterly propriety, with only the passing pangs of normal sibling rivalry and the unavoidable skirmishes that arise between children to slightly mar their relationships. Her repeated denials of the unflattering reports of her inhumanity caused toil and trouble to boil and bubble beneath Bea's normally placid surface, despite the friendlier overtones that had developed later in their relationship over the long distance between them. She had finally decided that Faye was really not conscious of having mistreated her when they were younger. Call it denial or selective recall, but those memories were missing, the occurrences doubted, and it was not a welcome topic of discussion for Faye nor an easy one for Bea to raise given her amnesia.

Bea had tried that one last time, years earlier, only to be met by gentle but mocking derision and Faye's laughing insistence that Bea must be imaging or distorting things that were long ago past. Bea knew such recollections didn't fit well with her sister's lofty self-image; a force for good, or at least good times, certainly a force and entitled to be held in the high esteem of others. She was assertive, not ruthless, a leader, not selfish, and much too busy with weighty matters or fun to contemplate the difference. In one sense, in that it was no longer an active grievance, Bea felt unafraid and somewhat forgiving. Faye had always stayed in touch with her, even if primarily to talk about herself, and, being oblivious to Bea's ambiguity, had increasingly treated her more as an equal as the years had turned them both into adults. Her fun-loving manner and vivacious charm made it hard not to like her, and Bea knew that despite the past they both shared an inherent love and respect for each other. She just didn't trust her not to be cold-blooded and callously self-serving if a contest of wills arose over anything.

Ironically, her experience with her younger sister had been much the reverse. They were closer when younger, though roughly seven years apart, and had sustained a friendship unstrained by early conflicts. It was only in their later years, in college and beyond, as the time came to enter the workaday world, that their opinions and sentiments began to clash while they struggled to live out their varied values and lifestyles. Polly had stayed a campus liberal well past college, and her far-left outlook had estranged her early on from Faye, fourteen years her senior, who preferred socialites to socialism, diamonds to love beads, caviar and champagne to yogurt and granola. With Bea as the middle girl, she had always been closer to each of them than they were to each other.

While she taught school in the infested inner city and her first husband suffered through the jungles of Vietnam, Polly protested and partied through college, feeling sympathetic with the oppressed mass of humanity and rooting for revolution. Her views grew sharply divergent from Bea, whose humanitarian instincts and distinctly nonpolitical outlook on life kept her friendly and kind to everyone, even her sisters as they grew further apart. The sad sense however of their emotional estrangement was not lost on her, and she had always hoped some day, some way, to reconnect and close those gaps – if it were at all possible.

Though the disparity in their ages created distance among them, especially for the oldest, surging ahead of her belated sisters in pursuit of her career, it had also served naturally to isolate their development, as though they were from different generations altogether, and that distance paradoxically had neutralized to some degree potential rivalries, allowing them to develop more fully as separate individuals. Each, for example, had been a cheerleader at the very same high school, yet so many years apart as to erase any comparisons of their identical heritage.

They had managed, along their separate ways in life, endowed with a strong kindred spirit from their parents, to maintain a tenuous web of filial contact, primarily by phone and short periodic visits. These held them connected if only by strands, even in the midst of distance and disagreements. They were different, yet still proudly conscious of being family, and drew strength from that fact, which in turned fed their differences. Could they ever concoct a greater feeling of closeness or was it only to be purely wishful thinking? She would soon find that out a few short days from now.

In the cold gray morning through the hotel window, high on the tenth floor, Bea watched the city natives go about their business briskly, crawling on the crowded wet streets below like little black ants engrossed in their primal purposes. Though she felt mildly nervous, it was less about her meeting with Perry – mere moments away if he was on time – than the telephone message she had retrieved late last night. Candy had called earlier, about the time Bea had landed, and had left as prearranged a summary of the day's office activities. They in themselves sounded manageable enough but her tone was a bit worrisome. She sounded upset, more tense than usual, as though something was bothering her besides the daily grind. Her singsong tone, heavier than normal, seemed pregnant with something felt but unspoken. And to Bea it felt ominous as she waited for her meeting time. She couldn't call there now, as everyone was sleeping given the three-hour time differential, so it was just another item to worry over while waiting. The hotel room phone rang in a short shrill burst of impatience.

"Hello. Hi Perry. I'll be right down."

She turned from the window, readjusted her vest, flicked some lint off her blouse, and prepared to join the ants. With a long last look at herself in the mirror, her plaid business suit in checkered fall colors – burnished gold, drab green, faded brown – she assessed her trim figure and round face approvingly….*older but still bulging in all the right spots*…She surveyed the image, from her mid-length blonde hair, parted at the crown, perfectly framing her soft hazel eyes, down past her square shoulders, firm bust and trim waist, to her rounded hips, tapered thighs, shapely calves and ankles tucked into her tan suede mid-high heeled shoes. She smiled bravely at herself to help quell the sudden butterflies fluttering slightly in her stomach, took a deep breath, then turned around, grabbed her briefcase and strode out the door to her meeting in the hotel lobby, a comfortable colony, with her errant or perhaps simply erratic employee.

Chapter 24

"Bill Clinton is an extremely good liar. Do you realize that? Extremely good."
(Senator John Kerry)

A s he unlocked his office door and closed it behind him, Jay frowned at the torrential rain splattering outside on the windowsills wildly in a frenzied drumbeat. He unzipped and hung up his tan leather jacket and matching cap on the back of the door and leaned over the glass coffee table to turn on the ceramic lamp with the lavender lampshade. It cast a welcoming pale lilac glow against the forbidding pallor of the dull gray morning gloom. He had clients to see and one call to make before turning to his prime preoccupation; the latest tape had arrived from Leroy for another dose of enlightenment lessons…*first things first*…Pulling a slip of paper from his shirt pocket he dialed the number on it and waited for an answer.

"Detective Clark, please." He sighed audibly without hearing himself…*might as well get this over with*…"Sure, I can hold." He peered out the speckled glass panes at the dark clouds enshrouding the unseen mountain in the distance. The rain seemed callously content to continue hammering away at its merciless message: no sun today – deal with it.

"Oh. Well, yes. Tell him Jay returned his call. He has my number. Thank you." He checked the clock radio whose large white digits gave him fifteen more minutes until his first appointment. He was torn between putting the tape on at the moment only to stop it for his impending appointment or waiting until later to hear it uninterrupted. He decided on the latter choice and instead turned his attention on his upcoming client, the flower lady.

It had been roughly two weeks since he had last seen her along with her new beau. They came together ostensibly for some pre-marital counseling but it had been to Jay's thinking a perfunctory gesture. They were caught up in the enthusiastic plan of going to Las Vegas the next day to exchange marriage vows. Jay's cautions to them about acting too swiftly – a headlong rush into a lifetime commitment – had gone blithely unheeded. They sought more his blessing than anything else and the rising tidal wave of their mutual attraction had washed away any reservations he had put to them. They were buoyed and bolstered by the fact that they had dated for a long time in high school, though that period had past by almost twenty years now. He presumed that if they were as happy as the last time he had seen them it was unlikely they would be coming to him again. The session had been set with the prearranged intention to focus on parenting skills for the boy Jason. He gave some thought to various points he had planned to cover during their meeting.

Glancing once more at the clock in a bit he saw it was just about time to begin. He looked outside again, hearing the relentless raindrops pounding out a steady stream of percussion sounds on the window ledge, as dirty dark puddles littered with dead leaves dotted the asphalt parking lot below. The small pools were pelted in synch to the incessant rhythmic incantation coming from the clouds…*green and gray…green and gray…green and gray… green and gray…*

He had never forgotten the words of a local friend, a former Californian himself, who had said to him jokingly, shortly after his move here, "Green and gray, Jay – that's got to be your favorite colors now". It had struck him at the time as an ominous warning, truly dark humor, and given too late to be of any help. He had hoped it was a tease, at worst a genial and gross exaggeration, spoken in jest. But the rain had indeed laid its claim to the northwest and he had not yet made his peace with that fact. He sighed quietly again as he turned away from the window, eclipsing the feelings that threatened to overtake him, by turning back to the business at hand. Rising from the swivel chair he made for the door and strode down the hallway toward the couple in lobby, grateful once more for the blessed opportunity to focus on the cares and concerns of another, thus temporarily forgetting his own.

On entrance he was stunned to see the tear-stained face of the flower lady sitting alone in the corner chair, looking like a shrinking violet, and as lost as Little Bo Peep's sheep. "Hi," he ventured, "are you alone?" He tried to soften the sound of his shock at seeing her normally perky persona as wilted and withered as an uprooted plant. She looked up with a flushed face, nodded her head, but gave no reply as she took his outstretched hand and moved toward the office as though in a trance.

"What's going on?" he asked with concern.

"It's a long story," she sighed, with tears welling up as she sank like a lead weight into the rattan chair.

"Okay, well why don't you start at the beginning – wherever that is – but first let me ask you; did you go ahead and get married?"

"Yes," she said, her voice breaking into a sob. "I did."...*oh boy...their first lover's quarrel...*

"What's the problem?"

"He's crazy!"

"What do you mean?"

"I *mean*," she started, staring at Jay with riveting puffy pink eyes, "he drinks too much and he fights too much."

"With you? Is he physically abusive with you?"

"No. Only with everyone else. But I'm afraid of him. With me he just wants to have sex when he's drunk." She shuddered. "Sloppy, ugly, gross"...she trailed off and looked out the window with glazed-over eyes.

"Okay, wait a minute. Start from the top. What happened after you guys left here last time? You went to Las Vegas. You got married, you say, so you're husband and wife. Then what?"

"We're not!" she exclaimed, and uttered an anguished cry before burying her grief-stricken face in her hands.

"What do you mean?"

"I got it annulled."

"No," said Jay in disbelief. "When?"

"Three days ago, as soon as we returned."

"Whew...how did Darin deal with that?"

"He can't stop me or do a thing about it," she stated flatly. She looked up, her usually soft features contorted with defiance. "Or he'll go right back to jail. I've got a restraining order on him," she continued. "He's already on probation for beating up some guys in a bar last year."

"Really? How did you find this out?"

"My lawyer found out by checking on his record."

"Wow." He looked at her searchingly, wondering what to say. "Had you any idea he was like this before?"

"No, not really. I mean I knew he had gotten into some fights in high school, but he said he had changed after becoming a Karate teacher. He drinks a whole lot more than he let on and he's not teaching at that school anymore either."

"How do you know?"

"Because my lawyer checked into that also." She sniffled and sat up straighter. "Darin was drunk every night since our wedding. It's been a nightmare. He started right after the wedding in the limo. Some champagne and he's gone. Every day in Vegas the week of our honeymoon he starting drinking by noon and went on through the night until he passed out. And at night, when he was really tanked, talked away like never before. He bragged about going into bars and picking fights. They never know he's got a black belt. He likes to hurt people. He went out one night in Vegas all by himself – to buy some more booze of course – and came back all bloody and scratched. He said he stopped at a bar and fought three guys at once and beat 'em all up."

"This is too much." Jay shook his head. "Look, this is shocking. You're probably in shock. But listen, one good thing is the worst is behind you. As hard as it is to bear, it is better, much better, to have found this out now rather than later. And, you were really smart to annul it. The nightmare is over. It could have gotten worse, for both you and Jason."

"I know," she cried aloud, "but I feel like such a fool. I don't know what's the matter with me. I can never find a good man." Jay paused, and then spoke softly and sympathetically.

"I know that's the thought people frequently have when they've been through something like this. It makes you afraid you can't trust your own judgment."

"Exactly!" she wailed hysterically, banging her tightly knotted fists on her thighs. "I know that I can't, and I'll never find anyone for me or Jason."

"Well, wait a minute. For one thing, you don't know that, and for another, that's the kind of thinking that got you into this."

"How do you mean?"

"I mean I think that the fearful thought that you'd never find a good mate was a large part of what drove you to rush into this in the first place. You thought your chance had finally come; that it'd been a long dry spell and you weren't likely to get another. You were desperate and though the romantic feelings seemed real, you let yourself quickly get caught up in the current before you really took time to test the waters. And when people do that, they stop listening to themselves – to that still small voice from within – which knows when relationships truly feel right or wrong."

"Hmm." She pulled out some Kleenex from the box on the table, wiped her eyes and sat back, looking more composed and attentive for the moment.

"Look…as painful as it is, as disappointing as it is, if you look at it squarely, knowing what you know now, wasn't there something, something you saw, something you felt, that early on said 'this is not right', 'this doesn't feel good', something you neglected to pay attention to?" He had asked this question dozens of times before to as many dejected and shell-shocked ex-lovers and the answer had always been the same time and again.

"Yes."

"Exactly. It's not so uncommon, especially in the throes of romance, to fail to see things or at least to acknowledge them. What passes for love chooses to be blind, even in the face of multiple opportunities to see. So, looking back on it now, what things did you see, what clues were given, that you chose to ignore?"

She looked at him darkly, a glimmer of guiltiness crossing her face. "Oh, I know things about him that I never told you," she said somberly.

"Like what?"

"Well…there was one thing he did, or had done, that especially freaked me out, but he did it for me…so I didn't know what to say, and at the time I thought it was an isolated case, and in a way, sort of proof of how much he loved me and would protect me." The change in her tone gave him pause, while eliciting his curiosity, and his left eyebrow lifted, wrinkling his forehead with rapt interest as he waited to hear more. She sighed, dropping her shoulders, and hung her head momentarily, then looked at him carefully, wary of his response yet intent on disclosing her revelation in coolly measured terms.

"Once," she started hesitatingly, "when I was younger, out of school, college age, I was raped by a guy, a guy that had gone to our school, in his car late at night. He was just going to give me a ride home from a bar, he said. Any way, this was over ten years ago. I never told anyone about it – I didn't want to talk about it – and then, in the midst of all this, this crazy fling or whatever it was, we were talking one night all about our pasts, and it just came out – I'd had some wine – and so I told Darin about it," she paused, "and he got really angry and said he wanted to do something about it. I begged him not to beat the guy up and he promised he wouldn't, so I thought maybe he'll just talk to him or something, scare him a bit." She stopped, looking reluctant to proceed.

"Go on," urged Jay, clearing his throat.

"Well, anyway, Darin was able to locate the guy. He's still around in the area somewhere. And he paid another guy, a big guy, a big burly mean guy, Hells Angels type, to get even with the guy who had raped me. So this guy found him, and he took him somewhere, and I guess he beat him up some." Her eyes and voice both faltered momentarily as she scanned the blue and white tapestry rug before meeting his eyes, "and then he raped him."

"Oh Jeez," said Jay quietly, feeling the hairs rise on the back of his neck.

Shortly after noon, Jay pulled up to the Taco Bell window and ordered two tostadas with Verde sauce, a favorite cheap lunch. Then he headed for the manicured park-like grounds of the nearby stately Ste. Danielle winery for a quiet picnic in a remote corner of the dirt parking lot where a gurgling brook bordering the estate rushed along. He often went there at lunchtime when going home was not as feasible for one reason or another. It offered a silent time to momentarily forget all the psychic aches and pains he had heard in the morning. He saw the irony in the cycle; being with others to forget himself, being with nature to forget them. Secluding himself in the familiar spot that he found so contemplative, he polished off his messy meal, wiped his hands clean, then slipped in a tape from Leroy and reclined the seat far back to listen with his eyes closed, as the rain tap danced overhead on the car roof.

"Okay, we're moving."

"Okay. Well, I think from my perspective what's most important to look at is that I've been back two weeks now from Europe and the first week after I got back was filled with people and activity and money and felt good and then this week has been more of a letdown and like the preceding weeks and it's hard for me not to experience depression and panic and just a general sense that's life not worth living."

"Okay, yeah, but first of all you have to, during this time, understand that this is just practice, just valuable practice. It's meaningless at the point that you are interpreting it. I mean that it isn't true that bad things are going to happen. But you see, the basic problem is that a thought is upsetting you. Thoughts should not upset you. That's the bottom line, and that's what you are learning to do. You're learning to let go of the thought attached to this experience of pressure so that you can begin to have the experience of pressure released unconditionally and then be able to be with any thought without feeling the least bit threatened by it. In a natural mind, in your divine consciousness, you would not be upset by any thought because your experience of integrity or wholeness would be uninterrupted. What you are doing now is to take time out from your experience of integrity to dally with this fascination, this thrill, of being tormented by thoughts. That's what the ego is.

"So what you need to do here is to realize that you are on a plane that's in turbulence and you are going to learn to get comfortable with the turbulence and the implications of it. Simply realize that you are going through this process of learning, of growth, and that it doesn't pose a real threat to you. But you have conditioning around you that is being let go of."

"Well, that's a helpful way to look at it."

"Right, because the problem with you, Jay, is that there are thoughts that upset you. Ultimately the reason you experience this is because you have allowed yourself to forget your experience of absolute invulnerable wholeness, this inviolable experience of Being, so that you can have this weird experience or distortion. Nothing in your life is going to change. You may go through this growth for a while fearing the demise of your good and eventually you'll notice that you do keep surviving despite these fears, and that begins to lessen your commitment to the defenses you have made and you begin to feel more free to trust the movement and integrity of life. That's what your freedom is about: totally trusting the movement of life and being there without any defense while feeling no vulnerability. It's not as though you are giving up your defense to feel excruciatingly vulnerable. It's simply just to be whole again and realize that there is no threat; that God does not intend for that to be your experience."

"Hm."

"It's just that everyone who is identifying with their ego has in effect opted to be independent of God and the first consequence of that is loss of freedom. You see, independence and freedom are not the same thing."

"You better go over that."

"Freedom is lack of restriction. It is the capacity to move without restriction spontaneously in any direction. And it always is a component of your capacity to express the will of God.

You learn that by spontaneously moving with life freely you are expressing the will of God. Independence is an attempt to live apart from your source. The original sin was a declaration of independence from God. The devil says to Adam and Eve, 'Well, here's an alternative to God – why don't you try it?' And they conspired to say, 'Well, we think we will – we're going to try this new thing.' And immediately they fell, because they were no longer connected to their source. And once grace was gone they had independence but they had no freedom. They had this terrible burden of responsibility to survive on their own. And what you are backing out of is that very conditioning that you have to survive on your own, as though that was a requirement of life."

"Hm. Do you mean by the devil our capacity to imagine ourselves as separate from God?"

"Right. That's the whole point of the story, which relates what's generally come to be known as the human condition. But look, joining with God and experiencing your freedom also include the experience of the sovereignty of your individuality. But you experience sovereignty as part of an overall experience of being connected to everything, to all of life. In other words, there's no independence in that, there's absolute connection, and yet you feel sovereign."

"Hm."

"In the political spectrum these aspects of individual Being are divided up as right and left. The right wing is attempting to uphold the sovereignty of the individual and the left is trying to get the feeling of unity, of everybody being joined. But where the left goes wrong is in trying to take away the sovereignty of the individual and the where the right goes wrong is in trying to be independent or separate from the whole. So both are flawed and both have some element of the truth, because in the kingdom of heaven you have sovereignty of individuality and you are absolutely connected. And that neutralizes the idea of right and left in politics."

"Hm. I always thought political solutions were inadequate, but that explains why more perfectly than I have ever heard it put. Views left or right are half-truths at best."

"Right. So, you're doing this right now. You're at a tough point where you're faced with standing right on the edge. And part of you wishes it could take a few steps back. But there is no going back when you have come this far. So then what you have to do is to feel safe and supported right now, right where you are. And understand that being comfortable with this is so valuable because it allows for any number of possibilities to occur seemingly from out of the blue. If you are less comfortable with this moment, then your possibilities are more restricted because you are still attempting to have a linear or cause and effect connection to life that the ego feels it can control or manipulate. If you can abandon any kind of edge of discomfort right now then you are really an open door and whatever desires you've set in motion can simply happen. That is they do not have to have a justification or intermediate cause that the ego would regard as reasonable and necessary. So being comfortable right now and trusting life is absolutely the best thing to do, as difficult as it is, as much as it goes against the grain of your conditioning to feel otherwise."

"Hm."

"And you will always have this in life, even when you are completely awake. You will always be in the vast unknown of Being. But it will be absolutely benevolent, it will feel completely safe and it will feel wonderful – literally wonderful if you understand that to wonder is to have curiosity."

"Alright. So, you're saying I'm at a point where it's uncomfortable for me to trust in life and thus I fill my head with fearful thoughts or imaginings?"

"Right, and you did it fine last week. What's the problem?"

"I don't know. When I came back from three weeks in Europe I felt relaxed yet enthusiastic and larger than life or larger than I used to feel. It actually seemed like I was standing taller. My problems seemed petty and unimportant, or at least quite manageable. Then it seems like once things started to fall away – I had a cancellation and some late payment notices – that I got back into the feeling of …well, like the first feeling wasn't really real and I got back into a negative vein. I guess that's just how dense my conditioning is."

"Right. And you are going to have to learn to be comfortable with this. And you are going to have to be very still at times and be very disciplined at not thinking but feeling instead; trying to find that feeling of safety right now – being disciplined with that. It may mean that you can't have any distractions in your experience while you are anchoring yourself in the truth. It may mean that you are going to have a place where this is easy to do; a place that is very quiet where people can't disturb you. You're going to have to trust that you are not alone despite the fact that this seems very scary."

"Okay. Those are the kind of nitty-gritty things that make sense to me – that I feel I can use."

"Right. And you will find yourself not being able to have a moment of extraneous reflection as you do this. This is the equivalent of going through the eye of the needle and you can't take baggage with you. The eye of the needle is a gate in Jerusalem and in order to get the camels through it they would have to unpack them and then shove the animals through, then take the bags in by hand and repacks the animals again. So what you are going through here now is a time when there is going to have to be an economy of thought, or a willingness to still everything as much as possible, to go through those moments when you feel most threatened. If you do that you will still feel safe, but it's carrying the baggage that's feeling difficult to you."

"What's the baggage?"

"Your conditioning or the attempt on the part of the ego to still uphold certain ideas pertaining to your fulfillment as real or relevant."

"I see. Well, could it also be the desire to drink or smoke grass?"

"How do you mean that?"

"Well, sometimes I get the thought that when I smoke grass my client load goes down. I only drink at night but during the day when I feel pressured or anxious I might have a few hits to relax me and it makes me feel better, but I fear it might affect things on a bigger level that I can't see; like maybe it works against my spiritual development or keeps me from just relaxing naturally. But I can get so uptight when things aren't going well, like these days, that I have a hard time finding any peace without it. So I go back and forth with whether or not I should do it. And at the end of the day I run, but then I have a beer and then I like wine with dinner, preferably great ones. And the whole thing seems like a bit of a vicious cycle, but it seems like life's going to be a bitch with or without them so I'd rather have them around."

"Well, the problem with the grass is that it really is still isolating. It makes you comfortable with feeling isolation because it brings a kind of relief to the nervous system from the pressure of the moment but it doesn't remove the sense of isolation. I suggest that you consider using the Bach flower remedies. They are very subtle because they are homeopathic and they are very helpful because they give you just a minor adjustment."

"Hm. I've heard of them, of course, but never thought they would be of any use to me."

"Well, I suggest you pick out one or two and try them."

"Thanks."

"Now, you are going through a filter or a strainer. Part of you is going to have to stay behind in the strainer; the part of you that isn't really you. And some of these beliefs, like the old belief that you have to be afraid of a lull in activity because if you don't keep going, if you don't keep being a rat in the race, you're going to have problems, must be left behind. You have to trust that there can be periods of no apparent movement at the discernible level of life and have it be no problem at all. That's the learning here."

"I feel like I wouldn't have any problem with that except that the bills keep coming and if I'm not paying them then my wife is or they're getting worse. And so it seems like I'm leaning on someone's else's period of activity."

"You have no choice but to lean."

"That seems to create additional problems."

"It wouldn't if you would see the integrity or wholeness of everything, and not believe that each thing is pulling it's own weight or acting independently. Your wife isn't doing anything independently either. Now, I could tell you that things are going to shift. They are going to shift. But that's not where I want you to find your comfort. I could tell you that the pressure that you feel will subside. And it may well subside when you feel a new burst of activity. But I would like it to subside right now, by you understanding that you can't do anything about being at this point of learning. Even if it made your life look like shit, there's nowhere to go but to yield to this. But do not think that it is designed to tear your life up."

"Well frankly, if yielding to it means giving up grass I'm going to be a little resistant to it. I'm having a hard time believing life would be any better without it, and I like the short episodes of peace it gives me."

"Right, that's the problem. You don't want to give up grass because you think it constitutes some kind of deprivation. And that's where you are. I would encourage you to look for other ways of feeling safe and grounded and unafraid, but even if you do use grass, you'll still get through this. It's not being held against you. I encourage you not to use it, but even if you do you are not going to stay stuck in the same place."

"Hm. I would just be less sensitive to the nuances of the movement of life as changes occur?"

"It doesn't do anything about your feeling and thought of being alone or responsible. The grass relieves you immediately because of what it does to the nervous system, but it doesn't do anything about the belief. It doesn't separate the feeling of pressure from the belief or thought, and that's the real problem. You see, the reason that you or anyone would indulge in any drug at all is because there are certain thoughts that upset you. If you had no upset around any thoughts, the last thing that you would want to do is to use marijuana."

"I see."

"So you understand what the topography of this is. Using grass has no benefit in getting you through this. It also doesn't stop you from getting through it either. But it's like going around the block an extra time."

"It has nothing to do that's essential to the psychological shift I desire to make?"

"No. The relief that it brings you is not enlightened. It brings relief to the ego, but it doesn't bring relief to you. It doesn't allow you to make the shift so that you no longer have to cater to the experience of the ego."

"It doesn't end the sense of being separated from God."

"Right."

"Hm. Sometimes I find myself thinking that there is somehow something different about me when I see so many images of other people either on TV or in real life who seem to be busily engaged in one fun project after another."

"Well, you're engaged in a fun project too. But you don't see it on TV, that's all. Not yet anyway. Believe me, there are a lot of people I speak with that are going through what you are going through; living this kind of strange life that you are living, in diverse forms, but essentially the same thing. It's a kind of life that is moving people from living a temporal existence to an eternal existence right while they are on the planet. It's just a big change, and what you will see on television eventually will be absolutely saturated with the subject of awakening."

"Good. When?"

"When the shift has been moved into more to the extent that it has been anchored by those individuals who are absolutely totally awakened."

"Hm. Uhhh…do you have a sense, a confident sense, that I am going to become awakened in this lifetime?"

"Oh, there's no question in my point of view about it. There's no debate here. There's not even a remote chance that you wouldn't?"

"Oh really?"

"No. It's like you are on a conveyer belt, like a bottle of Pepsi, who like a lot of others want to know if you are going to get to the final experience. And yes you are. That's all."

"You think so, huh?"

"You see, you think you have something to overcome. But you really just have to yield to the moment, yield to the movement, yield to your safety…and you're there."

"But I've got such a stack of unpaid bills that seem such clear evidence that I'm not there."

"Well, they don't have to be paid right now. Just let them be unpaid. All you have to do is be unconflicted about the subject. Be unconflicted about those bills."

"You mean my intention to honor them?"

"No, about the fact that you seemingly can't pay them at the moment. Don't have any conflict about the fact that they are as of yet unpaid. Next, be grateful for whatever the bills represent. And lastly be clear that the intent to pay them is there. There is nothing else you need to have in your consciousness. That suffices. You see, that's what you are here to learn: that that suffices. You don't need responsibility. You don't need urgency. You don't need to react to the pressure. You just need to feel peaceful, grateful, have the intent to pay them, and trust it will happen. And however long that takes, that's the right speed."

"Hm."

"And with respect to your practice, you will find that you will be seeing more people when you feel balanced and at peace, and less people when you are going through this kind of thing."

"Yeah?'

"But that's okay. You don't need to see people when you feel this way. You need to be attentive to your own shift because something new is being incorporated or embodied in your life. And it's hard, but if you don't see many people it's because you really have enough to do without seeing people. But when you are feeling safe with this movement and allow the shift to occur, you will be ready to see more people and they will come. "

"I sure hope so."

"It's just part and parcel of how this shift works. And on some level you have authorized it. On some level you desire to be functioning as an enlightened being."

"Is it this hard for everyone?"

"Quite."

"Hm. Uh, in regard to my practice, I'm considering getting another therapist in this office to share my expenses. Or I'm also thinking about getting another psychologist in here like I used to have years ago because I can bill on their license if they act as my supervisor. Or I just wonder if it's all just…sometimes I feel like there's not a damn thing I can do anymore except try to do what we're talking about."

"Yes, that's true. You see, the feeling of desperation that you feel comes from the thought of not having any slack. And what I'm telling you is that you've got so much slack that it's pathetic that you don't appreciate it. This is the whole point of view. You have slack that doesn't end."

"Well, you're the only one who seems to see that about my condition." (laughter).

"That's how I see everyone's condition."

"I understand."

"You see that's where your comfort is. You smoke marijuana because you want to feel some slack but it doesn't do anything to undermine your misperception."

"And so you're saying to practice undermining it yourself."

"Right. What does it feel like right now, Jay, to have no tension? What does it feel like to have a sense of all the slack in the world around all these issues?"

"If I truly believed it, it would feel very good."

"Well, that's the truth of it. And that's the feeling you can have if you don't kowtow to these thoughts of the ego to the contrary."

"I'm reminded of a line when Saul was talking to Rex in his first book and he was feeling very much like I am about his bills and he said sarcastically to Rex something like, 'You know I could be doing all of this in jail'."

"Right, and Rex says 'No, you're not going to be doing this in jail'."

"Right, but it was Saul's fears that not paying his bills was going to land him there."

"Right."

"Well, okay, and that brings up one more issue. I enjoy talking with you, it's very uplifting, and I'm aware that I'm not paying you and I know this is how you make your living."

"Well, don't sweat it. I know you will when you can and I'm willing to extend slack."

"Alright, good. That feels good. Whenever we have these talks I feel good, but eventually, like for instance after I leave my office today and drive home, sooner or later there will be a sense of something needs to be done, some bill needs to be attended to, and I guess what you are saying is make sure that you screen that sense of need for fear or pressure."

"Exactly. Make sure that what you need to have first is a sense of the slack around you."

"But even having slack around you, or a lack of fear and pressure, implies that you are free to do what needs to be done.'

"Yes, that's true, but that's the icing on the cake. But the first thing that you do is to allow your self to feel the slack. That's the foundation for the icing, which is the cake."

"Keep baking the cake."

"Right, because the slack you see is the sense of luxury again and this allows you to be able to do things naturally. If you feel the slack you'll just know what to do next. But you can't act responsibly, independently, out of the threat that this tension implies anymore. But you can act quite another way. And that is to feel the slack, no pressure, plus the desire and the intent, and that will work great."

"Hm. That would be great."

"Well, sooner or later everyone must come to this. Mankind is evolving to an enlightened point of view. And although the great majority of people are resisting it we'll all eventually come to this point. So give yourself a bit of an interlude of appreciation for the fact that you are serving a far greater purpose here and that people are going to benefit from what you are doing right now, and that you will extend it to others."

"Hm. Well, I feel I am a little, but I'd like to do it a lot more."

"Well, sure, and the answer to that is just give yourself some more slack. It's very simple."

"Good point." (laughter)

"Isn't it interesting how much resistance there is to easiness and how mistrustful people are of things being perfectly easy?"

*...time to go...*Slowly, ruminating over what he had just heard, he drove back to the office for his next appointment. After three more hours he could go home for the day. Hopefully Candy would be gone by then and if not he needn't go downstairs anyway. She had been so different without Bea there. Talking to friends or other private parties unrelated to work, she was sometimes very loud, brassy and sassy, and at other times almost whispering, as though being conspiratorial. He marveled at the difference in her behavior with her boss gone and especially resented that she sat at Bea's desk now, feet on the desk, pretending to be queen for a day. He was looking forward to Bea's return for more reasons than one but definitely to share his observations on Candy.

He had only spent one day in the office alone with her since Bea's departure and was amazed at how much personal time she had spent on the phone. He wondered if she was always this way in Bea's absence. He had called once from his cell phone to the second business line to see if she would end a personal call on the first line to get it and also to make a point. When she finally did pick it up on the fifth ring he said "I just wanted to make sure that these calls were being answered".

"They're being answered!" she shot back, resentful of the insinuation. He had also noticed, now that he was in the basement office thrice a week, that she had color photos of nearly naked muscle men taped under her desk on the side of the cabinet next to her and wondered about her apparent schizoid take on men. It looked like a love/hate relationship with the species...*poor randy...*

In general she disliked them, made jokes about them, and complained of her mistreatment at their hands to anyone who would listen or even if they wouldn't, and yet simultaneously deified or revered them, or their images that is, as objects of beauty, desire and adoration... *what a nut case...*He didn't trust her, and worse, feared her sanity questionable, but worst of all hated to be around someone who hated him simply because of his gender, while at the same the time being paid to work under his roof. Still he knew Bea depended on her and that she basically did her duties well, including the extra work load given her by Jay, without batting an eye or even opening her mouth. If she continued in that vein they could peacefully co-exist, but her recent behavior, with Bea out of the office, made him wonder if she was really worth having around at all.

He put her out of his mind as he prepared to welcome his next client, once again grateful to focus on the troubles of another.

Chapter 25

"All anger is nothing more than an attempt to make someone feel guilty."
(*A Course in Miracles*)

SHE SPIED HIM IMMEDIATELY upon entering the lobby, a large and lavishly ornate space, with classical art paintings gracing amber walls intermixed with ferns around whitewashed pillars, creating a number of clustered settings suitable for intimate conversations. He was by the far wall, in a wrinkled gray suit and tie, sunk back in a deep-cushioned leather couch. He jerked himself up quickly, tall and slender, as she approached him with a smile. Slicking back his thinning hair with one hand, he extended a nervous handshake with the other, exchanged greeting pleasantries while pumping her palm, then followed her to a corner nook where they sat in cushy leather chairs across a small cherry wood coffee table. Bea sat up straight, smiling politely while quelling her own anxiety, and noticed his blue eyes were wide with apprehension, while his body seemed to be slightly shivering as though he were cold. She turned aside and reached into her briefcase for a manila folder of notes, feeling fleetingly like a card shark about to play a confident hand. Wanting to be constructive, yet careful and wise, she wondered if his fright meant he feared her disapproval for his costly and careless, but honest, mistakes or if it were worse. Had he done, as Candy feared, something wrong, like embezzlement?

"Well, Perry," she began, in her best tone of professional friendliness, "my main concern of course, is what happened with the finances. So I guess the first order of business is that I wonder if you have found those unaccounted for receipts."

"Well, yes and no, frankly. Some of them I have found and some of them I have not." He squirmed in his chair, tightened his tie knot. "And I wonder what happened myself," he added sheepishly. "Are they misplaced? Didn't I get them in the first place? I'm not sure, but I do at least have handwritten ones for some of them."

"I really prefer – I mean for bookkeeping purposes – I really *need* to have the original receipts."

"I know, believe me, I know, and I've prayed to God for them, but I'm afraid some of them were just somehow lost or misplaced somewhere, especially on those days where we did several activities – all those kids to bus around." He bit his lip and cocked his head sideways like the sitting loyal dog, in the old RCA ads, listening to his master's voice on the phonograph. "I was so busy doing this all by myself that I may have just forgot to get a receipt sometimes, but mostly I think I did, so I think some were misplaced." He looked up at her in a hangdog demeanor like a sad-eyed bloodhound expecting harsh words for losing the trail scent, and mumbled mournfully, "I'm sorry, I really am. It was just so much work. It was so hard to find families. It was hard to keep everyone together and on schedule for events. I just didn't realize how busy it would keep me."

"Believe me, I know it is a difficult task, and I know that it was your first time," Bea said sympathetically.

"Exactly!" His spirits perked at the hint of understanding. "I had no idea."

"Right, I understand, I do, and I'm sorry I couldn't offer you more guidance." She paused and stared at him for a pregnant moment, searching for clues. "But it was difficult to reach you whenever I called. I did call a lot in the beginning and usually just got your machine or voice mail."

"I know – I'm really sorry – but I was just so very busy, running around with this, and the church and my family."

"I know, I know, and it was new, and you did your best, and in general, you did pull it off. I just hope you can account for all the money I sent you or…well… we'll have to figure something out."

"Oh of course, of course. One way or another I want to make everything right."

"Alright." Bea raised her eyebrows as she leaned forward to emphasize her point. "You said on the phone you could explain everything, so I'd really like to hear what you mean by that."

"Well I meant," he assured her, "that I think I can explain how some of the expenses went unaccounted for."

She studied his face, so prematurely aged and not yet forty, permanent forehead wrinkles and new crow's feet marking worry imprints…*is it character or lack of*…She nodded. "Please, go ahead. I'm listening."

As she heard him relate the many problems he'd encountered in the course of coordinating the summer program, she knew well the familiar truth of his complaints, having wrestled herself all season long with the same demanding work. It was a large task of many details; handling precious human cargo from their arrival to their departure and their active schedule in between. The sons and daughters of people across the sea had been entrusted to her company's care; foreigners in a foreign land, connected by a chain of trust, as strong as its weakest link. She had always intended to supervise him closer, to talk with him more frequently – and he *had* been hard to reach – but mostly her own demanding schedule had grown so overwhelming that she chose instead, as the season grew busier each week, to simply cede him more authority, including check-writing privileges on the Canadian account, trusting in the hope he'd pull it off, as she always did, one way or another. And in a way, he had, though barely, and way over budget.

While listening to him now she knew it was nearly impossible to validate all that he was saying. At some point she simply had to believe him or not. Overall it all sounded plausible. He had truly been overwhelmed, a feeling she knew well, along with under-trained and under-supervised, and as a result had gotten disorganized and fouled some things up. But, perhaps most importantly, he seemed willing to set them right, which was a very big plus. If she let him stay on, to try again, one more time, then she'd have a means of recouping lost funds plus wouldn't have to take the time and expense to find and train somebody new.

"So at least, as far as I see," concluded Perry, in his explanation, "overall, too much was probably spent at the welcome and sayonara parties. And at some of the excursions, well, I guess those receipts were either lost or not gotten in the first place, I'm sorry to say."

"Uh-huh, I can see that may be true. And all those things can be improved with experience. It's hard at first to get the knack of estimating everything. I've been at it awhile now. Look, I think you simply may be in need of some more training. We didn't have much time to train you last spring and there's a lot more I can cover with you, just in one day, that will help you next time. So I think it's best we do some training while I'm here. How's your schedule for today and tomorrow? Can you meet with me?"

"You mean you're not going to fire me?" asked Perry, incredulous at the desired but surprising good turn in his fortunes.

"No I'm not," said Bea firmly, "but instead I really want to train you further, in preparation for spring groups."

"Oh, that's wonderful. I was hoping you would feel this way. I really appreciate a second chance to do it better. Um…I've got some meetings the rest of today for the church, but tomorrow is good. I just need to check with my wife first."

"Okay, good, just call me tonight. Listen though, however, I want you to understand I'll need to deduct whatever unaccountable expenses we end up with from your next paychecks, till they're paid off. But I can do it over several paychecks. Alright?"

"Alright. You bet. That's fair, eh? I appreciate being able to do it that way."

"Of course we don't know how much it could be, but we'll tally it all up as soon as I return to Seattle and add in your new information. I'm afraid it looks like you may have gone several thousand dollars over budget, you know."

"Oh, I know, I know, and whatever it is I'll make it right. As long as I can do it in several payments."

"Right. Good. Then we agree. Okay. Let's get together tomorrow as early as you can. Can you meet here for four or five hours?"

"I think so – at least three or four, like I said, just let me double-check with my wife. I'll call you later today and set a time."

"Okay. Good."

"Thank you so much. I really appreciate this. You won't be sorry you gave me another chance."

"Good. I hope not."

"I hate to run off but I have a meeting with the elders on the new addition to the Sunday school. So if you don't mind, and we are finished here at the moment, I should be getting on my way. I will call you later today."

"Alright, go ahead if you have to be somewhere. We're done here for now. I'll be expecting your call."

"Yes," promised Perry, as he got up, bowed slightly with a broad grin then made his way swiftly through the ferns and pillars outside to the busy sidewalk.

Bea watched with a quiet satisfaction as he left and felt relieved for the first time since arriving in the city. She entered the hotel coffee shop and sat at a table with a window view of the sidewalk and street. After a cup of coffee, she ate a light breakfast of a bagel with cream cheese, strawberry jam and orange juice. She noticed through the window sunbeams bouncing off the buildings, bathing sidewalk figures in daylight shadows and decided to stroll about town to sightsee while getting some exercise in the fresh Canadian air. Tipping generously to match her mood, she returned her briefcase to the room and then headed outdoors, brimming with curiosity about her surroundings. She had been there only once before, briefly last spring when she'd first hired Perry. The streetlight turned red as she approached the corner and she waited patiently in the warmth of the sun, basking in weightless anonymity, an alien herself now, momentarily free of concerns and virtually on a brief vacation. A light breeze tentatively tickled her ankles and caressed her calves, as other pedestrians gathered at curbside waiting with her for the signal to change.

Looking across the street to the Starbucks coffee house she noticed inside three women, professionally dressed, laughing and talking in an animated manner around a corner table, covered with croissants and coffee cups. They looked like good friends, approximately her age, enjoying the moment as though in a commercial, and powered by finely roasted caffeine. Their apparent easy familiarity with each other was reminiscent of her sisters and the impending reunion a week ahead in Pittsburgh; her next big meeting. A flash of envy coursed swiftly within her, transforming itself into a clear keen desire. She wanted that closeness, that fun, that ease, with her sisters...*is it still possible*...

Bumped and jostled by people on both sides of her, she realized the light had changed and marched in unison across the street. As she walked by the coffee shop, past the three women, she noticed behind them two couples in the back. One pair was watching pensively as the other, a woman and man, seemed to be arguing. The woman's eyebrows were deeply furrowed in anger as she jabbed home a point excitedly with her finger while the man pursed his lips in grim disagreement. It reminded her of an incident one evening years ago, in the mid-80's, the golden era or the dark ages, depending on your politics, of the Reagan years.

In Seattle at a restaurant, over pizza and beer, she and Polly were chatting amiably, sisterly buzz, about friends and family, while their husbands' talk had turned from music to politics, with the volume increasing along with their beer consumption. Wade was a democrat but not a radical one and Bea knew the men were fond of each other. She also knew that when together they preferred the gentle art of conversation to the rabid sport of debate so was unconcerned about the possibility of an argument breaking out. She could hear the thread of their discourse while talking with Polly. Wade was astounded to hear that Jay had evolved over the years away from the left-wing of the political spectrum.

"How did that happen?" asked Wade, grinning broadly in disbelief. "You were like an original hippie."

"Well, I'm not particularly conservative really. I'm just less liberal in the political sense. I'm actually more liberal in the broad sense of the word than most people I know. My philosophy of life is still the same: live and let live. I just want the freedom to be, for myself and others. I mean I'm a vegetarian, I'm an astrologer, I smoke pot, I'm a jazz and rock musician. Those interests are more typically associated with a liberal lifestyle, but now I just regard myself as an individualist, and definitely no longer a political left-wing type."

"But how did it happen? What changed things for you?"

"Well, that's a good question. It took place over many years. I was raised in the fifties, in a conservative family, and went to high school in Orange County, a conservative place, and as I got to college the anti-fifties wave of the late sixties was breaking and I became liberal, extremely so politically, like much of my generation, and stayed that way well through the seventies. It's easy to do in an ivory towered place like college, and I was in college for nearly a decade. I got married as a sophomore, my wife got pregnant, and I started working full time for a headhunting firm. Then she had a miscarriage, but we found we liked having money so I just continued working and went off and on part time or full time all the way through grad school. And all during those years liberals on campus were always angry, self-righteously protesting with their little 'no war' signs, railing against the 'establishment', and generally hateful towards the right while proclaiming themselves for love and peace. And basically most of them were ideologues; people whose whole self-concept is wrapped up in being a liberal. If they didn't identify themselves as liberals, beyond being students, they hadn't a clue who they were."

Wayne nodded, smiled knowingly and took a draught on his beer. "I know what you mean. I went to school in Massachusetts."

"Exactly. It's like California that way. And so anyway, as I continued studying psychology and related disciplines, it just became clear to me that they were totally contradictory and counter-productive. Gandhi and King had it right, as far as political activism goes. You must be non-violent if you don't want violence. An angry war protestor is an oxymoron, only creating more anger and violence in the world. And so I gradually became disenchanted with the left, the tyranny of the left, as someone once called it. It felt just like when I was younger and had rebelled against what seemed like the tyranny of the right."

"I see," said Wade, with a noncommittal nod, as he tipped his mug to his lips.

"And then, at the same time, while learning more about the nature of the mind, of consciousness, I just came to realize that ultimately there are no political solutions. Democracy, for all its faults, is as good as it gets. Socialism sucks. I don't want the government telling me how to live or dumbing down the world for mediocrity. I want freedom. And so I saw the next significant development in human evolution had to be psychological. People must choose to have peace in their minds and love in their hearts and that can't be imposed through government. The left can pass all the laws they want for more government in our lives or try to control freedom of speech through political correctness, and they'll achieve nothing but a fascist socialistic system because these things can't be legislated. You can't get to love and peace through hate and controlling people."

Wade smiled, raising his eyebrows slightly, then slugged down more ale.

"To be a spiritual or a loving influence in the world, is an individual choice, whether or not you believe in a higher power. But it can't be mandated." Jay paused for a deep slug of his own. "So," he continued, "I realized only a psychological revolution will change the world. And thus the next step in human evolution is to realize that we are spiritual beings. So its not so much that I'm left-wing or right, since politics are ultimately useless, but I want the freedom to live with as few restrictions as possible. And as the left wants more government and the right wants less of it, I tend to favor the latter. Actually, if we reduce ourselves to political labels, I'm probably more of a libertarian. Oddly enough though, in social situations I'm often more comfortable being around liberals, if they're not self-righteous or politically correct twits, because I'm relatively unconventional. And if someone is courteous and respectful in discussing politics, I don't really care which side they're on if any."

"Mm-hm," intoned Wayne, as he nodded, pursed his lips and eyed the beer level in his glass.

"You know, when I was young, the first thing I did when I could finally vote was to register with the Peace and Freedom party. I *was* a hippie. And that's still what I want from a political party. But now I understand we can't have peace through anger, nor freedom through more government. So my creed's the same; live and let live. But be peaceful and loving, don't try to legislate it."

"I see." Wade nodded. "So," he asked with a wide grin, possibly pleased to shift the subject, "did you vote in the last election?"

"Yeah," Jay replied. "I did, but without much enthusiasm. I voted for Perot just to make the point that we needed something different. I hadn't voted for years. I didn't care much for Bush. He seemed so out of touch with common folks and I couldn't stand Clinton. He's not only a huge liar but a sexual predator." Jay paused for a refreshing swig and returned to the subject recharged. "And that's another contradiction from the left. They say they are all for women's rights and then they give us a sexual predator as their candidate. What a joke."

"I get your point," said Wade, slightly smiling with a shrug, as he took another sip. Looking perhaps again to steer the topic off politics he ventured another friendly question. "So did you become a vegetarian when you were a hippie?"

"Yeah, I did at age twenty one with my first wife; idealistic young hippies. I just tried it and was surprised to find I loved it and that was that. And that's another thing too, speaking of contradictions in the left. All them running around whining how they want to save the planet and yet very few of them are actually vegetarians. It is so contradictory for a person to say they want to save the world and not be a vegetarian. Animal agriculture, that is, breeding livestock, so they can be killed and eaten, is one of the worst contributors to water pollution, deforestation and climate change, not to mention heart disease. Also we could significantly reduce starvation around the globe and feed a whole lot more people by using the grain for them that goes to animals. And yet, instead of choosing to save the planet in a way that would be genuinely effective plus compassionate to animals, they eat flesh every day while bitching and moaning about the car someone else is driving."

"I never thought of it that way," Wade offered diplomatically, tipping his mug again.

"Well, most people don't. And right-wingers of course are even worse in that respect. I'm sure much less of them are vegetarians. But at least they aren't out clamoring for more government to save the world or angrily protesting for peace or clamping down on what words people can speak." Jay stopped and took a long deep draught of his brew and brought his glass down with a thump. "You know,' he continued, "if had been in places the last dozen years that were filled with conservatives, I imagine I'd feel as strongly critical of their views. I can't stand fundamentalists, but I don't know any. And instead I've been mostly on college campuses and now in the Seattle area, where liberals are rampant, and it's so easy to see their faults and fallacies. And most all the conservatives I know here are ex-liberals. And they're not all that conservative except when they vote."

"Kinda' like you," said Wade agreeably.

"Well, yeah, kinda'. But like I said, after you've attained democracy, politics are useless, so frankly I'm happy to disown them both. I don't feel I can relate to either side very well unless, like you, they are friendly, kind-hearted and open-minded."

"Well, thanks."

"Oh, you're welcome. I appreciate being able to talk with you, even though you probably disagree with some of what I said."

"That's true," Wade acknowledged, with a slightly elfish smile.

"I know you think of yourself as an environmentalist, and you're not a vegetarian, but that's okay with me because you're not like these angry self-righteous radicals."

"No, that's not my style."

"Exactly, so we can talk. But now, these days, if a conservative speaker goes to a college, they're likely to be shouted down by left-wingers, who of course claim to be oh so tolerant. What crap. They are truly oppressive and against free speech."

"Yeah, I understand your point."

"Right, and you're respectful, and I respect you, and you know, I think because I was so intensely liberal, or what that word used to mean to me – freedom, tolerance, liberation from dogma, an enlightened perspective – that I think I really hoped for and expected more of them. I guess I just got disillusioned. We all started out so idealistic. But now so often the ones I meet anymore or see on TV are just ideologues and their identity's tied up in hating the right. So actually it's just the extremists on both sides, the radical left and the fundamental right, that I especially disown. I just don't know any extreme right-wing folks, and they're not around protesting, screaming for peace, at least not here or on campuses."

"Yep, that's true," said Wade, taking another swig.

"And you know, I really have a hard time respecting anyone, and it's usually some self-righteous left-wingers, the self-proclaimed saviors of the world, arrogant and ignorant, who call themselves vegetarians, and then eat animals, like chicken or fish. I can't believe people eat fish and say they're vegetarians."

Wade smiled and nodded, causing Jay to wonder if he was being politely agreeable or just enjoying the beer, or possibly both, as both men lifted their mugs for another drink. Jay contemplated the empty pitcher beside him before continuing.

"And so all these radicals angrily protesting, trying to control people with their PC rules, hating Bush while espousing peace and love – hate your way to love I like to say – are really just phonies or shallow or both, but either way, they're definitely intolerant as hell."

Wade smiled knowingly and said, "Like they'll kill ya' if you disagree with 'em."

"Exactly," said Jay, as his voice rose in delight over having the point unexpectedly confirmed. "And so in a way, because they really do mean well – both left and right do actually mean well – our misguided brethren are just paving the road to hell with good intentions. And then they call themselves progressives. What a joke. They get that from the Progressive Labor Party, a pretentious name for communists, the most Godless party of all." Jay laughed scornfully and hoisted his mug in a mock toast. "And so it's all nonsense to me. A liberal dose of nonsense. They should call themselves regressives because all they want is to go back to Socialism. What a crock." And he took a long swig, draining his beer, then grinned broadly as he set his mug down with a satisfied sigh. "So anyway, I hope that answers your question."

"It does," affirmed his brother-in-law with a grin, as he polished off his beer with one long last swallow. He looked toward the bar as though considering another pitcher.

A momentary quiescent lull hung over the table like the last few seconds of life in Pompeii.

"Fuck you, Jay!" blurted Polly, startling everyone by her outburst. "Fuh-uck you!"

"Wait a minute!" asserted Wade, his sense of fair play in public discourse aroused and appalled by the sudden emergence of a scene. "You can't say that."

"It's not true what you said," she angrily insisted, oblivious to the others. "You are so wrong!"

"It's okay," said Jay to Wade, ignoring her remarks and smiling in vindication as he waved his hand dismissively. "See what I mean?"

"Enough!" said Bea, who sensed a spiraling conflict imminent, and because she so rarely ever raised her voice at all, even in anger, the others fell silent to the authority of her remark, knowing its prudence. After a smattering of disconnected small talk all soon went home to their respective corners thereafter. Still the unspoken tensions stayed alive well beyond that night and eventually became, along with other incidents, just another brick in the wall of their receding relationship. It had been a doubly frustrating experience for her, as the argument was not hers nor did she care at all for politics. And yet it still happened, despite her intermittent attempts, direct and indirect, to find common ground in their heritage if nothing else, that a pervasive undercurrent of uneasy distance grew slowly, inevitably, between them over time.

Politics tacitly became a taboo subject, after several misfires, and at no loss to her, but the loss of a familiar closeness with her younger sibling was felt, slightly at first, then vaguely more through the years as they both became consumed with their separates lives. Buried but alive, her desire for close sisterly relationships remained solidly in her heart despite the difficulties. Like her own mother before her, she felt deeply in her bones that "family was family" and wanted to sustain the security and strength she drew from the ties to her Ohioan lineage, her Midwestern roots, her family of origin, her two sisters.

Letting go the memory of that fretful incident she strolled about the area nearly an hour, window shopping some but people watching mostly, then returned to her room just as the bustling noontime rush of pedestrians foraging for food broke loose on the streets. Entering the lobby she noticed a group of smartly dressed men and women, all carrying briefcases, the mark of an executive. It reminded her of Faye, who also carried one, monogrammed with her initials, capitalized in gold. Upon entering her room she realized it was late enough in the day to call the home office and decided to check in. Candy answered on the first ring.

"Homestay Connections. May I help you?"

"Hello, Candy, it's me."

"Oh good. I was hoping you'd call. How was your meeting?"

"Oh, fine. I think."

"Oh?"

"Yeah. Well, we'll have to wait and see, but he was able to account for some of the money and agreed to pay back whatever's unaccounted for, so I decided to give him another chance."

"Oh."

"You sound disappointed."

"Oh, well, it's your decision. But I just wonder."

"Wonder what?"

"Wonder if that's wise."

"Yeah, well, we'll find out. I hope so. Like you say, it's my decision. I meet with him for more training tomorrow."

"Oh. I see. Well...we'll see."

"Yep. Look, I wondered what it was you called about yesterday. You sounded upset."

Candy sighed audibly. "Ohhh, I hate to bother you with this but... it's Jay," she said wearily.

"Jay?"

"Yes. He's been acting a little strange ever since you've been gone."

"What do you mean acting strange?" inquired Bea with curiosity.

"Well, for one thing, I think he's been listening to my calls."

"What? What calls?"

"My personal calls."

"Your personal calls?"

"Yeah, you know, like to my kids or the doctor or whatever."

"Oh. Well, why do you think he's listening?"

"Because I hear these little clicks on the line."

"That doesn't mean it's him. It could be something else."

"Oh I know. Could be, but he's been acting a little funny around me lately. Quieter. He avoids me. Just leaves work on my desk with little notes instead of talking to me about it."

"Well maybe that's okay. You know what to do, right? Ask him if you have questions."

"Oh, I know alright. It's just spooky."

"Okay. Well, I'll be back in a week or so. Just try to do your work and don't let little things bother you. Anything else?"

"Uh, well, just one other little thing. It's probably not so important it couldn't wait, but..."

"What?"

"Oh, it's probably nothing...except...well," she lowered her voice, "he's getting a lot of calls on the third line and doesn't want me to answer them. And I guess they are not for you, because he says they're for him but still – I mean if they were – I couldn't very well take a message because he always answers it so quickly."

"What?" said Bea, slightly taken aback at the shift in her intensity of her tone. "What do you mean?"

"Well, I mean, that's my job – answering the phone. That's all. That's my job."

"I see. Well, maybe he's got someone calling back on that number for a reason."

"Well yeah, that's what he says. He said he's having people call him back on that number and he'd rather take the calls himself just so he can get things done quicker, but…I don't know."

"You don't know what? You know Jay moves and acts quickly. It's probably just a way he's set up that lets him do that more. He's streamlining his operation."

"I know he likes to move along fast but it doesn't seem right that he bypasses us. What if someone calls for you on that line?"

"Well, they rarely do. Usually they come in on the first or second line. I'm sure he'd tell us if someone did. Don't worry about it. I know you're used to answering the calls when you're there, but this is a small adjustment. Hey, it saves you work. Look at it that way."

"I know, that's what he said too, but…"

"But what?"

"Well, it's probably nothing I'm sure, but a few times I've picked up on the line – accidentally of course – I'm just used to answering – and well, it seems like there's always some woman on it with him."

"What's wrong with that?"

"Nothing really, probably. It could be he's just making personal calls on the line. It's none of my business of course and I really don't care except …well, it just makes more phones ringing in the office and there's enough noise, you know, enough activity already without having extra and unnecessary…oh I don't know. Never mind. It just different than how it was. That's all. And it's kind of funny because I hear him laughing when he's talking with her and I just think 'well, I thought he didn't like to do this work'. That's all. It's noisier. It's different. It just seems funny. That's all. I don't know. Maybe it's his sister or a client or something. He doesn't want me to answer it is all I know, and then the laughter can be distracting."

"The laughter? Loud laughter?"

"Oh not too loud really, and not very often anyway. Just a little distracting at times."

"Oh. I see. Hmmm. Well, I'm not sure what to tell you. It's okay if he's enjoying the job. I'd rather he did actually. I guess you could ask him to be a little quieter if it's really a problem."

"Oh, that's alright. I'm sorry. You know, I guess I'm just used to being here alone when you're gone. It's so quiet then. Anyway, I just want to be able to do my job. That's all. And now it's gotten different all of a sudden."

"I see. Well, just try to think of it as a small adjustment. His presence could really help us grow."

"I know. Sorry, I don't want to seem nosey or cause any trouble. I'd rather you handle it when you get back. I guess I just wanted you to know how I was feeling. Sorry I mentioned it. I'll just try to get along and do my job."

"Thanks. I appreciate that. We all have to make adjustments for changes in life. It'll probably just take a little time for you to adjust to him being there."

"Uh-huh." She sounded less than enthusiastic.

"Look," said Bea, trying to sound sympathetic and reasonable at the same time, "I can't do anything right now about what's going on there, unless you want me to talk to him about it on the phone. Do you want me to do that?"

"Oh, no, never mind. Sorry I brought it up. I'll work on adjusting, like you said. After all, you're the boss."

"Okay," said Bea, sensing dark clouds on the horizon"...*and he's not, you mean...*

She heard the other line ring in the background of the office. "You'd better get that. I'll hold." She waited until Candy got back on.

"Sorry," said Candy, "just a student with some questions."

"It's okay. Listen, unless there's something else pressing I need to get off now to plan out the training for Perry tomorrow."

"Yeah, everything's fine. I'm getting everything done that you left me."

"Good. Is Jay there now?"

"No, he's not. He just left. I think to meet someone."

"You mean a client at his office?"

"I don't know. I guess so. Who else would he meet?"

Chapter 26

"I was conscious of a slight insanity in my mood, and seemed to foresee my recovery."
(Walden, Henry David Thoreau)

THE NOONTIME TRAFFIC ON the rain-slicked freeway was finally thinning out as back-to-work drivers crowded the exit lanes like stampeding buffalo through a chasm towards the cliff. Jay glided the Mercedes along the glistening arc of the oil-stained on ramp and slowed down to merge into the cramped flow of cars clogging the exit just ahead of him. Overhead in the darkened sky groups of mottled clouds loomed like large clustered mushrooms and scattered drizzle on the windshield in time with the wipers. He cautiously threaded through the pack across the first two lanes then accelerated quickly, nimbly negotiating a spot in the fast lane, and joined the procession speeding northward.

He was going to a university, about two hours away, to speak to a large gathering of Japanese students, here on a special one-semester program; something he had never done before. It gratified, amazed, and frightened him all at once. Suddenly he had two careers, two jobs, two sources of income, and found in turn that he had two opposing sets of feelings about it. He was basically uncomfortable with the thought of being a businessman, even with an idealistic enterprise such as this. It was just not his bent. But he loved the newfound feeling of relief he now felt in relation to his private practice. He no longer cared as much if his clients paid late and worried less than before over having a light week. He was finally feeling a little more slack and foresaw more of it coming if his role in the operation continued to be productive.

It was odd to feel good about succeeding at something he really didn't care very much to be doing, and yet it was also enjoyable in a way to exercise what flair he did have for commerce. It was fun as an independent entrepreneur to offer new services to large universities. He was truly on the international cutting edge of societal change by bringing cultures together and that thought alone made the work more tolerable. At times he'd even actually enjoyed it. He'd been doing it now for nearly a month with alternate days at his counseling office, and had generated immediate income through some local colleges that had welcomed his proposals to place their students with Host Families. The plan he intended to present today was far more ambitious; the one Bea had originally envisioned.

Local students could spend Christmas holidays with American or even Canadian families in many cities out of state, and all under his direction. Several schools had already given him the green light. Today's presentation was directly to the students. If they liked what they heard and signed up in large numbers for a winter Homestay, he could make a lot of money soon; exactly when he needed it. Beyond that the potential for profit was starting to appear unlimited. He'd learned that several universities in the state, not only this one, brought in large groups of Japanese students for a single semester each fall and spring. He could offer both Christmas and Spring Break programs for the new groups of students in rotation endlessly. Suddenly the future seemed bounded by only his ability to expand his programs to other colleges and perhaps someday even other cities throughout America.

In preliminary talks with college officials on the subject he had found a surprisingly welcome reception and for more than just holiday break programs. A Homestay was apparently a novel idea whose time had arrived; a crest on a wave of the swelling tide of multiculturalism, the trendy new movement sweeping colleges. Diversity on campus, excluding conservatives of course, was a popular and growing concept. Since colleges charged much higher admission fees to foreign students than to Americans, they were aggressively competing with other schools for that income, and were only too happy to make their campus more inviting to prospective internationals by adding a Homestay to their residential options. The ever-popular dorms were typically filled before foreigners had even a chance to apply for them and the only alternative – solitary living in expensive apartments – filled many a foreign parent with uneasiness; much better their children were with warm loving families. Aside from the possibilities of programs for the whole school year, right now the Christmas holidays were in play. They were difficult for students far away from their homelands and he hoped the new notion of a home away from home would be a welcome one to all parties; students, parents, and schools.

Along with the nervous anticipation he felt over whether or not the idea would fly – were his prices too high – could he answer all their questions – were his prices too low – could he deliver if they said yes – he felt an unusual gut-wrenching nausea in the pit of his stomach that stubbornly persisted with each passing mile. Since youth he'd felt crippled by a shyness that made it nearly impossible for him to address large groups. The same sensitivity that served him well as a therapist had arisen from a timidity that had made him wary of others since childhood, especially with his early teen years in the race-charged hostile climate of sun-baked San Bernardino. The move to Orange County in his first year of high school was a sweet breath of fresh air; the climate and people both being more temperate. Though he grew more social and out-going there in time and with age, learning to understand and so to handle other people, his abhorrence of public speaking had never dissipated. In one-on-one or with small groups he was fine, even thrived, but large ones were nerve-wracking, and he had never before had to address one of this size.

Twice in college he had taken speech classes to help overcome his inhibition, but he had failed the first one miserably and barely cked through the second. Today's test would be far more severe than addressing a dozen of his university classmates. He would speak to a hundred people, all of whom he had never met before, to persuade them to buy his services and trust him to provide them; something he had never done before. Looking down on the seat next to him at some notes he had scribbled on office stationary, he saw the logo of Bea's company – a pair of hands clasped across a globe – and reflected how important the success of this mission was to his wife, still out of town. If he could establish another substantially profitable avenue of business it would free them both from the fear of insufficiency. And with all of his hard work, at a task foreign to him, in the tense and hectic atmosphere of the office, he deeply wanted his profits to be substantial.

Feeling the butterflies still quaking in his gut, he glanced down at some tapes on the passenger seat he'd brought along to play. They were recordings of his last few conversations with Leroy...*a perfect time for some enlightenment*...

He gripped the wheel tightly in both hands to navigate the last long winding curve uphill to the summit towering above the plateau. Reaching the top suddenly revealed a broad vista of flatlands stretching below for miles on end. The breathtaking beauty of it gave him an instant's peace as he surveyed the crisscross patterns, greens and browns, of approaching fields and pastures spanning far into the distance; a panoramic patchwork in a vast and fertile valley laying just outside the rolling hills of suburbia. He slid back his seat another notch on the floor, set the cruise control at seventy-five, and reached for a cassette. Slipping it in the tape deck, he stretched his back and legs momentarily, then took a deep breath to relax while the car whisked downhill in the rain like a skier on a steep slope towards the stretch of open road that ran north through the farmlands.

"We're rolling. Go ahead Jay."

"Well, I'm listening to the tapes and am aware that doing so has a good influence on me. It tends to allow me to brush away whatever fears I'm entertaining. And I feel like I have to be persistent in this no matter what, uh, but there's a real strong undercurrent that keeps tugging at me."

"That's because you're in the middle of a voyage. What you're looking for is a place to land, essentially, a place to ground your self. And the work you're doing involves two things: becoming more and more conscious, and at the same time allowing always for the experience of peace. The tension arises when you realize that becoming more conscious sometimes seems like not much fun and it seems like it would actually be easier to become unconscious because peace would seemingly be very easy at that point. So what you are doing is hard. There is a gradual increase in what you see and its like the lights are being turned up and at every increment of increased lighting you see more things. Some of them don't bring you much pleasure. Some do.

"So what you're having to do is to still suck it up. Find some peace right there in your relative incapacity to do anything about the things you are now seeing that you don't like. This is a gradual humiliation of the ego. You keep seeing more, you keep feeling helpless, and you keep going for your peace. Now it's not all like this. But the moments that you're in where you find yourself straining to get a handle on something, straining for something familiar that feels like ease and control in the old way, which feels like success, it is not forthcoming. But you are going to see no problems, nothing threatening you, nothing breaking down, so that there is not anything that you'll really be able to complain about, tangibly speaking, but you'll still feel like that opportunity to gorge on control and independent ego willfulness is still not going to be satisfied. Do you understand?"

"Not exactly, no."

"Well, it's because you are so conditioned to think that you need an advantage of one sort or another in order to have your good. And just seizing that advantage and being able to move with it is very satisfying to a part of you that is basically being prevented from having that experience. You think in some way you need to qualify for your good. What you're going to find here, as you stay with this, is that your good will come to you without any satisfaction from the ego, because its not going to require you to be in any better position than what you are right now. So what do you do about that? Well, you let go and you enjoy where you are as much as possible, and understand that there is a process, a very real process, going on, of exhausting the ego of its energy, of its vitality, of its purported existence and it feels like something not very comfortable if you're particularly identifying with it. If you feel yourself lapse into separation and lack for example, and you feel this energy dissipation going on, you're not going to like the feeling."

"Hmmm."

"So it's real important to understand that you have an option now of changing stations, of listening to something else, when this is going on. You do have that choice not to get caught up in the work that's being done on you. Just imagine that you are in a dentist or doctor's office and they are doing something and you're under relative comfort and sedated in some way. If you put your mind to it, you can get into the fact that something uncomfortable is going on. But it's not appropriate for you to spend any time in that point of view. Similarly, now, it's really appropriate for you to enjoy yourself and feel as much freedom as you can, even though there is something going on that if you engage it from an ego viewpoint, won't particularly feel good."

"Well, is there any way I can pay bills on time now and engage that fact from a non-ego point of view?"

"Yes, you can say to God, 'If it's all the same to you, I'd like to do this' and just let that be, and not feel the pressure and conflict. That's part of the problem though. You're having to say uncle on this point of insisting that it be paid on time because it means something to you in the wrong way. There's nothing wrong with paying things on time but you have an agenda here around doing that that needs to be broken. You have a responsibility, your respectability, your trustworthiness and so on."

"Yeah."

"Now the question of trust is an important point, and what I will say will turn things around for you if you really embrace it. The more you trust what you're doing, the more trust becomes a factor in the expression of your good and how you conduct your business. And so from living from trust, having that be your mainstay, you're going to find that it will take that very form that you're asking, which is that the bills will get paid on time; that will be the tendency."

"Trust what?"

"You have to trust your safety right now. You have to trust that you're supported – those basic things. You see paying your bills on time as evidence of you being trustworthy, of being reliable in some way."

"Well, I cleaned up a big credit mess a dozen years back and if I don't pay these bills I'm afraid we're going to slip right back into it, and it just seems to create a lot of headache and heartache."

"Well I just have one word for that: 'tough'. Because it's not supposed to be a problem, but you're going to have to get past the point of making it a problem or feeling it as a problem. You're just going to have to do that without any accommodation to your error here in belief. You're just going to have to trust that however it looks at the moment, you're taken care of."

"Hmm."

"Look, you got on a plane and went to Europe. Did it ever occur to you how much courage that might take?"

"Well, it scared the shit out of me actually. I just don't think about it."

"Yeah, but you trusted them. You trusted the airplane, you trusted the people in the plane enough to get on the plane."

"Yeah."

"Alright. Same thing here. You're on a flight. You haven't landed. I mentioned that. That's what the ego is looking for, a landing right now, because this is an extended period of having to trust the unknown, to be comfortable in your suspense. And that is all that you have to do. Nobody is setting you up to have grief here. No one is setting you up to have an attack from your creditors."

"Hm."

"What if you believed everything that I've said, and just said 'Oh, well that's great, thanks'? What does it feel like to believe what I've just said?"

"Remarkably peaceful and joyous."

"All right. Well, that's all you have to do. It doesn't even matter whether it is true or not. If you believe it's true, it's true. Do you understand what I'm saying? We're not about objective reality here. We're talking about what happens when you make this shift. And the truth is that when you make this shift, reality becomes what you believe. It is according to your belief. So, you see, there isn't an objective here. It's all subjective. So you can make that shift, you see, and that's all there is; you live in that place."

"I understand. I guess I need to continue practicing it."

"Yeah you do, but guess what? You are going to do it. There is real movement for you to get this. That is what is going on."

"You feel that?"

"Yeah. That's all that's going on. You have clearly authorized this piece of learning, this particular unfoldment now and so you're going to learn it. You're going to learn to live right where you are with sufficient trust and with sufficient fulfillment."

"Hmm."

"See, this is important. The word sufficiency is really good because you have a problem here. You experience to some degree adequacy, which is less than sufficient. But sufficiency is a word really used to describe that which is appropriate for the balance of the situation. Sufficiency is what you need to be with. You need an abundance of sufficiency now, which means that you want things that express balance. You'd be quite happy with that. You'd be quite happy to see that the experience of imbalance that you call 'not being able to pay your bills on time' can be absolutely remedied by you feeling no imbalance in your self; by you choosing to feel at peace. Because by doing that you are already experiencing the essence here, which is sufficiency. Sufficiency is a word for the adjustment that is made in life at any point where there's a need to accommodate a shift or movement. And when something needs to be offset, it is offset to a degree that one calls sufficient. So you want sufficiency. Sufficiency feels like peace and balance. You don't want more than what is sufficient."

"Yeah, I don't feel like I want anything but to be free from fear."

"Right, but I'm giving you here an understanding of how little it takes from your end to play the game right now, which is basically: do what you can to be free from apprehension and fear, feel balance in your heart and feel no pressure there. That then is the internal experience of sufficiency and all you have to do then is say 'Yes, I agree with this, and I'm going for it'. And what will happen in your life is that there will be a manifestation of sufficiency in any area that it is needed, and you just keep doing this; you keep with the idea here of sufficiency."

"Okay, I understand….mmmm… I feel sustained, nurtured, tapping into the right part of me when engaging you and can draw upon it somewhat when I'm alone. And whenever I leave it I even can get back to it to some degree, sooner or later. I mean, I'm good for the moment, but…"

"Yeah, well you know what? The moment is enough. What you're doing in the moments while we're talking glides beyond the moment. Your needs are met at this time and the peace you are feeling is assuring your good."

"Well, I believe you, and yet it's hard not to believe the point of view of the stack of bills I have."

"Oh, right. But it does not matter because the feeling good that you have right now is the solution. Nothing else is the solution. But by feeling good like this you can trust."

"Hmmm."

"Okay, look at is like this. Suppose that you got this idea of how to be at peace and feel good and free all the time and the bills never got paid. You wouldn't care anyway. Do you see what I'm saying? I want to say that that scenario is not possible; it is not possible for you to feel good all the time and feel free and not be able to experience this particular issue unfolding well. But I'm trying to make the point that you need to be unconditionally in your peace. If you were willing to be carefree and have no bill ever paid again, well then, there is nothing stopping you from being at peace."

"Hmm…Well, I'm not there yet. Most the time I'm still pretty worried and upset, but what keeps me going is the thought that I'm actually genuinely awakening maybe."

"Well, you are, but that's also what I mentioned to begin with; you wake up a little more and you see a little more and then you see some apparent need to act and you can't find a way of acting and that creates some tension. You see?"

"Well, that reminds me of a kind of general feeling I get sometime, I can't quite articulate it, but it has to do with this sense of life that feels like we're just being these little beings in these bodies temporarily on this little globe in space – a sort of objective look at it all, like we're these little ants on a hill – it's not negative exactly but it's just a sense like there's really no words for what we're doing here. I mean, we've got this culture and this language, and there has been hundreds of cultures and thousands of years of them, but it still just seems like no one has any idea what were doing and sometimes I feel keenly the pain of other people like single moms or something and it seems hard to bear the …uh… so anyway that's how I read it and uh… so then I try to come back to 'okay, just be happy now' and uh…"

"Well, I can generalize on that just to tell you that it is no fun to be unconscious. It really isn't. And I mentioned earlier that what was going on was that you were getting little by little more conscious and having to adjust and allow for peace at greater levels of illumination where you see things that you cannot directly affect and the inability to directly affect things is very hard on the ego, though it isn't hard on you at all. Your bills you can't directly affect, you can't directly affect single moms, you can't -"

"You mean feeling other people's pain is a function of my ego?"

"No, not necessarily. It depends if you can distinguish between compassion and sympathy. Whereas sympathy joins in the suffering but compassion knows the truth of the individual and seeks to comfort and knows there is pain going on. You don't have to desensitize your self to the pain of others but it is not necessary for you to embrace the pain in order to recognize what's going on and be compassionate."

"I can feel peaceful and happy in the face of someone getting hurt, for example."

"Yeah, well you'll feel compassion but you also know the truth. Right now it is a little hard because you are acutely aware of helplessness."

"So knowing the truth will help me heal others?"

"Yeah. You see it's not always going to feel as helpless as you do right now."

"Good, 'cause I'm getting sick of this."

"Well, that's what I'm saying. This is the work that's going on, and it's like work."

"I hear you."

"And you are helpless because your whole concept of taking action is based upon having an advantage. It's based upon a less than innocent view of life. In your perfect innocence you would be able to act spontaneously without there having to be any right condition for it to be effective. In the world of doubt, in the ego's world, in the world of lost innocence, you need to have circumstances give you an advantage to provide the opportunity for this to take place."

"I understand what you're saying."

"So you're having to understand how it is like to be innocent again, and as your innocence is restored, you come more to the place of being able to act for any good purpose and have it be exactly what is appropriate. And it's hard work. It's hard getting to that point because the ego is looking for a way of having it occur in its old familiar pattern."

"Thanks. Okay. I feel good...ah... right now."

"You're present in the moment."

"Okay. Can you feel the difference in me?"

"Oh, of course. That's the whole point. You come to me and I am never sympathetic but I have some compassion and I see my job as coercing you into seeing it my way."

"Well, it doesn't take much coercion." (laughter)

"And I don't abide any disagreement either...(laughter)... I know that I'm formidable in this."

"Well, only because there's no room for any." (laughter)

"Okay. Hey, how's your friend with the bust by the way?"

"Barry? Oh, I'm not sure, but the last time I spoke with him he had a lawyer and sounded better."

"Good. He should be alright. You have about four minutes left. Are there any other questions you'd like to ask?"

"Uh, I was wondering… I got something in the mail yesterday, a little card from Seattle Pacific University. I don't know how they got my name but it said 'We're considering opening up a doctoral program and would you be interested?' and it really felt good. Maybe because they are local as opposed to these out of state programs I've been trying to coordinate and they're smaller, probably more personal than the UW, because – and this is kind of funny for me – but I thought 'And they believe in God'. And normally, not too many years ago, I would have rejected any kind of orthodox sort of thing or institutionalized God thing, but I just thought 'I don't have to put up with this clinical intellectual academic nonsense where you pretend everything's godless and you figure it out in your mind'."

"Hey, oh yeah, that's wonderful."

"So I wondered if it seemed appropriate for me to consider this over the Santa Barbara program, which Rex had been encouraging me to get in for years, and that may have been appropriate at the time, but I've remained ambivalent about it."

"Well, the Santa Barbara program still feels pretty strong, but this is something to explore. It has purpose in it and there's no way of knowing –"

*…shit…*The half-hour tape ended abruptly and the reverse side was blank. He had no recollection and there would be no way of knowing the last few minutes of that session. The anxiety that had dissipated while he was listening to the tape slowly started to resurface. He put the cassette away and slipped in his favorite Willie and Lobo CD; the one they had autographed for him at the jazz club in Seattle. The undulating cries of gypsy violin with the passionate pangs of Spanish guitar was a peaceful distraction for the next forty minutes in unrelenting rain until he saw the big green freeway sign for the college exit showing a mere ten miles to go. He started again to feel queasy and tried to settle his thoughts. There was nothing to do but take the bull by the horns and go forward.

He practiced deep breathing for the next ten minutes until pulling into the parking lot. The campus was larger than he'd realized. The downpour made it harder to see though he had an umbrella. He found the building after getting directions from a girl in hiking boots with a pierced tongue and stopped at the lavatory on the way in to freshen up. While washing his hands and face he looked into the mirror…*well, here goes nothing*…Fighting back nervousness he strode out the bathroom looking as confident as he could muster. As he approached the double metal doors to the auditorium he had a fleeting thought of Daniel entering the lion's den.

Chapter 27

"When you have learned how to decide with God, all decisions become as easy as breathing. There is no effort, and you will be led as gently as if you were being carried down a quiet path in summer." (A Course in Miracles)

THE FIRST RAYS OF sunrise squinted through the closed blinds of Bea's hotel window in thin lines of neon amber. Her soft blond tresses cascaded across the pillow as she instinctively rolled onto her other side, turning her back to the brightening aura. She had been blissfully lost in a dream until that very moment when the dawn's golden glow seeped into the room, sparking a subtle shift back toward wakefulness, her consciousness curling, climbing to the light. As the brightness grew bolder, she pulled the sheet over her face, gently struggling to stay unaware of it, even as she felt sleep slipping faster away. Try as she may to stay asleep, slowly, inevitably her mind moved on.

After a few minutes more of futile attempts to insinuate herself back into slumber, she blinked several times, eyelashes flashing like newborn butterflies, and glanced at the clock: 6:06. She yawned mightily, customarily her first morning movement, and while on her back stretched her arms high, straight up, palms back. This time would normally have been an hour too early but today was different and she felt the first fluttering of excitement already stirring in her heart as she made her way out of bed.

After ordering a pot of coffee from room service, she freshened up in the bathroom, then sat back against a pillow to sip herself awake to the morning drone of Canadian television news. Her flight wasn't leaving until the late afternoon so as eager as she was to head for Pittsburgh there was really no reason for rushing through the morning. The unfamiliarity of the local news stories combined with the pleasant cadence of the talkative TV hostess set her mind adrift, reviewing the last few days with satisfaction. The training with Perry had gone well, she had felt, and it seemed as though the prospects for his improvement were brightening considerably. She recalled the talk she'd had about him with Leroy just a few days prior to leaving for this trip.

Jay had been speaking with him, as he did now on a weekly basis, and wanted her to hear Leroy's take on her situation. A tape of the conversation had arrived in the mail from him the day before she left and Jay had stuffed it in her suitcase in the hope it might be helpful or interesting to listen to if she had the time. She flipped off the television and pulled her small portable tape player from the side pouch of her suitcase. The tape was already in it and she pushed in the play button. Leroy had just finished speaking with Jay and had stopped the recording, then started it again when Bea came on the phone.

"Okay, let's go."

"You're very good at shifting gears, I'll have to say, when you speak to people."

"Oh, yeah, yeah, I am. But you know that came because I sort of grew up doing this without know what I was doing, and it wasn't until I came across Saul that I understood what was happening and what had been happening all my life."

"Really? That people just talk to you, you mean?"

"I mean that in speaking to them I would suddenly connect and I would be someone else – or not someone else – but have such a different point of view and was so unequivocal, and I had no reason for being that way. It was just how it was."

"Ahhh. So it just sort of comes through you, huh?"

"Yeah. Yeah, it always did and it's now that I identify it and it's also that now I make a buck doing it too." (laughter)

"Yeah, right, and say 'thank you' along the way." (laughter)

"Oh you bet, you bet. So."

"So I have a couple of business questions."

"Okay."

"I leave Thursday and have to go back east and to Toronto. I had a man who was in charge of the Toronto programs this past summer and we had some problems with the programs and, uh, it came down to he wasn't being supervised closely enough and when questioned he would give me answers that were sort of right but not quite right."

"Yeah."

"And so it made me look to my clients like I wasn't telling a straight story. So I guess my dilemma is that part of me thinks I need to fire him and find someone new and train them and all that, and part of me thinks experience is the best teacher – he's very aware of all the problems – and should I give him a second chance?"

"Yeah, I would say give him half a chance."

"Give him half a chance?"

"Yeah. In other words, the moment that there's any collapse into inefficiency or chaos, go somewhere else. He knows how to do it; that's the truth. He's not incompetent, but he also is not handling the pressure and responsibility very well, partly because his own life is a little bit rocky. He needs to pay attention to his work, and that will make him feel better, but he's paying attention to other things, and that's why. But he is able to do it. He needs to be encouraged that to pay attention and be meticulous is going to feel good and that is what you would like him to do. But don't fire him at this point. You only have to do that if he begins to lapse again."

"Yeah, then my dilemma is that I'm halfway into the season without a back up. I'm thinking if I'm there I probably should be looking for someone to take his place if I need to let him go."

"No. You can't premeditate this."

"I can't premeditate it?"

"You can't premeditate it. You're going to have to trust that letting him proceed with his job is the right thing, and that if it becomes necessary to can him that there will also be support in the form of an easy solution here."

"It will become obvious that someone is there to take his place?"

"Right. There will be continuity of fulfillment of purpose here. Yeah, that is absolutely the point. So you don't have to start then becoming isolated and deliberative in your point of view, which is not any fun."

"No. Well, I would feel like I was deceiving him on some level."

"Right, yeah. You want to give him another chance and you don't want to compromise that with a hidden agenda. But if it becomes necessary to get rid of him, then trust that there will be continuity of fulfillment and that you don't have to do any of that now."

"Okay. Well, that's a load off. I have to tell you how accurate you were, in that he's been having trouble with his teenage son and I know – and dogs dying – and all of that, in his family life, and it got in his way when he was doing the job. So you were right on."

"Yeah, I could tell that there was just too much distraction, and that he's actually able."

"Well, I've had that feeling too, but everyone here keeps saying I'm making a mistake by giving him another chance. And if I give him a chance and he blows it, I'm going to lose a lot of business – half my business. So a lot rides on his performance and I almost hate to put that on his shoulders. But he knows that."

"No. You see, again that assumption that you're going to lose half your business, that's a concept that you are projecting out there. You aren't going to lose any of your business if you stay in the center, if you stay grounded here, if you trust. You see, you're not trusting him. You're trusting the integrity of your own Being to fulfill itself perfectly. It doesn't matter who the participants are, who else is in the cast here. Your good comes to you because you are centered, not because so-and-so is doing a good job back east or not. If you have that kind of burden, it's on you not on him, you see, and you need to be free of that. You need to say 'I trust that this works out perfectly and that I can afford to be present, at ease and unburdened in the moment and I will know exactly what to do at any point'."

"You're right." (laughter)

"That's how you get there."

"I know. (laughter) I forget."

"And every thing in your life is designed to teach you that, you see. It's all about that lesson. Of course every body gets it wrong. They misread the lesson. They think the lesson's about control and it's not about control. It's about trust. But you're not trusting people. You're trusting the very integrity of life and your own Being."

"Okay."

"God, that is supportive. I mean when you realize that that's what it's about and it's not about other people's performance…"

"Yeah, it puts everything into the right perspective."

"Absolutely."

"Okay, good. Well, my instincts were sort of aligned with what you're saying, so that's encouraging."

"Yeah, you need to feel the obvious rightness of that, and then you can afford to let go of whatever -"

"It's fear. I can feel it."

"- resistance you have to letting go like this."

"Um-hm, okay."

She smiled to herself and stopped the cassette as she sipped her coffee to contemplate the words against the experience of her trip. It did appear indeed that Leroy had been right, as she had been right, that Perry could be trusted, at least one more time because, wonder of wonders, life could be trusted, with perfect certainty. She wondered was it true? As she'd said on the tape, she'd forgotten all about the thought of trusting in life. She tried to be trusting in God but her way of doing that usually entailed working overtime all the time and hoping He came through in the tough spots. She recalled the little sign on her desk about making the effort and never being let down.

Feeling pleased with herself, her decision and her instincts, she imagined the disgruntled look on Candy's face on when she returned from Toronto. She knew her skeptical secretary would think she was making a huge mistake trusting any man, let alone life itself. Neither had proven too trustworthy for her. She was even insinuating Bea couldn't trust Jay. It was there implicitly, in their last phone dialogue, buried in a transparent concern for the operations in the office. She had suddenly felt uneasy from the subtle seeds of doubt sown covertly in Candy's snide intimation…*there's always some woman…i hear him laughing*… When she had spoken to Jay later that evening he was spoiling to introduce the subject of Candy.

They had ended up arguing about the situation. He was irritated on hearing that Candy had accused him of listening to her calls but he much more upset at the notion that he was talking to another woman unrelated to work. He declared Candy crazy but was begrudgingly deferential to the fact that Bea relied upon her heavily and did not want for her to leave. Her thoughts shifted back to the first one with Candy…*who else would he meet…* as she recalled the contentious conversation with her husband.

"What did she say exactly," he had asked, "other than things were harder here without you?"

"She said basically she thought you were avoiding her, as though you didn't want to have anything to do with her."

"Well, actually I don't, unless I really have to. But I'm not rude about it. I just keep to myself. I give her stuff to type when I need it and try to be civil. What else did she say? You seem rather upset just for that."

"Well," Bea paused, unsure about getting into it, "she said that she thinks you were listening to her phone calls."

"What? What phone calls? What is she talking about?"

"She said she hears little sounds on the line at times when she has a personal call, like with the doctor's office or her kids."

"Why would I do that? She spends a lot more time on personal calls while you're gone but I don't listen to them. That's paranoia. And I doubt they are just to her kids or the doctor. I'll tell you another thing. I came in once while she was on the phone with someone and she had her feet up on the desk. Course she took them right down – I surprised her – but still -"

"I don't care about that."

"Why not?"

"Because it's a little thing. She gets the job done and that's what I need. I don't want to get caught up in sweating the small stuff. I don't want to be distracted from work with this stuff."

"You really don't care if she does that?"

"No."

"Jesus, I can't believe this. It's sneaky of her. It's not right. You're paying her for her time and -"

"People come with baggage, Jay! I've learned that in this business. I don't expect them to be perfect, and Candy, despite her faults, has been doing a good job."

"Well, I know but – look, if she really thinks I'm listening in to her phone calls she really is paranoid. I mean, she is really nuts if she thinks that. Clicks on the line? Tricks in her mind."

"Okay, may be. Who knows? I'm not there." Bea sighed aloud. "She has not had an easy time with men. She doesn't trust them. She does not have an easy life."

"Who does?"

"I don't know. Not me, but I'm not complaining about it. I just need for you two to do your jobs and not make the office more stressful for all of us. She and I have been getting along fine for nearly two years now and I don't want to lose her or have any bad feelings there."

"Okay, okay, I know that. I understand. But listen. I get the impression she does not want me there. She doesn't like me and she doesn't like men. And I don't like being around someone like that. It's uncomfortable – and especially in my own home."

"Don't take it so personally. You always do that. It's not all about you. I think she can change. I think she'll adapt, sooner or later, to you being there. But she can do it a lot sooner if you'll be more cooperative. It's really not that hard."

"Alright, alright. Okay. I'll try. But it isn't going be easy." He frowned and pursed his lips in thought, considering the possibility of peaceful co-existence with someone he loathed. "Did she say anything else?"

"Oh, not really."

"What does that mean?"

"Oh…nothing…"

"What?"

"Well," Bea sighed audibly again, slightly softer, "just that you grab the third phone line before she can answer it, so she doesn't know who's calling. And if she picks up then you tell her to get off the phone."

"I don't tell her to get off the phone."

"What do you say?"

"I just say 'I've got it, it's for me'."

"That's the same thing."

"Why does she need to know who I'm talking to?"

"She's used to answering the phone when there's a call – all calls. It's always been her job. And she's frustrated you pick up calls from some woman before she can get to them."

"Calls from some woman? That's what she said?"

"Yes."

"Oh God. This is crazy. Look, I just gave that number – the third line – to several college people I'm working with so they can reach me easily. They happen to be women. So what? The first two lines are frequently tied up with Candy on one or both of them – especially since you've been gone, I might add – and I don't want to wait until she answers the phone to get a call meant for me. It might go unanswered. I just want to run my own show smooth and fast. There's a lot to do and never enough time."

"Well, why don't you just tell her this??"

"I did. I told her I'd be taking calls on the third line."

"Did you elaborate much on why?"

"No, not really. I don't feel I have to explain my business to her."

"You're a therapist, Jay. She's having to make an adjustment to you being there. Can't you communicate with her any better than this?"

"Yeah, yeah, you're right, I can, I can. She's just so hostile, so passive-aggressive. I know she doesn't like me there, so I minimize my contact with her as much as possible."

"Well, you can't do that completely. There has to be some interaction. What is she supposed to make of a woman calling often and you answering it so quickly?"

"Well wait, look, there are several people, not one, and they are all from local colleges. They just happen to be women. That's all. And if she's making something out of that, well, she is more screwed up than I thought."

"Oh, settle down. She's just upset you're taking over her job. She's used to taking all the calls, screening them, taking messages. We get a lot of telemarketers and she's suspicious of callers till she knows them or what they want."

"Suspicious of men, you mean."

"Yeah, well, that too."

"She hates men, actually. Is that really why you're upset? She gave you the impression that something funny's going on? I'm getting calls from some woman?"

"No, no, not really. I don't know what to think and I don't want to have to think about this kind of stuff. I just want the two of you to get along so I can work in peace. I don't want the stress. It's not good for me, or the office, or business, and I want it to stop. You're both adults. Can't you please act like it?"

"Okay, okay," muttered Jay, in a mixed tone of resignation and disgust. "Alright," he added, trying to assure her. "I'm sorry we made a problem for you." It was futile to pursue the topic any further now. "I better go get Phil. Soccer's about over. I love you. Bye-bye."

It had been an unpleasant way to end her day but she hoped in urging him to be more considerate of Candy that she might in turn not go off the deep end with unsettling suspicions. After all, that's probably all that they were. Baseless suspicions of a beleaguered mind…*maybe it was his sister*…The very word 'sister' reminded her of her own, whom she would be seeing very shortly in Pittsburgh. She wanted to relinquish the thoughts of the phone talks and recapture the quiet sense of eager anticipation with which she had awakened that morning…*i've done all i can*…Putting it behind her, she decided to listen some more to the tape. Leroy had been so right about Vienna and seemingly about Perry, what else could he shed light on? Recalling they had talked on numerous subjects she punched in the button, took a long sip of warm coffee and listened.

"Gosh, all my questions are based on fear. As I ask them -"

"They're all based on curiosity and mistrust."

"Yeah."

"It's fine not to know, you see. If you can, as I say, be at peace with suspense, you have got it made. So what I do is basically push you back to the point of accepting *not knowing* as natural; that curiosity leads to revelation and discovery. So what we're doing here is going through a process of your curiosity leading to revelation or discovery. That's what we're practicing here, and so on your own you're going to be more able to have the experience of not knowing, that is to say wonder, followed by curiosity, followed by revelation or discovery. And that's how life will have to be lived eternally."

"Hm. So, then my next thought is about my husband and I, and unfortunately it always circles around money, and uhh...his practice, and I know he feels...uhhhhh...oh, that's a ... and his music...and uh...I'm not very kind about uh...all that he contributes, sometimes I think that he should be doing more., uh... and again this is probably fear-based, I feel like I'm carrying more than half the load a lot. Uh...any suggestions or advice?"

"Well for one thing, who says it has to be fifty-fifty at any given time?"

"Right."

"So don't think that what he's doing is somehow insufficient. It's that he's in the thick of something where the block to his abundance is directly in front of him. And it's very critical in the sense that this is the moment that it can be undone. And so you have got to trust his process a little more. And yet you can say whatever you feel like saying. If you have a feeling, if you're not at ease with something, you don't have to inhibit what you feel. Yet, you also can feel trust in your own process, and understand that there is no requirement on a spiritual path to be denied your good. It appears that it might occur at times because there are certain beliefs, and when these beliefs come up for release, it may seem as though they are in fact becoming true. So he's at a point now where he's got these things right in his face and he is learning how to not connect his fear to the belief, to the thought. And what is happening is, for example the thought 'I've got no money coming in', if that thought no longer provokes a sense of fear, one is done with that block. Do you see that?"

"Yeah."

"So a lot of this work has to do with understanding that the upset one feels is not connected to circumstances, but the ego says it is in fact connected to circumstances. So one stays stuck in that place. And so what he is trying to do right now is to learn to not be afraid of that thought, which will take energy from this, and drain it, and ultimately he won't have any blocks around this."

"Uh-huh.

"And I mean ultimately isn't like way down the road either. Ultimately is relatively imminent."

"Uh-huh. Hmm."

She hit the stop button to ponder that last point...*that'd be nice...imminent...relatively imminent...*

Chapter 28

"I was supremely happy, for I had seen. Nothing could ever be the same. I have drunk of the pure and clear waters at the source of the fountain of life and my thirst was appeased. Nevermore could I be thirsty. Nevermore could I live in utter darkness; I have seen the light. I have touched compassion, which heals all sorrow and suffering; it is not for myself, but for the whole world. I have stood on the mountaintop and gazed on the mighty Beings. I have seen the glorious and healing Light. The fountain of truth has been revealed to me and the darkness has been dispersed. Love in all its glory has intoxicated my heart; my heart can never be closed. I have drunk at the fountain of Joy and eternal Beauty. I am God-intoxicated."
(Jiddu Krishnamurti, after three days of meditation in Ojai, CA)

JAY WAS SAILING HIGHER than a springtime kite as he left the college campus. Feeling oblivious to the dark skies he was suddenly inclined to celebrate with a beer, which he picked up at a corner store near the school before heading home. Sipping Corona without a slice of lime was a hardship he could now easily endure while flying down the freeway and feeling happy about his speech. He had surprised himself by projecting his voice louder in the auditorium than intended. He was very nearly shouting as he explained the program to them and though ironically it was due in fact only to his nervousness, it had come off like enthusiasm in the large theater space. To his amazement they had applauded enthusiastically at the end of the presentation and he was flush with the giddy thought that many of them might well try it. Nothing to do now but wait for the checks and applications to roll in, if he had read their response rightly, for Christmas Homestays with friendly Host Families around the nation. His sense of exhilaration was quite unexpected and he heard himself humming "Singin' in the Rain" as he barreled southward under the shower.

He looked over his CD's for some lively music and noticed a second tape from Leroy he had left in the console last week. He had not listened to it in its entirety. It was just a short segment but he wanted to finish hearing it. Each tape always helped to lift his spirits by reminding him of truths easily forgotten in the distractions of daily living.

"I was wondering what sort of attitude would be appropriate for Bea and I to have toward each other in relation to working together in this business."

"Well, who's the boss?"

"She's the boss."

"Well, then, in that part of your relationship you have to allow for that."

"Okay, I can deal with that. But what I think I'm really concerned about is that she has an undercurrent of resentment towards me not making enough money in my practice lately. And, uh…"

"Well, yeah, and she needs to understand – and I told her – that she needs to trust your process. That where you are does not afford you the opportunity to satisfy others' expectations for you."

"Boy, that's the truth."

"You just are not in a position to do that. You would if you could. It's not out of willfulness that you find your self where you are. And what I said was to trust the process. Where you are, you have a certain block right there, a certain fear, that you are learning to undo, and that's that."

"Okay. Well, uh, I'm wondering how you get this information."

"What information?"

"The information that you give to me."

"How do you get to feel as good as I do?"

"Yeah, that's one way of asking the question."

"Well finally, you just know that life works. The demonstration of the integrity of life has been consistent enough for a long enough time that the real active doubting ceases. It just does. At some point it just does. Now, there's a certain kind of micro-management of your consciousness that I encourage you to do, which is moment by moment you either feel okay or you feel pressure.

"And so recognizing when you feel pressure that something has got your attention, something is making you feel responsible, and that you have to let go of the pressure. It doesn't mean you ignore circumstances. It just means that you disconnect the feeling of conflict from the circumstances. So then what you have is the feeling of well-being and also a lot of clarity about what to do about circumstances as well. And a lot of times you don't have to do anything because there's already movement for fulfillment anyway. And so you get out of the way. You practice getting out of the way of the movement here, and you see that it's already taken care of things and it really wasn't in your hands anyway."

"Is that like saying, to borrow another phrase of yours, that you recognize that your good's set in motion?"

"That's right, yeah. Well, we talk about need. The feeling of need is really the presence of one's good but the incapacity or inability to discern that it's present, and so you don't see it there. You can't justify or rationalize that it's there, but the feeling of it being there is very strong and so it creates this odd sensation in your denial called need. Do you see what I'm saying?"

"I do."

"So when you feel you need something it's basically because it's there and you're not seeing it."

"So a lot of Psychology is just bullshit built around the ego."

"Oh, Psychology is all bullshit, yeah, I'm happy to say."

"So what do I want a Ph.D. in it for? (hilarious laughter) More BS Piled Higher and Deeper."

"Yeah, well, no. Psychology can be changed."

"Oh yeah, right. I tend to forget I'm a pioneer and not a victim of the system."

"Psychology's basic intent is good. It's to understand and to get to the heart of things. But you see the problem is that Psychology makes one fatal mistake. And that is that it does not acknowledge the reality and the sovereignty of the Infinite. It reduces everything to reasoning, to rationality. And rationality is always a way of describing cause and effect in terms of ratios or fixed relationships. And ratios are always finite; three to one, two to five. You see what I'm saying? They're always finite. And so what happens is you end of with a lot of confusion and the exclusion of the Infinite. And then what happens if you live entirely by rationality is that you end up with shortages of things, because you're not connected with the Infinite. And there's a word that is used to describe how one handles shortages, and the word is rationing. You see? (laughter)

"That's because the Infinite has been excluded, because the system could not provide for every need and every contingency. Well, God can. The Infinite can. So, reasoning is bullshit too. Reasoning is fun and is a way of describing how discovery and revelation sometimes occur, but it is not absolute, because it does not include the Infinite."

"It's like, 'The description is not the described' as Krishnamurti said?"

"Well, yeah, and I use reasoning right now to debunk it. So it has a use. It's just not ultimate. Anything that's relative is always going to be a sort of momentary glance at something and seeing some particular connection but it's not going to be fundamental."

"Hmm. What's it like after death?"

"Just like it is now, basically. The real question is 'Is it different when you are awake?' And yes, of course. Being awake is the answer, not dying because you just die into the same system that you've been living in on earth; an experience of limitation."

"How is being awake different?"

"What happens after death is that people realize, become aware, of the game much more and they do experience some regeneration and they go back for another round of the same experience of limitation again. But birth and death have nothing to do with waking up in that they don't happen after you're awake."

"Hmmm. Do you know what does?"

"Well, of course. What happens after you're awake is that you realize you are experiencing some wonderful eternal gift; that life is a gift."

"Can you be in touch with the giver?"

"You always are. You're always experiencing gratitude, yes."

"Is there is sense of knowing God other than yourself?"

"You know God as Self. You know God as mystery. You know God fully and yet you don't understand God. There's always that element beyond comprehension."

"Beyond reason?"

"Yes. It's the Infinite again. What you do is that you feel safe with this."

"Yes. Thanks. By my clock, our time is up. Did you want to say more? I'm very comfortable with trying to digest what's been said, though we could talk all day probably."

"No, we have enough here. Basically it's a question of trusting your process and you can't do any better than you're doing and that's the way it is. What you have to do is be comfortable with that and give up a sense of responsibility around anything and you'll see what's really there, you see."

"Mmm. Moment by moment."

"Right."

"Hmm…that helps."

He stopped the tape, knowing their conversation had ended…*moment by moment*…If only he could remember to take time to smell the hours…*breathe slowly*… The words were especially inflating at the moment, as he was already elated from his caper at the college. His feelings were also intensified in knowing that Bea would share his elation were things to work out well. Feeling lighter than a brightly colored hot air balloon he downed the last dregs of cold Corona, tossed the bottle on the floor of the passenger side and switched to the sweet strains of the sensual CD he was listening to earlier. Willie and Lobo were in tune with his spirits and he turned the volume up almost as loud as it would go, feeling the pulsations joyously pounding through him. The highway cut through chiseled cliffs of rugged granite, steeped in mountains of dense forest whose dark trees huddled together like crowded tents in a packed campground. It wound along a twisted river rushing madly in the rain, which splashed past boulders, bouncing forth frothy spray, and for the first time in awhile, as he hit eighty miles per hour, he felt mildly ecstatic. Things were looking up.

As he cruised through the raindrops, savoring the apparent good turn in his fortunes, he reflected on his other work, his real work in his mind, his passion, his duty, his destiny, his life's work or so he had thought. It did now seem more likely than ever he would have two careers simultaneously. It was a phenomenon he had not previously entertained; certainly not as a permanent state. To lower the expense of maintaining his practice, he was seriously considering renting office space from another therapist and relinquishing his own. This would be hard. He took great personal satisfaction as well as aesthetic pleasure, in picking and arranging the furniture, art, plants and lamps. He loved mixing and matching the colors and textures, and in setting the shadings that lighted his office; a safe and comfortable space for healing.

He had subleased his own office to many others during the years, for usually one or two days a week, and knew the arrangement could work easily enough. It was also his pride that had kept him from making inquires already to colleagues in the area. The new psychologist, Marianne, next door to him in the office building would probably be amenable to such an arrangement. She was certainly the closest potential option. She had relatively few clients as of yet that he could see, but she was armed with a recent Ph.D. degree and like all fledgling shrinks intending somehow to build a practice. Though seeming a little distant, perhaps shy or just reserved, she was still courteous enough in a professional way and if he didn't like it there he wouldn't have to stay long. She had after all been kind enough to give him the inside scoop on what to expect next from the managed care industry. They wouldn't be working together at all and these things were usually founded on a month by month basis, so...*oh God, i really don't want to give up my office...*

Chapter 29

"Detailed on the night of July 16, 1962, was their experiment smoking marijuana, when the president laughed and said, 'We're having a White House conference on narcotics here in two weeks'. They smoked their joints and then JFK told her, 'No more. Suppose the Russians did something now'."
(Seeds of Destruction, Ralph G. Martin)

THE DUTIFUL DRONE OF the school buzzer sounded, reverberating through the red-leaved maples on the hilltop like a distant swarm of honeybees, announcing the end of the day's last class. As young teens poured out of their classrooms into corridors, Phil walked quietly towards his locker to retrieve the many books required for that evening's homework. He filled his backpack with the customary load of thick tomes that made his slender frame hunch forward to balance the burden ever since school began. Walking on toward the parking lot to meet his father for a ride home he felt the November chill in the air on his neck send a shiver down his spine...*feels like snow*...Recalling all the fun snowboarding trips of last winter he felt anew his anticipation for the steep slopes of the impending season.

Crowded cars encircling the muddy dirt lot mixed into each other like fast and slow skaters on a chaotic ice rink. Older students, revved up and proudly driving themselves, dodged in and around the late model autos of parents arriving to pick up their progeny to the bass thumping backbeat of mesmerizing rap music; the kind Phil was just discovering... *Boom...baba-boom-boom...Boom...baba-boom-boom...Boom...baba-boom-boom...* His father's car wasn't there and he leaned against a nearby telephone pole to wait. He pulled up the collar of his gray woolen vest, tucking it underneath his thick dark locks to ward the breeze off his neck and stuck his fists in his pockets as he eyed the winding driveway and the avenue far below. No sign yet of a chocolate Mercedes amid the steady stream of traffic trailing in the distance. He was tired from another long day of learning and not looking forward to another evening's soccer practice on the marshy fields in the valley. As he played almost year-round on a private team plus the school one, his ball-handling skills were perpetually well honed and his quickness on the turf, especially agile twists and turns, was nearly unrivaled. Last year he had helped his first-place team advance to the state soccer play-offs where he had eventually, late into the final minutes of the decisive game, scored the winning goal that had crowned them state champions.

This year had been harder, with the loss of some key players, and though a feeling of team pride had remained a saving grace, with just a few games left the season was turning out largely disappointing. The practices were grueling, and his severe Scandinavian coach even more so. Even the weather seemed worse. Much of the year had been harder in several ways well besides soccer ever since early spring when his mother's basement office business had become big. Along with seeing less of her, which caused him to miss her – a strange new feeling – the challenging shift from elementary school to junior high had been unexpectedly overwhelming, especially with the strident curriculum demands of the new institution. High-achievement was expected and pressure a given. Overall it had made him pull more deeply into himself, still willingly shouldering his full lot in life but feeling the added weight of a much bigger world, not to mention the girls; the beautiful girls. His sparsely populated classes at the small Montessori school he'd previously attended had prepared him as best it could for the coming academic rigors, but the number of new female students in his presence had soared nearly as high as his hot raging hormones.

He spied a passing blonde girl, head held high, hair braided, with her own bulging book bag strapped tightly to tapered shoulders and swinging just over the swelling curve of her hips, as she slipped through the meandering mélange of vehicles…*nice ass*… Feeling that inescapable burst of unrequited desire that plagues most male teenagers he deliberately diverted his gaze back to the gravel driveway and the boulevard below to relieve his sensation. His ride was not in sight, but lumbering toward him with a crooked half-grin was a large familiar schoolmate in a long black overcoat, one grade above him, who was the red-headed goalie on the school soccer team and sported reddish-gold sideburns down his bright freckled cheeks. They had met earlier in the semester in jazz band, Phil's favorite class, and become friendlier in time as they shared both activities. Though he didn't know him well, he respected him as an athlete and musician, and looked up to him somewhat as a seasoned upper classman. The older boy sidled up to the telephone pole, leaned against the other side of it and slanted his head downward toward Phil.

"What's up?" he asked nonchalantly, the customary greeting exchanged between peers.

"S'up, Ryan?" nodded Phil, meeting his eyes.

"Waitin' for your ride or just holdin' up the pole?" Ryan's half-grin broadened into a self-satisfied smirk with the glee of his own clever jest.

Phil smiled through his tiredness, close-lipped in return. "Just waitin' for my ride, dude."

Ryan nodded, crossed his arms, and surveyed the busy parking lot. "What a mess – check it out." He shook his head and smiled sardonically.

"Yeah. You waitin' for a ride too?"

"Me? No way. That is, not now anyway."

"Whadda' ya'mean?"

"My ride comes later, man, so I don't have to deal with this mess."

"Ah." He could tell Ryan felt this a superior advantage and wondered if it had occurred by necessity or by design, as his attitude seemed to suggest. No further elaboration was forthcoming. Perhaps it was cooler not to talk about such things, not to lord his lofty status over the horde in the parking lot, jockeying for positions like common commuters on the clock. "So you just hang out here awhile?"

"Yeah," he said smugly, his smile widening on one side, while twisting his head around the pole to lean closer. "I just *chill*." Phil nodded knowingly in grudging admiration, aware that this particular activity was uniformly regarded by his peers nationwide as one of the most desirable states of mind a teen could attain in their limited lifespan. He felt a greater appreciation for Ryan's coolness of outlook and chillful demeanor. *Chilling* was something he could definitely use more of, and his curiosity began to kindle.

"So, like, what do you do?"

"Well, like, sometimes I go to the band room and play with the drums. Or some times I just hangout with some guys or girls, whoever's around…and sometimes, if I feel like it, I go for a walk in the woods."

"Really?" Phil had often observed a few students, mostly couples hand in hand, strolling towards there during lunchtime, but he ate in the cafeteria under crowded conditions that had left him little time for exploring the grounds as of yet. Roughly a square block of forest ran along one side of the campus, with two salmon streams and scattered paths running through it, and the backside bordering a large family farm tautly fenced with barbed wire for three generations. Once through a schoolroom window he had seen a class on an apparent field trip being led there by a teacher and had wondered what they could be observing that justified such a pleasant break from the tedium of the classroom. "What's it like there?"

"Oh, man, it's mass cool. Haven't you been there? There's lotsa' paths, some creeks and bridges. Sometimes there's even fish."

"Really?"

"Oh yeah, it's awesome. You never been there?" repeated Ryan with surprise.

"No," said Phil, suddenly feeling a little deprived. "Not yet."

"Oh man. You gotta' see it. You got a minute? We can check it out right now."

Phil looked down to contemplate the invitation. He didn't want to be late to be picked up and moreover, late in turn for soccer practice. That would likely mean extra laps around the mud-puddle track and harsh stinging words from his stern Norse coach. Still, he was curious and a bit bored with waiting in the cold… *just holding up the pole*… His dad was a little late more often than not. He turned again to view the drive and the line of cars leading to it down the hill; no brown bomber yet.

"It won't take long, man, really. Five minutes." Ryan searched his face for clues "Leave your books here – it'll be easier – we can just run right over there and back."

"Aw, I don't know." It was tempting.

"Who's pickin' you up anyway?"

"My dad."

"Is he pretty cool? I mean, will he get mad if you're not here right when he shows?"

"Yeah, well, he's pretty cool, but I got soccer practice later, and don't want to be late."

"Just five minutes, man. Hey, it'll take him at least five minutes to reach the lot in this line."

"That's true," conceded Phil, pursing his lips in reappraisal.

"It's up to you, man. At worst he'll just have to wait a few minutes. Hey, just tell him you were like talking with a teacher. That's what I'd say. What's he gonna' say?"

Phil scanned once more the long bumper to bumper line heading up the hill, seeing no sign still of the cocoa brown car, and mulled over the potential risk and gain…*just five minutes…*

"Alright," he snapped quietly with an adventurous look in his eye. "Let's do it."

"Alright!" exclaimed Ryan. He leaned forward and lowered his voice as his mouth flashed half his teeth in a sideways smile. "This is totally cool, man. You'll see," he said confidently, almost conspiratorially, like a member of a sacred sect sharing secrets with an initiate. "C'mon."

Slipping free of his burdensome pack Phil trotted alongside Ryan up the slightly inclined dirt walkway worn wide by students tramping to and from the gymnasium. It was a straighter trail than the sidewalk and while it ended at the front of the gym a narrow path forked off to the forest on the left side of the building. He was suddenly excited, not only feeling lighter from loosening his load, but delighted at the spontaneous indulgence of his whim, the sudden satisfaction of his curiosity, the thrill of discovery with a brand new friend, a respite from pressure, a real chance to chill. As they passed the gym and reached the edge of the forest Ryan's pace slowed to a fast walk.

"There's the first path right up here – the one everyone takes. But there's one more farther up that's even better 'cause no one hardly takes it at all." He pointed up the hill and looked at Phil for acknowledgement as they passed by the first path. Phil met his look and saw Ryan's eyes had a trace of dark circles, signaling he needed rest…*he's as tired as me…*As he looked forward again to the path less traveled, he noticed on the left a tall stately cedar; a weather-beaten beacon, carved by the elements; fired by summer, whittled by winter, cleansed by the constant caress of the rain. He felt impressed with its stature, its quiet nobility, simply wrought from withstanding what life had to offer while thriving in the process. It was clad in bright clusters of leafy lime green, at the edge of the woods, amidst a group of darker pines, all spared from an indifferent death by development for having grown up on the right side of the line. Its crusty ruffled bark, burnished golden brown by age, bespoke the proud fate denied its once lofty ancestors – the grand old growths beheaded by progress. They'd read about it in school. What the loggers did; killed them off like buffalo. He hated the thought.

"Nice tree," he said quietly.

"Yeah," answered Ryan, turning onto the second trail. "Follow me."

The second path curled left around a ripe cluster of huckleberry bushes, and then swerved down under a low-hanging cedar bough, where the boys ducked slightly to avoid being hit. It curved through the dense trees like a ribbon on the forest floor, unfurling through feathers of ferns, pine needles and tattered leaves until it reached a footbridge of small logs and a railing with a clear creek flowing underneath. A short distance across the bridge the pathway wound around and disappeared behind a small grove of pale slender aspens assembled atop in faded yellow leaves that fluttered in the wind above a tangled thicket of big-thorn blackberries.

"See," said Ryan with obvious satisfaction as he stood on the bridge. "Isn't it cool?"

"Cool," nodded Phil, as he took it all in; listening to the gurgling brook, scanning the multi-colored stones underwater. "Pretty cool."

"No fish right now," said Ryan, looking up and down the stream. "Just some old leaves floatin' by. Great place to chill though, huh?"

They stood still in silence, admiring the quiet spectacle of water effortlessly twisting by and listening to the chorus of the wind whistling through the woods. After a few moments of peaceful reflection, more than he'd felt in quite some time, Phil leaned on the railing and looked up at Ryan.

"So you come here a lot?"

"Yeah, when I feel like it." He laughed and spread his arms out, half turning side to side, like a car salesman extolling the bargains galore on the lot. "Great, isn't it?"

"That's for sure," said Phil as he looked around, breathing it in. He felt himself softening, shifting into a more relaxed state, and definitely starting to begin to chill. His curiosity returned about Ryan's situation. "So what's with your ride, man? You like hanging around here later? Your folks like coming later to miss the crowd?"

"Yeah, I like it fine – really – and it's not my folks, man." He paused for emphasis. "It's my brother." He peered at some crinkled leaves drifting under the bridge, and then added self-assuredly, "He picks me up – soon as he gets off work – and then we go home and work on his car. It's great, cause he hates waitin' in traffic anyway."

"Oh, I see." Ryan shrugged and continued.

"Course I'll be learnin' to drive myself next year."

"Oh, sure," said Phil, grasping the implication of his tone. If one wasn't driving one's self it was clearly quite cooler to be chauffeured about by a hip older brother than one's out-of-it parents. "What kind of car does he have?"

"He's got a Bronco, man, a red one. It's cool." Phil nodded admiringly, knowing Broncos reputation.

"Four wheel drive?"

"For sure."

"What year?"

"Eighty-five."

"Really?"

"Yeah, but it's in good shape, dude." He warmed to the subject. " My brother and me worked on it together. Tricked out the stereo. Totally. It's hot."

"Just you two?"

"Well, uh…," Ryan's enthusiasm faltered momentarily and he fumbled for words. "Actually my Dad, uh, helped us – he's a mechanic – uh, in the beginning…and …but then, uhhh, he's gone right now."

"Gone? You mean like left town or like –" He saw the sadness flash across Ryan's face. "Oh."

"Uhhh…" Ryan hesitated, looking somewhat crestfallen. "My parents are separated, man…my Dad's moved out for awhile."

"Oh…sorry," said Phil, not knowing what to say. He looked away from Ryan to the stream and focused on the smooth stones at the bottom. They both stared at the water winding downstream for a long moment as the wind whooshed through the trees above them. Ryan coughed abruptly, cleared his throat and spat to his far side.

"Hey man, it's no big deal." He shifted his weight back and forth on each foot, and then looked warily around the area, up and down the trail. "It's okay."

"Sure," said Phil, wondering if that was so and wanting to drop the subject as gracefully as possible. They watched more dead leaves glide by like tiny tattered sailboats. "Well," he intoned, "guess I better be getting back." Ryan looked at him and said nothing. "Thanks," he added.

"We got a minute yet." Ryan grinned wryly with his lips shut. " Let me show ya' one thing that's really helped me stay cool."

"What's that, dude?"

Ryan shoved his right hand in his overcoat pocket and proudly produced between his thumb and forefinger a fat wrinkly hand-rolled cigarette with one end twisted tight.

"What's that?" said Phil, suddenly taken aback, unsure of the gesture and feeling wary.

"It's weed, man," whispered Ryan with muted eagerness. "Grass, hemp, pot, you know… marijuana."

Although he had never seen it, he did know of it all right. He knew of it from the rumors of the exploits of other students, older ones, at wild parties that he had not been invited to. He knew of it from exciting footage of the media's turbulent tales of the sixties. He knew of it from the hints hidden in his parent's stories of their college days. And he knew of it most recently, most flagrantly of all, from every gyrating rap artist he'd ever heard and seen on MTV. Weed was the undisputed supreme currency of Chill, the treasured taboo of the coolest musicians on the tube. "Wow," said Phil, as though piecing together fuzzy parts of a puzzle. "You do that?"

"Sometimes," nodded Ryan, "every once in awhile." He peered at Phil as his smile spread slowly over one side of his mouth. He pulled out a lighter, flicked on the flame, and lit up the cigarette with a slight inhalation. "It's fun." He raised an eyebrow inquisitively as he tipped the forbidden fag towards him. "Wanna' try it?"

Chapter 30

"It is essential to realize that you are not alone, and to embrace guidance."
(Conversations with Raj, Paul Tuttle)

THROUGH THE FLYING WIPERS on his rain-splattered windshield Jay caught a fleeting glimpse from the busy highway of the two amber willow trees swaying in the distance in his back yard on the lake's far embankment. They were dancing in the wind like wet hula skirts on twin Hawaiian women as he passed them on the way to his office for an early morning appointment – the first of a half dozen clients today. He'd left home early that day as usual with Phil, heading south off the highway down a long tree-lined lane congested by road construction and traffic, for a twenty minute stretch five miles to the campus. Then he turned back, passing the lake again and his well-hidden house, this time on the left as he drove into town, which he now did twice a week. Moments after dropping off his son at school, he ejected the excruciating rap tape he'd tolerated on the way there, and plugged in the latest one from Leroy which needed rewinding. While it rewound, he thought of his schedule, anticipating his full slate of counselees ahead. Putting all of his appointments on two days a week had given him two busy periods of counseling. He had at one time conducted nearly thirty sessions a week. Now he was doing roughly a dozen. That thought and others were turning energetically in his mind like a fast spinning top reeling slightly out of balance.

He was also relieved to be out of the basement where he still felt ambivalent about being a businessman and tensions were growing between him and Candy. Thankfully Bea would be returning in a week. That would make life more livable again both downstairs at work and to some degree within the household. At least she would be there, even if unseen. In the past, before her work escalated, when she was home, they'd not only be sharing the endless onslaught of parental tasks – school rides, soccer practice, soccer games, guitar practice – but her very presence alone made home or work a more pleasant place. Now with her gone so much, downstairs or out of town, things were different. With this last trip spanning several weeks Phil no longer now spoke of missing her, but Jay thought he did and that spending more time in a bedroom wracked with rap crap was a weak substitute for a motherly touch.

Candy also had seemed worse off in Bea's absence and he wondered if she was upset because he appeared to be succeeding. It was still too soon to say, but talks with schools had gone well enough and he was feeling optimistic. She rarely looked at him directly in the eye and was matter-of-fact and curt when addressing him, which wasn't often. Though he kept his office door shut while making calls, sending faxes and writing emails, in truth he needed her help much more than she needed his. She did all his typing whenever he wanted and knew where things were, how they ran, and how to fix them. Yet he would rarely give her the satisfaction of asking her for or about anything. He'd rather figure it out alone or wait and ask Bea, though he was still smarting from the phone call with her yesterday. He winced as he recalled the intense conversation…*you're both adults…can't you please act like it…*

When he had hung up from that call, he'd felt a twinge of guilt from the thought he was mindlessly adding stress to his wife's life. He also felt a rising wave of anger that was tempered by a touch of near nausea from the thought that a mad woman was loose in his house, creating tensions and wreaking havoc on his marriage simultaneously. Though Bea had acted as though she wasn't troubled by the innuendo, he feared it stirred up uncomfortable memories from the past, decades ago, back in the heat of California in the seventies – the glory days of graduate school – when he had slipped up slightly, or almost anyway.

To have lusted in his heart, though briefly, for another, was a sad mistake he'd made at a group therapy marathon one weekend in the mountains. The night he came home from it she'd read it in his eyes; a strange look – a stab of shame. They had talked. She felt hurt. He felt guilty. Nothing had happened really, as he'd tried unconvincingly to explain to her then. It had been accidental.

She was another graduate student, a pretty brunette, who had become friendly with him earlier in the year as a classmate in Personality Theory where she'd confided that her three-year-old marriage was in trouble. Three months later she found herself languishing in the throes of being left by her husband for another woman, and had sought Jay's help as a confidential ear. He had listened sympathetically and offered advice the few times she had called, thinking it would somehow run it's course in due time. Sometimes they talked between classes or at lunch. Then they had both been group therapy members at that marathon session for a weekend. It was during a dinner break on the second evening, after a communal supper of pizza, that an incident had occurred later that night. He had simply been listening, while they went on a short walk, to another refrain of her sorrowful story when her eyes welled with tears and she suddenly turned, clutching him for support while choking up in grief.

He had held her automatically, a gentlemanly gesture, an innocent embrace. Such hugs were popular then in therapeutic circles. It would have been heresy to turn anyone away who had sought one, especially if they were crying. Nor would any white knight worth half his creed ever spurn a distraught damsel in distress. Perhaps it was the exhaustion of the of the long hours of the marathon – participants bonded, defenses were lowered – but instead of loosening her grasp after a minute, she sobbed harder, held tighter, her firm braless breasts boring into his chest, her breath heaving hotly. Taken by surprise, warmed by her perfumed body, he was too late to stop an unexpected erection from poking her momentarily before pulling back his pelvis, slightly escalating the upper pressure of their chests together. Her hardened nipples, flush with feeling, pressed into him like diamond drill bits and just for a second – a very long second – he felt overwhelmed, inflamed, with the pure heat of desire. She continued to cling to him, weeping her heart out, lamenting her fate, seemingly oblivious to his awkward stance, while staining his vintage blue tie-dye t-shirt with tears as she buried her sorry head in his shoulder. She felt he understood her. He was a sympathetic soul and she desperately needed one. Within twenty minutes they'd returned to the group. Her grief had subsided, his honor was intact, but his desire unabated. That was the wrongful rub.

It was the long brown hair strands still enmeshed on his shirt that had later led Bea to ask the hard questions that he'd answered so awkwardly. He was too embarrassed to admit that he'd felt so attracted to another woman's body that he'd pressed an erection into her crotch at the same time that he was trying to offer some consolation. He was ashamed of the fact that he had not kept his physical reactions controlled in an emotional moment. It was so undisciplined, unwholesome, and unprofessional. It could lead to trouble. And soon in fact it did.

The very night he came home she had sensed his discomfort in explaining why so many mangled fibers of her long mane clung to him. She knew about marathons and the release of strong feelings that could emerge within the safe confines of group camaraderie. It was well known how people shared their innermost feelings – revealing deep hurts, dark secrets, tragedies and traumas. She wanted to believe him that nothing had happened by design, or at least by his design, but wondered what may have happened by circumstance or even possibly the design of the woman. The reticence in his manner lent an air of lost innocence, which gave her the impression that something was wrong. His reassurances were weakened by the lack of the whole truth. He could not bring himself to admit he had been aroused. He explained the situation while leaving out that part. Despite Bea's uncertainty, her doubts might have evaporated, had the phone calls not started and then become more recurrent.

They were intermittent at first, usually in the evening, sometimes during dinner. She was usually crying and he felt compelled to listen, advise and console the best that he could. The last straw had come a month later when she called after midnight. Bea had answered that one, her sweet milk of compassion having curdled with resentment into sour cream over the previous calls. Bea had told her in terse unequivocal terms that enough was enough: stop calling her husband. She was bothered that Jay had let it go on so long, interrupting their meals, taking up his precious time, and suspicious of her motives ever since the marathon.

From that night on no calls ever came again but a fissure, a hairline fracture, had emerged; a tiny crack in the foundation of their trust. While washed over by time with the layers of their lives, it had never widened but never been filled. A tiny seed of suspicion was sown in the heart of their love. Forever after that, though on rare occasion, Jay knew by a look in her face or a tone in her voice that she wondered about his personal reactions to his more attractive clients; especially beautiful divorcees. He had hoped in time that all doubt would cease but feared now that Candy's madness was stirring up memories. The tape snapped to a stop as it finished unwinding and he hit the play button; glad to find a respite from his present plague of thoughts.

"I've got a different issue I want to run by you for a minute. Since Bea's working so much in her office or out of town now, we see a lot less of her and consequently I'm spending more time with Phil. And frankly that's okay because, well, it's just the way it is now, but my main concern is that I feel myself fussing or doting on him. And I try to restrain myself because it seems to me, in simplistic terms, that I'm doing to him sometimes what I felt my mother was doing to me. And I hated it and couldn't wait ….was glad to get away from it eventually, uh…a sense of being over-protected, over-controlled, over-prodded…and…uh…I'm just wondering if you could speak to that in some way that might be helpful to me."

"Umm, you're not doing that."

"Oh."

"You're not doing that. It's very nurturing actually, for the most part, what you do. And it's partly because it's coming from the father, you see. It's good attention."

"Okay."

"So I would tell you not to be concerned about it, and allow yourself to do what you do. And you can even say to him, 'If you ever feel that I'm putting too much pressure on you or am in your way or something, just say so – that's fine'. And then he can tell you."

"He does." (laughter)

"Well, that's the point. But it's good. It's mostly welcome."

"Well, it seems to be…but I wanted to check. Once, many years ago, when he was three or so, Rex, in a conversation with Saul, told me that I let him get away with murder and that it could prove problematic later on, like maybe in his teen years."

"Well, that may be. It remains to be seen. But the attention you're paying to him now feels mostly well-balanced and nurturing."

"Thanks."

"You're welcome."

"There's another thing with him. Phil knows that I'm talking to you – 'to a psychic' is how I put it – and he asked me to ask you the name of his spirit guide."

"I'm not going to say."

"Okay. Let me ask you this. At some point in time – it was several years ago, when I was talking to him all about this and he was interested in it and I was into Rex a lot – for some reason he came up with the thought or the feeling or the sense that the name of his spirit guide was Sebastian. Does that have any resonance?"

"Yeah, it does, and if he's curious about that then he can just address this presence as Sebastian and see whether he has further clarity. That's my best advice there. I'm not in a position to interrupt a natural acquainting process here, which includes the revelation of the name, you see. It's improper to do that."

"Okay."

"Part of being in touch with one's guidance is to come upon the name, to discover it."

"Mm-hm. I'm wondering if I'm sometimes neglecting this or how best to nurture that side of him more, or to help him move into that sense or dimension more. Should I encourage him to meditate… or… talk to him about spiritual issues?"

"No. Just encourage him to be at peace and feel unpressured in his young life. That's really getting to the point of the matter, right there; for him to be at peace, to feel open-ended. He's at a point now where the world begins to shut him down – shut young ones down – and so that being on the threshold or the verge of the Infinite all the time isn't as much an experience as it has been when he was a little child. And so keeping him open-ended is the best thing for you to do. Encourage him to be at peace, and to not feel any pressure about life."

"Okay, and even another step…I said something to him the other day about the beauty of a spirit guide was to help people realize they weren't alone."

"That's fine. That's very supportive Any thing that counteracts the encroachment of the perception of time. Because he's at a point where time is getting to be more and more of a factor. Not so much in a moment by moment sense, but in the sense of three year plans and four year plans and down the road when you're grown up and so on. It's beginning to densify him, and everyone in that group. So what you have to do is in little ways through suggestions, and by your own example, demonstrate that this does not have to be suffered."

"And would it be wise to encourage him to pay attention to his intuition or his inner feelings and to act upon the supposition that he is experiencing communion with this spirit guide?"

"To some degree. At his age and his position in life – being in the process of education – he's not in a position to have his life run by intuition and feel balanced with that. He's going to be at odds with a lot of things, you see, if he goes by intuition, and he's going to find himself in an isolated experience of rebellion because his intuition is going to tell him a lot of this stuff is crap."

"That reminds of the line in the Paul Simon song about all the crap he learned in high school."

"Exactly. So that's not a good step right now because that's going to polarize him from his world. So intuition and acting on it is not the step of the moment. Feeling at peace and feeling unpressured is much more important. It's more important for him to experience agreement with life in general than it is to act on specific intuition. He will find himself doing that anyway, you see, so that's not a problem. But mostly he's got to feel comfortable in the world and safe in the world."

"And he can do that through feeling at peace and open-ended and unpressured."

"That's right."

"Okay. Uh, I'm wondering, because I'm really struggling with it, how I might become more finely tuned in as you are and I'm wondering how you did that. Was it just sit still and say 'Thy will be done'?"

"You see, what happens is, as you become more who you are and as you give up being what you're not – and being what you're not includes all the fuss, all the righteousness, all the conflict, all the things that don't amount to anything – you're left simply being the door or the passageway from which the Infinite moves into manifestation and that's who you are – that's where you are. And what's left is you from the Infinite perspective, and that's all the tuning you need. So as you become balanced, at peace, centered, feeling safe more and more, there's also more inspiration going on. There's constantly inspiration going on. There's always an eagerness to express. And there really is no restraint around that expression, thus things are said in such a way as to be moving and triggering and profound because ideas that normally have to be thought out and analyzed and understood suddenly can be expressed without hardly any kind of real grasp and yet they are perfectly meaningful. Do you see what I'm saying?"

"Yes. It seems like I can do that as a counselor when I'm on."

"Well, that's exactly it, because you're out of the way and there's no ego there and there's no pressure and you feel safe and grounded. It's that experience constantly with more amplification, so there are greater nuances and chords and tones in the experience. You're doing what you're doing when you're with a client but more so."

"Yes."

"And I'll tell you, you know the expression 'Time heals all wounds'?"

"Yes."

"Well, nothing heals as well as not having time."

"A sense of timelessness – no pressure – 'Timelessness heals all wounds'?"

"Right. And what you find is that the experience of not having time is such an upper – a natural high – that what will occur is that everything will seem very obvious to you. Even things which are profound and sort of elusive now, will just seem very obvious, like there's nothing hard to figure out."

"Including computers?"

"Yes."

"Good. I'd like to learn ours. (laughter) Uh, is my spirit guide's named Jeshua?"

"I'm not going to comment right now on that."

"Okay."

"I want you to be with that. I want you to engage your guide in dialogue calling your guide Jeshua if you want to know."

"Well the reason I mention it is that – I almost forgot about this, I've been so out of touch with my spiritual side the last few years – I was in like a meditation a few years back, late at night outside on the deck alone, and suddenly had a sense that I was with someone. It was just like Tinker Bell going 'ting' and I just looked off to my left about ten feet and said 'what's your name?' before I even knew what I was doing and I got back kind of a rippled sort of a thing in the airwaves that seemed like it said 'Joshua' or actually like 'Yeshua', and that's the last close contact I remember having. It was sort of like it came from a body of light the size and shape of a man. It was like the first and last contact, and frankly I don't even remember what happened next, so I guess I shut it off almost automatically, like without knowing it – just sort of letting my conditioning take over again instantly or something and feeling alone as usual. I don't know. But I was never able to repeat it and eventually just regarded it as one of those isolated experiences you don't know what to make of and can't really tell anyone about. Actually it made me think there's probably a spirit here with me but I'm too damn dense to reach it, which after awhile just made me feel more depressed."

"Well, yeah, that was the most obvious face to face contact but actually there's contact going on all the time."

"Uh-huh. So is it wise for me to feel I'm in the company of someone who knows me and loves me more than I realize, or something like that?"

"Certainly, absolutely, and who's got his eyes open And that you are well in hand here. You're being taken care of. You're not in any kind of dangerous situation. Life is safe because of having this guidance."

"Okay, thanks. Uh, talking with you is so helpful to me that I think I'm starting to summon up the courage to smoke less lately – very lately. I usually go to my little music studio in the den after dinner. Bea goes down to her office, if she's around, and Phil's off to his room for homework and music. I take a glass of wine and some pot with me for company while I play or try to record music on my four-track recorder. It's a habit I like or think I do anyway. Or thought I did."

"Well, you're just starting to lose interest in it maybe."

"Yeah, well, perhaps you're right, but it surprises me because ever since the sixties when I discovered marijuana, I've always felt fascinated by being high, off the ground, up in the clouds, in ecstasy. And now for the first time since over a dozen years ago when I discovered the Course – only to abandon it later as I told you – I'm thinking maybe there's a sort of real way to be off the ground."

"Yeah. All that would provide you with after all while is a kind of jangly rush of the nervous system without any kind of experience of being high. The irony is that you find that the high part of it is something that was available in completely natural ways. And you start experiencing that constantly. Then when you do something that's supposed to get you high, it doesn't have a high anymore. It has a rush of some sort obviously, but it doesn't have a high."

"Is it like drinking a beer when you're on LSD? That is, it doesn't do much because you're way beyond any effect a little beer might have on you?"

"Yeah."

"Okay. Well, I just want to keep getting better and better, until I'm doing as well as you are. And it feels like – if I don't think about it – the feeling is like I just need to open my heart up to everyone, and so that tells me that somehow I'm almost habitually unconsciously really shutting it down a lot, and operating out of some thought image around other people, and I'm wanting to…not do that anymore. Does that make sense?"

"You're trying to be inclusive. Yes. You want to be inclusive. You recognize the need there to have that. And be patient with that. Just think 'inclusive', but don't strain to deliberately include someone. Just be aware that you want to be inclusive – that there not be any exclusion in your mind – and that's sufficient. You're open-ended at that point."

"Okay."

"So you don't have to work at it. You don't have to target people for special inclusion because you've been isolating your self."

"I understand. I was thinking today that if I allowed myself to be as open-ended, as you say, all the time, then some activities, like driving, would be dangerous because I'd be so into some present experience so deeply in my mind that I wouldn't be fully aware of the external situation."

"No, because part of the experience you'd be having would be the fun of driving the car, you see. And so you would be appropriate with that intent to drive the car."

"Okay. Well, where I'm coming from – and maybe you can help me with this – is that once, in college, I took some LSD and got into such a place that felt like centeredness, though in an almost sort of slightly groggy way – though I could function. It was probably cut with something, because pure acid is not groggy at all. And I was aware that wherever I went amongst people that I was very unselfconscious and hardly noticed them. I was so into feeling me and my little orbit. So there was a sense of being really aware of myself and yet not aware of others, and I really liked the feeling of being unselfconscious around others, and yet it seemed sort of dangerous in a way."

"It was a drug."

"Yeah?"

"That's not what we're talking about here. That's just the ego finding some refuge in some moment in time from its constant paranoia. It's sort of indulging itself in a little bit of fabricated peace. That's not waking up."

"Yeah, okay. Well sometimes it seems like the closest experiences I've had to that have been on psychedelic type drugs."

"Well, yeah, because there's a certain jolt or shift that occurs immediately, and there is a relief from the paranoia and the obsessive defensiveness of the ego. So that clicks for a while. So you're not as uptight. There's some rest. The ego's not as ragged or belligerent as it usually it."

"I usually felt very loving in those experiences."

"Yeah."

"So all this can be had naturally, yes?"

"Well, something better, because you get a false sense on drugs that the ego is divine. Because there's a shift in consciousness and there may be some appreciation of things in a different or abnormal way. And there's also a feeling of 'Gee, in this world there's a place for my personality'. So it creates ultimately a false sense of your divinity, because it includes your little personality and its foibles and limitations and whatever as part of the divine experience when it's not."

"So I don't really need to do anything but be happy, huh? Is that a fair statement?"

"Well, you are happy, yes, and you don't even do that. That's just your natural state of being."

"It's just happening?"

"Yeah, because when you're uncluttered with personality, then all you're doing is reflecting the Divine Self."

"So that's why happiness and happening have the same root word."

"Yeah."

"Because I get these feelings when we talk – it's like it makes me so happy that then it must be my ego or my conditioning jumps in and goes 'Yeah, we gotta' do something; let's open up a big sanctuary for the homeless or let's go out and hug everybody or let's go give away money'. (laughter) You understand?"

"Yeah, I understand."

"And yet on another level I feel something like 'Gee, that seems silly, or no, just sit and be'..."

"Right, well, there's a need to simply ground that experience; anchor it."

"In just being?"

"In just being, yeah."

"Hm."

He turned off the tape as he turned down a side street to the back entrance of the parking lot behind his office building. He pulled into a tightly sandwiched space between two glossy Cadillacs and sat motionless with his hands still on the tan leather-wrapped steering wheel. Contemplating what he'd just heard to the rat-a-tat-tat of rain on the car roof, he shifted internal gears in preparation to hear and hopefully help others.

Chapter 31

"This is an insane world, and do not underestimate the extent of its insanity."
(A Course in Miracles)

IN THE WELCOME WARMTH of the Toronto airport's international terminal Bea stood in line at the crowded ticket counter in the late afternoon, awaiting a seat assignment. Her eyes followed carefully the assortment of travelers traipsing about, lugging their luggage, carrying brief cases, towing their trains to their next sheltered stop, be it home or away. She observed them with an uncommon attention to detail but not from a lofty or critical perch. She felt comfy as one of them, no better no worse; one of the mass of women and men leading their lives of flight destinations. A tense young mother hurriedly pushing an overloaded cart with one hand held two little boys trailing behind her with the other. The kids' hands were tightly locked, clasped in a chain, clutching their lifeline while their minds were on the loose, wildly careening in kaleidoscopic curiosity at the collection of sights and sounds assailing their senses. In awestruck absorption they gawked at the uniformed flight crew, peculiar passengers, food booths and souvenirs, all to the anonymous announcements overhead. They wound their way through the scattered groups and individuals like a Chinese dragon on wheels with its tail flailing madly. Bea smiled with compassion at the cute tragicomedy and silently sighed with a twinge of nostalgia, while feeling a mixture of envy and relief...*ah the arduous days of early childrearing...*

She glanced up at the electronic board posting departures...*plenty of time yet...*and noticed an adolescent boy with a guitar case scanning the screen with a puzzled demeanor.

He was slender and muscled with close-cropped dark hair and appeared to her vulnerable in his apparent confusion. It reminded her instantly of her own sweet youngest son – steering through the muddled maze of the torturous teen years – and for a moment she forgot where she was while remembering him. A sudden sense of longing echoed up from the depths of her heart as she let herself feel what she hadn't in awhile. She missed her little boy, and not just this week. It was his whole teenage life going by she was missing. Tension covertly crept into her shoulders and she stretched her neck forward, slowly twisting it side to side, then moved it around in a circular motion. A spasm of anger suddenly resounded within… *someone's gotta' make the money* …

Feeling a rising tide of resentment, she stopped herself consciously…*don't think that way*…As much as her work took her far from her family she knew that she loved becoming successful and especially enjoyed traveling to faraway lands she'd never before seen. Even if Jay were to start making big bucks again she'd still want to run her own show, which meant travel. At least with the nearing of the end of the year she'd soon be able to stop – she hoped. Now that she'd settled her affairs in Toronto, she'd return home in a week and recover her motherhood, long lost since last spring to the demands of the job. In fact it appeared that Jay might indeed just make a go of it, providing more money, and maybe for her, more family time too. She paused at the realization of it all and let herself relax as she squared back her shoulders and stood taller to correct her stooped posture. Things were going well. No need to be negative. Wouldn't help a bit anyway.

After receiving her seat designation she walked over to a quiet corner of the waiting area and sat down to continue surveying the crowd till boarding was announced – a good half hour yet. She needed a new book, having finished the last one, but couldn't find the kind that she wanted at the bookstore in the airport. She wanted to continue reading something that dealt with women and empowerment, and not the strident left-wing feminist claptrap on corporate glass ceilings. She had surpassed any and all ceilings without any help from the National Organization for Women, thank you, and was seeking something deeper; something like the last book that spoke to the prehistoric roots of her womanhood and stirred the depths of her soul. Perhaps in Pittsburgh a bigger bookstore would have it.

As she sat there silently viewing the various individuals, couples, and families around her she noticed a woman with long purplish hair braided down the back wearing a calico skirt of similar hue; a well-coordinated outfit of nonconformity replete with black boots, black belt, turquoise buckle and beads. The waist-length braid was faintly reminiscent of how her younger sister's hair was once worn back in the sixties. It struck a chord in her mind of her own fling with hippiedom, short-lived as it was, and the contrast she saw between herself and her sisters. While the younger one had dallied about in the era, extending her liberal identity to the present, her older one had barely even given it a glance, except in disdain, while regarding it a passing fancy for malcontents, weirdoes and ne'er-do-wells. Bea had been able, through the balance point of the middle child, to relate to them both on each end of the spectrum without identifying wholly with either. She had tried in her way to bridge the gaps between them, but they had still widened anyway inevitably in time.

She hadn't seen Faye for several years now and wondered how she might have changed if she had at all. Certainly her style would be still much the same; fashionable, sophisticated – the flashy elegance of the big city. It wasn't her appearance though, but her attitude and behaviors which Bea had found disagreeable, at least when they were children, and the memories still stung as if from yesterday. It was the meanness she recalled most and the unkindly treatment that had bordered on cruelty, which had left her untrusting and wary of her big sister. She was such a damn bully, and to someone so sweet. How could she ever have been moved to do such heartless things?

Bea had never forgotten the incident with the swing chain that hung from the old tree on the hillside in their backyard. Faye had unhooked the swing's chair and pulled the chain up high and over to the edge beyond the railing of the elevated deck. Over the frightened protests of her age seven sister, the mean queen of fourteen had coaxed and coerced her to jump off the ledge while holding onto the chain rings. "You be fine'" she assured her, "and I'll do it next. It'll be fun, just hold on, and you'll swing back to me." When she refused to budge, paralyzed by fear, feet stuck in cement, Faye pushed her off the balcony and she swung out panic-stricken, sailing over the downhill slope. Though she grappled at the iron links her slippery grip could not hold and she slid to the ground in a painful crash to the sounds of her sister's brash laughter above. When her tearful cries brought her sister to her side as though she cared, Bea suspected it was only the fear of parental punishment that had moved her there.

Were it only one incident, it probably could have been forgiven; a faux pas out of character, a flash of bad judgment. But it was one of a great many such incidents that were repeated, in tone if not severity of consequence, over the years. The endless alcohol back rubs she was forced to bestow in summer as though she were Cleopatra's very own cooling slave. The nasty names she had endured, the spiteful looks, the cold rejections. She had learned one thing well from her haughty elder sibling – exactly how not to be – and prided herself on being a much better big sister when her opportunity eventually came to be one. The many years that had past since left Faye seemingly a kinder person but that was deduced primarily from phone calls and periodic greeting cards. How would she be in person now for an extended period of time?

The cell phone of a businessman in a three-piece suit nearby her went off and she listened to his terse responses to the caller. After a brief exchange he ended brusquely with "I love you too" and slipped the small handset back into his pinstriped vest pocket. It reminded her that now would be a good time to call the office and she pulled her own phone out of her black leather purse and did so.

"Homestay Connections. This is Candy. May I help you?"

"Hello, this is Bea checking in. How are you?"

"Oh, just fine – pretty busy. How are you?"

"I'm good. I'm tired, but I'm glad this is over. Now for a week of fun – I hope."

"Oh I'm sure it will be, and probably just what you need."

"Is there anything there I should know about right now?"

"Well, we've had several calls from families in Toronto saying they haven't been paid yet for that last group of students there."

"Hmmm. Well, Perry's going over the rest of his records and receipts again to try to account for everything, so hopefully we can get this all worked out as soon as I'm back."

"Hopefully."

"Anything else?"

"Yes, some faxes from Japan about a new group of high school students for next spring."

"What did they say?"

"Mmm, it seems another company has submitted a lower bid and they want to know if you'll lower yours."

"What? I thought that was all set. Did they say who's the other company?"

"Uhhh, let's see here. Yeah, it's Japan-America Student Exchange."

"Damn it. That's Kazuo's company. He's trying to get the business away from us. That jerk."

"Oh. Well, what should I do?"

"Did they say anything else?"

"Uhhh, yeah. The say they that it's been brought to their attention that you are not properly licensed or fully insured."

"Oh jeez. That jerk. I bet he did that. Well, that's not true, and I can prove it."

"Good."

"Anything else?"

"Uhh, well no, not really, just that they are concerned about these matters and would like your response as soon as possible."

"Alright. Look, I'll call you after I get to Pittsburgh and I want you to fax that letter to me. Maybe at my sister's office."

"Okay."

"Then I'll figure out how to respond exactly. That jerk."

"*Attenttion passengers for flight 1034, Toronto to Pittsburgh. We begin boarding in five minutes. Passengers for flight 1034, we begin boarding in five minutes. Please have your boarding pass out for the flight attendant to see as you board.*"

"Listen, I'm at the airport and don't have much time. Is Jay in?"

"No. He's at his office...I assume."

"Okay. Are you two getting along okay?"

"Oh, well, sort of."

"What's that mean?"

"Well, he does his work and I do mine. He's on the phone with whoever all the time and every other day he's not here anyway, so...."

"Uh-huh. But what's it like between you?"

"Well, he's still doing the phone thing, if that's what you mean."

"You mean you still think he's listening to your calls?"

"Oh I'm sure of it. But I haven't said anything. I'll let you handle it. I just think it's very very creepy."

"Uh-huh. Yeah, well, like I said, I'll talk to him when I get back. Say, uh, have you seen Phil around at all?"

"No. But I don't usually. Did you want me to give him a message?"

"Uh, no, that's alright. I just wondered." *"rrriiinnnggg"*

"There's the other line. Do you want to hold?"

"No, that's okay. We're going to board soon. I'll call you from Pittsburgh with the fax number." *"rrriiinnnggg"*

"Okay, you better run. Bye for now."

"Bye."

Bea clicked off her telephone and sat stewing over Candy's word...*damn that kazuo...i should have known he's too crazy to leave me alone...and perry...what is going on...all those families should have been paid by now...be glad when this is settled...and jay...is he really listening to her phone calls or...'he's on the phone with whoever all the time'*...She looked at her watch and considered giving Jay a quick call at his office when she heard the blaring announcement over the loudspeakers again.

"Attention all passengers for flight 1034. We will now begin boarding, starting with the last rows first. Please have your boarding pass out as you board the plane."

Realizing the time was too short for a call she resisted the impulse and gathered up her stuff to board the airplane. She decided to call him the very first thing after getting settled in Pittsburgh.

Chapter 32

"One night he went into the bathroom and fell down on his knees, as he had been taught to pray as a child. 'God, Jesus, or whoever the fuck you are!' he cried. 'Will you please, just once, just tell me what the hell I'm supposed to be doing?'"
(The Many Lives of John Lennon, Albert Goldman)

As HE MOUNTED THE carpeted steps to his office Jay felt once again the customary exhilaration that filled his spirits each time he approached a therapeutic hour. He always felt honored that he was in a position to assist someone with the inner workings of their mind, whatever their condition and circumstances might be. He was curious about the two new clients to be seen interspersed among the four others he had been working with awhile. After setting the lighting just so in the room – shunning the glare of overhead fluorescents for the soft glow of the lavender lamp shade – he turned on the fountain that gently bubbled water over rocks in a bowl and pulled up the blinds on the two tall windows overlooking the black puddles in the back parking lot. The distant view of Mt. Rainier was completely obscured by the early morning downpour and dark menacing storm clouds. Taking a moment to compose himself in readiness he sat at his desk, folded his hands in his lap and closed his eyes to focus on his breathing to relax.

Aided by the soft sounds of the cascading fountain on the coffee table he soon felt the growing sense of peace that he'd wanted to find before starting his day. Since talking with Leroy this had become his new practice. A glance at the clock showed a few minutes yet until the first hour began and he decided to check with his answering service for any new messages since last night. He identified himself to the woman on the phone and felt his peace disappear with her report of one call.

"A Detective Clark called about ten minutes ago. He said he'd called before. Do you need his number?"

"No, that's okay. I have it. Thank you. Good bye."…*oh shit shit shit*…He put his head in hands and thought for a moment about how to deal with the long arm of the law that kept reaching out to him. He suddenly realized that he didn't need to say a word to this officer about Barry at all. Their conversations were privileged…*hell with him*…It was merely the fact that he had never been in such a situation before that had given him concern. He hadn't considered that he could stiff the authorities because they had no authority over Barry's counseling sessions. He was a shrink. With a sense of near glee he quickly telephoned the police station and asked to speak with the dogged detective.

"Detective Clark speaking."

"Hello, this is Jay of Forestville Counseling. I'm returning your call."

"Oh yes, thank you. I was hoping to hear back from you today."

"Glad to be of service, sir…*like hell*…How may I help you?"

"Well, as I'm sure you must know, if you got my first message, it's about Barry Thomas, a patient of yours."

"A former client, yes, but not one at the present time."

"I see. Well, we have Mr. Thomas arraigned on some serious charges. He's due to stand trial next month for growing, possessing and selling marijuana from his home. I wonder if you could shed any light on his activities or background during the time that you were seeing him."

"Gosh, I'm terribly sorry…*almost*…but I'm bound by the strictures of the client-counselor relationship not to reveal any part of our discussions, unless of course he had threatened to be of harm to himself or others, which I can assure you he did not. Sorry."

"Well, I understand that and wouldn't want you to do anything that you shouldn't, but these are very serious offenses and anything you say might actually help him."

…*oh sure*… "Believe me I'd love to help you in any way that I could but in fact I am totally bound by the ethics of my profession – and of course the law in this regard – to reveal absolutely nothing of our conversations to anyone, that is unless Barry himself were to direct me to do so by signing a release, which I gather he has not."

"So if I get you one of those – a signed release form – you can answer my questions?"

"Oh certainly…*damn*…I'd be more than happy to."

"Okay, doctor – uh, by the way, are you a doctor?"

"No, I don't have a doctoral degree. I have a masters degree in counseling and am licensed by the state as a mental health counselor."

"I see. Well, okay then, uh – so what do I call you?"

"Well, you could call me master – just kidding. My first name's fine."

"Well, okay then, Jay, I'll go to work on that angle and get back with you."

"Great...*crap*...I'll be waiting to hear from you. Uh, sorry to rush things but if we're all done now I've got a client to see."

"Sure, just one more thing."

"Yes?"

"Uh, your name was in his little black book, which we suspect was used in his drug dealings with others. Any comment you'd like to make about that at this time?"

"I assure you I haven't the slightest idea about whose names are in his book, including mine or anyone else's, and for what purposes they may be there. Since I was his therapist it does not surprise me he would keep my number somewhere."

"But in his little black book?"

"I really don't know what to make of that and of course that is your job, but I can say unequivocally that I've had nothing to do with Barry on such matters. Now, I do have an appointment with someone I've kept waiting too long in the lobby already, so now if you'll excuse me..."

"Uh-huh. Well, I was just wondering. Just doing my job, as you say. I'll be getting back with you. Thanks for your help."

"My pleasure, sir.".…*asshole*..."Please call any time."...*not*...Jay hung up the phone and heaved a sigh of relief while simultaneously feeling a sense of foreboding. His peace had disappeared and there was no time to recover it as he headed for the lobby to retrieve his first client.

It was nearly midway through the session when the anguished flower lady was able to stop crying. For the first time that hour she slipped into a smile when Jay joked that it was wetter in his office than outside. "I was thinking if you kept this up we could bottle those tears to water the new plant you brought me today." She laughed as she sniffled and wiped her eyes dry with another Kleenex.

"I'm sorry to use up all your Kleenex."

"Oh, don't be sorry. That's what they're here for. You had to get it out. That's part of what you're here for. I'm not sure if you heard half the things I've been saying. Is the last thing I said what made you stop crying?"

"Yes, that and...I don't know, I just feel cried out."

"Is it more missing Darin or the dream that you had?"

"I really don't miss Darin at all. He was such a thug...and such a drunken one. I just didn't know. And our dream became such a nightmare so fast... really I'm relieved that it's all over. I just feel like a fool and I get so depressed now and I'm so lonely again. I try to hide my feelings from Jason but it's hard. I know he misses Darin and he's disappointed about it all."

"How did you explain it to him?"

"I just told him the truth – sort of – not as bad as it was really, but he got the picture."

"What did you say exactly?"

"That Darin got drunk too much and wasn't really the person that he seemed and… and…that I just didn't want to be with him. It wasn't good. It would have been bad."

"And how does he respond to that?"

"Oh, he says he understands. He believes me. He trusts me. But I can tell he's sad and confused. He never saw Darin drunk, and he doesn't know how mean he could be."

"Hm. Well, it's good your relationship with him is good enough to withstand this."

"Oh yeah, I know, and I'm glad for that, but there's pain in his eyes now. He'd like a good dad, and I feel so guilty. It's just like we said last time. I wonder if I'm ever going to have anyone to love who will love us."

"I know. And we don't know the answer to that question. Nobody does. But Darin wouldn't have made a good dad considering how he was with you, and I do know the one thing you can do, and you should do, and that's to focus now on loving yourself. There is simply nothing better you could be doing at this time."

"I don't even know what that means anymore. I mean, I'm not sure I even know how to do it. Or maybe it's just I've been doing it so long I'm tired of it."

"Well, it's not anything to be tired of doing. It should feel good, by definition. I think maybe you really mean you're tired of being lonely, and I understand that, but what I'm talking about is how best to deal with it, and ultimately how best to transform your situation into that which you desire."

"That would be nice."

"Look, I'll tell you a story – a true one – I once read in a book. A woman, a psychologist, who went through a very painful divorce, wrote it. Her husband left her. And it was her second divorce, and she felt like hell. So she was crazy with grief at first and then later with despair. She stayed that way for a while – I don't know how long – many months at least. Until one day – she had managed to get herself working again in her garden – and that was an act of self love because she loved gardening. And at some point during the course of doing that; hoeing, planting, weeding, etc., one day she reached a moment where she suddenly felt good. She suddenly – and this was probably the result of weeks of gardening and time passing – but that very day for the first time in a long while she felt at peace. She suddenly, unexpectedly felt at peace with herself.

"And she said to herself 'I realize I can actually be happy just being myself and living by myself. I don't need someone else to make me happy or complete me in any way'. And it felt good. And for the first time in a long time she was content just to be her. She felt good. And then later that night she went somewhere and met the man who was later to become her third husband. And she's still happily married to him – happier than she ever was – and probably wiser. And that's how that works. You understand? She learned to love herself fully, without any anyone else, and then the next step followed; a fulfilling relationship. It just happened. But only because she felt fulfilled in herself first. She didn't go looking for someone to fill her emptiness, like people so often do."

"I do understand, and it's a great story. But what am I gonna' do now? You know, I love working with plants, but I can't start a garden in the middle of winter?"

"It's not about that. That's just a metaphor really, though gardening obviously happens to be a nurturing activity. It's about feeling good – completely good – about yourself and your life on the most basic level without anyone else there to complete it. And the way to do that, and to engage in the most basic form of self love there is, is to start by refusing to dwell on the thoughts that hurt you, like 'I'm lonely or I'm all alone', and to focus instead, first and foremost, on just being grateful for what it is you are and what it is you have, right now. Just for your life as it is; for having a son, being a mother, running a plant shop, and everything else that you have, you are, and you love. Just for being alive. And let yourself feel how good that is, because it is. It really is. And just stay with that feeling, and don't let it go, especially when you're tempted to think thoughts that make you feel bad. And then of course your life will continue to unfold, but you won't be needful of something to happen to make you feel good. And in that state of mind, from that reference point, you can do whatever it is you feel moved to do. And that will constitute the next level of self-love. But you can't proceed without that base."

The session with Howie started out with the usual banter Jay had grown to expect from him. Though in past sessions they had seriously delved into the likely origins of his homosexuality, Howie's puckish delight in telling jokes and making wisecracks was still his standard way of being much of the time. Jay could not tell if it was a salesman's way of easing into a situation or a defense against his underlying psychic pain or both. They had discussed the implications of his dominant mother, whom Howie hated, and his out- of-town father, now deceased, whom he had adored but mostly from a distance. They had agreed that a critical factor in his choice to pursue a homosexual lifestyle had been when he was raped at age thirteen by an older cousin. At Jay's suggestion he had, while on a business trip in New York, confronted that man about the brutality, the humiliation and the consequences to which it had contributed. Though that had given him a measure of satisfaction, a chance to release long held feelings of rage, it had not brought about any change in his attraction to men, which he was struggling to resist.

"I'm wondering, Howie – I'm not quite sure how to phrase this – but when you have had sex with men in the past, are you the recipient or, shall we say, the giver of the sexual act."

"Uhhh, I'm the recipient."

"I see."

"Why did you ask?"

"Well, it may not be that important, but I'm curious somewhat, because your wife seems so much more masculine than feminine, to use those terms for moment, with her rough and tough cowgirl demeanor, as emotional as she is, and she has continued to complain that she must ask you for sex, and the nature of intercourse between you and her requires you to be masculine – requires her to be the recipient – and I was wondering how it feels for you to be switching roles, so to speak."

"I don't know why it is or how it happens exactly, but I'm able to go both ways without giving it any thought. It just seems to happen naturally."

"Well that's why I'm saying, as I've suggested before, that perhaps you are bisexual. What do you think?"

"I can see why you'd say that but the thing is for me that aside from with Sharon, I feel no sexual attraction to women at all. Only to men, and that's pretty constant."

"You feel sexually attracted to her on a visual basis?"

"No, not really. But when we go to bed she's pretty physical with me and manages to get me aroused one way or another. I mean she doesn't give up till I have an erection and she'll do anything and everything to get one going."

"I see. Well, she still complains to me that she thinks you're disinterested – that you don't make love with any passion at all."

"Well, I fucked her last night. I fucked the shit out of her."

"Now you sound angry."

"I am angry, the bitch. I wish she'd just leave me alone. I'm working my butt off to support her. I'm trying to work this out. I'm trying to abstain on the road."

"Are you? What do you mean 'trying'? Are you seeing other men or not?"

"Well, not quite as much."

"So that means you are."

"Hey, I'm coming to see you. I'm meditating every day."

"What's that doing for you? I mean, what's your objective? What's the nature of your practice exactly?"

"I just repeat my special mantra – the one the maharisha gave me – over and over, and keep going on with it until I feel I'm levitating."

"You mean getting off the ground?"

"Yeah, right. It's possible, you know. The maharisha has made this very clear."

…oh God… "How high do you go?"

"I'm not sure, but maybe a quarter inch or so. It takes practice to go higher."

…oh man…"You been doing this a long time?"

"Yeah, for years. It takes awhile to perfect."

"Uh-huh. Well, uh, I guess that would be quite a feat, but I'm wondering of what good is it in relation to your problems? Sharon just resents you going off into the closet for long periods of time. Seems to me that actually that could be making things worse."

"I thought you meditate?"

"Well, I do, but not to levitate. I do it for peace of mind and hopefully guidance."

"Well, the maharisha has contributed to world peace in my opinion, by just spreading vibes around the world through his meditations. That's practically documented by his foundation. And he says levitation is an important state to reach."

"Yeah, well, maybe so, but John Lennon, who studied with him, says he was just one big fake, who wanted to fuck Mia Farrow in the shower to boot."

"John Lennon was a drug addict who just didn't get it."

"Well, maybe you're right, I truly don't know, but I was struck by the tale he related when he said that all the Beatles were leaving, disillusioned with the maharisha, and he said 'Where are you going?' and Lennon replied 'If you're so fucking cosmic, you'll know'."

"Oh, fuck John Lennon. What does he know anyway?"

"Alright, good point. I don't know what he knows, and never will now since he's dead. I just know what he said. But my real point is this: that it seems to me that you're no closer to revealing to your wife what the real problem is since we first met months ago. Neither of you is any happier. And I cannot see that your form of meditation is helping you much either, though maybe it is. But sooner or later, for the sake of your sanity, your integrity and the integrity of your relationship, you're going to have to come clean. If these desires do not abate, and if you can't or won't stop indulging in them, you're going to have to be honest with her, and let the chips fall where they may."

His third client was a raggedy dressed blue-collar worker with thick tousled hair whom Jay suspected was stoned the very second he saw him in the lobby. Not only was his appearance ruffled and unkempt but also he smelled of an unpleasant earthiness which Jay assumed was from pot or his unwashed overalls; some sort of company work clothes. He listened to the wiry young man drone on in explanation as to why he was there. He complained about his marital difficulties and the rigors of his work. He was earnest in his scruffiness yet slightly inattentive as though distracted or lost in a world of his own. He was there at the behest of his wife who was unhappy that he seemed to be losing interest in their marriage and in life in general.

"I'm just tired when I get home, man and just wanna' have a beer on the couch and watch the TV."

"Well, after a bit of that do you start to feel refreshed?"

"No, I usually just crash there till Darla wakes me up for dinner."

"How about after dinner? How do you feel after that?"

"Honestly, that just heavies me out man, and I like to get back to the couch and relax."

"And then what happens?"

"I guess I fall asleep again till Darla wakes me up and then we go to bed."

"Do you guys make love?"

"Uh, sometimes on the weekend, but I'm too bushed during the week."

"Do you love your wife?"

"Hell yes. That's why I'm here."

"But there's virtually no time together except for sharing supper?"

"Yeah, well, I'm *tired,* man. I get up early. I work hard all day. And I'm just wasted when it's time to go home. She doesn't understand how hard my work is."

"Well, what kind of work do you do anyway?"

"I work in a factory with paints, enamels, stuff like that."

"So you work with toxic chemicals?"

"All day long."

"Do you wear a protective mask?"

"Oh yeah, gotta' do that. It's the rules."

"Listen, I don't want you take offense at this, because I'm not accusing you of doing anything wrong, but it seems clear to me you are stoned. Am I right?"

"Right now?"

"Yes."

"No way. No way in hell, man. Why do you say that?"

"Well, frankly because you're all bleary eyed and seem a little out of it."

"Really?"

"Yeah. You look that way to me."

"Well, that's bullshit, man. I am not stoned."

"Hm. Okay, I'll believe you, but I'm telling you, you look and even act a little out of it to me. You seem sort of drowsy or something."

"I don't know, man. I'm feeling like I usually do. I'm just a little tired."

"And you took this day off?"

"Yeah. I said I had a doctor's appointment. My wife's getting pissed. Said see a counselor or else."

"Hm. You know, maybe I'm wrong, but it's just hitting me, and primarily because I can smell the odor you give off. It doesn't smell like pot exactly, but it smells like something strong. It smells like some kind of chemicals, ammonia or chloride or something. I think you may be affected more adversely than you realize by the stuff that you work with all day."

"You do?"

"Are you breathing those fumes all day long in your work area?"

"Yeah, but I have the mask on all the time."

"Yeah, well, that may help, but if you really are not stoned, and this feels normal to you, I think that this job is taking a greater toll on you than you know."

"Well, I gotta' work, man. Ain't no way around that."

"I know that. But I'm saying that you may well be working at a job that's slowly killing you. Do you think that it's worth it?"

At lunch Jay decided to give Will Ringer, his colleague, a call. He had not heard from him since their last phone conversation and was wondering how their marriage was holding up.

"Northwoods Counseling Service. Dr. Ringer speaking."

"Will, it's Jay."

"Hey Jay, how are you? Sorry I didn't get back with you."

"That's okay, I understand we get busy. I was just wondering how it was going with Collette. Can you talk for a minute?"

"Yeah, it's cool. I'm just taking a lunch break after my last client."

"Yeah, me too. Well, what's up?"

"Well, we had a long talk. We had to have one of course. She was feeling terrible about me and everything."

"Yes?"

"And I just explained to her that it's hard in the therapy sessions sometimes not be strongly attracted to a beautiful woman client."

"Yeah?"

"Yeah. You know how it is. You've been at this a long time. Sometimes, I don't know why – probably a combination of things – you just lose it. I mean everyone makes mistakes. Maybe it's a mid-life crisis, I don't know. But somehow, this time, I just went too far. I crossed the line. That woman was so gorgeous, man, I mean, I just said to Collette 'Can you blame me for wanting to lick every inch of her beautiful body'?"

"Oh my God. You said that to Collette?"

"I did. I did. I wanted to be totally honest with her."

"That's honest, man. Maybe brutally so. Pretty graphic anyway."

"Yeah, well, it was a spirited discussion and I might have gotten carried away. We were speaking our minds. She was yelling at me and I was trying to make her understand, and that's just how it came out."

"What'd she say when you said that?"

"Well, she didn't like hearing it, but I just said 'Look, I'm being honest with you. I didn't love her. I didn't fuck her. We just had oral sex. I'm sorry. I fucked up'."

"And she was okay with that?"

"Yeah, well, eventually, yeah. Plus I swore up and down I'd never ever do it again. And we both cried. So…so there you are."

"Whew. Good luck, buddy. Maybe being that blunt was good. What do I know? I just hope you can reestablish the trust."

"We're workin' on it."

After his talk with Will, Jay bought a tostada and a bean burrito from the Taco Bell down the street and spent the rest of the lunch hour savoring his food and listening to the latest tape from Leroy to arrive in the mail.

"Okay. The tape's running. What's up?"

"Well, I'm aware for the first time in awhile of feeling some gratitude for my life circumstances, primarily from my involvement in Bea's business, which has been a big shift in my life. I'm running a Christmas program for foreign students while keeping my practice going on a part-time basis. And it looks like I'll be bringing in a substantial amount of money soon and I wonder if you see that I might continue to be involved with this."

"Yeah, you will be. It's as simple as that. And the programs will be successful."

"Good. Well, everything seems to be going pretty well, except that I'm no longer seeing enough clients in my practice now to justify the expense of the office...at least in my mind. So I'm going to move out and sublet from a psychologist next to me in the same building, which feels pretty lousy on one hand, but on the other hand makes me feel good that I'm still paying my way, so to speak."

"My sense is that this will be just a temporary move."

"Yeah, well I hope so. Anyway, it's happening. I've given notice and made arrangements so it's a done deal for now. I've gotten so behind in my bills – my office rent, my car payment, my credit card debt, etc – that I just can't justify keeping this office anymore. The money I'm earning through the other business will go quickly toward some of my debts and her expenses, so I've got to keep making a lot more one way or another. It looks like the next big chance to do that in Bea's business won't come until spring, for the college break week, when I can run a big program like the Christmas one, if I want to, and I will if my practice isn't generating more income, and without taking insurance I don't know how it can so anyway...so there you are."

"Uh-huh. Look, what is it that you have some clear desire for?"

"Well, feeling really secure in my work as a counselor would be nice. If I had enough appointments where I felt a certain security like I did for the last dozen years or so – say twenty some people every week rather than just half that or less."

"Okay. Now is the desire there really for security or to see more people?"

"Well, really for security, right now, I guess. I'm starting to wonder if I really want to see more people or not, since we've been saying that it's desire that brings about the results. But frankly as far as I can tell, I really enjoy doing it, so I'm starting to question now just what it is I am really desiring, uh...unconsciously you might say."

"Well, you have the opportunity here to see through something. You have a desire for an experience of surplus, shall we say. You have practiced being comfortable with less than enough. And this has been good. The perception of not having enough has been rendered less significant or less impactful to you. You've practiced finding your peace when it looked particularly unappealing."

"True."

"And so, given that the circumstances that appeared to be insufficient – given that the only purpose they might have served was to educate you – and given that that education seems to have taken hold – then the question arises: are these circumstances necessary in and of themselves or can they be transformed into something else? So your inquiry now is: how would you like it to be? Given that you have learned to be at peace with suspense, do you desire something? It isn't so much that you desire security. It's that you'd like to have more money. You'd like to have that which is necessary for your good to be there presently, without delay. Correct?"

"Yep."

"So since you have practiced being at peace with that which normally would have been very troubling to you, let us now see if there is a way of having more money simply for the asking. Is it going to be that simple? Is that what you want? Do you want to be able to say 'Yes, I'll have it' and simply have it be there?"

"Sure."

"Of course you do. Now that it doesn't secure or defend you, it still has value. And you want to have that value available to you without a lot of time wasted. So what we want to do now is to start to work more with the feeling of your desires. There are those things that are possible in theory and then there those things that are real possibilities. And I want you to understand the difference, because those things that are possible in theory just require an intellectual agreement. But for something to become a real possibility it has to be felt. What would it feel like for you to have this much money, you see? So much of your attention now has to be spent at the level of the heart and not the mind.

"So first what we want is for you to acknowledge exactly what it is that you desire. Then I want you to be able to agree with the desire, to join with it, so that there's a sense of intent being born of it. And I want you to be willing to ride this movement. This is a little bit like getting on one of those mechanical bulls, because when this agreement is experienced it tends to build up a great deal of energy. It is often called passion although it's not really that. Passion comes from the ego. But it is a very strong feeling around particular desires. It is the intensity of your intention. And what you have to learn to be comfortable with is the feeling of not taking no for an answer. You have to be comfortable or at peace with a very intense feeling; the feeling I call not taking no for an answer, or meaning business."

"You mean I have to feel at peace while simultaneously feeling the intensity of a desire?"

"Exactly. These are certain feelings of absolute authority and will that aren't yours. They are God's Will or the Movement of Life. But if these feelings get caught in the ego, they can become aggravating and cause you to behave in a conflicted way. So you're going to have to learn to be very comfortable or at peace, not in your ego, with intense feelings. After all, if there's real intention there, it's going to be intense. So I want you to be comfortable with what it feels like to mean business, understanding that it's not you, the ego, which means business. It's that degree of vision, of power, of authority that you need to allow to move through you in order for the mountains to move. Normally the ego tries to make desires come into fruition through effort. Otherwise it is basically stuck passively wishing and hoping for the mountains to move, and in the meantime you're doing the best that you can to be centered and tolerant of the wait, you see.

"But there's something else going on here. Though you haven't mastered it completely, you've learned to a significant degree to be at peace in suspense. So there's a crack in the wall that blocks you from your good, and if you can be comfortable with this very intense feeling, then you will find yourself being unequivocal and that will not allow circumstances, or their appearance, to deny you your good. Circumstances will yield to you. If you can be comfortable and at peace in this place, then circumstances will begin to conform to your will, understanding it is not your personal will."

"You mean to feel, for example, what it feels like to think I want enough money to build an addition on my house or buy a motorcycle, or whatever, without a doubt that it's possible?"

"Exactly. And then when you feel the intent of a desire in this manner, it will build up on its own, and at times you may find yourself becoming aggravated by the fact that the desire is not yet fulfilled. And those are moments where you need to understand that what is happening is that something very powerful is being moved through you and you need to be at peace with it. You need to be patient, which is the willingness to abide with your desire without fear. And when you abide in this state, patiently feeling the power of the intention of your desire to manifest, it feels like you're not taking no for an answer. That's all there is to it. And if you can express not taking no for an answer from an absolutely divine and unconflicted perspective then it will be, you see. That's when the mountain moves. And you're not doing it personally. You can't possibly get yourself to this point alone. But you learn to be gotten to this point nevertheless by virtue of willingness and yielding to God's Will and in that way you become the agent of your own transformation."

"Hm. Well, if you're not taking no for an answer then it's always yes."

"Right. So the point here is that you can start feeling your desires, not paying any attention to the reasonableness of them, but seeing just what you naturally and spontaneously can agree to which allows for the intent to be born for them. And once it's born, then you allow it to be expressed through you with all of its power, which allows it to happen. It's coming from God, right up through your heart, as the movement of Life, the movement of fulfillment, and is expressed in the world. And this is what is meant by the phrase 'to move mountains'."

"Hm."

"So you have to practice this."

"How do you practice it?"

"How do you *practice* it?"

"How do *you* practice it?"

"The same way that I'm saying to you; recognize what you desire, agree with it, and allow that agreement to grow. It's like the fertilization of an egg – it starts to grow. You see, when you agree with a desire while staying at peace, that's the masculine and the feminine coming together; the yin and the yang. And then what is born there is the intent. And then it becomes powerful. It seeks on it's own to be born. And you have to go through a kind of birth process here with it. You become the mother in the sense that you have to yield to it, and give birth to it; the Will of God manifesting on earth."

"I see."

"So this is your practice now. And this takes you out of the world of limitation, the world of the ego, of cause and effect, as you experience it now, where you have to work at the level of resources rather than go to the Source. You see, in the world you have resources because you are not at the Source. You have to make do with what is there and sort of move it around in a way, if you are lucky, to give you what you want. A lot of what waking up involves is being able to bring into manifestation those desires that come directly from the Source, where there aren't apparent resources available. And it takes singleness of mind, which is blindingly illuminated, in order for that to be. That's why I say 'What does it feel like not to take no for an answer and to be at peace with that?'. To be nonresistant to the idea of not taking no for an answer, to be able to abide with that particular yang energy, is what you need to do in order for these manifestations to occur. And you are at a point now where you are...getting ready to do that."

"Hm. Well, I sure hope so."

Chapter 33

"You who want peace can find it only by complete forgiveness." (*A Course in Miracles*)

L ONG AFTER THE PLANE had roared off the runway circling above and away from Toronto, Bea had stared out the window at the sprawling gray city that was shrinking beneath her, more distant each instant. Knowing there was nothing else now she could do but let everything run it's natural course, she had put back her seat, kicked off her shoes and reflected on her time there while munching the peanuts the stewardess had given her. She'd given Perry another chance and, through retraining him, her best shot at success, which left her feeling satisfied that she'd done the best she could. Time to let it go. If her inclination to trust him were as right as it felt, it would prove far more rewarding than the alternate choice. And she probably wouldn't know until the spring how right she'd been, when he'd have his next chance to coordinate another program.

She took a sip on her gin and tonic, letting the sharpness cut through her concerns, and breathed a quiet sigh of relief as the warmth filtered slowly down into her stomach... *mmmm that's better...*Now she could look ahead to the meeting that had been on her mind for weeks; the one that tugged at her heart in a way no business meeting ever had. As she thought of her sisters she felt again how strange it would be to meet as a threesome after all these years. With the oldest and youngest so many years apart and her in the middle it had been quite a span. The fact they had each been cheerleaders as seniors in high school had marked them as an enthusiastic trio – a trait they still shared even now she assumed. The last time they'd converged in one place together was at their mother's funeral almost seven years ago. That period was so marked with elaborate proceedings and widespread grieving that they'd had little time to be alone as a unit. It was said that more people had crammed into the church on that day than anyone could recall, for their kindly mother, who played the organ there, was a much beloved figure in the close-knit community and her first name, Grace, was thought perfectly befitting.

In recollecting the somber Episcopal service Bea warmly reminisced over the outpouring of care given her, her sisters and her stooped aging father, heart stricken with a loss from which he would never recover. Expressions of gratitude, respect and love were shown throughout the ceremony and the reception. She remembered with amusement an anecdote Jay had told her about an incident he had observed in the gathering that evening. He had just met an old high school girl friend of Bea's who was delighted to meet him and expressed it wholeheartedly. "All the sisters were great," she had said a little loudly in her sudden excitement and boosted by booze, "but I'm so glad to meet the lucky one who got Bea." Jay was tickled by her statement and understood what she had meant. Virtually everyone had sung Bea's praises from the past to the present ever since he had known her. She was the one sister most often regarded by others as possessing her mother's sweet and gracious attributes.

What had tickled Jay further, as fate would have it, was that the other two sisters were standing close by and directly behind the woman, unbeknownst to her, with one on either side and their backs to each other while conversing with guests. They had both turned around upon hearing her statement as if on simultaneous cue and frowned ever so slightly at the apparently implicit unfavorable comparison. Bea smiled to herself as she recalled Jay's amusement when telling her about it. "It was faintly reminiscent of the two sisters in Cinderella," he had chuckled. "And such perfect timing. I wish you could have seen it." Bea knew it was nothing at all but at most a moment of passing and mild sibling rivalry, yet appreciated the story. She had never really thought that jealousy or envy had particularly been a big issue among them, at least in their youth, and certainly not for her. She preferred to believe whatever conflicts they had came more from the differences in their temperaments and ages, which were later reflected in their values and actions. Clearly the most salient discrepancy was felt by the youngest and oldest, between the simple lifestyle of the back to earth hippie and the gratuitous excesses of the flamboyant jet setter. There had been caustic comments from Polly to Bea about Faye's extravagant Nieman Marcus shopping sprees while Faye had expressed to her withering criticisms of their youngest sister's counterculture ways. In any case now was an opportunity to heal and resolve any and all wounds and disparities like never before.

She mulled over in her mind exactly what she sought, what specifically she was hoping to recover with each of them. She had learned from her experiences in past business meetings that good preparation usually paid off. It was especially wise to enter a discussion with a clear understanding of the goals to be met. In general her goals with each sister were one and the same; to improve relations by building intimacy. With Polly it was a matter of restoring the closeness she had felt as a child on through to her twenties. Sadly it had gotten lost in adulthood and though she knew well the whys and the wherefores her belief was unshaken that it could be restored. It was with her older one that she felt more uncertain. That base had never been solidly built and whatever they made now would be a new start.

She thought about how she might venture once more to bring up the various hurts and humiliations she had suffered when younger. The one time she'd tried was so roughly rebuffed. Faye had scoffed at the notion she'd been less than loving and hinted that Bea had been imagining such things. It wasn't so much that Bea wanted the satisfaction of hearing Faye say she had made some mistakes. It was more that she didn't see how she could trust her if their earlier history were reduced to a myth. If their past reality wasn't a shared one, how could she trust they could share one in the present? Especially now if there were finances to sort out for their ailing father's care and ultimately his estate. Money could create more problems than it solved. She simply didn't trust her to be a fair person, a selfless administrator, an honorable sibling, and the best way to deal with it was to be very candid which seemed difficult for a conciliatory middle child.

She took another sip of her drink as she pondered precisely what words she might say to be clear. Her standard style was to be diplomatic while offering insights without giving offense. Yet this was a rare chance, possibly their last one, and she feared the thickness of her big sister's ego would be hard to penetrate without being blunt. The alcohol comforted her vague apprehensions and caused her to pause in the search for the right words. Perhaps it was better to be clear on objectives and let her expression flow freely at the time. Over planning could kill the best of intentions where pure spontaneity might just serve her well. Feeling an increasing sense of repose by adopting this balanced approach to the subject, she decided to give it a rest for the moment and move on to other new nagging concerns. What in the world was going on in Japan?

Recalling the sinister note she had found that was left in her box at the Vienna conference – *you will be sorry* – she had little doubt about who was behind these latest dilemmas; her nemesis Kazuo. The thought of a menacing force always shadowing her every move in Japan made her nervous. She knew he was ruthless, self-centered and cunning from dealings she'd had with him over the years. It didn't surprise her he'd try to steal business from any new customer that she might land. It was obvious at the outset of her recent break with him that he regarded her forays into Japan as betrayal. He would not recognize that she had a right to exist on her own as a separate company without him as the middleman, a dictating agent. As revealed in his threatening faxes to her office, he had a capacity for delusions of grandeur and a consuming sense of his own self-importance that was only exceeded by his facility for cruel and tiresome tirades. Her parting reply that he'd best check his dictionary, given his spelling and grammatical errors, had no doubt refueled his rants and his rage. He was a dangerous enemy, of that she was certain.

She had not expected that he would lie outright by telling her clients she had no insurance. That would be easy enough to remedy by showing the documents but she wondered if other potential new customers might hear of the rumor and even believe it. He was a pervasive evil lurking in the darkness and she felt ill equipped to counter his efforts to besmirch her reputation and destroy her company. Feeling the need for strong reinforcements she finished her drink and summoned a sociable stewardess for another. She was starting to appreciate the full meaning intended by the airline that had coined the advertising phrase of flying the friendly skies. While ruminating over the possible responses and protective measures at her disposal in dealings with Japan it occurred to her that Faye was probably the only other person she knew who had solid business acumen and her own streak of ruthlessness. Maybe she could offer some sage advice. A satisfying swallow of her second gin and tonic helped to persuade her that tabling the matter until then would be wise. Just like strong liquor poured over ice perhaps with some time it might mellow and dilute in intensity.

She thought of the office and Candy's dour comments and decided to refrain from focusing on them until she could talk first with her husband. Things seemed to be running along well enough in her absence despite their acrimonious attitudes towards each other. What she'd really like now was some reading material to cozy up with as she sipped serenely through the rest of the flight. Stuffed in the pouch of the seat in front of her was the same magazine she had read on arrival. Feeling keenly the loss of a captivating book she wondered if going back to the magazine rack was worth the effort it would take to get up...*next time i better eat lunch before drinking*...She leaned back and stretched, wondering what to do, then suddenly remembered that there was a small portion of the tape that she had not yet heard. Rummaging through her carry-on bag to the bottom she pulled out the cassette player, slipped on the headphones and sat back to listen.

"Oh, I know, something else just came to mind that I'd like to ask you. It's been weighing on me."

"Yes."

"I have a horse, and uh, he's pretty old and he has some foot problems. But he's getting better. But it's costing me quite a bit of money and I don't get to be with him a lot. But I can't bring myself to sell him. Uh, what do you think about keeping him and doing what I can do with him or do you think I should try to find a new... a new mommy for him."

"Well if you don't want to sell him, just keep him."

"Just keep him and pay the price?"

"Right. Well, yeah, learn that the price is not an expense, but that the good for that is there and you just have to be open to it."

"Hm."

"Don't feel responsible for the horse. Just accept the fact that you love the horse and you don't want to send him away. That's fine."

"Okay. Good. Uh, Jay's here behind me and he wants to know if you think I should expect him to get more involved in my business while I'm gone these two weeks on my trip."

"If it's his wish, and your wish, absolutely."

"Okay. Yeah. Yesterday he put in a full day and then he had a counseling appointments the next day and he said he thought that listening to other people's problems was going to be a really nice thing to do after spending a day in the office." (laughter)

"Yeah, right." (laughter)

"Jay wants to know if you have time now to speak to him a bit."

"Yeah."

"Thank you so much."

"You're most welcome."

"I'm sure we'll speak again."

"Okay."

"Okay, Leroy. Here's Jay."

Chapter 34

"As God sent me to you so will I send you to others. And I will go to them with you, so we can teach them peace and union." (A Course in Miracles)

A S THE LUNCH HOUR drew to a close Jay put his small cassette recorder in the bottom drawer of his file cabinet and escorted his next client, a new one, into the office. She was a tall, attractive, well-dressed young woman in her early twenties who had taken off her lunch period to see him. She worked in accounting at a nearby electronics company in the technology corridor, as it was called, in the adjacent valley to the north. On the telephone she had mentioned feeling ridden with anxiety during the holidays as a perennial problem. Settling into the cushy rattan chair, she pulled her pleated wool skirt over her knees, clasped her hands together, interlocking the fingers, and sat up very straight.

"You know, I've never done this before," she said with some trepidation, " and I feel pretty nervous about it."

"Well, that's perfectly normal, like the first time for a lot of things. I get many people here who are seeing a counselor for the very first time. But after they've come once, usually their fears are allayed and they find we can work together on whatever it is that brought them. So I suggest you just give it a try today and see how you feel as we progress along the hour. Does that sound okay?"

"Yes, thank you."

"Good. I want you to feel comfortable here and that you're in a safe place."

"I appreciate that."

"You said on the phone that you start to feel anxious with the onset of the holidays each year."

"Yes."

"And are you feeling anxious now?"

"Yes, a little bit."

"Because you're here or because the holidays are coming?"

"More because I'm here I think and we're going to talk about it."

"Okay. Well, maybe that's good in a way because it's just exactly what it is we want to work with."

"Yes, I guess so, but I'd still rather not feel this way."

"Sure. Well, aside from being nervous here now, how long have you had these feelings?"

"They usually start up in October in anticipation of the holidays."

"For how many years?"

"Ever since I moved out of my parents home, about five years ago."

"Do you have any idea what causes them exactly?"

"Yes. Basically it's because I have to go over to my mom's place for Thanksgiving and Christmas every year."

"You don't like that?"

"I hate it."

"Why?"

"Because of my step dad."

"You hate him?"

"Well, no. I don't really hate him, but he makes me uncomfortable."

"What's he do exactly that makes you feel that way?"

"Nothing really, that I can put my finger on. I just think he doesn't really like me. I've always felt that way. He was always whittling with a knife and it made me kind of nervous when I lived with him."

"Did he ever threaten you with it?"

"No."

"How long's he been your step dad?"

"Ever since I was eight. My real dad left us when I was six. We don't know where he went. Or even if he's alive. But my mom remarried two years later."

"I see. That must have been tough, losing your dad so young."

"Yes, it was at the time but I'm over it now."

"Uh-huh. Does your mom know you have these feelings about your step dad?"

"No, not really."

"Why not?"

"She'd think I'm crazy. That I'm just imagining that he doesn't like me."

"How do you know that?"

"Because when I was a kid I used to tell her and she'd say I was wrong – that he loves me really and I should give him a chance."

"Do you think that you did?"

"I don't know. I tried. I just felt he never loved me the way that my Dad did. He was never really bad to me actually. He was like..ummm…polite and all, but I always had these funny feelings around him. He was kind of distant. And he had that knife. I just never felt very comfortable with him. I always had the thought that he wanted my mom to himself."

"What was the worse thing that he ever did?"

"Well, nothing that I can remember exactly, but…but…well I always thought that maybe he might have been the one who killed my cat?"

"Really? That sounds like a sad thing to happen to a little girl. But you don't know for sure that he did it?"

"No. I was just suspicious. She was found one day in the alley. I know he never liked her. He didn't like animals in general. My daddy had given me that cat as a kitty for a Christmas present when I was five."

"I see. Is that still a pretty vivid memory?"

"What? Being given the cat?"

"No, I meant it dying. But do you remember getting it on Christmas?"

"No. I just know I did. It was like the one thing left to me from him. And I don't even remember its death at all. Just that it died one winter right after New Years."

"How do you know it was then?"

"Mmmm…I remember it was snowy and my mom always said it we found it on New Years Day."

"I see. Do you remember any details, like who found it or how it looked?"

"No, not really. I was only nine or so then. I just remember it happened."

"I see. Well, does mom know that you get these feelings about going to her house?"

"No. I don't want her to know. It would just hurt her feelings. She wouldn't understand."

"So how long are you there?"

"For Thanksgiving dinner, then later Christmas Eve and then dinner the next day."

"And you feel anxious the whole time?"

"Yes. It's always the same. I can never relax and my stomach's usually killing me. I always have to take Tagamet before I go."

"And it still bothers you?"

"Yes. Nothing works completely."

"How'd you handle being around your step dad as a kid?"

"Well, I spent a lot of time at other girl's houses. I didn't like going home right after school because he would get home earlier than her."

"Why's that?"

"Because she was a secretary and he was the foreman on the day shift at a manufacturing plant. He worked till 3:30 and she wasn't off until five."

"Uh-huh. So it was like this all the way through high school?"

"Yes, pretty much, and I always had school activities. Anything to stay away really."

"How about after high school?"

"I went away to college in Pullman and only came home for Christmas and summers. As soon as I graduated I got a job and have been living with my boy friend for the last two years."

"Did you ever consider leaving the area for good?"

"Yes, I did. But my boy friend's here and he's not sure if he wants to leave. He's got a good job, and family and all. It'd be hard."

"Okay. Well, how do you feel now?"

"Right now?"

"Yeah, right this minute."

"Mmmm…a little better maybe." She unclasped her hands and self-consciously sank back slightly into the chair.

"Why do you think that is?"

"Well…" she hesitated. "I guess that I feel like you want to help me and that…that sort of calms me down some."

"Yeah, well you're right about that. And I'm glad that thought has some effect on you. You remember on the phone I said that perhaps we could find some ways to dispel the anxiety by helping you relax?"

"Yeah."

"Good. Well, what I have in mind is a self-relaxation technique that I think I can teach you to help yourself with."

"Huh."

"You see, aside from being a regular psychotherapist, I'm also a certified hypnotherapist, and what we do is basically help people relax when dealing with anxiety."

"Hm."

"And I think that this might be a way to help you? What do you think?"

"Well, what do I have to do exactly? I'm not sure I want to be hypnotized. I don't think I could be, anyway actually. I'd be afraid of losing control."

"Okay. Well, right.. I understand that. It's not really supposed to be about losing control, but I know that's a popular notion. What I'm talking about is more about deep relaxation, and I'd try to teach you to do it with yourself eventually. Does that sound less threatening?"

"Maybe. I just don't want to be out of control. It's too scary."

"Okay. I hear you. I understand. Most of us don't want to be out of control. I certainly wouldn't. But what I have in mind is a little different than that. I think you'd find you can stay in conscious control of yourself. At least that's how I'd want you to feel. We would hopefully just be focusing on helping you relax and, in effect, easing your anxiety away. And then learning how to do the technique yourself."

"Yeah, well that sounds like it might be okay, but it still seems a little spooky."

"Alright. Well, we won't do anything that you're not comfortable with. The main reason I'm suggesting it is because it is one method commonly used to treat anxiety when that's the only problem that people present."

"I see. That makes sense."

"You see, sometimes people have a generalized anxiety around something in the present and they know it's related to something in the past but they can't quite recall what. So in psychology that's called repression, meaning it is being held back in the unconscious part of our mind, because we don't feel its safe enough to let into our consciousness."

"Oh."

"So the idea of using hypnosis in a situation like that is that we go back to the point in the past where the anxiety was first experienced and see if can get them to be aware of it in the present , while realizing they are now safe in the present, and thus allowing them to release the hidden thoughts so they no longer feel plagued by anxiety anymore."

"I see."

"Good. Well, what I'd really like to do now, is for us to just continue talking the rest of this session, so that I feel I know you better and you can feel the same with me. Hopefully we'll establish a greater comfort and trust level between us."

"Okay."

"Good. And if you're willing at the end of this session to schedule another appointment a few days from now, I'd like to see then if you are comfortable enough to try the hypnosis, the deep relaxation, and if you are, and you find it helpful, perhaps we can lessen or eliminate your feelings in time for the holidays. If you're not, we won't. And also, like I said, if we end up doing that, I'll teach you some self-hypnosis, some relaxation techniques, for additional help if needed. Does that sound okay?"

"Yeah, it does. I would really like to be rid of these feelings this year, that's for sure."

"I'm sure you would. I know that's why you're here. So look, let's just talk the rest of this session and see how you feel at the end of it today. If you want to come back, we'll schedule an appointment. If you don't, we won't. And even if we do you can always cancel it if you have second thoughts later, you know. Alright?"

"Yeah. I guess so. That sounds good for now."

"Great. Now, I'd like to learn more about your childhood."

His next to the last session was with a married couple in their early thirties that he had seen but once before. They were a racially mixed couple with the husband being a white Microsoft computer programmer and the wife a black elementary school teacher. The main stress in their busy lives emanated from the fact that they had four energetic young boys, ages five to ten, to contend with around the clock. He was intense, simmering with silent anger, over the level of rampant disorganization that he came home to each evening, night after wracking night, which made it hard to work on the research project he brought there with him from his job.

She was depressed, feeling overworked, harried and unappreciated by her spouse, day after busy day, which made life seem relentlessly demanding and bleak. He spoke in measured soft tones that belied his true feelings of exasperation and despair. Thinking he was being reasonable, he was unaware of the effects of his quiet fury. She felt his anger keenly and was uncertain how to respond to its hidden presence, and as a result had become distant and uncommunicative with her mate. Their sex life was non-existent.

"Well, how has it gone since I saw you last week? Any better? Any worse? I'm curious if you were able to make use of what we discussed last time. Who wants to speak first?"

"Why don't you go first," said the husband, legs crossed, arms folded. "You're the one who made the appointment."

"I don't know," said the woman shyly, looking over at the wall, "We tried to talk like you said, but it didn't help much. I'm afraid we're still the same." She gave Jay an embarrassed smile. "No matter what I do he's always unhappy. Anyway, it seems that way to me."

"Of course I'm unhappy," he retorted. "I'm frustrated with our life at home. It's always messy. It's always noisy. The boys are always going crazy and running around from room to room. The TV's on loud. You never do a thing about it. I can't get any work done. You don't even care to try and stop them."

"It's not as bad, Peter, as you think. I do try. It's just not that easy."

"How hard can it be? They have chores. They have homework. You just don't make them do it. I don't understand why you can't get it organized better."

She looked at Jay with imploring eyes, then shook her head and looked away again.

"He doesn't understand what it's like. They do their chores, not always on time but… they do their homework…sooner or later… but they're boys. They've been in school all day. I have to make dinner, do laundry." She looked forlornly down into her lap. "Things get done sooner or later."

"You sound like you feel overwhelmed," said Jay. "Like it's an awful lot to handle."

"Yeah…I do…it is. He doesn't believe me…he doesn't know."

"I know, Sheila," interjected Peter. "I come home to it every night. I know. I'm just saying it could be handled a lot better. I come home and the boys are running around…you're in the kitchen…"

"Then you do it,' she answered glumly. "You try and get them to be so perfect."

"I do, damn it, every night, after a long hard day at the lab. They listen to me. You're just too soft on them. If I got off as early as you do, things would be a lot different there at night."

"Yeah, well… that's what you think," she almost whispered. "But I work all day too. Just because it's not as long as you – just because it doesn't pay as good as your job – doesn't mean it doesn't count. I have to cook. I try to clean up."

"Yeah, well it sure is messy," Peter snapped. "You could get them to help more. It's so crazy everywhere."

"It's not as crazy there as you think," said Sheila quietly. "You're just a…a perfectionist."

"Okay, sure, it's my fault. That's what you always end up saying."

Sheila looked away as tears welled up into her eyes then trickled slowly down her cheeks. Peter wrinkled his nose in disgust and looked at Jay.

"This is what she always does. We can't ever get anywhere. We can't talk. And nothing ever gets any better." He shook his head form side to side. "I'm so tired of it."

"You sound angry," said Jay matter-of-factly.

"I'm not angry. I'm just frustrated."

"Okay. You're frustrated."

Jay reached for the box of Kleenex on his coffee table and handed them gently to Sheila. "Here," he said in a sympathetic tone, "use these." She took them from him, murmuring a thank you, and wiped her wet face while sniffling.

"Look," continued Jay, addressing both of them, "it doesn't sound like you were able to make much use of the communication skills we went over last time. And that's okay – or at least to be expected – because old habits die hard and you guys have been married now for almost eight years. I didn't expect miracles to occur overnight."

"We could use a miracle," snorted Peter.

"Well," responded Jay, "you could certainly use some changes and we didn't have much time last session to go over this method, since most of our time was spent with you both giving me your side of things. This time I'd like to use most of our session to go over again the communication techniques I talked about last time. And then I want you to practice them here, in front of me, so you can get a better sense of them. Okay?"

"Sure," sniffed Peter. "That's what were here for."

"Sheila, you up for this now?" asked Jay.

"I guess so," she said back softly and sniffled again. "Yes."

"Okay," Jay announced, "just to recap, remember last time at the end I summed up how it seemed to me you were feeling. You're both unhappy, but with a different tone to it. To make it simple, you're depressed Sheila, and Peter, you're angry."

"You said that before but I thought you were wrong. I'm not mad. I'm just sick and tired of the mess and things never changing."

"Okay, let me revise that for now. You feel frustrated, and it comes across to me as being mad. And I can't help but wonder if your wife senses that too. Sheila?"

"I guess so. I…I never really thought about that way before. He doesn't lose his temper or anything. He's just always complaining. Always criticizing, tense all the time."

"Right. Okay. Look it doesn't matter what we call these feelings exactly, at least for the moment. You both agree you're both unhappy and you'd like things to change. So let's start from there. Alright?" He looked at each of them for corroboration. Both nodded their heads slightly and looked back at Jay expectantly. "Alright. So as I said last time, communication is the key. You guys are so upset with each other, you've lost an important key to making things better. So here we go. Remember last time I mentioned that it doesn't really matter how people communicate when things are going well?"

Each of them nodded their heads slightly in confirmation.

"Okay. But like I said, it does matter when thing are not going well — when there's a problem. And a problem is defined for our purposes here as when someone has a negative feeling. Okay? And we don't even need to know exactly what that feeling is to use this method. Okay? That'll be clarified as we get into it, but to get started using these skills, we just need to recognize that when someone's upset in a relationship, there's a problem. The bad feelings are the problem. Alright? Now, the two parts of communication, as I said before, are the transmission and the reception of messages. Right? That's what it's all about." He waited for each of them to indicate they were with him. Peter nodded once and Sheila quietly said "Yes".

"Okay. So the method I'm teaching you is based on dealing with those problems. If there's no problem, talk any way you want. But if someone has a negative feeling — or if you both do — here's how to handle it through communication. The person with the problem — with the bad feeling — expresses themselves by using what is called an 'I message'. Okay?

"You can cover every possible thing there is to express under the sun by saying 'I feel, I think and I want' when you start your sentence and you have a problem. Alright?" He looked at them again for confirmation and each one nodded once more. "Basically what you think is a statement of the problem and what you want is a solution to the problem. The bad feeling itself is actually the problem but the thought is the context it occurs in, or why it is you feel bad.

"All right. So that's how you begin to communicate to another person when you have a problem with that person. You say 'I feel this and I think that and I want this or that'. It's as straightforward as it gets. It is not an attack. It is not a complaint. It is merely a statement of what you are feeling, thinking and wanting. Period. And it's important that when you say 'I feel' that you follow it with the emotion or feeling that you are actually feeling. If you say 'I think', then you must follow it with what the thought is that describes the problem. It is common for people to say 'I feel you're not listening to me' for example. That is not a feeling. That is a thought. It would be right to say 'I feel angry or sad because I think you're not listening to me'. And of course, when you say 'I want', you need to follow that with what it is you are wanting, which is the solution. For example, 'and I want you to listen to me'. Okay?" More nods.

"Good. Okay. People so often use 'you messages' when there's a problem with someone. 'You never do thus and so — you always do thus and so' — and that is usually taken by the other person as an attack. And when someone thinks they are being attacked they usually respond by getting defensive, and often they attack back. So on and on it goes spiraling out of control till there's a huge fight or a break up or in some way a worsened situation and a total lack of communication with no way out. It can stay that way for years sometimes, just repeating the patterns. You follow?"

"Yeah," said Peter, with greater interest in his voice. Sheila nodded her head slowly but her eyes were wider with more attention than before.

"Okay. So with 'I messages' offense is less likely to be taken. People may choose to take offense anyway but none is given in that way of speaking so it is much easier to defuse it if it happens. Frankly it doesn't usually happen. Instead a message – the feeling, the thought and the want of a person – is simply being communicated directly. And that is relatively easy to take or to hear because someone is just making a statement about his or her feelings, thoughts and wants to someone else. People are entitled to their feelings, thoughts and wants. It doesn't mean they are entitled to have others do something about them, but they are entitled to have and express them.

"Now, the next step or the other side of this – receiving a message from someone who has a problem – is called 'Active Listening'. Okay?" He did not pause to see if they would agree. They were clearly paying attention. "And this too is very specific, very simple, very direct. Active Listening simply means that you, as the listener, try to understand by reflecting back exactly what the other person is feeling. Not what they're thinking, not what they're wanting, just what they're feeling. Because the fact that they have a bad feeling is the problem.

"If someone says 'I feel like you're not listening to me', for example, an Active Listening response would be 'sounds like you're angry', or sad, or whatever feeling you think that person seems to be feeling. Okay? And why does this work? Because when people know that you want to understand what they are feeling, they feel valued, respected and ultimately heard and understood. They see you care enough about them to try to understand their feelings. You have then set an ideal climate for people to feel inclined to communicate what's going on with them. And things can then proceed from there in a positive manner. A constructive dialogue can take place. And the problem can be resolved, or at least understood in such a way that is not destructive to the relationship. And that's the point; to communicate constructively and to save the relationship from being hurtful or destructive or ruined. Are you with me?"

Peter nodded thoughtfully, "Makes sense," he said. Sheila nodded her head in agreement. "I think so, " she said. "But I don't know if we can do that".

"Well, it sounds like you have some doubts. If I were doing Active Listening I would say sounds like you feel apprehensive, which is a form of fear. Actually all negative feelings are an expression of fear. And all we are doing through this method is trying to help people express and release their fears in a constructive manner. And I think anyone can learn to do it," Jay stated reassuringly. "If they want to. And I think you want to. That's why you're both here: to heal and to save this relationship. And it's my job to teach you. And I will. Now let's use some real life examples from your own life and you'll see how it actually works. I want you to move your chairs around so that you are directly facing each other. And I'll guide you through speaking and listening to one another using this method. I think you'll be impressed with how well it works."

His final appointment was with a man he had seen weekly for three prior meetings. He was a big burly guy in his late thirties who owned his own construction company and was married to an unhappy woman twelve years his junior. He had always been a relatively humble person in their sessions, and Jay wondered if that were his characteristic demeanor of if he had simply been humbled by the recent downturn of his marriage. He was an active father with two young boys in fifth and sixth grades, whose sports teams he coached. She would not come into the sessions with him and was seeing a female therapist individually.

A few months earlier they had gone together to see that counselor but the man refused to go any more after two sessions as he thought no progress was being made on resolving their marital conflicts. He said they only focused on how angry she still was with him for slapping her months ago and could not seemingly get beyond it. He had hoped that his wife's individual sessions with her therapist might result in restoring peace and harmony to their marriage but that was not happening. He had then sought out Jay for advice on how to handle his wife's continuing anger and coldness towards him. Though they had discussed various ways in which to deal with the situation so far little progress was being made on the home front.

"So how did it last week go, Steve," said Jay. "Any better?"

"Well, maybe," replied Steve, looking wistful and pensive. "I'm giving her the space that she wants, like you said."

"Well, that's probably wise, given that she just gets angry when you try to talk with her about the relationship. No point in forcing things. Best to wait and see if she'll be more approachable as she continues counseling."

"Yeah, I know. So I'm doing what you suggested and just waiting for her to bring it up instead of pushing things."

"Good."

"It's hard though. I feel like I never loved her so much as I do now and it's killing me not to show it."

"Well, maybe the best way you can show it right now is just to respect her wishes that you not press her. Hopefully, if she sincerely wants things better, she'll let you know when she wants to talk about it."

"Yeah, I know. I know. And she does, but it's not very often. She seems happy enough to just be doing what she wants and most of that's without me. It's hard to wait for her to want to talk when I feel so bad." Steve looked as penitent as he had from their first meeting. "I'll do anything she wants," he said sadly. "Anything."

"I know you would. But apparently now this is all she wants. Is she still going to the gym quite a bit?"

"Oh yeah, she looks great. Works out all the time. She's a beautiful gal and she never looked better. It just makes it harder to keep my hands off her though."

"I bet. Does she still want to make love upon rare occasions?"

"Yeah, about once a week, and that drives me nuts. I mean I'm so glad for the opportunity to show her some affection, and she really seems to enjoy it and everything, and then when it's over she's quiet again. And the next day she's back to being distant and cold, or else just angry."

"I'm sure that's hard to take."

"Oh man, it is. One minute hot and the next minute cold."

"But mostly cool all the time."

"Yeah."

"Anything new or different happen this week?"

"Well, for the first time she brought up the possibility of separation."

"Whoa. How'd you deal with that?"

"I said that I didn't want a separation, but she said maybe if we had some time apart she might start to feel better towards me again. She's still won't forgive me for that one time I slapped her."

"Yeah, I know. You told me before. Since she won't come here I don't know what she's thinking, but I'm curious why she doesn't seem interested in forgiving you and moving on."

"Well, I told you I was probably kind of domineering in the past. I mean when we got married she was twenty and I was thirty-two, and she always deferred to my judgment, my way. And I think I got used to being the one who made most of the decisions and stuff. But we didn't argue about things much and I thought she was happy with the way things were."

"I know. You told me all that, and perhaps you're right. But eventually or lately that must have gotten old for her. It doesn't sound like it's that way any more now anyway."

"It's not, believe me, it's not. But she just started changing earlier this year. Anyway, now she does what she wants when she wants and I ask her opinion on everything. I'm willing to do things her way if she wants."

"You know, it's common when people marry someone much older than themselves, especially if they do it at an early age like she did, to defer to their spouse's wisdom, maturity, age, experience, and so on."

"Yeah, it was kinda' like that."

"And it's especially common that when a girl picks a great big strong guy like yourself who's a dozen years her senior, that she's probably seeking some protection and guidance in dealing with the world."

"Well, I think that's probably true. She left home at eighteen, always fighting with her parents, hated her dad, hated school. She always seemed to like that I could take care of her. I had my company going and so she was secure. With no education she couldn't get much of a job. Before we met she'd worked at cleaning homes for a few years, but she hated that too. Then when we married I said 'Go to school, I'll pay for it', so she did. She went to community college for almost two years but that's all. She stayed at home then with the boys for a couple of years but then said she was bored."

"Even before they started school?"

"Yeah. She was bored with just being a mom, so she started working out and then got a job as a receptionist at the club, and now she works there part-time."

"The athletic club where she also works out?"

"Yeah."

"Well, I can tell you it often happens that when someone, usually a young woman, picks an older man, a bigger man, or in some way a man that she sees as stronger than herself, and in effect is dependent on him to take care of her, after a while as she grows up and grows stronger, she comes to resent the very qualities she chose him for and wants more independence."

"Hm. Well I'm trying to back off. I'm trying to share the decisions. I don't want to be in charge. I'd rather just have a partner anyway."

"And she's telling you that it's too little too late, right? All because you slapped her once?"

"Yeah, and that was a good six months ago. I never touched her before and I haven't done so since. She's hit me before in the past when she was angry."

"Well, I know that seems unfair but she may have thought the differences in your size and gender made her actions justifiable. You said she's about half a foot smaller than you."

"She's five-ten and I'm six-two, so she's not exactly little."

"Yeah, but you're also kinda' thick and you say she's pretty trim?"

"Yeah, but she's all muscle. I slapped her without thinking because she was pushing me and yelling her head off. I just wanted her to stop. She was getting hysterical. Then of course I apologized immediately but she wouldn't have it. Just stomped off to the bedroom and slammed the door. I slept on the couch for two nights."

"And things have never been quite the same?"

"Right."

"Okay. You know, there's been a lot of focus on domestic violence the last decade or so. They've passed laws here in Washington State that somebody has to be arrested if there's a complaint and of course they like to think they are being progressive here, but I always thought that was a flawed law. It would be much better first to try to mediate with the parties. But anyway, the cops have to arrest someone and they tend to believe whoever calls them first, so either spouse can use it against the other one, and they sometimes do.

In that sense, you're fortunate she didn't call the police. I've seen many times where police have actually arrested the woman for being the violent one. Usually they have no record, having never committed a crime. And in most those cases frankly, I thought it was a travesty, because often she was being bullied in some way by the man before she struck out. You may have had a case of that in reverse."

"Yeah? Well, maybe. I don't know. I never thought about it that way before."

"Well, I don't know either, not having been there, but I wanted you to think about it because I see you're blaming your self for all this, but I always tell couples whatever's going on, it's fifty-fifty. They have both somehow created it, and each is responsible for one hundred percent of their half. That allows them to get past the abuser-victim mentality and work on healing their relationship, which is what most people go to counseling for."

"Huh."

"Now, the police weren't involved in your situation and that's not the point I'm making anyway. My point is that violence is more than pushing or slapping someone. It's a mindset. And people have that mindset when angry. It's a mindset of attack thoughts, which is violence; psychological violence. But if the cops come they have to arrest somebody and then the other person is encouraged by the legal system to feel like a victim. The prosecutor wants to convict someone. I've seen it do more damage than good to a couple. You understand what I'm saying?"

"Yeah."

"You must stay cool and never slap her again. And she hopefully will not push you either. Both are grounds for arrest."

"I understand."

"Okay, and so, and though there were no cops, you're wife seems intent on feeling like a victim. Now, refresh me on what that fight was about."

"Oh, she wanted to go out dancing with some girl friends – they'd had it planned – and I was supposed to watch the boys, but I had to go to a meeting that just came up at the last minute and we couldn't get a sitter and she was really pissed I wouldn't cancel my meeting. But I couldn't. I mean it was important. It might have meant the difference between getting a big contract or not and we pay all our bills on my paycheck, not hers."

"Okay, okay, I remember. And so she wanted to go out, ostensibly with the girls, and she's seen herself as the victim ever since then, right?"

"Uh, yeah, basically…right."

"So you go to this other counselor, this woman – who your wife first saw alone a few times – and the focus of the counseling becomes that your wife is a victim and you're an abuser. Right?"

"Yeah, in a way. Right."

"And it's supposed to take a long time for her to get over it, if ever, and in the meantime you're supposed to feel guilty about it all. Right?"

"Yeah. That's practically all we ever talked about there. She was always mad throughout the sessions. Always talking about how I'd really hurt her and scared her, and how overbearing I am and how she couldn't ever trust me again. That's why I stopped going. It wasn't helping."

"And so she's still just as angry at you as she ever was, despite all this time?"

"Yeah. That's right. There doesn't seem to be anything I can do."

"Okay. I know. Sometimes this happens. At least here's what I think it is that might be happening. I've seen it a fair amount, mostly with women therapists but sometimes with men too. Therapists are people too and they can be biased in all sorts of ways. A female therapist is more likely to be sensitive to a female client being abused by a man than a male therapist might be, just because she's woman and is aware through her own experience that there has been and can be a level of male dominance over women in the world. Actually it's a good thing to be sensitive to, because that needs to change. But sometimes, and I think this may be happening with you, it gets overdone, and becomes the main thing and the focus on forgiveness and healing and understanding and working things through is hardly touched upon, while, if people are serious about improving their relationship, that should actually be the main thing instead."

"Hm."

"By the way, you said you guys depend on your paycheck, but doesn't your wife pay some bills too?"

"Well, no, not really. Her money's for whatever she wants to do with it – go out to lunch, buy clothes, girls' night out, whatever. I pay all the monthly bills."

"I see. Hm. Did it ever occur to you that she may be a bit self-absorbed?"

"Well, not until lately, but yeah, I sorta' see her that way a little now."

"What about her seems that way the most to you?"

"Well, it's just that despite being unhappy with me, she still seems really happy with everything else she does. She loves going to work. She loves going out with her girl friends. She talks on the phone with them a lot. She loves going to the gym every night. She loves spending money on herself."

"Uh-huh. I see. What sort of stuff does she like to buy?"

"Well lately, the last few months, she's been buying a bunch of fancy underwear from Victoria's Secret."

"Really?"

"Yeah, all kinds of fancy stuff."

"Does that seem a little odd to you since she doesn't want to make love much."

"Well, she's getting in shape like never before. I mean she was always pretty trim, but now she's working out with the weights too, and I guess she just enjoys looking good, you know, at the gym and everywhere. Her leg and arm muscles are strong and well defined. I'm telling ya', she really looks gorgeous. More than ever."

"Hmmmm. Look, maybe I'm dead wrong, and I hope that I am, but I've been doing this a very long time. And when someone's partner is out every evening, plus working out hard and making their body more beautiful than ever, plus buying up fancy underwear a lot, which isn't for your eyes, and says they're unhappily married but doesn't really want to work on it – just wants some more space…I gotta' tell you that I get suspicious."

"What do you mean?"

"I just get suspicious they're having an affair."

"Oh, I don't think so. I mean that crossed my mind, and I asked her about it. But she said 'no way'."

"And you believe her?"

"Yeah, I do. I don't think she'd do that. I don't think she'd lie to me about it either."

"Yeah, well could be, maybe you're right, and I hope that you are, but it seems funny to me. And this other counselor may well have unwittingly, with the best of intentions, played right into her hands, because when someone shows up at your office and they're crying and they're saying 'My husband is such a brute, and he's a huge guy, and he hit me and I don't trust him and I'm so scared of him and I feel intimidated by him, and he's so suffocating, and I don't have a life and I never have since I left home as a teen and my dad was a brute too', the first impulse of many a counselor, especially another woman, and in this day and age, especially in liberal cities like Seattle, where it's basically politically correct to feel victimized, to take offense, is to sympathize with that person and work with them individually, until they feel strong enough to decide if they want to leave or stay in their relationship. If they elect to stay in it and make it better, then it's time to work on that. And it sounds like your wife is showing no inclination to do that at all. She's preferring to hold onto her grievance toward you while apparently having a good time otherwise, and having seen people act this way before, well, it's just very similar to other situations I've seen where people were having affairs. I certainly could be wrong."

"I sure hope you are."

"Well, since she says that she's not, you really have no choice but to take her at her word. But it's hard when she's not willing to work on things with you."

"I just think that if she has more time she'll come around."

"That's possible. That's certainly possible. And apart from moving out that's about all you can do, plus hope she'll eventually consider marriage counseling, or some way of working on things to better them."

"So what do you think about a separation? About me moving out?"

"Personally I think it's a bad idea. It would hurt you and your two children. Did you guys talk about them?"

"No, we didn't get that far. She just said she might feel better if I moved out."

"Well, it's the very last resort, and it often doesn't work. Also, if it turns out that she then wants a divorce it could well put you at a disadvantage in court. She could say that you left her."

"Do you really think she'd do that?"

"I have no idea really. I'm just speaking in terms of what I have seen happen before in situations similar to this one. If you leave for a separation you may never get back in."...*and if she's having an affair, guess who eventually does...*

"Hm. I never thought of that."

"Yeah, well it's something to consider. I'd like for you to ask her if she would come in with you for just one session together. If she's not interested, don't push it. Just let it go. But there's no harm in asking. Maybe we could make some progress in resurrecting your relationship."

Chapter 35

"Big sisters are the crab grass in the lawn of life." (Charles M. Schultz)

"M A'AM? MA'AM? MA'AM!"
Feeling a persistent touch on her shoulder like a faintly throbbing muscle contraction Bea mustered a sleepy-eyed sideward squint to the official smile of a stewardess in the aisle. She was leaning across two empty seats and staring down at her with a courteous sense of urgency. "We're about to land now, ma'am," announced the woman briskly, looking relieved she'd finally made contact. "Please bring your seat to an upright position."

While searching for the seat button she struggled to shake off the grogginess in her head and yawned deeply. When upright at last she fumbled around in her bag for the bottle of Evian water there. After a few swallows the wetness began to wash away the cobwebs of a gin induced slumber and she cleared her throat before yawning once more. She had slept so soundly that the pilot's announcement over the loudspeakers had gone unnoticed…*guess i needed that…*

Looking down through the window at a spattering of sparkling lights below she could dimly make out the undulating dark hills of Pittsburgh's suburban countryside. A subtle feeling of excitement suddenly seized her. This was the occasion she had been awaiting for weeks. A slight feeling of dread momentarily arose. What if it didn't turn out as she wished? She dismissed the latter feeling as quickly as it had come. This was going to be a special time, no matter what: a rare and precious moment in her life…*and that's that…*

As her senses returned to full power she started to revel in the anticipation of seeing Faye at the airport and wondered how different they might look to each other. In the distance on the freeway she could see the red and white lights forming their long lines as the five o'clock commuters began caravanning home like a steady stream of fireflies. Grateful she was spared such a fate in her life, she reflected on how it wouldn't bother her a bit if it took their car hours to crawl to Faye's home tonight; all the more time to chat and catch up. By the time the plane touched down and was rolling to a stop, she was filled only with gladness at the prospect ahead. Surely she could find a way to circumvent her feelings from the past and begin anew. After all, this gathering was Faye's idea. She was the one who had put out the call for a family meeting and proclaimed it a reunion. What could be bad?

On the second that the signal sounded to disembark she bounded readily into the aisle with an eager expectancy of what lie ahead. Stepping spryly through the shuffling crowd she boarded the packed subway that led to the baggage claim area. She held onto the metal pole while standing in the train and felt an inch above the ground as it raced noiselessly along the tracks. Faye had requested they meet at the curbside outside baggage claim after getting her luggage so as to avoid the parking lot fee. "Just look for a shiny white XKE", she had said proudly. "You can't miss it." Bea was pleased and amused at the idea of riding in her sister's sleek jag. It would be hard to find a more stylish entrance into the city.

She gathered her bulky suitcase and trundled through the glass doors out to the curb then looked about for the illustrious luxury car. It wasn't there yet but that wasn't surprising. She knew well her sister's predilection for being late. Punctuality was simply not in her vocabulary and the thick cords of traffic had probably played havoc with any attempt on her part to try to be prompt. She shivered slightly in the cold air, wishing she'd replaced her knee length dress with some slacks, and wondered whether to don her black leather gloves or go back behind the doors. Her enthusiasm was enough to warm her for the moment and she slipped on the gloves while staring up the line of cars briefly stopping or filing past… *probably be here any minute*…After ten minutes her enthusiasm failed to keep the evening chill from creeping up her bare legs and she moved inside to a point where she could still easily view the approaching vehicles…*better call her cell to see how close she is*…She searched in her purse but could only locate Faye's office number instead and called there in the hopes that someone could help her.

"Faye Mondavi's office. May I help you?"

"I hope so. This is Bea, Faye's sister, and I am waiting at the airport for her to pick me up, but she hasn't arrived yet. I wondered if you could give me her cell phone number so I could call and see how close she is."

"Oh, I'm so sorry, I can give you that number, but she was unexpectedly called into a late meeting with the mayor and wasn't able to leave as planned."

"What?"

"She told me to tell you she was terribly sorry and asked me to page you on your arrival, which I've been doing for the last ten minutes or so."

"Well, thanks, but for the last ten minutes I've been standing outside."

"Oh, I'm so sorry to hear that. I hope you're okay. It's cold out there isn't it?"

"Very. But that's okay. I'm just so disappointed."

"Oh I'm sure that you are and she was quite put out also, but she told me to tell you the best thing to do is to just take a taxi right over to her place where they're expecting you and the concierge has a key. She said to go up and just make yourself at home."

"Oh. Okay. Well, I don't know how to get there."

"That's alright, I have the address right here for you. Just give it to the driver."

"Okay, just a minute and I'll write it down."

"Yes, of course, let me know when you're ready. And again, she really regrets that this happened. But under the circumstances nothing else could be done."

"That's okay, I understand. By the way, do you know when her meeting will be over?"

"I'm afraid that's hard to say. Sometimes they run awhile and sometimes they're rather short."

"I see."

"I suggest you call her on her cell phone after getting to her place and perhaps she can advise you of that at that time."

"Okay. Go ahead and give me the address and number."

As Bea relaxed in the worn back seat of the polished yellow cab she was relieved to find that the traffic was moving along faster than it had seemed to be from the air. While disappointed to be alone she was trying to be philosophical about the matter and retain the upbeat state of mind in which she had landed...*these things happen*...The cabbie, a grizzled old man in a gray wool cap, gave a quick glance at the address and nodded knowingly. "Fawnzy playz," he said, winking with a mustachioed smile. "I geet you der queek." His short stodgy build and amiable manner reminded her of her father when he was younger. She had imagined nothing less than a fancy place from her sister but was more impressed than expected when they circled around the fountain in the driveway at the hilltop to reveal a vast vista of the city in all directions...*wow*...

The doorman's manner was impeccably polite as he extended his arm to help her out of the cab. She was mildly embarrassed as her tightened skirt rose to her thighs when she slid across the seat and saw him admiring her shapely legs in the process. Tipping the cab driver more than she might normally have seemed a fair gesture for such a classy locale. As he drove off and the doorman held the door open for her, she couldn't resist looking up at the huge edifice before entering; twenty tall stories of glass and concrete. She advanced into the lobby, as spacious as any fine hotel, and collected the key from the gentlemanly concierge sitting behind a curved jade-green marble top counter.

On her way down the wide hall to the elevator area she took in the various large paintings on the walls and other artwork. There was a mixture of contemporary and classical artists interspersed with clay and bronze pieces of sculpture. She stepped into the elevator, wheeled in her suitcase, and punched in the button for the sixteenth floor. As it whirred it's way upward she felt a mixture of admiration and envy for the plush surroundings and proficient service that encased her sister's luxurious lifestyle. Moreover she was grateful and relieved for the chance to settle there for awhile; a welcome and much needed respite.

The elevator opened a few yards from the door of the condo and upon entering the small foyer she was immediately overwhelmed by the suite's roomy opulence…*oh my God…*She looked around in wonder one hundred eighty degrees, down the long hallway toward the bedroom on her right to the balcony on her left just beyond the living room. Each end had its own panoramic cityscape scene. She left her bag in the entryway and set her purse on the glass dining table, then slipped off her shoes while examining the golden chandelier. Flicking on the light switch she slid gently across the white sandstone tile to the edge of the magenta living room carpet and dug her toes in to feel its cushiness.

She glanced over at the compact kitchen on her right, eyeing an empty cupboard, and leisurely sauntered into the whitewashed living space, appraising every detail of the interior with each step. It was filled with two overstuffed plaid charcoal chairs, two hefty lemon leather floor pillows, and a sumptuous maroon couch bordered by lavish leafy green silk plants on mahogany end tables with a matching coffee table. The real showpiece however was a dazzling red and yellow vase of spun glass that twisted nearly three feet high atop a walnut cabinet housing the television and stereo. She paused momentarily to gaze at some framed color photographs of Faye alongside it but felt drawn to the balcony on the far side of the room.

She drew back the sliding glass door to walk out onto a hard rubber-coated deck, crowded with lounge chairs and a patio table, and surveyed the vibrant skyline of the downtown in the distance. To the east giant skyscrapers were carved in myriad shapes and crowned by varied peaks and radiant colors that touted their dominance through their company insignias; Mitsubishi, Kaiser, GE, Kodak. Beneath them rambled a network of lowly streetlights and the dotted windows of lesser structures in the softened tawny glow. Streams of traffic, flickering neon signs, and bright billboards filled in the blackened landscape surrounding the sprawling city center. Past the business district toward the outlying hills rounded to the north and south were dimly lit houses and a few assorted high rises similar to the one she was in. She felt moved by the beauty of the immense metropolis but also knew from her remote high perspective that concealed within the silent city limits in the darkness lay unseemly assaults on the senses; grimy gutters, blaring horns, exhaust fumes, panhandlers, addicts, the homeless and an endless unforgiving pavement. As charming as it appeared underneath a beaming half-moon, she knew herself foremost a faithful country girl at heart and was glad she would soon be viewing contentedly her lovely lake in the woods in due time.

She leaned against the cold metal railing and looked down to the fountain sixteen stories below. The turbulent spurt of the upward surge and spray was barely audible and amidst the amber cross lights of the surrounding pool it looked like a small volcano erupting. Less than a mile to her left she could dimly make out the outlines of the 'Y' where the three rivers of Pittsburgh conjoined on their way to meet the mighty Mississippi. Just beyond them was the stadium, ringed with a string of lights but barren of activity. No games tonight. Farther on she spotted a bridge that crossed into an old section of the city; smoky bars, homey restaurants, cheap coffee shops, garish nightclubs, mom and pop stores. As her hands began to freeze on the frigid iron bar she rubbed them together and turned towards the beckoning warmth of the living room…*brrrrr*…From that vantage point she faced two framed glossy photos of Faye on the cabinet. She studied them intently, seeking clues to her whereabouts within in their gala background.

Leaving the evening chill behind her she went inside and strode to the cabinet for a closer look. The largest picture was of Faye gaily posing at some social festivity, the bread of her life, and she wondered if the man standing next to her might be her new beau. Ever since Faye's second divorce years ago, she had stayed resolutely single. That marriage had been a brief nightmarish affair best forgotten. Bea knew from their last talk she was dating someone named David now. The pair in the picture looked happy in their dressing gown and tux. She stared at the one next to it, a similar scene, a ball or party, with the very same fellow; tan, tall, a congenial smile. Perhaps things were changing. Farther back on the cabinet, almost hidden behind the others was a smaller black and white photograph; one of their family in Ohio.

A touch of nostalgia ran through her as she reached for it. She didn't recall seeing this specific picture before. She must have been about ten, with Faye a teen and Polly a tot. What a wholesome and dignified picture of normality; a midwestern family unified in the stable if slightly dull decade of the fortuitous fifties. To see the three photos juxtaposed now brought back memories of the tremulous times when as a curious grade school girl she'd spy upon her older sister making out with boyfriends on the sofa by the brick fireplace in the den. Knowing there'd be hell to pay if they saw her crouching on the stairway only added more exhilaration to her game. She'd be safe behind the locked door of her bedroom if she could sprint upstairs to it before they nabbed her. Fortunately she was never caught nor seen nor heard and so learned early on what the big kids did when mom and dad were gone away.

She observed her parents, looking noble in their naturalness, grand in their goodness, proud of their offspring and themselves as well in an unassuming way. An aura of hard work and humility hung over them both like a halo; two of God's earthly angels. It brought tears to her eyes, even as she smiled. Her little sister seemed lost or somehow listless as though she'd rather be playing outside with her toys; the languid look of a toddler forced to hold a protracted pose.

Her older sister was chubbier then and had longer hair, almost to her shoulders, but her smile was the same and her make-up was flawless. She snickered as she recalled all the intolerable times that the rest of the family was kept endlessly waiting for their eventual turn to use the one and only bathroom that they all had to share while Faye groomed herself to everlasting perfection. It seemed funny now but was not at the time. Dad could go outside in the woods if he had to but mom and the two girls were up the proverbial creek.

She remembered one time when she was pounding on the door, to no avail at all, and her father yelled up the stairs for her to stop banging on it, afraid that she might somehow cause damage. The only resulting damage was to her bruised fists and bursting bladder. Then she too learned to heed the call of nature outside. That wasn't the first time she'd thought that Faye was getting favorable treatment due to more than her age. Was it really just because she was the oldest? Yet she'd felt so loved and well treated by both her folks that favoritism had never really ever been a big issue for her. For the most part the girls had grown up distinctly as though in separate households due to the disparity in their ages. Her stomach suddenly growled in a display of desire and she sat the picture down, realizing she was hungry.

The refrigerator was almost as bare as the cupboards except for a motley assortment of items. On the top shelf was a stale slab of sharp cheddar cheese darkened at the edges from being carelessly wrapped in cellophane. Next to it was an empty carton but for one egg, a package of sliced ham rimmed in black with rot, an aged half-emptied jar of pimento-stuffed green olives, two unopened caviar jars, a bottle of champagne, and a carton of cream well past the expiration date. On the lower shelf was a casserole dish of macaroni and cheese that appeared to be in the latter stages of hardening along with a large baking tin of decomposing meatloaf. In the side door were bottles of mayonnaise, mustard and ketchup, each respectively encrusted with a film around their lids. Opening up the breadbox she cautiously pulled out an unopened crusty loaf of pastel blue sourdough...*ugh*...She wondered how anyone could stand such a mess and then recalled that Faye rarely prepared any food. She honestly, simply did not know how to cook, and in fact, had no interest or the slightest intention of learning at all. Why would anyone bother to with all the restaurants in the world?

A glance at the clock on the stove confirmed that despite the fact she'd crossed into another country her stomach was in still tune in with her basic biorhythms. It was almost 7:00. She wondered if Faye would be home soon and decided to give her a call on her cell to find out. Realizing she also wanted to call Jay, as well as Candy at the office, she calculated the time difference...*near 4pm there...better do it now*...She grabbed the pale yellow telephone hanging on the kitchen wall and used her phone card to place the call home.

"Connections. This is Candy. May I help you?"

"Hi, it's me."

"Oh hi, how are you? Good thing you called. I was just about to leave."

"Well, I'm glad that I caught you. Anything new since we spoke earlier today?"

"Yes, you got a fax from Spain. Mr. Hernandez would like to send some groups."

"He would? When?"

"This summer."

"Great! When this summer?"

"Mmm, one in July and one in August. For three weeks each."

"Terrific."

"Actually now he just wants a price quote."

"I know. Did he say when he needs it by?"

"No, just as soon as you can get to it, I guess."

"Right. All right. Listen if you wouldn't mind before you go, would you send him a fax saying that I'm out of town and I'll be home in a week and get it to him then?"

"Okay. I'll do that right now when we hang up."

"Anything else?"

"Oh yes, from Japan."

"And what's that?"

"Toshi wrote again and is wondering why you haven't responded to his first fax yet."

"Oh God. These people have no patience. Uh, I haven't been able to get a fax number here yet. Just write back and say I'll do it by tomorrow."

"Alright. Will do. By the way, how's Pittsburgh? Are you having a good time with your sister?"

"Well no, not yet. She had an unexpected business meeting and couldn't meet me at the airport so I've sort of been on my own for awhile."

"Oh no. Well that's too bad. Where are you?"

"I'm at her place. I took a cab. They let me in. I'm okay. I'm just getting hungry and there's nothing here to eat."

"Oh. Gosh. Doesn't she eat?"

"Yeah, but only at the closest expensive restaurant."

"Oh, well that's too bad. I guess you better go out for dinner, huh?"

"Yeah, well maybe. I'll see. There may be a store nearby. I getting tired of restaurant food."

"I bet."

"But anyway, as soon as I get her fax number I'll call and leave it for you so you can fax me that stuff from Japan and I can respond."

"Okay. Anything else?"

"No, I don't think so."

"Is Jay home yet?"

"No. He's not down here and I haven't heard him upstairs."

"Alright. Well, would you leave him a message I called? Let me give you Faye's number. I want you to have it too. Call me if anything important comes up, but I'll check in with you daily anyway."

"Okay."

"So. You think you two can get along in my absence?"

"Oh, well, I don't see why not. Like I said, he does his work and I do mine. He's on the phone so much with … well, with whoever…and I'm so busy with everything I've got to do, we barely notice each other."

…*oh right*…"What do you mean 'with whoever'? Do you think he's talking with the same person all the time?"

"Seems like it to me. Some woman, same line. It's none of my business. He's made that clear. He wants to answer his own phone on that line."

"Uh-huh. Okay, never mind. Just give him the message, alright?"

"Done. Don't worry, my dear. I'll put right it in the middle of his desk as soon as we hang up."

"Okay. Thank you. And don't forget to fax Mr. Hernandez."

"Oh I will. Don't worry. I'll get everything done before I leave."

"All right. Thanks. Here's the number. Ready?"

After she hung up she quickly called the concierge. The gnawing in her belly was growing worse and she couldn't tell how much was hunger and how much was Candy… *don't worry…sure…*

"Hello, do you have any grocery stores nearby?"

"The closest one is across the river into town. About two miles."

"I see. Alright, thank you."

"Shall I call you a cab?"

"Uhh, I don't think so for now. Thanks."

"Certainly, madam. Please don't hesitate to call if there is anything else I can do for you."

"Alright."

She hung up and looked around the kitchen, spying one more cupboard on the end by the wall. It contained a can of baby peas, tomato soup and some spaghetti. She checked the freezer. Just ice. Her stomach growled once again in its impatience and she decided to give her sister a call. Maybe she was on her way home and they could go out to dinner together.

"Hello."

"Faye? This is your sister."

"Bea! I was wondering when you'd call." As an aside she said, "Just a minute. It's my sister. I won't be long." A few moments of silence followed, then she spoke up, "Where are you?"

"I'm at your place."

"Oh good. How are you?"

"Starving. There's nothing to eat."

"Oh, I'm sorry. I know. I just always go out."

"That's what it looks like."

"Well listen, I can't talk now but we're almost finished and I should be home soon. Can you hold on? There's a fabulous French place, just minutes away, Chez Pierre's. You'll love their cordon bleu."

"I'm a vegetarian."

"Oh that's right. I forgot. Well, I'm sure they can do something."

"How long do you think you'll be?"

"Well, we're almost done here. Maybe another fifteen to twenty minutes or so. Then another twenty to get home, I should be there by eight or eight-thirty at the latest."

"That means we won't eat till nine. I don't want to wait that long. I'm really hungry."

"Okay. Well, there's some stuff in the refrigerator. And in the far cupboard to the right, I think."

"Yeah, I found it all. Not much."

"Can you make do?"

"I'll have to try, I guess."

"That's good. You're a good cook. Take whatever you want."

"Thanks. Guess you'll be here as soon as you can, huh?"

"Right. It shouldn't be too long. Just make yourself comfortable and I'll see you soon."

"Okay."

"I'd better get back into the meeting. It's with the mayor…. Sorry I couldn't meet you at the airport. Did you get the page?"

"No. I was outside waiting for you, I guess. But I called your secretary."

"Okay. Good. Well, I'll see you later. I can't wait."

"Okay. Goodbye."

As Bea hung up she felt her earlier disappointment returning. An agitated mix of hunger pangs and Candy's comments made the pit of her stomach churn even worse. She took three Tums from her purse and chewed them up while pondering her possibilities for a meal… *better make the best of it*…She pulled the cans of soup and peas down from the cupboard, found some pots to heat them in and a pan to fry the egg. When they were ready she sat down on the couch and ate her meager fare while watching the television news. Looked like the Clintons, America's longest running non-fiction soap opera, were in trouble again. Hilary's missing billing records from her previous law practice, long under subpoena from congress, had suddenly shown up at the White House one morning like magic. No one could account for it and she'd found them her very self. Somehow hidden behind a couch all this time. The mainstream media didn't seem to find it strange. Must have been the ghost of Eleanor Roosevelt...*what a circus...bet jay loves this one...*

When she finished the last morsels of dinner she lay back, snuggling underneath a furry black comforter, and flitted through the news channels chronicling the daily grind; murder, rape, robbery, accidents, corruption, more lies from the highest office in the land and colder weather on the way. The warmth of the food felt good in her stomach and along with the Tums it settled down her agitation. The handsome news anchors were professionally cheery, with occasional light touches of somber irony, while reporting the squalor and degradation of their broadcast between gaudy advertisements for things she didn't need. The combination of their buzz, the downy blanket and a full belly gave over to subtle waves of tiredness gently sweeping up and down her body, lulling her deeper into warmth and comfort. It was nearly two hours later when she was awakened by the sound of the front door to the condo closing with a loud click.

"Faye?"

"Bea!"

Chapter 36

"A sense of separation from God is the only lack you really need correct."
(A Course in Miracles)

THE DOOR CLOSED WITH a click as Jay locked up his office and walked the few steps to the back stairway leading to the parking lot. As he opened the door at the top of the stairs he saw through the large window facing west the dotted streaks of pink and orange cloud trails streaming out from the setting sun, unfolding like a pastel fan over the forested ridge. He stopped to take it in for a moment, mesmerized by the dazzling specter...*and another day ends*...before briskly skipping down the steps to his car. Though the lake provided a striking sunrise whenever morning clouds allowed the orb to shine, the tree-lined hills west of his property prevented a clear view of the sunset from his home and he relished seeing one whenever such a sight was possible.

Feeling the customary goodness he felt after a full day of counseling, he hopped in his car and headed toward the school to pick up his son. Though the school classes had ended almost an hour earlier he was comforted by the thought that the boy had made a friend to spend some time with on these late days while waiting for his father...*maybe they'll play in the band room*...He was more absorbed in reflecting on a sense he often felt when finished with a full slate of appointments; likening it to feeling of being a conduit or channel. He was a pipeline of purity, an instrument of integrity, a culvert of candor, a funnel for enlightenment and could take no credit for it at all whatsoever. On a good day like this one, a long stretch of straight sessions with person after person, he got into a groove, a rhythm or a current that seemed to simply sweep right through him as he strove to help those seeking his assistance.

It was as though the culmination of all he'd ever learned just naturally came to the forefront of his mind and poured forth through him as befitting each situation. What he once had learned, that he now regarded as true and helpful, he had not invented. They were principles and ideas handed down through the ages from others to him. Though he had honed his skills as best he could for speaking to, listening to and understanding others, he could not claim responsibility for the truths of human nature that he applied to help his clients and thus felt used by some unseen force. He was simply there to deliver the goods. The thought of a line from a seventies pop song ran through his brain as he recalled the melody: *if it feels this good being used…just use me up… bom bom bom ba bombom…just use me up…*

As much as he appreciated his education in retrospect the one thing none of his professors had ever touched upon was the fact or the concept, depending on your viewpoint, of God and the spiritual nature of humankind; the missing link in psychology. Thank God, he thought, enjoying the pun, that his own impulses had carried him further into reading theological and philosophical works. He'd covered virtually all religions and their history therein plus various spiritual tracts and ancient texts of a sacred nature that bore no covenant with religion at all. That thought reminded him he wanted to hear more of the tape he'd brought along and he plugged it in as he stopped at the corner of his office for the traffic light. It was glowing bright red in the shadow of the building that hung near his wood carved sign on the street and he imagined for a moment it was a beacon of hope for world-weary travelers passing his office on the long road of life.

"Well, I get the sense from listening to the tapes and reflecting on the last conversations, that what we are doing could be described as you guiding me into an understanding of how I can be my natural self and effectively operate in reality."

"By all means, yes, that's what it is."

"So, I think part of me is assimilating that and part of me is resisting that, cause I'm still concerned that I need more money to pay all these debts I've accrued. I have not yet gotten rich, or as you said, secure."

"Well, yes, you are resisting it, because there's a clash here – a clash in everyone – between the insistence of your Being for something and the ego's resistance to it. So it's insistence versus resistance. When that happens, it's an emotional experience of frustration, resentment, anything negative and it's always the ego telling you that life is saying no to you. Life never says no. The ego's the only thing that ever says no and it says no to life. What you have to get in touch with, when you're upset and having the kind of rocky experience that you know now not to extend, is an understanding that there's more to that experience than just your willingness to be pacified during that time.

"Now pacification is essential because what you want is to first feel at peace and then realize in that moment that intention is being expressed. But there's a high degree of intention – intensity – and that is what I call insistence, or as I said earlier, not taking no for an answer. So what happens is you become in alignment with that movement. When you take that position you're actually aligned with the movement and then it can be released. So you're going to find yourself very much at peace in a highly intense experience of will.

"But it's not going to be your will personally. The ego is not going to have any defense against this. If you opt to allow this to happen there won't be any ego left to quarrel with. Because the one thing the ego cannot coexist with is not taking no for an answer, because the taking of no for an answer is all the ego amounts to. It's a denial of life."

"An insistence on limits?"

"Right. It resists your good. So life is not denying you anything, and when you find yourself with that thought, you have wandered into that trap that the ego has set for all these ages."

"Hm."

"So, do you still feel that you are resisting anything?"

"Well…it kind of comes and goes."

"Right. And so when it comes, you want to make a shift. It's as though you are standing sideways but think you are standing straight ahead. And there's a kind of significant shift in point of view – a ninety degree shift let's say – that you have to make, realizing that no, straight ahead is this way."

"Hm. That reminds me of an episode with Phil when he was a little boy, where he thought it was early morning because he'd fallen asleep for a long nap, but it was really night time though and it took me quite awhile to convince him. He couldn't understand why I wanted him to take a bath and I had to take him outside and hold him there quite awhile to show him it was getting darker."

(laughter) "So what other questions do you have?"

"Well, I was thinking what else do you have to say."

"Pretty much that's it. There's always creation going on. And these moments that seem to be frustrating and uncomfortable are actually moments of accelerated creation, where the Divine Will is being expressed through you, but somehow gets blocked by the ego. And the ego has done this successfully and cleverly for all these years, all these lifetimes."

"Resisting my good?"

"Right. It's a clash between divine insistence and ego resistance."

"Okay. Well, I know you gave me this information before but I want to get this right. Are you saying that in order to allow intention to show forth, I need to agree with my desires?"

"Okay. Yeah, you do, but more than that. Whatever it is that you desire, that you feel your self attracted to, just agree with that, because that's the fertilization."

"That constitutes intention?"

"Well, it then becomes an intent. Once you agree with a desire it becomes an intention and it gradually becomes more and more compelling or energized. And that intention becomes insistence and that in turn takes form in the world. It's like a point of climax or an orgasm."

"Well, it seems like I'm not yet seeing evidence of manifestations of this. I do not have a lot of money in the bank, for example, though I've been focusing on that in my mind."

"No. Not yet. You're just not quite adept at this yet. I mean you're adept at waiting for your good and you're hoping it happens but you're not fully in the experience of your sovereignty yet to actually have the experience I'm talking about. But this is what you are moving towards; feeling or becoming the embodiment of insistence. Look, what does it feel like to insist on it right now?"

"Well, it feels happy. If I really believe in it."

"Right. I mean right now. Look at how your mind has still little pockets of doubt. The ego wants to explain or justify or account for how it could happen. I'm saying that there's nothing there you have to do to justify it at all. The insistence simply has to prevail over any three dimensional requirement. Now, there will be three dimensional movement – there will be change in your physical circumstances regarding this intent – but you cannot take that movement into account. When you are expressing this absolute insistence you cannot take how this will occur into account nor be concerned about it. This will be. This will be now. That's all you're saying there."

"It's like when people say that God or the Universe will take care of the details."

"That's right."

"Is there a point where one shifts from 'this will be' to 'this is happening'?"

"Right. A shift to this is happening now. It starts as this will be, as a desire, and shifts to this is happening now, as an intent."

"So I need to continue to allow myself to feel rich or secure now?"

"Right, and insist on it."

"Hm."

"Look, here's another way of saying how this works. You go into this experience with an image or reference point of what you desire, and you intensify it. Then ultimately all you are left with is an experience of intensity or insistence without the image because all of that imaging moves out of you into the world of form. You transfer the content of your desire through the power of your insistence out into the world where it takes form."

"God makes it take form?"

"Right. It's all God moving through you. Remember that desire, the origination of this process, means of God or from God, of the Father; de sire."

"How can you tell if they are ego desires or desires from God?"

"Your true desires are felt at the level of the heart. And you can feel them most clearly in your peace."

"Hm. Does one learn this through a series of successive steps?"

"Sure."

"Through successive creations? Like my first one is to have more money?"

"Your first step is to understand that you're never without this support. You're never without your capacity to experience the continuity of perfect fulfillment. What you also will learn is to experience sufficiency all the time. Sufficiency is a reflection of inner balance, you see. Balance is exactly sufficient. There's nothing more required because that's what is perfect. And so your equilibrium, your poise inwardly, is going to have an outer manifestation as sufficiency. So don't struggle with the idea of getting more money because what you need is simply to experience sufficiency. And I'm not talking about mediocrity or adequacy. I'm talking about that which is exactly a reflection of what is appropriate.

"So there's no need here for any kind of grandiosity. In other words, you don't want to see some large amount of money as grandiose. What that figure would be is that which you could easily allow from the basis of balance and sufficiency. In other words, if there were something that would require that amount of money, it would be there, as often as necessary. So you cannot have it unless it is on the foundation of balance, ease or complete sufficiency. You cannot try to acquire a whole lot of money first to achieve balance however. The balance has to come from the fact that you have set aside conflict inwardly. First you find your peace. Then you can freely experience your desires, and agree with them, and you then experience intent, and ultimately insistence, you see, and that's how this works."

"Hm."

"It won't seem so dramatic after a while. You'll just recognize what it feels like to have your way God's way all the time."

"Hm. Well, I just don't know if I can do this properly."

"Well, you are learning to, and you will."

He stopped the tape to ponder that point awhile just as he was passing by the lake in the distance on his right. The wind and rain had ceased sometime in the afternoon and the haggard yellow willows in his distant back yard drooped over the water's edge, dripping with moisture, resigned to another cold night...*the continuity of perfect fulfillment...that'd be nice...*It did seem as though his wealth was increasing but actually it felt more like he was earning it rather receiving it from a divine source. Perhaps he didn't get it but it seemed to him that clearly he was working his butt off for it. It certainly didn't feel like pennies from heaven. What felt especially odd was that his work in the business was increasingly generating more and more money while the income from his counseling practice was still relatively low. Very shortly he would vacate his office and move next door; a relief and also a humiliation. He looked out once again at the growing mist over the lake as the long line of five o'clock commuters ground to a halt. Circling above it was one of the two eagles that nested in the tall cottonwoods near the small park on the water to the left of his home.

As it circled close to a gathering of ducks they all bobbed quickly under the surface in fright, like synchronized swimmers, to escape the fate of being eaten for dinner. The white head and tail of the eagle glistened in the dying rays of the sun when he soared above the tree line and were all that was visible when he swooped down for the kill. Again the ducks disappeared as he dove like a determined kamikaze pilot toward their group. He pulled up at the last moment with a powerful sweep and veered south toward the highway as though scouring the lake for less attentive prey. Veering right as he reached the embankment to circle back Jay caught a glimpse of his beak on the turn and thought of the phrase 'eagle beak' that Bea's dad had applied to Jess as a child years ago. The moniker had stuck and had served as a good-natured bond of teasing between the grandson and his grandfather, especially since the old man actually had the more pronounced nose. Jay smiled to himself as he recalled the scramble between them whenever they met to see who would first get out the opening line: "Is that your nose or are you eating a banana?"

While the traffic inched forward like a constipated slug toward the street to the school, Jay reflected on his older son and his fortunes in the world. He had just found himself a job teaching Spanish at a local private high school and that was a blessing for which they were all thankful...*was it divine insistence*...Now if his bride-to-be could just find some work they would be well enough set to start a family if they wanted. Before too long he might be a grandfather himself. That thought seemed quite foreign to him. He was much too young to bear such an appellation when he hadn't yet made his full mark on the world...*have it your way God's way...all the time...how about now...*

He mulled the phrase over in his mind and what it meant to him, feeling the tug of war between his polarities. A part of him wanted to master the lessons of the tapes; learning to be enlightened, living in God's love, experiencing fulfillment effortlessly; Grace, in a word. Another part pulled him toward earning big money. The means was apparently emerging at hand. The stress of so many unpaid bills had taken a long toll and he longed for an immediate cessation of it all. As he turned down the avenue to the school, moving at a faster clip now off the crowded highway, he weighed for a minute what it'd feel like to throw in the towel on his practice altogether and just be a rich businessman working out of his home, dealing with colleges, different states, different countries, still being his own boss...*mmmmm...no...that's not my dream...*

As he approached the campus he felt again reconciled with his desire to be a healer and spiritual teacher and wondered how he might pump life back into his practice or at least keep it from diminishing any further...*maybe i shoulda joined those damn managed cares*...Though several doctors in town still referred their patents to him, that number was dwindling as many of them discovered he wasn't covered by their insurance. His last column in the paper had brought several inquiries and even eventually produced one new client; a single parent mom with no insurance, strapped for cash. He'd given her a low rate and was glad to be seeing her. Seeing someone for something beat no one for nothing. Perhaps it was time to write another column.

Since they were really advertisements written as information or advice he needed to pay the newspaper for running them and hated to add to his existing bill there. Yet his credit was good there, thanks mainly to his long time friendship with the editor, a former social worker, and if his efforts with foreign students ever panned out as hoped, he'd be able eventually to pay off everyone. If he was sincere in learning his spiritual lessons then the best thing to do was to incorporate them into his life in all ways possible, including his practice, trusting the capacity of the Infinite to provide. It was a risk he had to take. He'd planned to be writing on communication, parenting, anger and other topics, but had never had never thought of doing anything spiritual at all. Maybe now he should.

He had always avoided such references in his columns for fear that he'd be branded a "Christian" counselor, possibly causing many prospective clients to avoid him. With the Christmas season upcoming soon the timing couldn't be better to convey his true thoughts in the town's weekly newspaper. In two days was the deadline for the paper if he wanted to get it printed in next week's publication. He resolved to start writing it tonight when he got home, right after dinner, before he went into his room to make music. As tempting and habitual as his nightly routine had become, tonight he'd have to try his very best to stay clear-headed if he wanted to write anything worth reading at all.

Chapter 37

"Forgive the past and let it go, for it is gone." (*A Course in Miracles*)

BEA SWIVELED HER LEGS from the couch to the floor and stood up in excitement just as Faye reached her. They hugged in a tight clasp while laughing elatedly then leaned back slightly to examine each other while clinging tightly by their forearms.

"You haven't changed a bit," exclaimed Faye. "Except your hair's shorter."

"Well, I've gained a few pounds, but I gave up the long-haired look some time ago." She backed up a step and looked at Faye up and down. "You're actually thinner. How do you manage that?"

"Oh, I don't know," she paused as though thinking how to answer the question. "I stay busy, I guess. Don't have much time to eat. And like I always say: 'You can't be too rich, too tan or too thin'."

"That sounds like something you'd always say, alright," chuckled Bea. Their eyes met and locked, sparkling with curiosity and delight, feasting on their sisterhood.

"Speaking of food, did you round up some dinner? Here, let's sit down, there's so much to talk about." She sat on a charcoal colored chair facing the maroon couch and motioned Bea to sit down. "Relax."

Bea plopped herself back on the couch and smiled at her. "Yeah, I cleaned out the rest of what you have around here, which sure wasn't much. Did you eat already?"

"Yeah. We went out. That's why I'm so late. Sorry, but the mayor wanted a bite and we still weren't done with our meeting, so we went up the block a ways to Spazio's and finished up there."

"Sounds Italian."

"Oh it is and the most marvelous food. Their veal Parmesan is to die for, I swear. Maybe we can get in this weekend – I know the chef – and you can see for yourself. Mmmmm."

"I'm a vegetarian."

"Oh, that's right, I forgot." Faye frowned as though puzzled and perhaps mildly disapproving at such culinary antics. "Well I'm sure they can do something. What do you eat any way?"

"Jay makes most our meals. He's a gourmet cook. I don't suffer. I'll have their eggplant or something."

"Oh, you are so lucky. I need a gourmet cook."

Bea took the opportunity to introduce the topic that had been on her mind ever since she saw the photos. "Looks from your pictures here you've been with the same guy more than once. Is that David?"

"Yes, it is. That's him."

"Is it getting serious?"

"Well sort of, yes, semi-serious, you might say." They lost eye contact as Faye reached down to slip off her flats. "Ahhh, that's better. It's been a long day."

Bea wondered if she was being evasive or factual. "The two of you look awfully happy in the pictures," she ventured tentatively.

"Oh yes, well, those are just wonderful events. Everybody's happy there, because everybody's smashed." Faye laughed loudly.

"I see. So nothing too serious?"

"Oh," paused Faye, "he'd like it to be serious. He'd like to get married, I think, if I were willing."

"Married? I didn't know you were considering that!"

"I'm not. He may be." She stopped and looked around the room as though trying to sum up just the right words to express herself, then sighed. "He's sweet, but after going through two divorces I'm not sure I'll ever want to get married again."

Bea looked at her sympathetically, feeling her mixture of despair and disdain. The last one had been such a farce, a short glamorous fling, with painful consequences for Faye and her two children. He was a charming and impeccably dressed political lobbyist, comfortable in the congressional corridors of the nation's capitol; the town where she had lived since college. He had left her at six months and the spiteful sting of his pitiless parting shot – "I never loved you anyway" – had been a near death blow to her self- esteem, at least as far as relationships went. Bea had never heard her sibling sound so sad as the night that she called to share her heartbreak. Bea wondered if it still haunted her even now and decided it too touchy to mention at the moment.

"I see," murmured Bea. "Well, these things take time."

"I didn't think I'd ever get married again after the first one, and I probably never should have."

"Well…" said Bea reflectively, unsure of what to say.

Faye shrugged and snickered cynically. "It seemed like a good idea at the time." She looked around again, this time toward the dining room. "Want a drink? I have some gin." She stood up and walked to the liquor cabinet where she pulled down two glasses before Bea had answered.

"Sure, why not?" Bea wasn't sure whether to continue on or drop the subject and so she said nothing while watching her sister dump clinking ice in each glass and fill them up with Tanqueray Ten…*of course she'd have the very best…*

Faye's first marriage had been a good one or so it had seemed for almost ten years, until she discovered her husband was having an affair. She'd been angry then, stunned and livid at the infidelity, and the furious fuel of her outrage had powered her through a cold-blooded divorce in near-record time. Her ex had complained she was married to her career, but somehow, years later, after he'd remarried and she'd moved, they had managed through the children to eventually reconnect, first as noncombatants, then as acquaintances, and finally as friends, though from the safe distance of DC to Pittsburgh. They had both wrung their hands in collective dismay at the failure of their youngest child to adapt to the demands of his school and life in general. Now he lived with his father in DC as Faye had given up all hope of rearing him; another touchy subject.

"I probably should have just stayed married to Tony," she remarked wryly while returning with the drinks. "Just got some marriage counseling. Then maybe Todd would have turned out better." She handed Bea a wet glass and hoisted hers up. "Oh well, cheers."

"Cheers."

"Remember," snorted Faye, as she took a large sip, "how angry dad was that I was marrying a Catholic? 'God-damn dago!' he used to say." Both women chuckled as they recalled their father's capacity for righteous indignation when they were younger. It was all the more amusing because the dago, Tony Mondavi, had turned out in due course to be good friends with the old codger. Faye had kept his last name, even after her remarriage, and Bea had always suspected it was because of the snob appeal and lofty status afforded her through association with the famous wine magnate, though there was no relation.

"Yep, dad sure had a temper," affirmed Bea. "He could raise the roof." She took a sip of the gin and tonic and noticed it tasted better than the airline's offering. Her memory was being jogged. "Do you remember that summer when you and Tony rented a cottage at the Jersey shore and me and Mary, my best friend, came to spend the season with you?"

"Sure."

"And he found out that I was wearing a pin – that I had been pinned by my boy friend Mike – and he made me come home and give it back? I was so sad."

"Oh yeah," nodded Faye with a laugh, "I'd forgotten all about that. He could really be cantankerous."

"Course the only damn reason he knew about it was that you had called him and told him," jousted Bea good-naturedly.

"Oh, I did? God I'm sorry. I forgot all about that too." She smiled sheepishly, "I was just trying to be a good older sister, you know. Trying to protect you from boys."

"Yeah, yeah, yeah. Thanks a lot," teased Bea.

"Oh God," said Faye, moving to another subject, "did I hate working at that store with him and mom. He was always so grouchy. Do this, do that, not that way, this way!"

"Well, I worked there a lot more than you did. After you went off to Syracuse you never came back for the summers."

"I know. I didn't want to. I got jobs as a camp counselor. That was a lot easier."

"Bossing little kids around."

"That's right," chortled Faye, "and they did what I told 'em."

"You did come home for Christmas though, and I remember Mom saying that whenever you came home, our place was like a big kettle being stirred up with a spoon."

"Ha, ha, ha," laughed Faye, "she did say that didn't she. But I don't know why."

"I think you were always arguing with Dad about staying out later and needing more money. They didn't have that kind of trouble with me."

"Well, you were younger."

"And I was nicer."

"Yeah, well I had more fun."

They both felt warmed by their gin and reminiscences as Bea offered a toast across the coffee table. "To our childhoods." *Clink!*

"Do you remember," started Bea, "the time that dad let you drive the Kaiser, our beautiful family car, back to Syracuse and you wrecked it in an accident in the snow somehow?"

"Oh God, don't remind me," hooted Faye. "He was so mad. It wasn't exactly my fault. I hit a snowplow coming towards me. Skidded right into it. Brakes were useless."

"You totaled it!"

"I know! I know! And I remember thinking for just a split second before I hit it, 'If this wreck doesn't kill me then my dad sure as hell will'!"

Both of them laughed heartily, till the tears started to spill. It was such a relief to come together again, reliving the past tensions, crazy times and catastrophic events that didn't matter any more. Bea caught her breath first and settled down a moment, composing herself for further recollections, as her mind went spinning backwards like a fast clock in reverse. "You know," she said wistfully, feeling the nostalgia growing, " the best memories I have though, are of the times when we all went to the cottage at Lake Erie, when we were young, and all dad's brothers and our cousins would come from Cleveland. That was heaven. I loved those times."

"Oh, those were great times. I'm surprised you remember them. You were so young then. Polly wasn't even born."

"Well, I remember them alright. But I remember feeling very young – like being the youngest kid there. I remember how you all would go diving off the dock, that high one, it was almost like a pier, and I would have to just stand around and watch you, wishing I could join in, 'cause I hadn't learned how to swim yet. Still it was fun. I loved the family feeling – all those relatives. It was great."

"Yeah, it was," nodded Faye in agreement. "Every summer till I left for college."

"And I'll tell ya' another time there I remember, very well, when you dared me to sit on ant hill. Remember that?"

"What? You're kidding. I don't recall that at all. Are you sure about that?"

"Yes I'm sure! There was a big mound of sand with red ants going in and out and you dared me and then you double-dared me to sit on it."

"No. Really?"

"Yes really. And I wouldn't do it! So there." They both laughed again and had another sip of gin. "You were a bad sister," teased Bea, with a sly smile.

"Now don't start that again. I was not," said Faye, grinning back, but sounding adamant in her tone. They both took another drink and were quiet a moment.

"So," started Bea, "what's the deal with dad? How's he doin'?" Faye cleared her throat and her expression became serious.

"Oh, he's slowing down a bit."

"How do you mean?"

"Well, he's getting by okay. He's still physically healthy enough, and can dress himself, but he can't drive and he needs someone to be there during the day to keep him company, buy his food, wash his clothes, make his meals, read to him, walk with him, give him his medicine. All that."

"Oh, and you said on the phone the woman who's been watching him has cancer?"

"Right."

"That's too bad. How about the one who was with him before her?"

"No," said Faye with a scowl. "She was terrible. I don't think I told you about it. I went to visit him once and she said she'd been trying to help dad so much and how hard it was, and then she let slip that she had sold him some curtains to help him out. 'Sold him some curtains?' I said to her sarcastically, because I saw the new curtains, if you could call them that, and they were raggedy old things that she was probably trying to get rid of."

"Oh no."

"Yes. They were just trash, and so was she, damn it. So I fired her on the spot. And then I got Mrs. Schafly next door to watch over him temporarily."

"Good old Phyllis."

"Yeah. And then I hired the one he has had for a few years now, but she can't really do it much anymore. I don't blame her, with the chemotherapy she can hardly get around, and so Phyllis is helping out again, but we need someone else there as soon as we can find them, and maybe someone who should just live there with him." She spoke with an air of grim finality and the tone in the room was suddenly heavier.

"I see," said Bea reflectively. "I wonder what the best way to go about that is?" she ventured. "Maybe we should call a temp agency?"

"Well, I decided to run an ad here and see if we could find anyone willing to move in with him."

"Someone willing to move from here to there?"

"Well, it's possible. I stated the situation in the ad. There ought to be some old single ladies around who'd like to live rent free for being a caretaker of an older man. Don't you think?"

Bea pondered the notion for a second and shrugged noncommittally. "Maybe. I don't know. Seems to me it would be better to advertise there."

"I know, but I don't have time to go there. I'm too busy here with my work and everything."

"Sure," agreed Bea...*lots of everything to do...*

"Matter of fact, I've gotten several people who have responded already. Five or six, I think. And I was wondering since you're here, if you could interview them this week."

"Me. Why me? I mean I don't mind, but you're closer to dad's house and know better what's needed there. You'd be interfacing with them."

"Well, I can tell you. I just don't have the time," stated Faye seriously. "Besides work during the day I've got meetings and other activities in the evening. It'd be awfully hard and... well, you're here now with all this free time."

"Well, I was looking for a bit of a break. I mean, I've been on the road forever, and besides, I thought we'd all be spending some time together when you weren't working."

"Oh we will, we will. I've just got some things planned that I have to do. I mean we can have lunch every day – well almost every day – you can take a cab in – and I'll be home in the evening, pretty much, except for a few nights. But I have arranged to have the weekend clear, mostly, so I can be with you and Polly of course, except for one night. There's just this one function – the charity auction for the philharmonic – I really can't miss. I mean it's just expected that I'll attend it. I was involved in putting it together this year. I couldn't miss that. But anyway." She drained the last of her drink in one long draught. "So you could find some time to interview these women, don't you think? They could come here. You could set your own schedule."

Chapter 38

"The Holy Spirit must work through you to teach you He is in you."
(A Course in Miracles)

I︎N THE DARKNESS JUST before daybreak Jay sat in the sunroom staring at the golden lights streaming across the lake from the houses on the far shore as the mist began to lift. Crows and seagulls were starting to signal the glow of the sunrise from behind the heightened backdrop of the eastward evergreens. He held a hot mug of strong French Roast coffee in both hands settled in the lap of his gray woolen robe as he tried to fend off the sense of bleakness that he felt while contemplating his first day in an office that was not his own. Having moved all his furniture back home over the weekend, all that remained in his new workplace to remind him of the old one was his nameplate on the door, under the larger one of the psychologist, Marianne, and his guitar in the corner she had reluctantly allowed him to keep there, as long as it was stored out of sight behind her bookcase.

He had not been able to sleep well all night, in spite of two Tylenol PMs, and had tossed in bed beset by various black thoughts and visions. Though his new landlord was friendly enough when she stopped by to give him a key as he was cleaning out his office, her husband in the car, waiting with their new baby, had seemed uptight and was almost scowling when the two men were introduced. It was an unusually odd and uncomfortable sensation, as though he were threatened by Jay's presence in her office. Perhaps they'd been fighting as young couples sometimes do. It had a funny feeling, as though he didn't trust another man around his wife in his absence. Maybe the new baby had brought some serious new stresses. He groped for an answer. She had once mentioned to him it was adopted so he presumed that meant that they couldn't have kids, another possible sore point for the husband if he was insecure enough to imagine it a slight on his virility. Whatever the reason, whatever his problem, it had seemed an ill omen on the eve of his move into her suite.

He had felt no seductive vibes or flirtations from her in the least. If anything she seemed rather cool and aloof, and in any case it didn't matter, as they would have virtually nothing in common but alternate times in a shared space. It was strangely unsettling to encounter disharmony in regard to his working quarters after fourteen years. His space had been solely his private space before and he hadn't cared at all about what others felt or thought about it. He had decorated it to his own liking with complete disregard to any one else's taste and had enjoyed extending the hospitality of his setting to every client that had entered it. Now all that was gone and the new place was rather sterile. Her black and white etchings along with some degrees adorned the walls instead of beautiful Monet's. There were no hanging plants freshening the room, no rich tapestry upgrading the rug, and no peaceful fountain trickling in the background. Her chairs and couch were less comfortable than his, his guitar was now hidden, and to top it off her mate seemed threatened or somehow unfriendly toward him. It was a grave new world and his nameplate on her door was like a marker on a tombstone; just further evidence yet that his practice was dying.

He was further depressed by his failure to write a new column for the weekly community paper. He had tried for the last few nights in a row to craft a spiritual message for the holiday season but the words flowed awkwardly from his pen and he fared no better by trying to fortify his thoughts with some wine. If he was going to write it would best be in the daytime before he sought relief from his pressures in the night. Now that the most recent deadline had passed there was only one more chance to get in a piece before Christmas. Otherwise it would seem anticlimactic and he might as well focus on writing something different for the new year. In so far as he was trying to be more of a spiritual creature than he had in a long time, it felt imperative to contribute something to the reading public on a loftier note… *as you teach so you will learn…*

Feeling the sadness creep into his heart he closed his eyes and bowed his head in prayer…*Father please help me be the person i'm meant to be…the person you created…help me to be unafraid…help me to feel your guidance…help me to carry on… help me to be good… help me to fulfill whatever is my function………Thy will be done…amen…*He sat there with his eyes shut in the stillness clutching the coffee mug like a warm life preserver, feeling the sadness give way to an emptiness, feeling the emptiness give way to peace. When he finally opened them the sun was peeking over the crest of pine trees like a slice of fresh pineapple, casting long shadows of evergreen spires on the water aiming toward him. As so often in the past, the pure beauty of the morning on the lake aroused him aesthetically and he reached for the twelve-string guitar he kept at home.

He'd been working on a song for months now but had been unable to finish it and had put it aside. He couldn't seem to knock them out like he used to when his band was actively a going concern. The melody had been completed for many weeks and he was pleased with it but the lyrics had been difficult to work out. He wasn't quite sure what he wanted to say. Strumming it gently with his thumb so as not to awaken Phil yet, he sang softly what he had written so far in the hopes of furthering it.

> *Ever notice how a certain song can send you higher*
> *Till you think it might take you through the top*
> *Later you begin to wonder 'bout your latest blunder*
> *And you feel your spirits drop.*

> *I believe the music is a means to make us higher*
> *But when it's over we don't have to stop*
> *Often times it's understood that a quiet solitude*
> *Can lift your spirits up*

He stopped playing and rested his hand on his knee, watching the sun grow rounder as it rose. ...*boy that's the truth... now a chorus*...suddenly, effortlessly, it started to flow.

> *Don't ask me why this is*
> *I won't reply let's just*
> *Sail right on by and*
> *Soar skyward*

> *There is no need to quit*
> *When the music's all spent*
> *You don't need this tune*
> *Nor my words*

He pulled out the pad and pen he kept under the couch for writing down lyrics whenever he was moved to do so and hastily scribbled it all down... *now two more verses for after the bridge...first the bridge...*Humming the tune again over and over he worked out an instrumental section between the verses. Resting momentarily in reverie he felt the impulse of a rhyme starting to merge and began writing down the rest of the song as it flowed forth.

So if you hear some music and you really can't refuse it
Let yourself relax – enjoy the ride
Just remember – don't forget it – when the music hits it limit
You can keep rising inside

That's about as high as my melody will fly
So the rest is up to you
Hope that if you catch yourself sliding down the frets
You'll be gliding right back up soon

He paused and reread it all, feeling pleased with the rhyme and the message. Then he sang it from the start all the way to the end, repeating the chorus after the last verse....*that'll work*...He sat there for a few minutes feeling satisfied with his composition and grateful for being moved by the muse. Then he put the guitar back on its stand and looked out at the water. The lake was brightening with the reflections of different colored homes as sparrows and starlings encircled in rapid-winged flight and dipped toward its glassy surface nipping at bugs. A long legged heron stalked about on his neighbor's dock and croaked a loud announcement to the fish. There was still enough time for an early morning hot tub if he went down right now and then kept on the move afterwards. Once Phil was up there'd be no time to spare, and he had a new client, which was always interesting.

Later that morning he approached his new office door with a mixture of gratitude for the cheaper digs and humiliation that his name was posted below another's. There was however no time for self-pity as he had his first client probably waiting in the lobby. This one was a bit different, a court appointed counselee, and he had spoken last week with her lawyer before setting the appointment. She has gotten into an argument with her daughter and her husband after drinking too much at a family gathering one weekend. She was an old woman who didn't drive, an Alaskan Aleutian Indian, who had a history with her husband of domestic provocations with the law over the years. The judge had mercifully sentenced her to two years probation, instead of jail, with the stipulation that she attend weekly counseling sessions all of that time.

Though he agreed to take her she represented the least desirable of all possible clients; one who did not come freely of her own volition. Such people usually resented being in therapy at all and often made little progress due to a lack of motivation. When he greeted her in the lobby he was surprised at her diminutive stature, barely five feet, and when she smiled up at him her grizzled grin revealed some nicotine-stained teeth in long standing neglect and need of dental work. Her countenance was wrinkled with the deep furrows that frequently accompanied the worn faces of aging alcoholics but there was a sprightliness in her eyes that had not yet been extinguished, even as she ambled with obvious pain in a crooked gait down the hall. She was a survivor, if a haggard one, and fortunate enough this time to somehow escape the worst clutches of the law.

He asked her about her background and family history in great detail. Naimee had grown up in a remote fishing village of Alaska that sounded more like the outer reaches of Siberia. Her husband, Jim, had worked for the railroad for years, a union man near retirement, who was getting too old for the physical labor still required of him at work. They had raised their kids amidst a self-admitted environment of chaos and squalor, with fighting, drinking and drugging a common staple of their impoverished lives. One of her adult sons was homeless and retarded, wandering the streets of Seattle and its shelters. His father would not allow him back into the house. The other one had died of a drug overdose many years past. Her two daughters had married and moved away, though one of them visited occasionally, which had occasioned the latest fracas that had landed the mother on probation.

She smacked of lowlife and yet he couldn't help but feel a certain compassion for her spunkiness. It was the same combative quality that had gotten her into trouble through being abusive but he admired her fighting spirit and it was not turned against him. She understood with the street smarts of an alley cat that her provisional freedom lay in the hands of her counselor and treated Jay as though he was her savior or a long lost lover. When he stipulated that he wanted her husband to join them next time so they could work on the many still fuming disagreements from the past, she was more than willing.

"Oh, of course, sir. Whatever you say. I will have Jim come in with me. I will just tell him you say he must."

"Well, I'm not saying he must, but I highly suggest it. It sounds like you two have a lot of unfinished battles going on still."

"Well yes, I'm sure you're right. And I tell you, the biggest problem is, once he starts drinking, he gets out of control. I can't stop him. I just tell him 'Stay away from me' and I lock myself in the bedroom."

"Yeah, well, that's probably smart, because one more visit from the cops and one or both of you are going to jail, I'm sure."

"Oh, I know, believe me I know." She looked at Jay and winked and grinned broadly, showing her snaggle-toothed smile and rotting gums. "But that isn't going to happen again, I'm sure, 'cause I have the very best counselor in the world."

"Yeah, well, I'm glad you seem to think this is helping you. You're going to be coming here for a while, so we'll have plenty of time to cover plenty of ground."

"Yes, and I'm so glad. Oh thank you, thank you, for all of your help today."

"You're welcome. Now I'll see you and your husband next week. In the meantime practice holding your temper and remember that communication technique I taught you if things start to get crazy; I feel, I think, I want."

"Oh I will. I will. I can't tell you how much you helping me."

"Good."

She stood on her tiptoes to give Jay a warm hug before struggling with her ailing hip to exit the room. After she left he sat down at the unfamiliar desk and cleared away some of the psychologist's papers so he could begin writing his newspaper column. He had a two-hour break before the next client and hoped to get a good start on the article now since he had but a few days to meet the next deadline. Putting his tablet and pen on the desk he sat back in the chair to try getting comfortable in the new surroundings and with the new furniture. Most of all he wanted to be clear in his mind just what he was going to say in his message. If it was going to be spiritual he wanted it to be uplifting and generic enough so that he wouldn't be labeled a Christian counselor, the kiss of death to so many people seeking secular answers for their dispirited states. He closed his eyes and concentrated on the meaning of what it was he wanted to convey. He knew from past writings it would roll out eventually sentence-by-sentence just as long as he stayed relaxed and focused...*help me Father*...Slowly it came, tentatively at first, then building like a snowball as he let it emerge.

The holiday traditions of the winter season celebrate profound truths of the human spirit. As the year winds down to a new beginning, we rejuvenate ourselves by reaffirming commonly shared and dearly held spiritual values. Though most of us seem to have our hands full trying to live in accordance with them, these values do sustain us in our innermost heart of hearts and give us lights to live by in our lifetime.

It is especially appropriate that we precede the onset of cold dark winter with a lavish Thanksgiving ceremony to usher out the fading fall. Giving thanks, or expressing gratitude, is a perfect way to experience good feelings in ourselves. Since we always get what we give, it feels great to be grateful and appreciative towards life, other people and God. As we often lose touch with such feelings in the course of the months, the year's end is a perfect time for such a touchstone to reemerge. The following days of Christmas, Hanukkah and other religious holidays glorify humankind as spiritual beings and honor our relation of fellowship to each other and our connection with our Creator.

We are a community of people in communion with God, though much of the time we feel isolated and alone. To feel our connection to the Divine is a personal matter no one else can do for us but ourselves. Living with a sense of divine purpose gives us a perspective on life that transcends the ego sense of self we frequently lose our Self in. Beneath the limits of the rational mind, we feel the presence of heart, conscience and intuition.

To live by these impulses, as hard as it may seem at times, is the most gratifying way to live. Living by the dictates of our inner guidance is the true message of our winter "holy" days and it is a welcome one indeed. We can use the winter holiday time of this passing year to reconnect with our Selves and our Source, in our own personally meaningful way, as the New Year approaches. Doing so can make a big difference between now and next winter.

As he was finishing the sound of the bells from the church up the block rang the announcement of the noon hour and he stood up, heaving a weary sigh of contentment. His hand was cramped, his back was aching and his mind felt finished and ready for a break. Two hours had passed fast. He tossed the pen down, wiggled the fingers of his right hand and stretched his arms outward then over his head….*thank you Father*…Then he opened the door and walked down the hallway to meet Howie, his next client, wondering if he was ready yet to reveal his sad salacious secret to his wife.

Chapter 39

"She walks in beauty, like the night
Of cloudless climes and starry skies
And all that's best of dark and bright
Meet in her aspect and her eyes."
(Lines from 'She Walks in Beauty', Lord Byron)

THE TALL YOUNG MAN with thick ruddy blonde curls stood erect on the deck with his bride at his side against the backdrop of the lake on a cool October early afternoon. His handsome tanned face and muscular build seemed especially robust next to his slender fair wife-to-be as they waited for the wedding ceremony to begin under the two weeping willow trees. The quiet current slipped beneath the cedar dock that stretched behind them and rustled through the cluster of green water lilies gathered by the bank. Their glowing white flower petals were lined in pink and opened to reveal a tiny yellow center like a furry button of sun. The heart shaped lily leaves and pads floated snugly on the crowded surface covering their ensnarled roots that snaked into the murky depths of the mud below. Overhead the autumn sun glistened on the long auburn locks that lay upon the shoulders of the winsome bride's white wedding gown.

From the cottage up the path the soothing strains of a piano carried down to the platform where the guests and bridesmaids surrounded the expectant pair. The father of the bride, having strolled down the path to give his offspring away, retired to the side of his slender ex-wife; a woman he'd married and divorced four times, creating three daughters in the process. He beamed with radiance as bright as the sun off his shiny bald dome while the unseen pianist then ended his song to signal the start of the recitation of vows. The parents of the groom, serving as co-ministers, began speaking to the couple by taking turns in their statements, each one well versed in their methodical incantations that tied the knot of marital bliss and obligation.

When they had finished with their parts in the program the ceremony proceeded to the point where the bride and groom then addressed each other in separately prepared pledges of definitive fidelity and permanent devotion. As the groom slightly bowed his head to meet his loved one's eyes he gently took her hand in his and tenderly affirmed to plight his troth to their lifelong companionship, so help him God. The bride's blessed pact that followed was an exceptionally long litany of inspirational promise and rapturous betrothal that moved the throng of well-wishers almost as much as it moved her mate. Her mother and sisters could not suppress their happy tears and the blowing of noses was heard in the background. With an exchange of rings, thin bands of burnished gold, the closing benediction was given by the ministers and the transported twosome pursed their lips in desire and planted their first marital kiss. While they embraced to the delight of the ogling onlookers a wicked wind whipped swiftly through the tall pines on the far shore. It brought the silky waters rippling toward them and swayed the clump of cattails by the dock like flimsy flagpoles.

"Not a moment too soon," yelled the undaunted groom as he grabbed his bride's hand and sprinted gaily up the path to his parents' lofty abode. "Follow me before it rains!" He'd seen enough of sudden late autumn storms assault the lake throughout his years to know the early signs of one coming on. The breeze from the northeast picked up speedily and gray clouds gathered on the run like a swarm of vultures blotting out the sun. The merry group of guests trailed after him toward the shelter of the house where the music had begun again and tubs of iced champagne awaited. After the couple was hailed with hugs, regaled with toasts and hearty exchanges of congratulations, the entire entourage drove off to the restaurant reserved for the reception, undismayed by the ensuing drizzle that showered their caravan all the way there.

Luckily the patio housing the party was covered and heated with high adobe walls to block the whistling wind outside. The members of the party were seated around three long tables put together as one for a great and joyous feast. The last of the group to arrive was the mother of the bride who had taken the time to change clothes after the ceremony. Her flashy appearance caused a bit of a stir in hushed tones among those guests who happened to notice her delayed entrance. She was dressed in a see-through tight-meshed sarong that clung to her svelte figure like a linen sheet of skin. As she stood in the doorway of the patio surveying the scene to discern where her seat was, the bold outline of her underwear, starkly visible beneath her cream-colored clothing, turned more and more heads; glances from the women and stares from the men. One stunned woman was overheard by more than a few to murmur, "Oh my God, she's wearing a thong!"

The groom's new mother-in-law smiled at him broadly as he approached to escort her to a place between his grandfather and a sister of the bride. "Your dress compliments your blonde hair perfectly," he said courteously. She slipped her arm through his as he extended it and swung her head lightly from side to side to take in the affair as they marched to her chair, revealing a dangling pair of shiny gold earrings inset with large diamonds. As he pulled out her chair she smiled at his grandfather while taking the place beside him at the banquet. The conversations of the company all gradually resumed and the space was soon abuzz again with the gay chatter and gossip of guests growing festively intoxicated amidst clinking glasses, clanging silverware, and scattered bursts of oratorical praise for the newly weds.

Hours later the party began to break up very slowly with the oldest of the participants being the first to leave. The grandparents bade their fond farewells to the relatives, the friends, and the acquaintances and lastly to the young married couple themselves. There were tears in the older man's eyes as he hugged his square-shouldered grandson and hoarsely whispered, "Good luck" in his ear. Their eyes met and the young man's face broke into a wide grin when his grandfather pressed a hundred dollar bill in his hand.

"Gee thanks, Grandpa. You needn't do that, you know."

"Your Grandma and I want to, just to give you a nice start."

"Well, I appreciate it and I love you both."

"We know you do."

The grandmother reached up to hug her hunk of a grandson and said softly, "We love you. Take good care of each other."

"We will. Don't you worry. Hey, I'll see you back at the house. We're coming back to get some stuff before we take off for our honeymoon."

"Okay, dear. See you then."

As the grandparents ambled off arm in arm to their car, the woman turned to the man with a questioning look. "What did you think of his new mother-in-law?"

The old gentleman shrugged his shoulders and frowned. "She sat beside me for two hours and never said a word to me. Blabbed away constantly to her daughter on her right."

"You're kidding."

"No, I'm not. She totally ignored me."

"Hm," said the Grandma, wondering what to make of that.

"And I don't think it bodes well for our grandson at all. I give them two years."

Chapter 40

"Rather than love, than money, than fame, give me truth. I sat at a table where were rich food and wine in abundance, and obsequious attendance, but sincerity and truth were not; and went away hungry from the inhospitable board."
(Walden, Henry David Thoreau)

SPAZIO'S RESTAURANT WAS NOISY and packed with patrons when Bea arrived there for her luncheon engagement. It was difficult to worm through the overflowing waiting room without stepping on someone's chic high heels or smart Gucci footwear as she struggled toward the hostess. Dapper dressed clientele, all presumably with reservations, were stacked up outside on the sidewalk as though awaiting a fashion show audition and she'd felt slightly self-conscious in her casual slacks and cardigan as she bypassed them all when entering the eatery. The mustachioed maitre'd looked at her up and down somewhat skeptically as she approached him as though wondering if she was applying for work or just lost.

"Yes, madam?" he inquired as he raised his dark eyebrow and wrinkled his mustachioed lip.

"Uh, I'm with the Mondavi party. I believe she's already here."

"Mondavi?" His expression and manner changed immediately into one of unctuous understanding. "Oh yes, of course." He smiled and bowed, and with a suave wave of his hairy hand said, "You must be her sister. Please, right this way. She's expecting you." When he turned to escort her through the tightly teeming bistro she amusedly recalled the scene in *The Wizard of Oz* where Dorothy and her companions had reached the city gate only to be refused entrance by a stern guard who instantaneously turned welcoming when informed the witch had sent them. "Well, why didn't you say so?" He had sputtered responsively. "That's a horse of a different color." While smiling to herself at the similar situations she fleetingly wondered if her awaiting elder sister was going to turn out to be a good witch or a bad witch. She spied her at a corner table topped with fine linen and flowers in a vase lifting a wet glass of the house chardonnay to her lips.

"Well there you are," said Faye, looking impatient but relieved. "What took you so long? I've been waiting ten minutes." Bea shrugged then sat down and tried to smile sympathetically.

"Whatsa' matter? Getting hungry? I did the best that I could. That last interview ran a little longer than I wanted. The woman was talkative and I didn't want to be rude."

"Did she want the job?"

"No. Actually none of them did."

"Damn." She lifted her wineglass again and took a cold sip.

"You're telling me. I've been interviewing two days now, six people overall, and not one of them really wants to move to dad's place for the amount that you're offering."

"Oh God," groused Faye, "what do they expect? I'm not paying a penny more. Not a penny more. That's good money and it's all we can afford."

"Well, that may be," sighed Bea, "but I don't think anyone from this area will move there for that amount, and I think we'd be better off advertising in dad's hometown newspaper."

"That could be," countered Faye, "but I don't have the time to go there this month. And I want to hire someone soon. Immediately."

"I know," said Bea reflectively. "I've been thinking about that." A tall gray-haired waiter with a gentlemanly air of impeccability interrupted them briefly by placing a menu and a glass of ice water with a lemon twist in front of Bea. "Madam," he stated as though addressing an aristocrat.

"Aren't you going to order?" asked Bea, wondering if Faye were dieting. She looked so very thin.

"I already did," responded Faye. "Just before you got here. It was getting late," she added, sounding slightly defensive. "And I can't linger today."

"I see," said Bea, while perusing the bill of fare.

"Our specials today," announced the waiter with apparent pride, "include gorgonzola penne with grilled calamari, scallions and fresh garden herbs, pumpkin ravioli stuffed with ricotta and chicken in a sun dried tomato pesto sauce, and angel hair pasta with veal and wild mushrooms in a fettuccine sauce. I highly recommend the ravioli," he confided with a thin-lipped supercilious smile.

"I'm a vegetarian," said Bea as she continued to scan the offerings.

"Ah," spoke the waiter, looking somewhat disappointed for just a second. "Then perhaps you would like the asparagus risotto," he sniffed. "It's quite elegant, I assure you."

"That's just what I was thinking. That'd be fine, thank you."

"And will you be having the soup or the salad with it?"

"No, just a la carte, please."

"Very well, madam. A glass of chardonnay, perhaps, to compliment your meal?" Bea was not fond of chardonnay. She and Jay were confirmed cabernet consumers, or as Jay like to say 'ABC drinkers – anything but chardonnay'.

"No thank you. Just water please."

He turned to Faye. "Shall I serve them together madam?"

"No, bring mine when it's ready." She shot Bea an almost apologetic glance. "I really should get back to work as soon as I can. Busy day today at the office. Carnegie Foundation's coming by."

"Sure, I understand." Bea took a drink of ice water and cleared her throat. "Listen, just before I left your place today I called the paper in Ohio. We can get an ad in today if we call back by three and it will be out in two days. What do you say?"

"You mean run one back there?"

"Right."

"But who'd do the interviews? I really don't have the time. And you don't have a car."

"I think we could let Phyllis do it," suggested Bea. "I trust her judgment. She might even know someone."

"She doesn't," said Faye adamantly. "I already asked." She pursed her lips and studied her napkin. "Lemme think about this a minute."

"You know," offered Bea tentatively, "Polly is arriving in Cleveland tonight. Perhaps she could get away for a day from there to do it. It's only an hour's drive."

"I don't want her to do it," snapped Faye. "I don't trust her judgment in something like this."

"She's older than you remember," Bea interjected.

"No, I don't want her to do it. She's not used to hiring people like I am." She looked up at Bea. "Or like you are, for that matter." She took a stiff slurp of wine, set it down with finality and cocked an eyebrow. "Look, I've got it. The only thing for us to do is for you to go there and do the job yourself."

"Me?...*for us to do*...But how will I get there?"

"You'll rent a car. I know someone. We can get a deal." She paused. "And I'll help you pay for it."

Bea sat up straight in her chair and considered the thought. The idea of seeing Ohio again and especially her father held a strong attraction for her. She had figured all of them would pay him a visit later in the week but was waiting for Polly to arrive before bringing it up. It was just that she was still so tired from all her days on the road and had not really rested at Faye's as she'd hoped. Despite her fatigue though she felt strongly compelled, a siren call from her heart, to go the extra mile to help her dad if that were best for him. She squared her jaw and eyeballed Faye decisively. "Okay, I'll do it."

When she had finished with lunch Bea took a cab back to the condo, reserved a rental car, placed an ad and started packing for her journey. As Faye had eaten hastily and left Spazio's before her, she'd had time alone to reflect over her risotto upon the visit. She was wondering how well her once hearty father was faring in his advancing old age. Though they'd spoken on the phone every few months each year she hadn't seen him since they'd flown him out for Christmas several years ago. From her talks with Faye it sounded as though he was getting gradually more forgetful. It was difficult to say yet if it was Alzheimer's disease. He did seem a bit slower on the phone this last year. She had been so harried and rushed all year with her work that she felt guilty now that she hadn't taken enough time to listen to him more carefully. He'd become sweeter in his later years, that was certain, no firebrand now. There was no reason to fear his fiery temper or tirades again. If they were lost solely however because his entire mind was deteriorating, she'd gladly have put up with them to have him functioning well again. She suspected however it was the enduring loss of his wife that was really dampening his flame.

Later, while packing her suitcase, the same thoughts returned to her and she felt a worrisome sadness growing over his predicament. She was also feeling a gathering momentum to get going, now that she'd made up her mind to do it. If she could leave before the traffic started that would shave off some driving time. Her watch said nearly two o'clock, which gave her enough time to call her office and check on her affairs before departing. She wondered if she could possibly catch Jay as well, thinking it might be one of his days to be there. They hadn't talked in days – since they'd argued over Candy – and she was starting to miss the sound of his voice.

"Homestay Connections. This is Candy. May I help you?" came the familiar opening.

"Hi, this is Bea. How's it going? Thought I'd check in."

"Oh fine. Busy. The usual. How are you doing there?"

"Oh, okay. Busy myself actually. I've decided to go to Ohio to see my dad."

"Today?"

"Yep."

"Why? Is he okay?"

"Well, it's a longer story than I have time for right now, but he needs some help and I'm the only one who can do it, so…"

"Oh. Well, you've certainly been traveling a lot."

"That's for sure. Listen, what's happening in the office?"

"Well, Toshi called. He's been trying to reach you the last few days actually. And he's sounds pretty insistent."

Bea felt her stomach turn. "What's he want?" she asked anxiously. "If it's about the spring programs I said I'd call him when I returned." She had found Japanese men were a demanding lot to deal with in business, especially, she assumed, since she was a woman. Kazuo, of course, was such an insufferable taskmaster that she'd finally refused to work with him at all. It had been a courageous leap for her to take, and still somewhat anxiety provoking, but she had done so in large part because of her remaining ties through Toshi, her other main Japanese agent in the student exchange field. Though he was also frequently demanding and unyielding, he was never as abusive as Kazuo had been. Yet every time he called the office her stomach flip-flopped, as it was almost always stressful. The Japanese were perfectionists and if something wasn't right it was never their fault. She had learned early on that they hated to lose face, and expected lengthy apologies from all the imperfect Americans, those faulty foreigners, they had to work with in the business. If it wasn't to complain about a Host Family's treatment of a student, it was to remind her about an approaching deadline for information or to negotiate a less favorable contract on her end for an upcoming season.

Jay hated to see her anxiety break out whenever Toshi called. He had already worked up a full throttle of hatred for Kazuo over the mean and demeaning faxes sent Bea. He had barely been able to restrain himself from answering them in a tone that would have shocked "that little Jap bastard" as Jay had once called him, delighting in his defiant scorn of the oppression of political correctness. "Hey, it's just short for Japanese," he had added with a mischievous grin. Bea had insisted however that Jay stay out of it and out of respect for her he managed to do so. He had nevertheless developed a healthy disrespect for Japanese businessmen as a result of how he thought they mistreated his wife and referred to Toshi as "Oshit" whenever his name came up.

"Well, it's about the spring programs," said Candy, "and I guess he wants you to lower your prices."

"What? I barely raised them at all. About five percent. Our costs went up nearly that much."

"Well," said Candy in her sarcastic saccharine best, "I don't think he's concerned about your costs too much, sweetie. Also he said there's a complaint from a student to resolve from last summer."

"Oh God. Did he give you any specifics?"

"No. And he seemed more interested in talking to you about the prices."

"Alright, well, listen, tell him I'll be back early next week and we can discuss it then."

"I did that. I don't think he wants to wait. He wanted to know where you were and what the number was."

"Oh, I don't want to talk to him while I'm here. I don't have the figures here. Besides there's plenty of time to talk about it before spring. And we can settle their complaint, whatever that is. They waited this long to bring it up."

"I told him you left Toronto and were having some brief time with your family back east and would be home by Monday, and didn't want the number given out unless for emergencies."

"And what he'd say to that?"

"He said it wasn't an emergency but it was very important and that he wanted the number anyway. I got the feeling he didn't believe me that you weren't back in the office. He just sounded so suspicious."

"Oh, he's always that way. I think the Japanese don't feel they can trust us to work as hard as they do. They're a workaholic society and resentful of us lazy westerners. He probably thinks I'm at the desk next to you and avoiding him."

"What should I do if he calls back?"

"Tell him you've let me know he's trying to reach me and I said I'll call him next Monday first thing. This is just not a good time to talk to him. I'm not prepared and I've got other things to do."

"He's not going to like it."

"Well, tell him I'm sorry, but it just can't be helped."

"Okay. You're the boss."

"Right," sighed Bea. "Is there anything else?"

"Did you get the papers I faxed you?"

"Yes, thanks. I've decided they can wait till I return too. Any thing new?"

"Well, yes," said Candy with an overdone tone of great reluctance, "Are you sitting down?"

"What do you mean?"

"Well, I hate to say I told you so," she said, not sounding like she did, " but we've been getting a number of calls from Toronto Host Families these last two day saying Perry never paid them."

"What? How many families? Two or three?"

"At last count eleven, which is nearly a third of them, and I'm starting to wonder if he paid any of them at all."

"Oh no."

"I'm afraid so," she intoned in a high judicious pitch. "It looks much worse than you thought or than he let on when you met him."

Bea felt a reeling dizziness in her head and sat down in the nearest kitchen chair. "That's a lot of money that I sent him!"

"That's right. And I just bet the other two thirds didn't get paid either. The ones I spoke with all said he promised them you'd be paying them when you were in Toronto this last week. I told them you just left and they were wondering when they would get their money."

Bea felt it hard to talk for a moment as her mind whirred, trying to calculate the amount due the families. "That's over three thousand dollars." She felt faint and a sense of nausea began bubbling in her stomach.

"Right."

"Plus the two or three thousand he already owes us that's unaccounted for."

"That's right."

"Then he's really lied to me."

"I think so. Big time. You know, that's embezzlement."

"Oh God." She put her elbow on the kitchen table and rested her forehead in her hand. "I can't believe he'd lie so badly to me." Her heart fluttered and her pulse sped up as she wondered what to do next...*oh no no no damn it no*... Leroy was as wrong as she was. Well, actually that wasn't technically true. He'd said to give him a chance – actually half a chance – and if it didn't work out she'd know then what to do next. But she didn't. She didn't know at all. Actually to be fair, he hadn't said exactly that either. He'd said she could trust that the resources would be available if she needed to replace him. But she'd thought she *could* trust him. And now she didn't know where to turn. She didn't know anyone in Canada to trust. And she wasn't sure she'd ever trust anyone there again anyway. "I don't know what to do about this. Have you called Perry?"

"Yes I did. Twice. He hasn't returned my calls."

"Oh God."

"Men," pronounced Candy, like a judge delivering a death sentence...*oh God...don't start that again*...That reminded Bea she wanted to talk with Jay. Maybe he could talk with Perry man to man, counselor to sick person, employer to embezzler. "Is Jay there?" she asked weakly.

"Sure, " said Candy, sounding surprised. "You want to talk with him?"

"Yes. Put him on please." Candy put her on hold and called out to Jay. "Bea's on the phone for you. Line one."

"Hi honey," Jay said, picking up the phone. "How's Pittsburgh?"

"Not so good at the moment."

"How so? What's up? You don't sound good. You and Faye aren't fighting I hope."

"No, we're fine. I just found out from Candy that things are a lot worse in Toronto than I thought."

"How's that?"

"Perry didn't pay a bunch of the Host Families and I'm wondering now if he even paid any of them."

"Oh no. Is that a lot of cash?"

"Could be over three thousand. And he already owes us at least two or three more."

"Oh man. I was afraid he couldn't be trusted. What are you going to do?"

"I don't know. I just found out. I was just leaving to see my Dad. I don't know what to do."

"Oh God. Well, why don't you call Leroy? He always has an answer."

"He was the one who told me to trust Perry."

"Did he actually say that?"

"Well he said to give him a chance and if he did the slightest thing wrong to fire him."

"Well, he has. So now what? Did he say what to do if you had to fire him?"

"He said something like I could trust that God would make the necessary resources available at the time."

"Hm. Well that probably doesn't sound too helpful at the moment, but it is the way Leroy thinks, and he might be right too."

"I know, I know. I just feel so disappointed. I can't believe he'd lie to me like this. I feel so stupid. You guys both said he was untrustworthy. I don't know now why I ever trusted him. And he's a Sunday school teacher!"

"Yeah, well, so much for religion. Look, I like that quality about you, and so does everyone else, so don't be so hard on yourself. But if I were you, I'd give Leroy a call right now. He's never let me down any time, on any subject, at all. He's always got an answer, a positive one, a spiritual one and a practical one. I mean if you want, I can call Perry. Tell him we'll sue his ass off if he doesn't square this. But even if I reach him he'll probably just lie to me too. And I can go back there too, if you want, but it's a long ways and I don't know how easy it'd be to prove that he's cheated us. It's a different country. I don't know how helpful they'd be. I'm afraid I'd forget to be spiritual and just want to punch his lights out."

Bea sighed. "I don't want you to get angry. That won't help. I don't know what I want. God, I just can't believe he's doing this. I was just with him."

"I know. I know. People are crazy. Let me tell ya'." *rrriiinnnggg* "Hey, I'm sorry, but I gotta' get this. It's my line. Could be important. Can you hold just a sec?"

"Is it that important?"

"It could mean money."

"Can't Candy get it?"

"No. I told her to leave the third line alone for me." *rrriiinnnggg* "It's got to be one of the colleges. They can't reach me every day 'cause I'm only here every other day and they there are hard to reach too. I've got a proposal that could mean big bucks! Big bucks! Which I need! And with Perry's rip-off we'll need it all the more." *rrriiinnnggg*

"Oh alright! But make it quick. I don't have long here."

"I will, and in the meantime I'll give you back to Candy. Oh, and here's Leroy's number." He rattled it off, put her on hold and yelled to Candy to get back on with her.

"This is Candy."

"Hi. He had to take that call. Guess he's been waiting for an important one from a college."

"Uh-huh," said Candy in a dubious tone. "He sure jumps when she calls."

"Whenever who calls?"

"Why the woman from the college, I guess. So he says. Who else could it be?" Bea felt her nausea rise up again, spreading into her chest and throat. Between Toshi and Perry, Candy and Jay, Faye and her father, life was suddenly getting very stressful. She hated the feeling of distrusting people. She glanced at her watch – now almost one-thirty. She'd hoped to head out on the highway in a half hour and still had to get to the rental car agency. "Look, will you just tell Jay that I had to get going? Tell him thanks for the number and I'll make the call now."

"Thanks for whose number?"

"Oh, Leroy's. You don't know him. He's a …he's a friend who might be able to help us with Perry."

"A lawyer?"

"No, no, just a…he's just a friend. I don't have time to explain right now."

"Another man. Well, good luck's all I have to say."

"I thought you were seeing more of Randy lately?"

"Well, I'm not really seeing him exactly. He's just fixing up some things around my house, which is something my ex could never find the time to do."

"I see. Okay. I better go. I'll call you later."

As Bea got off the phone she felt as jittery as she had as a little girl when fearing a wrathful outburst from her father over some infraction she'd committed. She paused before picking up the receiver to call Leroy and saw that her fingers were shaking like a hummingbird hovering at a flower. She closed her eyes and took a deep breath. She wanted to scream. She wanted to cry. She wanted to go to sleep for a long, long time. She wanted to call Perry but the thought of hearing his voice made her feel sicker still. Had he really simply fleeced her and then just lied to her, boldfaced as a bulldog? Was that why he'd seemed as frightened a cornered mouse? Why hadn't she seen it? Was she really so softhearted as to be that softheaded? She gripped the phone with her trembling hand and dialed the number that Jay had given her.

"Hello."

"Hello Leroy. This is Bea. How are you today?"

"I'm wonderful."

"Well, good for you. I'm afraid I'm not doing so good."

"What's up?"

"It's about my business unfortunately."

"And what exactly?"

"Remember I talked to you before about a man in Toronto. Everyone was telling me that I should fire him, and I didn't want to, and you sort of validated how I was feeling."

"Yes. Right."

"Um, so I was just there last week with him and ended up not firing him and we reckoned that he owed me some money through mismanagement – maybe two thousand or so – and I gave him more training and he promised to pay me back and do better and so I left thinking things were good. And now I'm in Pittsburgh but I just talked with my secretary and she said a bunch of Canadian families have been calling the office lately saying they were never paid – which he didn't tell me – and so it looks like he's mismanaged – or taken – a whole lot more money than I thought. I'm so I'm starting to feel sort of sick about the whole thing. I think maybe he's really fooled me."

"And how much money are we talking about?"

"Oh, about three thousand dollars…but really, with the other two or three thousand, maybe closer to six thousand dollars."

"Have you spoken to him?"

"Uh, no. I just learned about this."

"And you gave him the money?"

"Yup."

"And when was the last time you spoke with him?"

"Well, not since last week when I was with him. But I didn't know about this then."

"Alright. What you want to do is you want to contact him. Tell him these things have to be paid, and that they have to be paid today. And just let that go."

"Well, uh, my secretary tried to call him twice now these last two days and can't reach him and he hasn't returned her calls. I guess I should call him next but the whole thing just makes me feel sick frankly."

"You need to pursue this. You need to bring this up with him. You need to say we've got to do this right now."

"Well, I think he would pay the families if he had the money."

"Well then, you're going to have to just see what has happened here. You're going to have to call him up and say 'Where's the money I sent you?'."

"Uh huh, I know you're right. But I feel like I don't want to talk with him at all. Why is this so hard for me?"

"To confront him?"

"Yeah."

"Because you feel the situation is more chaotic than it is. All it requires is that you be clear. You have to see that your authority is not impeachable. I want you to be able to comfortably call him up and say 'Now what's going on here? We need to talk about this and I need to have an absolutely truthful answer right now.' That's all that you have to do."

"Mmhm."

"You have to understand something here. I want to inspire you in a particularly empowering way. And that is, it doesn't matter what he's done with the money. You'll get it back, one way or another."

"Mmhm."

"Do you know what it means – and I've spoken to Jay about this – to not take no for an answer?

"What if you knew that by calling him up you would still have all of the money that you rightfully should have and there was no way anyone could violate that? It doesn't matter what he's done with the money even. Whatever's yours will be there. How does it feel to have that kind of authority and to express that kind of will without resistance?"

"Uhhh…it feels much more peaceful."

"It does. It has to do with being able to express insistence and being absolutely at peace with it. Not taking no for an answer. There's no possible resistance to you here. If you can find that vibration, that internal frequency, you'll have your money. It's not lost."

"Hm. Well I don't quite see where it's coming from because right now I'm still thinking… you know, it's lost…"

"Yeah, you're thinking."

"And I have to pay some more."

"What you have to feel is that you cannot possibly be violated. And when you talk to him, you need to talk to him from that place and not the place of feeling victimized. That's important for you."

"Uh huh. And I don't want to do the guilt thing either. I don't want to try to make him feel guilty."

"No. Just say 'Where's the money I gave you? Did you steal it? I just want to know. And if you did, just put it back.' That's all you have to say."

"Oh that sounds so simple…You do it."

"I would be happy to do it. And the money would get back to you too."

"You know…I want to believe that the man has integrity. And I think that's why this is so hard for me, because I really can't believe that he'd steal money from me."

"Well, that's why you need to almost, almost – and I say this just so you get the feel of it – almost not mind that he might have stolen from you."

"Well, I can almost not mind that if he'll admit it and give it back."

"Yes, of course. But just insist that he admit it and give it back, if that be the case. Insist on having the whereabouts of the money made clear and if it's not where it's supposed to be, insist that he put it back where it is supposed to be."

"Mmhm."

"Just absolutely insist on your good here and be of good cheer while you're doing it and very firm."

"Mmhm."

"You see, it's important to distinguish between discernment and judgment. Judgment is when there is an assertion that harm has been done. Discernment is realizing that there's something amiss or inappropriate going on and it's got to stop, and that's all there is to it. And that's perfectly benign. It's benevolent. It doesn't accuse and thereby keeping the ego dynamics going.

"But you also recognize that if there's not an expression of integrity here, that's going to change and in a hurry."

"Right. Alright."

"So you get to be powerful here. You get to be unconcerned, not frightened by this..."

"All the things that I am."

"Right. And you get to set the thing straight. This is very good practice for you."

"It is, yeah."

"And I want you to look at the blessing here because once you do this, if it ever arises again or even if it doesn't, you will have acquired or allowed a certain aspect of your Being, or your divine authority to be expressed. And you won't be subject to this any longer."

"Mmhm. I know. I'm sure that...you know...well, when I met him he was shaking – his hands were trembling. It just seemed weird. I mean I'm sure this is as hard on him as it is on me."

"Right."

"But he didn't come clean then, and … I don't know."

"Well, he can come clean now. Just say 'Where the hell's the money and why didn't you say something?'."

"When we met I did bring it up and he said he thought he owed me money. But then now I see it was probably far worse than he let on."

"Right. Well, you can say, for example, without even batting an eye, 'Perhaps you can get it from a credit card'."

"Do whatever you have to do."

"Exactly. That's not that hard to do. It's not that hard to find three thousand dollars."

"I know, I know. It just seems so bad. I mean my secretary's going 'that's embezzlement'."

"Sure it is. It is. But the problem here is that you are learning how to set things right with a minimum of conflict, no matter what the circumstance. This is very good practice for you. You see, one opinion might be how nice it would be to avoid all this stuff. But you're living in a world where this stuff goes on all the time. What you want to see is how you can experience no loss, being in a world that is as dysfunctional as it is, and to understand that there is divine justice always available that sets things right and that does not include recrimination or retribution. It just sets it right and says go on with your life. It involves forgiveness but it also does balance things."

"I see."

"So you get to be firm and magnanimous."

"Well, those are things I'd rather be than angry or …unkind."

"Well you can be those things. But you must pursue this. You cannot let this go, to learn these things and to have it this way. You really need to call him."

Chapter 41

"It is only because you think that you can run some little part, or deal with certain aspects of your life alone, that the guidance of the Holy Spirit is limited."
(A Course in Miracles)

FROM THE SMALL WOODEN stool by the front door Jay looked out at the lake as he put on his mud smeared jogging shoes and adjusted the earphones of his portable tape player on his head. Over the brown withered leaves left on the willows he watched a seagull sailing into the encroaching mist that crept slowly across the water as the nighttime neared. Having just left Phil at soccer practice he had barely enough time left to run, shower and make the long drive back through the throttled early evening traffic to pick him up again. The daytime drizzle had waned to the point where he would only get soaked from whatever puddles he didn't dodge while jogging on the dirt-lined asphalt lane and he was grateful for that minor miracle in rain soaked November. Beyond that he was even more grateful for a major miracle that had come his way lately. Several Washington State Universities had called, one today and one yesterday, to say they had accepted his proposals for Homestay programs to be offered their foreign students. They were both sending major deposits to the company right away.

He had initially been ecstatically elated with the news only to have it tarnished by the fact that Candy had told Bea about it before he'd had a chance. When the first call had come yesterday he'd interrupted Bea to take it and when he'd called back twice to tell her, the line was first busy and then he got Faye's machine. He'd left messages there and on Bea's cell but none had come back from Bea or Faye. Then the call from the second college had come today while he was counseling and Candy had taken it in his absence. That caller had incidentally told Candy about the other school also as the two university programs were coordinated. She had thought the news significant enough to warrant calling Bea on her cell phone "to balance out the bad news about Perry." She informed him of her call to Bea when he'd come downstairs right as she was going home. Though he'd managed to dismiss the disappointment he felt over not being the one to deliver the good tidings, he was sorely rankled by the developments that had followed.

On hearing the welcome news, Bea had felt, according to Candy, for some reason, a generous urge or sudden impulse, he wasn't sure which, to share the wealth by paying Host Families a larger sum than usual. Perhaps it was Christmas spirit. Perhaps it was guilt over the Toronto families that Perry had screwed. But whatever it was, it had rankled him first that his newly made money was being given away before he got it and secondly that Candy had actually had a say in it. He knew this because she had told him that she and Bea had "discussed" it at length on the phone in his absence. Candy thought it would be a great idea. Not only had it outraged him that her opinion was even considered, but the whole thing was bothersome from a standpoint of which they were ignorant. He was deeply in debt under a mountain of bills that he had minimized to Bea for well over half a year.

Though he had shared with her his worries and the miserable fact that his practice no longer covered his expenses, he had kept the worst from her out of pride and a concern for her peace of mind. She was burdened enough with her own load of worries and moreover he was determined to make good on his accounts without asking for her help or adding to her fears. She had no idea that he was so behind in his payments. He owed two months on his old office rent, phone bill and answer service, three months on his Mercedes, and was thousands of dollars in arrears on each of several credit cards, from which he continually borrowed cash to make payments on his share of household bills and lately his new office. It had been driving him crazy for so long that it dominated nearly every waking minute of his time when not working. It was why his purported enlightenment lessons with Leroy always revolved around money. He asked for it in meditation. He fretted over it when trying to sleep. He sweated over it in his jogging workouts. He was consumed with a compulsion for compensation.

Aside from his not telling her, the main reason Bea didn't know the extent of his obligations was that his creditors primarily contacted him at his office. He had given his cell phone as his home phone when buying the car and to the credit card companies, so no calls as yet came into his home. His cell and his office numbers however were constantly plagued by calls from creditors condescendingly reminding him he was overdue again. He was continuously worried if collection agencies might soon be set upon him and what numbers they might unearth through their subterranean sleuthing. Though some of the bills did arrive at his home, Bea never gave the slightest thought to looking at his mail and assumed though in debt he was keeping his ship of state afloat. She had no idea he was drowning in a pool of sharks.

He snapped a tape in his machine, slipped out the door and trotted down the brick sidewalk that connected to the long gravel driveway leading to his street. Still seething with indignation at Candy's intrusion in his affairs he hoped to calm himself by listening to the tape of his latest talk with Leroy, made less than an hour ago. He had purchased a device from an electronics store that allowed him to tape their talks so he needn't wait for Leroy to mail them anymore. The moment she had left the office he had called him in the hope of becoming composed and finding guidance before picking up Phil at school. As he turned onto the slick road his worn shoes began to pound the pavement and he felt his tension subside with each outstretched stride. He'd been jogging for exercise since they'd moved there and always thought of it as his personal therapy. Falling deeper into the hypnotic rhythm of his accustomed cadence, he focused solely on his breathing and relaxing as he listened to the tape.

"Hello."

"Hi Leroy, this Jay. Can you talk for a few minutes? Sorry to surprise you."

"No problem. I'm free at the moment. What's up?"

"Well, there's a potential conflict brewing in the office between me and Candy and Bea; me against them. Just happened a few moments ago actually."

"What's that?"

"Uh, well I've been doing this one branch of Bea's company – running it by myself – creating it actually – it's a new venture – and it's turning out to be sort of wildly successful all of a sudden. We just heard today – well, yesterday and today – that a whole bunch of money's going to be coming in from two universities I've been working with to establish these new programs, and…I'm feeling really good about it on one hand because it's been so nice just to sink my teeth into something and have it work out on a grand scale rather quickly, and… I especially feel good about making a lot of bucks for Bea's company and just doing a good job on something in general."

"Sure."

"But at the same time suddenly there's this tension around it because I'm really worried about money – as you know – 'cause I've got such a big stack of bills and uhhh…mostly I haven't really shared with Bea how bad it is and what I've been going through because…I don't know…I just don't like to…I don't feel good about it. So ahhh…to make a long story short I just heard from Candy that she called Bea to tell her about these college deals I just closed and uhh…they talked about it and uhhh…well basically they decided since it will be such a ton of money, to give a lot more of it than we usually would to the families who'll be hosting the students over the holidays."

"Uh huh."

"So...I feel kind of torn about that because on one level I think well, that's great – let's be generous – and another level it seems like all I've been focusing on is getting rich – in my meditations and in this business – which is demanding and absorbing when I'm in the office – and then finally, all of a sudden, I'm getting rich, just like you were saying and uhhh...I don't want to be greedy but at the same time, this week I got a message from the Mercedes folks saying they're going to repo my car if I don't catch up and the bank sent me a shitty letter saying they are tired of my bounced checks and ...and I just feel attacked on all sides by this stuff and I'm sick of it, and I've been trying to fix it for a long time and..."

"Sure."

"And the other tension I have is that when I'm around Candy, on one level I can tolerate her okay, but she's really hyper-reactive to all the tensions in the office and kind of emotional and opinionated and thinks she needs to put her two cents in on everything and...it's hard for me to concentrate when I'm around her, so I close my door – which I think she resents – and I take a lot of my own calls on the third line, and I really don't like her involved in my projects at all, except in a kind of secretarial way; to type and stuff. I don't want her opinions. But Bea likes her opinions and she's always asking her 'What do you think of this, what do you think of that?' so anyway I guess they started discussing this money and I don't know how much of this is Candy, but I wish Bea hadn't talked with her about it at all, and...well I guess I just feel torn I guess because I'm thinking 'Okay if it's God's will that we pay these people the money then so be it' and on another level I'm thinking I'm so sick of this poverty and...on another level I'm thinking it's none of Candy's damn business. Bea should only be talking about this with me. But they've been working together a long time without me there, so...so... anyway...you get the picture?"

"Well, yeah. There's several things going on here. For one thing you're feeling excluded or isolated. For another, you're feeling responsible. And a third thing is you have some apprehension that you have to make a decision here. Also it is disillusioning for you to finally have some degree of success going on and at the same time still feel isolated. People always have the belief that if something happens – that if circumstances change – they will feel different. And the truth is it doesn't work that way. So you're having to recognize that it's really what you're feeling that matters, you see. It's really becoming more embedded in reality – capital R Reality – that will allow you to enjoy everything. So the kind of special relationship you had in your mind with having more money didn't pan out. With respect to your feelings, it didn't make anything better. And your feeling of inclusion isn't very strong. You feel walls between you and Candy and you feel walls between you and Bea. But there's a pressure to join them that is hard for you to respond to because, well, let's just say there's plenty of ego going on with all of you around this at the moment."

"Okay."

"Now, as far you feeling responsible, the truth is you have no responsibility here. If you understand that and can feel what that is like and let go of it, you will relax into this moment more easily. The real question here is this, and that is, if you don't have responsibility, what do you have? And the answer is you have gratitude. Gratitude is what always has to be where there once was responsibility. That allows you to act spontaneously and lovingly but in a carefree way."

"Gratitude for the circumstances I find myself in?"

"Gratitude just for being. Forget the circumstances. Your ego is having problems with the circumstances but you are not. If you can be in touch with the gratitude you will recover your identity."

"Hm."

"Okay. So there's no decision that you really have to make. You don't have to control anything, in other words. So you can be grateful, feel included, and you don't have to exercise any control. But what you do get from this is a wonderful sense of your own stability. You feel unshakeable. You feel unassailable. And that's all you want right now. The banks can send you letters about this or that, and in this state, if you want to you can go down to the bank and be absolutely clear with them and they will say 'Thank you, sir'."

"That'd be different."

"Right. So that's all that's needed here. You need to find your stability; your peace. You need to feel anchored in your capital B Being here. So again: you are not excluded, you don't have to control anything, you are not responsible for anything, you get to feel grateful. And it doesn't matter what anyone else is doing. It doesn't matter if Candy or Bea are at wit's end or are feeling righteous, or whatever. It doesn't matter. It doesn't affect you."

"Well, it almost seems like I would be deferring decisions to other people because everything would seem so inconsequential no matter what way the decision went."

"No, no, no. You just don't make decisions from the ego's point of view. You are neutral until God selects a gear for you, and moves through you."

"Will I experience that as making a decision?"

"You will experience it as knowing what to do and having absolute clarity about it and not taking no for an answer, because the clarity you have will be so indisputable that people will say 'Yes, that's right'. But it's not because you thought it up or that you were trying to uphold a position here."

"Because I felt it out?"

"Because you were listening. And yes, you will feel it. It's like what Rex says: 'I don't know anything but I listen'. Only the Father knows. The Son listens."

"So I'll know what the right movement is at the time?"

"Yes. Here's something. I want you to spend some time – in this time now when it clearly seems like your needs are starting to be met – I want you to spend some time in meditation just feeling your ever-increasing capacity for your good, for your fulfillment. Capacity is an interesting word.

"Capacity is that which contains; the ability to contain. I want you to look in every direction right now and realize that in every direction there's no end. So there's no end to the capacity for your good. In your ego concept of reality those directions are limited. Your good is limited to the world or what you see on this planet. So you begin to put limits on the first three dimensions and because of that you start coming up with a limited capacity for fulfillment. That's in effect how the ego was born. The ego believes life is limited to the first three dimensions rather than seeing life is fully infinite. So abide with the idea that there is enough capacity for your fulfillment, not the fulfillment itself, but the capacity. And let your embrace of infinite capacity be unreasonable. Now what this does is to eliminate the necessity for you to have personal capacity, which I'll refer to as capability. If you cannot experience the infinitude of the first three dimensions – the infinite capacity for being and fulfillment – then you have to resort to personal capacity or capability, which comes from the ego. And if you happen to not have that, then you are shit out of luck.

"So spend time getting clear about the infinitude of the first three dimensions so that you begin to carry the big picture with you all the time. Then your good can come to you easily. You still express your desires and have moments of intensity. That doesn't change. But you don't struggle any more with the question of where it will come from because you know that it comes from the Infinite."

"Hm. Well…that sounded good. I think I'll have to listen to this tape a lot to get it though."

"Well, it's real simple. You limit yourself to the first three dimensions – the dimensions of the ego, of physical reality – and they seem final or finite. But actually they extend infinitely. If you can feel that – this is not something to reason out, because it doesn't work that way. But if you can feel no end to the capacity for fulfillment then you are aligned with the Infinite. You see, the problem is that if you see yourself limited to the finite then there's competition for the capacity available. So someone else may have some good but you don't, for example, because there is not enough capacity. But in God's kingdom the capacity is infinite and doesn't follow those rules of logic, of rationality, leading to rationing or competition. But you have to feel it. This is what it means, Jay, to seek the kingdom first and then all things will be added unto you."

"Well, uh…that sort of gives me a sense of being aware that everything's in continual motion. Does that relate?"

"Well, yes, in that there is always momentum and also constant transformation."

"But the other way of seeing things is as though everything is fixed."

"Exactly."

"It's like looking at this building and realizing that the molecules are alive in it and that's actually its reality, more than the fact that it appears to be fixed."

"Right. It's alive and can be transformed into something else."

"Uh…what I'm thinking of is that light actually is running through me and light is running through the building, though at different frequencies, you might say."

"Yeah."

"Once in *A Course in Miracles*, Jesus said 'You are really just light'."

"Well, right. That's all it is anyway. Just frequencies of light. But look, here's a good phrase for you to dwell on, and that is 'infinite capacity' because you really want to know that there's the capacity for this fulfillment and you have not yet fully grasped this."

"Isn't that the same thing perhaps that I've been asking for lately when I say the one desire I want to focus on is feeling rich or having riches?"

"Not quite. You want the capacity. Exactly. But capacity is literally what you want, not capability. You see what I'm saying? Riches is an interpretation of the recognition you have that capacity is necessary. See, students of metaphysics have often been told in the past to ask for what they want, to focus on their desire, but without the understanding of how it is that it manifests. But to truly understand the process it is important to have a full comprehension of the big picture; of how it actually works. And the how is not a method. It is just the fact that there is infinite capacity for it. God, as the Source of Life, has infinite capacity. So if you can experience consciously that infinite capacity, if you can extend yourself beyond your limited ego view, then your capacity is extended as well, and your good can happen, simply by that act."

"So you're suggesting I be aware of …uhh…walking around in, sitting around in, operating in infinite capacity?"

"Right. It's always going on anyway. It's just a slant that you have adopted that has put you in limitation. Make no apparent reality matter right now, when you're doing this. And get into the feeling that it doesn't matter."

"It's hard to reconcile that with a practical situation – like going back to this problem in the office. I mean, if I'm staying in this space I think I'd say 'Well, just give everybody the money – let's just spread it around – let's just throw it at everybody and have fun and not think about it beyond that' – kind of like feeding the chickens or something."

"Right. What happens if your capacity is unlimited? If you can feel that your capacity is not limited then you are free to do what is appropriate or meaningful or loving."

"Well, generosity is the word that comes to mind. And…I feel like I have two very different feelings. One's like input and one's like output. And it's like I'm needing to experience or believe that there's this infinite capacity, which I also think of as riches – maybe from an ego standpoint – that is feeding into me, all around; I'm living and breathing it. It's like I'm taking or receiving. And then there's another side of me also, that feels like I want to give. And I want to feel like they're both at a hundred per cent. And I get it set up in my mind, or my ego somehow, where I'm only receiving so much so I can only give so much."

"Well, is it that you want some of that money for your self?"

"Well, yeah. I want to pay the bills. I don't want to be getting these calls and letters from people saying you owe us money."

"So you might have a point here that where instead of those families getting the extra money, that you get it."

"Yeah. Well, it seems totally justified to me."

"Well, then do it."

"Well, I want to but I want to take Bea's feelings into account too somehow. I mean I wonder if she feels guilty about making so much money – 'cause she's making a ton – I mean she gets checks for like sixty thousand dollars at the end of a season plus other big checks during it, though she works her butt off for it. But basically she's making this money through the hospitality of these families, who do this for a fairly nominal fee, though supposedly that's not why they do it. And, well, I know her well enough to know she has some genuine humanitarian instincts – more than most people frankly. I mean she worked as a teacher for two decades for shit pay and now she gives to about any charity that contacts her, which kills me since I could use it. And she has some good business instincts. And she's honest. And she comes from her heart a lot. And I just wonder if she isn't also feeling a little worried or guilty that if people – these families – find out how much money she's making, their egos will take over and say 'Hey, we want more of the pie'.

"And I think Candy maybe plays into that – judging by her comments today – that it would be nice to give the families more money – and makes it a problem that needn't be one. I mean, she gets paid and treated very well by Bea, but it's nothing compared to what Bea makes and I just wonder if Candy doesn't fan the flames a little out of her own bitterness at feeling like one of the 'have nots' in life. And she doesn't like men – hates her dad, hates her ex, hates having a man in the office now, though she'd never say it – and I think, especially since I made this money, she's particularly motivated, though perhaps unconsciously, to give it to people she's identified as 'have nots' like herself."

"Well, that's not your problem."

"Well, it's like I'm going to be putting pressure on Bea, saying 'Don't think of it that way – 'cause I've got this stack of bills'… which she doesn't really know about completely."

"Have you ever heard the expression 'Charity begins at home', Jay?"

"Yeah, right. Okay. Well, see I'm thinking like what if later there is a problem, maybe someone says 'Hey I heard you made a lot of money on that program and I think you should have paid me more for being a Host Family' and then Bea says to me 'I wish you'd let me pay them more that time'."

"Well, if that would be her argument then she would be doing it out of guilt or unworthiness, you see."

"Well, I'm not sure what she's feeling and it could be a very mixed bag of good and bad feelings. But now I'm thinking, God, if I were really enlightened or awakened I'd be saying 'Hey whatever, there's plenty for all of us'."

"No. You don't know what you would say. You might have absolute clarity to say 'I feel this'."

"I feel worried about my bills?"

"You don't need to put that slant on it. It may just be appropriate for you to say 'Well, I think I should have this, before this gets sent out in some gratuitous way – it feels balanced to do it here first'. Maybe the next round of incoming money will be appropriate for that other particular way. You see, if there's money coming in then it's likely to continue. But you'll have to see how you feel then."

"Well, that brings up another question, which we've covered in a way here, but it's about more money coming in. Once you referred to the process of having your needs met, of sufficiency, as like having a riches button on a VCR remote control. And so I've been focusing on that in my mind. I read in a book recently called *Conversations with God*, where God, presumably, tells this guy, the author, that you don't say 'I want' something because the universe or universal mind or consciousness at large or what ever the hell we call it, picks up on exactly what your mind puts out there and if you say 'I want' it says 'Okay you're in a state of want – fine, you have that' and in effect you stay there because that's what you're putting out: I want, which is really a way of saying 'I lack' and God or Mind at Large or whatever says 'Right' I understand that's the mind set you have and are putting out and so you get that state of mind'. And so you stay in a state of want. Matter of fact that really helped me understand when they say in the bible, 'those who have get'. If you think you have it you're not wanting it, you're just getting it 'cause you got it and it keeps on coming as long as you stay in that state of having it. And I gather that's what you meant about if money's coming in and it's likely to continue."

"Right."

"Anyway, I'm trying to work the riches button on the remote in my mind. And I wake up every day and say 'I'm rich and getting richer', rather than I'm wanting riches. And it suddenly it seems to be working, but it's not a pure thing where I feel like an angel. I mean I still attend it with thoughts, decisions, calculations and I'm basically working hard for it also, and ...so I kind of feel like I'm in the middle. I mean, it's like 'Wow – this is working' and then I wonder if it really is working or is it just me working hard?"

"Well, you see, if you think that there's a moment when you're on your own actually doing it yourself -"

"Well, by doing it, I'm mostly just trying to agree with the desire to experience riches, but also I'm working for it. I'm wanting it. I'm trying to earn it. I feel fear over not having it, which is in effect, why I called today, really."

"Right. Look, if you were really feeling just led to take every step and just grateful to do it and not being tempted to feel responsible, then it would be very clear to you that this was the movement of your good."

"I see."

"But because you aren't in that place you have lapses into personality, where you feel responsible. You feel it's you that's making the decision and that maybe your guidance is helping you to do that. That's not it. There's a movement of Life that's just taking care of everything. It always is for fulfillment. It always is for good. It always is for success. And you have to trust it. And you never will get any clearer than that. It always is a mystery. But it always is there."

"It's a mystery you learn to trust?"

"Yes. Exactly. Peace with suspense. Remember that?"

"Mmhm. So you really are encouraging me to stay in the now, with the realization that that's all I have."

"Yeah."

"So I don't need to go back to this issue with Bea or Candy with an attitude or a thought or a plan. I more just need to see how I feel at the moment when it comes up again and just say what I feel moved to say then, which may well be 'Well, I think we should just keep it', or maybe not."

"Yeah. And you need to allow generosity to be extended to you, to the sufficient meeting of your needs, which would create balance. How much better it would be in your house to have balance. You're doing the best you can internally to have it, and so the money may come in such a manner that it doesn't look like it's your money, as though you don't deserve it. You think you've got to earn it. But really you'll never be able to earn your good. It's there. It just shows up. Be grateful for it. Ask for more. But don't think you must earn it."

"Yes. Okay. Okay. That sounds good."

"I told Bea that this was a tough lesson and that you were the one learning it. I made it clear that this was hard, that it was a hard thing to do and that you had come upon the occasion to learn it, and that she wasn't. It wasn't her particular thing, and that I knew you could do it, but that she needed to be mindful of what you were doing, of what you were going through."

"Yeah, well, it's not easy for her either if she feels she's carrying the load. I'm sure she's doing her best."

Breathing heavily now as he rounded back into his driveway he pushed the off button on his cassette and slowed to a walk. There was a little more to hear but he could catch it on the way over to get Phil. His brief cool down period was always the last fifty yards up the gravel drive and the twisting brick walkway leading to the cement patio and front door. His anger had subsided, just as he knew it would, but it had also left earlier after his conversation with Leroy only to rise again after he'd dropped Phil off at soccer as he recalled talking with Candy. Thinking of it now he felt it rising again, throbbing in his psyche, like a fresh bee sting…*that damn meddling twit*…This was going to take some practice.

Chapter 42

"Remember thy creator in the days of thy youth. Rise free from care before the dawn, and seek adventures. Let the noon find thee by other lakes, and the night overtake thee at home." (Walden, Henry David Thoreau)

THE HARDENED SNOW BANKS on the sides of the highway were dripping into dirty gray slush puddles on the ground as Bea sped through the countryside on her way back to Pittsburgh. She'd stayed two nights in her Ohio childhood bedroom where a moderate snow had swept in the first evening. It had not hindered her interviews with applicants and she was feeling good that she'd accomplished her mission. Several older women had answered the ad and one of them, a retired nurse named Carrie, seemed perfect for the job of caring for her father, who obviously needed nearly round the clock care now. Although a widow living alone, the woman preferred not to reside there, but did live close by and instead would work a twelve-hour shift starting at eight in the morning. That covered all meals and the day's activities, plus she and the old gent had seemed to click well. She was pleasant yet prescient, warm-hearted and thankfully knowledgeable about the pertinent medicines crucial to his health. They had struck up a friendship from their very first meeting when he appeared to brighten at the realization he was going to have constant company around. "Can ya' cook?" he had rasped with a twinkle in his eye a moment after Bea had introduced them.

"You'll have to be the judge of that," she'd retorted good-naturedly. "But I fed my husband and four boys for forty years with nary a complaint. I think you'll be right pleased."

He'd nodded slowly while leaning on his cane, conceding the possibility and seeming to enjoy the sprightliness of her response. She offered to make dinner for them all the next evening and the old boy was heartened by the sight of a pot roast, baked potatoes, string beans, biscuits and gravy. "I guess ya' can cook," he pronounced after swallowing his last morsel of sauce-covered meat. He tried to conceal a slight burp with his napkin.

"I reckon so," she responded, pleased at his declaration. "Glad it suits your tastes, Gabe. Wouldn't want you to go hungry. Maybe we'll put some meat back on those bones."

He shrugged nonchalantly in the comic deadpan Bea had witnessed for years then arched a bushy white eyebrow while scraping his plate with the fork for a last line of gravy. "Guess we'll have to keep ya'," he replied hoarsely, licking his lips, and the deal was sealed and off to a good start.

Bea had observed their interaction throughout the meal and was amused at the gentle banter that flowed easily between them. Though twenty years his junior the nurse had lived in the same county all her life with the customs and cadence of the Ohio valley drummed as deeply into her bones as into his. Reflecting on it now while barreling down the road she felt relieved she was entrusting her father's care to capable hands. The cordial yet competent manner of the widow had reminded her of her able mother's agreeable style. For her father it was definitely just what the doctor ordered and actually better than anything he could have prescribed. She was certain her sisters would be glad to hear the news.

Roaring down the road she reflected bitter-sweetly on the precious time her task had allotted her to be with her father. She thought his memory seemed fine enough. It could well be due to isolation not Alzheimer's if it had suffered some. They had gone on a walk each day to the spacious park that spanned beneath their hillside home and she enjoyed the long conversations to which his leisurely pace lent. One day she drove him to the shore of Lake Erie, which he enjoyed immensely, having not seen the water for almost a decade. They had also spent two evenings reminiscing about the past with countless tales of people and good times. At one point after a glass of sherry by the fireside they had both become tearful as they recalled fond memories of Grace, wife and mother; an irreplaceable loss to them both. Yet overall he seemed content that his life had been well lived.

Bea's parting to Pittsburgh was an especially emotional moment for them. Though it went unacknowledged, the loving look between them was poignantly laced with the aching awareness that time was lessening while lengthening between visits. She had hugged him warmly and kissed his cheek gently, whispering in his ear "I love you, dad" as he stood mute. She assured him all three sisters would be back soon to visit him while they were together at Faye's. As she climbed into her car at his curbside he shuffled over the sidewalk under Carrie's watchful eye and rapped on the passenger window. Opening the window she smiled at him sweetly.

"Just tell my little girls that I love them all," he said in a husky voice. That eternal twinkle was still in his eye.

"I will, dad," she answered cheerfully, trying to stem the tide of tears that swelled up from her heart. "I promise I will."

He nodded his white-haired head up and down, bit his lip, then smiled kindly and sent her off with a faint wave of his well-calloused hand...*i promise i will...*

Seeking a shift in her mood she blew a sigh through puffed cheeks and glanced about casually on either side of the road at the combination of rolling farmlands and stark leafless maples all around for miles. Dotted with scattered patches of mushy snow in the fields she would love to take Cheyenne for a leisurely ride through them. They were a far cry from the thick crowds of dark evergreens, like tall serrated knife points, covering and choking the hillsides of Washington. She'd noticed also that the lakes of the two states were different, in size as well as in texture and tone.

Lake Erie, which she had often frequented as a child, had a gray sandy shoreline and a vast choppy expanse reminiscent of the sea. The lake she now lived on was serene and contained, bordered by calm abodes with no mototorized boats allowed; a picture of tranquility. Even Lake Washington, twenty miles from her cottage, and crowded in summer with sail boats and motor crafts, still seemed small by comparison to the Great Lake. Also the beaches of Washington's waterfront were relatively barren, more rocky than sandy, virtually uninhabitable, and especially in contrast to the ones in California. But that state had never really touched her as deeply as the other two had...*too glitzy*...and she let out a little sigh. As she contemplated the contrasts of the states she had lived in, she was aware of feeling a sentimental attachment to the fertile soil of her native Midwest, her beloved homeland, yielding gently to an emergent yearning for her faraway northwest home.

She'd been on the road the greater part of a month now and was missing her family; her boys – her three boys. She was concerned about Phil's progress in his new school and the pressures such a distinct transition could entail. Such a quiet and sensitive boy, a courteous young gentleman, she worried if the switch to such a larger campus would prove difficult for him with students and teachers alike. At the Montessori he had known but a handful of instructors and the same small group of kids year after year. Plus these kids were rich kids, mostly Microsoft brats from upscale Bellevue, and she was slightly apprehensive that they might be snobbish and unsociable to newcomers. Though Jay was a good dad he wasn't a mother and she felt a twinge of guilt over leaving them both for another long spell on the road.

She wondered also how Jess was adapting to marriage and whether his wife had found a permanent job yet. Such a bright young thing but with no computer experience beyond college she had found herself adrift in a job market swarming with computer savvy engineers laid-off from Boeing, which made competition stiff in her preferred field. Perhaps more work would open up after the year's end. While Jess had just landed a job at a private high school, it was hard for the young couple to make it on a teacher's salary. Thank goodness there were short stints of work for her through a temp agency. At least they seemed happy, as far as she knew. As soon as she got home she'd have them over for a festive dinner to catch up on their lives. She'd returned to cooking for herself this week, almost a lost art, as Faye had been late most every night with one thing or another that couldn't be helped. It'd be nice to get back to Jay's great meals again.

She was glad for the short but friendly conversation with him yesterday, though surprised at how much he had wanted that money. She was willing enough to comply with his desire but disappointed that no extra Christmas cash would be paid the families beyond their normal stipend. Candy had been so enthusiastically in support of the idea that Bea had been convinced of it before talking with Jay. Though Candy was taking a student herself for the holidays this year Bea was sure her motivation had not been strictly personal. Candy had wanted to give all of the families a greater share of the profits the program was generating and Bea appreciated her generous instincts. Still Jay had a point that if he needed the money, his needs should come first. After all, he had made it. She recalled the near desperate but firm tone in his voice when she had asked the key question, "How much do you need?"

"I could use all of it, to tell you the truth."

"Really?" she had said, dumbfounded to hear it. "Are you that much in debt?"

"Well, I've just got a lot of expenses and bills, especially with the move to the new office and all. It's nothing I can't handle over a period of time but with Christmas and everything coming up now…well, it would just make things overall a lot easier."

Though she had thought to bargain or negotiate the matter he had sounded so serious and, as he had never previously pressed for a slice of the pie, it did seem appropriate to grant his request. "Alright," she'd consented. "Go ahead if you must." His gratitude and relief were clearly evident and the regret that she felt was assuaged by that alone. Candy would just have to understand the situation. Maybe they could pay her a little extra Christmas bonus.

In thinking of Candy she wondered about the office and was especially nettled with her insinuations about Jay. She hadn't the wherewithal yet to ask him outright who exactly was ringing him so frequently. It would all seem so silly if her suspicions proved false to have ever entertained them at all in the first place. Still she wondered why he was so adamant about taking his own phone calls. It didn't seem right, kept Candy on edge, and that was another reason it'd be good to get back in the office. Not to mention Toshi, her impatient agent, and God only knew what Kazuo was up to. But the worst one was Perry, at least at the moment, and the rest of the worries would just have to wait.

Yesterday she'd dictated a letter by telephone to Candy, who'd typed it and faxed it on to Perry's home. He'd responded with a fax that was indirect and noncommittal, citing 'mismanagement' as the innocent culprit. Despite Leroy's urging she still wasn't feeling the gumption to call him. A letter seemed a cleaner and more formal way of dealing with it for now. Conversations such as these could be so emotional and messy or worse, perhaps confrontational – not her strongest suit – or even worse yet, just more lies. She excelled in situations where reason, trust and diplomacy were in play but had never been comfortable with anger or guile. This was new territory, better suited for Jay, who regarded erring mankind with greater suspicion. Maybe this experience would teach her discernment, as Leroy had stated, and with luck without losing a small fortune in the bargain.

She had called Leroy right after sending the letter, just to see what he thought of that measure. She hoped he wouldn't be disappointed she hadn't called Perry as he had counseled her to do. While whizzing past fenced-in pastures and undulating hillsides strewn with barren trees, she recalled their conversation.

"Hello."

"Hello Leroy. This is Bea."

"Hi. What's up?"

"Well, it's about Toronto."

"Sure. What's going on?"

"Well, it's not resolved yet."

"But what is the level of communication right now?"

"Well, I sent him a letter saying that we're combing through the numbers. Actually I'm having my secretary call all the families to see if they got paid and then I thought I'd just lay it out to him in a whole package; what it is he owes me."

"And did he respond?"

"He sent a fax back saying he's talking to his accountant about the 'apparent mismanagement'. So that's the last we've said to each other."

"So you haven't determined yet how much he owes you?"

"Not until Candy's done, but at the worst it could be around eight thousand."

"I see."

"So I don't know if I'll get it back or not."

"Well-"

"But you think I will, so maybe I will."

"You have to stay with this. That's the thing."

"And not let it slide."

"Right. You see this thing has been going on for a while..."

"Yes."

"... and if you had canned him earlier like you were considering, you would have discovered it in a different way, and you might not have had him right there to work with."

"Yes, that's right. So I think it ended up fortunately and I just haven't finished it yet."

"No, it's not finished."

"I don't know why this is so hard for me."

"To..."

"To just call him and confront him and say what did you do?"

"I'd say that you imagine that what would come back with you being clear would be something that would be threatening and somehow destabilizing to you."

"Yes. I guess you're right."

"But you know what? You will learn to speak with authority and know what it means to be unassailable."

"Umhm."

"And that's your birthright; just to be able to be unassailable, so that there is no argument."

"Umhm."

"And no one will give you any shit. All the shit is given by you." (laughter)

"Oh, imagine that. You laugh like you knew me."

"Well, I laugh because I know how good that feels." (laughter)

"I'm a shit saver not a shit giver." (laughter)

"Yeah, right…No. You'll learn just how to give it out and let it be known in no uncertain terms that none is to be given back."

"Umhm. Well, the last time we talked you encouraged me to do that and instead I sat down and wrote him this letter that said pretty clearly that I knew he owed me money and I didn't know how much and that I knew he would want to make this right too…and that after I got it totaled I'd get back with him…and that felt pretty good. I mean at first I stewed about it and then it just rolled right out of me."

"There wasn't any kind of accusation?"

"No. It was just like 'Let's straighten this out – the sooner the better'."

"I see."

"I hope he has the money to pay me back. That's what I wonder about."

"Well, he can get it. He got your money. He can get somebody else's money."

"Good point."

"I feel he might be able to get it on a credit card or something."

"Well, I'll keep you posted."

"Oh, please do."

She felt a pang of anxiety returning along with a feeling of regret. …*how did i ever get mixed up with that guy…why can't i just call him*…She realized now her greatest mistake had been simply giving him the money and trusting him to disburse it. Having had a father who was as honorable as they come and a mother as an organist at the church for many years, she had simply assumed that most men were honorable and especially those who taught Sunday school. Her dear old dad, as crusty and high tempered as he could be, would never have stooped so low in his life. She'd once thought his high standard was the rule and not the exception for men everywhere. Now she was wondering if any man could be trusted. Perhaps Candy's cynicism was justifiable after all. Maybe women were the only adult creatures you could trust, though spending the earlier part of the week with Faye had left her ambivalent about that proposition too.

She was much the same as always; fun and laughs one minute, selfishly calculating the next. It was a hard combination to trust completely. You never knew when she might want you to do something to save her from doing it, like driving to Ohio or taking a taxi or leaving you to eat lunch all by yourself, while she went about her affairs. Her purposes always took priority over yours. That had been also the complaint of her children as well as her husbands. Bea wondered if her new boyfriend might feel the same way...*he'll find out*...All through their childhood she had been the bossy big sister; hoarding the bathroom, demanding massages, teasing about freckles, pushing her off the porch, daring her to sit on ant hills, telling dad she was pinned and calling her cruel names.

She'd never forget the time the two of them were riding in the car alone, just shortly after Faye had gotten her license. She was practicing her driving, mostly parallel parking, and had begrudgingly taken her kid sister along at their mother's behest. Grace had wanted the youngest to go along just to get her out of a stuffy house for some air on a cold winter weekend. It had started out well enough when they first hit the hamburger stand for some cokes and fries. But later, after an hour of precise parking practice, over and over in the school parking lot, when Bea had protested she had to go to the bathroom, Faye had turned to her with a short stinging blast that had since been forever burned into her mind. Curling her lip into a menacing snarl, she had spat at her hotly, "Just shut up! You ungrateful dog!" And she had, but not without hurt feelings and a brooding resentment at the cold-blooded fury which her sister could vent.

That incident reminded her of a anecdote told by her nephew Todd, Faye's youngest child, who'd said that his mother had once taken him out for a special lunch. Early in the month she had set up an enticement as a special incentive based on good behavior. She had told him if he could just get through one week without a telephone call from the school principal or a note from his teacher detailing his customary troublesome conduct, he'd be rewarded on Friday by going out to lunch at any restaurant that he chose. The boy had successfully struggled through the week to control himself by setting his sights on McDonalds, the golden giant of junk food. But when they left to go there they ended up driving past it as Faye imperiously declared that it looked so crowded that eating there would certainly take way too long. They landed instead at her favorite Italian eatery, much to his unforgiving and unforgotten consternation. "And that," he had said with resigned indignation, "is what it's like to go out to lunch with mom." Although the scholastic lunch offer remained standing for the rest of young Todd's rocky academic year, the program was never again successfully implemented as no week went by without a disciplinary notice or call from school authorities.

She remembered her niece, Faye's daughter Mary, complaining her mother always came home so late from work, especially after the first divorce, leaving her in charge of her hyperactive young brother for not only dinner but homework, bathing and often bedtime too. The children grew accustomed, though bitterly so, to their mother's consistent absence at school activities and related functions. While it created a close bond between sister and brother, it had also over time created divergent effects in them. The son became belligerent, being fatherless and hyper, worsening with age, and was a constant source of problems to his mother unto to the present. Even though she'd eventually shipped him off to her first ex-husband, he'd barely finished high school, became enamored of street drugs and lived a vagrant lifestyle between periodic menial jobs. Their relationship was rancorous whenever they connected, which usually was only when he called her for money. Lately she'd been threatening to write him out of her will if he wouldn't assent to a drug rehabilitation program. It troubled Bea as she knew he had a good heart and was probably suffering from maternal neglect more than anything.

Mary, on the other hand had proved a model of decorum, growing stronger and poised under the premature responsibilities thrust upon her at an early age. She had chosen to stay in DC after college, near her father and his new wife, when mother and brother later moved away to Pittsburgh. Ultimately she had married an affable young carpenter, whose unrefined social status was regarded by her mother with undisguised disdain. But the union proved a happy one and they were busily engaged in making a good life for themselves, raising three lovely young daughters and building additions to their small home. Her niece had confided to Bea on more than one occasion that at the very least she had learned firsthand from her mother exactly how not to be with her own children.

Reviewing the past, both recent and distant, of her big sister's life left her feeling a little saddened. She didn't want to judge her unkindly or unfairly and certainly their relationship was better now than in the past. For one thing she couldn't boss her around – at least not brazenly. Still she'd had funny feelings, unwanted and uncomfortable ever since arriving in Pittsburgh this week. Starting at the airport where she'd felt neglected, continuing through the week where often their only time together was lunch – if Bea arrived promptly – continuing with interviews that she hadn't planned on or known of, and culminating with the hastily arranged trip to Ohio. Though she was glad to see her father that was really beside the point. No, Faye hadn't really changed much, it didn't appear. They were both just much older. Making changes in their relationship would probably be difficult if not impossible. Perhaps they just needed more time together to talk. She hoped when Polly got there that would finally happen.

She was feeling an eager anticipation of her younger sister's arrival growing stronger with each day. While with her father in their hometown, Bea could sense the woman's presence just an hour away in Cleveland. With the three of them gathering at Faye's for the weekend not only was the prospect of time together certain but she also thought it'd be easier to find intimacy with Polly. They had been so close as children and even through Bea's college years...*such a dear child...so fun loving...*It was only in the divisive sixties that the span in their ages had materialized as something akin to a generation gap. She didn't then or now give a hoot about politics and though the Clinton burlesque could be somewhat entertaining – the Jerry Springer Show of politics as Jay liked to say – she couldn't care less for any of it really. Her family and her work consumed most of her mind and anything left over could gladly be given to friends and her horse. Well, actually tennis, gardening and the piano would be of great interest if she could ever get to them. But for now at least briefly she could focus on her sisters.

After revisiting Ohio she was starting to believe with increasing conviction that if given the time to show Polly how she felt, a new understanding could be forged between them. Finally at last they could have enough time, even if she would have to insist. They had always been able to communicate so easily that if Polly and Jay hadn't disagreed on the subject, the specter of politics would have never been an issue. She resolved to make this weekend the time to reclaim her long lost heritage with her sweet kid sister. Politics be damned! Polly wouldn't be acting like Faye, gadding about, with places to go and people to see. Neither would she have an ulterior agenda, as Faye had about dad, which might take precedence over being together.

On the phone shortly before leaving Seattle Polly had emphasized to Bea how much the reunion really meant to her. At the time they had been welcome words to hear but she'd been so enmeshed in the affairs of her work that she hadn't taken time to reciprocate the sentiment. Now would be the time when she would make up for that moment and a lot more as well. She wanted to make up for all the lost years that had lapsed in Seattle while they were living mere miles and minutes away. If Faye were going to be difficult to reach – driven by duties, demands and desires, not to mention distance – at least she'd resurrect the easier one. She wasn't leaving Pittsburgh without giving it her best.

She felt the desire accumulating power, growing keener and stronger, with each passing mile as she soared down the stretch. It heightened and heartened her awareness of herself. There was plenty of love to offer and recover. They'd talk about old times. They'd talk about new times. They'd make plans to meet more – a quick drive over the big lake. They'd embrace each other with a new understanding and a reinforced wish, nevermore neglected, to be so very close, a family once again; two sisters indivisible, under God, amen. As she zipped through the landscape she no longer saw it. Consumed by a vision of what lie before her she accelerated slightly and focused straight ahead on the narrowing gray line in front of her windshield; a car load of hopes hurtling down the highway, drawing nearer a destiny whole-heartedly desired.

Chapter 43

"Today I resumed my practice and saw my first batch of nuts again."
(Sigmund Freud, in a letter to Carl Jung, upon returning from a vacation)

OUTSIDE THE MOISTURE LINED windows of Jay's office the downy snowflakes drifting onto the parking lot looked like tiny feathers falling from heaven. They appeared to have burst from huge celestial cushions as if some wild angels were having a pillow fight. He watched them settle lightly on the asphalt area forming a thin white tarp on the parked cars and ground. The weatherman was saying it would be gone by this evening. It was not quite cold enough yet for it to stay long and no more was forecast for the foreseeable future. Still it had been a lovely sight to discover in the morning.

It had fallen slightly overnight and the brilliant reflection of the bright sun off the snow had hurt his eyes when he first beheld the layer on the roof of the deck as he peered through his bedroom blinds on awakening. Beyond the willows the still surface of the lake was shiny flint black like a flattened field of metal. A thin film of powdered sugar dusted the trees and rooftops beneath them while ringing the water in an eerie silence as though the birds were watching and waiting. Dark clouds arrived later, carrying the snowfall he was observing now, though the sun was expected to return again shortly and melt away whatever residue might remain. Before it had vanished he'd wanted to recapture his reaction to the beauty and for the second time in a week he'd felt moved to write a song. He sat with his guitar in his lap while leaning over the coffee table with a pencil in his hand, trying to finish it before his first appointment.

Awakened to the quiet
of a bright light dawn
Snow draped all around me
like a white nightgown
A winter land of wonder
with its mystery underground
What a day
What to say

Glistening like pearls
silver snowflakes dwindle down
Listening to the swirl
of the wind that softly sounds
Fields and treetops meet
to share a sheet of sacred ground
What a day
Got to play

He glanced at the clock on the wall and saw it was time to retrieve his client from the lobby...*better finish this later*...Leaning the guitar against the desk he looked for a place to put away his notes. He and Marianne had not talked about which if any drawer of the desk might be his to use. It was her desk in her office and she hadn't been inclined to offer him a file or a drawer, nor had he thought to ask her for one. He opened each drawer hurriedly seeking an empty one. They were all crammed full of papers and related office paraphernalia until he got to the bottom one on the right. It was empty but for some letters stuffed in a tattered envelope. He laid his pencil and yellow tablet on top of it, closed the drawer and rose to meet his first appointment; the flower lady.

She was looking better than he had seen her look in weeks and holding a potted red poinsettia in her hands as his payment. Her cheeks were flushed pink from the cold and her blue eyes shone like stars at twilight. Her nightmarish marriage was just a memory now and one that was dimming with each passing day. He thanked her for the flowers as they walked back to the office and placed them on the coffee table as they settled in the chairs. She talked excitedly about her plans to visit her parents in Minnesota over the Christmas holidays. Her son had not seen his grandparents for many years and they were all looking forward to a snowy celebration together. She and her boy had been making the most of his Christmas vacation by traveling to the mountains. She had made a new friend with another single mom whose folks had let them stay in their cabin over the weekend.

"Oh it was great," she was relating to Jay. "We made a snowman and went sledding. And at night we built a fire and sang Christmas carols. Jason and her son are almost the same age and they got along fine. In fact they never argued. Just played and played the whole weekend long."

"I'm glad to hear your having so much fun now this winter. I was concerned you might have a lonely Christmas this year. How'd you turn this situation around so quickly for yourself?"

"Well, I really didn't want to get depressed for the holidays and especially not to spoil it for Jason. Having him there helps keep my mind off myself. And I thought a lot about what you'd said about taking care of myself, and I just started thinking of all the ways that I could do it."

"Good. Like what?"

"Well, like I said, I started thinking of my family. I've been kind of estranged from my parents for a while. My mom and I used to fight when I was younger. She's kind of bossy and I'm kind of headstrong."

"You?" teased Jay.

"Oh shut up," she said with a smile. "So anyway, I decided to give them a call and see if we could just let bygones be bygones. And, well, to make a long story short, it worked."

"Great."

"Yeah. They had disapproved of me getting married in the first place, thought I was too young, and when I got divorced and tried to raise Jason on my own they were there with financial support, but they were always giving me advice too. And a lot of it was kind of critical. Like they didn't think I knew what I was doing."

"That can get old quick."

"Yeah, it did, and I got more and more tired of it and so eventually I decided to move out here, about four years ago, and haven't seen them since."

"I see."

"Since I'd worked for a florist I was able to make a go of it by living above the flower shop here and renting the whole house but, as you know, things have always been tight."

"I know."

"Anyway, I had a good talk with my mom and dad, and at the end of it dad surprised me and said he'd like to fly us back there for Christmas."

"That must have felt wonderful."

"It did. It really does. And Jason's up for it too."

"Great. Does he ever talk about Darin?"

"No, he hasn't, except once, that is."

"What'd he say?"

"He said 'Mom, I'm glad it's just you and me again'."

"Really?"

"Yep."

"Does he seem alright?"

"Yeah. Actually lately he's been great. No problems at school. Got a new friend. Enjoying vacation. He's okay, I think."

"Well, I can talk with him if you want."

"I know."

"But it sounds like he's rebounded."

"I think that he has."

"Well, how about you?"

"I'm feeling better; a lot better. You know, I know it's early in the year but I started thinking about that story you told me about that woman and her garden and all."

"Yes?"

"And I knew that basically I had to do the same thing; just focus on taking care of me and Jason."

"Right."

"And I've always had a garden, not just flowers, but vegetables too. And for next year I decided I want to make it bigger – bigger than it's ever been in the past. And I just felt it would be good for me to start looking ahead to spring. So I got a bunch of seed catalogues and spent a lot of time going through them, ordering all kinds of stuff, and planning out the design of what and where I wanted to grow things this year, and it really helped me keep my mind occupied."

"Great. But do you ever think about Darin?"

"Well, I did. I did. I did a bit at first, and though I felt sad about how things turned out, frankly, overall, I'm relieved to be rid of him. It was just a mistake."

"A learning experience."

"Yeah. And I'll tell you something that sort of really clinched it for me."

"What's that?"

"I was driving through Kirkland the other day. The gal who cuts my hair is there. And on the way back from seeing her I saw Darin in the lot of this used car dealership."

"Really? He was looking for a car?"

"No. That's the thing. He was selling them. I could tell by the way he was dressed and talking to this couple. And he was wearing a tie. Darin never wears a tie. Not even for our wedding. And he was gesturing with his hands and smiling away. And I just thought bullshit, bullshit, bullshit. It was so fitting. He'd become a used car salesman."

"Has he ever done that before?"

"No, at least I doubt it. He's just been teaching karate, as far as I know, but I think his drinking was getting in the way. I bet he just walked in there and gave them a line of bullshit that he had done it or that he could do it – he can be so charming – and they gave him a try. And that's what he doing now for a living – what he's so good at; bullshit."

His next client was the young female accountant, Jennifer, with the electronics firm, who was stricken with anxiety each holiday season. He had taught her a self-relaxation technique in the first session and they had discussed the possibility of trying light hypnosis in the next one, depending entirely on her comfort level then. As they took their seats across the coffee table from each other Jay thought she looked less nervous than before.

"Well, how are you feeling today?" he inquired congenially, hoping to put her at ease from the start. She sat up straighter in the chair as she laced her hands together in her lap.

"Not too bad," she replied, managing a forced smile.

"Are you feeling less anxious than you were last week?"

"I'm less anxious with you, but not about the holidays."

"I see." Jay nodded and smiled back. "Did you have any success in practicing the relaxation technique we did last time?"

"Oh, a little." She sounded mildly exasperated. "I tried it every day before work, during work at lunchtime, and after I got home, and it did help me relax some but overall the feeling in the pit of my stomach is still there whenever I think about going to my mom's."

"I see. Well, I commend you for trying. You wouldn't know how much it would help unless you tried it, but it sounds like we may need to do more to help you find peace. You mentioned last time you'd rather not take medications."

"Yes, that's right. I don't want to get drugged out or feel dependent on something."

"Well, I completely agree and rarely recommend them to anyone, but sometimes people are just so anxious that they may be useful on a temporary basis. If I do suggest someone take Valium or whatever it's always with the idea that it should only be a temporary measure. I'd rather help people get past their fears without resorting to medication."

"Good. I don't want to do that. I just want to stop feeling this way. I want to feel normal. Do you think I can do that?"

"Well, yeah, I'm sure you can, but it may take some work. Look, we talked last time at some length about the nature of relaxation and finding relief from anxiety. I know you have some fear of losing control and I was trying to make the point that there are levels of relaxation that don't involve the kind of apparent loss of control you might see in an entertainment show with a professional hypnotist, for example. Remember?"

"Yes."

"Okay. And so what we're talking about are different degrees of relaxation, and getting comfortable with the process of going gradually deeper. And that's why I wanted you to practice it yourself, to see how far you could go and still feel safe. And what I think we need here now is a level of relaxation that is a bit deeper than you've been experiencing so far, but one that still feels like you are completely in control. I think we could call it light hypnosis. I wonder if you'd be willing to try to achieve a state like that today."

"What do you mean exactly?"

"Well, I mean I'd like to see if you can get deeper into a relaxed state by letting me guide you there, while at the same time have you feeling safe and in control of yourself the whole time."

"Do you think we can do that?"

"Yeah. That's how I normally do it with people. No one loses their mind. No one gives it to me. They just close their eyes and listen. They go deeper into a relaxed state. But they do it because they choose to. They make it happen, with my help, and at the same time they learn how to reach a deeper level on their own. Then they can practice it without me later, which is what I'd like you to do. I've also brought you a copy of a self-relaxation tape I've made for folks to take home. It should take you deeper than the technique I taught you. So what do you think?"

"Well, I'd be willing to give it a try. I want to do something to get rid of this feeling."

"I know you do. And I hope this will help. So let's find out."

"Okay. What do I do?"

"Alright, in a minute I'll ask you to close your eyes and let yourself relax as much as you can in the chair. I'll continue talking to you the whole time, giving you suggestions or thoughts that are intended to help you relax more and more as we go along. But you should feel in control of yourself the entire time. Eventually we'll reach a point or a level of relaxation where you feel very deeply relaxed and at peace, though still in control of yourself and in contact with me. Then I will start to talk about the holidays – about your past memories of Christmas over the years, leading up to the present. I'll start with various associations around it, sort of working up on it a little at a time, step by step, all the way to the point of imagining yourself having Christmas there now.

"It's a technique that's called systematic desensitization. It's used a lot with people that have phobias or fears about something. Maybe they're extremely afraid of bees or spiders or snakes, for example, or leaving their home, or whatever; any kind of phobia or extreme fear of something. Anyway, the way it works is that you essentially hold the relaxed state consistently and consciously as we move up to and eventually through things that cause you to be anxious, and we gently, systematically, move right through them till you're not afraid any more."

"I see."

"Along with that I want to teach you the means to relax yourself – to reach a deep enough level of peace when you want to – so you can do it without me ultimately. Plus you'll have the tape. And eventually, hopefully, you won't have to do it at all because you'll have worked through this thing. That's our overall goal."

"That's sounds okay, but does it really work?"

"Well, yeah, for some people, for a lot of people actually. We'll just have to see if it works for you. You ready to give it a try?"

"Yeah, okay, I will. Let's do it."

"Good. Okay then. Before we start I want to mention that part of the process includes you having what is called a safe place. It's usually a place that you recall when you felt safe and secure sometime in the past. It acts as a relief valve or an escape hatch. It you ever get uncomfortable you can always move out of whatever we are doing and into your safe place. Understand?"

"Yes, I think so."

"Okay, then. Good. So let's begin. Close your eyes now, and relax into the chair, resting your head back on the cushion and begin by taking a few deep breaths." She unlocked her hands and folded them in her lap, laid her head back slightly, and breathed a quiet sigh. "That's good. That's a good start. Now see if you can breathe a little deeper for a bit." Jay shifted his voice into a calmer intonation with a steady drawn out rhythm to his words like a chant or a recitation of a poem.

"Inhale deeply, exhale fully, feeling peaceful and relaxed, peaceful and relaxed. You have really nothing better to do at this moment than to let yourself relax as deeply as you want to, as deeply as you will… As you continue to breathe deeply, inhaling deeply, exhaling fully, just let go of all the residual tension you feel within your body, your neck and your shoulders…your entire upper body…your hips and your pelvic area…your legs and your feet…just let go all the tension that you are aware of holding, sinking deeper into the chair… deeper into relaxation…feeling peaceful and relaxed…peaceful and relaxed…just giving over to gravity now…simply because it feels so good to do so… peaceful and relaxed…

"Now as you sink more deeply into a relaxed state I want you to imagine, if it feels comfortable to do so, that your entire body is limp and totally at ease as though you were floating on a cloud, totally supported, totally at ease, just floating along, feeling at peace…Now I want you to imagine if you will, if it feels good, that a ray of warm light is pouring down from the heavens, a gentle warm ray, that touches your forehead, and the feeling of the warmth spreads gently over your face, warming your face and feeling good as it does so, warming your eyes and your cheeks and your chin, relaxing the muscles there, then slowly moving down over your face onto your neck and spreading across your shoulders and down along your arms, through your biceps and triceps, through your elbows, wrists, your hands and through your fingers, allowing your arms and shoulders to feel completely relaxed, peaceful and relaxed…

"Then feel the warmth spread from your shoulders down over your chest, and over your stomach, enveloping your whole upper body in the glow and the radiance of the warmth, feeling peaceful, feeling relaxed, simply because it feels so good to do so…Then feel the warmth spread down through your abdomen, into your hips, into your thighs, into your knees, rolling down into your calves, on into your ankles, into your feet, through the soles of your feet, and out through your toes, feeling peaceful and relaxed, and imagine the warmth just keeps on going right on down to the center of the earth…leaving you feeling connected to the heavens above and grounded to the center of the earth below, feeling centered, feeling balanced, feeling peaceful and relaxed…

"Now imagine, if you will, that the warmth sinks in deeper, starting first with your forehead, then caressing the top of your head very gently, and moving slowly down the back of your neck, caressing your head and your neck and your face in the warmth, basking in the warmth, and feeling the warmth sinking deep into your muscles, into your shoulders, into your arms, all the way to the bones, through your elbows, wrists, hands and fingers, down through your chest, your stomach, going deeper, feeling the warmth going deeper and deeper, relaxing you even more completely than before, with each breath you take, feeling peaceful and relaxed, peaceful and relaxed...Feeling the warmth spread deeper into your abdomen, into your hips, into your thighs, deeper and deeper, down through the muscles, down into the bones, moving through your knees, down into your calves, more deeply into the muscles, down through your ankles, on through your feet, through the soles of your feet and out through your toes down to the center of the earth...Feeling relaxed, peaceful and relaxed, connected, grounded, and totally at ease...

"Now I want, if you will, for you to indicate to me, that you are hearing me clearly... and I want you to do it without disturbing your peace or opening your eyes, by simply raising the first finger of your right hand when I ask you to do so...would you do that now please...thank you...that's good...that's just fine...now I want you to imagine if you will, a place where you were, perhaps either recently or in the distant past, where you felt very safe, very secure, very peaceful... we'll call it your safe place, some place you felt happy and completely undisturbed, either indoors or outdoors, it doesn't matter where, just some place, some time, where you felt entirely safe and totally at ease...and when you've found such a place I want to signal to me that you have by raising again the first finger of your right hand...very good...now I want to share with me where that place is and you will find that if you want to, you can speak to me softly, slowly, without disturbing at all, the deep sense of peace and relaxation you have now...so when you're ready to do that just tell me the place..."

"My grandma's house."

"Good. Your grandma's house, good. Okay, and now, about how old are you then?"

"Six."

"Six. Okay, good. And where exactly are you at your grandma's house? Are you indoors or out?"

"Out."

"Out. Okay, out. Out where?"

"I'm out in a tree house my grandpa made."

"Great, okay, great. That sounds like a very nice place to feel safe. And I want you to take a minute now and feel what its like to be there again. Notice the color and texture of the wood, and what it smells like and sounds like to be there again, and what you can see. Can you do that for a moment?"

"M-hm."

"Okay. What's it like? Tell me a little about it?"

"Mmm, it smells like cedar, cause it's made of cedar wood, and I can hear the birds singing, and there's a soft blanket with a pad to lie on, it's very soft, and I can see over the orchard where grandpa grows apples. And it's warm because it's summer."

"I see. Thank you. And so it feels safe, and warm and loving there. Is that right?"

"Yes."

"Good, thank you. Now I want you to unlock you hands in your lap and put each one on your thigh, and then I want you to make a little circle with your forefinger and thumb of your right hand…can you do that?…good…Now I want you to know that you can go to this safe place, this place in your mind, whenever you want to, whenever you desire to be peaceful and safe, any time during this relaxation session, or any other time as well, and all you have to do, wherever you may be, is to take just a moment, to close your eyes, take a deep breath and relax, and make a little circle with your thumb and forefinger, to remind you of how you felt safely encircled, safely encircled there, and you'll be there again, though only in your mind, but the feelings will be real…and you'll feel peaceful and safe once again at that time…Do you understand?…Just nod your head…Good…Okay…

"And you can go there, to that place, to your safe place, any time that you want to, if you ever start to feel uncomfortable about anything that happens, whenever we do these relaxation sessions or any other time…now just let your hands lay flat on your legs for now…and again, know that you can return to your safe place with those safe, warm and loving feelings you felt as a child at any time during this relaxation by simply making a circle with your thumb and forefinger…so be there a moment, in that safe place at your grandparents… and simply feel how good you felt…that's right…can you do that now? … good…remembering it as though you were actually there now…just be there now… and gradually soon we will gently move forward…on up through the years…and we'll just take our time and see how that feels for you…by the way, I'm wondering, do you go to grandma's often?…just nod or shake your head…I see…very often?…okay…can you say why?"

"Because daddy's gone and mommy has to work on the weekend."

"Okay. So that was a good place for you to be when that happened. Do you ever remember celebrating Christmas with grandma?"

"Yes."

"Very often?"

"Two times in a row after daddy went away."

"Uh-huh. And do you remember those occasions?" Jay spoke more now in a normal tone and cadence…."Good, okay, and were they fun times?…Good…Even without daddy?…I see…Okay…Because you felt so very safe there?…And loved?…Right?…Okay…Okay…I understand…I see…So feel safe there now…Do you feel safe there now?…Good…Now, I want you to remember, as we move through the years, as best as you can, what Christmas was like after your mom got remarried…Christmas at your mom's…Just relax…It's okay…Take another deep breath…That's good…Now remember, what was it like…Can you see the Christmas tree in your house?…Good…You're breathing a little bit shallow right now…Are you feeling uncomfortable?…You're shaking a little…What's happening?…What are you seeing?"

"My kitty."

"You got a kitty? That's right…For Christmas…A few years ago…Okay…Why are there tears starting to stream down your face?…Why are you sad?"

"It's dead. It got killed. It's in the alley. I see it! It's all bloody! Bloody snow! Somebody cut its throat with a knife!… aahh, aaahh, aaaahh, oh no no no no… poor kitty, poor kitty, poor kitty."

"Alright, stop. Wait a minute. That's enough."

"Its all bloody. My white kitty, all bloody and red, ahhh, ahhh, its terrible, its terrible. I want my daddy! I want my daddy! I want my daddy!"

"He's not here. He's not here. But you can go to your grandparents. You feel safe there. Go to your safe place. Go to your safe place. Go to your grandma's house right now. Go to the tree house. Circle your thumbs and fingers and go to the tree house right now…That's right…That's better…That's good…Take a deep breath…That's right…That's good…That's better…You're safe…You're safe now…In a few minutes, after you are feeling completely safe and peaceful again, in the warm and loving place of your grandparents, eventually you can open your eyes…and relax…and we'll talk…"

As Howie strolled down the hall ahead of him toward the office Jay noticed his step was less bouncy than usual. He walked with the heavy stride of an overburdened man. Howie plopped onto the couch and looked at Jay with sad eyes. "I don't think I can go on like this for much longer," he spoke in a voice that was filled with despair.

"What exactly is happening now? Are you still keeping your secret from Sharon?"

"I don't know how to tell her," he said in exasperation. "I know if I do she'll just go through the roof. I know it."

"What if you tell her you're trying to get help? What if you tell her your desire is to stay married? What if you tell her you are really confused? Because along with your homosexual urges, you're really also feeling genuine heterosexual ones. That's what it is that drives you to have intercourse with her. I mean this is not a simple case of you've decided you're gay and want out of the marriage. You're seeing me because you really want to save the marriage."

"I know, but I just can't get rid of these urges. And I'm not attracted to other women at all – just other men. All of the time."

"Okay, I understand, but as far as your marriage is concerned you're still heterosexual, by definition. You're still having sex with her. How do you explain that?"

"I don't know," he said flatly. "It makes no sense to me. But frankly I'm away on the road more often than I'm home these days. And when I'm gone it's only toward men that I feel any desire."

Howie's eyes darted around the room nervously, taking in the difference in the new surroundings. "I know this one's bigger but I liked your old office better. You're a lot better decorator with colors and everything."

"Thanks," said Jay, feeling embarrassed and appreciative at the same time. "It's just a temporary move till I get a new place."

"Oh," said Howie nonchalantly as he looked around the room. "Still got your guitar I see."

"Yep. Couldn't do without it."

"Hey, that reminds me I heard from some friends there's a jazz club nearby; the first one on the Eastside. Supposed to be really cool. You like jazz?"

"Yeah, I do," replied Jay, "but let's get back to you."

"Okay, okay." Howie sounded almost hurt. "I just thought you'd like to know, being a musician and all. You should go check it out."

"Okay. I might. What's the name?"

"Jake's Place, in Redmond, just twenty minutes away."

"Okay, that's easy to remember. Thanks." He nodded…*a local gay bar…*

"I appreciate it." He cleared his throat. "Now look," he asserted, changing the subject, "I think there is no way around this any longer for you. You've got to come clean with her about what you're going through. It's driving you both crazy and she doesn't know why. I saw her twice as you know, this last time you were out of town, and though I can't share with you the content of our meetings I know that you know she is highly upset. It can't be a very good experience for either of you to be there together, not to mention for the kids."

"You're right," he assented. "We're fighting most all of the time. The same old shit but worse than before. Yesterday she actually came out and asked me if I was gay. I couldn't believe it."

"And you said?"

"I lied of course." His eyes widened with horror. "I'm tellin' ya' she'll kill me. You don't know how mad, how crazy she can get."

"Maybe it'd be best if you moved out while you worked through this."

"Maybe," Howie sighed. "I just hate to leave my little girls. And I know if I do she'd just poison things with them."

"Well, look, that's your assumption. You don't know that for sure. Perhaps she can be made to realize how destructive that would be to the children. That's certainly a point I'd insist on making to her."

"I'm tellin' ya', you don't know how insane she can be. When she gets really angry it's worse than a hurricane."

"Well, we'll just have to weather it," said Jay with finality. "I know this is probably the most difficult thing you've ever attempted in your life."

"You can say that again," chuckled Howie nervously, as perspiration appeared on his brow. "I might as well shoot myself. Otherwise she will." He paled noticeably and swallowed hard.

"I'm fucked. I'm just a fucking queer and I'm fucked! My fuckin' mother! My fuckin' cousin! Fuckin' everything! Just fucked!" He looked around room desperately, seeing nothing.

"I know you're scared," said Jay, as soothingly as he could, "and she has her suspicions, but the fear and the tension that you're living with now is really terrible and it's just growing worse. As hard as it may be to imagine, it might be a measure of relief for both of you just to get it all out. At least then you can deal with it openly finally. It's not going away."

"I know. I know. Part of me thinks you're right." Howie's eye rolled in panic. "But the rest of me is scared shitless. She's gonna go nuts!"

"You cannot be responsible for her reaction. She'll have to do what she does. But at least you'll finally be giving her the gift of your honesty. You'll have restored your integrity – at least have stopped lying – and be giving her an honest chance to reckon with it all. She doesn't have that now. The way you're going you could both end up with AIDS. How'd you like to tell her then?"

"Aw shit! I know. I worry about that all the time." Howie took off his glasses and rubbed his face in consternation. "I just don't know how to tell her. Do you think I should do it here?"

"You can do it here if you want to. Whatever feels best." Jay reflected on the question seriously for a second. "Yeah, frankly I think it may best for you both if you do tell her here. Perhaps with me present we can be somewhat more constructive than if the two of you were alone. I'm willing to do that. But I'll leave it up to you."

At lunch Jay decided to run next door to the 7-11 for a bean and cheese burrito rather than taking time for Taco Bell. He wanted to finish the song he had started. When he had finished eating he reached down into the drawer where he had stowed the tablet and pulled it up. His fingers were still slightly sticky from the burrito and he accidentally pulled up the envelope underneath the tablet, faintly staining both with orange fingerprints in the process…*damn*…He rubbed the envelope with a paper napkin but the stain would not wipe off. Feeling badly he had besmirched her property he examined the envelope and saw that it was a unmarked piece of her office stationary, of which there were several boxes on a nearby shelf. If he replaced it with another one she would never know the difference.

As he dumped the contents of the envelope on the desk he noticed they were handwritten notes on various sizes of sheets of paper, some folded, some not. A tattered page torn from a small composition notebook landed face side up and he glanced at the words without even thinking. The fervor of the first words riveted his attention and he read the whole note captivated by its intensity.

Marianne, my lover, I'm missing you so much I just had to write. Two days since I saw you and I can't hardly stand it. I love you so much, so much more than I've ever loved anyone. I'm burning with desire for you all the time.

Feeling mesmerized...*oh my God it's a love letter*...he kept reading.

I can hardly wait for next Friday to see you. I think of you always, day and night and in my dreams. I still feel your hot hands all over my body, driving me crazy, your lips melting mine. No one has ever touched me the way that you do, all over my body, all through my mind. When we're together I feel so alive I could jump out of my skin. Your eyes burn a hole through me right through my brain to my heart to my soul. Our ages don't matter. It just gives you wisdom. Dying to see you again. Till then, love, Lisa

*...oh my God it's from a woman...*Although he was awestruck by the passionate prose, he felt even more so by the startling discovery that Marianne was having a serious and searing lesbian relationship. Taking a deep breath he paused for a moment and wondered if he dare take a look at the rest of them. Something inside him insisted he stop now. This first time was obviously simply an accident, mere happenstance, a slight quirk of fortune, a twist of fate that just crossed his path on the way to a good deed. He'd innocently sought only to replace a soiled envelope; a purely altruistic gesture in itself. Surely that was clear and overall excusable, likely to be forgiven by a jury of his peers, unless of course they were perhaps lesbians. But to go to further now would be insensitive probing, spying in fact, like a common voyeur, into the innermost private domain of a sovereign individual, a trespass, a burglary, a scurrilous violation of all that was right; a veritable offense against human dignity. *...i really shouldn't read these...* He picked up a second note.

Marianne, my lover, my wonderful new friend, I was just thinking about you today, all day long. I love how you know so much more of life than I do. I was remembering how when I first came to see you for help as a therapist and you -

*...oh my God she's a client...*He sat down the note and reflected for a moment on the realization of what was happening. The notes were dated October and November. This was apparently happening now. Marianne was in the middle of a homosexual affair and heterosexual marriage; a torrid relationship with an infatuated young woman – a client no less – and an infertile bond with her husband and their new baby...no wonder the bastard looked so damn miserable...*wonder what he knows...if anything at all*...He read through the rest of them, about a dozen in all, and found the same tone; devoted declarations of love and lust. He put them in a new envelope and placed them in the drawer under his tablet precisely as he'd found them, then went out for a short walk.

The snow had stopped falling and lay thin on the sidewalk as he trudged around the block, absorbing the meaning of what he'd just read. By the time he returned his ears were starting to burn with the cold and he came up the front stairs into the lobby where Naimee, his Eskimo lady, as he had named her, was waiting expectantly. "Oh hello, doctor," she said

admiringly. "I'm surprised. I was expecting you to come down the hall from your office."
She smiled at him brightly with discolored teeth.

"Oh, I went for a little walk, just to get out."

"You must get very tired, listening to people's troubles all day." Her sympathy was
evident. "I'm sure it's very hard."

"No, no, not really. I just wanted a little air." He kept walking by her on his way to the
office. "Come on back now, and remember, I'm not a doctor, so just call me Jay."

After the appointment with Naimee was ended, a cheerful recitation of her inconsequential
week, his mind returned to the notes he had read. What a twisted tale he has stumbled
upon. Although he had violated her privacy by reading them he felt no desire to tell anyone
about them. He had for so long now systematically followed the hallowed principle of
confidentiality in his work, especially with all of the anguish, woe, sordid stories, and
general craziness that he'd encountered, that this seemed like just another human drama
best kept secret. Still it titillated him to behold it; another unhealed healer on the loose…
who does a shrink see for help and advice…That thought reminded him that the last talk
he'd had with Leroy, his source for healing, had covered the topic of psychologists briefly
and he recollected the exchange they had had on the subject.

"I recently wrote a newspaper column about the holidays and took a more spiritual tack
than I normally do in these writings. And I'm wondering if I might be alienating people or
if you think it was wise for me to do that so openly."

"Oh absolutely, absolutely. Look, the problem with psychologists, psychiatrists and
the whole lot of these therapists is by and large they don't know the first thing about
consciousness. They know everything else, but they don't know the first thing and that is
that consciousness is unified and infinite and that people are really just individuations of
that one infinite consciousness. There are no personalities or egos to deal with actually, since
they are all just illusions, there's really only that. And if you don't know that, then what are
you doing? What are they doing?"

"Earning a living?"

"Earning a living, right. Well, they are trying to understand the personality but since
the personality doesn't really exist it would be far better for all of these therapists to turn
their attention to dismantling the personality and finding the individual. They'd have to do
that to themselves first of course. But indeed, that's where all of this is heading eventually
and in time they will find their real occupations."

"I was just joking. You told me once earlier not to be earning my living."

Maybe that was where this was all leading to eventually but in the meantime it seemed
there were a lot of crazy shrinks around…*thank God for the sweet healing powers of the
muse*…With that thought he reached for his guitar and pulled out his tablet from the

drawer to work on his music. He remembered the jazz club that Howie had mentioned and contemplated visiting it this weekend to check it out. Just because Bea was off somewhere out of town again didn't mean he couldn't enjoy a little entertainment by himself once in awhile. For now he just wanted to finish his song. Staring out the window at the light traces of snow that were still left below in the far corner of the parking lot he recalled how he'd felt on first seeing it in the morning; an unforgettable flash of blinding white light, then a holy stillness all around and over the lake. He felt the lines coming.

Rising without warning
to the snowdrifts round the pond
Taking off the morning
just to write this song
When winter comes a calling
springtime won't be long
What a day
Got to pray

Chapter 44

"Beware the temptation to perceive yourself unfairly treated." (A Course in Miracles)

FROM ATOP THE ARTIC perch of Faye's modest balcony Bea gazed out at the expanse below her. The snow swathed over Pittsburgh like a rumpled silk sheet covering the spires, squares and streets of a vast toy town. A light coating had swept in overnight from Canada giving her a magical white vista from a height of which she had not formerly observed. She had seen many an inevitable Ohioan snowfall; sometimes drifts piled high against buildings, up and around trees, over cars, on rooftops and roadsides in the city, stretching out to the fields and barns in the open countryside. But her typical viewpoint was from her second story window overlooking the front yard from her bedroom as a child. Before now she had never beheld such a massive white span of winter's cold cloth from such a towering height and she found it a beautifully breathtaking omen with which to begin the brand new day.

It was a day of promise for a night of celebration as tonight her younger sister would finally arrive and the three of them would happily be united at last. Faye had left earlier than usual for work as she planned on leaving early so the two of them could go to the airport together. She was to pick up Bea at the condo in the late afternoon and head to the terminal before the five o'clock traffic would throttle the freeway. It was always worse on Friday as everyone wanted out, wanted away, to the bar, to their home, to a getaway or a gathering; somewhere to rest or play and put the week behind them. The plane was due in shortly after seven, but the girls knew they'd be wound up in a very festive mood and planned to enjoy a few drinks in the airport lounge in joyful anticipation of its landing before the three of them were off together to Spazio's for supper. Bea was actually tiring of restaurant food, but was glad to have an occasion to join with Faye in what she knew would be a highly spirited time.

Since returning from Ohio they had spent relatively few hours with each other as Faye had been working overtime and their first night together had been marred by her concern that Bea had offered their father's caretaker too much money. With a note of irritation clearly in her voice she had questioned Bea's judgment on the matter as soon as she came home late from dinner out, waking Bea up from a snooze on the sofa.

"I told you we could only afford so much. I hate it when people ignore what I tell them. Don't you understand I'm in charge of his budget?"

"It's not that much more," responded Bea in defense, unappreciative of the rude awakening. "I couldn't find anyone for the money you were offering and this woman is perfect. She was the best of the lot. She'll be great for Dad."

"Maybe so," countered Faye, "but still he's got other bills and I just wish you'd consulted me before doing this."

"Listen," said Bea, her voice rising with urgency, "I took on this whole thing with no help from you. You were too busy and dropped it in my lap. The money is not the most critical item. Dad's care is. And in fact the increase I offered her is relatively insignificant. What's fifty bucks more a month?" She waited a second for that fact to sink in then followed up quickly with another point, sharpened for emphasis. "I don't think this is about money at all. I think, as usual, you just want the power of decision, of control, in your hands."

Faye scowled at her and tightened her lips in a frown as Bea continued. "And furthermore, I think you should trust my judgment at a time like this. You weren't there. You don't know what this woman or the other ones were like."

Faye put her hands on her hips and glared at her. "How dare you say that? It is not about power, it's about making good decisions, and *I'm* the one who's entrusted with making them. I trusted you all right. I trusted you to work with the figure I gave you. You need to trust me and accept that I mean what I say when I say it."

With that, she turned and stalked off to her bedroom, leaving Bea flooded with resentment and frustration, plus the partial satisfaction that she'd hit Faye where it hurt – with the truth – which was why she had stomped off. She lay on the couch awhile wondering if she should go back to the bedroom and try to make amends. She couldn't help noticing that the bad feelings she felt now were all too reminiscent of those she'd felt as a child in similar confrontations. Although the struggle for Faye was always over power, for Bea it was a matter of being respected, but the most troubling part was the total lack of gratitude. It grated on her mind like sandpaper on cement *…how can she be so damn insensitive…i've busted my butt to make this thing work and she acts like it was nothing…the nerve…*

The next morning Faye had seemed softer in her tone, but if she had any regrets none were forthcoming. She moved more quietly than usual in the kitchen while making coffee and left Bea a note for the first time that week saying she'd try to be home early enough for dinner and had a new café in mind. As it turned out she did make it home earlier than usual and had taken Bea out to a stylish French restaurant. They had dined without incident and the issue of Gabe's caretaker had not been mentioned, but in the back of her mind Bea still felt some irritation. She decided to let it go by the wayside for now unless Faye brought it up again. They both shared a growing sense of excitement over the impending arrival of the baby of the family the next day and that topic dominated their conversation while they ate. As they finished the last of their sugar crusted crème brulee, Bea lifted her glass of Chateuneuf du Pape for a toast.

"To sisterhood," she smiled, "through the good times and bad." Faye seemed to wince slightly at the subtle inference that all was not good, but raised her chardonnay for a celebratory clink and repeated the sentiment as she squeezed out a smile.

"To sisterhood," she nodded, and downed the rest of her yellowish wine with a gulp.

As Bea stood on the balcony overlooking the city, she was reviewing the events of the previous two days. It appeared she was right that her relationship with Faye was going to be difficult to forge into a closer one. They had certainly had their moments of closeness or at least fun, but when push came to shove Faye still wanted her own way, still wanted to be the boss, and that wasn't going to do. They were both big girls now and Bea wanted her respect. For the time being her hopes lay in the thought, stronger than ever, that the intimacy she wanted, a true sisterhood, would have to start first with her younger one, tonight. She sighed in a mix of resignation and anticipation and placed her hands on the frozen rail in front of her. The frost-covered bar sent a chill through her spine and she shivered then turned back indoors to the living room warmth.

Looking about the room she felt a sense of exhilaration growing with the thought of Polly's impending arrival. She spied the picture of their family on the cabinet, barely noticeable behind the larger one of Faye at her gala. She picked it up and examined it, then placed in front of the other one...*tonight's a family night*...Suddenly she knew that she wanted to fill the room with a party atmosphere. They'd have their own gala. Her mind whirred vibrantly with instant merrymaking possibilities; crepe paper, candles, champagne, a great meal. Why go to a restaurant when this place was so beautiful? No restaurant in town had such a magnificent view. She'd make them the very best Fettuccini Alfredo that they'd ever known...*who needs spazio's*...

She grabbed a pad and made a quick list, then called a cab to get to the store, feeling uplifted with each passing moment at the pleasant prospect lying before her. No matter that Faye was a challenge to connect with. She'd start with the youngest and work her way up. Nothing nor no one could possibly cast the slightest shadow upon this imminently brightest of moments. When she returned from shopping the phone rang in the kitchen just as she closed the front door behind her. Setting her packages on the dining room table she decided to grab it in case it was either one of her sisters.

"Hello?"

"Faye?"

"No, this is Bea."

"Oh, you sound just like her. I knew you were in town."

"Who's this?"

"This is David."

"Her boyfriend?"

"Well," he laughed, "I don't know if she'd call it that. But I am her current steady date. I think she would admit to that."

Bea laughed in response to his self-deprecating humor. "I think you aren't giving yourself enough credit."

"Well, that's good to hear. I hope that you're right. Are you enjoying your visit? I know you've been here all week."

"Why yes, it's been great. For the most part anyway."

"Only for the most part?" he joked. "Don't you like it here?"

"Oh sure, I like it fine. I just mean there's been things to do besides sightsee and play with my sister that I hadn't anticipated."

"Oh," he said, sounding curious but uncertain if he should inquire further.

"I had to go to Ohio to help out my father."

"I see," said David, with some hesitation. "Is he doing alright?"

"Well, I guess, yes and no. He is getting older." Bea paused, then offered by way of explanation, "I had to go there to hire a caretaker for him."

"Oh, I see. Yes, Faye mentioned she was seeking one. So you found one okay?"

"Yep. It all worked out well."

"Great. Well, welcome to Pittsburgh."

"Thank you. I like it."

"Yeah, it's a nice town." David cleared his throat. "Is your other sister in yet?"

"No, she arrives tonight."

"Oh, I bet you're all excited."

"Oh yeah. In fact I was just out buying some things to spruce up the place for our reunion tonight. I just came in as the phone was ringing."

"Ah, okay. Well, I was just calling to leave Faye a message. I rarely call her at work because she's always so busy."

"Oh, would you like for me to give her a message?"

"Well yeah, if you would, just tell her I was able to get those Super Bowl tickets."

"The Super Bowl? Wow! That sounds exciting."

"Yeah, well, you know Faye, always wanting to party at the biggest one around."

"Yep," Bea laughed. "I know Faye."

"Okay, well thanks. I'll let you get on with your reunion preparations."

"Well thank you, and it was nice to have met you. Do you think you might be coming around while I'm here?"

"Oh, I don't know." His voice sounded wan. "Maybe, if she wants. She'll call me if she does. She told me she wanted this time alone with you two."

"Oh," said Bea, wondering if she had introduced a sensitive topic. "Well, I hope we get to meet sometime in the future."

"Yes, I'd like that too. You do sound just like her. And I'd like to talk with someone who's known her for as long as you have."

"Oh yes," chuckled Bea, uncertain what he meant. "The stories I could tell."

"I hope I'd want to hear them," he laughed back nervously. "Well, nice talking to you."

"Same here."

"Enjoy your stay."

"Thanks."

"Bye."

"Bye."

As she hung up the phone she felt a subtle twinge of sadness...*he seems like a nice guy... hope she's nice to him*...Her reflection was forgotten as she returned to the sacks of goodies on the table. Feeling submerged in the delight of decorating the condo for the evening, she began tacking crepe paper trails to the walls of the dining area out to the larger living space, connecting the rooms with red and white streamers in lavish gaiety for a feast with a flourish. Unloading the groceries, she lay the champagne down in the refrigerator, set the pasta on the counter and opened a dusty green bottle of Bordeaux. She had bought an old vintage, spending more than she usually would, and the merchant had said to give it several hours to breathe. On spotting a crystal decanter on a cabinet shelf, she took a little sip before pouring the wine in it, solely in the interests of quality control, and rubbed her lips together in warm satisfaction...*mmmm...seems promising...*

Searching the cupboards and drawers for holders, the setting was completed as she set out tall candles, tapered and matching the crepe paper colors. At home she had strung twinkle lights in the crease where the walls met the ceiling for an enchanting effect at night in the sunroom overlooking the lake. But she doubted that Faye would appreciate such a measure. Her rooms must reflect the right look, the proper touch, the current trend. Bright twinkle lights might not quite cut fashion muster with Vogue or Vanity Fair, and were anyway too expensive for a simple one-night stand. They'd settle for crepe paper and candles tonight. Such decorative highlights in Faye's snazzy interior might seem a bit garish for her snobbish taste but they were mercifully temporary and easily removed when the party was over. Unlikely she'd resent the homey if intrusive bright style of a good old-fashioned get-together for some gals from Ohio; at least for a night – the night of all nights.

Wondering at the time she glanced at the clock on the stove – four o'clock...*might as well start getting ready*...As she headed to the bathroom to wash up and change clothes, the kitchen phone rang again and she ran back to get it.

"Hello."

"Hello, Bea. Listen. I'm sorry but it doesn't look like I'll be able to get away from the office in time for the airport."

"What? Are you kidding? We had this all planned."

"I know. I'm sorry, but something's come up. The mayor is calling a meeting of department heads and he'll expect me to be there."

"Oh jeez! I can't believe it. Are you sure you can't leave?"

"Yes. I think it wouldn't be wise to do so. At least not for awhile."

"Oh man," said Bea, feeling stunned with disappointment. "I can't believe it, " she repeated. "Polly will be so disappointed."

"I know, but she'll get over it. You're going to be there,"

"It's not the same thing as having us both. And how am I supposed to get there? Take a taxi, I suppose?"

"I guess so. That's probably the best thing to do. It's too late now to get the car to you. Just come over to Spazio's after you get her and I'll meet you both at eight."

"I'm sick of restaurants. I bought some great food. I was going to make us a nice dinner for a change."

"Oh. Okay." Faye sounded taken aback. "If you're sure you want to cook."

"Some of us like cooking," said Bea with a noticeable trace of sarcasm.

"Okay. Well, whatever. I'll be home by eight, or shortly thereafter. Really. I promise. I'll tell them I have to. By then we'll have had time to go over the important stuff."

"All right," sighed Bea in exasperation. "I hope that you mean it. I've got a great wine, champagne, candles."

"Candles?"

"Candles. And crepe paper too. I've gussied up the joint. We're going to have a party. A reunion. Remember? You invited us to one."

"I know. I'm sorry. It sounds great. It really does. But there's nothing I can do. But I'll be there for dinner. I promise – by eight. Count on it."

Chapter 45

"A lake is the landscape's most beautiful and expressive feature. It is earth's eye;
looking into which the beholder measures the depth of his own nature."
(Walden, Henry David Thoreau)

THE SUN STREAMED THROUGH a wrinkled seam in the fading lilac clouds of dawn like a flashlight in fog as it peered over the hills. It spilled onto the thick solemn mist covering the lake like a weighty woolen blanket buffering night's receding chill. All remnants of the snow had vanished, leaving no traces but damp stains in the shadows. Gray vapors wafted upwards curling gently into the morning air and obstructing the view of homes across the water before gracefully disappearing into the disguise of day. Jay in his robe held his hot coffee cup tightly to his chest as he surveyed the scene from the sunroom, noting the sharp contrast between the vermilion cumulus clusters and the insistent arc of piercing light on the rise. The steam of the coffee left a light film on his glasses and he removed them momentarily to clean them with his robe and rub the sleepiness from his eyes.

A few minutes earlier, before the sun had shone, he had been in meditation, hoping, groping, for some peace and guidance, preferably from a voice, the Holy Spirit or his Guide. It had become his latest preoccupation when meditating, which he tried to do daily. In the silence he could hear the sounds of Phil sleeping softly in his bedroom plus the birds outside excitedly announcing the break of day, but no celestial voice had as of yet entered his head. Feeling a growing mixture of disgust and disappointment he thought of Paul

Newman's character in the movie *Cool Hand Luke* when he had yelled aloud to God to make his presence known or strike him dead. "Just standin' here in the rain talkin' to myself," he had muttered in disdain and Jay was starting to appreciate the sentiment…*don't go there, idiot…this isn't the movies …patience, patience, patience God damn it…*

He sniffed humorously in recognition of his ridiculous thought processes – impatiently demanding patience, pressing for blessing through damnation – and sipped more coffee as he saw the sun become a brass ring, melting the rest of the mist on the lake into invisible ether; new clouds in the making. Watching the lavender heaps on the horizon transformed by the light into pinkish puffs balls he took a deep breath and tried to think positively. Things were improving in some ways for sure. He'd had a rush of money, a flush of success, though in business not counseling and there was the rub. The money had come in. The money was going out.

More of it would come, if Leroy were to be believed, and Bea was making plenty. Although there was pleasure in relieving the pressure of bills to be paid and achieving success in an entirely new discipline, he still felt lingering dissatisfaction on a much deeper level in turning away from his life's work and dream. If this was a period where he'd rediscover God and then return to the task he'd always felt made for – the healing of humankind – then he was ready for the turnaround to start.

Because it seemed impossible to do it at present, since he'd boxed himself in by scorning managed care, it appeared that only a miracle would suffice to bring him enough clients to eke out a living as a therapist again. And as everyone knew miracles only emanated from God, he was hell bent for the Lord with no time to waste. From speaking with Leroy and rereading *A Course in Miracles* it was becoming clear to him that meditation was the best avenue to spiritual awareness; the fast track to awakening, wherein every moment was communion with the Creator as creation rolled on, revealing his unique part in it to him each instant. He watched the sun burn off the last smear of smoky haze lying on the lake, its light extending out like an accordion spreading open over the pale face of the water, tinting the treetops on the far shore a bright green as it streaked toward Jay's cold embankment.

Though today was another one set aside for counseling, he wanted to put the finishing touches on a business idea that had emerged in the basement office yesterday. He had discovered through literature mailed to Bea's company that a convention of college administrators who worked exclusively with foreign students was being held in San Francisco in January. It seemed to him the perfect venue to market his program of placing students in homes for the holidays on a national scale. With the advent of his current venture well established on a local level, he hoped to translate the same model into successful programs with more out of state colleges. He was making enough money now to afford the airfare and the lodging for the weeklong convention. Thinking to pleasantly surprise his wife with the impressive scope of his marketing savvy, he was considering making the arrangements alone without her knowledge or consultation. It was a bit of a risk but his confidence had grown in his ability to make sound business judgments, especially lately as he had been functioning without her. Aside from that, he'd like to travel himself and San Francisco was beautiful place to visit.

Refilling his mug he ambled down to the basement and found the application forms to fill out for the affair. Through the window above his desk he looked out at the long leafless tendrils of the willow trees below, bent like thin bony claws curling in the meager warmth of winter's stark light. The clouds that had billowed about the sun when it rose had dissipated into fluffy gray ruffles rolling across the eastern sky as though upon a ribbon. Even in the barren sterility of December the lake exuded a serenity and fascination for him like nowhere he'd ever been. Not the ocean, not a river, nor a waterfall would do it in the way that the lake always left him enchanted. He felt a softening in his heart as he gazed at the water rippling by and suddenly realized he was missing Bea. It had been too many weeks of her absent and away; working without her, parenting alone, no one to share the elaborate meals he once made.

Cooking for Phil was an entirely different story, as he had no use for fancy pasta or appetizers, preferring a platter of hamburgers and fries. And cooking for himself had curtailed his appetite for nouveau cuisine and elegant wines. He ate less and drank less when left to his own company and looked forward to the times when they would wine and dine together again.

A lone crow flew over the willows croaking as it landed in the huge cedar to his right and the sound pulled him back to the paper task at hand. Quickly he completed the form for attendance, stuffed it in the large brown envelope and sealed it, then addressed it and ran it through the postage machine. He bounded upstairs, feeling the effects of the coffee plus the encroaching press of time, and slipped into the shower to get ready for the day. After trimming his short beard and dressing for the office, he woke Phil up and made breakfast for the both of them while the lad got ready for school. There was one final thing he wanted to do before leaving; make reservations for himself tonight at the new jazz club. He located the number in the phone book, placed the call, and listened to the recording, then left a message as instructed…*no point in sitting around home feeling lonely…bea's having fun tonight…*

After eating a silent and fast meal at the counter with Phil, they sped off to school accompanied by the usual gyrations and grunts of the hip hop generation; a loathsome indulgence he still allowed his intrepid teen. On the way back from there he punched out the CD and replaced it with a tape of his latest talk with Leroy.

"Hi Leroy, it's Jay."

"Hello, how are you doing?"

"Well, in one sense I'm fine. I'm making money through the student-exchange business and though it's already gone, the promise of more seems likely."

"Good."

"Yeah, well, I guess that's good, but frankly I'd rather be doing therapy for a living and I still feel frustrated about that."

"I see."

"I'm questioning why I'm not receiving many new clients. I mean, I think that I desire them and I express that in my meditations. So I don't understand why I'm not getting them, if this stuff really works, unless somehow it's operating on a timetable unbeknownst to me or there's some other factor that's going on like I'm so impatient it's a form of demand that's getting in the way or I wonder if God's just trying to teach me patience. If so I wish to hell he'd hurry up about it. Just kidding. It does make me wonder how much we influence what is going on and how much is just being done to us that we cannot influence."

"Where do you feel pressure right now as you're asking the question?"

"All over really; in my heart, my back, my shoulders, everywhere. I feel disappointment, sadness, frustration, tension in my body."

"Right, you see, what's underlying this is the assertion that something has caused the body to lose its integrity. And where you have to go with this is to the true remedy, which is to ask for those areas to be restored to their integrity or allow your perception to be clarified that they are whole and not subject to this tension; this subtle violation of your integrity."

"So my body's not subject to it?"

"Right, that's conditioning there, felt in your body. Those points of discomfort are conditioning and nothing more."

"Hm. I don't get that."

"Well, you see, if you jab at a one celled organism, an amoeba for example, it springs back a lot and then finally it stays contracted. It's been conditioned. It now relates to conditions, where before it related to the truth, it's divine nature."

"Oh, I see what you mean. It's frightened. Hm."

"Right. So when you ask a question why something hasn't happened and you are bothered by it – if you're bothered by anything - "

"I'm bothered by a lot of things."

"Right. Then there is an experience of your conditioning at work."

"Hm. I never thought of it that way."

"Right. So it's important to see that the content of your bother isn't as important as how it affects you, how it feels, what it feels like in your body."

"Hm."

"So if you will spend some time thinking 'I want to get clear of that sensitivity or tension in my body', pretty soon you'll get to the point where you recognize that you have zones or areas in the body where you chronically flare up when conditions are a certain way."

"You mean like when people talk about getting their buttons pushed?"

"Yes, but you'll recognize it less as emotion, and more as your bodily feelings. And when you can do that, you're getting close to working it out."

"Interesting. That means you are withdrawing from the thought and just noticing the sensation?"

"Exactly. You're recognizing that the discomfort is what it is and it doesn't really have to connect to circumstances. If you are connecting it to circumstances, then you're still in the human game, or the world of the ego."

"Hm. It seems like when we talk that things take a little different shift as to what I'm to do next and now I feel like you're saying pay attention to your body."

"Oh absolutely. There's nothing more important to waking up than the body."

"Really? I would have never thought that."

"Yes, because ultimately we are talking about what you are feeling, which you do in your body, and you are getting closer to being able to recognize your sore spots. And your sore spots can be remedied. See, if you were in the middle of a situation where something undesirable was happening – let's just say that not getting more clients is undesirable – and you were bothered by it, and suddenly you allowed your body to be restored to it's integrity, you wouldn't be bothered by it."

"Really?"

"Yes, you'd be feeling fine; peaceful, happy, no negative feelings in your body. You could then say, 'Oh well, God's will be done', you see? And then what happens is – if it's appropriate for you, and when it is – clients will show up. Or whatever God's will for you is will happen."

"Hm. Do you mean that the thought incites the feeling and the feeling in turn incites the thought?"

"Say that again?"

"Do you mean that the thought of lack, for example, incites feelings of fear which are felt in the body as tension or discomfort, and that the remedy is to choose to feel at peace, for example, and as that feeling is felt in the body, the thought that things are okay is restored to the mind?"

"Yes, exactly."

"Well then, I understand the importance of paying attention to the feeling, but it seems that a more root awareness would be to pay attention to the thought at its inception."

"You ought to be able to reflect on anything without it making you feel uncomfortable."

"Oh, that's your point?"

"Yes. You ought to be able to reflect on anything without becoming edgy or squeamish or upset in your body."

"So you start to find truth more in your body sense than in concepts?"

"Absolutely. It's the body that's becoming transformed."

"You mean I just say 'Well I don't know what the hell to think but I'm feeling good'?"

"Right, because it is your body that's becoming transformed and your body includes everything, all the form around you."

"I do not understand that. Can you elaborate? Do you mean a body of thought or a body of feeling?"

"It's a body of substance, the whole of creation, all of which comprises the expression of divine meaning. As you undertake the transformation of your self into an awakened being, you begin to experience the transformation of your body, in the way that I was saying. By disconnecting the tensions from the circumstances, you recognize that your body is just not your form, but is connected to everything, because you are no longer separating your self from the whole. And as you notice improvements in the way you look and the way you feel, you'll notice improvements in other things as well. Your life becomes easier and more agreeable. You understand?"

"Well, not exactly. Maybe if I listen to the tape a few times I will."

"Well, let me try it a different way. You see, when Jesus said 'As you do it to the least of these, you do it to me', he wasn't just saying it to discourage people from bullying the weaklings, but actually he was stating the truth that he did not know the distinction. Everyone is connected through the unity of consciousness. It is all the mind or creation of God. And I can tell you that as anyone approaches awakening and they see improvement in the body they are going to notice improvements in all aspects of their life. All form becomes more harmonious and integrated, not just your body, but including your body. A lot of people think that they can become enlightened and be sickly, but that is not true."

"Huh. That reminds me of a line from the Course when he says 'To heal is to make whole'."

"Right. You realize, as you awaken, or heal yourself – restore your wholeness – that you are connected to the whole of everyone and everything as well."

"Hm."

"So as you spend some time in regenerating your body, in the way I referred to, disconnecting the conditioning, be aware that that transformation includes everything around you – all the things you think you're stuck with, all the snags you think you're caught with in your life – and that by allowing the regeneration of your body you are going past those snags."

"Hm. Is trust still the key element?"

"It's the only thing that's going to make you sane, in your position."

"Well, I find myself wondering who's trusting who."

"You're trusting you. And you don't have to know what that means."

"Well, I don't."

"Right. You don't know what it means. And all you have to do is listen."

"And who am I listening to, me?"

"Yes, but you are listening to the part of you that is unfathomable, that is connected to the whole of Divine Creation, and can only be experienced as revelation, not as thought out information."

"Hm. Well, I still must be thinking way too much and reacting more than I realize, because the part of me that wants to access that unfathomable part just feels disappointed at getting no response most the time."

"Right, and the moment that you find yourself going into disappointment you need to back out of it. You see, it is unintelligent but quite understandable to take a position of disappointment. It's one thing to feel it in the moment and then recognize the discomfort of it and to move beyond it. To stay in disappointment is exactly what the ego has in mind as a diversion for you to keep you from moving on to awakening."

"Hm. So is anything in the realm of thought merely ego?"

"Nearly ego?"

"Pardon?"

"I'm trying to I understand your question."

"Uh, it seems to me that you're saying that once you sense you're in disappointment, or a negative place, just move into a good feeling place. Now earlier I would have thought 'Okay, that means I need to counter the negative with a positive thought'. Now it seems like you're saying 'No, just feel good'."

"Right. I would rather that you ask just to feel good and recognize that it doesn't matter what you think."

"Right, I got that. And so then I wondered is that because what one thinks is merely always coming from the ego state of mind. So I said is it merely ego?"

"Oh, I see what you're saying."

"Because if that's true, I'm going to stop thinking."

"Well, do that anyway. But I want to get clear on this answer… just a moment………. okay. Any mental process that is going on while in the belief of private consciousness would be called thinking. If you think – if you think – if you believe that your consciousness is a private area and exclusive territory, and you happen to be reflecting on things from that perspective, that's called thinking. When you are connected or awake, and aware of the infinitude of consciousness and the commonality and sharing of consciousness that really exists, what you do then is not think but instead you listen and reflect.

"So, thinking is a word that describes a distortion of listening and reflection that occurs when there is a misunderstanding about what consciousness is. Remember I said that therapists as a rule don't know the first thing about consciousness. And when you skip that first step, then you are engaging in thinking, and it's based on the assumption that consciousness is going on privately in individual organisms. So that's ego. It's not that you give up being alert or being discerning or learning or cognizant. It's that you just know how it is. You know the score. Whereas people who think, and don't know the score, are still unenlightened. The problem with society or the people who are running things and earnestly trying to make things better, is that they don't know the score."

"Maybe that's why things seem to always be getting worse; more government, more problems."

"Right."

"Okay then, well, using that definition of thinking that you just gave me, could we call that neurotic?"

"Would I call it neurotic?"

"Yeah. I'm always thinking that most people are 'normal neurotics' and if I want to define that in full depth, it seems to me that I would have to go as deep as you just did, meaning most of us are not aware of our full state of mind, which is God."

"Well, I would say an accurate definition of neuroses would be the kind of conditioning of the nervous system that makes one feel the kind of discomfort we've been speaking of, in the body. So everyone's neurotic in that sense that they have acquired an impairment in their nervous system, which is then in effect, connecting the thought with the feeling. That is what it means to be neurotic"

"Great. So you're saying 'Drop thoughts, be aware of your feelings, and accept nothing less than feeling whole and at peace'."

"Yes, but when I say drop thoughts, I mean just sever the connection between the thought and the feeling in your body, and ask for help with the feeling."

"I see."

"As I said, you ought to be able think anything without any discomfort."

"Is that what you mean by reflecting?"

"Yes, exactly. Ideas are still going to be there. It isn't as though there's a big blank all of a sudden. There are still, for example, punch lines that are delightful."

"So in effect you are asking me to disconnect myself from the neurotic state."

"Exactly. You have it."

"Okay. Good. Well, I've another issue, unrelated to the previous one – well maybe not. But anyway, every year we typically give a New Year's party. And this year's the same thing, but it is in one way different, because before I used to love providing live music entertainment with my band, but now that we've broken up, I only make music by myself, with my synthesizer or guitar, mostly making recordings, and I feel too shy about it to try to entertain the crowd. A band's much louder and easy to be anonymous in. And I'm not too good at chitchat, so I really don't enjoy parties too much. So…I wonder if you have any perspectives about that."

"About whether or not you should play?"

"More about just feeling good or comfortable at the party. I'm concerned I'll feel uncomfortable there. I usually do at parties. I don't like to, but to me they usually seem kind of meaningless and I have a hard time hiding it, but I'm not very interested. I mean I love making music or even watching another group but most people don't have live music and often they don't even think to play some on the stereo. And I enjoy cooking and serving people great food and wine, to a lesser extent, but my experience is that most people don't have great food and wine at parties, at least according to my tastes, being a vegetarian and a wine snob, I guess. Anyway, this one's at our house, and we give a lot of parties, living on the lake and all, and I'll have great food and wine, but since I'm not making music I think I'll just be pretty bored with what seems like a bunch of superficial chatter."

"Consider not going."

"It's at my house."

"Yeah, well just consider spending time in quiet."

"Gosh, that's funny. I actually had a thought like that. That I could just go downstairs and watch a movie or something and then I thought 'Oh how absurd'."

"You see, you need to have the right to do what you have to do. That's where you're struggling. It's not about whether or not you would enjoy the party. What you are really dealing with is the abridgement of the right to do what's absolutely appropriate for you because of social obligations. If you know you can do what you feel moved to do, then being at the party is not going to be as much of a millstone as it is. It's the selling out of your freedom there based upon the perceived expectations of others and it would be good practice for you here to take a stand for your comfort and recognize that as soon as you're comfortable you can bop in and out. It's not going to be difficult."

"Thanks, ha ha, great answer. Sometimes I get caught up in thinking that I'm crippled somehow in that I'm not appropriately sociable in gatherings like this. Bea thinks is just because I've done so much therapy with people that I don't enjoy what I call chitchat and that I just want to get to a deeper level with people's thoughts and feelings."

"But it's just a game though, Jay, like square dancing. If you could do it because it was an interesting game wherein nothing more was called for than just allowing your self to be spontaneous and be you in those situations, you'd be fine. You see the real issue here for you is self-consciousness. And self-consciousness is one of the consequences of loss of innocence. You see, all problems are born of that, starting with Adam and Eve – 'Oh my, we're naked, we didn't realize that before because we felt whole'. So it's important for you to do what you feel moved to do innocently."

"Well, how do you do that? I mean I'm aware of feeling self-conscious and this does relate to what we started with today but…"

"Well, you just basically surrender to it. And it's important to recognize that your comfort is important."

"It's like I shouldn't give a care about what others are thinking then, because I tend to operate with feelers out to others' reactions."

"Right. It's about making being comfortable more important than being sensitive."

"Ah. Got it. Thank you. That feels good."

"Absolutely. I talk to people who are very smart, just as sharp as can be, and very sensitive, and are not quick enough sometimes to recognize the need not to be sensitive, but just to be who you are, maybe even be obnoxious. (laughter) And you do this by listening."

"Listening to your deeper self?"

"Right. It's not that I decide to be laid back or be firm with someone on the basis of thinking. I just know it from listening, from paying attention to my inner self."

"Okay, well that brings me to another thought. I was imagining what it might be like to withdraw from being concerned about what others might be expecting of me at a party, and if I were to put more emphasis on just being comfortable, in tune with myself, do you also feel a sense of oneness with someone in the spiritual world or do you just feel alone in a physical body but relaxed?"

"You feel the kind of lack of inhibition you would feel if you were drinking, but without any kind of distortion that accompanies that."

"Hm. But you don't feel …um, what I guess I'm saying is that if I don't have feelers out for other people, then I want to feel connected to God or Jesus or the Holy Spirit or my Guide, feel connected to some other body beyond my own sense of individual consciousness."

"Well, if that helps, that's fine. That still means you can have a good time though. Connect with the people. Connect with the divinity of those around you, if not the egos of those around you."

"Thanks. That helps perfectly."

"If you see the divinity of someone and yet their ego is alive and well, you can have an easier time with it. You can get past its lack of awareness and connect with the divinity by coming from that point in yourself, which again, just requires staying comfortable and listening to your self. And then you don't feel any sense of separation from them. I do it all the time in my work with people on the phone."

"Hm. Okay, I'll try it – after I feel comfortable."

"Have you any more questions?"

"Yeah, actually I've got one in relation to the Ph.D. thing. An out of state school I applied to, whose program can be done in this state through their coordinators, called me recently and said 'Hey, you never called this guy – our local northwest coordinator – so it looks like you're not going to get in this semester'. And of course that's kind of funny from one perspective because I did call him and left a message saying 'I'm going to Europe for two weeks so call me soon or when I get back' and he never did call me. It's a local psychologist they've hired to run things here for this school in Santa Barbara. And so I said to her 'No that's a mistake, I did call him, the ball's been in his court, he hasn't called me back'. And she said 'Gee, that's too bad' and sounded surprised and went on to say that I probably wouldn't get in this semester now but should try for the next one, and I'd felt uptight with them before about not just admitting me immediately, but this time I just felt like 'That's okay with me', and I even had to suppress saying 'Frankly I'm not sure I want to get into your program anyway'. So then she'd called back yesterday to say 'Dr. so and so, the northwest coordinator, wants you to give him a call to set up your appointment for an interview'. So I called him yesterday and left a message, since he was out, to call me anytime, and I haven't heard back from him. So I don't know what to make of it all."

"Oh just go with this."

"Well, what helps me go with it is what you said about just allowing it to be easy because I have a lot of bad feelings or concepts around this whole thing so I have to be careful, as you say, not to get in the way of my own good."

"Well, don't resent anything here. You see, it doesn't make any sense to resent being given the opportunity for a Ph.D. Here's the problem though, you don't have much respect for the institution and people involved. And you have an idea that being involved with them and with they having the authority would be a kind of unpleasant, demeaning, dysfunctional experience. And I just want to say not to bother with that idea. Don't allow your bitterness to intrude here, because this situation simply calls for you to be innocent."

"So it's just like practicing what we talked about with people at a party? Just pull back from assessing them and being sensitive to them and just try to relax?"

"Right. Because if you can feel connected and allow them their foibles, and see that they aren't harmful no matter what they're doing, you'll be fine."

"Just connect with their divinity?"

"Right."

"Insist on seeing them as harmless?"

"Yeah, though you might feel the need to tell them to shut up sometimes. (laughter) You see, if you are awake, if you are feeling your integrity and it cannot be violated by anything because you are past having that neurotic experience, then no one's apparent malevolence can do anything to you. So your tendency is to handle it compassionately but firmly. So you might say, for example, 'Shut up'. But understand that if the Christ in someone said shut up that would be it, because the Christ in the other person would feel the genuine authority of it. They would feel the connection."

"So just dare to be yourself, at a party or a Ph.D. program."

"Absolutely."

Chapter 46

"A little while, a moment of rest upon the wind, and another woman shall bear me."
(The last words of The Prophet, by Kahlil Gibran)

As THE CAB SPED swiftly down the freeway toward the airport Bea sat in the back seat, torn between two emotions. She was elated at the emergence of the moment coming nearer when her sister would arrive and their mission would be met. But haunting her euphoria like an itch she couldn't scratch was a sense of irritation mingled in with disappointment that her older sister once again had failed her in some way. Along with feeling miffed that Faye had bailed another time in the face of other pressing matters was a growing overwhelming sense that it might be impossible to ever have her see the problem, let alone find a solution. Mulling through the grim consideration that her sister's self-centeredness might never be negotiated or ever even recognized was giving her some second thoughts about their chances for a closer tie. The prognosis seemed dim. She felt that she now understood better than ever how her niece and nephew felt and wondered if Faye's boyfriend felt the same sad quiet desperation. Perhaps that's why he wanted to talk...*too bad he's been banished...*

She looked out of the window at the stretch of rolling mounds a mile beyond the freeway fraught with snowcapped rooftops, lawns and trees. Underneath a cloudless cobalt sky they mirrored back the sunlight pouring down like golden oil anointing the landscape from a cosmic cistern. She wanted her mind shining true blue now with the clarity of the heavens, sweeping out the feelings that darkened her joy, like a strong wind whisking away black clouds. As she stared up at the atmosphere, absorbing the color, a large passenger airplane appeared on the horizon, making its approach to the airport ahead. It gave her a rush of excitement that flushed out the negative feelings like rain down a gutter and she decided to deal with one sister at a time. This was the moment to deal with youngest.

The cab reached the curb of the baggage claim area and she climbed out from the back seat feeling inspired. On passing through the glass doors she sought out a monitor with flight information to check on the plane's arrival. The board noted that the flight was due to land on time at 7:10 pm. Bea glanced at her watch, which read 6:20…*nearly an hour …time to have a gin and tonic…* She walked down the corridor that led to the gate where her sister would deplane and looked for the nearest bar to kill time. Her excitement was growing and she felt her heart racing, silently pounding with the eager beat of expectancy.

Down the hallway a flashing pink neon sign shaped like a tilted martini glass caught her eye and beckoned with the seductive promise of refreshment. The dark bar was packed with chatty business travelers, mostly men. With neon palm trees alit on the walls, it resembled a shady watering hole in the desert at a hot day's end for a camel caravan of traders. All of the small rounded tables with black vinyl tops were taken, along with the red leatherette booths against the far wall…*just as well I'm alone – no room for faye anyway…*She spied an unoccupied seat at the bar between two men in suits and wound her way there through the talkative throng. An overhead television set blared above her, broadcasting a professional tennis match somewhere. Since playing tennis was one of her pastimes, at least when she'd had some time to pass, she looked at the set with a mild sense of interest, grateful that it wasn't football or hockey. As she stepped up to wiggle herself onto the bar stool her snug skirt slid back on her smooth tapered thighs revealing her shapely legs to the guys on each side of her. They glanced down simultaneously in muted admiration while scooting a bit sideways to accommodate her space.

She tugged self-consciously at the hem of her dress while seeking to make eye contact with the bartender at the far end of the bar; a short man with a bald spot in the back of his curly hair. He also soon noticed the blonde woman in a room filled with mostly dark-suited men and winked as he approached her with a wide toothy grin.

"Whatcha' have, sweedee?"

"A gin and tonic please, with a slice of lime."

"Right. Beefeaters okay?"

"Uh, I'd prefer Tanqueray."

"Right."

She focused on the tennis match while awaiting her drink, recollecting what it felt like to be playing on the court. Last year before things had gotten so hectic she was over at the sports club at least twice a week, enjoying doubles and singles with all the other women.

Funny how life had changed suddenly so soon…*and they call it success…whop!* A black woman belted a serve to her opponent, a high-cheeked European.

Clink!

"Der' ya' go."

"Thanks."

"Run ya' a tab?"

"Yes, please."

"'Kay sweedee," he said with a smile and another wink. "Ya' lemme' know when ya' ready for anudder."

"Thanks."

His friendly and informal attention struck a welcome chord within her. She sensed he was appreciating her presence in the bar…*probably glad to see a woman…*He set a bowl of peanuts down in front of her, cocked his head sideways and raised an eyebrow as though taking her in.

"Ya' muz' not be widda' convention."

"What convention?"

"Lawya's convention. Some group o' udder. Dat's who deez guys are."

"Oh, that explains it."

"Whut?"

"Why it's so crowded."

"Right. Flight to Boston's been delayed two awahs, so dey piled in heah 'bout twenty minutes ago. Been talkin' up a stoam eva' since."

"They sure are." She smiled. "That's how they make their money."

"Right." He gave her a wink while wiping off the bar with damp white towel. "Let's jus' hope dey tip big."

"How'd you guess that I'm not with them?"

"He leaned closer toward her, shook his head and then spoke in a confidential tone so as not to be overheard. "Ya' don't look da' type." He grinned and winked again, then threw the cloth under the bar as he turned to respond to a patron down the way. "I heah ya', pal. I heah ya'."

As he walked off she wondered how exactly to take his comment. She figured it was probably meant as a compliment…*don't i look professional…*She took a good look at herself in the mirror behind the bar and brushed her hair to the side with her hand. She had been feeling festive and dressed up for the occasion; gold earrings and necklace to contrast with her black sweater and skirt… *just don't look like a lawya'*…She lifted her icy wet glass off the bar and took a long drink. It felt good going down.

A glance at her watch showed at least thirty minutes yet before she would head off to the gate to meet Polly. She imagined what their initial meeting would be like; all smiles, probably laughter, even giggles as they chattered away endlessly, all the way to the condo. There was so much to catch up on and so much to look forward to. She couldn't wait to show the girls how she had transformed the rooms into a sparkling and sprightly high-rise party palace. Never mind that Faye had missed the chance to unite at the airport. At her home they'd be together like they'd planned from the beginning...*sisters – sisters – sisters...party!* Pop the champagne and let the good times roll with all the wild enthusiasm they'd shown as cheerleaders. She finished off her drink and felt the excitement growing within her.

"Wun' anudda'?" The bartender sidled up and leaned towards her slightly.

"Yes, please."

"Cummin' up."

Though the noisy blather all around her seemed to have increased a notch, she felt anchored on her bar stool in joyful anticipation and not distracted in the least by any of the commotion. She watched the tennis players scrambling back and forth about the court and though she couldn't hear a thing she saw the black gal was ahead. Remembering her own fun competitive matches made her miss the sense of free time that her life no longer allowed. Just last year she'd been more carefree with not only the tennis but also some trail riding on her temperamental horse. Now she was so busy trotting the globe, making big money, pulling off grand deals, that it was starting to feel a touch like a giant treadmill. She needed a break.

Clink!

"Der' ya' go sweedee."

"Thank you."

"Ya' betcha'."

The bartender moved quickly on past her this time. Things were heating up. The hectic activity in the room seemed to parallel her thoughts about her work. It was getting too big. She needed more help. Though Jay was an asset his heart wasn't in it and though she could trust him with the business since he was family, who knew how long he could be counted on to stay there. She needed an assistant, a trusted lieutenant, whom she could send in the field to spare herself the long trips. Candy was handy, at least to a point, but she was needed in the office to run the computers, and besides she couldn't leave her two children to travel. She pondered for a moment her dilemma and decided perhaps she could advertise on her return. It had worked for her father and Faye believed in it. She'd had a highly successful career as an executive in magazine advertising before landing this latest job with the mayor.

Bea took a small sip so as to bide her time...*no point in getting too tipsy before the party starts*...Her watch indicated that a good twenty minutes must pass before it would be time to leave. A slight swell of joy swooned again in her heart as she envisioned their meeting as Polly disembarked...*less than twenty more minutes...yahoo!*...She munched on some peanuts and looked up at the tube when it suddenly hit her...*i've got it!...of course!...right in front of my nose*...She stopped chewing for a moment and paused in her delight...*polly can be my assistant!...she's nearby, she needs money, she likes to travel...and she's family!*...A smile slowly widened on her face as she considered her idea. It had that good feeling that her best ideas did. She took another sip – this time a larger one – and thought through the pros and cons of the possibility. With no children to leave behind, no careers yet carved out, no commitments existed to keep her from the job. It could be a godsend to both of them at the same time…*i'll just have to train her…that's easy…do it all the time…*

Feeling pleased with herself for discovering such a perfect solution, she started to imagine the details of it all. She pictured them both in the office at the lakeside with the work as a vehicle to bring them together. They could take turns traveling whenever it was called for. That would give her more time at home for family and fun. And not only that but the work would be more enjoyable. They could get rich together; a dream come true. She finished her gin, leaving cash on the bar with a nice hefty tip, and decided to go to the gate a bit early. A few minutes to seven she strolled down the corridor, light-hearted, light-footed, and lifted by her spirits like a box kite rising in a warm summer breeze as she relished the pleasure of sharing the prospect of unexpected glad tidings with her long lost little sister…*i'll tell her tonight…oh God she's gonna' love this…*

At precisely the same time a pilot in the aircraft returning from Cleveland radioed the tower to clear his descent.

6:56:57 pm US Air: Approach US Air 427 is descending to ten.

6:57:19 pm Tower: US Air 427 Pittsburgh approach heading one-six-zero vector ILS runway two-eight right. Final approach course speed two-one-zero.

6:57:27 pm US Air: We're coming back to two-ten and uh one-sixty heading down to ten thousand.

6:58:31 pm Tower: US Air 427 descend and maintain six thousand.

6:58:34 pm USAir: Cleared to six USA 427.

7:00:14 pm Tower: US Air 427 turn left heading one-four-zero reduce speed to one-niner- zero.

7:00:19 pm US Air: Okay one-four-zero heading and one-ninety on the speed US Air 427.

7:01:03 pm US Air: Did you say two-eight left for US Air 427?

7:01:06 pm Tower: Ah, US Air 427 it will be two-eight right.

7:01:08 pm US Air: Two-eight right, thank you.

7:02:22 pm Tower: US Air 427 turn left heading one-zero-zero. Traffic will be one to two o'clock six miles northbound Jet stream climbing out of thirty-three for five-thousand.

7:02:32 pm US Air: We're looking for the traffic turning to one-zero-zero US Air 427.

7:03:10 pm US Air: Oh (unintelligible) Oh God.

7:03:14 pm Tower: US Air 427 maintain six thousand over.

7:03:16 pm US Air: (unintelligible) traffic emergency (unintelligible) oh shit ahhh (unintelligible) ahhh ahhh ahhh

7:03:24 pm Tower: US Air 427 Pittsburgh.

7:03:30 pm Tower: US Air 427 Pittsburgh.
7:03:47 pm Tower: US Air 427 Pittsburgh.
7:04:09 pm Tower: US Air 427 Pittsburgh.
7:04:38 pm Tower: US Air 427 radar contact lost.

Chapter 47

*"Write as if you were dying. At the same time, assume you write for an audience
consisting solely of terminal patients. This, after all, is the case. What would you
begin writing if you knew you would die soon?"* (*The Writing Life*, Anne Dillard)

JAY UPENDED THE BOTTLE and sucked down a long slow satisfying swig of a lime-flavored
Corona as he stood on his deck trying to wash away the daily cares of the weary
world of work from his shoulders. He'd just finished showering after a thirty-minute
jog and was feeling the high that comes from long distance running. Between that and
the beer plus the beauty of the lake, surrounded by fresh budding bushes and trees in
the magic of early spring, he was beginning to relax. With Phil at soccer practice and
Bea below in the basement, he was alone with his thoughts overlooking the willows just
starting to sprout on spindly tendrils that arched down to the lakeside, like dangling
daddy longlegs.

As he surveyed the water reflectively, noting the mirror image of trees and rooftops
pointing towards him from the other side, he suddenly he felt moved to write in his journal.
He went back to retrieve it from the desk in the corner of his bedroom and brought it
outside to write on the deck. Although it was slightly chilly he was flushed with warmth
from jogging and the alcohol was starting to add a light but discernible glow. He sat down
on the wooden bench of the picnic table facing the lake and opened the journal to his last
entry...hmmm...*haven't done this since september...*

3/15 I haven't written to myself in six months but so much has happened I now feel moved to do so. My practice is still running at a low level but I have been so busy with other work it seems I hardly have time for it anyway. The Ph.D. option is no longer available. I could pursue it but missed the first semester's admission and actually feel relieved. Instead I started working for Bea's student exchange company in the fall and have assumed portions of it that I essentially run alone. In one sense it's been fascinating to do something so different and succeed with it so quickly. Though rewarding financially, and personally in another sense, it lacks the heartfelt satisfaction and intellectual stimulation of counseling. In the business I now run two kinds of nationwide programs. One for colleges who want Homestays for their foreign students during winter and spring break and one for college kids who come over here individually for a few weeks in spring or summer to learn English with a tutor while staying with a Host family.

Since the end of the year, after the winter break program, we have been busy marketing to other countries in the hopes of expanding. In January I went alone to San Francisco to represent the company at a student exchange convention of international agents and national college reps involved with Homestays. I was able to expand our network through new business. More colleges and countries are interested in Homestays so the timing and position of Bea's business is excellent. Not only now will my summer programs expand, but Bea will have more high school groups then too. Last year we mainly lived off her summer groups, which was tight, but with the influx of my work our finances are better. It has been a roller coaster ride in more ways than one. At summer's end there was enough money to coast through fall, then my Christmas program tied us over till now. My spring work will cover summer and the cycle continues. Bea needs a lot of money to keep her company going so I still haven't caught up on all of my debts. Her copy machine alone is over $600/mo, plus the fax, phones, supplies, postage, Candy, program costs, teacher pay, family pay, a nationwide network of coordinators, etc

He paused for a moment, reread his entry, then looked out at the lake scene...*what else to say...*

A V-shaped horde of Canadian honkers sailed in high over the water, veering around and splashing down to the right at the far end of the lake by the large layered spread of lime-green lily pads. The wind chimes hanging from the glass roof on the deck clanged lightly in the gentle breeze picking up from the north. He felt the coolness brush his forehead and cheeks as he chugged down the last of the icy beer. Still his body burned hot like a furnace from the run and the drink felt like fuel to the fire. In the middle of the lake he saw concentric rings welling out in the water where a fish had jumped up to snatch an unsuspecting insect. The sky was a pale blue topaz canvas with the pointed tops of pines arrayed against it on the far bank. A smattering of small birds, at least fifty, burst out suddenly from the distant trees as though shot from a cannon. They flitted about over the lake in all directions at once as though lost, before careening out of sight in an instant of orchestrated chaos. He looked down at his open book and resumed writing.

She has no idea how in debt I still am. From January on I've sent new proposals to many nations hoping to get other business than Japanese for spring. So far Spain and France have indicated an interest. I hope to have confirmations soon. Meantime I wonder or worry about money flow. I am scheduled to go to California again; this time to extend our Host family network into LA, San Diego and San Francisco. On the home front my efforts to revive my practice through meditation and enlightenment have shown poor results. I can't help but wonder if it's all just a fraud, if I'm way too impatient, or if I am simply not doing it right. It's hard to be at peace when I'm galloping through the day with extensive business matters racking my mind. In the mornings I feel pressured to keep my meditations short and at night I'm so exhausted I just want to relax. One bright light that's brought some fun into my life is the discovery of a local jazz club. If Bea and I could get there more often it could easily become that special place for just the two of us.

Another bright spot has been to have Jess back from college, though we don't see him much. Marriage and work seem to take up his time. Bea's been gone a lot too this year. In late January she went back to Toronto to hire and train a new Area Director. In February she went to Japan for a week. At least both trips appear to have been successful, as we feel driven by the race for the almighty dollar. Our relationship suffers from the time apart as she travels about. I believe Phil misses her and she him too. She seems more emotionally withdrawn than last year, no doubt from the endless demands of her work, but probably especially from the death of her sister. In December a plane crash near Pittsburgh brought a terrible end to their reunion at Faye's. I don't think she has had the time to fully grieve. I'm sure another loss of a different nature, the ten thousand dollars embezzled by Perry, has also weighed on her. Though she says she hasn't given up, she hasn't had the time or the heart to aggressively pursue the matter.

He felt the tension tightening in his stomach as he wrote those last words...*that bastard...* He took a deep breath, sighed and stretched his shoulders back in an effort to release the tension threatening to return. He had tried at times to intervene in Toronto on Bea's behalf but the distance between the cities and the division between the countries had made it difficult. Even with Leroy's single-minded insistence that they continue to pursue it, the ensuing complications had made it unfeasible. Though neither she nor Jay would call it quits, it looked like Perry might well get away with it. Jay only hoped he was suffering from guilt, but had periodic fantasies of making him suffer far worse... *someday...*

The grandfather clock in the living room chimed six bells, indicating it was time to go pick up Phil. He closed the book, went back to his bedroom and put it away in the lower desk drawer. On closing the front door on his way to the Mercedes he noticed the evening sky was darkening. The temperature was dropping with moisture in the air and he turned on the heat as soon as the car started. As was customary now, whenever driving alone anywhere, he rummaged through the glove compartment for a tape from Leroy. Though some of their talks had not been recorded, usually because Leroy had run out of tapes, the majority had been and Jay listened to them often. The most recent ones were in the house to hear when jogging, so he chose one from early January and slipped it in the slot. He recalled it reflected his growing despair and impatience.

"And how are you today?"

"Oh, about the same, I guess. On one hand there's enough money at the moment because we're still cruising on the Christmas program, and on the other, I'm concerned about what we'll do when that runs out if my practice doesn't pick up. Also Bea is still sad of course over her sister's death, and that's somewhat of a heavy shadow in the background. But I already talked to you about that."

"Right."

"You didn't tape that call did you?"

"No, it was so sudden and you we're so upset I didn't think to."

"That's okay. Like I said, it's sad, it's tragic, it's horrible really, and I really wish it hadn't happened, but we really weren't very close. I feel like I hardly knew her. I mean I think she was probably a really nice person, because Bea loved her dearly and my brother-in-law's about the nicest most sweetest guy you could ever hope to meet, but I just didn't get to know her well at all. We initially has some disagreements over politics and I rarely even saw her over the last few years. Mostly I just feel sorry for Bea and her family and my brother-in-law. And anyway, frankly, I'm simply more consumed at the moment with the continuous worries about my practice."

"How is your practice going?"

"About the same; lousy. I keep having to turn away most new inquiries I get since I'm not doing managed care. People who don't have insurance usually can't afford one hundred bucks an hour either so I've cut that in half, which makes for less money. I was hoping that by meditating, doing the stuff we're talking about, that that would manifest more business, but it hasn't happened. Sometimes I wonder if it ever really will. It doesn't exactly present God as a benevolent force."

"Oh, you never want to make that assumption though. If you go for that then you've still got a problem in basics. The truth is you don't know what is happening and you're just going to have to trust the unknown with more patience."

"Yeah, yeah, I know, I know."

"There is always an ongoing display of grace and meaning. It's much like a kaleidoscope."

"Do you mean I need to have grace when I can't discern meaning?"

"Exactly. You want to have balance. Another good word for where you have to be is equity. Equity is a good experience of balance and having equity also means being out of debt."

"Yeah, well is there any thing I can do about achieving equity?"

"You have to have an inner experience of balance. There's nothing that you can do externally on your own. And you have to assume that the inner experience of equity is sufficient. That's what you are willing to stake everything on; that the inner experience of equity, which is quite easy to allow, is sufficient. In doing that you then stay on whatever path God is unfolding as your life. And as soon as the perception of insufficiency is released you will have external manifestations of sufficiency. So that internal feeling of grace and balance is key to the experience of external equity. In the beginning, as you practice this, before things really shift, what happens is that you are no longer afraid of what you call debt. You won't feel the need to escape it. You'll just be where you are and you'll see that every step you take is in grace. There's always an automatic adjustment so that there is never any imbalance somewhere."

"That would be nice."

"Right. So what are your questions?"

"Well, lately I'm feeling drawn again to trying to get another band together and maybe doing some writing on a book about …mmm…spiritual psychology…maybe a collection of essays on different topics modeled after my newspaper columns. I'm hoping it might be transformational for me in becoming awakened. But those feelings are sporadic and then most of the time everything feels rather chaotic or scattered or routine or meaningless."

"It does? All right, well that's okay. The first thing I want to address is that with your experience of chaos, if you are conscious of your responsibility to stay on track, to stay at peace, even if you are not feeling peaceful, that is, if you are not buying into the drama of what you are going through – the bad feelings you're having – you will see that life maintains orderliness. So it's not necessary to have total peace and trust in order to have the demonstration that there is continuity of fulfillment. It's nicer if you have peace, of course, because then you realize that it is divine. But even if you have tension and anxiety, if you can be clear at some level of intelligence, even if it's only at the intellectual level and the emotions are chaotic and stressful, if you will remind yourself that even while you are going though this that you know on another level that you are safe, what you will see happening is that even while you are feeling dysfunctional and upset, things will somehow still be okay.

"This is an important lesson to understand. Even if you feel like shit, as long as a part of you is willing to be grounded in Reality, even if it is only that you are holding to the right concept, that will be sufficient. It's just when you break ranks with that and go back into the drama of your feelings that you start making up frightening ideas based on those emotions and you then run into trouble. You don't have to feel grounded in Reality entirely as long as there is a part of you that is claiming that to be true; that you are in fact grounded despite the evidence. That's very powerful. It is the first lesson in the Course; nothing I see means anything."

"Hm."

"So, you need to realize you are safe, no matter how it appears. You're safe even when you are having your turmoil. It's just the work that's going on in your consciousness, untying knots and eliminating debris, so that you end up with a sparkling illuminated view of life."

"Hm."

"And the second thing I have to say is for you to go ahead and pursue your musical and literary interests. Allow the genuine enthusiasm you feel for those pursuits to be expressed and just see where it leads without expecting either fantastic or dismal results. Just be open to doing them, enjoy doing them and be open to the possibility that they may well lead to the satisfactions or answers that you are seeking."

"Well, it seems like the only answer I'm seeking is wanting to feel connected with God."

"Right. And that's all you need. That desire is what is carrying you through. I want you to understand that your life is not going to fall apart. You are already invested in this sufficiently."

"You think so, huh?"

"Yes, but you are having to do the lessons here just where they occur, that is, in the context of which you have been living. It's not as though there is a need for there to be sweeping change in your life for you to have a greater connection with God. You'd like sweeping change anyway, and it can occur, but first there is going to have to be a total acceptance of where you are, so that where you would like to be will seemingly arise out of that. And not as a contrast to what you have now but as a natural unfoldment of what God is willing for you. So by being in agreement with the status and details of your current life while maintaining your desire and willingness to move forward, you are putting that continuity in alignment.

"Take a train, for example. If you want to build a train you need more than one car. And in order to bring the cars together you have to connect them by their couplers. Now let's say that your desires, namely freedom and peace if we generalize them, are the dining car, and you are in the coach. In order for those trains to connect they have to be on the right track. The dining car has to be on the track you're on. And in order for the dining car to be yours, to be connected with you, you have to be in your coach, so that there can be this alignment. The more you are at peace now, the more you will be aligned with the very thing you desire; total freedom and peace. The more you can experience the foundation of what you desire, even if you don't apparently have it, the more you are aligning your self to receive it; the easier it can be switched over to your track and coupled. So it's about alignment. It's about recognizing that where you are is the only place you can be and that somewhere else is really just the next car on the train and you have to relax and accept where you are so that that car can be coupled rather than you getting off the train and trying to find the dining car on your own. You see?"

"Yeah, and then I wonder if I need to feel passive to allow that to happen. I don't think I'm being passive enough."

"Okay. It's true that the first thing you do is to yield. You yield to peace, but I wouldn't say to be passive."

"Good, because passive feels boring."

"Passive is weak. But yielding is different. You can yield, for example, to the energy of chopping wood. So yielding must be done first and that's always yielding to the will of God. Then what you will feel is an immediate recognition as to whether there is action to be taken or not."

"Hm."

"Now, I want to suggest to you that you spend the day with no conflict about where you are. And I want to push you up against your sore spot here by saying to make yourself be willing to live just as you are for a thousand years before your dining car is coupled. I'm not saying that it will take that long but I know you have limited patience. And because I want your patience to be infinite, I want you to totally embrace all that you have, even while recognizing that you have some desires which are not presently manifest, and understand that it is all that you have that will be the basis of transformation for those desires to come into being."

"Hm."

"You see, you always have all of your good. It is transformed into different meanings at different times, but it is all there all the time. Do you see what I'm saying?"

"Not really. Do you mean my good shows forth when I feel good, like when I'm playing the flute or doing therapy?"

"No, I mean it is there in the form of everything that you have; a house, a practice, a family, a car, a phone, etc. It is there as everything and it is constantly there. The form it takes is based upon two things. First of course its form is based upon Divine Will. Secondly it takes whatever form you will allow it to take from the defining and limiting perspective of your ego. The problem is that the ego does not understand it is all there. It believes in scarcity of resources and is busy trying to reasonably, rationally, ration out God's abundance in ways that make it appear that there is lack or insufficiency. The ego also does not believe that God's abundance, your good, has the capacity to transform itself miraculously, irrationally, into fulfillment. But it does, and that is the ongoing activity of creation.

"Now, creation will work in accordance with your desires, because God has created you as a creative being. That's what the phrase 'in His own image' means. So, there are times when you desire something you do not have. But rather than get into that grasping feeling of the ego and its condemnation of life for what is apparently lacking, you appreciate totally all that you already have and along with embracing that, you have some anticipation of transformation, of your desires, and that's all you have to do. And I want you to do it for a thousand years. I want you to extend your patience while remaining at peace. You see?"

"Hm. Well, it reminds me a bit of feeling that way when I was younger. Though somehow along the way – I think when I got married at age twenty-one and my wife got pregnant right away – it seemed like things shifted and it felt more like things were happening to me. And that I suddenly had a lot of responsibilities."

"Well, sure."

"Well, would it make any sense to ask the question am I going to see any evidence of financial stability in this new year?"

"Absolutely. It makes sense to ask the questions and the answer is yes, absolutely."

"How do you know that?"

"Because I'm going to insist on you getting the point here. There is no financial stability that you need to be concerned about. What you are being asked to do is to have an inner experience of stability, and as soon as you have that, you will feel you have financial stability, and there will be a clear indication that there is never any exhaustion of your resources. That will be the difference. Right now, you feel that as possible, but you are still fearful that your resources can be exhausted. I suggest you not think so much about being rich, though that's fine. But what I suggest you think about more is that your resources are never exhausted. And once you feel that peace, that balance, that equity, that grace, then you don't see yourself as having those problems and your capacity to access resources that never diminish is immediately there."

"So if I wanted to write a check for an overdue bill I could do it?"

"You could only do it if you were guided to do it. And the step would be clear and it would be supported. You would have evidence of the support as you were doing it. This is not about jumping off cliffs and hoping you land safe. This is seeing that the integrity of life is now at a level where you actually have tangible evidence of the appropriateness to take a step. In other words, the money shows up. You don't have to go on blind faith that you are hoping that if you write a check that somehow it will clear. It's much more substantial than that."

"You mean as opposed to where I'm at now?"

"Right. There's always the experience of movement, of things converging and coming together at the appropriate time, even when you are apparently not being productive enough. You are not going to find yourself struggling with this kind of lack. It's going to be an experience of doing all that you are doing now while seeing better results but not because you are more productive. That will be the most astonishing aspect of it. You won't feel you are any more productive. You feel as though you are just enjoying yourself and feeling grateful for it. There won't be that sense of struggle and accomplishment, but you will be seeing that things will be closing themselves off with greater finesse. There will be resolution occurring all the time. And it is the apparent inexhaustibility of your resources that will be your great comfort."

"Hm."

"It's more about seeing that your resources never end rather than having a big ton of money."

"Well, it seems also that it would be more about a feeling that there is a meaning for the use of the resources beyond the ego's purposes. I mean like I would feel what my purpose was in being alive."

"Oh yes, absolutely, and the resource will only be there if there is an appropriate purpose for which it is to be used. But you will know, you will have a clear feeling when it is appropriate for it to be used and there will not be any sense of self-denial. You may, for example, purchase something that someone else may consider junk or a waste of money, but you'll know, you'll feel the appropriateness of how the resources are to be used."

"Well, that sounds great, but I'm really tired of not paying my bills on time and it's hard not to believe that this won't be just an endless state of affairs."

"I know. You going to have to come to a point of embracing things just the way they are right now and say, in effect, this seems to be the best I can do. I'm grateful for my life, I'm desirous of change, I'm accepting that God is having it this way at the moment for some good reason I cannot discern and I'm just going to yield to it. Again, it's more important to just yield to the reality that you are facing, even if it seems kind of shitty."

"Yeah?"

"You have tried everything else. If there were an award for struggling you would have gotten it. So struggling isn't helping you. It's in embracing and yielding to the present circumstance, with some compassion for yourself because you know that doing that is difficult, that you make way for and align yourself with transformation. You need compassion rather than judgment for your self here."

"How so?"

"I have compassion for you here. You see, I know it's hard. But I also know that if you yield to it fully, that you'll begin to see it moving. You'll begin to see it change. You'll begin to see that the resources can start coming through you and that there are these wonderful cycles of fulfillment working everywhere. At a certain time it will look like you are paying and at a certain time it looks like you are receiving, but it's just a cycle."

"Hm."

"So it's very important here to be with the idea of the inexhaustibility of your resources. That is how you realize you are immortal. That is eternal life. It cannot be exhausted."

"Hm. So it's like practicing being at peace in the moment so there is no sense of need in the moment."

"Right. Okay, look, try this. How much money do you need at present to pay your bills?"

"Oh I don't know. A few thousand right now would be good."

"Alright. Now I want you to be with the feeling of having that few thousand; feeling the gratitude of it, allowing yourself to feel grateful and happy for those that are going to be receiving the money from you. Just spend some time with that; making the shift from one of responsibility to one of gratitude. You are at a point where it's got to be shifted to gratitude for it to happen. You can't do it from responsibility anymore. There is no way for you to be more conscientious than you have been. You're trying to do responsibility here and I want you to do gratitude instead."

"Alright. I got it. I'll practice it."

"Good. Fantasize if it helps. Imagine how nice it would be just to have an armful of money to give to all these people. You see, it gives them something to feel grateful for. It's part of the cycle. Your creditors need to feel honored at the level of the heart, because they're people too. It's about all humanity."

"Sure."

"So it wasn't a dumb question at all."

"Good." (laughter)

"I like dumb questions, but that wasn't one of them."

"So just practice that feeling of gratitude over having the money now."

"Right. First of all start with the gratitude. The basic thing is to recognize that God extends gratitude to you. That establishes your worth. So you are not responsible for generating your own gratitude."

"It's like the warmth of the sun."

"Right, exactly. You simply absorb it and you reflect it. You extend it out. So once you feel that gratitude, and warmth is a very good companion word to that feeling, then you can begin to extend it elsewhere freely, because it keeps coming to you, and there's no need to hold on to it. You can't hold onto it because it doesn't feel like gratitude if you hold onto it. It feels like pride. And pride doesn't feel as good as gratitude. So you extend it right and left, and in this case you want to extend to those people to whom you owe money."

"I recall you once saying that nothing's going to change until you have peace in the moment."

"It doesn't have to change is the point. You see, the assertion that it must change is mistaken. There's always going to be transformation. You can't stop that. But full transformation comes when you can be at peace with what you have and embrace the fullness of it because full transformation, which entails complete fulfillment, cannot occur if there is a belief that you lack substance in any area. Do you see that?"

"Not entirely."

"In other words, there is the vast mass of substance, your good, love, the infinite and eternal creation of God known as life, which can take any form. And it happens to be taking a certain form now. But you cannot have complete transformation if you think the problem is a lack of substance, with which to make a new form. There has to be recognition of the fullness of substance in order to allow it to change form. It can do that, but that's the problem in the world. There is a belief in the lack of substance; not enough money, not enough love

– a belief in scarcity of resources, a disconnection in the mind with the Source. Whereas if people were awake, they would realize that they have all the substance there is. It happens to be forming itself in a particular way according to, as I said earlier, both Divine Will and the precepts of the ego. What you want is to eliminate the precepts of the ego, recognize that you have the substance, then let it take off and do its thing."

"So where does the desire of the individual fit in?"

"Desire is absolutely crucial, in that true desires, heartfelt desires, are of the individual, not of the ego personality, and are in essence of the Father, literally; as I've said before, 'de sire'."

"Okay, so I don't need to search around for desires to feel."

"Right, but what you have to have is to be at peace with what you have so that the foundation for the desire is established. It is not easy to try to promote a desire if you don't have the foundation for it, which is your basic peace and agreement with what you already have."

"So it's like I need to feel like I have plenty of substance all around and I'm just kind of curious as to what's God going to transform it into next and I'm aware of my desires."

"Right. If you can do that – if you can find that your life is already founded in God's love and that all the substance is there and that all you are needing to have is transformation rather than acquisition of substance, you will find this much easier. Then what happens is that your desire is felt as an attraction to a certain meaning and you agree with that meaning. You agree with your desire. Then it moves into a feeling of intent."

"Do you mean it's kind of like a waiter came up and said 'Red wine or white?' and I said 'Red's fine'?"

"Yes. And then you know that you intend to have red wine. Once you agree with it you say 'Yes, I'll have that'."

"I see."

"Prayer, effective prayer, is always an agreement with God's will. It never is 'God, give me this, give me that, 'cause I don't have it'. It always is, if the feeling is connected, it will always be 'Yes, I'll have that, thank you'. It is an acceptance or agreement. It is not coming from a place of lack. It is always coming from the recognition of having and what you always have is substance. Your life is always filled with something, and recognizing that is the basis for transforming it into something else that you desire."

"So you are always saying yes, never no."

"You say no to the ego. That's the only word you ever need to say to it."

"Uh-huh, what is written in the Course as the appropriate use of denial."

"Yes, exactly."

"So life is a series of graceful yeses."

"That's it. Life is always yes. It's always positive."

"Even yes to suspense, or suspended activity."

"Absolutely."

"And it seems like you are never motionless."

"That's true, although you can be like an ice skater who is standing still but also simultaneously in motion. There can be movements that are like glides of conveyance, where you're not actually animated in any way, and you feel yourself being conveyed. Sometimes you will be in suspense in that place where you are aware of conveyance but you don't know where and you are not doing anything; there's no animation to it."

"The thrill of a different kind of motion."

"Exactly. There are lots of different varieties of movement."

"Okay…well, to sum up then, I never need to feel passive. I simply yield, actively, to the feeling of peace…and then gratitude…I'm just in and out of these states…and we've been through this a lot…and I get so despairing still…and so I need to stay in them better."

"Yes. You need to stay in them. Of course."

"You're assuring me that I'm practicing what is to become a natural reality?"

"As soon as you understand and begin to trust the fact that your resources are plentiful, there will be a significant relief. You will realize that you don't have to project endlessly, and you won't. You'll give that up. You'll just say 'I'm not going to do that any more, because doing that never did me any good and in fact it always made it worse and harder than it really is'. So you will begin to trust living in the moment. And there will be a time where you are stepping back and forth, not like you are doing now because you know how it works, but you are curious and say 'Well, can it possibly do this one?'. And of course, it does. But I'm not talking about you being at peace and not seeing anything get better. That will not be the case. But what will occur is that there is no exhaustion of the availability of your good and it comes in accordance with the apparent demands for responsible action. Only it won't come out of any responsibility. It will come because you are grateful that you see how this works. You're grateful for the fact that you've gotten that clear."

"I see."

"Listen. Here's a good place to put your gratitude. How grateful would you be for seeing that things are easier than you think, and that you can be who you are and moved the way you are, but suddenly you realize you are able to see continuity here where you hadn't been able to see it?"

"Endlessly grateful."

"Right, and that is the essential point. You don't want to work hard, you don't want to be a slave, you don't even want to have to be a success. That's how profound this is; you don't even need to be a success anymore because you've really gotten the game right. Of course it is a success. It is absolute succession; one thing after another – a sense of constant movement. So if you can be in this place, you'll see that at each meaningful point your resources reconfigure themselves in an appropriate way, which will feel like success, because it is. It is literally success; a succession of events. It is that rhythm of movement called success."

"Hm. Well, it seems like coming from the heart, where success isn't a concern."

"Not the kind of success the ego is seeking. No. That feels like stressful goal-oriented behavior. What we are talking about is where you see in any particular situation there's no end to resources. That will feel like success plus you will be at peace and totally unstressed because you know that you are not doing it. The ego's form of seeking success includes the fear of the threat of failure. But this is about the recognizing that the basic movements of life are to move ahead and then to reveal, movement and revelation, constantly, endlessly."

"Well I'd like to believe that even being in suspense doesn't mean you can't pay your bills on time."

"Yes. You will be in suspense constantly, as part of the rhythm of the movement, and the bills will be paid and then you will have the next move. As you learn to trust the process, your experience of suspense will become more peaceful and you will find yourself simply observing it happen. You will trust the suspense to guide you to that point of discovery where you already know you will find your good. You will not question the integrity and intelligence of the One who moves you through suspense to provide. You'll know that suspense is the way to it. Suspense works."

"It reminds me of being in the air when you're on a trampoline."

"Right. It is understanding that your foundation is everywhere and that you are safe at all times, even in circumstances where there is no revelation yet occurring as to the outcome of something that is moving."

"Yeah, well, I suppose it is ludicrous to ask when will my circumstance change since the process is a function of being here and now, but…"

"As far as that is concerned let's just say today is the best time to forecast that, because there is no need to put off having evidence. Having said that, then you just do the best you can. If you are distracted still that is still okay, because as I mentioned earlier, your feelings of chaos and dysfunction are not blocking anything anyway as long as you are willing to recognize the process."

"Yeah, well, okay. I'm going to take in a check for my rent today and it's for December so I'm many weeks behind, which I hate to be, and frankly I'm not sure if it's going to bounce or not, but I refuse to delay it any longer. So I'm going to try to maintain this state of mind that the evidence of abundance is available and that there's no lack and whatever happens, still stay with that, even if it bounces. Does that sound sane to you?"

"I want you to do it with gratitude. Be aware that you are grateful for having the office."

"That sounds good."

"And if you want to talk to more people, to see more clients, then put that out too, because that's what you enjoy doing."

"Well, I guess I'm not putting that out clearly or in the right way somehow because if the results are evidence of my intentions…well, I don't understand what's happening."

"I understand, but I don't mean to say this as a problem. Some of this is simply very hard to do. I want you to do something here. I want you to forgive yourself that maybe you can't do it any other way. That maybe you feel like not talking to more people than you are. Maybe there is a need for it to be this way and you want to forgive that so that you can experience ample support regardless of whether or not you are counseling enough – so that you experience your ability to provide and to pay for bills regardless of whether or not you are seeing enough people."

"Hm."

"You see, you cannot will yourself to see more people. You are either able to do it or you are not. And for one who is doing what you are doing, intending to become awake, there has to be a sufficiency of support, ample somehow, regardless of anything else, even if you don't see anybody."

"Well oddly enough, that does seem to be true. I mean money just keeps coming in, despite our fears that it won't or we can't imagine from where it will next. But it's still hard to trust. I know of virtually no one who thinks this way. They're all consumed in the struggle, caught up in the rat race. And I just wish I was pulling in my share through my counseling practice rather than another business."

"I understand. And you will have to trust that this will change, and that what we have been talking about today is the best way to facilitate that."

"Yeah. Yeah, I hear ya'."

The tape came to an end as the slow crawling traffic approached the soccer fields; muddy turf torn by the cleats of many players. The March sky had darkened, threatening spring showers, to the point where most drivers had turned on their lights. It was difficult for Jay to make out his son in the scrambling swarm of kids at scrimmage. He veered off the road onto the gravel drive, eased into the dirt parking lot and pulled up to the big log barrier. Spotting Phil at the far goal wearing thick goalie gloves he watched the boy jump up and down to ward off the cold while keeping his attention fixed on his teammates rioting at midfield; a commotion of kickers with occasional head butts. The slick ball banged and squirted about wildly as though careening around in a wet pinball machine. Shrill impatient barks of the coach pierced the sharp air at short intervals but Jay hardly heard them as he gazed at the boys' sloppy but frenzied fights for ball control...*the best way to facilitate that... the best way...peace...gratitude...desire...intent...bingo!*

Chapter 48

"Why should we be in such desperate haste to succeed and in such desperate enterprises? If a man does not keep pace with his companions, perhaps it is because he hears a different drummer. Let him step to the music which he hears, however measured or far away." (Walden, Henry David Thoreau)

THE OVERHEAD SLAM OF the upstairs front door jarred Bea out of the state of concentration she'd been engrossed in, hunched over her desk for almost an hour. She glanced at the glossy black clock on the shelf, an ornately enameled gift recently given her in Japan, the second one over the years...*must be going to pick up phil...he's either leaving early or the clock's running late*...She turned back to the thick stack of bills she was reviewing and laid them down on the desktop for a break. She yawned, rubbed her eyes, and then looked blankly out the window, staring at the lake. The reflection on the water of the lengthening shadows of evergreens from the shore was fading into an amorphous blur, as the somber gray sky grew darker overhead...*looks like rain*...The dull roar of a faraway plane sounded like an airliner and she felt the faint familiar stab of pain in her heart as the thought of her sister slipped in unannounced...*no no no don't go there not now not now*...

She pulled a Kleenex from the nearby box and dabbed the tears welling up, then looked back to another clock plugged into the far wall and decided the Japanese one was indeed running slow...*time to change the battery*...With a deep breath she tossed the tissue away and regained her composure. Fumbling through her top desk drawer among the paper clips, pens, and assorted paraphernalia she found a spare battery and took the timepiece down from the shelf, holding it in her hands like an open book. The unusual feel of the rich polished surface caused her to examine the fine brush strokes of the hand painted picture on the clock's inner left flap. It was a tranquil scene of village huts huddled in a valley under a shining half moon hung over the surrounding hillsides; a typical oriental pastoral setting, primitive and exquisite. It gave her pause to marvel once again at the intertwined dual themes she'd observed there so often during her eye opening visits. A country so deeply steeped in antiquity, tradition and reverence for the aged, transforming itself into an emerging economic superpower, newly marked by models of manufacturing excellence and conspicuous consumption by crowded commuters, overworked and intent on indulging their offspring.

She smiled inwardly at the memories of her last trip there in February; the huge and ancient wooden temples of Osaka, the busy but manicured streets of Tokyo, the rice paddies in the lush but shrinking countryside, the speedy bullet train rumbling over and underground, clogged with hushed and polite passengers, always on time. There were fond remembrances of the teachers and officials who treated her with sincere if exaggerated respect and the school children that unabashedly regarded her with eye-popping curiosity. A blonde in their society was a spectacle to behold, a successful businesswoman virtually unheard of. Each year she had enjoyed every minute of it, nearly, anyway, except for the agents. Despite warm receptions given her at each public turn when it came time for private talks she had to deal with agents and the cold facts of business.

The two agents she had been dealing with for the last two years, Toshi and Kazuo, represented different clients and separate venues of business. Toshi worked for JTB, Japanese Travel Bureau, a monolithic company who had a near monopoly on sending student groups to America, primarily in the summer for three or four weeks. Kazuo ran his own small company as an independent agent, representing high schools that sent students to study for a semester in America during the academic year. His biggest client was Hundai high school in Tokyo, a large prestigious school. She had inherited both agents in the process of starting her own company from the ruins of her former employer; a California-based student exchange corporation that unexpectedly went bankrupt. She had been their northwest coordinator for several years and when they abruptly folded she decided to risk going solo with her own outfit. She still worked with Toshi but had eventually severed ties with Kazuo as he grew more belligerent, demanding, and degrading in the last year of their partnership. It was a daring move since the Japanese were used to working through established agents.

Business was done there through the matrix of tradition, which meant layers of middlemen, all Japanese men. It was the Japanese way; inefficient, expensive and unnecessary to Americans, but until they learned better, innate, ingrained, and indispensable to the Japanese. They didn't trust foreigners and were willing to pay the cost of excessive representation by their own countrymen to ensure what they thought was a safe and secure process in dealing with outsiders. When she'd gone there this winter her purpose had been twofold: to strengthen ties with Toshi and to court Hundai high school in the hopes they would work with her directly, sans Kazuo. She would have loved to have had another local representative; someone who worked for her company in Japan. At the moment she hadn't a clue how to find one.

In recent years the Japanese had acquired a deserving reputation among American companies in all walks of business as being tough negotiators and she found that to be true in each of her encounters. They were unfailingly courteous on first meeting and then became serious, often taciturn, after making their points with inflexible grace. As she learned over time what the agents were charging schools and students compared to what they were paying her company, she realized an unspoken but enormous disparity was lining their pockets. Agents were getting rich, very protective of their turf, and hard to do without in a competitive field. She also knew that part of her trouble in dealing with them was that she was a woman. Japanese society long held a tradition regarding women as second-class citizens. As she was an American it gave her a slight edge. They valued Americans, or their stature in the world, and as they were driven to reach the heights of success, they prized most highly the learning of English. They were sending their children in droves to America to learn the language so that all the right doors would be opened for their futures. She knew her timely operation rode the breaking edge of a cultural wave.

Bearing that in mind she traveled each year to Japan to recount the past season and negotiate new programs. It was the expected thing to do. Her competitors came calling and she feared losing her foothold if she didn't show up. Dealing with agents was difficult but it had to be done. Along with their toughness and chauvinistic bias, they were also demanding and expected a level of excellence that Americans often thought unrealistic or impractical. There were a variety of ways for a variety of reasons that any number of things in a Homestay situation could come off less than perfectly. And not only was the Japanese way perfectionistic, but the students whose parents could afford to send them to America were the ones from the richest strata of the country. They were used to living in favorable conditions, being treated as special, and sometimes, in the eyes of Americans, spoiled.

A student might not like the food prepared by the Host Family. They might not feel a Host Family paid them enough attention. They might not think the living quarters were adequately furnished. To compound the difficulty in solving any such problems, students normally, due to their custom, would politely withhold their complaints – until back in their homeland. Then the agents would raise hell. Though Americans might point out that the problems could have been solved if they had been made of aware of them, to the Japanese such problems were simply inexcusable in the first place. If a student was unhappy, they had somehow been wronged.

Any action that resulted in a Japanese student being upset was considered unacceptable and demands for a refund were a commonplace penalty for any kind of upsetting experience. This cultural difference in attitudes permeated all aspects of the programs and since the Japanese were paying and competitors did abound they ultimately had the upper hand in negotiations. Bea had learned early on the condition she was faced with and had adopted an attitude she called ESAD (eat shit and die). She would argue a point until it seemed pointless and then accede to their demands as graciously as she could, while negotiating any slight advantages possible. The overall payoff was that she was hugely successful but the big bottle of Tums on her desk emptied quickly. When Toshi called she usually jumped or felt a little jumpy at least, knowing that he rarely did so except to complain. And when he did he expected complaints to be resolved in the Japanese way, meaning his way. If things were going well enough he had no reason to ring and usually they were. Still it kept her on eggshells to know that he might.

Jay had objected to her ESAD policy shortly after joining her business, but his attitude served only to increase her tension. She knew it'd be just like him to tell a Japanese or any other agent he found objectionable to eat shit and die themselves, which would not go over well. He was bullheaded enough to take on the whole culture, which though admirable in a way, would not advance her company's interests. She had kept him apart from Toshi and Kazuo completely, fearing the worst if they ever should speak. It would just take a little bit of Japanese arrogance or impatience for Jay to let them know where they could stuff it. Aside from their perfectionism the culture was deathly afraid of losing face. If there was a mistake it simply couldn't be their fault. That would be too embarrassing and profuse apologies with lengthy explanations were expected with complaints, even in cases where refunds were not. Thus Jay took delight in pointing out errors any time they were made on the Japanese side. He seemed intent on single-handedly revising the centuries-old attitude of the country. Oddly enough he was getting their respect by running successful programs. But for her as a female and by nature conciliatory, it was a more trying task.

She recalled her last meeting with Toshi in Tokyo. In his small but smartly decorated office they had gone back and forth in tense but smooth tones. She'd tried to stand firm in the face of the imposition of his new terms. He had wanted her company to expand into more cities so he could offer them to more students to attract more business to make more money. She insisted that staying small was key to ensuring quality programs and keeping capable help. It was his demand the previous year that had forced her to extend her operations into Toronto, ultimately resulting in the fiasco with Perry. She was too embarrassed to tell him of the embezzlement scandal for fear that he would merely think less of her business expertise.

Now he wanted her to extend into three other cities for the spring of next year; Los Angeles, San Francisco, and San Diego. Since being burned in Toronto she was hesitant to take on so many new locales at once. It took a lot to organize new operations in each place. Hiring and training people, bankrolling the entire set-up, required money and time, neither of which she ever seemed to have enough. She felt a sense of dread come over her in recollecting their discussion.

"I understand," she had said tactfully, "your desire to offer more places, but it takes time for me to find and train reliable staff. I'd prefer to add just one city each season."

"Do you say you cannot grow fast enough to meet our clients' need?" Toshi sat erect behind his desk squinting piercingly at her through his Armani designer glasses.

"It's not that so much," she countered, trying to sound very reasonable, "but that I simply want to be certain that the programs we offer them will be run by competent people. I want your students to be ensured of having a good experience."

"Our students have good experience so far. That is why we want use your company again," he stated stiffly.

"I know, and I appreciate that very very much, but I am concerned that it may take some time to create good operations in each city. With new staff in several new operations at once we run a greater risk. Once we have had a successful season somewhere, I know that I have staff in place that can be trusted for the next year."

"I understand problem," said Toshi icily, tightening his resolute jaw. "But we know other companies, our competitors here and yours in America, will offer program soon in these city. We must not fail offer same. You must develop program in all city if you want keep our business. It is your choice."

She had reluctantly agreed to launch the new operations but felt the need for some Tums from her briefcase upon leaving his office. On the train back to her hotel she felt worried and wondered how she possibly could pull this one off. The thought of traveling extensively out of state was exhausting and the prospect of being burned again in several cities simultaneously was utterly nerve-wracking. She couldn't survive another disaster like the last one in Toronto: a ton of work for a total loss. In the bathtub in her hotel suite as she relaxed in the steaming water it occurred to her that possibly Jay could do it for her. He had pulled off the programs with universities last year. He had ventured into San Francisco earlier this year, successfully marketing their programs in January at the convention. And he did like to travel.

On her return to the states they had discussed the matter and he agreed to fly south again down to California. Not only would he hire and train people to run her groups but also he proposed that they extend his programs into the area, to which she readily agreed. She appreciated his willingness to help the company grow. Might as well kill two birds with one stone. If they were going to expand she liked having him to help. Too bad he didn't really like doing it much. He seemed to have a knack for it...*wish i could trust him to deal with Toshi or Kazuo*...She shuddered inwardly at the thought of Kazuo. It had been in the back of her mind during her whole trip. She feared he was lurking somewhere in the shadows; watching her quietly, waiting to strike. He'd been furious when she'd told him she'd no longer work with him and when he learned she was approaching Hundai alone she feared he'd stop at nothing to destroy her chances, and possibly her business. As far as she knew the only thing he had done yet was spread the rumor to the school that she was not properly licensed nor insured. Since she was able to demonstrate the falsity of those charges on her visit to Hundai they had tentatively agreed to work with her on a trial basis, without Kazuo, for one semester. She was overjoyed at their decision and had come back enthused to prepare for the spring.

She sighed in satisfaction at the memory of it all, reset the clock and put it back up on the shelf. It was a gift that she treasured partly just because it had come from Hundai, signifying her greatest success so far, but also because of the way it had been presented to her. She'd been invited to a dinner at a fancy restaurant where speeches were given in her honor by the principal and the teacher in charge of the exchange program there. She had never before been feted in such a ceremonious manner anywhere. As she sat there reliving the glory of that moment her thoughts spun back to the first day she had entered their school, a massive ten-story brick structure surrounded by athletic fields and asphalt parking lots. The first person she had met there, the principal's secretary, had impressed her with the sparkle of kindness in her eyes. She was a diminutive slightly built elderly lady with soft gray hair, an air of humility, penetrating eyes, well-worn smile wrinkles and a slight stoop. She remembered how the woman's face brightened when she saw Bea enter the office and the respectful way in which she had addressed her.

"The principal is most happy to welcome you," she had cooed excitedly as her lips formed a sweet smile. "I will tell him you are here. Please wait just a moment." She clasped her delicate hands to her chest and gave a small bow of deference before exiting the room. She reminded Bea of her favorite aunt, Sophia, with whom she'd had a close relationship as a child. Though all of her time in Japan was spent with male teachers, male officials and old boy businessmen, she'd had several occasions to converse with the woman through the weeks of her stay since her work entailed multiple meetings with school personnel. Each time they had met in the principal's lobby she felt a kinship with a woman she could not fully understand. It seemed to her the secretary admired her and she assumed it was because she was such a rarity; a young businesswoman, dealing as an equal with men whom the secretary had known only as superiors for many long years.

She felt the woman's respect and saw the gleam of admiration in her eye but most of all appreciated the kindness she exuded. On the day of her last visit to the school before returning to America she had taken the old lady a bouquet of flowers. It brought tears to the woman's eyes to receive such a gift. She'd regarded herself as a humble secretary, a lifelong devoted servant to the office of the principal. She shared with Bea that she had seen many principals come and go there, and while none of them had treated her particularly unkindly, none of them had ever thought to bring her flowers. It had strengthened a bond of affection between them and they had hugged momentarily by the old woman's desk...*what was her name...her name...ah yes...tomoko...sweet tomoko...wonder how she's doing...* "rrriiinnnggg"

As Candy had already left for the day she needed to answer the phone herself. To be honest with herself she had to admit it was frankly easier to function alone in the office.

Candy had become more tight-lipped lately, which would have been fine, but was abuzz with more static than a high tension wire whenever Jay was there with them; Monday, Wednesday and Friday. Her suspicions about his phone calls were questionable to Bea but still somewhat distressing. Her relationship with Randy, having taken hold, seemed to go up and down and her emotional tenor in the office went with it. Even on up days she wasn't the same as she'd been when it was just the two of them. Still she was essential to decipher the computer. She was the central processing unit...*oh well*...

"Homestay Connections. Bea speaking. May I help you? Oh hello, Toshi, what a pleasant surprise. How are you doing? Good. Yes, I'm fine thanks, just busy. What? Oh yes, yes, we have that underway. Uh, well, my husband is flying down there shortly. Oh yes, he can do it. What? Should you talk with him? Oh no, but thank you anyway. I doubt it's necessary, really. I think it's probably best if I just coordinate between the two of you. But thanks for asking. I appreciate it. What? Ah, no, we haven't set the exact date yet. Yes, soon, very soon, to be sure. Okay, yes, that's fine. I'll call you back shortly, as soon as we...what? Tomorrow? Um, well, okay, I'll call you then. Uh, tomorrow afternoon, with the dates and details. Right. Alright? Okay. Alright. Yes. Talk to you then. I will. I will. Okay. Thanks a lot. Good-bye."... *oh boy...must talk with jay tonight...get it all straight...*

She hung up the phone and sat back in her chair, feeling her stomach starting to churn. Along the far shore against the darkening trees, white plumes of smoke sputtered up from a big brick chimney like steam from a teakettle and spread sideways through the forest. From the upstairs deck she heard the faint tinkling of metal wind chimes ringing in the evening breeze that blew off the water. It fluttered the newborn leaves of the aspens like little green hummingbird wings in the tree. Two ducks from the south streaked in fast and low to land on the lake, skidding in like water skiers, squawking their arrival. The sense of impending darkness and rain, plus pressure from afar, made her want to go upstairs and call it a night. She looked at her stack of bills...*oughta finish these now*...Taking a deep breath, she turned on her desk lamp as her eyes caught the message on the small piece of paper dangling down from it on a short golden chain: *Remember, as long you are making the effort, God will never let you down.* She felt a subtle quickening of resolution within her and picked up the stack of bills in her left hand while reaching automatically with her other one for the Tums.

Chapter 49

"Jesus knew he was a drop in the ocean but he also knew he was the whole ocean."
(Anonymous)

AFTER DROPPING OFF PHIL in the school parking lot, Jay circled down slowly along the narrow asphalt lane in line with all the other parents heading for the highway and the day's tasks before them. The crisp air was cold but the sky was bright blue and promised a sunny if chilly spring day. Proud skeletons of young and old deciduous trees were sporting the fresh growth of leafy green patches on their branches; new medals earned for enduring another winter. The stoic evergreens seemed to take it all in stride as they continued to stretch silently upwards, pointing into space like elongated pyramids. Jay shared their silence, mercifully relishing the absence of rap music, as he turned onto the highway and accelerated back toward the lake on route to his counseling office.

As was his practice now, each and every school morning, he reached into the glove compartment and pulled out a tape from his talks with Leroy. It was the one following the last one he had listened to most recently. He was going through them all now, repeating the sequence in which they were made, to glean anything that he may have missed earlier, to possibly absorb deeper what he'd already heard and to mark his forward progress, if any. He knew that the tapes from January reflected a certain disillusionment he was starting to have with the whole idea of becoming awakened. Even months later, now in late March, he was still feeling periods of doubt and desperation as he doggedly pursued his course of speaking with Leroy once a week. All that he had read and learned in his lifetime had led him to believe that Leroy spoke the truth. It had that simple feeling, that ring of authenticity, and if his life wasn't yet an experience of grace he was still willing to believe that his mind, not the teaching, was really the culprit. He slipped in the tape.

"Hello Jay. How are you today?"

"Well… I'm somewhere poised between feeling fine and feeling frightened, in its various manifestations, depending on what's happening. It's interesting to me that I'm feeling good sometimes and then suddenly I can lose it, my temper that is, in any given situation, so that tells me I'm pretty unsettled underneath despite how I may seem on the surface."

"I see."

"I mean, there's the potential of financial security through what I'm doing in the student exchange business and that's good, or it relieves some pressure, but that business requires intense, demanding sort of days wherein there's a lot of phone calls and faxes and deadlines, and just pressure in general, which I handle. I will do it. I do do it. But I'd still rather be counseling instead and my practice is not picking up yet, which frankly bugs me, and I guess that's the undercurrent. I don't know what to do about it."

"You need to confess your fear to God, in moments of surrender, in moments of realizing you haven't really any other choice."

"You mean in moments of meditation?"

"Yes, but also anytime you are feeling an urgent fear to respond to apparent demands of the world. You need to realize that whatever your fears or your circumstances seem to reflect to you, you are safe and you are forgiven. You have a direct line to God. So there's no need here to abide with the fear and to try to find what responsibility you can assume and carry out to placate that feeling. But it does require you to be quiet and to go deeply within and confess that you feel this way and you don't know really why you do. You know you have ego suggestions that the circumstances or conditions do reflect certain things, but you need to go beneath that and ask that the slate be wiped clean."

"Well, I do know why I feel frightened. It feels like a lack of support. But you're saying don't get attached to that. Go beneath that."

"Go through it. Go right through that fear to the point of confession."

"To God?"

"To God, to Jesus, to the Holy Spirit, to your Guide, it doesn't matter, because they are all aspects of the Divine. But connect with your divinity and confess that this is troubling you and that you want so much to be beyond that particular level."

"Just say that I'm tired of being angry?"

"That you are tired of being angry, you're tired of being afraid, you're tired of feeling hunted, you're tired of fearing what happens next. You need to take the time to go beyond that level and it requires a wholehearted embrace of the Holy Spirit, for example, for its power to absolve you of this feeling. And it will take you through what looks to be unresolved conditions; conditions that the ego will say are dangerous."

"Yeah, conditions are terrible."

"So, you see what I'm saying?"

"Yeah, sort of. But I'm feeling kind of…I don't know…"

"You're afraid."

"Yeah, and I'm getting sick of it. I'm not reacting as strongly as I might have in the past but I'm ready to."

"This is a deep part of your psyche that you are going to have to connect with. You are feeling up against it. You want to go to the point where you feel your absolution, you feel your sovereignty, you feel you are unassailable -"

"The question for me seems to be in what way is it appropriate to be active and in what way is it appropriate to be passive. Sorry to interrupt you, but does that make sense?"

"It's a good question and what you must understand is that yielding can either be active or passive, in the sense of being peaceful, but you want to start out with it as capitulation or inner stillness so that you may move through this density, this place in your mind where there is fear still being felt and the thought that peace is unavailable to you. So you need to be with this quietly and confess 'Help me'. You can do the mantra of breathing 'Help me, thank you' as you inhale and exhale."

"Hm. I don't know if I can go that deep into meditation."

"You can, and sooner or later you will. There is no better time than now. You must recognize that you are safe. And if you are in a place where you really feel terror and rage and similar feelings, you can confess that that is still there. And in a most intimate way, with that One who is most intimately connected with you right now, confess it. And understand that there is no judgment but there is the capacity to undo not only the fear but any kind of energy that might be afoot that would seemingly cause you problems."

"Hm."

"This is the intent of the Lord's Prayer – 'Forgive us our debts as we forgive our debtors, lead us not into temptation, but deliver us from evil'. You can go through the Lord's Prayer and feel the meaning of it, which is to connect you with God and to make you feel safe and to make you feel and recognize your support."

"Hm."

"You see, you want heaven on earth, that's what the prayer is about, and as long as you feel the way you do, you can't really recognize heaven on earth."

"Daily bread."

"That means anything."

"Right now it means money to me."

"Yes, well, it means sufficiency of needs. You see, with any problem that you are having around the issues that are brought up in the Lord's Prayer, you can confess them and say 'I need help here – I can't arrive at that place without your help'. You are not meant to do this prayer in isolation. It is supposed to feel like you have been set free."

"Hm."

"If you go through that prayer and you do it with a conscious connection, you are to feel your freedom from what you feel troubled from right now. There really is no more powerful declaration that you can make than what is in the Lord's Prayer."

"Just say it?"

"Yes, but say it with a sense of your conscious connection with God and also with a sense of warmth."

"Warmth?"

"Yes. That's important because if you can allow the feeling of warmth then the meanings that you are stating in the prayer are turned into intent and into action more easily and it is easier for you to experience them as fulfilled. Then when you say 'Thy will be done', God's will is set in action more easily through you and you are more likely to recognize the evidence of it, plus if there are steps for you to take you feel more clearly what they are."

"Hm. As a teenager I used to body surf a lot in California and as you were talking I got the image of a state of mind that was attuned to the riding of waves, flowing from a long way off and eventually building."

"That's right, it is like that. It is the experience of being conveyed and on top of something."

"They used to come in sets and you'd get a succession of about half a dozen waves – you'd catch a couple of real whoppers – then you'd wait for awhile. Seems like an example of how consciousness moves through us; succession, suspension, etc."

"Yes, that's a good example of what the movement of consciousness feels like. It also has a lot of different rhythms and contours."

"Seems like the ocean is a perfect metaphor for it."

"Yes, it's great. It's also a perfect metaphor for the experience of conscious individuality. It's been said that Jesus knew he was a drop in the ocean but he also knew he was the whole ocean."

"Hm. I like that. If I happen to use that in one of my writings do I need to give credit to anyone in particular?"

"You can just say that it's been said."

Jay stopped the tape as he cruised by the lake and looked over at his house, a few hundred yards away. It was too bright now to see which room lights were on and he wondered if Bea were upstairs or down...*probably already working away*...He was glad to be away from the basement today. Not only was he looking forward to a full slate of clients but aside from the fact he had little interest in the demanding business of student exchange, Candy had become so difficult to be around he was delighted to have a day without her in his presence. No doubt she felt the same, but even without him there Bea also had noticed that Candy was a drag; quieter, moodier, with intermittent heavy sighs. It was apparent she was not adapting well to a male in her vicinity, violating a once sacred male-free safe haven. The conundrum as Jay saw it was that Bea could hardly afford to do without either of them. Candy's knowledge of computer workings and how the business was stored within it made her virtually indispensable to the running of the operation, while Jay's contributions had expanded the business in profitable ways that were helpful to its survival and essential to its growth...*oh well...free today...*

He glanced at the plane of ultramarine water, glistening, gently rippling, reflecting the ring of tall trees and quiet homes on its shore in placid perfection, all caught in the bright slant of early morning sunlight. Even from the road the distant dew on the budding leaves of the willows in his back yard sparkled like tiny emerald chains hanging down over the embankment, hovering lazily in the cool stillness. He felt the subtle flush of well being that inexplicably filled him whenever he saw Cottage Lake, from his home or the road.... *something about water...a body of water...just feels so good...*He let the mystery of it go and returned to his tape.

"Okay...Well...Oh God...I find all this so damn challenging."

"Right, it is. Not really, in the sense that you are recovering your real self, but it is so much to the core of the ego. So to move through this particular threshold, which offers the opportunity to undo the ego's whole scheme of things – all of the concepts that the ego has – and to embrace something else, that is very challenging. And in fact you wonder how you could possibly survive it. Well, you know what, you do, by staying warm. By allowing the experience of warmth you will find yourself traveling first class here and not coach. I mean the difference between a smooth comfortable ride and a ride which is not so easy is really warmth."

"Warmth generates comfort?'

"It does. As I have mentioned before, the Holy Spirit is often called the Great Comforter."

"Coming from the heart releases bodily tension?"

"It releases bodily tension. It releases love. It release judgment. It expresses the will of God and it regenerates."

"By allowing one to be open to the process of regeneration occurring?"

"Yes, that's right."

"So I'm being regenerated here, even though I feel like I'm dying." (laughter)

"Yes, because, you see, as I've said before, the ego is engaged in preservation and what you want is regeneration. So by surrendering at this point, where it seems that there is nothing that you can do about the way you are, about the contents of your mind, about your emotions, by saying instead that you need help and by allowing there to be a feeling of warmth – just asking for that and opening up for the warmth – you are immediately put in the right place. And there you just stay. You continue to listen to what goes on at that point, whether there's anything specific being said at that point or whether you're just simply enjoying the fact that there's something other than conflict as the basis of life."

"So you're just going back and forth between 'Help me, thank you' depending on what comes up in your life?"

"Absolutely, whenever you need help. Trust that it's powerful. Trust that surrendering and feeling the warmth and declaring the truth that's in the Lord's Prayer can move through this feeling of being up against it. That, in fact, is as powerful as you can get and is certainly as powerful as you ever need to be. Trust that what happens from that point on will be justice and equity and grace."

"It's going to be hard to relinquish that much control."

"You are becoming meek, by realizing that there are certain feelings in the ego or certain blocks that comprise the ego that you cannot rationalize away. Some of it you can. Some of the blocks you can undo through reasoning, which is helpful, but ultimately you come to the point, the core or the more deeply entrenched part of the ego, where you can't do it all that way. Then there comes the need to surrender and to confess 'I can't do it any more. It's still there. I recognize that whatever block I have is a block to my full trust and I need help in setting myself free'."

"I simply need more help?"

"Yes, and you have to come to the point now of saying that and allowing the warmth of the Holy Spirit to be felt."

"Well, that's quite a leap. I guess I have to believe it's here."

"We're trying to get you beyond belief and into the experience of moving through this threshold where you have gotten to by virtue of belief and the commitment you have made. Now the time has come to move more deeply."

"You think I'm ready to do that?"

"Yes. You see, when you find yourself struggling with the same old question all the time and you are not getting an answer, then you need to stop asking the question and go for the experience of warmth or moving into a felt communion with God or the Holy Spirit."

"Well, I must be going up against a lot of conditioning because I have to focus hard to consciously allow warmth rather than feel…say, sadness or boredom or irritation or frustration."

"But you don't want those feelings."

"No, I really don't."

"Right. So what you want is to say 'I can't do anything to get these monkeys off my back'. They are really monkeys on your heart. You really cannot reason them away. You cannot justify getting rid of them yourself. You are going to have to trust that there is such a magnificent power and glory that sets you free from the trials and tribulations of the world, and not only that, but also allows you to still participate in the world."

"Great. That's what I want (laughter)....Well, I must be going through a period of suspense or else I'm really resisting succession by trying to have it on my terms."

"You are asking the same question again, you see? You keep going back to that point. And I'm saying there's a need to capitulate here. To what?"

"Feeling warm-hearted through communion with God or whatever."

"Right. Now I could call it gratitude but I want it to feel as visceral as possible and warmth will generate a feeling of love, of safety and greater clarity in your consciousness, promoting you to ask the right questions."

Jay punched out the tape as he rolled into a space in his office parking lot...*catch it at lunch*...He unlocked the back door, dashed up the flight of stairs, entered the new suite he now sublet from Marianne and glanced at the clock while pulling up the two window blinds...*five more minutes*...Looking at Mt Rainier far to the south he admired the sharp clarity of its chiseled white slopes majestically set against the crystal blue sky. He scanned his appointment book, noting his schedule, appraising the list of new and returning clients. The flower lady was gone now, off on her own. Maybe he'd hear from her – one never knew – but somehow he doubted it. She had reached a plateau, had experienced a breakthrough, was off to a new start. He did have a visit though from the Eskimo lady, as he had dubbed her to himself in the course of their meetings; another character he enjoyed, a perky individualist, as gnarly in appearance as the florist was pretty. There were also several new ones plus two men with their wives, Howie and Steve, which promised to be challenging. All of the day's clients had no mental health insurance and were willing to pay cash; his current modus operandi.

He decided to check in with the answering service to see if anyone had cancelled or called for any reason.

"Hello, this is Jay. Any messages?"

"Just one, sir, from a Detective Clark. Said he had a document to fax you and wanted your fax number."

"Oh."... *damn*...

"Would you like his number?"

"Ahhh, yes. Go ahead please...*shit...shit...shit...*"

He suddenly felt nervous as he jotted down the number and hung up the phone. The thought of counseling others while experiencing anxiety was a dismaying prospect. It was a disservice to his clients to be so distracted while attempting to focus on them and their problems. He decided to call the detective immediately and, if possible, get past it all before counseling.

"Is Detective Clark in please? I see. No, that's okay. I'll call back. Thank you."

He hung up the phone and sat down in his chair, contemplating the potential import of the call. The long arm of the law seemed to be inevitably inching closer. Sooner or later he may well have to talk to the police about Barry. Whether or not he was a suspect himself in the world of drug trafficking was not being made clear but it felt awfully close; too close for comfort. Nevertheless, he was not selling drugs. He had nothing to hide. Nothing they would know anything about anyway, unless Barry told, except for his stash…*better bury it outside…don't want them showing up at my house…*He closed his eyes and took a few deep breaths to recover his peace…*there is no urgency here but the urgency to get back to God…* then marched down the hall to meet his first client.

In the lobby sat Howie and Sharon reading magazines, which they put on the coffee table as Jay approached them. Howie looked anxious as he flashed Jay a grin. "Good morning, my good doctor," he said teasingly. Sharon looked serious, as she stood up, and gave a tight-lipped smile as she nodded her head to Jay. "Good morning," he replied, sensing their tension. "Please, come on back." As they strode down the hall ahead of him he was struck once again by their contrast as a couple. Sharon walked with the heavy-footed gait of a field hand, lumbering like farm animal, her huge hands hanging at the sides of her jeans. Howie stepped lightly in his wingtips and slacks, sauntering as his thin tapered fingers brushed by his slender frame nonchalantly, reminding Jay of Woody Allen in a movie.

"Alright," said Jay, as they settled in their seats. "What's happening with you folks?"

Howie looked at Sharon tentatively and spoke. "Why don't you start, dear?" She glared at him then turned her gaze to Jay. "It's just the same damn shit. He's out of town almost all the time, leaving me here to take care of the kids. When he comes back he always wants to be with them but he doesn't want to be with me."

"I do too!" Howie blurted out. "How can you say that? Of course I want to be with you."

"Oh that's what you say alright," Sharon's voice was rising. "But you don't really want to be with me. I can tell."

"What are you talking about? You're nuts to say that. I can't believe you think that."

"Then why don't you want to fuck me?" She shot a glance at Jay with a wild look in her eyes and then turned back to Howie. "Huh? Huh?"

"I told you. I told you. I'm tired. I'm just tired. Being on the road so much takes it out of me. Give me a little time." Howie suddenly seemed like a cornered animal fearing for his life. He looked over at Jay. "Can't you make her understand?"

Jay raised his hands up from his lap with fingers extended in a gesture to quiet them. "Let's calm down a moment. We've got the whole hour." He looked at Sharon. "You sound pretty upset."

"I am," she shrieked. "Wouldn't you be, if your wife wasn't ever interested in having sex?"

"Sharon," interjected Howie, "that's not true and you know it. We have plenty of sex once I'm adjusted to being back. Jeez."

"Oh I see," she spat back in disgust, her dark eyes flashing lightning. "You need to be away almost all the time and then when you're back you need more time to adjust!"

Howie shrugged, shook his head and then meekly, like a trapped creature, looked at Jay for help.

"Like I told you before, I can't win. I can't win."

"You mean I can't!" countered Sharon.

"Calm down," asserted Jay. "If you want to yell at each other why pay me for watching?" They both looked at him silently, Sharon fuming, Howie frightened. "Now let's start at the beginning. How long have you been home?" Howie brightened in relief to field an easy question. "A day and a half. And I'm beat, from hard work, a long flight and jet lag."

"Alright," Jay said softly, "and how long does it usually take you to feel okay?"

"About three or four days."

"He's only here for two weeks," Sharon growled, "and then he's off to New York again."

"It pays the bills, darling," said Howie sarcastically. "I don't hear you complaining about all the money you get to spend. A new horse, a new barn, a new truck, a new everything! What about a little appreciation sometimes? I break my butt and you're off breaking the bank!"

"I'm running the household, you jerk! While you're off running around the country!" Sharon started to sob. "Just, just you try it! You try taking care of everything by yourself."

Howie's winced as his inflection grew higher. "I know. I know. It's not easy for you either. I do try to help you when I come back. That's why I take the kids. It's not cause I don't want to be with you at all. I'm just trying to help." Sharon sniffled and wiped her face when Jay passed her the box of Kleenex. She looked at Howie, then at Jay, then back to Howie. "I don't believe you," she muttered.

Howie threw his arms up in exasperation. "I can't win! I can't win!" As Sharon started sobbing again into the Kleenex, Jay addressed her. "Why don't you believe him?"

"Be...be...because...because..." she stuttered, then wailed. "Because I think he's gay!"

"That's crazy!" spurted Howie. "You're nuts! You're nuts!"

"I wish I was!" She yelled, and flung the Kleenex box at his chest with a vengeance. "You're lying! I can tell!" She sprang for the door and flung it open with a bang against the wall. Turning with tearstained cheeks burning red she glared at him piercingly through hot coal eyes. "I can tell, you bastard! You're lying! I can tell!" She slammed the door behind her and marched down the hall.

Howie slipped down in his chair and sighed, looking up weakly at Jay.

"I'm sorry, Howie," said Jay in a low voice, as he felt the shock waves subside in the room. "But it's like I said before. I really think you need to come clean with her. There's no way around it. You're gonna' have to come clean."

Howie and Jay talked about how best to reveal the truth to Sharon and the possible consequences that might ensue. He left the office shaken and worried while promising Jay he would try his best to share his secret soon. Privately Jay wondered how many days or weeks soon might add up to be. With Howie leaving town every few weeks for long stretches at a time this could go on indefinitely. As Jay strolled pensively up the hall to the lobby for his next client he was still thinking of Howie till he encountered the Eskimo lady. Her crooked tooth grin and wide eyes of adoration brought him back to the present and he thought it was the sweetest tobacco stained smile he had ever seen.

"Hello. Where's Jim?"

"Oh he'll be here. He just ran next door to the 7/11 to get some cigarettes and beer while we were waiting."

"I see. Well, come on back."

They settled in the rattan chairs with Naimee's short legs causing her feet to swing above the ground as she crossed them at the ankles. She pulled some old photographs out of her purse.

"I got some pictures here from my village. I thought you might like to see them."

"Sure."

"They're my family; mom and pop, and my sisters, and my brother. He's dead."

"Are your mom and pop still living?"

"No, they're dead too."

"Oh." He examined the scratchy black and white photos. They were dog-eared and wrinkled, looking very aged. "You must have had these a long time." Naimee swelled with pride and grinned.

"That's right. That's my people. That's where I'm from."

"I see." The pictures included one of a small village with scattered huts on a dirt roadway, with old and young villagers in tattered heavy clothing. In another were a group that seemed like a family with two girls and a boy, a mother and father. Behind them in the background there was a polar bearskin being stretched as if to dry and a kettle on some stakes hanging over the remains of a rock circled campfire. "Did you mostly survive off hunting and fishing?"

"Yeah. That's my father and my brother."

"I see," he nodded as he thumbed through the stack. "Is that you?"

"Yeah. How'd you know?"

"Just a lucky guess. How'd your brother die?"

"Oh, he drowned," she said matter-of factly, with just a trace of sadness. "He was fishing, with my father."

"I see." The older people in the photos looked grizzled and ancient, maybe old before their time, thought Jay, and while most of them looked solemn, one old woman smiled to reveal that poor teeth apparently ran in the family.

"That's my mom," said Naimee, pointing with a gnarled finger.

"Yes, I see the resemblance."...*worn and haggard...snaggle-toothed*..."You do look alike."

"Thank you. She was a good cook, like me. I love to cook."

"Really? Me too. What do you like to cook?"

"Oh, everything. How about you?"

"I love Italian," said Jay, as he handed her the pictures back. "Thank you for sharing that." She smiled and tucked them back in her purse. "Well, how have you and Jim been getting along lately?" Her face darkened under a scowl and leaned forward to make her point confidentially.

"He's been drinking a lot again lately."

"I see. And have you been joining him?"

"Oh no, doctor, no. It's against my probation."

"Glad to hear it. I know you don't want any more trouble."

"Oh I know, don't worry. I no drink anymore."

"Well, I am not lecturing you and you are free to do as you want. But if you do drink, and you guys start fighting again, if the police are called, I cannot help you any more. I want you to realize that."

"Oh, I know doctor, I know. But it's Jim," she said in a guttural voice thick with concern while leaning forward again. "I tell you it's him, that make me worry. He's slipping back. He's a bad, bad man when he drink too much."

"Well then, I think we had better talk about this today."

"Oh no." She looked panicked. "Not with Jim here. He get angry I told you. Who knows what he do then."

"Well, I don't just want to ignore it. The whole point of meeting here is to deal with this kind of a situation. That's what got you here."

"Ohhh. I'm afraid he get me later." Jay sighed, and stroked his short beard thoughtfully.

"Maybe I can bring it up in such a way that he won't realize that you actually told me."

"Mmmm, maybe, if you can. If not, I'm afraid of his temper." There was a hard knock on the door. "That's him!" She whispered hoarsely. "Please, be careful, for my sake, please."

"I will," he assured her and turned his head to the door. "Come on in, Jim." Jim entered quietly with a nod to Jay and sat down. By contrast to Naimee he had long lanky legs. His lined face was tanned like leather and weathered with wrinkles from years of cigarette smoke, hard work for the railroad, and hard drinking afterward. He still appeared somewhat handsome in a worn out rugged way and his dark sideburns and mustache reminded Jay of a gambler or a gunslinger character from the old West. He slouched back in the chair and grimaced slightly as he got comfortable.

"Back still bothering you, Jim?"

"Yeah, but not as bad. Should be able to get back to work soon."

"Good. Must get boring with nothing to do."

"Yeah, well, I been doin' things 'round the house but I'm 'bout caught up." He laughed gruffly and glanced at Naimee. "Mama here's been keepin' me pretty busy with chores."

"Oh yes, I believe those are called Honeydew chores; honey do this, honey do that." The couple both laughed and Jim coughed raucously; a deep throated smoker's cough.

"So how the two of you getting along anyway? Any problems?"

"Nope, not really," said Jim, "unless she hits the sauce hard."

"Jim!" broke in Naimee, eyeing him darkly. "I'm not drinking these days. You know that!"

"Woman!" exclaimed Jim incredulously, "you gonna' sit here and lie to him? He's your counselor. He ain't the law. You don't hafta' bullshit him no way." Jay looked at Naimee. She appeared nervous and upset.

"Is that true, Naimee?" he asked. "Have you been drinking some again?"

"Well, maybe a little…sometimes… only at night though." She glared at Jim as though daring him to contradict her. He coughed again with a low wheeze and covered his mouth with his shirtsleeve. She turned back to Jay with a guilty face. "I was afraid to tell you."

"I see. Well, I'm glad you did. I need to know what's going on to be of any help to you." Jay sighed, cleared his throat, and spoke carefully in an understanding tone. "Look, the court didn't say you couldn't drink anymore. It just said you couldn't have any more incidents of domestic violence, like the last one when you slapped your daughter and a fight started and the cops came. If you can drink a moderate amount and keep things pleasant, there's no problem. But if you can't, and things get out of hand, like I said, I won't be able to help you. You're going to jail."

"I know," nodded Naimee, looking contrite as her eyes watered up. "I'm sorry not to tell you. I'm just afraid of more trouble. I don't want you to think bad of me."

"I don't," insisted Jay. "But I need the truth to really be of any help to you. So don't be afraid to tell me what's going on. I'm not interested in calling the cops. I'm interested in helping you."

"Oh, thank you!" she gushed, beaming like a little girl on her birthday. "You are the best counselor. The best counselor in the world!"

"Well, I don't know about that. But I'm your counselor and the fact is my job is to help you."

"Oh, you are! You are! You're the best!"

"Uh-huh. Okay, well what's Jim referring to when he says there's problems when you start in on the sauce?"

"Oh, he's exaggerating." She stared at Jim. "Tell him, Jim. Tell him!" Jim looked sheepishly at Jay and shrugged.

"We're not having any problems right now," he stated reluctantly. "I just don't want any more." He gave Naimee a meaningful look, lifting one furry eyebrow.

"Don't look at me and say that!" she snapped. "It's not my fault all the time! How about all those things you did before: all those drugs, all those other women. Giving marijuana to the high school kids – your own son's friends! Having sex with those drunk girls!"

"I never did that!" interrupted Jim angrily. "You're crazy. You're imaging things. I told you a thousand times. I never did that."

"Yes you did!" she retorted. "I know you did! You were bad. Bad bad bad! And you always blame - "

"Stop!" said Jay forcefully. They both looked at him wide-eyed, their mouths open in mid-argument. "What's the point in fighting about that now? How far back are you talking about, anyway? Sounds like many years ago."

"It was," said Naimee excitedly. "But he never change. I can't trust him with other women."

"You're crazy," said Jim flatly, and crossed his arms in a show of stubbornness. "You imagine all kindsa' things that never even happened."

"I know," said Naimee with quiet conviction. "I know what happened." Jim looked to Jay and shook his head back and forth with an air of resignation as his bushy black eyebrows narrowed down fiercely.

"She's always gettin' jealous for no reason," he mumbled huskily. "No damn reason a t'all."

Jay sat wondering who to believe and where to start. He concluded for the first time since their sessions had begun that it was probably a good thing after all that her two years probation included mandatory counseling for the entire period. "Maybe," he said calmly, "it would be helpful to go over what happened in those early years, but to do it in a calm atmosphere – not fight. I think you're both still carrying them around with you a bit."

They finished the hour recounting old memories, some vague, some contradictory, many painful, of the earliest years of their marriage; the child-raising ones. They were dim memories plagued with dark shadows like a musty basement shrouded in cobwebs. They were filled with tales of drugged and drunken figures, unsettled arguments, and undying jealousies. They disagreed as to the details and who was at fault, who got the worst of it and who made the best of it. As they reached the end of the hour, while Jay listened to their recriminations, he felt amazed that they had stayed together through the bitter years while their children left one by one. The sharp pain of fighting, he finally surmised, must have seemed preferable to the dull pangs of loneliness.

His next client was a young woman, Lee, in her early twenties from Seattle. Being on the Eastside he rarely saw people from the west side of Lake Washington but someone he had seen previously had referred her to him. Specifically her newly acquired stepmother had been in marriage counseling with Jay several years ago. Though the marriage crumbled anyway she had felt he was helpful in getting her through it. The woman had advised her new husband of this when she learned that his daughter was having some problems. The husband had come first just one time to see Jay himself to determine if he would be suitable for the job. He had concluded that he was by the end of their session, during which he had confided that his daughter was flirting with lesbianism. This rankled the man to no end and his agitation was evident throughout the course of their talk. He was a wealthy businessman with a computer-consulting firm that had boomed with the recent rise of the industry. The bearded and burly intense individual stoutly refused to accept homosexuality in his child and spoke with the demanding tone of a man who was use to getting his way.

"I raised her by myself from age ten to eighteen. Her mother up and left us for another man back east," he explained. "I just can't accept that she can't be normal. I think it's just all this crap in her head from the crowd she hangs out with; a bunch of young city liberals, artists and the like. I would feel that I'd failed her."

"Do you think there's something wrong with being homosexual?" Jay had asked.

"I don't know if there is and I don't really care if anyone else wants to be one. Just not her."

"Why not?"

"Cause she's my daughter and it makes me think I might have done something wrong. That's really what kills me."

"I see."

"I just want her to have someone to talk to. Someone that can listen and maybe straighten her out."

"It's not up to me to determine or not if she should be a lesbian."

"I know that. I agree, but I just want her to have somebody she can see. Maybe through therapy you can help her find herself."

"Does she want to be in therapy?"

"She says she's willing to talk."

Now, a week later, she was sitting in his office. A light skinned freckled person of medium size and build she wore black jeans, a sweater and army combat boots, with her short reddish brown hair tucked tightly under a scarf. She was friendly and talkative, peering through black-rimmed glasses while chewing gum nonstop as Jay listened patiently to the story of her life.

"So after my mom left us it was just me and my dad, and now I've been on my own for the last couple of years."

"You live alone?"

"No, I've got two roommates."

"Are they friends or lovers?"

"Just friends. One of them's gay and the other one isn't."

"She likes guys?"

"Well, actually she's bi."

"I see. But are you a confirmed lesbian?"

"Well, I'm not sure. I think I'm bi at the moment."

"Are you dating any guys?"

"No, but sometimes I see some cute ones at Starbucks – that's where I work – and I think 'Wow, I might like to do him' – maybe."

"Okay. I see. Do you have any career interests yet beyond Starbucks?"

"Well, yeah, sorta'."

"What?"

"Well, I'd really like to be an announcer or something like that on MTV. You know, like those babes they have that talk between songs and stuff."

"Yeah, I think I know what you mean. How do you apply for that?"

"They go around to different cities and interview or audition people."

"Really?"

"Yeah, and they're comin' to Seattle soon – in a few months."

"No kidding?"

"Yep."

"I bet you're excited about that."

"Definitely. I'm getting ready for it already."

"What do you do?"

"Well, they just ask you questions and have you say stuff, like a presentation sort of, of who you are and what you do and stuff like that. See if you're their kinda' person."

"You mean like 'cool'?"

"Yeah. Hip. You know. Together."

"Uh-huh."

"But not too pretty."

"Oh?"

"Yeah. They want people that are kinda', you know, flawed or have sorta' irregular features or somthin' unusual about them. Not just another pretty face."

"I see."

"Somebody that's got a schtick or somethin'. You know, a way about 'em."

"Charisma?"

"Yeah, I guess, kinda, but in a funky or offbeat way. You know, like bad, but good. Somebody different."

"But not too different?"

"Yeah."

"Someone groovy?"

"Yeah, kinda', except nobody says that word anymore. You musta' been a hippie."

"I see. Yes, that's true. Long ago. So is that person you?"

"Yeah. I think so. Kinda'. I mean, I guess I'll find out."

"Well, I admire your courage. Good luck."

"Thanks."

"So what brought you here?"

"Uh, my dad."

"Do you get along with your dad?"

"Kinda'."

"Is he kind of overbearing?"

"Yeah, you could say that."

"Do you want to talk about that relationship, or are there other things, more pressing concerns on your mind?"

"Um, maybe later. I wanna' talk about some other things first."

"Okay, like what?"

"Well, I guess my sexuality."

"What about it?"

"I don't really know if I'm gay or bi or what."

"Well, there are only three choices, and one's all-inclusive."

"Yeah, I know. But I feel pretty confused sometimes."

"Well, let's start at the beginning. When we're you first aware of being attracted to another female?"

"Uh, just recently really. Maybe the last two years, ever since I started hanging out with my roommates."

"Where'd you meet them?"

"Starbucks."

"I see. So you were interested in boys before then?"

"Well, really, I was just sort of neutral for a long time."

"Neutral?"

"Yeah, well I mean in high school and college, I just wasn't really attracted to anyone?"

"That's strange, or I mean, it's rather unusual."

"Yeah, I know."

"Do you know how you got that way?"

"Umm, no, not really"

"Well, then that's something we want to find out. Our time's about up here. Do you want to come back next week and explore this stuff with me?"

"Umm, yeah."

As she left the office he felt the faint rumblings of hunger growing in his stomach. He wanted to continue with the tape that was in his car, so he got a microwave-heated bean burrito from the 7/11 and brought the tape up to his office to play it on his portable player. Leaning back in Marianne's big leatherette chair reminded him how much he missed his own office with his own choice of furniture. His own desk chair felt much more comfortable to him and now it sat lonely in his garage at home…*someday i'll get my own again*…Refusing to think further on a troubling subject he fastened on his headphones, bit into his warm burrito and turned on the tape from where he'd left off.

"Yeah, well…boy…It's going to take a lot of energy for me to go to the depth of focusing on being warm-hearted. I mean I am just so busy all day long with one business or another plus running Phil here and there. Nights are for music, wine and dining and I just don't ever really have time to relax, except with wine or weed, let alone meditate deeply or focus on the warmth of the Holy Spirit."

"Right, I know, but it's why you're suffering now. And that's why I'm saying to confess your conflict. There's no judgment about it. All the Holy Spirit will do is to balance things in a way where there's no longer conflict."

"So it seems like to do this you have to feel passive, like you're doing nothing, and that's really hard because I feel like I've just got to do something."

"Yes, but I would say yielding, inactive, still. We've gone over this before. To be passive and in conflict or tense is useless.

"I am so unused to being still. I think if I did it I would then think 'Now what am I supposed to do – oh yeah, be warm-hearted'. I mean, it's all so foreign to how I'm used to dealing with worldly problems."

"Right. All your demons, you see, rest in that conflict, in that unforgiven experience, and it is forgiveness, or letting it go, that takes you past that point. Remember that all of this right now is to be seen as an internal experience and that you don't have to attend to the world. But rather say 'I can't attend to it – I don't know what to do – please help me'."

"Mmmm…Sometimes I wonder about continually asking for help around the same things. I mean, I wonder why having said it once isn't sufficient."

"But you are not in your peace. And if you were in your peace, trusting, not conflicted, you would not experience lack or have the experience of separation. You would feel connected to the movement of life and feel receptive to that which was being given. And you would accept it with gratitude. But to continue to ask for something while continuing to have the experience of separation reinforces the idea that you do not have it instead of allowing you to experience receiving it."

"I see. So what I said was just another form of doubt or mistrust."

"Right."

"Okay…well…I wonder if there's any point in asking what I consider to be practical questions at this point."

"Well, you can, but you do need to get to the point of capitulation. You need to know what the heart of the matter is."

"Yeah…okay…well then… ahh…I have a lot of bills that are probably worse than they've ever been, yet I'm not indulging in such a crazy negative reaction than I might have in the past, though I'm feeling like it, and I realize this may be something you can't speak to in linear terms, but I'm wondering if you have any sense when it's going to turn around, or if it ever is at all."

"Let me help you. You're still stuck on the same point. Let me go back to what we're saying here. If right now was the last minute you were ever going to spend on earth, what would you do?"

"I'd hug people."

"Yes, but beyond that. I'm going to answer the question for you. You would really embrace God as much as possible."

"Okay, that may well be."

"You would seek to have love, peace and forgiveness with regard to everything as well as safety for your journey. And what you must do is to do that now. Do it constantly. And allow there to be a genuine urgency about it; an urgency in regard to your plight. Not in how the world reacts to you but just urgent because you are tired. You are tired of standing apart from the truth. You are tired of standing away from God. You see? You want to feel that urgency. You have put your urgency into other things. You have put your urgency into the world, into your bills, and it's more important that you put your urgency, if you have any, into your embrace of God."

"Alright, I can try to do that. I have often lived with a sense of urgency or intensity. I've put it into music, into politics, into sports, my work, my kids… just every day life…"

"You need to put it into your embrace of God. That's where your safety is. Whenever you feel that you are putting it anywhere else, recognize that you are putting it in the wrong place."

"Reminds of the line from the Course 'I'm not upset for the reason I think I am'."

"That's right."

"Okay, I feel like I can do that right now, while speaking with you, but I also know that I can lose it easily sometime after we finish talking. Of course I guess I can get it back again."

"Right."

"I just have to believe that my footing is sure…as I edge along here on this precipice."

"No, but you see, even if you don't believe that, there is an urgency that you must recognize in yourself that you do have in some way. And it has to be expressed to God. You see, you go back and you say 'Well I just have to believe my footing's sure'. No, don't. There's an urgency here that you're feeling that you cannot skirt by trying to find the right handle. And that is the urgency to get back to God right now."

"I get it."

"You see, when you are alone in the world and there is urgency of some kind, if you are not clearly at the point where you realize that embracing God is really the only thing to do, you feel urgency around other things, such as your apparent responsibilities. And so you are going to have to practice that, to be with that; the urgency to be with God right at this moment."

"I understand, but I fear it will be hard to remember to do."

"Remember the Lord's Prayer. When you are feeling urgency to deal with the world and you are at your wit's end about it, start to cultivate the practice of realizing you urgently need to get back to God. Say the Lord's Prayer; Our Father who art in heaven, hallowed be thy name, thy kingdom come, thy will be done, on earth as it is in heaven, give us this day our daily bread and forgive us our debts as we forgive our debtors, lead us not into temptation but deliver us from evil, for thine is the kingdom, the power and the glory.

"Those utterances are what you want. You are acknowledging the Source. You are acknowledging it's not in your hands. And you are acknowledging that God's will is heaven on earth. And then when you say 'Give us our daily bread' you are saying, in other words, let there be sufficiency around the meeting of present needs. Forgive our debts as we forgive our debtors means, in other words, let there be equity and balance in all areas of life and let God's justice prevail. Lead us not into temptation but deliver us from evil means let there be no trials, let there be no challenges or temptations. For thine is the kingdom, the power and the glory forever. Amen. That's the truth of it. That's your Father. That's your God, right there."

"So there's never a moment when I'm not being given to?"

"Never a moment."

"Well, if I stay with this long enough…at least at the moment… I feel a sense of peace… and then… (laughter)… temptations arise."

"Temptations arise if there is a sense of lack. That's why the prayer is set up in the order that it is. First your needs are met. Secondly there is equity in your affairs. So by the time you reach the temptation part you are not suffering from the illusion that you lack anything. And when you don't lack anything, temptation does not affect you, you see. Temptation occurs when you are close to something that would apparently fill some lack you are feeling and you feel an urgency to take it."

"Are you saying there's no temptation really?"

"I'm saying you don't feel it if you are feeling whole. You simply are in alignment with the will of God. Again, that is why the prayer is given in the order that it is. The part about temptation is not before your needs are met – your daily bread is given – or there is equity in your affairs – forgiveness of debts and debtors. That is why those parts precede the part about temptation – because at that point you are experiencing greater wholeness. You are not meant to be experiencing temptation while you are experiencing worldly misery. The order of the prayer and the order of your experience is not set up to work that way, you see?"

"Yes. Well, it seems to me that if all this is true, then as you go along it eventually becomes clear that things work. That is, evidence of good material circumstances show forth."

"That's right. But you need to feel something first. You need to stop it, first of all, about how things look. You are at a point now where you need to feel more embraced by God and to hell with the circumstances. That's what this is about. There is that kind of urgency right now for you to feel that, so that you can surrender the status quo essentially. This is a change of heart. This is born again right here. This is regeneration."

"Well, I feel like if I'm going to go with this, I'm just going to be crazy happy."

"Sounds good to me. I mean that's what people need to be. It's what the world needs."

"It reminds me of the Beatles song 'The Fool on the Hill'…or a spiritual teacher whose book I ran across once. I think his name was Laughing John or Happy John or something…I don't know. But his school was called The Laughing Man Institute…Don't know what happened to him…Hope he didn't starve to death." (laughter)

"Mmhm."

"No one's going to relate to this but you." (laughter)

"No one's going to relate to it but me?"

"I don't think anybody else who knows me will think that I have any reason to be so happy. If they knew my material circumstances they sure as hell wouldn't. (laughter) Sorry… that's okay, never mind."

"You see, all that you are saying is that you are still struggling right now."

"That's right."

"And you are going to have to take the time after we speak to lie down and feel exactly what I'm talking about here. You are going to have to feel the warmth. You are going to have to realize that you can't do anything of your own and that you would rather feel your peace. You would rather feel love. You would rather feel the absence of concern than any change in your material circumstances, you see. That's where you are coming to. You want that. You want what is absolutely fundamental and what expresses your birthright in the most exalted and impeccable way. You want that. Period. That's the choice. Up until now, though you have made progress, there has been an imposition of your conditions upon your peace, still. You are looking for results. Of course. And where you are right now is in having to forego any more consideration or concern about that and trust that the connection to and the declaration of the Lord's Prayer as it was given by Jesus is the only thing you need. Go through it step by step. Go back if you lose a part. If you find yourself out of your peace and in conflict at any given moment, go back to the part that applies and ask for help there. What you want is to be a living example of what is stated in that prayer. That's what it means to be a disciple."

"Hm. I read once where the word disciple comes from the Latin 'disci', meaning 'to know'."

"Right. To learn."

"Hm."

"Well, after we get off I'll do the Lord's Prayer lying down and practice this."

"Good, but remember to start with the warmth, before you even say anything, so you are not feeling that you are struggling to get at the truth of it. Be willing to experience the feeling that what is stated in that prayer is what you want for your life."

"Being that prayer is being fully aligned with God's will."

"That's right."

"Well, that's just what I want."

"Yes, and maybe you need to spend the weekend doing it. Maybe you need to have a weekend or a day of being quiet and lying down and reflecting on the feelings and the commitment there, reflecting on the trust. Understand that God is trustworthy. God is faithful. God can deliver. So if you will do that, if you will be warm and go through the meanings of those words, you will recognize that God is faithful."

"Well…sounds good…I guess I need to do this."

"Yes. You do. You need to take this to heart. You want all of the stuff that's causing you discomfort to be dispelled right now unequivocally, by you being appreciative of the power of the word of God so that you understand that there is refuge and that once you seek refuge in that place, everything is set right, but in ways that are sublime and wonderful."

"Do you feel that your life is magnificent?"

"It's getting there. I too am still working on these things."

"Well, you sound very confident about what you are saying to me."

"Well, when I'm saying it I sure am. There are times when I need to say it too, sometimes."

"What do you mean?"

"Sometimes I have moments where I'm struggling, when I need help, and what will happen is that I will get in a position where someone calls and I will have a chance to speak the truth and it helps me. It lifts me up."

"Oh yeah, I understand how that works. I've experienced it many times as a therapist. Nothing like being a voice for truth to feel good."

"Exactly."

"Well…we're about done here, so I want to say I trust you and I appreciate you, even though I often feel riddled with all this other stuff; the fear and the doubts and the urgency."

"I know, but remember that the urgency goes only in one way: back to God. Surrender to and embrace God."

"Yeah, I hear ya'."

He clicked off the tape while mulling over the message. His voice sounded pretty desperate in that conversation, even cynical at times. A glance at the clock showed another ten minutes before his next session. He pondered the value of meditating versus taking a brisk walk and decided there wasn't enough time to do either one justice. As he stared out the window at the parking lot below he suddenly remembered the letters in Marianne's drawer and decided to peruse them again, just for the lurid satisfaction of it. He opened the drawer and reached for them in the back of it. They were no longer there… *she took 'em outa' here*…He closed the drawer and wondered if she wondered if he knew…*a little too late*…He thought about where they might be hidden now…*home's more dangerous than here*…*maybe a safety deposit box*…*better yet to burn them*…

Recalling Marianne's cool composed demeanor he felt slightly amused …*no different than any of the clients i see*…*sex sex sex*…*maybe freud was right*…He thumbed through his appointment book to see who was next. It was Steve and his wife…*oh boy*…Though it had been like pulling teeth, she had finally consented to join them in therapy. Jay had a strong suspicion, as he had shared with Steve earlier, that she was having an affair. It simply made sense. He had learned through the years the simple telltale signs; new underwear, working out more, staying out more, needing space. They were the four flaming horsemen that infidelity rode in on. If he were wrong it would be a hard lesson to swallow and a reminder not to be so sure of himself in prematurely judging others. He strode down the hall to the lobby brimming with curiosity.

Steve sat next to his wife with his huge hands clenched in his lap as though in prayer. He jumped up as Jay entered and stuck out his palm to clasp Jay's in a big grip. On the seat next to him, still reading her magazine, sat the slender blonde lady, tall, tanned and muscle toned. She sat the magazine aside with deliberate poise and slowly rose from the chair to extend her hand gracefully. Jay noticed the light silver sheen on her long painted fingernails as he took her hand in his and squeezed a gentle greeting. Though her smile seemed tense and altogether contrived he couldn't help but noticing the striking beauty of her face; soft blue opal eyes like large painted almonds set apart the thin aquiline nose curving down to thick lips coated seductively pink. Her long face was accented by finely trimmed eyebrows, golden hoop earrings, and framed like a portrait in the long shiny tresses curling over her shoulders…*God she is gorgeous*…

"This is Amanda," said Steve somewhat proudly, though his eyes looked weary and ringed with sleeplessness.

"Hello," she said, with a tight-lipped smile.

"Pleased to meet you," said Jay, returning her smile. "Please come back," he added, with a sweep of his forearm to point the way. As he followed them down the hall he was once again struck by the difference in the couple, but just the opposite of Howie and Sharon; a hulking bulk of a tousled haired man, head hung humbly as he hunkered along beside a deft graceful doe, slinking on high heels like a cool wayward angel. He was still in his work clothes, taking a late lunch hour, and his faded blue jeans and grease smeared long-sleeved navy shirt, rolled to the elbows, contrasted oddly with the pale yellow sleek skirt and silk blouse of his wife with her golden-chained necklace and watchband. As he squatted slowly into the rattan chair, lowering himself as though by a crane, she skillfully slipped her serpentine frame into the seat facing across from him. He stared at her blankly while she adjusted her skirt, nimbly tucking it back above her knees as she crossed them to reveal svelte muscled bronze calves. They both looked uncomfortable.

Jay looked at each of them, one on each side, giving them his best professional smile while sensing immediate discordance in the air. "Welcome," he said, "I'm glad you're both here, and thank you especially, Amanda, for coming. I've heard a lot about you from Steve and have been looking forward to meeting you for some time now." Her eyes flashed angrily as though she'd been slapped and she responded tersely, "Well I'm not glad to be here!"

"I see," said Jay. "Well I'm sorry to hear that. I prefer to have people come here because they want to."

"I'm only here because he wants me to. As far as I'm concerned this is a waste of time!"

"Amanda!" broke in Steve, "you said you'd give it a chance."

"I am giving it chance. I'm here aren't I?"

"Yes, you are," interjected Jay, "and I do appreciate it." He paused and observed her seething in silence. "And we might as well make the best of it. It's only an hour." He turned to Steve, saw the dismay in his face and turned back to Amanda. "Since I have already heard Steve's side of things perhaps it would be best if I talk with you first."

"Go ahead," she said as though welcoming an anal probe.

"Well, I wonder if you would tell me what your thoughts and feelings are at the moment with respect to your marriage."

"I feel suffocated," she answered resolutely. She added resentfully, "I just need space and he won't give it to me."

"How much space do you need?" queried Jay.

"I want him to move out!" she snapped back. "I'm sick of him, always crowding me, always asking where am I going and when will I be back and do I want to make love and when am I going to forgive him and-"

"Do you think you will forgive him?"

"What?"

"Let me put it this way. Do you want to forgive him?"

"For what he did? Slapping me?" She scoffed, "Are you serious?"

"Yes, I am. I'm very serious. It seems to me that if you don't forgive him, or try to forgive, or consider forgiving him there's no hope for your marriage."

"Well I'm sorry, but he should have thought of that before he did it!" She took turns glaring at each man back and forth.

"I told you I was sorry," lamented Steve. "I am sorry. What more can I do?"

"Yeah, well maybe sorry's not enough this time."

"What do you mean," he cried. "I've never done it before."

She sighed, a mixture of contempt and resignation, and looked him in the eye while cocking one finely stenciled eyebrow sharply upward.

"I've told you," she said, as though speaking to a whining child, "I'm am tired of living under your heavy-handedness. I'm tired of you being the boss. I'm tired of you always being right."

"I'm sorry," he exclaimed, sounding hurt. "I've told you. I didn't know. You always seemed happy to leave the decisions to me. I've let you do whatever you want. I bring in the money. I pay the bills. You'd never had to work. Just take care of the boys."

"Well maybe I wanna' work!" she hissed like a snake who's tail was being stepped on. "Maybe I'm tired of taking care of the boys so much. Did you ever think of that?"

"Then we can change things," he pleaded. "You know I'm willing to change." She stared down at the floor.

"Maybe it's too late," she muttered quietly. An air of grim finality hung in the room like death as Jay watched the two of them cease talking. Steve fumbled with his hands, looking beaten and discouraged while Amanda gazed absently out the window behind him. They both turned their attention to Jay simultaneously. He was looking for an opening, a point of intervention, which might reverse their course, a trajectory to hell. He decided to back up and try to take a broader view of things.

"How long," he asked thoughtfully, "have you two been married?"

"Too long," parried Amanda, with a harsh despairing laugh. "I should never have married him."

"Oh Amanda, come on!" countered Steve. "It's been good in the past."

"I was too young!" she snarled, curling her upper lip slightly as if baring a fang. "I didn't know what I was doing. You're so much older than me."

"You said you liked older guys. You wanted an older guy. It's not my fault I'm older. You wanted someone to take good care of you. And I did. And I will." Tears welled in his eyes.

"Maybe I just don't want that any more." She uncrossed her legs and stamped her foot soundly on the floor. "I'm sorry, Steve. It doesn't feel the same."

"How much of this," interrupted Jay, directing his question to Amanda, "is about what happened and how much of it is about just not feeling the same."

"It's both," she said defensively. "It's both. I haven't felt the same ever since he hit me."

"Slapped you," said Steve. "C'mon now. It was just a slap."

"Just a slap huh?" she said contemptuously. "Whatever."

"It sounds to me," continued Jay, "like these feelings have been growing over time."

"So what if they have!" barked Amanda. "Maybe they have. I don't know. I just know I need some space. And he won't give it to me! If he loves me so much why won't he give it to me?"

"Perhaps," said Jay softly, "he's afraid he'll lose you forever."

"Well," she said haughtily, titling her chin up, "he is going to lose me if I don't get what I want."

"Have you considered," said Jay in a kindly tone, "that perhaps you may be being a bit willful and self-absorbed in this matter?"

"Absolutely not!" she replied indignantly. "Are you saying that?"

"No," said Jay politely. "I'm just asking because I know you were seeing another therapist before and I wondered what she made of your unwillingness to forgive."

"She said," spoke Amanda with firmness in her voice, "that no woman should ever have to live in an abusive marriage!"

"And I agree. But is that what this is?" asked Jay. "An abusive marriage?"

"I'm afraid of him. Don't you understand? I don't trust him. I don't trust him not to hit me again. He's big. He's a brute. I'm afraid to be around him."

"We've been married twelve years," wailed Steve, "and I've never hit you. What are you talking about?"

"I'm intimidated. You're intimidating Don't pretend that you're not." She pointed an accusing forefinger at him. "I'm the victim here! You always lorded it over me and I'm sick of it.! I need my space."

"I haven't. I haven't." Steve stared at her beseechingly. "And if I did I didn't know it. You should have told me. I'm sorry. Please forgive me." His voice cracked as tears began streaming down his face and Jay handed him the Kleenex box before then turning to Amanda.

"What do you want?" he asked her quietly.

"I want him to leave." Her lips tightened in determination. "I want him to leave the house and give me some time. I want a separation. I need to find my own identity."

"Leave you with the boys?" said Jay.

"Yes."

"I can't leave my boys," cried Steve. "It isn't fair. They mean everything to me. I coach their teams. I do their homework with them every night, when you're out at the gym. I can't leave my boys. It isn't fair. It isn't right."

"Perhaps it would be better if you left, Amanda."

"What?"

"Well, I mean why should he leave," inquired Jay earnestly, "when you're the one who wants the freedom to create a new identity?"

"I can't believe you said that!" she snapped, looking furious. "Are you on his side?"

"I wasn't thinking of it as a matter of sides. I was thinking more that if you want more space, as you put it, and want to be going out a lot, it seems almost logical to me. Just a thought." Amanda didn't answer, as though considering the idea. She pursed her lips and looked at nothing, transfixed inwardly. "I don't know," she said cautiously. "I never thought about it before."

"Well, Steve would rather you give some thought to working out your marriage. But that seems to have very little appeal to you at the moment."

"I just need space so I can think!" she said exasperatedly.

"Yeah," said Jay. "I know. I hear you."

"Well he doesn't!" she steamed. "And I'm tired of it, damn it. I deserve some space."

"I'll sleep on the couch," offered Steve weakly, his eyes sinking deeper into dark rings of sleeplessness.

"That's not what I mean." She gave him a dirty look. "You know what I mean."

Steve sighed in hopelessness, looked down and scratched his head in silence. Amanda crossed her legs again to emphasis her stubbornness and gazed once more out the window. Jay watched them sit in silent opposition, a tug of war of wills, a stalemate of sour souls, and thought of the line from T.S. Eliot's poem…*this is the way the world ends…this is the way the world ends…not with a bang but a whimper…*

"I'm just wondering, mmm…" he said with a curious inflection to Amanda. "Have you met other people at the gym, or wherever you go out, that have given you a sense of having more a world of your own apart from Steve? More space so to speak." Steve blinked and sat up with renewed interest as he studied her.

"Do you mean am I having an affair?" she asked incredulously.

"No, I didn't mean that necessarily."

She regarded Jay with amazement as she pulled her shoulders up and he saw a spark of rage go ablaze in her blue eyes.

"Are you?" said Steve quietly.

"I can't believe," she said with cold fury, glaring at each man, "that you would go so low as to ask me a question like that."

"I'm sorry," Steve mumbled.

"I take it," Jay offered, "that's a 'no'."

His next client was a new one; a dentist from a nearby town. He was in his mid-forties, with a medium build and well dressed in a pinstripe suit of dark brown with a russet tie on a pale yellow shirt. The stems of his thin-rimmed tortoise shell glasses were lost in the thick curls of his neatly trimmed sandy hair. It was evident he had money, a successful professional, and Jay wondered what it was that could have brought him to therapy. He seemed nervous as he sat down looking very uncomfortable.

"I'm not sure where to begin," he spoke in a flustered manner.

"Then just tell me what's bothering you the most."

"Well," he began, his eyes darting about the room, "this is confidential, right?"

"Absolutely," Jay assured him, "unless you are homicidal or suicidal."

"I'm not either of those, but I'm at my wit's end."

"What's the problem exactly?"

"Uh," he hesitated, and then continued tentatively, "have you ever been to one of those sex clubs?"

"You mean topless bars?"

"Right, those kind of places."

"Yes, once…*at the behest of a japanese group escort*….I know what they are."

"Well, there's one near here, at the north end of Seattle called Naked Ladies. Do you know it?"

"I know of it. It's right off of City Way if you take the long way around to Seattle."

"Right, that's it."

"What about it?" The man swallowed and looked guiltily into Jay's eyes for a judgment.

"I've been going there."

"So what?"

"I've been going there a lot."

"I see. Okay. How much is a lot?"

"Almost daily."

"Every day?"

"Yeah, just about."

"Why?" A faint film of perspiration appeared on the dentist's forehead and his lower lip trembled as he struggled for composure.

"Because I'm in love with one of the dancers."

"I see. Okay. How long ago did this happen?"

"About six months ago." He patted his forehead with a white handkerchief from his pocket.

"Are you married?"

"Yes."

"Does your wife know?" More sweat broke out on his face and he dabbed it again, this time touching above his mouth and under his eyes.

"She knows that I'm going there, but doesn't know about the dancer. She just thinks I am addicted to sex."

"I see." Jay paused and thought for a moment. "When do you go there?"

"Mostly on my lunch hour."

"And how is it that she knows that's what you're doing?" The man looked desperately forlorn as he raised his voice.

"Because more often than not I end up staying there the afternoon. I call in to cancel patients. I do it all the time. And over the months when she's called to talk to me about some thing or another, usually about the kids, she's found that I'm always out. She knew that something's up and she's been asking me about it. So I confessed to her a few nights ago, except for the part about the girl. And now she thinks I'm a sex nut. And she wants me to see someone. Do you think you can help me?"

"What exactly do you want help with?"

"Getting over this girl – the dancer. I'm crazy about her."

"I see. What's her name?"

"Sierra, that's all I know. She won't tell me her last name."

"Is that her real name or her stage name?"

"I don't know. I just know she's young and ...well...she can really dance."

"Naked you mean?"

"Right."

"How do you know this is love and not just lust?"

"I don't know. I'm hoping you can help me sort it out. I just know when she dances for me I go crazy with desire for her."

"Doesn't she dance for everyone who's there?"

"On the stage, yes, but she does special dances for me in the private booths."

"Aren't those expensive?" The dentist nodded vigorously.

"That's the problem," he said in anguish. "I'm spending a ton of money there."

"And you're closing down your business to stay there."

"Yes." He looked tormented, lost and confused. "Oh God, I know," he cried defensively, "I know that it's wrong. I just can't seem to stop it. She's on my mind all the time, all the time. I can't help thinking about her."

"You're obsessed."

"Yes, I guess so. Obsessed. I guess that's what you call it."

"Have you considered leaving your wife?"

"Yes, but I'd never do that, especially with the kids. I've got a boy and a girl, eight and ten."

"I see. Well, what does this girl feel for you, if anything?"

"I don't know. She says she likes me. She lets me touch her, behind the curtains. She even kisses me."

"But all for money?"

"Yes, but well, that's her job. I mean if she goes back there in the booth with me her time is being watched by her boss."

"Exactly."

"What do you mean? That she doesn't care for me?"

"Well, you gotta' wonder. Sounds like you are her sugar daddy."

"She's something special. Not like the rest of them. I think she likes me."

"Maybe so."

"I've offered to get her out of there. Put her up in an apartment. Send her to junior college. She could have a different life."

"Sounds like you want her as a mistress."

"Well, in a way, I guess you could say that."

"What does she say?"

"She doesn't want that," he said gloomily. "She says she hates school. She likes dancing."

"Well, then, there you are."

"I just can't accept it. She could be better. She's just a diamond in the rough."

"Have you had sex with her?"

"No. We can't do it there and she won't see me after work. I've tried and tried. I've given her presents; jewelry and clothes. But she won't have a relationship with me because I'm married. Won't even tell me where she lives. Says she needs her privacy."

"That's what she says?" The dentist looked hurt and made a wince like he was sucking a lemon.

"Yeah, that's what she says." Jay leaned back in his chair and looked squarely at him.

"How do you know your not being taken for a ride?"

"I don't know. But I just can't believe that about her. She's so beautiful. She's so sweet. She's so, so …"

"Sexy," Jay added.

"Yeah, yeah, okay, she's sexy. That's true, but she's more than that. She's really… special."…*i bet…*

"Look," said Jay soberly, as he leaned toward the harried dentist, "you don't really know what she's all about. You don't know where she lives. You don't even know her name. In the meantime, you're throwing away a practice that you've worked years for to establish. You're risking losing your family. You're in a mess with your wife. You're losing money left and right. Do you disagree with any of that?"

"No," said the dentist, sighing. "You're right. It's terrible. What should I do?"

"Stay away from her awhile and see what you feel in your heart then."

"I don't think I could do that. Every morning I go to work and I think 'Today I won't go there' and then lunch rolls around and I just can't fight it. Then I go there saying to myself 'Just for an hour' and then the hour is gone and I don't want to leave."

"So you end up canceling patients?"

"Right."

"And everything just goes to hell."

"Right."

"It's amazing you've let it go on this long and still survived."

"Well, she usually has two days off a week," he explained. "And on those days, which change every week, when I see she's not there I just eat lunch and go back to the office."

"I see. So you get some work done in the afternoons."

"Oh yes, definitely. At least two days a week."

"Okay, well listen. Here is what I suggest you do. I think you should take your wife and go away on a short vacation. Maybe a week or so. Can you do that? Get out of the area. Far enough that you could not drive back to Naked Ladies. Then tell her what you are going through." He looked at the man intently. "Are you sure you will not leave your wife?"

"Positive. She's a good woman. She's a good mother. I just couldn't do that to my wife or kids."

"But you're willing to have a mistress."

"Yes," his voice faltered. "I guess so."

"Don't you see that's a path to heartache? You'll want to spend your time with her. You'll want to spend your money on her. Don't you see how that's going to impact your relationship with your family? It already has." The man lowered his face as it darkened with shame.

"I know. I know you're right. I just don't know if I can forget about her."

"You love your wife?"

"Of course."

"Do you have intercourse with her on a regular basis?"

"No, not really. Actually not really since the kids."

"Why not?"

"I don't know. We just both got busier; me with the practice, she with the kids. And she got fatter."

"How much fatter?"

"Oh, not a lot really. But she's just sort of out of shape now, compared to how she used to be, and compared to, compared to…."

"Compared to Sierra you mean."

"Yeah."

"Think Sierra would make a better mom for your kids?"

"Oh no, absolutely not. Never. My wife's a great mom."

"Well, there you have it."

"What?"

"You will not leave your wife and family for this girl. She will not be with you while you are married. And you're going to hell in a handbag trying to accommodate both situations. The only sane thing to do is to stop seeing her. And since you have a hard time doing that, go far away awhile, so you literally have no chance of seeing her. Then to top it off, tell your wife, so she knows what's really going on. Then come in here for some marriage counseling when you return."

"You really think that's what we need to do?"

"Yeah, I do. Can you think of anything better?"

"No, but it sounds hard."

"I didn't mean to imply it would be easy. It just seems to me like the best thing to do. Are you afraid she'll leave you?"

"I don't think she'd do that. Especially if I say I want to make things right with us."

"Well, then let's try to do that."

His next to the last one for the day was a young man in his twenties, tall and slender, with long black hair and a hangdog look on his winsome face. His sensitive countenance was pained, wrinkled with worry, as though deeply troubled by some hideous thought he dared not speak. After introducing themselves they sat down in the rattan chairs facing each other.

"Well, Skyler," said Jay, "what's on your mind? You look pretty unhappy."

"Does it show that bad?" inquired Skyler. "I thought I was keeping it to myself pretty well."

"Everyone is potentially readable. I can just tell you are upset over something, and of course otherwise you wouldn't be here. Go ahead and get it off your mind. Let's see what we can do to help." Skyler looked at him and frowned, then spoke softly.

"It's just so hard, and it's so damn crazy."

"Well, then you're in the right place," quipped Jay. "What's the trouble?"

"Ah, it's with my wife," he said begrudgingly. "It's all about our relationship." Jay nodded understandingly.

"What's going on?"

"Well," he said slowly, as though it pained him to say the words, "last year she left me for another guy."

"I see. Well, that happens. But now she's back?"

"Yeah. She came back. But she was with him for about six months."

"That must have hurt."

"You don't know the half of it."

"I'm sure I don't. But I know it can be pretty painful."

"No," he groaned. "It was worse than that."

"How do you mean? By the way, what's her name?"

"Melanie, and what I mean is, this guy was crazy. He thought he was Jesus Christ."

"Oh."…*God he was crazy*…That's a…a bit bizarre."

"You're telling me!" Skyler cringed and shook his head. "That's just for starters."

"I see," said Jay, his curiosity growing. "How else was he crazy."

"Oh, man…" The young man gazed at Jay with a tormented look in his eyes. "He was built like a bulldog, real strong, kinda' short and he had a beard and he shaved his head. He had some followers, kinda' like Charley Manson, and they lived together in this house out in the country; the back woods of Duvall. Nobody around for miles. Kinda' like a commune." He stopped as though at a loss for words.

"Yes," said Jay, "go on. So what happened?"

"Well," he sighed, with grief entering his voice. "He used to call me up and say shit like 'Your wife is such a good fuck', and man, it just drove me crazy. I hated that bastard. But I couldn't do anything. I couldn't reach her by phone. She wouldn't call and I couldn't get his number. He told me they had guns and mean dogs around, pit bulls, and if I ever tried to come around they'd kill me. So for about six months there was nothing I could do and it was…it was a bad scene."

"I see," said Jay softly, feeling slightly stunned by the revelation. "That *would* be a bad scene. A very difficult situation." He stopped and waited for Skyler to go on, but the young man seemed sickened by what he'd just said. "So," encouraged Jay, "then what happened? I mean how did she get back with you?"

"She just showed up one day, a few months ago, and said she wanted to get back together. She said she was sorry. She'd made a big mistake. She said he was crazy and she just didn't realize it."

"So you took her back?"

"Right."

"So what's the problem now?"

"I don't know," said Skyler anxiously. "But I just can't seem to get over it. She's having to have some kind of operation because she has cysts in her vagina, and we can't have sex. And I can't help wondering if it's because of having sex with him. I mean he used to call me almost every day or night and just say that in that deep voice of his 'Oh I just love fucking your wife'. Then he'd laugh and hang up. I hated him. I hated her."

"Does she know he tormented you like that?"

"I don't know. I haven't said anything about it to her. I don't like to remember it."

"Whatever happened to that guy?"

"We heard he killed himself. Shot himself in the head about a month ago."

"I see. Well, he's out of your life forever. What do you want to do now?"

"I don't know."

"Do you want to stay with your wife?"

"Yeah, I think so. If I can get over this. I think we love each other."

"Do you trust her?"

"Yeah, actually I do. Pretty much anyway. She did come back, and of her own accord. He was pretty charismatic. He broke away from the church they both attended. That's where they met. I never went in the first place. She's got some real spiritual values, but she's impressionable. I think she was just misled. Plus I had been pretty busy with my work and my band, and so I wasn't home a lot."

"You got a band?"

"Yeah."

"What do you play?"

"Guitar. Got a Gibson."

"That's a nice make."

"Yeah. I could never have afforded it. John Wayned a guy's door once who owed me some money on a drug deal and took it as payment."

"Wow. You got gigs?"

"Yeah, we play at some bars and stuff, private parties mostly."

"I see. That's great. I used to have a band."

"Yeah? I see you got a guitar over there."

"I play flute and keyboards too."

"Cool."

"Used to be. We broke up."

"Too bad. What was your name?"

"Terra Mystique."

"That different."

"Yeah. We wanted to be. What's your group's name?"

"Grunge Guys."

"Hm. Seattle style music, huh?"

"Yeah. We're trying to cut a CD."

"I see. So how long you been at that?"

"A couple of years. But it just took off shortly after we got married and it meant I was gone a lot after work to practice and my wife ended up being alone at night. I know it was hard on her."

"I see. You sound pretty forgiving."

"Yeah, well, I try to be. I don't want to hold a grudge. I've changed things so I'm home now a lot more. It's just that she is so lovely and when I come home from work I just see her and I think 'Damn, I wanna' make love' and she always says 'I can't – wait till after the surgery' and I just think 'Fuck! He didn't have to wait!'."

"So what happens? Do you argue with her or let it go?"

"Well yesterday I just said 'Then how about a blow job, damn it!'."

"And what happened then?"

"She gave me one but then later she cried and I felt like shit."

"She doesn't like giving you a blow job?"

"It's not that, really. I don't think she minds. She just knows that I'm angry and I'm hurtin' and I want to have her love and she can't fully give it to me."

"She can give it to you in other ways."

"I know that. But the fact that we can't make love drives me crazy because I wonder if it's because she had so much sex with that other guy."

"Have you told her that?"

"No. I think she knows. She's not stupid."

"She may not be. But she may not know fully what's on your mind. I know you don't like thinking about it but talking about it is the best way to get through these things. You don't even know what really happened between them. Maybe it's not as bad as you are assuming."

"Whatever it was, it was bad."

"I understand," nodded Jay. "But it's gotten better, and you want it to get better yet. Sounds like you both want that. Why don't you come in with her? Perhaps it would be easier to talk about these things here."

"Yeah, we could try. We gotta' do something."

"Does she know you're here?"

"Yeah. It was her idea. She said I oughta' talk to somebody."

"I think you both do. I'd like to see her alone once first. Can I have your permission to share with her anything that you've shared with me?"

"Sure, if you think it will help."

At four o'clock he saw a new person, and his final one of the day. Named Lynette, she was a tall fair-skinned woman in her thirties with long yellow hair and sad brown eyes. She wore sneakers, levis and a sweat shirt and stated that she worked in a large nursery and garden store just up the street. The moment she sat down she started weeping profusely, making it difficult for her to talk. Jay offered her the Kleenex box and sat quietly with her as she gasped for words between choked sobs.

"I'm...I'm sorry," she managed to say, while wiping her streaked face with a tissue.

"That's alright," Jay responded, "that's why there here. Just take some time to compose yourself. We have the whole hour."

"I...I didn't want to come here and cry," she lamented. "I've been doing enough of that at home for the last few days." A fresh round of tears welled up and streamed down her face as she reached for another Kleenex. "I just can't seem to stop," she wailed.

"It's okay. Get it out. Crying is cleansing. You've got to express the sorrow." He waited for a moment as she gushed another few sobs then ventured a question. "Has somebody you love died?"

"Oh no. It's not that bad," she said mournfully. "Or maybe it's worse. I don't know." She cleared her throat and looked through her tears at him. "My...my... my husband's had an affair," she bewailed. "And I just feel so bad about it I don't know if I can ever get over it." With that she began crying again and sobbed into the wadded up tissues in each hand.

"I see." He paused respectfully as she released her sorrow. "And so is it over with now?"

"Yes," she nodded, looking at him through reddening eyes.

"How do you know that?"

"Because she's gone home."

"What do you mean she's gone home?"

"She's gone back to her country to be with her family."

"She was a foreigner?"

"Yes."

"And she's married with a family in another country?"

"No," she said insistently, contorting her face in anguish. "She was a foreign exchange student. She was just a college student."

"Ohhhh," said Jay slowly...*oh no*...He cleared his throat. "Was she Japanese?"

"No," she murmured. "She was Swedish. A beautiful blonde Swedish girl!."

"Ah," said Jay with a sigh...*at least not one of bea's*..."And was she living with you?"

"Yes!" wailed the woman, as she began weeping harder again. "She was...she was...like my own daughter."

"I understand. I understand completely. We've hosted students before. It's no wonder you feel so crushed."

"I do!" she sobbed and touched her chest. "And my heart hurts so much!"

"I know. I know. I know it feels like the end of the world," spoke Jay reassuringly as he watched her cry some more. "Do you still want to be with your husband?"

"Yes," she whispered. "I do."

"And does he still want to be with you?"

"Yes. He does. He says he's sorry. He feels terrible."

"Well, then it really isn't the end of the world. At the moment it just feels like it. But these things can be healed."

"I know," cried Lynette, struggling for air as she talked. "I want to believe that. That's why I'm here." She moaned low in her grief. "I just don't know how to do it."

"Yeah, well, that's why I'm here."

They continued talking for the rest of the hour, focusing on what had happened, how it had happened and what could be done about it now. She agreed with Jay's request to meet with her husband alone and then to come in as a couple after that. A dozen tissues later she left the office with her heart still feeling like shattered glass, but buoyed by the shaky hope that the love she still shared with her husband could ultimately mend it. From his upstairs window he watched her cross the parking lot walking as in a daze and clutching her handbag under her arm with both hands as though hugging a teddy bear. He turned to his desk and reached for the phone...*just one last person to talk with ...*

"Is Detective Clark there please? Thank you. Yes, hello, this is Jay, the counselor. I understand you wanted my fax number earlier today. I was wondering why...Oh, the consent form from Barry. Good for you...*damn*...Okay. Well, if he signed it then I just need to see it. But I don't have a fax number...*not one I'm giving you anyway*...You'll just have to mail it to me...Yeah, that's right, and then we can talk. You got my address? ...Okay, thanks. I'll look forward to it...*like hell*...Bye for now."

He sat down in his desk chair and rotated back to the window. Outside a cold evening was steadily descending and though the sky was darkening it still remained cloudless blue. A block away five o'clock commuters in wheeled cages were starting to group in long lines at the corner stoplight, gearing for the grind of their homeward trek. To the farthermost point in the south he could still see the craggy pale bulk of Mt. Rainier in the distance, indifferent to the traffic or the time of day. Aside from being mildly distracted by the detective's dogged persistence, he felt overall a deep sense of satisfaction at completing another full day at a job he loved. He drove home in silence without radio or tapes, anticipating a jog, a Corona, some cabernet, perhaps a toke or two while overlooking the lake, and though he felt drained he was also aware of feeling quietly elated.

Chapter 50

"Our brothers are forgetful...Your mind is so powerful a light that you can look into theirs and enlighten them, as I can enlighten you." (*A Course in Miracles*)

ASTRIDE HER APPALOOSA BEA loped along loosely on a well-worn trail in the mid-morning warmth of an early April Sunday. It wound through the tall stately pine trees in the woods near the stable where she boarded her horse. That property belonged to a friend named Jeanne whose husband was a wealthy psychiatrist. They lived in a Tudor mansion on a hill above the town. More than half a year had passed since her last ride in September and she savored each step in Cheyenne's gentle trot. Usually she rode with her friend on their horses together but today the woman wasn't available. Though she liked Jeanne's company, this morning she was relishing the pleasure of being alone in the healing milieu of Mother Nature in spring. Aside from the clip-clop percussion of her mount on the hard forest floor, the only other sounds to be heard were birds whose sweet songs, chirps and trilling sang out in the woods like a chorus of piccolos, whistling to a drumbeat at an outdoor concert.

Scattered amongst the mixed shades of green were pink pastel blossoms recently popping from the wild rhododendrons spread near and far throughout the woodland. She broke into a clearing on the grassy pipeline that served as a firebreak twenty yards wide between sections of forest. It extended in a line for miles on either side of her; sloping up and down the hills that rippled out eastward from Seattle to the lush rough and tumble countryside. On a good hill and a clear day she could see the silver silhouette of the city's proud skyline set starkly against the Olympic Mountains staggered to the west. Cheyenne halted; snorting his contentment as she reined him in to let him munch on some grass. She gave a momentary glance toward the far-away buildings but her senses were more entranced by the scents, sounds and sparkle of springtime surrounding her on the hillside. Lost in a reverie to the remedial powers of being borne on horseback through a Garden of Eden, she was content to let her mind meander winsomely along as undisturbed as her sturdy steed. It felt slightly strange to be so alone and at peace in the glow of the sunshine finally once again.

For so many months she'd been busy at a hectic pace, sometimes alone, but never relaxed and rarely in the sun. In hotel rooms and offices, airplanes and taxis, she'd toiled, scurrying from one task and town to another. Now it was Jay who was off for a torrid tour of duty to the capital cities set along the Californian coast…*wonder how he's doing*…She shielded her eyes from the glare of the sun then spun her horse around heading back to the east, feeling the heat on her shoulders as he sauntered up the slope. Purple crocus flowers and wild yellow daffodils burst forth from their bulbs through the crust of the earth, dotting the landscape like fresh spots of wet paint. The radiance of the sun reminded her of California where she'd first met Jay in a crazy college psych class, taken as part of her continuing education. The professor was a psychologist, bearded and longhaired to the tune of the sixties, and had turned the class into a group therapy session devoted to the principles of Gestalt psychology and its insistent focus of how you were feeling in the ever-present Here and Now.

It was a night class, the only kind that she could attend, since she worked as an elementary school teacher in the daytime. Jay was there getting his graduate degree and through the context of the classroom, the caring and sharing, the crying and sighing, as she witnessed her classmates baring their souls, it dawned on her how unhappily married she really was. Through the course of the semester they got to know one another and gradually he too admitted similar feelings. They had both married young without fully appreciating the depth and complexity of their respective mates. Bea married a man who had been a fun playmate in Ohio in their college years, but he'd returned from Vietnam as a more distant person, preferring to hangout with other war veterans and their dirt bikes. When not working late as a mortgage officer he was gone on long weekend trips to the desert and though he was not unkind to her, he had become relatively uncommunicative; a likely case of post-traumatic stress. Jay had wed a college girlfriend who soon became pregnant then suffered a miscarriage and the feeling of romantic compatibility between them had been steadily lessening with each passing year.

By the end of the semester both Bea and Jay were in love with each other and increasingly committed to ending their marriages. Oddly enough, and thankfully too, both spouses had been less resistant to the idea than was originally anticipated and the separations actually went fairly smoothly. They had simply done their own divorces with the help of a workbook and even had a harmonious gathering of the four of them wherein they signed their final papers together. A year later they married and upon Jay's completion of graduate school, moved from California for a brand new start in the bold fresh frontier of the northwest. When they returned in six months to visit Jay's parents they were both unfavorably struck by a notable contrast; the absence of greenery.

Clogged freeways, new power lines, condos and cul de sacs were continuing to converge on California, converting orange groves to smoggy asphalt jungles and covering the hills with cookie-cutter housing tracts; the cancer of city suburban sprawl. And they knew then their move was likely to be permanent. At least there would certainly be no going back. The pull of the sun was not a strong enough magnet and the Southland worsened, at least by their standards, each year they revisited. Now that he was down there again on the mission to court the expansion of her company's contacts, she hoped he was having a blessed April day as bright as her own. She recalled their conversation just two weeks ago when they had finalized the trip.

"Toshi called today and wanted to know about California," she began, over a dinner of whole wheat linguini with Puttanesca sauce plus an aged Chianti. "I told him you were going soon so I think if you're willing we should buy the tickets now." Jay looked at her over his wine glass as he sipped his first taste.

"Oh nice," he announced quietly. "Eighty-eight was really a great year for Italy."

"Are you still willing to go?" asked Bea, undeterred.

"Oh yes, most definitely, mustn't make Toshi unhappy." He cocked an eyebrow and smiled sardonically. "He might commit hara-kiri, before writing us a check."

"Very funny."

"Sorry, just kidding. Of course I'm still willing. When do you want me to leave?"

"If we buy them tomorrow you can leave in two weeks and we'll still get the discounted price for the tickets."

"Sounds good," agreed Jay, as he twirled his noodles nimbly through the red sauce. "Mmmm," he added. "This sauce is yummy too. Do you know, by the way, the origination of the name Puttanesca?"

"No," replied Bea, with half-hearted interest. "And if it's a long explanation I'd rather hear it later and focus on the trip at the moment, if you don't mind."

"Well, I wouldn't mind a bit but it's a short explanation and somewhat colorful to boot – no pun intended on Italy's shape."

"You're rather witty tonight, my dear. Has something happened today to lighten your mood?"

"Yeah – the wine's unexpectedly good and I got it on sale to boot – whoops I said that."

"That's nice to know. I'm glad for you. And now if you don't mind, about this trip. Can we discuss it please?"

"Yes darling, as soon as I finish my story, unless of course a tale about Toshi is much more important than one of mine could ever be."

"Oh, that could never be, at least not at the moment anyway, so hurry up please and tell me. I can't wait. What's the story?"

"Thought you'd never ask. In Italy it's a sauce that was made late at night in the restaurants by adding ingredients left over from dishes made earlier in the evening like olives, capers, peppers and garlic to the basic tomato sauce. That made it rather spicy. Then they would serve it primarily to the prostitutes who weren't free to eat until the late hours of the evening. The root word for prostitutes is puta." He swallowed a spun forkful with an air of satisfaction. "Hence, Puttanesca."

"Thank you, that was fascinating. Now can we talk about the trip?"

They proceeded to do so and to outline it in detail, and she smiled now as she recalled their entertaining exchange...*sure loves his food and wine*...On a more serious note she remembered how she had impressed upon him the disastrous consequences that could potentially happen if Toshi were disappointed. "Yes, yes, I know," Jay had assured her with some sarcasm. "Whatever Toshi wants, Toshi gets. Pressure, pressure, pressure. Maybe," he added, "somebody should tell him to back off. Adding three cities is a lot and could easily backfire if someone screws up. What if we get another Perry?"

"I know. I'm worried about it, believe me. But at the moment we really can't say no."

"I'd like to say no to him just to see what he does."

"I'm afraid if we do that I'll lose half my business."

"I know, I know, I know. Still...you'd think with all the good work you've done for him he would pay more attention to your concerns."

"Well, when you come back from this trip we may have some greater influence. But if we can't line these cities up...well, I hate to think what he'll do."

"I hate working for people that you are afraid of."

"So do I, Jay, but it's just the way it is. If you can pull this California trip off, our position will be stronger, we'll be more valuable an asset to the Japanese and the next time I go to Japan to see Toshi, I should have more leverage in future negotiations."

"I sure as hell hope so. I hate it when he calls. You always act so nervous."

"Yeah, well, I make it work."

His comments had given her some cause for concern. She agreed in principle that it was best to feel equal and unafraid with your business partners, but she was new at this game of student exchange and the adage her father had handed down from his store was paying huge dividends; the customer's always right. Moreover the Japanese agents had been so exacting, so insistent on certain conditions that she feared if she did not agree to their terms, they would simply look elsewhere for another company. On the good side it was well known that once they established a working relationship they strongly preferred not to change partners. If you could do the job you were in for life. That is, presuming the job didn't kill you. She longed at times to speak her mind more forcefully to Toshi, and for that matter to any other agents, but the timing wasn't right yet; she didn't feel strong enough. If she got these new cities and had another good summer season, then maybe she could say no when she felt it was warranted. Until then she'd appease them and keep them away from Jay.

She let Cheyenne slow down to a walk as he dipped down a steep long slope on the pipeline. He was starting to sweat and he swatted at flies with his tail as he carefully sidestepped through the rocks and grass...*ah this is the life*...Feeling appreciative she leaned forward to pet him with a friendly slap and wiped her wet hand off on her faded jeans. Usually she was chatting away with her cohort and did not take the time to notice her horse or the surroundings as fully as she was right now. Jeanne was a talkative though pleasant companion but today it was nice just to enjoy the solitude. When they had met many years ago there had been some hope that a couple's friendship would develop, since both men were therapists, but Jay had not found the other man to his liking, so the women had forged their own alliance on horseback.

Once at a restaurant, early on in the relationship, the four of them had gone out for dinner where the psychiatrist had proudly declared that he'd finally bested his record, seeing for the first time fifty clients in a week. In a humorous but biting tone Jay had inquired, "Did you help anybody?" and the relationship had never really gained ground from there. Jay knew from Bea who had learned from Jeanne that the doctor had recently had three clients commit suicide within a month's time and though the man was well off and obviously successful Jay couldn't help but wonder how great he really was. Since Jay was just starting up his practice at the time, Bea wondered if jealousy had sparked his remark and questionable assessment of the man's therapeutic skills, but nothing she could say would sway Jay to consider a relationship with him, either personally or professionally. They had argued about it but to no avail.

"He's already established, successful and rich. He could probably help you get set up in your practice," she had plaintively intoned. "Why make him an enemy?"

"I'm not making him an enemy," Jay had stubbornly replied, sounding irritated. "I just don't want to be friends. I don't really want anything to do with him. I'll make it on my own."

"But what's wrong with networking? It could save you so much time."

"I will do networking, but just not with him."

"Why not? Are you jealous? Why make this so hard?"

"I'm not jealous!" He paused. "Well, maybe I am, I don't know, but he's just not the kind of person I want to be around. He's more of a businessman, or at least so he seems. It's all about money. It's all about status. Or maybe it's not, but I don't think he gives a damn about spirituality. When I mentioned the Course to him he said he thought it was a cult."

"A lot of people find the Course hard to understand. He must be good to be so successful."

"Maybe he is and maybe he's not, but I just don't click with him. He's much older than me. He likes to recommend pills to people. He gets a lot of referrals from that hospital by his office. I bet he pushes Prozac like its candy. I try to get people off pills. We just don't mix. Being around him just doesn't feel good to me."

"Alright," said Bea, acquiescing at last. "But I don't see why you have to argue with success."

"If I ever have three suicides in a month, remind me to tell you how successful I feel!" And with that retort the subject was closed.

The next year, as Jay's private practice progressed, he'd bought her Cheyenne as a spectacular surprise for Valentine's Day. Ironically as circumstances would have it, the nearest and nicest place to board the animal was up on the hill at Jeanne's property. Though the men stayed distant the women had grown closer through riding the trails. They shared similar interests in literature, particularly themes on the spiritual roles and influence of women past and present, leading them to trade and discuss many of the same books. They also both appreciated the restorative power of nature, especially on horseback, taking trail-riding excursions and camping together for weekends at a time when weather permitted. But because of the recent boom in Bea's business it had been many months since they had gone on such outings.

Even while enjoying her solitary ride now she was aware that she missed their growing friendship. Good women friends were hard to find and harder yet to keep...*just like my sisters*...For a second she felt a sudden pang of loss as she remembered the plane crash and the numbing pain of grief. Cheyenne felt the lessening of tension in the reins as she absently rested her hands on the saddle horn and feeling the desire to run in his blood he broke into a trot down the grassy pipeline. "Whoa, boy," she said to him firmly, and pulled hard on the reins to keep him in tow. As a pony he'd been a champion in the wild sport known as Play Day where his speed and intensity had been harnessed to good use. She knew from his former owners that he'd been the best of the bunch in barrel racing. She'd also learned from experience that when he got a head of steam he could be hard to stop and riding alone was the worst time to flirt with danger. Sensing she meant it he complied immediately and slowed to a walk once more while still descending.

She thought once again of her sisters and focused this time on the remaining one. Their mutual loss in the tragedy had brought them closer at the time but now that they were off again living separate lives they had hardly spoken to each other since the winter. Faye had called once to say she was thinking of taking a trip, combining business with pleasure, to Seattle in late summer and Bea had warmed at the prospect of reconnecting. That trip was still tentative though and she hadn't yet heard back from Faye as to if and when it would be...*perhaps we could bond then...if she has the time...*

She continued to muse on the subject of women friends and how they kept changing or seemed hard to keep. Once she'd felt close to Candy in the office but that was deteriorating ever since autumn after Jay had joined them. She felt pessimistic about the likelihood of improvement. Maybe she ought to take Candy out to lunch and see if it were possible to have a good talk. She was certainly the best secretary that she'd ever had. It was sad to Bea to lose the closeness of their friendship simply because she didn't like men. The entire situation was growing more perplexing, especially with Candy's insinuations that Jay was flirting or possibly worse with a contact from a college. Although overall she felt she could trust him, there had been that one incident years ago with that woman from the college that had lasted for months until Bea protested. Being away so much of the time lately had made her feel keenly that she was neglecting her son. Now she considered if also her husband had been feeling neglected. Stranger things had happened. Men had their needs. Or so she had heard. Once on a trail ride Jeanne had confided that her husband insisted on having sex at least twice a week.

Though she and Jay had never quantified it she knew that he was, at least in comparison to her first husband, highly sexually charged...*wonder what he does with all of those feelings*...Sooner or later they'd have to talk too. The whole office tension was becoming intolerable and now that she was home it was hard to avoid. At least on the road she didn't have to bear that. And besides Candy's innuendos about Jay, when things were not going well between her and Randy she also complained unhesitatingly about him. Randy had no time for her, he was insensitive to her, he didn't take her out enough, and he was stubborn, unreasonable when they disagreed. Though Bea had thought earlier that Randy seemed a nice guy, listening to Candy she couldn't help wondering if he had a darker side; insensitive, selfish, colder than he seemed...*maybe she's right...maybe you can't trust them...*

That was certainly true of Perry, and also she'd learned that with Japanese men. Kazuo, the scourge of the earth in her universe, was up to no good, she could be sure of that. He was a silent invisible enemy – the worst kind – and she feared she hadn't heard the last of him yet. And Toshi, reliable as he was in many ways, could always be relied on to be demanding about his needs. Perhaps it *was* time to be more assertive with him, especially if Jay's trip went well, as expected. She felt her mood darkening as she contemplated the challenges posed by the men and the women in her life. The decline on the hillside leveled out and turned upward. Suddenly she dug her heels in sharply to Cheyenne's sides.

"Giddyup'" she shouted, abruptly deciding to shift moods swiftly with a quick change of pace. In an instant Cheyenne was bolting up the hill, happy at last to be free from constraint. She knew that he fervently loved to run fast and an uphill climb was the safest place to do it. He bounded through the thick grass with reckless abandon, trampling flowers, scattering stones, with his mane and her hair flying in the wind. The rapid shift to a gallop loosened one of her boots from the stirrup and she bounced about briefly on his back until finding it again. The breeze blew off her cares like a blast from an air hose as she crouched in for balance. She flew through the air secure in the saddle as though in a seat belt on a bumpy plane ride and grew more excited as they neared the hilltop. Normally she would have been reining him in as they approached the crest but the thrill of the speed was a welcome respite from the weight of her worries. While gripping her legs tighter like a vise on his body she lowered her head into the wind and let him charge to the peak at full tilt.

His momentum carried them into the air and he landed on all fours then tore down the next grade. For the moment she knew there was nothing to do but clamp on like a crab and pray he didn't stumble. Luckily the angle was a gentle decline and it ran as long as a football field before sloping up to the next apex. He was still running strong when she began to slow him down but he'd gotten enough of it out of his system where she knew that he would not resist her. Pulling the reins back with all she could muster brought him to gradual halt at the summit. As Cheyenne stood there heaving and panting she sat up in the saddle, feeling relieved and exhilarated. She turned around to look at the faint Seattle skyline, feeling for the moment on top of the world.

As solid as the high-rise silhouettes against the mountains, she felt at that instant the best thing to do. As uncomfortable as it seemed, she couldn't forever forestall an encounter with the people and problems plaguing her now. Sooner or later she'd have to take action, with the women around her as well as the men. If she wanted to change or at least clarify her concerns with her friends, relatives, and business associates, she would need to take the bit in her mouth and run with it. The idea of doing so half scared her to death. She had always given cooperation precedence over confrontation. But now the latter way seemed definitely better than a gradual demise through worry and pressure; starting immediately with Candy in the office. Perhaps with Jay gone she could soften a bit. Perhaps they could have an old heart to heart talk. Then later when Jay returned she'd speak with him about the woman at the college. She had put it off knowing that there was trouble either way. If Candy was right, she'd have a problem with Jay and if Candy was wrong he'd have a problem with her, which was bad enough already.

She thought of her sister, on the distant east coast. She hoped that her visit would definitely pan out. If not, she'd find another way to fortify that bond. While Faye, her last sibling, remained here on earth there was always the chance for them to get closer. Giving up was not an option. As for the key men in her hard world of work, irrespective of whatever Jay's trip achieved, she felt a resurgence of purpose in seeking to strengthen her position in her dealings with them all. She wanted more than anything to strengthen her character and courage through the challenges that arose in that realm. Though Perry had proven extremely elusive, at times seeming futile to continue pursuing, she wouldn't let it go, as much for her own growth as well as the money. By contrast Toshi, who was always unavoidable, was offering her a different kind of lesson in confrontation. As threatening as the thought was of losing half her business, the tactics of ESAD were becoming rather tiresome. Though his interactive style had left much to be desired Jay had demonstrated that tough talk could clearly impact the Japanese. Perhaps it was time for some straight speech of her own. If Leroy was right there was nothing to fear. Her fulfillment was not contingent upon another person. As for Kazuo, well, he'd have to make the first move; an unsettling thought but probably inevitable, as he seemed quite thoroughly obsessed with her ruin. Until he did something, she would focus on the others, beginning tomorrow in the office with her secretary.

Chapter 51

"Clinton was not the worst president the republic has had, but he is the worst person ever to have been president." (George Will)

AS THE HUGE JET lifted off the runway in a roar Jay took a last look at the sprawl of Los Angeles surrounding the airport in a hot smoggy haze. The busy boulevards most notably sported high-rise hotels in the immediate area interspersed on the perimeter with a jumble of steel gray industrial sites. They were infused with a vast scrambled network of billboards, shabby stores, parking lots and dreary neighborhoods. The aircraft circled slowly towards the north while heading higher and as the suburbs became visible the brilliant sheen of blue swimming pools dotted the landscape like wet turquoise stones shining in the sun. The long sandy curve of the coastline came into view as the plane crossed the shore and rose over the ocean. He noticed the boats becoming dimmer as the craft continued upwards till they were merely tiny specks in a measureless sea whose rollicking surface swayed freely in all directions.

He leaned his seat back when the plane leveled out and reclined at rest for a moment without thinking, feeling the low-level vibrating whirr of the engines on the wing. As he relaxed in his seat a feeling of satisfaction came over him while he reflected on the completion of his task. Starting in San Francisco over a week ago he had journeyed after three days on south to San Diego before finishing up his trip in the LA basin. The time in the first two cities had been fruitful in the effort to find local Area Directors. The time in

LA had been unproductive however in locating good candidates to run an operation. He'd reached the tentative conclusion that perhaps they were better off eliminating that city anyway as a destination for Bea's foreign students. It was such an ugly jungle. If anything bad could happen to a foreign student it seemed that the likelihood was greatest in a congested conflagration like the misnamed city of angels.

Not only was it a snarling snake pit of traffic but the nicer areas, those appropriate for students, were a ways from the airport and scattered about in different vicinities. The suburbs were the ideal neighborhoods for the kids but they were far enough apart that it would require many supervisors – one for each area. That meant little work for a lot of different people and it lessened the chances of finding good help. Even those seeking part-time work usually wanted more than a few hours a week. Along with that it would be logistically rigorous to have the members of a student group spread all around the suburbs. It would take a bus driver several hours to pick them all up for a single group excursion. He had come up with what he thought was a better idea, and hoped that Bea would concur with his assessment; better to place them all in Orange County, midway between San Diego and LA. A few people from there had responded to his ad in the Los Angeles Times, planting the seed in his mind. That community was safer, friendlier, cleaner and easier to navigate than LA would ever be. Plus Disneyland was there, and it wasn't that far for a bus trip from there to LA for a day of activities at Universal Studios or whatever other venues.

San Francisco had been different. It was suitable for students. Many families had nice homes in or near enough to the city that it was not necessary to rely on the suburbs. His visit had been the second one he'd made this year, having traveled there in January for the foreign student convention. It had been exciting then to be among so many people, mostly college administrators, trying to woo the foreign student business to their university. Since having a Homestay program to offer those students was considered an asset by many schools, he had found a ready audience with most school personnel. As a result he'd been successful in gaining new contracts with colleges in Oregon, Idaho, Arizona and Washington. Plus other states were considering it yet. Bea had been beaming upon his return, grateful for his bountiful marketing success.

The city itself had been a memorable experience; beautiful buildings, bridges and ballparks, colorful characters and costumed performers down by the waterfront. At night there were block long throngs of Italian cafes spilt out on the sidewalks under the streetlights, filled with chattering patrons and pasta, wine in straw bottles, candles in glass. A hint of the city's wild side was never far away and there were hordes of the homeless strewn in disarray, plus street people, crazies, bums, beggars, junkies and jive-ass punks who preferred the art of panhandling to an honest day's work. Most of the time he was at the convention site, a mammoth structure, visiting booths of the various colleges; sharing his wares, making his pitch. The week had gone so well that toward the end of it he'd relaxed a bit and taken in the sights; Candlestick Park, the Mark Hopkins hotel, riding the BART, walking through

Fisherman's Wharf and Golden Gate Park. He'd strolled the city, amazed at the contrast; so much degradation amid such beauty. Every night he had eaten alone in the Italian sector and once on the way back to his hotel, a few blocks from the restaurant, he had witnessed some black teenagers chasing another up the outdoor stairs of an old apartment building, carrying two by fours and shouting they would bust his butt when they caught him.

This trip he'd been too busy in the brief time he was there to see much of the city. He interviewed prospects throughout the day and trained those he hired during the evening. In the end he was pleased with the new employees and felt that the time had all been worth it. The San Diego effort had gone equally as well and if Orange County could be substituted for LA, as he would recommend, then the programs in California were ready to roll. He only hoped Toshi would okay the deal. His reputation as a tough negotiator was an abiding concern. Along with that it bothered him how much Bea seemed to fear the man. She lived in constant apprehension that he could destroy her company by taking away half of her business at a moment's notice. It still disturbed him to see her become nervous whenever he called...*i'd love to talk to that guy some time...*

He felt himself getting tense and thought about having a beer. Disdaining the canned crap they served on the plane, he instead he took a deep breath and tried to relax. As he did so he remembered that he'd brought along a tape with him from Leroy to listen to whenever he had down time. This trip had been so filled with interviews and training he'd never had time to play it. He pulled out the cassette tape recorder from his bag in the overhead compartment, put on the headphones and listened to the conversation.

"It's Friday the twenty first of January and we're all set."

"Okay, well, the first thing I want to say is that my son, Jess, is interested in renting a house out in Duvall and it's a wooden dome structure and he's not sure if it's appropriate and the owner is in a hurry to culminate the deal and he wants six hundred a month and it has outdoor plumbing, but he and his wife are living for free at her father's house and there's some tension around that but I wonder if they should offer this guy less or even if it is appropriate for them to live there at all."

"No, it's not appropriate."

"Can you expand on that?"

"No. There's no reason for it. It's just not where they are to live. They need to seek something more conventional."

"To make their life easier?"

"Of course."

"Well, what's their attraction to the unconventional all about?"

"The attraction in general is the desire for adventure and fun and I recommend that. I'm just not recommending this place. What I do recommend is that they listen, and they step back from this and see where the current is really taking them."

"Let it unfold?"

"Right. I just don't recommend this place. I see it as challenging. I see it as having a leaky roof or something."

"Okay. So they should step back and continue to search for housing but with an openness to see what unfolds."

"It could be just as fun but more conventional. I do recommend indoor plumbing. That is something the lack of which could get old real quick."

"I bet. Think they should consider paying more than five hundred a month wherever they go?"

"Of course. I mean, you are asking someone who is encouraging people to explore limitlessness. I'm not suggesting that they will spend more than that but they need to pay attention to the movement and not what they think their budget is."

"Are you saying that if they continue this search in an open minded manner that they will know the right one when it happens; that there will not be even the kind of questions or tensions they have around this one?"

"It could be that way but it also could be something that they do not see as special because the appropriateness of it is obscured because it may not be something that seems particularly remarkable. It may not be absolutely illuminated. It's nice when it happens that way, but a lot of waking up is about just paying attention and asking what step to take simply based upon your common sense. You see, they are not ready, nor you quite yet for that matter, to vacate all of the mechanisms of perception and reason that serve one; to be able have one revelation after another. They live in a mixture of reasoning and occasional revelation, and until you are past the need to reason you don't experience constant revelation. So, it's nice to have revelation in the midst of your rational mind, but as long as they are still relying on common sense and thinking, it may well be that they will simply see something that meets the need and there's nothing greatly moving about it. But that's still what they need to do. They need to take what's there."

"Okay. I get it."

"What else is on your mind?"

"Well. What you are saying about being open to things reminds of my consideration of a Ph.D. program."

"How so?"

"Well, I think about how you have said to me to just be open to the possibility of a Ph.D. program and I have not been very much open to it at all and I just recently went to the interview with a psychologist, an older guy, the local representative of the college I applied to, and I got through the interview and the guy liked me and said that I was just the kind of person he was looking for and then he went on to say that he thought the college had not been very honest with me because they have a glut of applicants for at least two years in the northwest and so I realized I may not get in there forever. But when I went there I was ready to basically do battle and bash the whole establishment and be defensive, but when I saw this guy he seemed like such a harmless and nice old man that I unexpectedly just sort of relaxed and allowed myself to be open, just chatting with an intellectual and kind person, and we got along fine and I felt no tension at all and although the information about the school was disappointing, I actually felt good upon leaving the interview because I just stayed open and at peace and he said, in effect, 'You would be perfect for this'. I felt vindicated without realizing I was seeking that."

"Right."

"So now, I wonder what will happen next. I mean he basically said that he accepted me and would like to work with or teach someone like me but that unfortunately I would not get admitted because the school had already accepted their applicants for this semester and perhaps for years ahead and he was angry with the school for misleading people and I said 'Gee, don't be angry on my account' because I felt so good being peaceful and open, and, I suppose, knowing I was totally fine in his eyes. It was very validating to me personally. I mean, I was ready to reject them, but now I see I was perfectly acceptable to them – just the type of person he wanted – and that made me feel great. So now I wonder if I will ever get into that school at all. In effect, the interview was a sham. For some reason the school just wanted the appearance of interviewing me."

"I cannot tell you what is going to happen next because it feels in flux to me at the moment but I can say that there was some value at the very least in having the experience of the interview and you will have to see where it leads from here."

"Frankly I don't really care what happens with it. I'm really happy that they – he – found me to be a such desirable candidate, but I still really have little interest in doing it. It was good to be valued or validated, and that made me aware that I hadn't expected that, but I think that was the main value of this experience. I'm ready now more than ever to forget about it, especially now that I'm more at peace with it, but the real thing is still that I'm just tired of being unhappy with my life."

"Right. That's it exactly. This is a time when things are still in flux and your happiness and your sense of constantly being connected are being revealed to you as the only important experience there is."

"That's true. But when I'm not having that I'm hell on wheels."

"Well, the problem is that when you are not having that you are experiencing urgency and urgency is really only the urgency to get back to God. That's what you have to remember when you find yourself in circumstances that are irritating or problematic. The urgency is only to get back to God. It isn't to fix the problem."

"I know. I understand that, and I've been saying that statement to myself, ever since you said it to me a few weeks ago. It really hit home, and so I say it a lot. There is no urgency here but to feel the presence of God."

"Right, and so you get back and there you are."

"But I forget that sometimes and then I'm just ready to kill everybody."

"You don't forget it much, and you don't forget it for long periods of time. You have minor episodes."

"But I'm concerned that the minor episodes are so intensely angry. I mean, it's like I have some people that pretty much I'm just ready to go ballistic with at any given time, like Clinton or far-left types in general. If there were any far-right types around I'd probably detest them as well but I don't know of any. This area is glutted with hate-filled radicals. It's funny, because in college and all through my twenties I was a liberal. And I lived in Orange County, a right-wing bastion. But I gradually kept shifting, and now it's more the reverse. But the simple truth is that all these political ideologues seem so shallow and counter-productive to me."

"Clinton?"

"Yeah. It seems I could feast my whole mind on hating him. I've got a bumper sticker taped to the back window of my car that says 'Honk if you're related to Clinton' as a comment on his character, or lack of that is. But my point is that on another level, in a corner of my mind, I know that Clinton just really doesn't matter, liberals and conservatives don't really matter, in terms of the true meaning of my life. My happiness or peace of mind isn't contingent on someone else's beliefs or behavior. It's just that they all seem so clueless about the spiritual nature of life that I seem to find them appropriate justification for these expressions of anger. So many ignorant arrogant people. And of course the worst thing is I realize that I am no better or different than them when angry."

"That's true. But look, any time that you feel injustice, it's because you are feeling some present lack."

"Hm. You mean a lack of fulfillment or an apparent scarcity of resources?"

"Yes, either one. If you didn't feel that lack, then the behavior of someone else wouldn't bother you. You would still be having your experience of peace, balance, grace, etc. You might want to say something about it, but the fact is that it wouldn't bother you. The fact that it bothers you means that you really are experiencing some lack."

"You're right. I am. That's why we talk about money so much of the time and peace of mind. And it's true that there are times when I have moments of clarity when I realize I don't care what Clinton, or political ideologues, or other people in general do – that my responsibility for my happiness lies solely in my hands irrespective of what anyone else thinks, says or is doing with their life."

"Right. So divert your attention whenever you have an episode of righteousness or injustice. Instead, pay attention to the fact that you are experiencing lack. And that has an easy remedy."

"Good. What's that?"

"Then you say, to God, your Guide, the Holy Spirit, whatever, 'Help me – I don't want to feel this way'."

"That works?"

"It works. You feel relieved. You see, the experience of lack is just another imaginary or illusory feeling based upon being off center."

"Feeling unbalanced is madness."

"Right. And so in the moment you allow grace back into you life, you don't feel it. Again, we talked about the Lord's Prayer. And all of that is about asking for grace. All of it is about balance. If you look at it, it says 'Give us this day our daily bread' i.e., let there be sufficiency; balance. Forgive us our debts as we forgive our debtors, i.e., let there be equity; balance. Lead us not into temptation but deliver us from evil, in other words, let there be an evenness of unfoldment so there aren't these moments of drama or trial, you see, in other words: balance. And balance is grace. See, that's the whole point. So look at these episodes as just moments when your ego still has got some little bit of life in it."

"Raging away."

"Yes, and if you can understand that you can go deep at that point and undermine its outrage, and if you are willing to do that, the help is immediate, and then you are free. And then you find yourself back on track again. And all of your life right now is about divine justice. In other words, it's about being restored to grace no matter how many times you slip out of it until the point is reached of absolute acceptance of God's will and your divinity; your own divinity as a creation of God. When that acceptance has become unequivocal then the grace is never seen to be lost, so you won't have those episodes. You will not waver. Lack or imbalance of any sort is just the perception of insufficient support or loss of grace."

"Well…okay…but…well, let me put it his way. I've been trying to practice being this way ever since we began talking. And I think I'm a fairly imaginative and energetic person. And I can dream up all sorts of things to do or buy. I mean right now I'd like to order up season tickets to half a dozen plays or sporting events. I'd like to buy a motorcycle. There's like a million things I could get or do, and so I practice feeling the peace and I'm willing to stay with this but some times…because there's not more evidence of the ability to do these things, I start to feel that this is somehow fraudulent. How do I get out of that?"

"You are still under the dominion of time. You feel you are waiting, and waiting is always done in the experience of time. And I'm sorry to say but you can wait forever and these things won't happen. So there is a need to accept what you have with greater appreciation and greater awareness that it is fully substantiated; that all of the substance that you need is already there."

"Uh huh. Somehow I knew that was going to be the answer. In other words I'm not feeling enough gratitude for what is. I'm focusing on what isn't."

"Right, because you think that you need more substance in order to have those particular things that you are saying are desirable, when in fact you don't need more substance. Somehow the appreciation of the substance, of which you have all that there is, is not wholehearted enough. There's a subtle complaint being leveled at the Source. And that is because, quite understandably, from the perspective of the ego you seem to lack substance. The ego wants to be able to fulfill itself through season tickets and motorcycles by having more substance added to it, and the Laws of God do not allow that. And where you have to go is here: you have to go with a complete wholehearted appreciation of exactly where you are with the awareness that it is fully substantial. You may then have a desire for a transformation of the substance you already have, but you do not require more substance. That's the whole point. So what you want is that you have a clear desire that you agree with; that you feel the intent for certain things to be. And in the mixture of that with the full appreciation of what you have, not as form but as substance, you then allow the movement of spirit through that substance to transpire and then transform the substance into whatever form identifies fulfillment."

"By substance you mean the whole of creation."

"Right."

"Hm. It's amazing to me how forgetful I am."

"Well, that's true. Whether it's amazing or not you do get forgetful, but you are not ignorant of the truth, which is a hell of a lot better than if you didn't know about it."

"That's true. (laughter) I started to say 'What would I do without you' but it seemed like an expression of lack."

"But you aren't without me. So, in effect, you have here the art of alchemy; the transformation of substance. Alchemy is considered a fake discipline but true alchemy has always been a spiritual art based in physical science. The problem with alchemy is that they did it by trying to combine opposite substances to synthesize something new, and that's not how it works."

"You mean they were trying to play God?"

"Yes, in a sense, but how the transformation of substance really occurs is by how I've just outlined it. You have the full recognition of the presence of substance in your life and the acceptance and recognition of the desire you have for particular fulfillment. That combined leads to the transformation of substance."

"Hm."

"This is what Holy Communion is all about; eating the wafer and drinking wine as the body and blood of Christ. It's about the transformation of substance, and the church refers to it as transubstantiation."

"Hm."

"So this is how you spend your time with respect to your desires; in appreciating what you have, not as form but as substance, as the presence of good."

"Out of that then, being at peace with what I have, legitimate desires will arise? I mean, maybe if I'm at peace, appreciating what I have and feeling I have all there is, then perhaps I won't feel like getting season tickets or a motorcycle. I won't feel I'm lacking anything."

"Right. In the beginning, when you are trying to do this, you don't want to be trying to do it so deliberately. It's more important that you understand that along with this is an ongoing movement for you to recover your innocence. So trying to use this as a way to manipulate things is not going to move the mountain. But instead what I suggest you do now is to contemplate just the first part of this; that the substance of life is all present, and it is not static. It endures simply because God wills it to endure. As I have said before, there is God's will and the precepts of the ego or your beliefs about life. Sometimes conditions in your life endure because you are not willing to accept the readiness or immediacy of transformation because your perceptions or reasoning will not allow it. In effect, they block it. They tell you that you do not have the means for certain desires to be met. So you back away from that position by going to the first thing, which is the acknowledgement and the appreciation that everything is fully substantiated, that the substance is there, regardless of whatever form it is currently in."

"It's all here now. I've got plenty of everything."

"You have everything. You have absolutely everything. This is not a personal thing. This is an acknowledgement of the world, the universe, from the unique perspective known as Jay. You are the wholeness of life looking at it itself from that particular perspective that you call you. And from that vantage point you say 'Gee, there's a lot of stuff here, endless substance, and I'm a part of it', you see, and that's the fundamental experience of Being. Now, be with gratitude for that. First, be grateful for those things that you personally have particularly. Then acknowledge that you are a part of all of the rest of it as well."

"Hm. You mean like the earth, all life forms, like the trees or something?"

"Everything; Clinton, liberals, conservatives, trees, whatever. They all need to be seen as God's creation, or substantiations of the intent to create. You see, if the intent to create is substantiated it becomes reality. So it is very important to acknowledge the basis upon which something can be created. That is what Jesus means, as I've often said, in seeking the kingdom first; by acknowledging there's stuff, there's endless substance, all of God's creation, and you are grateful for it also. Then, when you feel clear that you are not seeing things in the same old way, through the ego, through a perception of lack or scarcity, you reflect on the desire to have something occur, realizing that desire is an expression of God's will, and you agree with it; you accept that it is to occur. And you understand that the desires move out into the stuff, into substance, into creation, by moving through it; they transpire. Transpiration is the capacity to move through a membrane. So the desire becomes the intent, and then transpires or moves through the substance or what you were thinking of as fixed form and transforms it into something new."

"Hm. I've been trying to practice this, but I think I've had difficulty in being intent without being in an ego state of mind. It's simply very hard for me to be at peace, meaning out of the ego state and feeling at one with God."

"I know. But you keep at it. You continue to practice and that's always the first step; the necessary step. Then, if you feel a desire and you agree with it, you can yield to it, but you must be coming from that state of mind."

"Is it more like a thought will come up and I'll think 'Yeah, that would be nice, a motorcycle ride would be nice'? Is that what you're saying?"

"That's a step. But intent feels like you know something's going to happen; like there's an intent for night to fall and daylight to follow. When a desire has been fully agreed upon it will move to that stage where it becomes intent. And you yield to it. You don't have to hold it. It's just there. You don't have to hold the idea that you have to will the sun to rise. You just know it's going to happen."

"But I don't intend for the sun to rise, while I might intend to see more clients or buy a motorcycle."

"The difference here is in the degree of knowing or trust. You trust the sun to rise. You know it is going to happen. You know it is inevitable. So, if you felt that way about your various desires, if you felt them as inevitable, you wouldn't have any difficulty with whatever you had to go through or endure in order to experience their fulfillment. You see? You would just know, beyond question."

"So it's doubt that's in my way over seeing more clients or buying a new motorcycle?"

"Yes. You don't fully experience the intent for that to be, because you are not allowing it to happen based upon the fact that it is simply the movement of life. There's seems to be still, in your mind, some degree of responsibility for it. You want to cause it. You don't cause the sun to rise, so why the hell should you have to cause anything to happen? Do you see what I'm saying? Well, of course, the conditioning of the world is that that can't possibly be."

"I'm not quite entering the mind state that you are speaking of."

"But you understand what I'm talking about. Whether you have entered into it or not isn't so important at the moment. What I want you to do is to be clearly aware of the distinction I'm making; how clear you are about the sun rising without you having to do it. Use that as a reference point for regarding your desires and intentions with the same degree of ease and conviction you have about the sun rising, and let that be. That's trust."

"Trust and gratitude replace responsibility."

"Absolutely."

"Well…I'll go through the day practicing that – I hope."

"Or don't do it all, but just don't take on more responsibility. Don't look for something more to be responsible for. That will be a subtle way of your ego insinuating itself into the process. There's a tendency to stop doing what you were doing and then to conscientiously try to do something else. It really does need to be more deflating than what you have done. Do you understand?"

"Less conscientious or responsible?"

"Just really letting the wind out of the ego by not assuming anymore burden and instead trying to find how you can be at peace and ease with no responsibility for doing something to make your desires happen."

"Hm…you mean really just relax into the moment?"

"Right, and just say 'Well, if I don't worry about that, if I don't do this, if I don't do that, if I don't make any of this a problem – I'll just see what happens'. Of course the ego will say 'What about me, I want something', want, want, want, you see. See whether you can settle down more deeply so that that crook of the ego, that hook of finding a new conflict, a new process to try hard at, doesn't get you."

"Easy does it?"

"Right. Easy money. I like that one too. (laughter) You are not experiencing easy money because you are not really getting with easiness. See if you can really let go of it, totally absolve yourself of responsibility, while at the same time staying with appreciation, you see, and see if life doesn't start serving you. That's how it works."

"Hm."

"Sometimes people flake out and they become inactive, but also they isolate themselves. I'm saying for you to yield to a feeling of no responsibility, but with no sense of isolation."

"You mean withdrawal is just another ego trip?"

"Right."

"I think I'm getting a little better at this."

"Oh, of course you are. How do you know you are not great at it?"

"Did you say 'How do you know you're not great at it'?" (laughter)

"Right. You see, your reference point here is that you see yourself as one who is slowly pushing through the mire, but maybe you are someone who is really advanced and close to awakening. And the fact that it doesn't feel easy and progressive right now simply means that there is no partial awakening. It's just all or nothing."

"Got it. It seems like partial awakening would be something like where your ego would like an accolade for the awakening work going on." (laughter)

"Right, and your life would look good to other egos, who would then be inclined to adopt your point of view as the way to go. (laughter) And it's amazing how it doesn't work that way, how, despite everyone's wish, and I mean everyone, myself included, who is going through this or has gone through this, everyone wants for it to work partially, at some point, so that it looks like you're on the right track. And what you begin to get is that you are having a pretty easy time of it, even though it may not look like it's all that great. You realize it's certainly gotten a lot easier and it seems to have the capacity to maintain itself without your anxiety. And that's the big part of it; to trust that this works."

"Hm."

"Again, I go back to the Lord's prayer as being so fundamental here, because you are learning to experience grace. And what you have with that learning is disengaging from the urgency around life. You are learning that more than anything right now. You are disengaging from the idea that life requires urgent response."

"Hmmm…I love this stuff."

"Yes. It makes it easier to live."

"More fun. Hm. Do you think that when one feels gratitude, that is, sometimes I feel gratitude, and want then to express it in perceivable actions and I was just wondering if it might be sufficient merely to hold a grateful feeling toward someone? In other words, sometimes I feel gratitude towards someone, something will touch my heart and it feels so good that I want to give them gifts or hug them or have them over for a meal or, I don't know, I guess just some expression of the gratitude. And then but it also all feels so futile at the same time, and I wonder if just feeling the gratitude is enough, and I don't know. Make sense?"

"Yes, it does, and there's a little bit of feeling responsible in that. You do what you can do. And if the best thing you can do is simply smile or say thank you, then that's it. You don't have to be concerned that the form of expression might not be worthy enough. It's the genuiness of expression that counts."

"Thank you. Well, I reach points in these conversations like this, where I feel peace. I feel blank. I have nothing to say. I'm open and willing to hearing more, but it seems that asking a question would be an unnecessary interruption to the peace being experienced. It's more like I'm wanting to go through the course of the day being this way."

"That's all you need to do then. You don't need to look for irrelevancies and try to make them relevant so that we could then continue talking in the manner that we have. This is not a therapy session." (laughter)

"Are you sure? (laughter) Maybe it is but we don't have to spend the required amount of time. (laughter) By the way how are we on time, speaking of irrelevancies?"

"Oh, we have a few minutes yet. We started about ten minutes after. You were late. That's what we can do. I can scold you for not being on time."

"Well, I already went through that one with my last client who arrived late, which made us late."

"You should have just cut that one off." (laughter)

"Right. Well, I let her scold herself for it and then I let her know that I didn't have any judgments around it, so I'm not going to buy any from you." (laughter)

"Good. How is business anyway?"

"Oh, well, not so good, but I guess it could be worse. I'm trying to appreciate it, I guess. Frankly it's hard not to feel angry or sad, or complain to the Source, as you said."

"If you are feeling the need to complain, then there is a need for an adjustment in your point of view, so that you do not have to feel guilty or responsible for the situation."

"Yeah, well, I'm not sure quite how to do that."

"Be grateful for not seeing more people."

"That's a thought. I forgot you said that." (laughter)

"Only because then you are in perfect accord with what is going on."

"Hm. Sometimes I think I must not want to see more."

"Well, you aren't, whether you want to or not. I don't want you to take it into the realm of responsibility here again. I don't want you to keep digging up that same old garden again, because you can't know what the seeds are going to do if you keep digging them up and looking at them."

"Alright. I get it."

"Just be grateful for the amount you are seeing, and not with that bogus humility like 'Well, it's not so much but I'm trying to appreciate it'. You are seeing as many as you are seeing and be grateful for that amount and no more. Be grateful for the fact that you aren't seeing any one else. And this takes all the subtle striving out of the situation that you maintain. Do you see that?"

"Yes."

"So be grateful for what you are seeing and no more and then simultaneously you can also still have the desire to see more. You can have that kind of paradox or irony and be very unconflicted about it. It may not make sense to your reasoning, but to your Being it makes perfect sense. Your Being comprehends exactly what you are doing when you desire to see more and you are perfectly grateful for not seeing more. Your Being knows that this is enlightened or awake. It knows how to unfold that perfectly, more than it does trying to rationalize a paradox. When you do it the other way you don't have any thing. You not only don't feel good about the number of people you are seeing, you also want to see more and can't."

"Okay. I understand. Thanks. I better get off now. It's about time for my next appointment. I'll call you next week."

"Alright. Take care, and be at ease, but be connected."

"Got it. Bye."

Jay took off the headset and sat up straighter in his seat. He noticed the drone of the airplane again as he returned the cassette to the bag overhead. He always felt good after listening to their talks and yet, months later, things still had not picked up much in his practice. He had long term clients who were continuing to come, like Howie and Sharon, and Naimee, among others. The problem lay mainly in attracting new clients. Upon learning that he didn't take insurance, prospective new clients, at least those with insurance, simply called around to other therapists and he never heard back from them... *be happy for those i have...while desiring more...*

Hearing tapes from three months prior made him realize he was neglecting to practice what was being preached. From the moment he awoke he did a brief meditation, followed by a frenzied pace of all day activity. By evening after his run, he was more than ready for happy hour to start. Occasionally he tried to meditate at midday but was usually too preoccupied and found that the weekends were the best time for serious practice. He considered meditating now but felt too distracted. The pilot would be starting his descent soon, blaring loud announcements on the speaker system. The flickering thought of another doctoral program flashed through his mind like shooting star, but he knew in his heart it was a dead issue now. He doubted a Ph.D would enhance his skills. That thought was supported by the many psychologists he had met or worked with throughout the years. He knew he didn't want any more college knowledge. This was purely about making it now through becoming aware as a spiritual being.

He reflected on Leroy's phrase: easy money. It sounded great but seemed such a hard shift. Here he was traipsing all around the west coast trying to rev up Bea's money machine. When back in the office he was up to his neck in business activity and any spare time went for tracking down Perry. It seemed like the more he was caught up in this work, he was losing the focus to advance his practice. It was a Catch-22; a rodent's race in a circular maze. Needing the work to make money now prevented him from concentrating much on counseling and made him too tense to meditate consistently. Such thoughts brought back the tension felt earlier in the flight. He considered just saying the Lord's prayer for a moment, but decided instead for a tried and true mood adjuster. He summoned a stewardess and ordered a beer, although not without misgivings about the available choices. Sipping an uninspired taste from a Coors can he kicked off his shoes, sunk into his seat and pondered his predicament...*gotta' get out of this rat trap somehow...* He chugged down the watery swill without pleasure, crumpled the can up and ordered another, feeling a flush of growing determination swelling evenly alongside a rival sense of futility.

Chapter 52

"One attraction in coming to the woods to live was that I should have the leisure and opportunity to see the spring come in." (Walden, Henry David Thoreau)

THOUGH THE SUN HAD not quite risen yet, the sky was blue and brightening above, while pink dimpled clouds on the horizon were perfectly reflected, like long floating feathers, in the lake beneath the gauzy mist. Several currents were flowing through the middle of the water like little rivers; alternating dark and light streams running side by side. They moved in undulating ridges like a line of endless dragon scales in smooth succession rippling left to right. Cutting neatly across them were three distinct v-shaped patterns gradually merging their fading waterlines in the distance as three ducks, roughly fifty yards apart, paddled steadily toward the shoreline trailing wedges behind them. A lone seagull circled high above the water before dipping down to cruise low over the lake.

Bea sat in silence, a hot coffee cup clasped in her lap like a porcelain heater, warming her hands as she surveyed the changing scene. The sun rose partially peering through the pines, sending radiant shafts across the surface like far-away searchlights. Gliding like a balanced boomerang in flight, a goose with widespread wings angled through mist and then settled lightly on the water motionless. A red-winged blackbird abruptly lit on a willow tree in front of her, flashing its bright orange marks as it landed. It warbled a brief song and was gone in an instant like a bird on fire. Yards away to the right she noticed a robin swaying on the flimsy tiptop of an evergreen. As the sun became round it reflected at the lakeside like a luminous ball glowing underwater. A man sitting in a small fishing boat by the far shore slipped along leisurely dragging his line.

She raised her mug for a drink while enjoying the sights and looked down at the beautiful bushes in her yard. Two orange and two yellow azaleas were mixed in with numerous rhododendrons, mostly shades of pink and purple. A soft stream of steam was rising gently from a corner of the hot tub beneath her, evaporating before it reached the huge cedar spreading its limbs overhead. As she looked up four white geese or swans sailed gracefully by like ghost birds or angels; an unusual spectacle. From the cottonwood trees, near the park on the left, an eagle emerged, gaining height as he soared toward the thick mass of pine trees lined across the way. For a moment the sun shone yellow on the bird's belly till it tucked into the woods and disappeared from view. A few seconds later it suddenly reappeared, flapping its large tapered wings vigorously. There were two squawking crows giving chase on its tail and they stayed in pursuit till it circled half the lake. Bea sat amused at the wonder of it all but knew with the sun now up it was time to get to work.

She thought for a moment at the agenda before her. Another day with Candy which, after their talk, was tentatively better, though Jay had not yet been back in the office. Further exchanges with Toshi were certain, as he continued to press her on California. So far their communications had been by fax. While satisfied they'd set up two new operations, he balked on the decision to reconfigure LA. They hadn't said Orange County. They had said Los Angeles. They wanted a program in place there for next spring. He had stopped short of threatening to cancel her contract, but had been insistent that she do their bidding. Furthermore, he had written, his company was now also considering sending a small group of students to LA for Christmas. Even a small group was something that Bea was reluctant to accept without having staff there. And as busy as they'd be from now through September, she didn't even want to consider the thought.

She also wondered what was happening with the program for Hundai high school. She hadn't heard from them recently but that didn't necessarily mean anything bad. No news could be good news and it had seemed things were slipping neatly into place for their students' trip to Seattle in August. She had received the student applications several weeks ago and her coordinators had already placed many of them with Host Families. It was just that she didn't trust Kazuo, her evil adversary, to give up on trying to railroad her business. She knew he would take a fiendish delight in taking it back or derailing her project any way possible. The very thought of him gave her pause for a Tums wafer, but they were downstairs in the big bottle on her desk. His cryptic warning from Vienna still resounded in her mind like a murmur in an echo chamber...*you will be sorry*...

A light breeze picking up from the north rang the hanging chimes and brought her back to enjoying the spring beauty of the lake. Just left of the willows the slender quaking aspen quivered in the wind, shimmering its leaves in the sunlight like spangles. She thought that April was possibly the loveliest month in the northwest, given the proliferation of flowers with the blossoming shrubs and trees. Jay had planted hundreds of tulips when they first arrived, lining the long driveway as well as grouping them in various beds. The first year there he had spent months landscaping the property, creating mounds, or raised flowerbeds, planting all kinds of bulbs, bushes and trees. He added groundcovers, birdbaths, birdhouses, while building brick planters and retaining walls. Eventually he rounded it all off by creating a large vegetable garden, which gave a harvest they could not have grown in California. It was their heaven on earth and when the dismal months of winter were ended by spring it always came forth the next year in full regalia, a celebration of profuse colors; their patch of paradise adjoining the lake. Friends, neighbors and visitors had often commented that it was like walking through the grounds of a finely contoured park.

Lately she had gotten so busy with work that she had hardly even noticed it. With that thought in mind, she took in a long last look at the scene from side to side, drank the rest of her French Roast, breathed a quiet sigh of contentment, felt some growing apprehension, and got a refill from the kitchen before heading downstairs…*down to the dungeon again…* Though the phones were not yet ringing off the hook, the fax machine held a thick stash of communiqués, a common occurrence in spring and summer. She culled through the pages, reviewing each one. Most of them were dealings that Candy could handle…*funny girl that one…may have her quirks but she sure knows the computer…couldn't live without her…*She set a stack of paper on Candy's desk and recalled their conversation of few days ago.

Knowing Candy's fondness for Mexican food she had taken her out to lunch at Pablo's, a popular place for the lunch crowd and townsfolk. In the past Bea's family had often dined at the restaurant and Jess had honed his Spanish skills there as a bus boy while in high school. Now it was an unusual treat, as they rarely had time to leave the office for a midday meal. But Jay with still in California, she'd decided ever since her wild horse ride to take the bull by the horns and confront the office atmosphere. In hopes of simultaneously lightening hearts and loosening tongues she had taken the daring step of suggesting they have a beer. After drinking about half of one and munching on tortilla chips she decided to take plunge, though as gently as possible.

"Well," she started, raising her glass, "here's to another successful season together."

"Cheers," said Candy, clinking her glass in response. "To another year."

"Course this year is different," offered Bea diplomatically, "since Jay has joined us, and expanded things somewhat."

"Yep," Candy nodded. "He sure has alright." She gulped down most of her lime-laced Corona.

"Want another?" smiled Bea.

"On a work day?"

"It is Friday." Candy paused then shrugged.

"I will if you will," she finally said.

"Let's do it. What the hell. We've worked hard all week."

"We always do."

"That's the truth." To punctuate the point, Bea drained her mug with a flourish. "Ahhh, tastes good." She looked at Candy and smiled...*here we go*... "Speaking of work, I was... uh...wondering how you feel about how you and Jay are getting on."

"Oh, it's fine," she said quickly. "We're both so busy, you know." She reached for a chip and held it above the salsa. "Honestly I can't help but wonder about you two?"

"What do you mean?"

"Well, I just mean – I mean it's none of my business, of course – but doesn't it bother you that he talks to that college woman all the time?" Bea drew back slightly at the unexpected response. The power of alcohol was cutting both ways, opening negative and positive lanes.

"Well, frankly, no. I mean, after all, I trust him. If they need to talk, I assume it's for good reason." Candy eyed her sympathetically.

"Yeah, I used to feel that way too." She stopped and then continued. "Until I learned I was being a fool." Bea had heard the long version of this tale before, many times; how her first husband cheated on her, secretly sold drugs, and later left her when she objected, for a woman he'd been seeing on the side.

"Well, I don't believe all men are alike."

"Oh yeah, I used to think that too," said Candy knowingly. "Now I'm not so sure."

The waiter, a handsome Mexican with a muscular frame and confident grin, appeared with his pad and asked with impeccable Latin charm, "Are you ready to order yet, senoritas?"

"Yes," they answered together. They ordered their lunch and two more beers. As he walked away Bea noticed Candy observing his derrière attentively.

"Well, anyway, you have a hard time trusting men, I know."

"You bet I do and for good reason too!" exclaimed Candy. "I learned the hard way what liars they can be."

"Yes, I know. Still I think that that's such an individual thing. You know that everyone isn't the same. Take Randy for example. You do trust him, don't you?"

"Well, no, not really. I haven't known him long enough. I'm still getting to know him, and until I do, well..."

"Seems you've been dating him for quite a few months now."

"That doesn't mean I feel I can trust him."

"I see. Well, he seems like an awfully good-hearted soul to me. Jay says he's one of the kindest and most sincere people he's ever met."

"Oh yeah, he seems okay, most the time. But he has his moments. I'm convinced it takes a long time to really know a man. If you ever can at all."

"Yeah, well, I've known Jay for a very long time now, and I think I can trust him."

"Uh-huh." She angled her head sideways, eyeing Bea skeptically. "Hasn't he ever done anything to make you suspicious? Ever? In your whole lives?" Bea felt herself flushing and hoped it didn't show.

"Oh, I don't know," she replied, hearing the barest hint of doubt in her voice. She smiled bravely. "I suppose you could always conjure up fears if you want to." Candy stared at her blankly, resolutely unconvinced.

"Well maybe those fears are not always wrong." She frowned skeptically while lowering her voice to a conspiratorial tone. "It just seems funny to me they talk so much *and* especially that he doesn't want me taking her calls."

"But he doesn't want you taking *any* of his calls. I've talked with him about it. He likes to be able to operate independently on that line. He likes to respond fast. You see how he is there; bam, bam, bam, always in motion with ten things going on."

"Yeah, I see him, or hear him anyway, behind the door. And it would sure make a good cover, wouldn't it, if something was happening." Candy finished the last of her beer and set the glass down with impact as her voice rose in insistence. "That's all I'm saying, woman to woman. It doesn't pay to be naïve. I learned the hard way."

"And it doesn't feel good to be suspicious," declared Bea firmly. "I don't want to live that way. I'd rather be trusting."

"Okay," said Candy in a falsetto pitch. "You sure trusted Perry, don't forget." Bea winced but said nothing as Candy shook her head in resignation. Then she smiled sweetly with a touch of pity in her voice. "I just don't want to see another woman get hurt."

"I know you're trying to help…*so to speak*…I see that, and I appreciate that." Bea cleared her throat. "But, actually, because I work with you both in the office, my real concern is about the two of you just getting along."

"We get along alright, in our own way," she sniffed. "We mind our own business."

"I know, but Candy," Bea stated flatly, "the tension in the office is still so thick between you, I could cut it with a knife." Candy returned her look with widening eyes.

"That's not my fault," she protested. "He's the one who started it all. Closing his door, not wanting me to answer the phone, and…and ..worst of all, listening to my phone calls when you were gone! The nerve!"

"He says he never did that."

"Of course that's what he says. You expect him to admit it?" she exclaimed indignantly. Bea sighed, looked down at the table, then raised a level gaze to Candy.

"Look, I don't really know what's happened with the phone. I'm just saying that whatever happened is amounting to too much tension in the office. It makes it harder to function. *And* it's also impacting our relationship, yours and mine, which was always so good. I hate to see it deteriorate. So I'm asking you please to just be aware of it – the feeling there – and see if we can make it be just like it used to be. I want you to try to not let it bother you that he's there, which is only three days a week anyway."

"I feel like you're putting it all on me."

"No. No, I'm not. I don't want you to feel that way. I've had the same talk with Jay some time back. I just decided it was time to have a talk with you too because, well, things don't seem to be getting better and, as you know, the summer is approaching. And that's such a demanding and hectic time. I don't want to turn it into any more of a hassle than it has to be. And besides that, I miss the fun, the camaraderie that we used to have. So I'm asking you, as a friend, not just as your boss: can I count on you to help me make this a better situation?"

Before she could answer their smiling waiter appeared with two sizzling platters of enchiladas on a tray. "Senoritas, your food is ready, por favor!" The women looked up expectantly, with hungry gleams in their eyes, and felt their ale-inspired appetite rise up as he placed the sumptuous plates in front of them. "Enjoy, amigos!"

"Don't forget the beers, please," Bea reminded him, still hoping to create a festive climate. The waiter apologized and wheeled off to get them.

Again Candy let her gaze linger on his departing form before turning to her meal. She raised her eyes to Bea, nodding as she placed her napkin on her lap and slid her fork into a molten mound of frijoles.

"Okay," she said, with guarded determination. "I'll try. But I can't guarantee it'll help very much. It takes two, you know." Bea smiled and reached across the table to pat her idle hand reassuringly.

"I know, and I thank you. That's all that I want. Just try your best to keep it lighter. It will be good for all of us. We can do great work together."

Since then the atmosphere in the office had been noticeably lighter, though the real test would be when Jay was back among them. He had flown in two days ago in the late afternoon, feeling pleased overall with his accomplishments. They had talked into the evening and all the next day he was gone counseling. Today would be their first time in the basement as a threesome.

As she had awakened earlier than usual today, she had used the quiet time to contemplate everything. She had faxed Toshi the night Jay returned, spawning a series of communiqués between them. The fact that no fax had been received last night meant a phone call today was virtually inevitable. She felt her customary surge of dread as she contemplated his likely demands.

She recalled the conversation she'd had with Jay on his return; how LA was tough going, a potentially inhospitable and unworkable place. She appreciated his original thinking on the matter; Orange County might work. But she was pessimistic on selling it to Toshi. The Japanese hadn't requested a feasibility report. They just wanted a program established there now to run by next spring. She recalled her anxiety on hearing Jay's conclusion.

"Are you really sure," she had pressed, "that it isn't doable somehow?"

"Well, it may be, in the long run, maybe next summer, if we take another trip down there. But the response I got to the ad was really disappointing, virtually useless. Most of the people who were interested in the job lived in poor sections of the area, dangerous for students who can hardly speak English. And those from the suburbs were too far from the airport and each other to coordinate with the situation easily. And none of them were confident that they could get the number of families we would need to run a program in their particular suburb. I really do think we're better off by basing it in Orange County. It's a friendlier, less crowded and overall safer. Several prospective coordinators I spoke with from there seemed to think that they could find a sufficient number of families. And it's not that far to bus a group from there up to LA for full day excursions."

"I can see that, but I also know, knowing the Japanese, that Toshi probably has his mind firmly set on LA."

"But we can do that to a great extent. That's what I'm saying. They can visit there all they want. Just not base their Homestays there. You know that it's less than an hour driving time."

"You don't understand," explained Bea patiently. "The way the Japanese think –the Japanese Way – is very inflexible once they've decided what should be done."

"You mean Toshi."

"It's not only him, but he's the one I've got to deal with."

"Well, let's just help Toshi learn to think more like an American." Jay was starting to feel exasperated. He was fed up with the idea of a one-sided relationship. "He can learn to loosen up a little, can't he? Welcome to the good ol' US of A."

"I'll try to convince him of the soundness of your plan. I'm just telling you that he may not be willing to take no for an answer."

"It's not really no!"

"To him it may be."

"Maybe I should talk to him then. Man to man. I was there. I made the trip. I know what the scene was like." Bea quaked slightly at the thought.

"I don't think that's wise," she said firmly. "I'm the one with the relationship with him."

"Well, maybe we need to change the relationship a bit," said Jay sarcastically. "Broaden it a little. Maybe he could eat shit and die for a change."

"It's not just him!" Bea raised her voice in intensity. "It's probably his boss, his boss's boss, the whole company! It's a big organization – the biggest one of their kind. Stop thinking you're going to change their whole world single-handedly!" Jay frowned and crossed his arms.

"Maybe somebody should," he muttered.

Bea left that conversation feeling frustrated and concerned, sending Toshi the first fax shortly thereafter. She awoke the next morning to an adamant reply, dismissing her proposal and still insisting on LA for spring next year. He also reiterated the portentous prospect of the Christmas group for this year as well. She responded by suggesting an LA summer program for next year rather than spring and added that Christmas would be very difficult. In the absence of receiving a return fax this morning she had an ominous sense about the call she now expected. Mulling over that thought, she reached for her first Tums of the day, knowing it would probably not be her last.

An hour later she was still alone in the office when she received a surprising call. She answered the phone on the very first ring and almost jumped out of her skin at the response.

"Faye! I can't believe it's you," she said merrily. "How are you, anyway?"

"I'm good," she responded, "and trying to plan a trip to Seattle."

"Really?"

"That's right. The mayor wants me to investigate the possibility of a sister city arrangement."

"Oh good...*of course...business with pleasure*...It would be great to see you. When are you thinking about?"

"I wanted to ask you. What's a good time? He'd like for it to be done this summer but I know you get so very busy then."

"That's for sure...*how unusually considerate*...It would be hard to have you until after then. Can you wait until September?"

"I don't know if it's possible. I'll ask. I'd prefer you be free to show me around."

"Of course...*aha*...Well, I'll be glad to do that. I'd love to do that. And you can stay here in the extra bedroom."

"Good. I thought you'd say that."

"Oh definitely. Actually September would be ideal. My summer groups will be almost ended by then, and the earlier in the month, the warmer it is. September's a month that usually still has some sun."

"That sounds good. I'll check with my boss and get back with you."

"Good. So how are you doing?"

"Oh, I'm still very busy. In fact I can't really talk now. Got a meeting to run to with the mayor very shortly. I'll talk to him about this. I just wanted to check what time was good for you."

"Yep, September's the best...*always on the go*...Would David come too?"

"That I don't know. Maybe. We'll see. I'll let you know that when I call back to confirm things."

"Okay. Can you talk now for a minute?"

"No, I'm sorry. I really do have to run. I'll call you soon. Bye!"

With that she hung up and was off on her way, leaving Bea still holding the phone. Still, she was glad Faye was coming. It was just what she'd wanted; a chance at close range to get better connected. Maybe now that there were only two of them it would be easier to be intimate, like she'd hoped for in Pittsburgh. The funeral had been such a miserable affair; unexpected, rushed, so sad and so final. The ashes of Polly's cremated body had been scattered on the wooded hillside beneath their childhood home except for some given in an urn to Wade. Both he and Gabe were so overwhelmed by the loss that they had been virtually silent throughout it all. The sisters had both been so beside themselves with grief and so caught up in coordinating the arrangements that they had not really bonded as tightly as Bea would have liked. But Faye had stated then that she would like to visit this year and now it was actually coming to pass. She felt excited at the prospect and set about her tasks with a renewed zest to her efforts.

By lunch break the day had gone relatively smoothly. Candy was busily engaged in typing, faxing, filing and answering calls while Jay was quietly bustling out of sight, hard at work as usual behind his closed door. They both seemed content to be enmeshed in their separate tasks. Bea had just finished her peanut butter and blueberry jam sandwich when the anticipated telephone call from Toshi came. He was faintly more reasonable than she expected. Though insistent that an LA program be done next year, his company was willing to forego spring for summer. However they really wanted a Christmas one there this December. When Bea mildly objected, he cut her off with the dire statement that they would be extremely disappointed to have no program there till next year. If she wanted to continue to do business with them, it would be a wise option to accede to their "request". Feeling amazed but buoyed by their rare willingness to bend, she decided to assert herself ever so slightly more. She told him she would need some time to give it consideration. Stiffly he replied she could have a few days.

Though still feeling pressured, in a small way she was pleased. For once they were actually postponing one demand and giving her some time for consideration of another. She had prevailed a little bit, if only temporarily, which was distinctly different. If they'd relent about spring perhaps they might even back off on Christmas; perhaps at least keep it small. Even if not, her spirits were brightened by the fact that, however uncommon it was, she could sometimes actually have it her way. Her mood was dimmed quickly however by the other call that arrived from Japan later that day.

The principal from Hundai high school had called her personally to say that they were reconsidering the summer program in Seattle. He apologized respectfully but explained that another company had just offered them a similar program in Australia. The programs were virtually identical in content but the price of the Australian program was much cheaper, given the rate of the yen to the dollar. Simply put, the school could offer the students a better deal.

"But don't your students have a greater interest in seeing America over Australia?" she inquired. "I mean I'm sure Australia is a nice country, but at the risk of sounding arrogant, don't you think America is much more fascinating?"

"Yes, I understand your point," replied the principal, "and I do not think you are arrogant. But you see, it is the children's parents who are paying for this trip, and ultimately we must consider their wishes very seriously. Of course, please understand, I personally would prefer our students go to your country. It is the best educational experience for them, I believe. Still, we cannot force them. We do not want to have angry parents. You must remember we are a private high school and cannot risk to alienate them. I'm sure you understand." Bea felt devastated and uncertain what to say. The man almost sounded like he was on her side.

"You know," she managed to say with a modicum of composure, "that we already have placed most of them in good homes. The American families will be very disappointed to hear this."

"I understand," he said gravely, "and I regret it very much to cause you such disappointment. I do not see however, that we really have any choice in this matter. I hope you understand." Bea felt herself sinking into a profound state of sadness and for a moment felt like crying.

"I just don't understand how you can change your plans so late. We had an agreement. We have your deposits. Surely the parents will object to losing their deposits?"

"A sensitive matter, I agree. We were wondering possibly if you would be willing to refund all or part of them. Is it possible, do you think? It would surely help with any relations in the future." Bea felt struck by an invisible blow to the stomach. Here he was canceling the program at the last minute and actually had the temerity to request the repayment of a nonrefundable deposit. He even seemed to be implying future deals hinged on it. She was feeling flabbergasted, when it suddenly hit her like a bolt of lightening…*kazuo!*….

"May I ask you which company is offering you Australia?"

"Oh, so sorry, I am not at liberty to divulge that information at present," responded the gentleman in a tightly formal tone. "It does not matter, no?"

"Just curious," she said, "about my competition"…*that jerk…it has to be him…*

"Of course," he said, oozing understanding. "It must be very difficult for you. I believe the school would regard it to be improper for us discuss such matters. I hope you understand. However, I can assure you that our only interest in the Australian program comes from the difference in prices, and of course, the desire of our students' parents for the best bargain. As you probably have heard, the economy is getting slower in Japan and people are spending less on traveling than before."

"Yes, I have heard the economy is tightening there," she admitted. "Still, these programs have already been committed to financially by your parents."

"Yes, I agree. It is most unfortunate. Please accept my apologies." He paused respectfully for the sentiment to be felt. "And I ask that you please let me know of your decision regarding the deposits as soon as you can. Thank you very kindly. Again, I am very sorry. I hope we can possibly work together in the future."

"Well, I appreciate you saying that but frankly I am very surprised, shocked actually, that the school would do this. I'll have to think about everything and get back with you on the deposit."

"Yes, please do. Thank you very much. Good-bye."

"Good-bye."

Bea reached for the Tums as she hung up the phone. She felt shaken and crestfallen, with a subtle nausea growing in her stomach. Candy stopped typing and their eyes locked across the room. "I can't believe they would do this," said Bea in amazement. "They're canceling."

"I know. I heard," said Candy with a loud sigh. She frowned and shook her head wearily. "Men."

Chapter 53

"Grace is the natural state of the Son of God." (A Course in Miracles)

THE SOFT GLOW OF track lighting from the ceiling in the jazz club highlighted the poster-sized photos on the walls of former jazz greats; John Coltrane, Miles Davis, Ella Fitzgerald, among others. The lively but gentle rifts of a sultry saxophone wafted through the darkness in the background from speakers mounted high on the walls. Small tables converged at the edge of a hardwood stage in the near corner and spread back across the carpeted floor all the way to a small bar protruding from the wall in the far corner. Jay watched from his table on the side of the room as patrons entered, mostly in couples, through the glass-paned doors. The owner, named Jacob, greeted most of them warmly with hearty hugs instead of handshakes and it seemed to be more a gathering of old friends than club members. Jay felt comfortable but a little out of place. He'd come once alone and once later with Bea, each time too early to be greeted by Jake, who was apparently backstage tending to last minute details. Tonight they had shaken his hand upon entering. Though this evening was their second time there as a couple, they still felt like newcomers to the festivities. He was in the jazz club that Howie had suggested, Jake's Place, a rarity; a hot spot in the suburbs.

It was an amazing location that defied conventional standards. Jake had taken his modern two-story home on a hill in a residential area, nearly an acre in a woodsy neighborhood, and turned the bottom floor into a contemporary nightclub. Upon entering his winding gravel driveway, which was hidden from the street, his clientele found ample parking in a section he had cleared. Next they climbed up concrete steps leading to a brick patio; an enchanting arena surrounded by twinkle lights in the trees. A gushing waterfall in the far corner added a romantic touch to the scene. The ground floor entryway on the left opened into the cozy ambience of the dimly lit club. It was reminiscent of a magic hideaway in Casablanca with a no smoking policy; a clean air cabaret.

The quiet chatter of the customers and occasional clinking of glasses accompanied the upbeat tempo of the music. It was a happy crowd, anticipating a repeat performance of a happy time. Jake somehow managed to bring in class acts; notable talents in the northwest jazz scene. Tonight there was a well-known guitarist with a standard three-piece combo behind him; piano, bass and drums. They were popular enough to have a good local following, judging by the comments Jay had overheard from those around him. He leaned over to Bea and spoke into her ear.

"Looks like a pretty cool happening overall."

"I know. I really can't believe how he's converted his house into such a great place. You'd think there'd be zoning laws or something to stop it."

"The client who told me about said that the owner is able to get away with it by applying each week for a private party permit."

"Wow. I had no idea such a thing was even possible."

"Me neither. It's unreal." They suddenly became aware of a hush in the room as Jake strode up to the microphone on the stage. He was a muscular thickset man with short-cropped reddish hair bordering his broad forehead and deep set blue eyes that sparkled with the expectant pleasure in the air. He lifted the mike from the stand and grinned at the audience.

"Hello everybody!" he said in a rousing yet charming voice.

"Hello, Jake!" came back the chorus. It seemed a well-rehearsed but enthusiastic routine. He scanned the room and rested his gaze momentarily on Jay and Bea. "I see we have a couple of newer people this evening. I want to extend a warm welcome to everyone. Though many of you are familiar with the group tonight, I want to share with you a few things you may be unaware of."

As he continued to talk Jay looked about the room at the various people packed into the place. It appeared to be an assemblage of adults, mostly between thirty and fifty years old. It was a well-heeled crowd of suburban yuppies, of which he was pleased and proud to be one. The atmosphere was festive and yet subdued, as though everyone knew to behave themselves out of respect for the fact they were in someone's home; a very special home designed for their entertainment by a man with a big heart, everybody's friend. One young woman, whose reddish hair made Jay guess she was Jake's daughter, was cheerfully serving drinks to each party. She turned to Jay and Bea to take their order.

"What kind of wine do you have?" asked Jay, hoping they had broadened their selection.

"Just Columbia Crest." The young woman smiled. "Would you like a glass or a bottle?" He tried to hide his disappointment by sounding polite.

"Do you have the Cabernet?"

"Yes, we do, along with the Merlot."

"Do you know the year?"

"No, but I can check." Jay waved her off.

"Never mind. We'll take a bottle of the Cabernet, thank you"...*damn*...He turned to Bea as the waitress left turned away. "Oh well, it'll have to do."

"Columbia Crest isn't that bad, is it?"

"No, not really. Actually it's pretty good for an inexpensive wine. I just didn't want an inexpensive wine." Bea reached over and patted his hand.

"You never want an inexpensive wine, my dear." They were interrupted by the applause of the audience as the musicians were introduced and took to the stage. The lights in the club were dimmed even more and the stage shone softly in pink and blue pastels. The group began playing a series of well-known jazz standards, starting with their uniquely imaginative version of "My Favorite Things". The stand up bassist started the song as he deftly slid into and slapped out the opening bars, followed by the pianist's nimble echoes of the number till they were joined by the vibrant brushstrokes of the drummer, laying the way for the guitar to lead. They moved without pause through a medley of classics. The tunes were familiar and the lyrical touch of the guitarist gave a light and lilting quality to the music that allowed Jay to slip into a relaxed mood of reflection. He was glad to have another week of work well behind him yet was feeling frustrated about his unchanging world. At Bea's acquiescence they had listened to a tape from Leroy on the way to Jake's. It was one that had marked his frustration by a decision to cut his hour-long sessions with Leroy in half. He had listened to the track many times before and it ran again through his mind with the music as background.

"Hello Jay. How are you doing?"

"Well, frankly I hate to say this but it's the same old stuff. I'm still feeling pressed with respect to my bills and the lack of my counseling practice picking up. I am making money in the student exchange business and that's nice but it's really not what I want to be doing, and it's high-pressure work. There's always a lot to do and not enough time to do it. Right now it's mostly marketing but there's plenty of that to do as well. I mean there are more countries in the world than I have time to address regarding the possibility of having some kind of work relationship with them. So there's constant pressure, or as you would say, urgency, and not much time for anything else."

"Well, it may sound like the same old stuff from me, but there's really no more relevant thing I can say to you than what I have said before and that is that all urgency is merely the urgency to get back to God. Where the confusion arises is when urgency is applied to something conditional or circumstantial. Once you have felt your connection to God, then you can look at your conditions and circumstances with an underlying trust that whatever appears to be unresolved will come into resolution at an appropriate moment. That's how problems are solved."

"Say that again about trust."

"What happens when you are connected again, when you are with your Source, you feel trust. You are founded in trust, an underlying trust. You then can look at your conditions or circumstances and trust or know that whatever appears to be unresolved, will be resolved at the appropriate moment."

"Um-hm. That's what I'm into now about all these bills, etc."

"Right. There is a distraction here to solve problems, rather than feel the urgency as a need to get back to God, to feel peace, to feel balance right now."

"Hm. Well, it seems to me that I'm continuing doing this, or trying to, and maybe achieving a bit of success at it, but it seems to be reflected in the material world erratically. One day it seems that I'm just getting profoundly into debt like hell, and then the next day a chunk of money will come in from somewhere."

"Well, what you have to trust is the ongoing continuity of it. You know when you are learning to drive a stick shift, as opposed to an automatic, and you are learning to coordinate the clutch and the gear shift and gas pedal well, and it's jerky at times?"

"Yes."

"Well, it's like that. You haven't yet learned the integration of this. It hasn't become comfortable or natural for you. There's still some tension, some responsibility, that you hold onto, that makes the shifting seem rigorous and disruptive."

"And the antidote is to continue yielding?"

"Yes."

"So I'm just needing to practice what we're been talking about for that last four months; continue to be consciously yielding."

"Yes, you have to do that. And as I've said before, the whole point of the Lord's Prayer is to provide you with a sanctuary of grace while you are living. It's where you have to be in order to see life as divine, as self-balancing, as self-renewing. You need to pay more attention to that rather than your problems. You pay too much attention to the details of your problems rather than how good it feels not to have problems. That's the real thrust here: how good it feels not to have problems. You tend instead to go back to what you think the problem is and stay stuck there, waiting for the ship to come in, whereas it would be so much better right now just to say 'God, it feels good to have no problems'."

"Nobody knows I have no problems except you. Everybody else tells me I have problems; my bank, my wife, I mean it's just…I hear ya' but…it's so damn inconvenient."

"If that's the case then you need to get earplugs."

"I went to the bank yesterday because I saw that this check bounced for the second time for four hundred and forty bucks, plus I owe eight hundred and eighty to these other guys, plus my rent's two months late. It all just seems like it's just getting worse and worse in one sense, but on another level I'm not allowing myself to get into that as much. So I went there to pay off this bill in cash because I happened to have some cash, and they said in effect 'No, the machine says you're paid up' and I said 'No, the check has bounced, believe me' and they said 'Well, we haven't caught up with you, but that sure does cause a lot of confusion'. I mean, it's like, everyone's going to say to you 'Hey, if you're not paying your bills on time, you're fucked up'. It's a problem. It even applies to the relationship between us, it seems to me. Here I am getting in deeper and I don't feel I can send you any money. If I do, it'll probably bounce. If it doesn't, other people who are breathing down my neck don't get paid. I don't like this. I don't see how it cannot influence our relationship. Seems like you're up against it if you have to trust that I'm going to pay you eventually. So…"

"But you will."

"I know I will. I think I will. I know I'm intending to."

"Alright. Here's what you need to do. You need to say 'I can't stay in this circle of confusion'. What you have to say is 'Thy Will be done' and step back from the ropes. You think you're up against the ropes. Just step back from that and just not know anything. You see, your problem to a great extent is that you think you know something about your circumstances and you hold that knowledge as a condition which grace has to honor in order to be successful in balancing what it going on. It has to somehow balance it through what you think is true. So you have assumptions about a lot of things. You have assumptions about what your mounting debt looks like. You have assumptions about what your capacity to bring money in is. You have assumptions based upon past experience. You have all of those things that you are arguing for as true. And that makes it difficult for grace to get past these rigid forms of thought or beliefs. So if a little bit of grace trickles in, 'Praise God', but the fact is that's there's too much assumption of truth here when there has to be an admission of the degree to which you are really ignorant."

"I know nothing."

"You know nothing. What you think is true isn't true. It's what you have assumed to be true based on your past experience and your interpretation of that experience. So all of it has got to be set aside, momentarily, because it only takes a moment, and then you must stay with it. You see, if you have an erratic pattern now that you notice it's because to some degree you set it aside spontaneously and then you pick it up again, over and over."

"Yeah, it's erratic, but it's not nearly as painful as I normally would have been experiencing things if I didn't set it aside at times."

"Right. You assume that the bank has this idea and someone else has that idea and the problem is that there is too much organizing of the situation in your mind."

"Just let it go?"

"Let it be chaotic, but at the same time be asking for grace. It's one thing to let go and just see where the shit hits the fan. If you don't ask for grace you'll have chaos. But if you let go of it all and are asking for grace, that is, if you are asking for those things that I've mentioned are stated in the Lord's Prayer – sufficiency, equity, harmony – while letting go of your organized view of things, you are allowing there to be renewal at that point."

"Let go and ask for grace."

"Right. Let go of what you think is true, because you've interpreted your circumstances so that you can keep some consistent definition of things and what I am saying is, let go of that, forget what you think is true of your life right now and simply ask for grace."

"Okay. I understand that, even though it's hard to do, but I have a question around the meeting of desires. It seems tricky to me when I get to the point about desires and intentions. It's like I'm thinking 'I better envision some good clear desires regarding how things are going to get better here'. And I wonder if I need to take responsibility for manifesting the desire. It's like I'm thinking 'I better imagine having ten thousand dollars in the bank and keep imagining that until it gets there'."

"No. You are at a different point in the process now. You are at point of needing to let go of an organized point of view that defines what is going on. For you, ten thousand dollars may be the remedy to what you think is the problem. Right?"

"Yeah."

"Okay, that was good, and it has brought you to a certain point. But what you really need to do at this point is to erase your organized view of the situation and just ask for grace."

"I don't need to feel responsible for envisioning a solution?"

"No. You've done that, and that was okay, but it has brought you the point where something has to be released. And that is what you think is going on, what you think you have to solve, what you are being told, what you believe, and what you have assumed. And in that place you are going to have sanctuary. You are going to have to feel safe in letting go of your mental constructs, and then you will be asking for nothing but grace. And in doing that you can have it. And you can have it in a particularly fulfilling way if you are not defining your circumstances."

"Hm."

"So you don't know what debt is, you don't know what any of it is. You just don't know anything."

"But I just trust that it's on its way to fulfillment."

"You don't even trust that it is on its way to what seems like fulfillment because you have an agenda then. You just want grace."

"You mean I can kick back and say 'Oh I don't care if I ever pay my bills as long as I feel okay'?"

"It's more humiliating than that. It's not with contempt. It's with the realization that you can't do any thing else; that you can't solve this thing, that you can't struggle with it, that you can't know what it is. Saying that you're not going to pay your bills and that you're just going to feel good is not the same thing as asking for grace. Grace is more than that, but it also requires that you recognize the helplessness to do anything about it from the point of view of the ego, or of being in the problem. All you are being asked to do here is to surrender what you think you know to be true."

"Um-hm. Hard to let go of the thought that it is causing others problems."

"Well, if it is, they have to learn to deal with it just as you are. They need to find grace within themselves. This is not easy. But again, it only takes a moment. It only takes a moment of saying 'I don't know what's going on, but I want to feel safe, I want to feel warm, I want to feel nurtured, I want to feel sufficiently balanced', all of that."

"Utter humility."

"Absolutely. It's humiliating not to be able to solve your problems."

"It's interesting how the two words 'humility' and humiliation' have such different meaning. It's humiliating to my ego but you're saying my real self will find humility in the process."

"Right."

"Okay. Well…you know I listen to the tapes all the time – in the car, jogging – all the time, and so I get a lot of us. And it's very helpful, and it seems like you're just telling me the same stuff over and over in different ways as though I just need to continue practicing it until it is my reality."

"Well, yes. What else could there be other than grace?"

"Well, I guess I'm saying maybe I shouldn't even be talking to you. Maybe I should just be listening to these damn tapes over and over all the time. On the other hand, I feel like the finest time I have during the week is our time together."

"Sure."

"And, I don't know, I'm just feeling funny about…after I while when you hear the same things, even though they're moving, they're beautiful, they're useful, and they're helpful, there's also a sense of 'Gee, this guy's been telling me this stuff for a long time – when am I going to get it?'."

"Well, you do have to get it, yes. You do have to do it. What you do get from me directly is the fact that's there's no amount of complaint, of anxiety or of being off balance that I can't assist in balancing for you."

"Yes. Well, I'm thinking that I'd like to stop talking now, at a half an hour. There's no real reason for it other than I don't want to run up a bill, but on another level it just seems that you are so clear on what needs to be done that I don't need to be keep going around and around with it or I'll find excuses. I simply need to be doing it. I probably don't need to talk another half hour when I can go sit in the car and listen to the tape without causing myself the anxiety that I'm raising my bill."

"Right. If you can't be at peace while you are talking to me because you think the bill is getting too high then it would be useless to continue to talk."

"Yeah, and frankly it's really hard for me to believe that this isn't stressful for you to be doing this while counting on being paid later."

"No, my approach is different. There are times when I call up people and insist on getting paid, but it's not in a situation like this. Whenever I do that it is only when I know that people have been unconscious about it; when they have neglected to pay any attention to paying me."

"You don't have those concerns around us?"

"No. I foresee you paying me. I don't see that as a problem. I know that you will. I know that you'll find that easy to allow that to be. It's not going to be hard for you to do that. It's more of an issue for you that it is for me. I am comfortable with my resources. I don't need to go into reaction."

"Okay. Well, another reason for stopping now is that there is just a sense that, while the talks are perfectly nurturing, I need to do this when we're not talking."

"You certainly do."

"And I'm kind of hottest and freshest right after we stop talking."

"Right. And of course we could talk about other things that would be enlightening. But you tend to come to the talks with exactly the same issue, and that's not always the case with other people with whom I talk a lot. And since there is a particular issue that comes up every time, it may well be that you need to spend some time by yourself sorting that out."

"Yes. I do. I mean after a while it feels like we're student and teacher and I'm failing."

"Right. You need to feel that you are getting it right."

"Yes. Internally, I do feel that there is some growth, but externally…"

"Right. That's what I'm saying. I recognize here what is at the heart of the matter and that is that you are holding onto your definition of your problems way too much."

"Yes. So if I let go of this stuff and move into this deal then I'm assuming I'm going to be as enlightened as you, and as much as we would enjoy being together there's no need for us to have a paid relationship."

"That's true."

"Though I get the implication from you, from what you have said earlier, that it's almost as though there are phases of growth. As if, you do this, then there will be more stuff to do."

"Well, there will always be curiosity for the next step, but this step is very close to unfolding for you. But it is not about talking with me at all. It is really about your need to practice this. You need to go into that place where you don't hold onto the circumstances and you don't fear that chaos will result by letting go of them. What looks to be chaotic is coming from holding on to them."

"I understand. I do. Well then, let's stop here. Say, do I owe you three fifty or four fifty?"

"Oh no, it's not much. I think it's maybe three fifty. At four fifty I would have told you then. (laughter) You would have crossed the line." (laughter)

"Oh that's good." (laughter) Well, I'll call you at the same time next week – for a half hour."

"Sounds good. If you want to go to a half hour, that's fine. Maybe that's what you need. It may help by allowing you to feel that it is safe to talk to me, even in these circumstances. Do you see that?"

"Yes, I do. Thank you. So, I'll see you then."

The audience applause reached its loudest point in the evening as the group concluded it's first set. Jake took up the microphone to schmooze with the crowd and make some announcements, then the sultry saxophone was turned on again for the intermission. Bea turned to Jay.

"You've hardly touched your wine."

"I know, I was just chilling out, I guess."

"How'd you like the music?"

"Not bad. Not bad at all. It actually got me in a pretty relaxed place. One thing I like about instrumental music is I don't have to listen to any words. Mostly I was just sort of lost in thought."

"Thought about what? Work?"

"No."

"Good, because I came here to forget about work. I don't want to think about Toshi or Kazuo or Perry, or even Candy. I want a break."

"Honestly, I wasn't thinking about anything related to your business. I was thinking about what Leroy said on the tape."

"On the way here?"

"Yeah."

"You sure listen to those tapes an awful lot."

"Yeah, well, they're the best thing I've got going for me at -"

Jay felt a heavy weight resting on his shoulder and looked up to see that Jake was at their side and beaming. "Welcome," he said warmly. "I think you folks are fairly new here." He extended both beefy hands to Bea and Jay at once. Jay had noticed them when Jake had greeted them with genial handshakes at the door. They were perhaps the only couple that he hadn't given a hug, simply, Jay surmised, because he didn't know them well enough yet. And now he was here at their table so as to do exactly that. Jay appreciated the personal touch.

"Well, I was once here alone," said Jay. "And this is our second time together."

"I thought I recognized you," Jake nodded. "Are you enjoying the show?"

"Oh it's great," said Bea. "We're having a good time."

"Good. Mind if I sit down and chat with you a bit?"

"Of course," said Jay. "Please join us."

They chatted amiably for several minutes; disclosing and discussing occupations and backgrounds. Jake recited the history of the club. He had founded it as fledgling enterprise with a core network of friends he had made as an amateur singer with his own band several years ago. He had given up singing to devote himself to the enterprise and maintained contact with a growing base of private members through the internet. He seemed sincerely interested in their feedback about the operation and was impressed with Bea's statement that Jay was a wine connoisseur.

"So, how do you like the Columbia Crest?"

"Oh it's fine," Jay assured him, "for an inexpensive wine."

"Doesn't sound like you like it a lot."

"Uh, well no, not really, very much, since you've asked."

"Well, what would you suggest that we serve instead?" Jay pondered the question.

"Oh, I don't know. I think a good way to go might be to take a survey of all of your customers through the internet and ask them what their favorite wines are."

"That's a great idea," exclaimed Jake gratefully. "I just might try that. I'm always looking for ways to improve things." He looked at his watch and rose from his seat. "Time to start the second set." He cleared his throat. "Now's the time when everyone, including me, starts to get hungry."

"Why don't you serve food?" inquired Bea. "Does it require a special permit?"

"Oh the problem is," said Jake, leaning his heavy frame on the chair, "that I can't get a caterer to take on this place. They all say it isn't big enough for them to make enough money at it."

"My husband," Bea said sweetly with a note of evident pride, "is a gourmet cook too. Perhaps he could help you in that department also." Jake looked down at Jay with interest.

"Really?" he asked. "You're a chef too?"

"Forget it," said Jay with a dismissive laugh. "She's exaggerating. I'm just a good cook, like a lot of people. Besides, I'm a vegetarian, and most of these people are probably carnivores, like everybody else. But I'll help you with wine selections any way I can. Let's see what response you get from your people first."

"Thanks," Jake nodded, as he moved toward the stage. "I'll call you on that real soon. Leave your number here for me after the show."

Chapter 54

"A bush of May flowers with the bees about them,
Ah, sure no tasteful nook would be without them,
And let a lush laburnum oversweep them,
And let long grass grow round the roots to keep them

How silent comes the water round that bend;
Not the minutest whisper does it send
To the o'erhanging sallows: blades of grass
Slowly across the chequer'd shadows pass."
(Lines from 'I Stood Tip-Toe Upon a Little Hill', John Keats)

A T ONE IN THE afternoon the phones and the faxes were going nonstop against the blue backdrop of a sunny day in May at the office on the lake. Outside the window, oblivious to the busy activity indoors, two gray squirrels and a pair of Goldfinches were furiously involved in a drama of their own; a fight for the bird feeder hanging from the cedar. When the squirrels approached the container the birds would flit away, only to quickly return to dart at their furry foes with irate chirping, trying to dispatch them. The squirrels would hastily fill their cheeks with seeds and scamper up the tree to perch on a limb. They would digest their mouthfuls, then dash back down to scare away the feeding birds with animated chattering and gorge themselves again only to be chased upward.

Like squirrels in a cage, oblivious to their natural counterparts outdoors, Bea and Candy were rapidly running through the repetitious motions required to turn the creaking wheels of commerce. It was pace they were used to, multi-tasking in tandem, adapting interchangeably to joint and separate jobs as the need arose. Candy seemed less moody than in past months and especially on days when Jay was at his private practice. It was obvious to Bea that she was trying, in accordance with their talk, to be aware of letting the office atmosphere be as free from gratuitous stress as possible. It reminded Bea of how it was before Jay joined them; the good old days. Yet his joining them had made things so much better – more business, more income, more sharing of assignments – that she actually preferred how it was now; the good new days. Overall she was hopeful this level of functioning would be maintained.

"*rrriiinnnggg*"

Candy grabbed the phone while Bea continued writing an email. She had a short conversation with the caller, then hung up the phone and turned to Bea.

"That was another Host Family in Toronto," she intoned with an edge, "calling to say they never received the stipend that was promised them by Perry from last year. I told them that we would be sending them a check, like you said to."

"Okay," said Bea, without looking up from her computer screen. "Just check the amount that they were expecting and make sure that it squares with what they should have received."

"I will," declared Candy, "and I'll get it out today." She reached for the books to look up the figures. "I wonder if you're ever going to get anything from that scumbag."

"Who knows?" Bea sighed. "I sent him another letter the other day, in care of his church this time. We'll see. Mostly I hardly have time to think about it, but I'm not letting it go yet."

"Men," muttered Candy, as she reached for a file. Bea considered ignoring her. It was an unprofitable and endless subject to explore. Still she was trying to be better in the office. Best to keep things light and friendly.

"I though you and Randy were getting along well lately? You've been dating for months now."

"I take it day by day," said Candy philosophically. "Never know how he will be." Bea looked over at her quizzically.

"Uh-huh," she finally said…*or you*…"*rrriiinnnggg*" Candy answered the phone again, then covered it with her hand. "It's your sister. Do you want to talk with her now?"

"Oh good," pronounced Bea. "Yes, I'd like to take it." She picked up the phone sitting on her desk. "Hello, Faye. How's my sister?"

"Well, I was just wondering that very thing myself."

"Ha. I'm good, just busy as usual. Summer's almost here you know."

"I do, and actually that's why I called."

"To remind me?"

"Very funny. No, you nut. To say that I've decided to visit you earlier than I thought."

"You have? When?"

"We're coming in August."

"August? We? You and David? That's great but it's the worst month. What happened to September? What about the sister city thing?"

"My boss called it off. Timing's not good. Maybe next year. We'll just come to visit."

"Oh."

"Anyway August's the best time for me. My scheduled looks booked for the rest of the year."

"Oh. Well…I'd love to have you, and we can make it work, somehow I guess, but I'm afraid I won't have the time to spend with you that I would like."

"Well, that's okay. We'll do the best we can. If we stay at your place we'll manage some time together somehow, I'm sure. Is that still okay?"

"Of course. It's just I'll be so busy…*and going half crazy*.…It's just going to be harder. I may not be able to show you around too much."

"I understand. Well, we could always just see the sights by ourselves. David and I are pretty good at getting around. Just give us directions. We'll get a rental car."

"Yeah, but I'd like to show you around."

"*rrriiinnnggg*"

Candy picked up the new call on the first ring. After conversing for a moment she turned to Bea. "I'm sorry to interrupt. But you might want to take this. It's from Japan." Bea immediately felt a slight surge of queasiness.

"Is it Toshi?"

"No, it's the principal from Hundai high school."

"Oh," she mused. "I wonder what he wants now…*maybe they changed their minds*…Faye, I'm sorry, but I better take this call. Can I call you back later? Okay, thank you. Good-bye for now." She took a deep breath and punched in the other phone line

"Hello, this is Bea. Good morning from America."

"Good morning to you also. I hope you are well."

"I'm doing fine, thank you…*depending on what you have to say*…and how are you?"

"Very good, thank you. We are of course very busy with the end of school near, as I am sure you are also, with your summer season approaching."

"Yes, we certainly are."

"Yes, of course. Ah, I am calling to see if you have decided that you will, ah, refund the deposits we had made earlier for the trip that was, ah, cancelled."

"I see…*shit*…well, actually I have decided that I really cannot afford to do that. I have to pay my coordinators for all of the work that was done in your behalf – recruiting Host Families, scheduling itineraries, and so forth. I had placed a deposit on a fifty passenger bus that I am unable to get back also, so you see, we still have many expenses to cover even though you cancelled."

"I see. Of course. I understand it is difficult for you. You may understand, of course, that we have much pressure from the children's parents to recover their money if possible."

"Oh, of course...*you could tell them that's why they're called nonrefundable*...and I feel very sympathetic for them and for you. It is a difficult position, to be sure. Surely, however, they can understand our position as well. We have done a lot of work for their children to ensure a good program for them."

"Yes, of course. I understand your position very much. And I personally would not even ask you to consider a refund in this matter, except that I am getting much pressure as principal from the board of directors, since we are a private school, and the parents too. I fear it may affect our ability to work with you in the future."

"Oh really? I see."...*sounds like a threat*...

"Yes, I am afraid so. And that is a matter that is out of my hands. I can of course recommend that we work with your company in the future. I do recommend you very highly. But I think the board may be unhappy if they believe you are uncooperative in this matter. I am very sorry to say."

"Uh-huh...*uncooperative?*...Well, hmmm. Maybe I can take a second look at the figures and try to work out a partial refund. I don't know. I can't promise anything. I don't want to take a loss on it."

"No, of course not. I would regret that very much. I'm sure the board would feel the same way. But I thank you for your consideration. Anything you can do will be appreciated here and help us to possibly work together in the future. I hope you understand."

"Yes, I think I do. Thank you."

"Oh, thank you very much. Ah, do you know, ah, when you will come to your final decision?"

"Oh, well...I could probably try to go over everything later this week. Is that soon enough for you?"

"Yes, that would be fine. Will you call me please then by the end of this week with your decision?"

"Yes, I will. I will do that."

"Thank you very much. Good-bye."

"Good-bye." She reached for the Tums bottle and shook out several wafers. From the corner of her eye she saw Candy staring at her and turned to face her.

"So he still wants his money back, huh?" said Candy.

"Yep. I'm afraid so," Bea replied. "And soon."

"The nerve of that man, and after all that you've done." Bea sighed and rose from her chair.

"I know," she said knowingly. "Don't tell me – *men*." Before Candy could respond she added, " I'm going upstairs for a quick bite of lunch."

She went up to the kitchen and made a peanut butter and red raspberry jam sandwich on whole wheat bread. After pouring herself a glass of milk she went out on the back deck with her food and sat at the round glass table by the hanging wind chimes. An intermittent breeze delicately clinked the dangling metal tubes together. The pink and white honeysuckle bordering the corner post was in full bloom as it spread out along the left and right rafters under the glass roof above her. A shiny green hummingbird poked its long beak into the flowers as it floated like a tiny helicopter, buzzing briskly from blossom to blossom in sudden short bursts. As the sweet smell of the plant wafted by her in the wind, she inhaled slowly and deeply to savor it. She gazed at the water over the two willow trees and took in the lake for the first time today. Near the bank beneath the willows she saw five baby ducklings swimming behind their mother in a tight row. The fuzzy brown creatures were so close to her and each other that they appeared to be knit together by an invisible thread. She finished her sandwich, leaned back in the chair and stretched out her arms to relax in the sun's warmth as she heard the screen door slid open from the office down below.

"Bea!" yelled Candy. "Another call from Japan. Do want you to take it or should I say you're at lunch?"

"I'll take it!" she replied, and she leaned through the railing to take the phone from Candy's outstretched hand. "Who is it?"

"Toshi," she said with marked trepidation, as though handing off a live grenade. Bea sat back in her chair and took a deep breath.

"Hello, this is Bea."

"Hello," he replied. "How are you?"

"Fine," said Bea, not really meaning it. "And how are you?"

"I am fine, thank you," he said curtly. "I am calling to confirm that you will be doing the Christmas program in Los Angeles. We need to set the dates to advertise now."

"Oh, gosh…*so much for your understanding that i need some time*…I haven't yet decided. I'm just not sure we can pull that off. We are so busy now with the summer programs and, as you know, they tend to run into September if there are any complaints. I would rather focus on doing LA next summer, with San Francisco and San Diego happening too. How about an LA Christmas after that?"

"My company wants Christmas program in Los Angeles this year. Otherwise…"

"Otherwise what?"

"Otherwise we may need to seek another company to help us."

"I see."…*must be getting pressure from above*…Silence lingered between them for an interminable pause. "Well,…I guess…" she faltered momentarily. "I guess we could give it a try. I really can't promise anything."

"I'm sorry," he said unsympathetically. "I need your promise on this matter."

"Oh, boy." She tried to think of how best to respond…*just stall*…"Well, I'd really like to think this through, give thought to the planning, the dates, the size and so forth. Can I get back with you on it next week?"

"We need an answer as soon as possible. What you need to think?"

"Well, I'd like to talk to my husband about it. You know he did the last trip."

"Yes," said Toshi icily. "And he did not do the job. He did not do Los Angeles."

"Well, yes," responded Bea tentatively. "But he did set up operations in the other two cities. And the only reason he did not do Los Angeles was because there was such a poor response to our advertising. It's such a big and diversified city. You already know all this. And besides, as I told you, he's certain we can run a good program from Orange County to include LA activities."

"When my company say Los Angeles, they mean Los Angeles, not Orange County."

"Yes, yes, I know, I know," sighed Bea. "But it is a lot of new cities to add at once in such a short time. Don't you see that if-"

"We do not want excuses!" he blared. "Either do the job or we work with someone else! We are willing to wait until next summer for program in Los Angeles only because your company has done satisfactory job in other cities. But we need a Christmas program in LA this year. You must be willing to grow with us. We cannot be held back by your refusal."

"I'm not refusing," she protested. "It is just a matter of time and timing. I appreciate your company understands that the timing is not good for an LA spring program next year. And I am perfectly willing to try a summer program there then. But for this year, I am concerned we simply haven't enough time to ensure a good Christmas program. If we set up a program I want to feel confident we have good people so it is successful. Surely you understand that."

"I do understand. But you must understand that we must have a Christmas program there this year. There is no question. I would like your response now." Another long excruciating silence went by.

"Uhhh," said Bea hesitatingly, eyeing the Tums. "Is it possible to do it for a relatively small group of students?" A tense pause hung in the air like Skeet about to be shot.

"Yes," he finally answered. "The size is negotiable."...*hallelujah*...Bea breathed a sigh of relief.

"I really want to speak with my husband first, as he will probably make the trip. I am simply too busy to do it myself. I will call you as soon as we have talked."

"How soon will that be? I would like to have your answer later today and as soon as possible."

"Well,...*oh geez*...I will try to settle it tonight. He is not here today. I can probably let you know tomorrow. Is that soon enough?"

"We really need to know today. Please call me tonight as soon as you can so it will not be too late here to advise my superiors of your decision."

"I'll try."

"No, do not try. Please do. It is very important." He was quiet for an instant as though to emphasize the point. "Thank you and good bye."

"Bye'" she responded, but he was already gone...*damn...so much for small victories...* She sat still and felt the anxiety growing...*gotta' talk with jay tonight...*

Chapter 55

"We are born at a given moment, in a given place and, like the vintage years of wine, we have the qualities of the year and of the season of which we are born. Astrology does not lay claim to anything more." (Carl Jung)

THE MORNING SUNBEAMS BOUNCED brightly across the hood of the Mercedes as Jay circled down the hillside, leaving Phil's school behind him. Heading toward his office for full day of appointments filled him with joyful anticipation as he drove. Many of the front yards that he passed were freshly tinted with pink, white, red and purple clusters of rhododendron flowers. Vivid yellow forsythias had already turned pale, but before long the lilacs would burst forth in profusion as the unbridled procession of spring colors continued. Though the spring days were sunny, at least half the time, the temperatures were still cool compared to California and he eagerly awaited the return of the summer, that short span of warmth and radiance he loved...*you can take the boy out of the sun...* Feeling pleased with the sunlight he reached for the tapes that were designed to enlighten even his darkest of days.

"Well, good morning and how are you?"
"I'm okay and just want to go a half hour today, alright?"
"Of course, that's fine. Whatever you want to do."

"Good. I'm slowly catching up with my bills but I'm way behind still in a number of areas. Aside from that, I'm not sure actually what to say to you, but I have been trying harder to trust this peace. I suppose I never really was doing that before or I wouldn't have been trying to find it in artificial means like pot or wine or whatever. Anyway, I guess I will say, what do you think is best for me to do next in terms of advancing my progress towards an enlightened state?"

"You are right at a point here where you are going to submit to being at peace as the foundation for your life. You are gaining the awareness now that peace and freedom are essentially the same thing. But in order to access freedom, you first have to go for the part of this experience of grace that is peace. As you come up to the assumptions, the thoughts about circumstances, that seem to limit your freedom, you will recognize more clearly that you have the option of moving through them by choosing to be at peace. As you continue then to yield to this peace, you will be moving in accordance with the divine intent to move through the apparent limitations, and circumstances will be transformed. You don't struggle anymore to get through the limit. You will be tempted to struggle, but you will also be aware that you have lost your peace and you will choose to return to it. You are approaching this point, where you realize peace and freedom go hand in hand."

"You mean, for example, like say I feel pretty good and I think I'd like to get a motorcycle today. Well, then I decide I can't go buy a motorcycle today, but instead of feeling bothered about it just say 'Well, so what'. That is, I recognize a sense of limit but don't let it bother me. Is that the start of it?"

"You have to be at peace and comfortable with where you are; grateful for where you are. At the same time you allow for the presence of a desire for the motorcycle, but you do not feel conflict about not having one. You do not energize the sense of limitation around your desire. You stay grateful and gracious about accepting where you are, because it is the capacity to accept that allows you to accept the motorcycle. The rejection of where you are, being that you are in the kingdom of heaven, is a great failure to recognize the truth and puts you in a place where you cannot see or do not believe that the motorcycle could happen. So it is good to be accepting, because then there is no gap between the motorcycle and what you happen to be enjoying right now."

"So the acceptance mode or state of mind is a readiness to receive?"

"It is. Anytime that you are in the experience of gratitude you are also receiving. It is when you step from that threshold of receipt that you then find yourself trying to determine and analyze how things can happen on your behalf. One step back from the Source, from the full acceptance of where you are, makes you seek out resources on your own. Everything is here. You are alive. Accept it."

"So pervasive gratitude rather than selective."

"Absolutely. It has to be infinite. It has to be gratitude for life itself, for your very consciousness."

"Well, I'm not at that point yet. Is that something which emerges naturally from a peaceful state of mind or do I conscientiously need to try to be grateful?"

"Don't try to be grateful. Just recall what gratitude feels like. If it is helpful, remember what it feels like when someone is grateful to you. And you want to feel grateful all of the time, because if you are not, you are basically wasting time. If you are trying to struggle with problems and are not in that place, you are basically wasting time."

"So you sense that I'm growing in this direction?"

"Oh, of course, very much so."

"It's funny, but I feel like I can feel it more right now as we talk. And, you know, as I do, the more at peace one feels, the less important so-called desires seem to be."

"They don't seem like problems, but they are still there in a gentle, interested and innocent sort of way."

"It feels sort of like 'Well, a motorcycle would be nice'."

"That's exactly it. And instead of saying 'Please give me this', you end up saying 'Yes, I'll have that'. And that means that you already feel some sense of having. And that's what it means in the Bible when it says those who have, get."

"Yeah, I got that. I suppose, hopefully, we could apply it to money."

"Yes, exactly, and you'll have a lot of money. If you feel connected in that way, then it is very simple and you basically affirm that you'll have a lot of money. The beautiful thing is that by being in that place, spontaneously acknowledging that you will have this or that, without specifically striving for particular things, you'll notice that things come to you quite easily. In general there will be a sufficiency of needs being met because you are affirming you are in the kingdom of heaven on earth."

"Hm."

"And it is very important not to be smoking grass, because you are powerless when you do that. I mean you are spiritually powerless to be in a place where you can see the miraculous transformation of life continue to occur."

"Well, the other night I was with some friends and one of them offered me some pot and I just said 'No thanks, I'm feeling okay like I am', which is a bit of a change for me."

"Yes, and that feeling will continue to grow where you will no longer have any interest in that whatsoever."

"Hm. That would be nice. Look, you know I'm into astrology, though we haven't talked much about it, but I have a transit coming up here, a significant one, that pertains to reaping what you sow in a big way. Transits are what predictions are based upon. It's different than using a chart to discern personality. It's using the cycles of the planets as they move across the points or mathematical degrees of where they were when you were born. Saturn is approaching the point where my sun sign was, one degree Pisces, when I was born, and I wonder if you have anything to say about that."

"Yes, I do. You were not born at the particular time that your horoscope is geared to. That was the moment of incarnation for this lifetime, or your personality in this lifetime. But the true self or higher self that you are abiding with now and referencing in our work together is not subject to those planetary movements."

"Astrology only applies to that particular sense of self called personality?"

"Yes. When you are identifying with your personality or ego structures, then it applies. But if you are identifying with your eternal essential Being, what Rex calls your Individuality, then it doesn't apply at all."

"Interesting. Okay, thanks. Well, do you think there's any value in astrology in the manner I've been using it?"

"Well, to the extent that there are egos around it helps to get some insight for people."

"Hm. Well, I prefer to be done with egos."

"Yes, but you are dealing with many people who are not there yet and in the understanding of their personality you can help them move along to a higher place."

"Well, it does seem I've been able to use it in my practice to help a lot of folks understand themselves better. People may say they don't believe in astrology but when they're alone in my office they certainly are interested in their particular chart if I bring it up."

"Good."

"Well, our half hour is just about up. I'm good to go for now. Thanks for everything. I'll call you next week."

As if on cue, Jay punched out the tape as he turned into the parking lot. The leafy birch trees bordering the lot were shimmering in the soft breeze. He unlocked the back door to the building and bounded up the back steps to the office. Once inside he sat at the desk and pulled out his appointment book, scanning the day's sessions. Content to be busy the entire day but for lunch, he drew up the blinds and looked to Mt Rainier. Its glistening white peak subordinated the surrounding landscape like a gigantic floating glacier dominating the sea. The aesthetic majesty of the spectacle moved him to drop into his chair and meditate for a moment. He closed his eyes, touched his thumbs and forefingers in a circle on his thighs and tried to feel completely at peace. It was a difficult experience in that his mind wanted to think... *peace...peace...peace...... ...wonder if howie's waiting for me in the lobby...peace...he probably – peace...peace...peace...... ...tonight we'll have that eggplant before it goes bad...peace... peace...maybe drink that barbaresco...mmmm...maybe a little caesar salad to go – peace... peace...peace...... ...now maybe try a little gratitude...thank you Father...for everything...just feel it...peaceful...grateful...peaceful...grateful...peaceful...grate-* "rrriiinnnggg"

He jumped at the interruption, then reached for the telephone.

"Hello. Forestville Counseling. This is Jay....Oh hi, Detective Clark ...*shit*...Fine, how are you?...The form?...Oh, the authorization form...No, I haven't seen it...You mailed it two days ago?...Well, then it's probably here. I haven't gotten the mail yet...I'll look for it today and give you a ring if it's here…Yes, that's right. I can talk to you about Barry then, assuming it is signed…I see, okay…I'll check and call you later…You're welcome…*not* …Goodbye."

A glance at the clock showed that it was almost time for his first appointment. He decided to give up meditation for now and invite Howie in a few minutes early. He was curious what had happened since their last explosive meeting. It seemed that relationship was nearing the edge. He strode down the hall and found him in the lobby, frowning while reading the Wall Street Journal.

"Is it stocks or your personal life that's giving you that look?"

"Both," said Howie, as he rose to shake hands.

"I gathered from your phone call Sharon wasn't coming with you."

"Oh, no. No, no, no. She may never be coming back – at least for awhile."

"Come on back and tell me about it." They entered the office and set down across from each other. Howie looked tired, a little pale and perspiring. "What's going on? You're sweating."

"I drank too much coffee. I haven't had much of an appetite lately – just coffee and water. I've been too nervous."

"Coffee will probably make you even more nervous."

"I know."

"Tell me what's happening." Howie paused, looking unsure of what he wanted to say.

"I told her!" he blurted out. "I finally told her!"

"Wow," said Jay. "Well, how does it feel?"

"It feels horrible and good at the same time."

"How so?"

"Well, it feels good in a way to finally get it off my chest, but it feels horrible too because she really went crazy." He wiped his forehead with a handkerchief from his suit pocket.

"I see. How crazy?"

"She threatened to kill me. Is that crazy enough for you?"

"Do you really think she'd do that?"

"With Sharon, believe me, anything is possible."

"So what did you do?"

"I ran out of the house while she was following me screaming and I drove over to Seattle to say with a friend."

"A lover friend?" Howie turned his head sideways and wrinkled his brow in consternation.

"I knew you'd ask that."

"I don't care. I have no judgment. I'm just trying to understand what you are doing."

"Okay," Howie sighed. "He's a friend and a lover…or a past sexual partner. Alright?"

"I really don't care."

"Just don't tell Sharon."

"I won't."

426 Cottage Lake Soliloquy

"Thanks. So anyway, I'm living there for the last three days."

"Do you have any clothes and living-type items; toothbrush, etc.?"

"Yeah, I went back when I knew she'd be out and got a lot of my stuff."

"Have you talked to her since?"

"Are you kidding? There is no way I could talk to her now."

"Maybe she'll settle down in a while."

"Yeah, in about a year maybe." He wiped his forehead again. "Oh God, what have I done?"

"You did what you had to do. You came clean with the truth. You couldn't live a lie forever."

"I'm not so sure about that. Right now it looks pretty good."

"Yeah, well, you both were pretty miserable and she was sniffing up to the truth like a bloodhound on a hot trail."

"You're right," Howie sighed again. "I know she was. Still…"

"There's no going back. What do you want to do?"

"I don't know." He sounded exasperated. "I guess wait for her to cool down a bit."

"Do you want to continue the relationship with her?"

"I do. I really do. I just don't know if I can get over this attraction to men. Do you think you can help me?"

"I don't know. But I'll try. We can work together individually for a while and see what happens. Anything's possible."

"That doesn't sound too optimistic."

"This is one of those issues where there are a lot of opinions, several different schools of thought, and when all is said and done, who's to say what's really right for you? To my way of thinking that decision rests with you. But I'll help you explore it, the best that I can. I can't say where it will lead. If you want assurances for something beyond that, you may as well find another therapist. I'm sure some people specialize in sexual orientation. I'd completely understand."

His next client was the Eskimo lady, who had been coming weekly for months. She hobbled into the room, sat in the same chair as always and crossed her short legs as they dangled above the floor. She grinned at Jay with her usual mischievous twinkle.

"How are you today, Doctor?"

"I'm good, Naimee. How are you doing?"

"Oh, very good," she said, nodding for emphasis. "Everything is very good."

"Great."

"But I have a little problem now that is different." She squirmed in her chair as though to get more comfortable.

"Well, and what is that?"

"Jim has been called back to work at the railroad for the day shift. So he can't bring me here anymore for counseling."

"Ohhh," intoned Jay. "That is a problem. You cannot drive, right?"

"Right. I don't have no driver's license."

"Why is that anyway?"

"Oh, I don't know. I don't really like to drive. In the beginning, Jim didn't want me to drive. He say a woman should just stay home and raise the kids. Now, we don't have kids but I am afraid to drive. Everyone goes so fast. I don't see so good. And I got used to Jim taking me everywhere." She laughed. "It's not so bad. I kind of like it now."

"Yeah, but the court has ordered you to have mandatory counseling for two years. It was your only option to keep you out of jail. You've been great at making every session for the last few months but that's not really long enough for me to tell them you have completely handled all of your issues."

"Oh, I know, doctor." She looked anguished. "And you been so good to me and Jim. You are the best counselor. I tell everyone, my counselor is the best."

"I appreciate that, but there's still very little I can do about reducing your sentence this early in the game."

"Oh, doctor. I understand. I don't know what to do."

"Can you take the bus here?"

"Oh, the bus stop is very far from my house, and with my back – its hurts me, you know – I don't want to walk so far."

"Are there any friends or neighbors who could take you?"

"Oh, we sort of live far away from everyone. I don't have any friends here, just my daughter, and she lives too far away, I think." As Jay pondered the situation an unusual idea came to him.

"How far exactly do you live from here?"

"About five miles or so." She looked at him quizzically. "Why?"

"Well," he started slowly. "This may be a crazy idea, but it may be the best one for the moment, and depending on where you live, I might be willing to do it."

"What are you thinking, doctor?"

"You know, I've done this before – not very often – but at times I have gone to the hospital at someone's request or gone to see a sick person at their home or even in some case where someone was simply afraid to leave their home, I've done a home visit."

"Oh. That's a good idea." Naimee spirits perked up. "And you could do that with me, yes?"

"Well, we could try it. I have enough freedom these days where my client load doesn't keep me at the office all day, every day…*though I sure wish it did*…and possibly I could get away from the office once a week to see you."

"Oh, that would be so wonderful, doctor. You are so good. You are the best!"

"Yeah, yeah," said Jay, with a self-deprecating smile. "Don't get carried away. And just call me Jay. I said we'd try it. Just give it a try and see how it goes. No promises."

"Oh, thank you! Thank you so much. If you want to come at lunchtime I could make you food."

"No, that's not necessary, but thanks."

"Oh, but I love to cook. I be happy to cook for you. Really." She stressed the word with great earnestness. "I mean it."

"No, no, no. I appreciate it, and I know you love to cook – I do too – but it's not necessary. Thanks anyway, really. Let's just do the counseling."

"Are you sure?"

"Positive. Now, let me get some paper and note the directions to your house. When does Jim go back to work?"

"Next Monday."

"Okay, we can start next week. We'll see how it goes."

His third client of the day was an eighteen-year-old boy named Ray, from a nearby rural town. He talked and carried himself in the unpretentious manner of a country boy and slouched in the chair upon entering the office.

"What are you here for?"

"I dunno'," he said casually. "My ma said I had to come."

"I see. But why?"

"Said I needed some help."

"Help for what?"

"Help with my attitude, I guess."

"What's wrong with your attitude?"

"I dunno'. She don't like it none. Says I'm lazy."

"Do you think you're lazy?"

"No, not really."

"Why does she think you're lazy?"

"'Cause I'm not workin'."

"I see. And why aren't you working?"

"I tried. I even had a good job there fer awhile, but they laid me off."

"How come?"

"Said they had no more work. Weren't my fault. I worked hard. Digged ditches. Ran the back hoe. Did whatever they said."

"Does your mom understand that?"

"Yeah, I guess. I tol' her."

"What seems to be the problem then?"

"She wants me to get a new job."

"That sounds reasonable. Are you looking for one?"

"Yep. Cain't find one though. Been looking all over town. Nobody's hiring." Ray shrugged defensively. "Ain't my fault."

"I see. And so what have you been doing with your time when you're not seeking a job?"

"Workin' round the house mostly. In the yard. Rakin' leaves, pullin' weeds, mowin' the lawn."

"Doesn't that give your mother some satisfaction?"

"She says I need a real job."

"I see. For the money?"

"That…and to keep me out of trouble."

"What kind of trouble?"

"Oh, all kinds I guess."

"Are you using alcohol and drugs?" Ray looked suspiciously at Jay and didn't reply.

"It's okay. I won't tell anyone. That's my job; find out what's happening, keep it to myself, and try to help out."

"Alright," assented Ray. "Then I'll tell ya'. I like to drink beer and smoke pot."

"That's all?"

"Yeah."

"Have you gotten into trouble with your use?"

"Not really."

"What's that mean?"

"Well, I got in a fight at a party the other night. Weren't my fault though. Guy called me a name."

"What was it?"

"Doan' 'member."

"Anybody get hurt?"

"Not really. I got him a coupla' good licks an' he got me some. Then they broke it up."

"I see. Well, what else is going on in your life? Any girls?"

"Yep. I got me a cute lil' girl friend."

"That's nice. How old is she?"

"Sixteen."

"She live around here?"

"Yep. 'Bout two miles from my house."

"I see. Is that going well?"

"Yep. "Cept her ol' man doan' like me."

"Why not?"

"Says I'm too old for her."

"What do you think?"

"I doan' think two years is much."

"Does that make it difficult to see her?"

"Yep, kinda'. She sneaks out though. We can still see each other pretty much."

"I see. Well, do you think there's any value in your coming here to see me awhile?"

"I doan' know. Maybe. Ma says I hav'ta till I get a job."

"You feel comfortable in talking with me?"

"Yeah, you're alright, I guess."

"Good. Any idea what you want to do with your life?"

"Whaddya' mean?"

"I mean do you want to go to college, or would you like to learn a trade, or would you like to see the world, or is there anything you'd like to be doing that you are not doing at the present time?"

"Well, I don' know. Hadn't really thought about it much."

"Perhaps that's something we could explore in counseling."

"Sure. It's okay with me."

"Perhaps your mother would be glad to know you were trying to get a clearer sense of some direction in your life."

"Yeah, …probably."

After Ray left he had an hour to kill for lunch. He decided the best use of his time was to get a warm bean and cheese burrito from 7-11 and continue listening to tapes on the cassette in his office. Leaning back in his desk chair he put the earphones on his head and gently unwrapped his meal, savoring the aroma of spicy frijoles and melted cheddar. He gazed out the window at the noontime traffic chugging slowly along the avenue. The morning breeze had slackened as the day wore on and the trees around the parking lot stood as still as soldiers at attention in formation awaiting a command. He sank his teeth into the bulging flour tortilla, enjoying the zesty mush, then turned on the tape.

"Okay, we're on. How ya' doing?"

"Well, at the moment I'm fine, I guess. I guess I'm always feeling fine when I talk to you, from the standpoint that I have seemed to learn, or am realizing, the value of staying relaxed in the face of what appears to be utter meaninglessness and chaos. When I look back on when our talks began, I have learned to do that, but there still must be some things I'm not doing right though, because basically things are still financially in a shambles. I'm way behind on my bills and my credit has probably gone all to hell and I'm always worried about somebody, some debt."

"Well, you have to understand something. There is something here to learn that hasn't been learned, and that is that you assert that the picture is bad. It is not bad. You give the meaning to what you experience that it is still bad; that it hasn't improved. It certainly hasn't changed to accommodate the ego's idea of what should happen, but you must not think that you are in any kind of peril because you happen to be stepping out of the realm of the ego and into something new and wonderful. That fact that you are doing that puts you in a place of sanctuary or grace. So whether you are behind or not isn't the point. What you have to realize is that there is no problem with what is going on. You still have a problem with it. You still resist the fact that things are the way they are and to the degree that you still do that you impede the natural spontaneous transformation or generation of life into new forms of fulfillment. You have to give up the idea that there is something wrong with your money situation or that there is something wrong with your life. That's where you have to step now."

"Somehow I thought you were going to say something like that."

"Yes, and by embracing what you have with peace and without judgment, then it is free to be anything. When you make a judgment about something it is like taking a snapshot it and holding the picture up and looking at it and saying, 'This is reality. Look at it. It's bad.' Meanwhile things are moving."

"You mean I damn the flow by condemning it."

"Right. You insist upon defining in a still or static way something that is in motion."

"Hm. That reminds me a bit of an incident that occurred the other night. I was sitting at the table in the kitchen with Bea and was looking at our newly painted wall and cabinets, and was thinking 'I don't like this – I don't like that' etc, and I decided for some reason to play a little game with myself and I elected to look at the kitchen through eyes of gratitude, or with an appreciative rather than a depreciative viewpoint, thinking 'I'm grateful for this kitchen', and all of a sudden the kitchen seemed to actually beam back at me, and a whole feeling of 'Yes, this kitchen is beautiful' came over me. It was fascinating. Is that a microcosmic example of what you are saying now?"

"Right. That's exactly what we are talking about. You see, whatever it is that confronts you at the moment is divine. It's not a problem. That's the truth of it. Your bills are divine. Your money in your checking account is divine. If it doesn't appear to be a balance that seems appropriate then what you must not do is struggle to change that or put pressure on the situation to change that, because pressure on the situation – even mental pressure on the situation such as concern – tends to keep the balance from happening because pressure is always the experience of being out of balance. So more application of pressure is not going to restore balance. Now, in the realm of the ego, where that is experienced unconsciously, people struggle to prevail. People fight their sense of lack of grace by focusing power and will to overcome what seem to be obstacles. And so when you are concerned about something, in the sense that you feel pressure about it, you are reacting to the circumstances as an ego. The alternative way or an enlightened response would be 'Gee, so you owe money – it will get paid someday – isn't this a wonderful life – isn't this a wonderful place – isn't this a wonderful moment'. And let it be that open.

"Now your ego will go crazy. I mean it will not be able to survive, which is of course why I'm suggesting you do it. And then what happens is that you find yourself at ease. And being at ease means that you are going to be in synch with what is happening – the ongoing movement of God – and your interests will find support in a way that they don't seem to right now while you are locked into the idea of struggling for self-support. You do not have to be self-supporting when you experience ease. You just have to be grateful, because the support keeps on happening. Your interests and your well-being are absolutely supported. And when you recognize that, then you tend not to bother trying to deal with things that seem capable of being unresolved in the moment, because the fact that you are in balance is the resolution, and it always will be. So by staying in that place, nothing that supports you and advances your life is impeded."

"Hm. Well, uh…I don't need to continually articulate my needs to this thing we are calling God do I, as though he's got a poor memory or if I lose focus he doesn't get it? I mean it seems like I've been so damn focused for so long on what I need that if there is a God he ought to have it down by now. So can I just go around feeling relaxed and assuming that he'll know where to channel the money?"

"Yes, but you also can be aware of whatever you desire simply on a daily basis. Acknowledge your various desires and feel gratitude for them, because that is how you are supporting your good, by expressing your willingness to have it. As you identify with the willingness to receive in diverse ways on a daily basis, you get off the problem you are creating by continuously insisting on a certain desire as though it were a demand, and that allows the movement of life to flow unobstructed in an appropriate way to you."

"Hm. Well, I guess you're saying that the state of mind that I'm coming from, which is focusing on lack – not having enough money – keeps me from appreciating whatever may be coming to me in other ways."

"I'm saying that it is important to realize that you have it all right now. What you are not experiencing is balance. It is not a question of having more. It is a question of altering the state of consciousness where you imagine you experience something called lack. Lack is really just another word for not experiencing grace, or being unbalanced, which feels like pressure. And the ego says that you have to remedy this lack by trying to figure out how to apply pressure – the pressure you feel coming in – back out into the world to make it conform to your intent. That's where you are stuck: with turning the pressure you feel into pressure onto the world to resolve your apparent problem or to have fulfillment. The ego says you must do something constructive with this pressure. And I am saying 'No, you must have this pressure taken from you'."

"By being in a state of mind that says 'Isn't this a wonderful moment'?"

"Right, and through realizing that there are powers around you, God, the Holy Spirit, whose purpose are to restore you to grace. So when you are feeling that pressure, you need to say to God or the Holy Spirit, 'I don't want to feel this' and if you are sincere, the feelings are gone instantly. As you reaffirm your divine nature in this way you restore your sense of balance."

"Just like the experience I had in the kitchen the other night."

"Exactly."

"So to the degree I'm not doing that I am still operating out of my conditioning."

"Yes, you must realize you are fine the way you are. Your circumstances are fine. Nothing needs improvement. If you can get past the thought that improvement is necessary, then you realize that life is always transformational and that your good comes from not improving but transforming what you have. And the full acceptance of what you have with gratitude and no resentment or judgment about it will facilitate the transformation more spontaneously.

"One subtle problem that people have who are at this point in their development is that they are starting to trust and believe that this is possible. But the ego is so firmly rooted in consciousness, or the conditioning is so pervasive, that there is a tendency to say 'Well, I'll give up ninety percent of the control'. That's because the ego wants to be around to see it happening. But that's not really giving up, and that allows the problem to persist of thinking that we are in control and so hinders or does not allow for immediate fulfillment."

"Well, what's tricky to me about this is that there is no real support from seeing others do it. Everyone I know that seems to be happier than I am is working their butt off and they seem to be happy enough that they get to be working their butt off and pay their bills. So I don't really want to be that way, but sometimes I think it would be better."

"You don't have a lot of support. But look at yourself as a pioneer. You are on a different wavelength altogether and they are not in their peace. They may be on a roll, but they are not at the point of being able to embrace the eternality of their life. They are still living in the world of polarity or duality. They are doing well now and they could be doing adversely later. And they feel subject to that pressure. And what we are trying to do here is move you past ever feeling subject to pressure. So that the good that you have is not a contrast to adversity, but simply all that there is."

"Yeah, okay. I understand. And I believe what you are saying because it sounds true and yet…yesterday for example, I went downstairs and Bea said 'Well, my fifteen thousand dollars is all gone. I just paid all my bills but now I'm dead broke and Perry's probably going to screw me out of another ten thousand' and it seems so fatuous for me to say 'Oh everything is wonderful for the moment, you know, and that just means more wonderful stuff is coming' and everyone's just going to say 'Oh fuck you'. I mean no one's going to want to hear that. No one's going to believe it. I can handle the fact that all the realtors downstairs in my office building seem to be happy and successful and the main guy, who I pay my rent to, looks at me like 'Why don't you pay your bills on time?' cause I don't love them or care what they think anyway, but when someone I care for is suffering out of those beliefs in scarcity and I say to them 'Oh believe me, this works' and then they're going to say 'Well if it works, why are you so fucking broke'?"

"Just let her be. You don't have to argue with her ego. She knows the truth. She's not looking to be embittered by what is going on. There is a moment of concern, that's all. She's not making a case against the truth here. She's at a point where some limit to her capacity to feel her good has been arrived at, and it doesn't feel good to believe there is a limit to your capacity to feel at ease, to feel your good, and to feel your support. But this isn't about saying to her that things are bad but they will get better. It is all right now. You do not want to define your circumstances. The way to deal with this is to say that you really do not know what is happening and you are not going to give up your peace over it."

"Just stay with feeling okay now?"

"Right. This is where miracles occur. When you realize that no matter how things look, grace and balance are never lost – that they are an uninterrupted experience – then you realize how free you really are. And you are able to go through this experience and find that recovery, adjustment and resiliency are present and that you had nothing to do with it."

"Hm. Bearing that in mind, should we continue to go after this guy in Toronto or just stay happy now and let God work it out?"

"My feeling is still that is appropriate to insist on getting your money back."

"Yeah, well, I've been handling this at times since she's been so busy. So I talked to the Royal Mounted Police the other day and they said that people could get off in Canada, in situations like these, by saying that it was a misunderstanding and mismanagement of funds. So I was reviewing the faxes he'd sent her and I noticed in the very first letter he sent her that he said 'Gee, I'm sorry, but I'm sure it was a misunderstanding and mismanagement of funds' so that tells me he's been stringing her along with bullshit from the beginning and probably has no intention whatsoever of making good on this. So I'm wondering what to do next."

"Just sue him."

"But then I have to put up several thousand dollars for that."

"If you decide to sue him you will find the money to do so. You need to remember that this is good for him as well as for you, because you are restoring balance. But you need to stay in your balance, your peace, right now while you are handling this with him."

"But this guy's such a lying sack of shit, and he's lying to everyone there. I mean I spoke with a woman from his bank that he said was going to send us some money. He kept calling us for several days, leaving messages when we weren't in, and saying that she was experiencing some delay. Finally I cornered him and got her name and the bank's number. Then I called her and said what's the delay and she said, several times, that she didn't know why I was calling her and that she couldn't discuss her client's finances. So I said that I was going to fax her some of his faxes to us which referred to her supposedly sending us money. And I did that but I didn't hear back from her and when I called her back she wouldn't take my calls, so really I get the feeling no one in Canada cares to help us fix this mess."

"Look, you can only do what you are moved to do as you stay at peace with this. If you do not get your money back, then you will still be okay, because by virtue of staying centered, at peace, in grace, you will not experience lack. The movement of the fulfillment of God will continue with or without Perry's willingness to operate with integrity."

"Hm."

The tape ended abruptly at that point. He reflected on how nothing had happened with Perry as of yet. The man had changed his phone number and could only be reached through leaving messages at his church, which he never responded to. Bea had opted not to hire a lawyer, fearing it would just be good money after bad. Jay had written every Host Family in Toronto that Perry has not paid and had told them the situation. Several had responded to say that Perry would not take or return their calls. The money had disappeared into a black hole and Perry along with it. Jay still felt strongly enough about it to imagine doing something though he didn't know what. Bea seemed content to address it periodically when she felt moved to…*someday maybe I'll go there and find him*…He sighed in frustration…*always some jerk in her business giving her a hard time…perry…kazuo…toshi…someday…* Knowing the time had come for his next appointment, he put away the cassette player and sat still with eyes closed to let go the growing anger. After a moment he felt composed enough to see his next client; Steve.

It had been several weeks since the session with his wife and the relationship had seemed to be worsening since then. Steve had been growing more despondent each successive week while persisting in his efforts to placate and to woo her. In the lobby he appeared tired and dispirited in his work clothes and shuffled back toward the office with a hangdog look.

"You look really down today, Steve. I take it things aren't any better?"

"They're worse."

"What do you mean?"

"She moved out this last weekend."

"Oh wow! Sorry to hear that. Left you with the boys?"

"Yep. Said it was the best thing. Said if I wasn't going to move out then it forced her to and she didn't want to take the boys out of their home."

"Hm. How do feel about it?"

"Like hell." He lip started to quiver and Jay automatically shoved the Kleenex box across the coffee table to him. "I knew that things weren't getting any better, and yet…I just kept hoping. I just kept hoping." He started to cry. "Now there's no chance. No chance at all."

"Well, you never know exactly how a separation will go. Perhaps with some time apart-"

"No. I know her too well. When she's made up her mind she never changes it."

"I see. Well maybe in some way, it's actually for the best. You were suffering a lot these last few months."

"There's more!" he sobbed. "You were right. There is someone else. She had another guy. Somebody at the gym."

"I see. I was afraid of that. All the earmarks were there."

"I know. And you told me. But I didn't want to believe it."

"Do the boys know?"

"No. I don't want them to find out. I think it would just make things worse."

"How did you find out?"

"She told me…on the phone…after she had left." He stopped talking to wipe his tears and grabbed a second tissue. "Said he was so nice to her. Younger than me. Said she's happier than she's ever been. Oh, that hurt." His crying intensified and Jay waited a moment before talking again.

"Yeah, well, that honeymoon feeling tends to wear off real fast when the forbidden fruit isn't so forbidden anymore. Things could change."

"I know," he sobbed, fighting back more tears. "It just hurts to hear it now. It just hurts to lose her."

"I know. I know. But if she's not happy with you then you can't be happy with her, and that means there is someone else out there whom you will be happier with. This is just the hardest period, when the sense of loss is keen. It will pass. Time will heal. And we can do things to accelerate the process."

"Like what?"

"The first thing to do is to see the situation you are in as a good one, not a bad one. You've got yourself, you've got your integrity, you've got your boys and your work, your home. You are free of someone who has been lying to you, cheating on you, and blaming you for it. There's nowhere to go but up. Be grateful for what you have; all those things I just mentioned. That'll be the basis for a more fulfilling transformation in your life. And that's exactly what you want. You're just stuck on the thought that you need it with her, but that's not true. You're going to have to trust in life now. And that trust, along with your integrity, will carry you through this."

"That sounds good," said Steve feverishly. "But it seems really hard to do."

"Yeah, well, like I often say: it's simple but it ain't easy. And right now you need the clarity of simplicity. You have to keep things very simple and straightforward now as you tend to your self and your boys. And I will help you with that. And you will find that other resources will become available, as you need them. And the way will become easier and easier as you restore the balance to yourself, your home and your sons. You will be healed. Your sons will rebound as well. And if you do not reconcile with your wife in the process, you will go on to love again."

"Thank you for saying that."

"Oh, sure. It's my job…and it's true."

"I really hope so."…*you and me both brother…*

The next meeting was with new clients; a woman and her husband, who had been frequenting internet pornographic sites, much to her dismay. The man was large and extremely overweight. His wife was slightly overweight but attractive enough in a plain but wholesome way. She was very distraught over finding her husband masturbating at his computer, late one night after they had gone to bed. He had thought she was sleeping. A few days later she found a stack of pornographic magazines in the trunk of his car while searching for a battery charger. The combination of the two incidents had pushed her to edge of demanding they seek counseling or else a divorce. They entered the office with signs of strain evident in her face while the man appeared downcast and deeply humiliated. Jay listened to their presentation quietly, mostly given by the woman, until they were finished.

"And that's when I said 'We're going to se a counselor or a lawyer – take your pick'."

"And so here you are," offered Jay.

"Exactly," she said firmly. Jay turned to the husband.

"Are you glad you are here?"

"Well, I'd rather be here than in a lawyer's office, if that's what you mean," he said hesitatingly.

"Do you think you have a problem?" queried Jay.

"Yes, actually I think I have two of them. I'm vastly overweight and I'm addicted to pornography."

"Do you want help with each of them?"

"Yes. That's why I'm here…and to save my marriage."

"Are you not attracted to your wife? She's a rather pretty woman, I think." The man looked at his wife in the chair next to him.

"Oh, she's beautiful. Yes, I'm attracted to her."

"Then why were you hitting these pornography sites?" The man squirmed uncomfortably in his chair and looked embarrassed.

"I don't know, really. I feel sort of self-conscious about my fat body and I guess it just seemed easier…I don't know."

"Do you think you can have a more satisfying sexual experience with an image in a book or on the net?"

"Well, no, but…"

"But what?"

"Well, the girls on the screen seem sort of dirty, you know. I mean, really sexy…kind of wild…I mean…you could probably do anything with them…and…"

"And what? You couldn't do anything you wanted with your wife? You don't think you can find sexual satisfaction with her?"

"It's not that exactly. She's just so…so…"

"What?"

"Nice."

"Nice?"

"Yeah. She's nice. She's good. She wouldn't …I mean I wouldn't want to ask her to do some of the things…you know…" The woman's eyes widened and she leaned forward in her seat as though to make her point stronger.

"I just want my husband to know," she voiced in an almost shrill tone, "that I can do anything any other woman can do in the service of pleasing him. Anything!" Jay cleared his throat and paused momentarily to see if the husband would respond. As the man sat there silently, perhaps stung by his wife's statement, Jay felt moved to press forward.

"What do you think of that?"

"Well," stammered the man, looking at Jay sadly, "I…I…I…don't know what to say. It's not just her."

"Tell her, not me," said Jay, motioning to the wife with a finger. The man turned to her.

"It's not just you. It's me too. I don't like how I look. I can't see how you'd want to make love with someone so fat."

"I don't care," she insisted. "I love you. Period." The man looked abashed and thankful at the same time.

"Would you like to start a weight loss and exercise program?" asked Jay. "You can change your physique if you really want to."

"I do. I do. I just don't know where to start," he said plaintively. "It seems like such a big job."

"You start," said Jay, "like the joke about eating an elephant – one bite at a time." The couple both smiled with some relief. "Look," he continued, "you are not alone. Millions of people are dealing with weight loss all the time. I have to jog every day just to keep from gaining weight."

"Is it hard to find the discipline?"

"At first it was. But now it's pretty easy. It becomes self-reinforcing because it feels good. And there are other benefits that make it worthwhile. You sleep better, you get a half an hour all to yourself, your metabolism goes up and you feel more energetic. I listen to tapes when I run. You could listen to music, books, whatever. And the other thing is to be aware of your diet, your nutrition."

"Yeah," he admitted. "I've been eating a lot of junk food."

"You are a junk food junkie!" exclaimed the woman. "You always have been."

"It's time," said Jay decisively, "for this to stop. Are you ready?"

"Yes," mumbled the man, looking at the ground. "I am."

"Are you sure?" questioned Jay. "You don't sound too convinced." He looked up, first at Jay, then at his wife, then back again to Jay.

"Yes," he asserted. "I am. How should I start?"

"Go home," Jay advised, "and make out a menu of healthy meals for the next week. Go get yourself some jogging shoes when you leave here and start running tonight. Do it daily. Vow that you will not eat any junk food between now and the next time I see you. Will you do all that?"

"Yes, I will."

"Good." The woman sat back in her chair and glanced at each man.

"But what about our sex life?" she asked. "And his desires?"

"Let's not rush things," Jay cautioned. "His self-conscious body image is tied to his behavior in the bedroom. I suggest that for now you focus only on cuddling, on holding each other close and feeling the warm feelings. If further action emanates from that, so be it. But don't push anything. Cut your self some slack. See what happens and we'll meet here in a week to discuss it all. Whatever happens, don't fight about it. Okay? Bring it here instead."

As the afternoon gray grew persistently darker, slowly drifting and deepening through subtle shades by the hour, Jay felt the impending release from his day as the next to last appointment began. It was Skyler's wife Melanie, the woman who had had a six-month fling with a man who had mistaken himself for Jesus. She was shorter and thicker in contrast to Skyler, who was tall and slender. She had thick flowing hair, softly beautiful features, a curvaceous body and sensitive eyes marked by their pain. Her eyes also reflected a certain shyness and she seemed reluctant to converse as he questioned her in the beginning.

"I'm not really sure why I'm here," she began. "It's really only because Skyler asked me to come."

"I thought you suggested he come."

"I did, but for him."

"Don't you think that counseling could help heal your relationship after what you have been through?"

"Yeah, maybe. But I'd rather just do it on our own. It's hard for me to talk with a stranger about these things and we don't have much money."

"I understand. Well, since you're here, we might as well make the best of it."

"I suppose that's true, yes."

"What do you hope to accomplish by being here?"

"I don't really know. Maybe you can help us get past the past."

"That's my intent. How much is the past affecting you in the present?"

"Me? Not much at all really. It's Skyler that's still upset. I made a big mistake, but I learned from it and I'm glad to be back with him."

"What seems to be the biggest problem now for you?"

"I guess that he's upset I can't have intercourse with him."

"But all that will change when your operation is done, right?"

"Yeah, assuming all goes as planned."

"Right. Well, I think a deeper problem may be his feelings about your relationship with that other guy."

"Oh I know that bothers him. But what can I do about it? It was a mistake. It's over." She started to cry. "I'm sorry. I'm really sorry."

"I know. And I get the impression he knows that too. I think the problem is that he thinks your condition, the one that prevents you two from making love, has something to do with that relationship."

"But it didn't. I'm sure."

"Well, I don't know if you can convince him of that, but whether it did or didn't, you both need to move on with your lives together."

"I know, but I just don't know how. I don't know what to say to him that I haven't already."

"Yeah, well, sometimes it just takes time." Jay paused for a moment. "Have you gotten completely over that other guy?"

"Oh yeah. He was nuts. I don't know what was wrong with me to ever see anything in him in the first place."

"How'd you feel when you heard he'd killed himself?"

"Actually kind of relieved. I mean, I'm sorry for him in one sense, but in another, he was just so crazy, and he could be mean."

"So I heard."

"What do you mean?"

"I understand he used to call Skyler and taunt him."

"Really? Oh my God. I didn't know that."

"That's an indication of how hard it is for him to talk about it. He gave me permission to share that with you. He used to say really cruel sadistic things to him, about you."

"Oh God. I didn't know. Like what?"

"Really sick sleazy stuff and that's all I'm going to say. I really think it's better if you hear it from him. Ask him to be utterly honest. I think you guys need to talk more about that episode, that period in your life, more than you realize."

"Oh God. I'm just so sorry about it all. I just lost my head. I was so stupid."

"Aside from dealing with Skyler on this, I think perhaps you have not fully forgiven yourself for what you did also."

"Maybe you're right. I hadn't thought of that."

"Do you still feel guilty about it?"

"Yes, of course. I mean, I've only been back with Skyler a few months."

"Well, sooner or later, for you guys to move on, you're going to have to forgive yourself, not only wanting to have Skyler's forgiveness."

"I guess you're right. I'm not sure I know how to do that though."

"Well, we'll get into that today. Also, I think coming here together, at least one time would be a good start. How about if you both come back next week as a couple?"

"I'll do that if he will."

"I think that he will. I think it would be helpful to dig into what was going on between you two before you ever left in the first place. Somehow that played a part in it all."

"What can I do in the meantime to make him happier?"

"For now it's best just to focus on recovering your own peace of mind through understanding and forgiving yourself. You can't really be much good for the relationship until you do. Let's use the rest of the session going over your background and see if we can uncover some of the clues, some of the reasons why you ended up doing what you did in the first place."

After Melanie left the office Jay retrieved his last client of the day from the lobby. He was Lynette's husband, Michael, who had been a Host Father for a foreign student and become her lover in the process. Tall with dark hair, he was boyishly handsome with a reticent manner and a sheepish look on his face. He sank into the soft cushioned couch across from Jay and looked at him expectantly as if awaiting bad news.

"Well," started Jay, in a soft tone calculated to put him at ease, "sounds like things got a little out of control at your house."

"I'll say," answered the man as he breathed a quiet sigh.

"And now," said Jay, "we're trying to put things back together."

"I sure hope so," mumbled Michael. "I feel like shit."

"I bet you do, and your wife's just dying."

"I know," he said, wincing. "That's why I'm here. Do you think you can help us?"

"Yeah, I do. I think so, if you want to save the marriage. But what the hell happened? How did you move from father to boyfriend?"

"I don't really know exactly, and I do want to save the marriage. It just sort of happened. We just kind of slid into it, me and Eva that is."

"Her name was Eva?"

"Yeah."

"And what was she like?"

"Oh God, she was a blonde beauty, just like you might imagine, a poster girl for Sweden."

"I see. Okay. Well, give me some details about how this slide occurred."

"Well, when she first came I was working – I'm a trucker – and never really saw her if it wasn't in the company of my wife on weekends and in the evenings at dinner time."

"Uh-huh, and then what happened?"

"I got laid off – just a temporary thing – I'm back at work now, but suddenly I was home, all the time, and Lynn was working. And that was lousy – being out of work – I felt so useless at first. And then it got better for a bit because I started doing some projects inside the house and out. And then shortly after that she – Eva – was out of school for Spring break, and I was finished with a lot of the projects and it seemed like a good idea that I would show her around a little bit. You know, take her to Seattle and stuff – the kind of things you would do for out of town guests. And that all seemed okay. Lynn was all for it. Everything was fine."

"How did it start to change?"

"Toward the end of that week, Spring break, I could tell – we had spent every day together doing something – I could tell that she really liked me and once when she was lying out in the sun in her swim suit on the weekend – I don't know – something just clicked and I felt aroused, and I had started sort of just loving her as a daughter and all and then – whamo! – it just hit me that she was gorgeous and sexy and really sweet and friendly and all of a sudden I knew I was really attracted to her."

"It probably didn't hurt that she had that exotic air of being from a another land and had an accent."

"Oh exactly. Her voice was beautiful. But anyway, the next week, when she came home from school, I was sort of dying to see her. And when she came into the house and she looked at me I could see that she was really wanting to see me too, and we just sort of hugged like, you know, welcome home and all, and then without really meaning too, I just gave her a little kiss on the cheek and she turned her face and gave me one on the lips and then before I knew it I kissed her back, and then I kissed her some more, and then I couldn't stop kissing her, and she kept kissing me too and we sort of sunk to the floor and were kind of burning for one another and one thing led to another and we ended up making love."

"Right there on the floor?"

"Yeah, right inside the front door. And then afterwards I felt bad, maybe worse I think than she did, I don't know, but she was just so beautiful, so warm, so everything, that my feelings for her were stronger than my conscience and …well..that's how it happened."

"Does your wife know all this?"

"Not exactly. Not all the details. Do you think I should tell her?"

"No, she knows enough. Why rub her face in it?"

"That's what I thought."

"And then what happened?"

"Oh basically, every day then I was there when she came home from school."

"And you made love every day?"

"Yeah, basically."

"You mean definitely?"

"Yeah…every afternoon before Lynn came home."

"And how long did that go on?"

"For a few more weeks, until I was called back to work."

"And then?"

"Then it was pretty much over, except for our feelings. But even those died down a little bit after that, since we were mostly around each other when Lynn was there too. And she's such a nice person – Lynn that is – that we both started to feel guilty, even though we still felt like we wanted each other and it just made the whole thing kind of tortuous all the time."

"I bet. So how did it end?"

"She had to go home prematurely, that is, before the school year was over. Her mother got sick and had to be hospitalized, appendix or something, and there was some concern she might die, but it all worked out okay. But when she got home, at some point, she confessed to her parents or to her father what had happened. It was probably weighing pretty heavily on her heart. And he called us, he called me and he said "I sent you my daughter to be her father, not her lover" and he was pretty angry, and he threatened to tell the organization that had sent her, and I felt really bad then, and really scared, and I must have looked really shitty while talking with him on the phone – thank God I answered it – and Lynn was watching me and she said "What's wrong?" cause she could tell, and I couldn't hide it, so I got off the phone – I said I was sorry to him – I felt like such scum – and then I got off the phone and kind of broke down and just told her. And then she...and then she wanted to be mad, but the tears welled up in her eyes, and then they started streaming down her cheeks, and then she couldn't stop crying and crying and...and I just felt like shit."

"And you still do."

"Right. I do. So here we are." He looked at Jay bleakly. "And I'm afraid that I'm always going to feel this way, forever. So, what can I do?"

"Time heals all wounds. But we can accelerate the process. Have you ever done anything like this before?"

"With another girl? No, never. Not since I was married. I thought I was happily married."

"You like your job?"

"Yeah, it's great. I got my own truck. I like driving. It's good money."

"Ever been laid off before?"

"No, that was a first. That sucked. I didn't like it."

"How'd you feel?"

"Like a failure. All of a sudden I felt like a dumb shit, useless. It brought home the fact that I was basically uneducated, after high school that is."

"So those were new feelings for you to experience?"

"Yeah, totally. I felt like half a man."

"Right. So it was humiliating, embarrassing. You felt like a loser."

"That's true."

"But being around Eva gave you a different set of feelings."

"Well, yeah. She took my mind off it, especially since we were doing things."

"Sure, but also, I venture to say, it restored a sense of your manliness, your virility, to have such a comely young beauty looking up to you, respecting you, admiring you, depending on you."

"I guess that's true. I never really thought of it that way."

"Well, I think it's important to understand, to account for, what you were experiencing that led you to drop your defenses, to cross a boundary, that you normally would not."

"I don't want any excuses."

"I'm not giving you any. You made a mistake – pure and simple. It was a fuck-up. A big one. You shouldn't have done it. You hurt a lot of people, including yourself. But I'm not interested in making you feel bad. You're already doing a good enough job of that yourself, thank goodness. I just want to provide you with a mechanism of understanding, an explanation of why you were moved to do what you did, so you can learn from it, grow from it, and never ever do it again."

"Oh I won't, believe me. I won't."

"I believe that you mean that, but I want you to profit from the experience in self-knowledge, not just wound yourself with guilt and try to hide the scars."

"I see. I get it. I think I understand what you are saying."

"You see, when people feel weakened significantly in their self-esteem, when they think less of themselves by virtue of losing their job or whatever, they are more vulnerable to temptation, to easier fixes, in whatever form they present themselves; alcohol, drugs, inappropriate relationships, et cetera. You understand?"

"Yeah, I do. I see what you mean. It's true, I know. Do you think that's part of my problem?"

"I think it was, from what you've shared with me. It doesn't excuse it, but it offers some understanding. You didn't set out to hurt anybody. And for that matter neither did Eva. That's why it weighed so heavily on both of you eventually, once Lynn was back in the picture, once you started working again, once Eva got home. Do you understand?"

"Yeah, I do, but I still feel so bad."

"Well, that's natural. It's even good. It shows you do have true remorse. And those feelings, the regret, the guilt and the sadness can help motivate you to make it up to Lynn and to yourself. Did the father turn you in?"

"No, apparently not. I don't think so, because we never heard from anyone."

"Well, thank God for small blessings. You didn't need that to complicate matters."

"That's for sure."

"Do you love you wife?"

"Most definitely. I do. She's wonderful. I don't deserve her."

"Well, I don't know about that. But she wants to be with you. And you want to be with her. And that's basically all it takes for the two of you to work this out."

"Thanks." Michael paused, looked at the floor, then back to Jay. "Where do we go from here?"

"The only place there is," Jay smiled, "upward and onward. I'd like the two of you to come together to my office sometime next week."

"Okay."

Jay traipsed down the stairs to the parking lot lightheartedly, feeling the wake of a good day's work behind him. He stopped at the gray metal block of mailboxes and extracted the mail from his narrow cubicle. Thumbing though the letters as the cool evening wrapped around him, his light heart turned heavier when he found the one from Detective Clark. The envelope was large and had been bent to fit in the box. He fought off an impulse to toss it in the trash bin at the corner of the lot and opened it up to greet the bad news. It looked to be in order; an authorization to talk about Barry, signed by both parties. Now nothing could protect him from talking about Barry, unless his memory proved to be selective…*or unless I never got this*…Stuffing the document back in the envelope he flung it like a Frisbee and watched it sail neatly into the bin.

Chapter 56

"His mother forbade him to drink wine at table, 'not a single drop'."
(*Coleridge: Early Visions*, Richard Holmes)

"A LITTLE MORE, MY dear, to wash down the last of your pasta?" Bea nodded her assent and watched the red wine rise slowly in her glass as Jay drained the last of the decanter. Through the glass panels of the sunroom she could see the tall shadows of the evening creeping upwards on the houses facing her from across the water. Huge cedars flanked several homes near the middle of the lake's far shoreline, hovering over an ivy-covered bank strewn with shrubs. They beamed a golden glow, a lime green florescent, back to the sun as it settled in the trees of the forest behind her. Though the meal of linguini in pesto sauce was tasty, her appetite had been tempered by the thought of telling Jay of Toshi's demands. She felt caught between the two of them as though in a human vise and had delayed sharing the inevitable announcement during dinnertime. She put her napkin by her empty plate and took another sip of Chianti....*guess it's now or never...*

"You've been quiet tonight," said Jay. "Something on your mind besides the ever present fact of work?"

"No actually, it's just work," replied Bea with a sigh as she set her glass down. "I talked with Toshi today."

"Oh boy. And?"

"And, well, he's really pleased with the work you accomplished in California."

"Good."

"Also, for the first time we've gotten a small concession. They are willing to forego or at least postpone a program in LA until next summer."

"Well, I guess that's a plus but how about Orange County?"

"He couldn't sell that idea to his superiors."

"Oh."

"And, even though they're willing to wait for next summer, they're still adamant on a December program there this year."

"Damn."

"I thought you'd say something like that."

"He's just never satisfied, is he?"

"Well, he's under a lot of pressure. The competition's stiff there. Companies are expanding."

"Yeah, yeah, yeah. I know, I know. Still, we just did a big expansion. Since I added two cities you'll be busier than ever this year through winter preparing for next spring. Plus now I've got my own Christmas programs with the colleges. To do an LA Christmas program would require more work in October and November."

"I know," said Bea. "But we haven't much choice. If we don't agree to do it we risk losing all we've gained with him."

"I hate this damn business."

Bea said nothing and just stared at Jay without expression...*then you find a way to pay the bills*...

"I know how you feel," she finally said. "And I'm sorry it's that way for you. But I think we'd just better go ahead and do it. If anyone can, you can. You've shown you've got a knack for pulling these things off. Why not take it as a challenge?"

"I can do it. But I hate it. I'd rather be shrinking heads."

"Well..."

Jay finished the wine in his glass and stood up. "Shit." He turned around to leave.

"Where are you going?"

"To get another bottle."

"You've had more than half of this one."

"Yeah, well that was before Ohshit. Now I really need a drink."

He headed downstairs to the cellar and returned to the table with a Syrah. He uncorked it and started to refill Bea's glass.

"I've had enough," she stated firmly, covering her glass with her the palm of her hand. "And so have you."

Jay didn't respond as he refilled his own glass, then poured the rest of the wine in the decanter. He raised the wineglass to his nose and inhaled deeply. "Needs air," he commented.

Bea could see that look in his eye emerging; that glint that usually preceded an outburst of temper. She leaned across the table and touched his arm gently.

"Look," she said. "I'm sorry to be the bearer of bad tidings, but it's the nature of my business. We either grow or die."

"You mean eat shit and die," grumbled Jay. "The everlasting motto." He took a big drink and set the glass down wearily. I'm sick of this pressure, especially from the Japanese. They don't own us. Why don't you sell this damn company?"

Bea gave him a look that cautioned him to stop. She spoke resolutely. "This is my company. And I'm proud of what I've accomplished with it. I'm grateful for your contributions but I need to do what I think is best.".*...it's not my fault that your practice isn't working...*

She watched Jay take another drink without replying, looking sullen. Wanting to avoid an argument she rose and took her dishes to the kitchen. "Thanks for a great dinner, again," she called. "I've got to get downstairs to make some more calls." She paused and looked at him decisively. "I'd really like to let Toshi know tonight and get him off my back. If you don't want to do it then I guess I'll have to. One of us will. I was planning to return to Japan in the fall. That won't leave me much time to set up an LA program. You should probably go to LA in October. Will you do it or not?"

Jay shook his head, muttering something unintelligible under his breath.

"What?" she asked.

"Oh all right," he acknowledged. "I'll do it. But I won't like it, God damn it."

"Thanks," offered Bea with a smile. "I do appreciate it. I better get downstairs now."

Jay stared at the lake as she left the room. The shadows now completely covered the far side of the lake, as the sun was long gone. Small birds were twittering, flailing over the water in the growing gloom. He observed ever-widening concentric circles here and there as fish intermittently broke the surface for an instant. A cool breeze from the south sent the wind chimes clanging softly and rippled the new leaves of the aspen like wispy green feathers. The stillness of the scene was not enough to still his passions and he drank another long draught in the hope of diffusing them...*that damn bastard...never good enough...always more pressure...*

Bea switched on her desk lamp and rifled through the papers stacked in front of her. She felt a lingering tension from the exchange with Jay, but was heartened it had ended in his acquiescence. It would have been nearly impossible for her to do it. She was eager to let Toshi know the good news, but first had to make a pressing call to an unhappy Host Family. Hoping to avert a problem with them now before their student took it back home to Japan, she glanced at the clock...*midday in tokyo...plenty of time to reach tosh...*She dialed the local family and reached the Host Mother. While engrossed in their conversation the second line on the business phone rang. She decided to let the voice mail take it and continued talking with the Host parent.

"Oh, I know how frustrating that can be," she commiserated. "So often the Japanese are uncomfortable in showing their true feelings. It's usually not rudeness, just shyness. It's not," she laughed, "the Japanese way."

A moment later the home phone rang out...*jay can get that...get his mind off his troubles...*

Upstairs Jay sat and drank, continuing to gaze at the lake. When the home phone rang he didn't respond, as was his custom, and instead listened to see who was calling. After three rings the machine clicked on and the caller's voice came through.

"Hello, this is Toshi. I am calling for Bea. I need talk with her as soon as possible. I call your work phone but there is no answer. Please return my call immediately. I need to know if –"

After a moment of stunned silence Jay leapt from his chair to intercept the message. His blood was boiling like a hot pot of pasta as he grabbed the receiver.

"Hello, Toshi. This is Jay," he said forcefully, squaring his shoulders and standing up straighter. "May I help you?"

"Hello, Jay. Please to meet you. Is Bea there?"

Jay felt the upsurge of his anger pouring out like a horde of mad hornets emptying a hive.

"No, she's not. You'll have to deal with me. And why the hell are you calling on our home phone anyway?"

"Ah…" ventured Toshi, seemingly taken aback. "Very sorry, but I have important matter to discuss with her. Can you tell when she will return?"

"No, I can't. She's busy. But you can talk to me," he nearly shouted. "What's it about? LA?"

"Yes. So you know?"

"Yeah, I know. I'm the one who fucking has to do it. I was just down there for your company last week. Guess that wasn't good enough."

"I know. Thank you. We very grateful. Hmmm. Is Bea free to talk soon?"

"No, she's not. What's wrong? You afraid to talk with me? I'd like to talk with you. I've been wanting to talk with you for long time. What's this insistence on LA in December? I was just down there. It's not a good place. It sucks. It's dangerous. Students can get hurt there. Don't you believe me? Do you think I don't know my own country?"

"Ahhh, please I want to talk to Bea. Can you get her please now? It very important."

"Yeah, I know how you talk to Bea. Listen you damn bully –"

"Jay!"

Jay turned around to see Bea glaring angrily as she strode towards him. "Give me the phone!" He handed it to her and backed up a step.

"Hello, Toshi. It's me."

"Ah, your husband very angry."

"Yes, I'm afraid so. I'm sorry."

"Why he so angry with me?"

"Oh, I guess because he just came back from California and your company wants him to return."

"Mmmm. But he call me bully. I am not bully. Do you think I am bully?"

"Oh no,...*duh!*...Of course not. I'm sorry. He's still very tired from his business trip and under a lot of pressure like all of us and unfortunately he's been drinking a little too much wine tonight."

"But he must think I treat you unkindly."

"Oh I'm sure if he has that impression it's simply a mistaken one he's gathered from hearing me talk with you in the past. Usually when we do there's a problem to solve and a lot of pressure involved. He probably sees me looking worried. I'm really very sorry this happened and I will talk with him about it."

She walked toward the sliding glass door, opened it and went out to the deck, closing the door behind her. Though she wanted no more intrusions from Jay, secretly she was surprised to discover that she actually felt some satisfaction in hearing Toshi sound so defensive and off balance. He had lost his usual cool to cold demeanor and seemed to want her assurance that he was a good guy. She had never thought of him as a good guy and it was funny, both odd and amusing, to reassure him that he was.

"I don't think I deserve to be talked like that. Do you think I mean to you?"

"Oh no. I don't feel that way at all," she lied. "I think Jay just doesn't understand that you are under a lot of pressure. He probably just thinks that sometimes you're a little hard on me and feels protective. You know, like a husband might."

"Well, I think I not deserve to be talked like that."

"Oh no." She could feel a hint of a smile forming on her lips. "Absolutely not." She turned to look at Jay through the window, unsure whether to scowl or smile. If this wasn't going to result in a loss of business and apparently it wasn't, it was great to see Toshi taken down a peg for once. As she stayed on the phone she watched Jay pour the rest of his wine into the kitchen sink. He capped the decanter and went off towards their bedroom. A moment later, on hearing the front screen door bang shut, she surmised he was going for outside to calm down.

They stayed on the telephone for another five minutes discussing the details of the proposed trip to Los Angeles with intermittent references by Toshi to Jay's remarks. He was clearly shaken from the usual proud decorum in which he cloaked himself. The inscrutable oriental façade had sprung a fissure. He was taking pains to explain himself.

"I never call you on home phone before. You know that."

"Oh yes, you've never done that before. I know."

"And tonight I call on work phone but get only your recording."

"Oh yes, I see. I was on the other line and Candy is not here this late of course to pick it up."

"So I only call because so important. Not to be rude."

"I know. I understand, and again I'm very sorry. But we will definitely do Los Angeles for December. You can count on that."

"Okay. Thank you. You know I do not want to be like bully. I just doing my job. You understand, right?"

"Yes, yes. I understand. Don't worry. I'm sure Jay regrets his words already and just lost his temper for all the reasons I mentioned before. Too much pressure on all of us. But I'm sure he'll do a good job in LA and then we'll all feel much better. Okay?"

"Yes, okay. Thank you. Good bye."

"Good bye. Thanks for calling."

"She came inside, hung up the phone and looked out the window for Jay. She saw his car was gone. Standing still for a moment she noticed that darkness had descended on the lake. Yellow lights shone from the windows across the way, shining shafts that widened on the water as they stretched toward her. She pondered on the experience she had just undergone. On hearing Jay's voice rising from down below she had come upstairs curious and slightly alarmed. When she realized it was Toshi he was raking over the coals, she panicked, feeling anger and anguish simultaneously. Yet on sensing that Toshi sought reassurance from her and not recrimination, she had suddenly felt powerful with him, a strange sensation. Though he was distressed by Jay's comments, like usual he was focused on the business task at hand and seemed somewhat content that her company would do his bidding. Ruminating on the conversation left her feeling better overall that they had somehow managed to weather a potentially catastrophic storm. Perhaps he would even treat her a little nicer in the future. For now the important thing would be to have a flawless summer and then cap it off with a good program in December. Hopefully Jay was still up for that.

Chapter 57

"Everything there seemed fabulous to me, especially Italian simplicity – the olive oil, the bread, the local wine."
(Pablo Neruda, Neruda: An Intimate Biography, Volodia Teitelboim)

THE LATE AFTERNOON SUN was at its warmest point as Jay drove back from Naimee's house. The appointment had been his first house call since making their arrangement and his first house call with anyone in years. It reminded him of when he used to feel like a country doctor. He had been the only therapist around for many a mile in the early years of his practice.

The Eskimo lady's home was old and worn, much like her, and off a dirt road in an unpopulated area a few miles from the nearest community. Though it was rundown on the outside the inside was neat and tidy with various knick-knacks and photographs on the walls and shelves to highlight the plain and simple furniture. The thick shaggy rug, a faded burnt-orange, that once had been modern, looked sadly dated and lent an air of days gone by. Still they had managed to be comfortable enough in some frayed overstuffed chairs. It was just difficult to conduct a clinical session in such an informal environment.

Naimee had been excited, as most homemakers would, to show off her things. She was especially proud to show off her kitchen and referred to it as "my room". She had a wide array of cookbooks including a large selection of Italian ones that Jay thought looked interesting. When they finally sat down in the living room to talk they initially discussed Italian cooking as a way of breaking the ice before settling into her counseling issues. Jay had mentioned that a new Italian restaurant had opened up in her town. As he had already been there twice he had developed a fondness for their eggplant parmesan, his favorite dish, that was prepared in the mezzanine or thinly sliced style.

"Oh, you should go there. I wish I could take you there. It's so wonderful."

"Really?" She grinned broadly with her eyes brightening considerably at the prospect of yummy Italian food nearby...*she must be hungry*...

"Yep, really. It is so great. And the owners are really nice. It's a husband and wife team. She cooks and he seats people and talks about the wine. And it is so close to your home." He laughed. "We could be there in five minutes and do your session there!"

"Really?"

"No, just kidding." Jay grinned impishly. "It'd be impossible to talk because we couldn't stop eating. I mean it'd be nice to show you the place and introduce you to the owners. So when you go there with Jim, tell them I sent you. That'll work. You'll love it."

"That sounds good." Her eyes twinkled with delight and she winked. "But I'd rather go with you."

"Yeah, right." Jay laughed again. "Well, I'm sure you'll like it." He paused for effect, ready to delve into the business at hand. "Okay. So anyway, how are you doing?"

"I'm doing good. My only problem lately is I get a little lonely with Jim gone, but we can use the money so really I'm glad he's back working."

"Does getting lonely tempt you to drink sometimes?"

"Oh no, no, no. I know that could be trouble so I am very careful not to drink so much any more."

"I hope you're right. I can't help you if things get crazy again."

"Oh, I know. Don't worry. I'm getting better with your help. You are the best counselor in the world. And I really appreciate you coming to my home. That is wonderful. I feel you really care to do that."

"Oh, it's okay. It just seems like the best thing to do...*and if you knew how much i need clients*...

He winced as he recalled that point of their conversation...*that poor sweet old thing thinks i'm going there just because i care so much when it's at least in part simply to keep a client*...The sudden onset of guilt made him reach automatically for the one reliable thing, besides certain substances, that made him feel at peace; a tape from Leroy. Pulling it from the glove compartment he noticed it was a compilation of three short talks in February and March. He had gone from talking for an hour to a half hour and then, most recently, down to fifteen minute sessions. As he slipped it in the tape deck he reflected on the fact that things had improved some since then. He was now seeing a slight increase in his client load, though not nearly as many as he used to. Whether or not it was helping it always felt good to hear Leroy espouse on the pursuit of enlightenment.

"I think I'll just say 'What do I need to know now'?"

"Okay. Well, I'm going to surprise you by asking you a question. What prayer do you say all the time?"

"Hmm, well, I don't know but the thought that crossed my mind was 'This is not enough'."

"Yes, that's true. You perhaps do that, but that's not the answer. The answer is that you breathe."

"Oh, the 'Help me/Thank you' prayer."

"Right. And the beauty of that is that it's a prayer that's always answered, as you ask. And what I'm going to encourage you to do is to become very mindful of that as the truth and that as your support, so you have a basis of understanding who you really are and who really supports you, and after that becomes more clear, then allow yourself to have your desires piggy-backed on that basic prayer so that you are constantly praying and the prayer is constantly being answered. What better place is there to also include other desires?"

"It sounds like you are saying to reflect on desires while breathing."

"Yes. It amounts to that, as well as feeling the anticipation of your good. As you breathe in you are receiving it. Now I want to say something else too. When you find yourself desiring something, it is wise to allow for the fact that that thing also desires you. When there is mutual desire, when there is reciprocity of desire, there can be something received. It is useless to desire something that somehow doesn't desire you. If you think that something like an automobile or a bank account is something lifeless, you might not realize that it too is capable of knowing its fulfillment. It will desire you because it is meant to. It is important to realize the reciprocity of desire. It is not a one-way street. The fact that it is a two way street allows for both points to be fulfilled. So when you find yourself desiring something, allow that to be part of your recognition; that there is also desire coming from the other direction."

"It reminds me of a book title I saw once called *Money is My Friend*."

"That's right. That's it exactly. And so what is important to realize is that your desire also desires you. And that puts you in a good experience of agreement to have with a desire. Then the yielding that you do, which allows that feeling of agreement to be transported on your breath, puts you in the perfect place to realize your desires for fulfillment without a lot of process."

"You mean they materialize through inspiration along with respiration?"

"Exactly. You are so clear about this. You hear the truth and you immediately know where to take it. You see?"

"Well, I seem to fall down at some point. It seems like I go back and forth between two states of mind."

"You are still in the world of pressure and emotion a lot of the time. And when you are there, it just seems hopeless. There is no leverage to be gained there. You are, in effect, learning to walk through walls. And occasionally, as you are in the middle of walking through one, you think 'Oh my God, I'm stuck in a wall – what am I going to do – I can't get out!' And then you think 'Oh no – this is fine – I can do this'. It's that you get a bit of self-consciousness in the middle of your awakening."

"Okay. That fits. Look, there's something else I need to tell you. Ah, Bea left town today to go to Japan for a week and I've been trying not to get high lately, to genuinely do this shift, and uh, I got high and felt an immediate shift to a peaceful place, that I really seem unable to come to grips with naturally – from that area of emotion and pressure. And so I felt both a sense of blessedness and unhappiness over the fact that I felt so peaceful but did it artificially. I mean, I thought 'I sure dislike having done it this way but it is the sort of peace I am seeking' so …well I'm just wondering what you might have to say about that."

"The only thing I can tell you right now is to let go of any conflict over what you did today."

"Just let the peace be as genuine now as I will allow it?"

"Right. And don't struggle to be righteous when it's really about grace anyway. You see that's the problem. There's so much attempt to build a righteous world based on a foundation without grace and it is going to fail."

"Hm. Thanks. I see that. I felt the need to share it since we are working in the area of my consciousness."

"Right. There's no call for judgment here. It isn't recommended, but so what. I'm not going to judge you for it."

"Hm. The only confounding thing is that the feeling actually felt gratifying, or peaceful."

"Yes, and that's fine. The important thing is that it's good to remember that. And to remember something means that you keep it a part of you. So you have remembered your peace."

"Integrated it."

"Yes, exactly. So just keep it there. You can keep remembering it now. Don't struggle with what could be called a lapse. It is just you living your life and doing what you felt moved to do and finding the pressure not tolerable and seeing that a certain remedy would be better than tolerating the pressure. I understand."

"Well, okay, but I'm just wanting to do what we are trying to do here."

"I know. And so it is important to recognize that breathing is prayer. If you will remember that, you will forget your problems. You can't be having a fulfilled prayer all the time and still think that you are having much of a problem. It's another way of understanding the declaration of Jesus to seek the kingdom first. If you acknowledge that your breathing is prayer and that it is being answered, then that's that."

"It reminds me of having bad feelings and saying to the Holy Spirit or God 'Take these feelings from me'. Same thing, right?"

"Yes, it is the same thing, but also what prayer as breathing does is that it makes it hard to feel isolation from God."

"Yeah. I see that. It gives a constancy of connection."

"Yes. It is an immediate experience."

"Got it. Okay. Our fifteen minutes is up and actually slightly over. Thanks very much. I'll send you a check when I can and I'll call you next week."

"Okay. Take care. Good-bye."

There was an approximate thirty-second break in the tape and then the next segment came on from a week or two later.

"How are you doing?"

"Well, I guess I'm doing okay on one level and on another level, I feel terrible. I've got one client this week which is I think the worst I've ever had in fourteen years of business; one hour. And as I look at my blank schedule it's hard not to get a lot of negative thoughts around it."

"How can you be comfortable now? That's the most important thing."

"Well, what helps a little bit is what you said to me earlier that if I am not seeing a lot of clients at the moment just be grateful for that, as I'm working on being awakened, but it does seem difficult to do."

"Okay. The first thing I want to say is that you are not in any danger here. There's no real threat. There's an implied threat."

"Yep. There's plenty of those."

"Yes, but nothing real. The problem that you are facing is an illusory or imaginary one, and it is a belief still active that there is a world out there, an objective world, a world which is not subject to the dominion of consciousness. Everyone who has an ego suffers from that; from the curse of objectivity. What objectivity feels like is a feeling of your good being opposed."

"Right."

"Okay. So whenever you feel in any moment that your good, the intent for your fulfillment, is blocked or opposed, it is because you are still maintaining your objective or ego point of view. What you want to do is to take a moment here to feel the intent that is always there for your good. It is always moving you. You want to feel that intent as being completely unopposed. What does it feel like to have no opposition? Even five seconds of that feeling causes things to shift and to realign. What does it feel like not to be opposed? Now, there's a word for that, and that word is sovereignty. When your good or your will is not opposed, that's sovereignty. And that's where you need to put yourself right now."

"It's another slant on just keep practicing what we've been talking about."

"Yes, and there is another thing that I recommend that you do, so that you do not have to go anywhere or get anything to have your good manifest right now; to set yourself up for fulfillment that is immediate. Envision that what you desire is in a place called 'there', and where you are is here. And what you want is to feel that there is also here. And you do that by arriving at a point of complete acceptance and gratitude for the here. And then allow your attention to include the there, so that the there becomes here. It is a shift of attention that comes out of an unopposed point of view.

"If you use those moments of sovereignty to recognize that the good that you desire that is not yet manifest can be included in the full acceptance of what you have, without conflict or a sense that there are blocks and problems to overcome, then you will have constant indications and manifestations of the fact that you are on track and that miracles and support are always going to be evident. You lack evidence right now because you are not feeling sufficiently unopposed and confident enough to say 'I will have this' or 'That will be great, thanks'. It is time for you to be more forthright or expansive in what you are doing. And all it takes is first of all not to feel opposed. Have moments where you recognize what that feeling is.

"It will always feel like a connection, like gratitude and like success. It will feel like transformation, which can be radical but is always harmonious. And this is hard to do because there is always this other agenda going on, which is the ego's participation in what's happening, in that it wants to apply pressure to what it says is an objective reality. There's always the temptation to want to continue the objectification of reality and then manipulate it in some way. And you cannot do that. You have to understand that you cannot fall into that.

"That will always feel like pressure because you will not be able to succeed at it. You can only do this when you feel no pressure or the absence of opposition. And the absence of feeling opposition is the signature of having entered the subjective realm or the kingdom of heaven. When you feel no opposition you know you are in the place where you can ask for miracles. You have entered the kingdom. But when you still feel pressure you are still entertaining the idea and the feelings of objectivity, as though reality were out there and not connected to here, in consciousness."

"Well, that gives me a couple of thoughts. Every day when I rise I say 'I am rich and getting richer'. And that seems to be happening through the student exchange business. Then I am pretty much caught up in the busy-ness of the day and that is pressure. I am not feeling peaceful but apparently that is working. Secondly, it seems contradictory to me to ask for a miracle because it seems that when I am in the kingdom that that is a miraculous state of mind and that somehow everything should simply be as it should be."

"It is as it should be but there is always movement and you asking for a miracle is simply an acknowledgement of something that is to come into expression. You get to ask for things all the time, not out of a sense of need but out of a sense of desiring to have them. Those desires are given you by God. They are meant to happen as an expression of creation. You get to participate in this by acknowledging your own desires. The fact that it isn't just the way it should be is an ego ideal about what life is about, as though everything could be unacknowledged and unspoken, but you are going to have to continue to acknowledge what your desires are. What we are doing is just removing only this little experience of conflict, pressure, doubt and need from the experience of living and life continues to be what it has been; always new, always adventure, always revelation. But you continue to function with the same expression of desire, delight and gratitude that you always have had."

"So everything is the same but you remove the sense of separation though this shift."

"Yes. The shift is to recognize that the kingdom is subjective and that you get to participate in creation in a fully conscious way. You are a full participant in creation, which means that you get to be asking for things that you desire and having them manifest."

"But the desires I feel then are coming from being in alignment with God rather than my ego."

"Yes."

"So I'm really just feeling what God is intending to give me, which is always fulfillment of some sort."

"Right."

"So that's why it's important to desire the essence of it, like a new car without specifying the exact make and model and so on, because the details of the form it takes in material reality are up to God."

"Exactly."

"Okay. I get it. This seems like different information than before, or actually a different slant or nuance of meaning. So practice feeling unopposed."

"Yes, and that will do wonders for you, because you truly do feel opposed. And it will be such a relief to recognize your ability to come upon that feeling of being unopposed, because that then will be your shift. The other thing is to not take issue with your present circumstances, but rather allow them to be fully accepted and see that your desires for transformation will occur right out of what presently is going on."

"Got it."

"You see, people always want to reform things rather than allow things to just transform. There is always the judgment that we have to make it better – we have to make better forms – whether it is pollution, homelessness, crime, etc. If people would just simply see the divinity of what is going on, of life as it is, the very next moment would begin a radical but harmonious transformation of the world without any chaos at all. But people are not willing to do that. They see, egos see, reformation as its salvation and everybody wants to reform in different ways so all of this energy is going on at odds with itself."

"Left versus right for example, and the constant call for political reform, though things keeps staying the same or even getting more screwed up no matter how many laws are passed."

"Yes. So it is important that you want to have transformation and not reformation."

"Stick with the subjective not the objective."

"Exactly, because people who are insistent upon reforming something are still caught in objectivity."

"Okay. This might be enough of an enlightenment hit for now. I'd love to talk with you for longer but at this point it feels like it is more valuable for me to have short doses and just do it."

"You just do what you have to do. You're okay."

"Well, I have had such a hellish day feeling opposed."

"I know. It's hard work. And you need to feel grateful for two things. One, that you are as comfortable as you are, going through this; that you are able to do it with considerable comfort. I know there's not as much emotional comfort as you might want but you are doing it with personal comfort."

"Creature comfort?"

"Yes, but you have that. And if you were just grateful for that, it might bring you into more alignment with the fulfillment of the things you'd like to have. But you are going through a significant change, and it's brave of you to do this. You are getting support for doing it. And it's hard to find where to be grateful when you are going through something that feels like you have absolutely no say in what's going on and yet you can't seem to grasp it. So it would be good for you as a way of grounding yourself and feeling more connected to be grateful for the level of creature comfort that you are able to experience while doing it. And that might be enough to alter your position so that you feel these things coming in easily now."

"Well, that's difficult for me in two ways. One, I can accept what I have but I feel somewhat worthless that I haven't really earned it, at least not in counseling."

"Yes, I know it's tough. Just allow your self to be humiliated by it."

"And then secondly, if I say 'I guess I'm worth all this so how about some more', and then that doesn't seem to happen."

"You have to understand that there's still that pressure of objectivity that's causing you to demand more right away."

"Okay. I see that. What was the second thing I'm supposed to be grateful for besides creature comforts?"

"You are doing what you are doing. You underestimate the value of what you are doing. Just because it makes the ego feel worthless does not mean that this experience is not absolutely glorious. You see, it does make the ego feel worthless and as long as you are identifying with the ego you will feel worthless. You have to lighten up about this and just see that this is what people have to go through when they are doing this and be willing to be appreciative of the fact that you are doing it without enduring physical hardships. Nor will you have to. You are being provided for. And the more you get with this, you will not be able to stop people coming to see you. When you get through this thing, you will have something about you that is unshakable. And that will be what supports your life and your work. So don't fret about this. This is to be easy."

"Well…alright. I don't really have any more questions. Just practice being unopposed and feel grateful for the level of comfort I'm at."

"Yes, and have enough confidence when I say you are being taken care of. Do you understand?"

"Well, I do, but it really is almost impossible for me not to translate that into 'Yeah, I'm being taken care of by my wife's business and I resent having to do it and she'd resent it if I stopped', so it seems like really a kind of shitty thing; a double edged sword."

"I know. And you have to forgive that. And I know it's hard. But better it look that way than it look like you are not being taken care of."

"True."

"And when you make this shift, you'll be able to provide for, let's just say, at least sixty percent of the family income."

The tape stopped suddenly…*sixty percent of the income…that'd be nice*…He flipped it over to hear the other side. It was the start of a new session, which meant there was no more to be heard from the previous one. That tape had ended in the comment about the family income.

"The main reason I'm calling today is that I'm feeling like doing some writing, a novel specifically, but part of me feels like maybe it is a waste of time and I should be thinking about making money somehow instead."

"Well, what else would you be doing now anyway, given that you feel moved by the spirit to do this? You are willing to do it and you are yielding to the movement so there's no better thing to do than what you are moved to be doing. You can't be concerned about the consequences of being congruent with the movement. See that's where your separation begins to reveal itself. It's the idea that you might know better than the movement of life. So, just go with this and trust what feels easy as contrasted with what feels effortful. If you find yourself unable to do this easily or find you need to press yourself to continue to do more writing then pay attention to that and recognize that you need to stop and ask what is going on now. If you are not moved to write, then what are you moved to do? There's no way of knowing until you come to that point. Then you ask what is to be done now. What you have to do is stay with the movement all the time.

"You see, what's going on with you is more about discovering the foundation of your existence. What you don't always experience is having that foundation, that invisible but evident experience of safety and support, of permanence. Foundation is the thing underneath you; the thing that supports you. The world is based upon the idea of self-support, little s or ego support. And if you can't do that then you hit bottom. In God's kingdom you can't do that. You literally can't hit bottom because there is a foundation supporting you. And the more you feel that, the less inclined you are to engage the thought of self-support as the only way. I will tell you this is hard on the ego.

"It's hard for the ego to stay with the idea of being supported when your mind is arguing otherwise. And what you have to do here to stay with the truth, is give up the places in your mind where you still consider yourself to be independent, because it is being offered you in those areas. Every thing is being offered to you at the level of connection or joining with the giving up of the notion of independence. As you begin to give up the independence or self-support you begin also to realize that you are not seeing the world as objective so much. And when the world becomes less objective in your moment-by-moment experience, your inclination to struggle with issues is much less, because you are already in that place where you are more naturally inclined to experience the wholeness of things rather than the division of things. As this happens your life is just supported always and you are less inclined to be concerned about the results of your work. You can't be doing anything else because you would be outside of the movement if you weren't doing it."

"Hmmm. Okay, well it does feel good to consider writing, but the thought that there's no money in it feels like a concern."

"You need to feel balanced in that area. If it looks to you like there's not enough money then just allow your innate support to come to you in that area. There is a belief you have that the support is not somehow there; that somehow there needs to be a compensation or adjustment. So ask for that. There is an experience of something being deficient that you want erased. Go to the feeling of not having that deficiency. Go to the feeling of having that balance, of feeling that support. Then, as you feel that support, allow yourself to trust that feeling and be curious as to how it begins to be expressed in form. Don't ask for 'I want this to happen – I want that to happen'. Just say 'I do want to feel support where I don't feel it right now' and then allow for whatever adjustment inside is necessary so that you actually feel something real inside of yourself; a conviction, a trust, a lack of concern."

"Ask and ye shall receive?"

"Exactly, but ask for the kingdom. And don't go any further than that. Let life take care of the details. What you have to learn here is that your support does not require you to come up with answers yourself. What is required is for you to learn that by an adjustment of feeling, and that alone, will put you in alignment with your good where you have perceived it not to be there."

"So this could take the form of work or money coming to me through Bea's company?"

"It could take any form. But it will feel like support. It will be movement and tangible experience that conforms to the experience of support that you are allowing yourself when there's nothing visible. Don't look for an answer beyond having the feeling that you want to have; the sense of support, agreement, communion, and balance. Just say 'This is what I want, thank you'. And allow yourself to have the feeling unconditionally. Do not insist on the conditions. That is always your salvation, to work from the level of unconditional experience, because God can then translate that into conditions. But if what you are dealing with is conditional living, that is, if you are insisting that your good come through certain conditions that you impose or insist upon, then it is a lot harder. If you stay at the level of conditions that you regard as reasonable to expect your good to work through, then it is a lot harder for your good to come because that may not be the way it is intended to come. It is better to be unreasonable, to go to the level of unconditioned experience and ask to feel support in whatever area you don't and then God can move things around effortlessly, as God does."

"Okay, I'll try to do that. Thanks. I think our time is about up. I'll call you in a week or so."

"Sounds good."

Turning off the paved street onto his gravel driveway as the tape came to an end, he felt his spirits lift as usual after listening to Leroy. Looking past the side of the house up ahead, he caught a glimpse of the lake beyond it. He rolled past the tall hedge of evergreen spires that lined the driveway on his left and took in the pink rhododendrons around his yard. They gaily festooned his cedar paneled yellow dwelling like fresh boutonnières pinned on a summer sport coat. The crackling sound of gravel underneath his slowing tires seemed to call out welcome home like a chorus from the earth. As he pulled to a stop gently, underneath the carport, he breathed a sigh of satisfaction and momentary relief…*still time for a run…*

Later that evening, after dinner, in his room, he received a call from the answer service while playing music on his keyboard synthesizer.

"Sorry to disturb you sir, but there is a caller, a woman, who sounds rather upset and says it is urgent she speak with you."

"Did she identify herself?"

"No sir. She wouldn't. She just says she's a patient of yours and wants to talk to you right now. She sounds like she may have been drinking."

"Put her through."

Chapter 58

"I am the daughter of Earth and Water,
And the nursling of the Sky;
I pass through the pores of the ocean and shores;
I change, but I cannot die."
(Lines from 'The Cloud' by Percy Bysshe Shelley)

THE COTTON BALL CLOUDS of a pretty May day were perfectly reflected in the lake as they sailed slowly over it against the blue canvas backdrop of sky. Amid phone calls and faxes Bea caught an occasional glimpse of the fluffy forms in flight as she focused intently on the incessant tasks at hand. At the moment she was absorbed in writing another communiqué to peripatetic Perry, her Canadian crook. She had not heard from him in over several months, when he had left a terse message on her voice mail saying he was still trying his best to resolve things…*whatever that means*…At Jay's bidding she had been gratefully willing to share with him the tedious task of trying to recover the funds, but their efforts so far were fruitless. Aside from occasional letters to Toronto, she had been so fraught with other business concerns that she barely had time to be thinking about it. But there were those moments, usually late at night, when unsettling thoughts about the unsettled issue crept into her consciousness. Despite her best efforts to compartmentalize it, the persistent sense of a problematic situation gnawed away unabated in a corner of her mind as protracted unfinished business. It was something she knew she had to attend to, for her own satisfaction, until it was resolved or she could let it go. And neither of those options had emerged as of yet.

The last letter she had sent him had apparently gone unheeded. At least as usual there had been no reply. She had addressed him in the manner that Leroy had advised; direct, firm, unyielding but magnanimous. She had offered to set up a payment plan with him, any plan at all, but to no avail. It still galled her that she lacked the wherewithal to confront him by phone, person to person, and though while not excusing it, she fully understood her own unwillingness. The realization that she was dealing with someone who had so deliberately deceived her, not to mention the Host families, while posing as a do-gooder, a Sunday school teacher, a family man, a righteous man of God, merging divergent cultures through the medium of her fine company, actually made her feel nauseous. How could someone ever sink so low? She'd given him a second chance, refusing to believe the worst, only to be fooled again while learning just how badly he had cheated her and his countrymen out of their rightful due. She had felt so badly for the Toronto families deprived of their stipends, that she had paid them with funds earmarked for other projects, thus increasing her losses substantially.

As she struggled now for just the right wording, a perfect way to insist on the return of her money while also respecting his dignity as a person, she found it challenging. Having never been in such a circumstance before she had never had occasion to write such letters. Pausing part way through the correspondence, she stared absently at the lake, awaiting inspiration. A large puffy cloud cruising across the water's surface seemed to reflect the agonizing slowness of her mental processes at the moment. She felt an abiding and growing frustration, not just with the letters, but the process as a whole. It had been nearly half a year since learning that Perry had duped her. The only changes in the process had been ever worsening ones as it was continuously revealed that many families had not been paid. Plus he had apparently gone into hiding. His old phone was dead, his old address no longer good. Her letters were now being sent to his church, the only way she thought that they might reach him. So far anyway they had not been returned.

Alongside her frustration and chafing reluctance she felt again the gnawing sense of disappointment in her self for her disinclination to speak with him directly. She knew that she should do it. But the very anticipation of the sound of his voice, knowing that she couldn't believe one word he said, left her feeling revolted as though embracing a leper. She also feared her sadness would break through her attempts to be impersonal and professional, as she took it so personally. She loved her work with an idealism that shone through every aspect of it. To encounter someone who had cynically and systematically rifled and besmirched it, in her good name no less, simply left her feeling utterly heartsick. To confront such a person was almost more disgusting than she felt she could bear.

Yet at other times the crime was so galling in her gut, so impossible to forget, that she felt moved to address him and this morning had decided to write him once more. It was one thing to fear an unpleasant confrontation. And another to be repulsed by the depth of his betrayal. And altogether a different matter yet to have been in equal parts so busy and so devastated by her sister's death that she was driven to distraction. A feeling persisted that there must be someday a final point of reckoning or her self-esteem would continue to suffer endlessly. As she contemplated these thoughts she felt a rising tide of dissatisfaction swelling keenly within her. Why write another letter to that despicable cur? It was a waste of good paper. She took a deep breath, set down her pen and said a short prayer. It was time to talk turkey.

She reached for the telephone and called his church in Toronto, hoping for the best … *try to be as tough and as tricky as jay…* Posing as a long time friend of his wife's – a bit of a stretch but not exactly a lie – she fortuitously managed to get a well-deserved break. The church secretary who answered the phone, while relating that she was new on the job, was happy to give her his new telephone number. Her newfound determination overrode the upsurge of her heart's palpitations as that phone began ringing.

"Hello," came the answer over the line from Canada. It was Perry's wife, Molly, who Bea had met early last year when she'd first hired him. They had invited her to dinner and she had spent a pleasant evening in their home that one night.

"Hello, Molly, this is Bea, Perry's ex-boss in Seattle. How are you?" She heard Molly gasp.

"Oh, hello Bea. How are you? I'm okay, I guess."

"Well, I'm okay too, considering the circumstances. Actually I called to talk with Perry. Is he there?" There was long pause and then Molly replied in a very flat tone.

"Bea, Perry's dead." The stillness between them was deafening for a moment.

"What?"

"I said he's dead. He died…about a month ago. I thought maybe you knew."

"Why no. How would I know? No one that I know there knows how to reach him." She stopped to let the news sink in, feeling shocked and flushed with curiosity, compassion, and confusion. "Oh my God. I'm sorry, Molly. Jeez, what happened?"

"Oh God, it's a long story. But I guess as much as anyone, you deserve to know. For quite a few months it's been really crazy here, at least until he died."

"What do you mean?"

"Well, I guess he owed people money. I don't really know the whole truth. Somehow he eventually got involved in gambling."

"Gambling?"

"I think he was trying to make some fast money to pay our debts, but he just got in deeper."

"Oh, God. That's terrible. And you didn't know about it?"

"No, not really. He would never tell me anything, except maybe half-truths. But people around here, some of them friends of ours, through the church and so forth, who had been

Host Families last year, would call him up and sometimes even come by the house, saying that he owed them money."

"Yes, I'm afraid he did."

"Well, I'm sorry about that. I didn't know anything about it. He told me that you were supposed to be paying the families and I never knew what was going on really."

"I hate to tell you this Molly, but Perry stole a lot of money from me, at least ten thousand, that was supposed to go to families and various student activities."

"Oh God. Well, I'm sorry if he did. I didn't know what was happening. I only knew he was getting hounded by more and more people. After a while he wouldn't even take their phone calls or answer the door. He'd have me do it and say he wasn't home. Eventually we sold our house and moved to an apartment on the outskirts of town. He told me you were supposed to be paying them."

"Well I did, but that wasn't the way it was supposed to happen. He took my money and then I had to pay the families with other funds."

"I'm sorry. I really am. It's all been so crazy. He started staying out late, going to bars or I don't know where. He often wouldn't come home, afraid people would find him, and towards the end he even started sleeping in his car."

"Oh my God."

"Yeah. It was pretty bad."

"So what happened exactly?"

"Well, one night he slept in his car in the church parking lot. I guess he thought he'd be safe there. But in the morning someone who was on their way to work – someone he owed money to – spotted it in the lot and for some reason went over to it and saw Perry inside sleeping. I guess he banged on the windows and woke Perry up. And Perry jumped out of the other side of the car and started running."

"Oh no."

"Yes. And the man started chasing him and he ran across the street, right through the morning traffic on that boulevard by the church, and he slipped as he reached the other side and he smashed his head on the curb, and he… and he…" Her tone became muffled with sobs. "And he just died right there. Right there on the street." With those words her voice broke into a high pitch and then she began crying quietly.

"Oh," said Bea, feeling saddened and stunned. "I'm so sorry Molly. I really truly am. I had no idea. What a shame." Molly sniffled and regained her composure somewhat.

"I know. It's terrible. But we're carrying on as best we can." That reminded Bea that Molly and Perry had a teenage son and younger daughter…*what a mess…now what?…*

"How are you…that is… how are you getting by?"

"Well, the people at the church have helped and I've got some family here, but overall it's tough. It's tight. It's day to day."

"I see. Are you working now yourself?"

"No. I can't yet. I can't think well enough to work. And I've got my boy and little girl. I'm not qualified for much of anything but motherhood."

"Yeah, I understand," said Bea consolingly. "It must be tough."

"Oh God, it really is. I'm in the middle of claiming bankruptcy right now."

"I see," responded Bea…*well there goes my money…and i thought i had troubles…* "Well, I'm sorry. I do wish you well."

"Oh thank you," cried Molly in anguish and gratitude. "And I'm sorry too, for all the problems he caused you. I really am, believe me, but I can't help you at all."

"I know. It's okay, Molly. I understand."

Chapter 59

"Believe me it requires no little Confidence, to promise Help to the Struggling, Counsel to the Doubtful, Light to the Blind, Hope to the Despondent, Refreshment to the Weary...But it is my earnest wish, I confess, to employ my understanding and acquirements in that mode and direction, in which I may be enabled to benefit the largest number of my fellow creatures." (On the Life of Solitude, Petrach)

JAY WAITED TO BE connected through the answer service with growing concern that Naimee and Jim had fought again.

"Here you are, sir," spoke the operator. "Go ahead."

"Jay?"

"Hello, Naimee. What's happening?"

"Oh Jay," she slurred, sounding drunk and very serious. "Jim is very mad...very mad... very mad."

"Uh-oh," Jay replied. "What's going on? Have you had another fight?"

"No...no," she said emphatically. "He very mad at you...because...because...you want to take me out. I told him. I had to tell him."

"What?" Jay's mind spun faster than a fishing reel on the loose, trying to get a line on her meaning. "What are you talking about?"

"Oh, I told him. I had to tell him. I told him about the restaurant. How you wanted to take me there. Now he's very angry...because I'm his girl. I'm his girl."

"Oh, God. Are you nuts? I don't want to take you to a restaurant or anywhere else for that matter."

"Oh, you say you did. I know. I remember. I know you did. You did!"

"Oh God." Jay's mind spun back, recounting their time together...*oh Jesus*... "Look, when I said that, if I did, it was just an expression. I meant like, when you say to someone 'Oh I'd love to turn you on to it', meaning, you know, I'd like to show it to you. I'd like for you to see it. I meant I thought you'd like it. I couldn't care less about – I mean, no offense but it never even crossed my mind to -"

"No, no! Don't you deny it, Jay," she yelled. "I heard you! You said it. You said you want to take me. You want to take me out. You know you did! Jim knows it. I told him! You lying! You know you did!"

"Oh, Jesus. Look, I only meant...never mind." Jay felt irritated, saddened, frustrated, panicked and at a loss for words...*how do you reason with a drunk*..."Is Jim there?"

"Oh, yes! He here. And he plenty mad. Plenty mad at you!"

"May I speak with him please?"

"Jim!" she said hoarsely. "He want to talk with you. He trying to deny it. He's lying! He's lying! He's lying."

"Hello," came a deep gruff voice. "This is Jim."

"Jim," said Jay, feeling slightly relieved. "I really can't believe this is happening. I hope you don't believe what she is saying."

"Well, I don't know what to believe."

"Oh man. This is crazy. She sounds drunk."

"She's had a few."

"Do you really believe I would want to go out with her?"...*that gnarly hag...that crippled ugly toothless low life*..."Do you really believe that?"

"I don't know what to believe," he repeated, sounding stubbornly petulant. "She said you came over. She said you wanted to take her out."

"Yeah, okay. I know she said that. You knew I was coming over, I assume, for the counseling appointment. You were in on that. We got to talking about cooking, Italian food, and I said something like 'There's this new restaurant and I'd love to show it to you' or maybe I said 'I'd love to take you there', I don't know. But whatever I said it was to communicate the idea that she should go there – that she would like it, etc. Do you understand that?"

"Uh huh," he intoned noncommittally.

"Listen, no offense, but I am not attracted to her in the slightest. Okay? I mean not even a teeny tiny eeny weeny little bit. Okay? I hope you understand that without taking offense. I am happily married"...*and even if i weren't i'd rather die than have that ugly piece of garbage touch me*..."I haven't the slightest interest in doing anything with her but counseling."

"Well," he drawled, "she seems awful sure you do." He paused. "I don't know what happened but I don't think you should come over here anymore, at least when I'm not here."

"Don't worry, believe me"…*you moron*…"I don't want to have anything to do with her. I can assure you that I wouldn't dream of having anything to do with her again whatsoever. Listen, she is screwed up. She's drunk. She's crazy. She's either making things up or imagining them but in either case I want absolutely nothing to do with her."

"Uh-huh," Jim grunted.

"And that's actually going to be a big problem for her"…*not for me you twits*… "because she is legally mandated to be in counseling for another year and a half. I was doing her and you a favor by coming over there."…*and good luck finding anybody else to do that*…

"Yeah," he admitted begrudgingly. "I know." Jay sensed his irritation was diminishing.

"So look, no offense, as I said, but I'm done with her. I'll call her lawyer tomorrow and tell him to find her another counselor or see what can be done. I'm sure he'll call you."

"Okay," he said matter-of-factly. He seemed to be just listening, taking it all in, unsure of what to think.

"So, good-luck. I wish you well." Jay sighed with relief. "I just wonder if you believe me. I want you to understand that she is either twisting this or imagining it. I really don't know which. Do you understand that?"

"Ahhh," he said slowly, "I really don't know what to make of it exactly." Jay heard Naimee yelling in the background.

"I'm going to call the police, Jay! I going to tell them what you did!" It made his heart flutter with fear while arousing his animus.

"You know, she can do whatever she wants. I really don't care. But if either of you think I am in any way even slightly attracted to her, you are both sadly mistaken and totally out of your minds. I'm hanging up now," he said bitterly and hung up…*shit…now what if she calls the state and complains…going over to her house…doesn't really look too good…shoulda' never ever offered…goddamn nut case…underestimated her craziness…shit…*

He turned off the synthesizer and stood there biting his lip while reflecting on the mess. There was really nothing else to do tonight but try to forget about it for now. He'd call the lawyer tomorrow, first thing in the morning.

Picking up his empty wine glass, he strode over to his dresser and pulled out a small glass pipe with a green bud stuck in it. As he left the bedroom and walked through the house he was aware that Bea and Phil must be in their separate quarters. He stopped by the small bar next to the kitchen to refill his wine glass and paused deep in thought. It was tempting to resort to his typical vices, artificial help, temporary aids. He decided to bolster them with words of wisdom. It was too late to call him but a tape might help out. He set down the wine glass, went back to the bedroom, and put the pipe in the drawer. From the top of his dresser he took a recent tape from Leroy, along with his Walkman. Then slipping quietly outside into the cool of the evening, he strode down the pathway in the dark to the water's edge. He lay down in the hammock stretched between the willow trees, adjusted his headphones and listened to the tape.

"How long did you want to talk?"

"Oh, maybe fifteen minutes."

"Okay, that fits. Go ahead."

"Well, ahhh, I was thinking to day how much I enjoy taking with you and yet how it feels like I'm getting nowhere and uh, I was thinking this morning of the story *Of Mice and Men* and I was thinking how I almost feel like Lenny, the retarded guy, saying to George, his buddy, over and over again 'Tell me again George, how it's gonna' be when we're awakened'. And of course, as you probably know, they never reach their version of the Promised Land, so to speak. And sometimes I just wonder…"

"Well, the thing is that getting somewhere is the problem. You are not getting anywhere. And you need to be disabused of the notion that there is somewhere else to be; that the circumstances have to be different somehow. Certainly the feeling that you have about things, the disillusionment, needs to be gotten through into something else. What happens then, once you are through that, you are going to find that you still have no control over anything, but that your level of trust is greater than it has been and that you have evidence of your good or of needs being met. And if you could accept that what you are going through is okay and there is nothing you can do about it except be at peace and feel somehow that you are on a roll, despite the fact that the world doesn't look that way, you would be exactly where you need to be. You are going to have to come to that point now or later. And talking with me is intended to get you to that point somewhat sooner. But there is nowhere else to go except that point where you feel your connection to life and you feel the basic regenerative movement of life unconditionally."

"Hm."

"You see, the basic movement of life is revolutionary and progressive. And you see this everywhere in creation. The basic forms in creation are spheres. They rotate around things, from the planets to the atoms. The basic movement is both revolutionary and progressive. So it encompasses both going around in a circle and linearity at the same time. They rotate as they move forward. And what you want to do is to know what that feels like, because to be connected to that is where you need to put your attention, not in the relative world. Now what does it feel like to be in that movement? There's a perfect expression and I've already used it: being on a roll. That's what life really feels like when you are connected. But being on a roll is an eternal thing. It's not something that you happen to experience only when circumstances are appropriate or adequate for some occasion. Being on a roll is something you have to feel all the time, and allowing that to be felt unconditionally is the only way out of your situation.

"And then when you are on that roll, you find that you have the opportunity to dance, which is the secondary kind of movement. There is first the primary movement of being on a roll and then there is the secondary movement of dancing or self-expression, which occurs once you are already feeling that primary movement. You see the problem is that people in an ego state of mind forget the primary or absolute movement and get absorbed in the secondary or relative things, the dance, the interchange between individuals without feeling that primary connection. So you are going back in order to feel that. It's a wonderful feeling and it prevails or endures even when there is no dancing or no particular activity going on. It is still going on. That's what you want to do. It's a sense of an eagerness for life and an openness towards it."

"Hm. Okay. I'll try to remember that. Staying in touch with a feeling that I'm on a roll with the basic movement of life."

"That's right. It could be compared to riding on a train, in one of the cars, where you still get to get up and move around even as you are being moved along on the tracks."

"I see."

"Now, one more thing. We talk about peace all the time. What the peace does is provides the axis for the roll. You see, if something rolls and doesn't have an axis it is chaotic. An axis is like an axle in a wheel. What you want is to be balanced so the roll is experienced as purposeful, creative and intelligent. So your participation in that is to have your equilibrium and peace. That is the axis. And when you are not that way then the perception is that first of all there isn't a roll, but a lot of chaos. You don't experience the roll as a roll but as chaotic random movement. And the fact is that the movement of life is always in balance."

"So being at peace is my part in regeneration."

"That's right, and then feeling the forward and revolutionary movement of life, in the sense of being conveyed."

"I got it."

"Good. You know, it's interesting to me that I used to be a figure skating coach when I was younger. And only now is it beginning to dawn on me that all of figure skating is based on revolutions and having an axis. All of these principles were being given me in a different way."

"What's the axis in skating, the skates, the ice, your balance?"

"In figure skating – you actually skate figures in the ice – the axis is the midpoint of everything. It is where the circles meet, at the center, and it's also the dividing point between the right and left side of the circle so that if you have a turn that you are putting on one end of the figure, it's going to be on that axis so that things are lined up. Alignment is very important in figure skating. In free skating – in doing the jumps – where you have to rotate three times around in the air, being on axis is crucial because you can't spin fast enough and be able to land a jump without having a clear axis for the body to be on. The body can't be wobbling around in the air."

"Hm. Well, I hear what you are saying, but I had a thought, a fearful one I guess, that if I feel like I'm on a roll then I'm thinking what do I do now. And I thought, in response to that, that if I don't try to think of what I should do next and just sit here it will come to me. I'll feel moved by the movement."

"Right. There is no pressure to act coming from being connected. That will not feel like pressure. It's more likely to feel like a real pleasurable inclination. You might find pressure when there is a desire to override an inhibition that you have kept for too long. Let's say, for example, there is something that you really feel you ought to do but you are also feeling reluctant or resistant to doing it. You might be on the verge of discovering that doing it is easy. Let's say, for example, that you don't want to get into doing something that seems somehow too challenging or whatever."

"Like writing a book?'

"Sure, or perhaps even something more apparently noxious like doing your income taxes, because you think you owe a lot of money or it's too tedious or complicated. There's this feeling of resistance. But suppose then you realize that you are not going to be responsible and that in choosing peace you become unafraid to take any steps. And then you get into it and find it somehow is relatively easy and it all comes out in perfect order."

"I've had those moments."

"Right. So sometimes you are led to do that, which is not the same thing as spontaneously doing something, but it is nevertheless a part of this movement, that you will be called upon to release inhibitions that serve no purpose."

"I wonder if that would apply to quitting smoking."

"Well yeah, just don't smoke."

"Just don't smoke."

"It's a matter of losing interest in smoking."

"Well, I've got to be enjoying doing what I'm doing when I'm not. Which is relaxing and having peace, I guess, like you are saying today. Yesterday was a tough day in that I found out I have a lot more hits on my credit report than I thought. I'm afraid it is going to negatively impact our attempt to refinance the house."

"Stay with the intent to finance the house and be at peace with it. You are then the axis for the roll that you feel going on which is intending in a revolutionary way to manifest the refinancing of the house."

"How long do I have to stay with this intent?"

"For as long as it takes. There can't be any pressure around it. It should not be uncomfortable. You have to be totally indifferent to the outcome of it at the same time that you are aware of the desire."

"Well, that may be, but something has to shift in order for me to make more money and I don't know what I should do."

"You have to trust the balance of your life just as it is even when it looks like you are not making money. You see, you have to work beyond what you perceive to be the problem, because the problem, as you see it, is that you are not making enough money. I can't tell you to do anything about that. I wouldn't know what to tell you, you see, except I can tell you how to shift your position so that anything else can happen besides those circumstances going on now. And that entails feeling your balance just where you are, and whenever the ego says there is a problem here of insufficiency, don't feel out of balance. Feel in balance. And then what happens is you are in a position where something radical can occur. But if what you are looking at is a problem and you are looking for a specific remedy and trying to create a rationale for it to occur, you are going to be stuck."

"Alright. I understand. Actually by just listening to you, and trying to feel what you are saying, I am starting to feel good, oddly enough, even though everything in my life looks bad."

"But it doesn't matter. It just temporarily looks that way. That's all."

"Alright. Out time is about up. Thanks."

Jay lay in the hammock staring through the willow branches at the stars above as the tape came to an end, wondering if he would ever integrate Leroy's wisdom...*i sure as hell hope its temporary all right, because it sure as hell looks awfully hopeless right now...*

Chapter 60

"You are a child of God, a priceless part of His Kingdom, which He created as part of Him. Nothing else exists and only this is real. You have chosen a sleep in which you have had bad dreams, but the sleep is not real and God calls you to awake."
(A Course in Miracles)

As THE SCHOOL BUZZER sounded the end of lunch, Phil emerged from the woods with a small group of boys who parted with a wave or a nod to each other while shuffling off to their various classrooms. In the sweet air of spring he felt buffeted by the breeze as he ambled down the path toward his favorite class: music. He pulled a small canister of Binaca from his pocket and sprayed in his mouth to allay the dead taste of smoke on his tongue. On reaching the building he ducked into the bathroom, went inside a stall and dripped a few drops of Visine in each eye, blinking like a bird while it washed the red out. After carefully washing his hands and face at the sink, he ran damp paper towel all over his shirt to wipe off any traces of the odor of pot that may have clung to it.

Feeling light-headed if not entirely light-hearted he headed for the band room just before the last buzzer and entered the room feeling ready to play. While buzzing like a bee at a honey-filled hive he felt somewhat smug in the fact that he was flying in the grand old tradition of the greatest jazz artists of the century. Satchmo, Bird and Trane to name a few had all caught a buzz to augment their playing. It was common knowledge. It was the hip way to play, the cool way to be, and as those in the know knew, the only way to go.

Along with other students in the room he extracted his instrument gently from its case and began to tune it to his little pitch pipe. Playing bass guitar in the jazz band had been the most delightful and satisfying experience of his school year. Not the sports, not the girls, not even the dances had been as much fun as his one hour a day class in music. And the concerts they had given at the two school assemblies had increased his popularity plus his pride in himself.

It had been a good way to make friends at a new school where he'd initially felt alien and isolated amidst the mob of new faces. Ever since Ryan had originally befriended him his circle of contacts had grown with each month. Because they were Ryan's friends first it had turned out that smoking marijuana was a common denominator. That had proven useful in obtaining it frequently. Someone in the group was always likely to have some and willing to share it with others at the school. After the day he'd first tried it last fall, it became available with increasing ease. Ryan especially seemed to have an inexhaustible supply, primarily because of his older brother. Getting high at lunchtime and then getting down with the sounds was their regular pastime by the end of winter. Though the rest of his studies had not gone so smoothly he felt in a groove when it came to making music.

At night he would practice in his bedroom by himself, alternating hip-hop with standard jazz classics. With his dad relegating himself to his room each night with his own instruments and four-track recorder he felt like a chip off the old block, as his mom would say. And what with her either out of town or working most the time, he was glad to have music to take up the slack of an otherwise relatively lonely existence. Ever since his brother had gone away to college he had been an only child. Since his private elementary school had been very small, most of his friends had come through sports teams but virtually all of them attended public schools. At least pot stilled the pangs of adolescent loneliness and mixing it with music was a cure for all ills.

The only drawbacks he noticed were that he had less time or inclination for his other subjects and also that he got more easily winded on the soccer field. He was getting by fairly well with his academic studies; mostly average grades for now. His parents weren't especially pleased with his winter grade average but thought it probably due to the tough transition to a much larger school and broader curriculum. They understood an adjustment took time but found it puzzling he'd missed so many assignments. He said he'd do better. More than school however it was the soccer that bothered him. He used to be a star. Now his gruff coach often used him as a goalie in the starting line-up, which involved much less running. He'd then exchange positions with another boy at halftime, assuming his normal position as a forward. With all the other kids being worn out from the first half of play his lessening of endurance was not all that noticeable. Though the coach had explained to his parents that the switch to goalie was because the former one had quit, he felt that the coach had observed a slight slackening of his stamina on the field. At practice the man had barked more often at him to dig in. Aside from that, he was fooling the world, most the time.

The teacher stood tall at the front of the classroom, holding his baton in a ready angle of attentiveness as he surveyed the group. "Let's start today with the new tune I handed out yesterday, 'A Night in Istanbul'. Everyone got their sheet music?"

As Phil finished tuning his instrument he looked in the guitar case for the sheet music handout he had looked over last night. He shuffled through several papers for different tunes but couldn't find it...*damn...musta' forgot it...shit...not again...*

"I hope," the teacher continued, "everyone practiced this piece last night. We don't have much time before the next assembly and it's a difficult song." There were appreciative murmurs from the students in concurrence with the last statement.

"It's damn difficult," mumbled Ryan from his perch behind the drum set in the back of the room.

"What's that?" said the teacher, arching an eyebrow toward Ryan.

"Nothing, sir," offered Ryan apologetically. "Just agreeing with you."

"Uh-huh." The teacher cast a look around the room. "Everyone got it?"

Amid nods and voices of assent from the group the instructor looked directly at Phil and said pointedly, "How about our bass player? Got your music this time?"

"Uhhh, yes sir. I think so. Just finding it now." He placed the sheet music of a different song on the music stand and lied. "Yeah, I'm all set.".*..guess i'll have to fake it...*He glanced back nervously at Ryan who smiled and shook his head knowingly.

"You're fucked up," he silently mouthed. The teacher looked at both of them suspiciously and then raised the point of his baton toward the ceiling, indicating it was time to start.

"All right. Okay. Here we go then. A one, a two, a one – two – three – four."

The piece started off at a fast pace weaving percussion, bass and piano from a burst of sound into a snazzy solo on the saxophone that barely got going when the leader yelled, "Stop!" He glared at Phil. "The bass switches to double time here. What's the matter? Can't you read your music or don't you even have it?"

Phil looked up at the teacher then down to the floor as anxiety overtook him. "Uh, I'm sorry. I thought that I had it but actually I don't. I must have left it at home last night."

"Again?" came the thinly veiled sting of sarcasm. "That's at least four times in the last few weeks. Are you losing your memory? Premature Alzheimer's?" Laughter arose from the ranks of the class.

"I'm sorry, sir, really. I had it all set out." He felt himself flushed with humiliation...*shit...* The teacher stared at him in exasperation for a long speechless moment, seemingly trying to comprehend the problem.

"Well," he finally said in a slightly softer tone, "we don't have the luxury of time to waste on poor preparation by anyone in the group. We need this done right and we need it done soon. I don't want to have to speak to you about this any more."

"I - I'm sorry," Phil stammered. "I really worked on it hard last night," he lied again. In the course of the evening he'd gotten distracted by hip-hop and only given the piece a cursory read.

"Well, you could have fooled me," said the teacher tersely. "Alright," he commanded raising the baton. "Move closer to the piano and read off that music for today." He paused for effect. "And then I want to see you after class is over."

Chapter 61

"Fear of the Will of God is one of the strangest beliefs the human mind has ever made…You have set up this strange situation so that it is impossible to escape from it without a Guide Who does know what your reality is. The purpose of this Guide is merely to remind you of what you want. He is not attempting to force an alien will upon you. He is merely making every possible effort, within the limits you impose on Him, to re-establish your own will in your awareness."
(*A Course in Miracles*)

IN THE BLUE-GRAY DARKNESS of an early May morning Bea sat at her office desk sipping hot coffee and blinking her brain to arousal while scanning the still water for signs of life. Its unbroken plane was as clear and as flat as a mirror, reflecting some yellow-tinged windows lit across the lake and a few gloomy clouds overhead. The clock from Japan registered 5:45, an earlier time than she usually arose. Her mind was filled with endless thoughts about work, especially the recent turn of events with Perry, Toshi and Hundai. She was coming to grips with the sober realization that no money would ever be recouped from the Toronto fiasco. She hadn't the heart to go after Molly. Although it was disappointing she also felt relieved that the protracted ordeal was finally even if abruptly ended. It would have to be a matter best learned from and forgotten. Never again would she trust anybody with check-writing ability on her company bank account. In spite of her losses she couldn't help feeling painfully sorry for Molly…*that poor woman…married to such a liar…a good man gone bad… and left in the lurch…*

Searching for a silver lining in the dark clouds of her mind she ranged through the host of positive homilies that she had found solace in previously. Automatically she glanced at the little card hanging from her desk lamp…*God will never let you down…God will never let you down*…She thought of Leroy's continuous insistence on pursuing Perry. When she had intimated her waning interest in doing so he had told her that either way she still had her good…*i still have my good…i still have my good*…She wondered wistfully just what that might exactly mean. Was her good going to be contingent on doing Toshi's insistent bidding? And what about the high school? Would Kazuo do her in? Taking another sip of the steaming brew she gazed at the motionless lake again. Near the middle of it was the reflection of an object in flight, gray-bellied and big, perhaps an eagle she surmised. Whatever it was soared too high above the water for her to see it except as an image mirrored on the lake's surface. As she focused on the moving shape suddenly four bright red lights flickered from its underbelly, blinking in unison, and she realized she was looking at the reflection of an airplane high above. It amused her to know she had mistaken a plane for a bird and chuckled to herself in the comforting recognition of a forgotten truism…*all is not as it appears…*

"Thank you, God," she said aloud and took another sip, feeling better. It would be an hour yet before the boys awoke and even longer until Candy arrived. She turned to a stack of papers awaiting her attention on the desk, then paused and changed her mind. She felt drawn to pray or actually to meditate, just to listen, to feel close, to connect with the heavenly powers that be. Between Jay and Leroy her interest had rekindled in a practice she had once done when they first moved to Cottage Lake.

Setting her steaming coffee aside she closed her eyes, composed herself and took several deep breaths. Letting go of the tension that was mounting in her shoulders she tried to feel open, receptive in her heart. Though she often forgot to do it amidst the hectic pace of her day, she had once felt when meditating, several months back, a sense of someone, a presence, there with her. She had asked then for a name and subsequently felt answered…*Alahee*… seemed to be the sound that came through the airwaves; a feminine presence. When she had mentioned it to Leroy he had verified her intuition. She had felt it again sporadically, rarely, vaguely; on those few times she had tried to meditate before the day began.

She tried to settle now into a quiet inner space, a stillness, hoping to evoke the same experience again…*Alahee…are you there…Alahee…sounds hawaiian*…A feeling of sweetness and calm began to sweep over her as she listened for a response when the ring of the home telephone shattered the air. She grabbed it immediately so as to avoid awakening the boys upstairs…*who's calling so early…*

"Hello."

"Bea, it's Faye."

"Well, hello. My, aren't you up early."

"No, not really. It's almost nine here."

"I know, but you don't usually call me this early. Is everything alright?" She sounded very businesslike.

"Yeah, everything's fine. I'm just calling early cause I've got a busy day and won't be free until late tonight. Listen."

"Yes?"

"My boss, the mayor, told me yesterday that he definitely can't spare me in August after all. There's to be too much to do. If I want to visit you we really will need to do it sooner."

"I see....*oh no*...Well, sooner is difficult. I am so busy in the early summer."

"I know. But we really have no choice. I've checked with David and he can get away."

"Well, I'd love to have you both. And we'd do our best to try and make it work. But the timing does suck. When exactly are you thinking?"

"My boss says June's best. How does that work?"

"June? ...*oh God*... Well, frankly, I guess it's as good as any other time, as far as summer goes. The whole season's hectic. We're just overrun with students. And the summer programs start to take off in mid-June, right after school's out."

"Well, how about if we come out in early June then? That's actually best for me."

"That's just weeks away!"...*best for you*...

"I know. But it's our best shot if you're busy from mid-June on. Will you have us or not?"

"Well, of course I'll have you. I just won't be able to be as hospitable or have as much time with you as I would like."

"I understand. That's okay. David and I can make do on our own when we have to. We're good at that." She paused for a moment, then added in a kinder tone, "I'd really like to see you."

"Alright...*that's different*...If that's the only time you can. I guess we'll figure out how to have some fun together somehow."

"Oh yeah, we will. Don't worry." There was a pause for an instant.

"Are you still there?"

"Yeah, I was just thinking," Faye said hesitantly.

"About what?"

"Oh, nothing."

"No, what?"

"Well, only that I'm having some medical tests being done soon and maybe there's an outside chance they won't be finished by then."

"Is anything wrong?"

"Oh no, nothing really. Just a check up. I've been feeling tired a lot lately."

"Well, no wonder with all the work and running around you do, Auntie Mame." Faye laughed.

"That's right," she affirmed, brightening at the mention of her namesake. She'd always loved the flattering comparison. "And Seattle's next on my list."

"Okay," sighed Bea, feeling resigned and yet also pleased. "It'd be good to see you. You sure there's nothing serious going on with your body?"

"Nothing that David can't fix," she cracked, then stated more seriously, "I'm just getting older. Listen," she added, changing the subject, "I've gotta' run. I'll get back with you as soon as I can confirm the dates."

"Okay. Let me know."

"I will. Bye for now…I love you."

"Good-bye…*that's different too*…I love you too."

Bea hung up the telephone, with mixed thoughts and feelings circulating in the high speed blender of her brain…*so much to do…so little time…still it'll be good…i hope…* It had been roughly six months since she had seen Faye in Pittsburgh…*another reunion… just the two of us now…*She winced at the idea. Sitting in a sweet melancholy of reflection, she ruminated on her siblings and the headlong rush of time…*getting old…being apart… getting together…dying young…* She shook off the invitation to drift into despair and sought out the brighter side of still having a sister.

Though the timing was difficult at least it afforded that chance of which she was so desirous; to forge a strong relationship with her remaining one. She sensed that Faye might well be feeling the same way and was cheered overall that despite the added pressure her big sister seemed very insistent on visiting…*with david here we'll have some couples fun…* She sighed and looked at the messy stacks of papers around her desk. There was so much to do with June around the corner, especially now with Faye on the horizon. She let out a long low sigh…*now…where was i…oh yeah…*

Feeling caught between the temptation to work and the desire to meditate she sat still for a moment and just let herself be. Her coffee had cooled but the overcast clouds had brightened as the sun simmered near the horizon. She decided to indulge in another try at tranquility. Closing her eyes once again she took a deep breath and let go of all thoughts into a feeling of peace. A few more deep breaths and she felt herself relaxing, her thought-provoking tensions subsiding into nothingness. From within came the feelings, like gentle waves of warmth, swelling, rippling, softly through her mind and body. She eased back into her large chair and felt the soles of her feet grounding her on the rug. She let the urge to connect rise up from her heart…*Alahee…are you there…are you there…*

The sputter of the fax machine broke the momentary silence. She could not ignore it and watched with curiosity as the flimsy paper peeled out of the chute like a thin sheet of onion skin rolling ominously towards her. The markings across the top were Japanese characters indicating another missive from her oriental counterparts. She stifled a near instinctive move to grab the Tums bottle…*could be good news…*As the paper piled out she lifted and read it, feeling a growing dismay with each sentence. The principal from Hundai was writing to inform her that they were going to sue her for the deposits they had made. Her dismay grew to shock as she finished it and laid it down. They were suing on the basis that she had misrepresented her ability to handle such a sizable program. Information had been given them that also cast doubt on the integrity of her company in past business dealings. She must refund the deposits immediately and in full or suffer the consequences of being sued. Those would include compensation for the expenses incurred by the school due to her misrepresentation of the program as well as damages to the school's reputation for the cancellation of the program and lastly remuneration for the school's legal fees...*that damned kazuo...it's all his doing...i know it...i know it...but i can't prove a damn thing*...She sat in stunned silence, not knowing what to do and feeling very numb.

Chapter 62

"If you put me to death, you will not easily find anyone to take my place. The fact is, if I may put the point in a somewhat comical way, that I have been literally attached by God to our city, as though it were a large thoroughbred horse which because of its great size is inclined to be lazy and needs the stimulation of a gadfly…If you take my advice you will spare my life. I suspect, however, that before long you will awake from your drowsing, and in your annoyance you will take Anytus's advice and finish me off with a single slap; and then you will go on sleeping." (The finale of Socrates' speech to the 500 member jury of Athens who then sentenced him to death)

ALL THE WAY TO Phil's school Jay had been preoccupied with the crazy phone call of the previous night. He had driven along as though lost in a fog and had barely heard, let alone minded, the cynical sounds of the rich black ghetto boys pounding out their pulsations. After dropping off Phil he turned back towards the office in town and slipped a tape from Leroy, made earlier in the year, into the dash. As always he was ready for an enlightening word.

"Okay. Shoot."
"Well, I was recently reading this book called *The Jeshua Letters* and was impressed with a part that said Jesus is with us now, so it made me think that He actually is with me now."

"Good."

"And it reminded me of that time when I thought some invisible entity said that word to me."

"Sure."

"So, anyway, I thought that's maybe all I need to remember. I guess. Because I feel paralyzed on another level, or chaotic."

"You see, what you would want to do is to get to the point of realization that your paralysis really doesn't block your good. You at this point still think that you have to be activated in some relative way in order to have your good. And so, more and more, what changes in your life is that you realize that the process of awakening, such as you are experiencing it with all of the moments of being confounded and thrust into feelings that are difficult to bear, really has nothing to do with your good; that the experience of stability and grace, once allowed, stays with you. It is there and it provides. So that's what you're coming to and if you would relinquish the demand that your mind makes around becoming active again you would began to start to see this.

"You see, this is like what I mentioned the last time we spoke. There are two aspects to the movement of life. There is the primary fundamental aspect that is the roll, the revolution and progression, which is always going on, and that's the real foundation of all good, of all creation. And then there is the dance; some form of human activity. Egos are preoccupied with the dance. And when there's no dance going on they feel desperate because they are not in touch with the fundamental movement. They feel excluded from that in their point of view except when the dance is apparently succeeding at doing something. Then they feel the roll. They feel that energy. But you need to feel it right now anyway. The anticipation of your good in a casual and off-hand leisurely way right now is all that is required of you and not so that then you become successful at dancing a new dance. That will happen. But you have to realize that you can be in this lack of activity, this apparent freefall, and experience your foundation of support just where you are. That's all that's going on here. And so you really don't have a hard lesson to get. You just have to get comfortable and not grind yourself, not flagellate yourself, because things are not happening the way you might want them to happen. You need to forgive that. You need to forgive the fact that you are not able to do what you would like to do or the way you would like to do it. You need to give that one up and say 'Okay, I forgive it'. That would help."

"Forego it?"

"Yes. Okay, so you don't have things your way, and yet you have support right now. You have a roof over your head and you are doing the best you can. You have to acknowledge that. It's difficult because there are no guidelines to waking up. It's unprecedented. And you are really just moving back out of something that you got into that was not appropriate to get into; the ego. And so the only way out is really just to back out. And as you do that, you go through all of the impact that you experienced going in, only this time it's the feeling and not the circumstance that is the issue. On the way in, the circumstance appeared to be causing the feeling. That is, the dance of the ego, or favorable circumstances apparently independent of God, made you feel good. But that does not last because there is no movement but God. And when you realize that, usually when circumstances become unfavorable, then you start to move back. And on the way out, or back to your connection with God, it's the feeling that has to be released in connection to the circumstances. And that, given our conditioning, is difficult to do.

"You have all these bad feelings that are caused by apparently bad circumstances and you are used to, conditioned to, thinking that if the circumstances would just change you would feel good again. But the trick is to realize that the truth of the matter lies in recognizing or feeling the underlying movement of God, or the roll. And when you do that you are aligned with the movement of God, which is the movement of fulfillment, and your life is fulfilling in all respects. Only this time you realize it is God and not you, as an ego, that imaginary presence apart from God, that is the movement, and it stays fulfilling, in whatever form it takes."

"Yeah, okay, that sounds good, but it seems awfully hard to do when I'm feeling so badly."

"I know. Believe me, I know. And yet, you do it anyway. You have your peace. You know what that feels like. You know what gratitude feels like. You know what the support of the moment feels like. Remind yourself of what is really going on instead of what is imagined or projected to be going on. Remember that projections are just imaginary experiences in the moment even though they may be taken quite seriously by the mind. Continue to practice feeling that you are on a roll and trusting into it and watch what happens."

"Hm. That sounds good but I'm obviously having trouble doing it. It's a shame I don't remember this stuff all the time. I briefly wake up and then go back to sleep."

"Yes, that's true, but you tend to remember it more and more though, because you are finding yourself more and more undefended and exposed all the time. You are becoming more conscious."

"Yeah, well, I sure feel exposed alright. I'd like to relate being more conscious to being able to pay more bills."

"But you see, that's just it. As you wake up through a limit you are going to be uncomfortable for a bit as you realize you have been in limitation. Like for example, if you have been sitting on your foot and you get up and realize that your foot is asleep. When it starts to wake up it tingles and is very uncomfortable, which is not its normal feeling. But it then recovers and becomes normal again. So you come to a limit that you have accepted as a fact in your ego state of mind. And as you are awakening you realize it is not a fact but just an imagined limit and it is usually experienced as uncomfortable. But that passes, and it passes into freedom, order and wholeness."

"Well, I'm afraid that point's not coming."

"But you see, that's just it. You are making yourself suffer here because things are not looking the way you would like them to look. What if things are never going to look that way?"

"Be patient for a thousand years?"

"The point I am making is that you are being righteous here and it is hard on you. It is out of compassion that I want to say 'Don't do it'. Don't be righteous about how things look. Just enjoy the fact that you are alive and, despite all of these things that you object to, that you are still moving on. Life is still going on and if there is any temporary insufficiency or imbalance, that's going to be adjusted. That means you don't have to do anything."

"Hm."

"In one sense it is interesting to me in that I know people who are at the opposite of this situation, which is that they tend to be perfectly content in a situation like you are in, but also they are resistant to paying attention to steps to take. Do you understand what I'm saying?"

"Sort of."

"They like their inertia. They like it to the point where they are not getting the message to take steps."

"Well, I wonder if I like my inertia, because I don't feel like I'm taking steps."

"No. Your situation is about peace. It's about ease. You are more than active or willing to be so. But what you are having to do is surrender the notion that you can accomplish anything on your own. You are under the heading of Type A personality, I believe; triple A." (laughter)

"Well, I used be kind of a fighter going through life. So, maybe that's what you mean about me objecting to things."

"Yes. You are becoming meek. You are becoming one who is simply aware that you don't know anything."

"Oh, that's comforting." (laughter)

"It's helpful, because it is what you think you know that is stopping you right now. If you could make friends with the unknown and choose that over what you think you know, you would be on the faster track at this point."

"That makes sense."

"You see, it is what you don't know that is where your answers lie. And by being at peace with the unknown while relying on its innate goodness – because it is really just the mystery of God – if you could stay with that you would find yourself seeing a new world. You see, that's really what it is, Jay. It's really ultimately about wanting to see a new world, not just a better version, a more successful version of your own life. It's about a new world. It's about everything new."

"I was thinking today about Jesus saying 'Behold, I make all things new'."

"Right. That's important. The apostle Paul said 'Be ye transformed by the renewing of your mind'. If your mind or your point of view is one of renewal or regeneration then everything around you is transformed. That's really what it means to be born again. People who say they are born again because they have a little catharsis are not really being born again in sense that Paul meant it. Being truly born again means that everything and everyone in your experience is also born again. It is totally inclusive. You can't be born again in the true meaning of the phrase and still be an ego."

"Uh…I understand what you are saying, but it sure is a challenge to be in this space all the time."

"Yes, it is. I acknowledge that. It is hard to disregard so many assumptions that are held to be true, you included sometimes. It is hard to disregard that much personal and cultural conditioning, though it is easier than it might have been at another time, because there is more genuine movement in the world for there to be freedom from what isn't real."

"So it's like being on a different wavelength. Like picking up vibrations from the sky or the center of the earth."

"You are getting it from the center, but it is your center; the axis. What you want to feel now is that you are on a roll and you want to feel the center of that roll, the axis, which is your peace or inner balance. And in doing that you will find you have sufficiency of needs being met. And in staying in that place you can forget your problems forever. Staying with the peace and feeling that you are on a roll will align you with the ever present regeneration of life or creation."

"Hm."

"But you are really going to have to do it. You are going to have to spend some time in quietude, where you recognize that you have a relationship to your problems. And I want you to focus on what it feels like to sever that relationship. And then feel what it feels like to become new. Realize that life is transforming right now and allow yourself to identify with that process. Practice shifting from one feeling to the other. This will work for you. But you are really going to have to spend some time doing it."

"Sounds like getting high naturally."

"Right."

"Well, the only problem I have is my lack of material means or paying my debt. I mean your point seems to be that aside from feeling well, my material problems would clear up."

"Right. But the problem is not getting out of debt. It's feeling movement basically. But the impediment to the movement that you could feel right now is this insistence that you have, through your conditioning, on a relationship to your debt. This is relativity."

"You mean as opposed to the realm of pure consciousness?"

"That's right. Whenever you have a relationship with something, like lack, and you do not have the underlying subjective point of view of your relationship with God, then you are in the objective world. Debt or your problem is irrelevant. That is your point of view."

"Well, I don't know if I could get into any Ph.D. program if I told them I want to enter the realm of pure consciousness." (laughter)

"Just say that you want to be at peace. You don't want to have to struggle. You want to feel comfortable and a sense of equilibrium."

"That sounds good. Um, I was starting to feel good talking with you here a few minutes ago and then as I thought about getting off the phone I started thinking in terms of all the things I need to do today and that's when all the little trickles of anxiety start creeping in, and that sense of objective reality..."

"Why don't you take an hour to do nothing?"

"God, that would be so hard to do. I'd really be...ah..."

"Just take an hour to do nothing and sit, and see what it feels like to be free."

"Hm."

"No demands."

"That's all I want anyway isn't it."

"Yes. You might as well practice it now."

"It feels like dealing with insanity."

"Well, yes, except that when you feel gratitude, when you feel connected, that's not insane. And so the answer is always close by. It's not so much a matter of anything except a little bit of discipline. It's not that your problem needs analysis of any sort. It's that basically you need the discipline to recognize when you are not in your peace and to allow yourself to have the luxury of finding your peace right then, no matter what is going on."

"I understand."

"That's discipline. You could be more disciplined. You tend to be undisciplined and then think that the disorder you are experiencing is happening because of something else, because somehow it doesn't work. It being waking up, which somehow apparently doesn't work. The fact is you are not all that disciplined yet. And discipline just means that you recognize what is going on, what you have to do and you don't spend a lot of time thinking it is something else."

"Got it."

"It's like you start thinking about a problem, let's just say your debt, for example. And you are uncomfortable. Somewhere along the line you simply realize that you are uncomfortable and you let that go. But you aren't doing that. You tend to take the question of debt and you run with it. You make it heavier and denser as you do that. You need the discipline to recognize that you are not comfortable in doing that so why do that. By now you know that ruminating on these things has no effect or value. So if you can, be disciplined enough to realize that you even feel uncomfortable thinking about these things and are better served instead by finding your peace, feeling the movement, and that by trusting into that, things will change. Transformation will occur. And you will enjoy the process. End of reprimand." (laughter)

"Oh, it felt great. (laughter) I like it. Straight talk."

"Exactly."

…wise words but i don't know how well i can use them now… He had sat in his car of the parking lot of his building listening to the tape for the last five minutes. When it ended he climbed out, entered the building, ascending the steps briskly as usual. Striding past the door of his former office he advanced a few feet to the one he was now subletting. While fumbling for the new office key he noticed that his sign was missing from the Marianne's office door…*strange…must have come loose…*As he entered the office and closed the door behind him he saw a note on the desk. Marianne wanted him to call her. His first client was Howie but he had well over thirty minutes before the appointed hour. He decided to ring her now.

"Hello, Marianne, this is Jay. You wanted me to call you?"

"Yes, thanks, I did. I heard from one of your clients last night."

"Really?"

"Yes, an older woman. I believe her name was Naime."

"Oh."…*uh-oh…*

"She said you had visited her at her home and had engaged in some inappropriate behavior."

"Oh boy, listen, I can explain that."

"I'd like to hear your explanation."

"You see, she's been mandated by the courts to have counseling once a week for two years. I've been seeing her regularly for maybe six months. She doesn't drive so her husband has had to bring her. He was laid off from work for a while so it was no problem. But recently he just got called back to work so she had no way of getting here anymore. The closest bus stop is apparently quite a ways from her home and she has a bad hip – she walks with a limp – so I offered to do home visits for awhile."

"Home visits?"

"Yeah, you know, a house call, like doctors used to do."

"A house call?"

"Well, yeah, I know, I know it's unusual, but I have done them before, especially in the early years, when I was the only therapist around for miles. Primarily it's just been in situations where people couldn't leave their homes for one reason or another, either physically incapacitated or simply too scared."

"Oh really?"

"Yeah, not often, just a few times basically. It may sound strange now but in the early days, the early eighties, I was kind of like a real country doctor around here. This was just before the big migration here. There was a recession then for a while and a lot of people here really suffered from it. They were poor. It felt like a malaise on the land. I did what I could. It was a way I help people and get compensated somehow too. At times I did things that I rarely do now like barter my services with a contractor or a masseuse."

"A masseuse?"

"Yeah,…*whoops*… a masseuse. I mean in the old days, when I was starting my practice, sometimes people just didn't have enough money for my fee. It worked out okay. I traded services for goods from the people that ran the health food store. I did the same thing with the bookstore owner. These were Forestville merchants. Forestville people. My neighbors. My community. Even now, frankly, I've got a woman I see who owns a flower shop and is on a tight income. She brings me plants for counseling. I don't care. I'm glad to help her. I'm glad to have the plants."

"I see." He wondered what it was she really saw. "But a house call is different. Surely you see that. And with a woman, alone in her home."

"Look, they live out in the sticks, fairly isolated. They don't seem to have many, if any friends. They seemed to be at a loss for how to deal with the situation, so I just volunteered to do it. It seemed like a good idea at the time."

"Uh-huh." She didn't sound too convinced. "And what about her accusations that you were inappropriate with her – that you asked her out."

"Oh God, I can explain that. It was just a misunderstanding. I mean, Jesus, have you seen her?"

"No, but I would like to hear your explanation."

"Well frankly, I don't know how much of it she misunderstood or how much she has imagined or even deliberately misconstrued. Honestly I don't get what she's trying to do here. It could be she's attempting to get out of counseling by manufacturing this. I was talking with her about food – Italian food – we both love it. We both love to cook it. And I said something about a new Italian restaurant in her town. I think I must have said something like 'Oh, I'd just love to take you there'."

"You said that?"

"Well yeah, maybe, something like that, I guess, but I didn't mean anything by it. It was just an expression. I meant I'd like for her to go there. But I wouldn't want to take her there. I wouldn't want to take her anywhere."

"Then perhaps you shouldn't have said it." This was going from bad to worse. Jay was starting to feel nervous and indignant at the same time.

"If you had seen her, I'm telling you, you would not be so incredulous. Look, I'm telling you she is gross. She is ugly. She's a hag, a pathetic one. She's a gnarled up old lady with bad teeth and a bad leg. I mean, I can't believe it. If you saw her you'd understand, I think, immediately. You'd have a hard time believing I would want anything to do with her aside from being her counselor."

"Well, I only know she said you came to her house when she was alone and that you asked her out to a restaurant. Both of these things you have admitted doing."

"Admitted? Look, I'm trying to explain -"

"It doesn't sound good to me. She may file a formal complaint with the state."

"Did you suggest she do that?"

"No, but I told her she could if she wanted to. She called me to complain and she was very upset. As a matter of fact she asked me to be her new counselor."

"Great. You can have her. Believe me, she's all yours."

"Well, that remains to be seen. But I wanted to talk with you because it sounds very serious."

"Oh yeah, it's serious. It's a serious pile of bullshit. Is that why my sign's down?"

"Yes, it's in the closet. I don't feel comfortable having it up under the circumstances."

"What are you saying? That's crazy. I have done nothing wrong."

"That may be. But it may be up to the state to investigate it and if your reputation is being tarnished, or at least under suspicion, I don't want to be linked to you in any way that could reflect on me."

"But what about our arrangement? We agreed to have my sign up."

"You can continue to use the office, for now at least, but that sign stays down."

"I cannot believe that you are doing this."

"I'm sorry but I need to protect myself from any sign of impropriety."

...*oh sure*..."So are you saying it's never going back on your door?"

"We'll have to see what happens."

"Oh, that's not right. That's not fair at all."

"I'm sorry. I've got to go now. We can talk about it more later."

After they hung up Jay pondered the situation. He felt inflamed with anger, beset with sadness, and flushed with anxiety all at one time. Though in no mood to see him he felt an obligation to be fully present for Howie. Maybe there was enough time yet to find a good perspective on this.

As he fumed and fretted over the mushrooming dilemma he decided he needed to call Naime's lawyer and did so at once. He felt fortunate to reach him and they talked for several minutes. The attorney was a young man and they had spoken once before at the outset of her counseling in regard to her court order. He offered to call Naime and then ring Jay back. Within five minutes he had returned the call.

"What's up?" said Jay, on the edge of his seat.

"Well, in talking with her she essentially said what you said she would. I mostly just listened."

"I'm telling you she's nuts. You've seen her. You've met with her. Do you really think anyone in their right mind could be attracted to anyone who looked like that?"

"Well," he laughed, "I don't know about that, but I do believe that you aren't. I can tell you two things. I did try to say to her perhaps there is another way of looking at this and she just got hysterical with me like she did with you. She started yelling how you were lying. I'll tell you something else though. I got the impression from the way she was talking about it that it really had to do with making her husband jealous."

"Aha! That's it! That actually makes sense. I knew this was too weird to be true. Oh man," breathed Jay with a sigh of relief. "I can't thank you enough for that insight. I really can't. Thank you. Thank you. Thank you so much. God, that really fits, believe me, if you knew their history."

"Ah, don't mention it," he said with a laugh. "I guess we both get our share of crazies."

"Boy, that's the truth. But what are you going to do? I mean what about her counseling sentence?"

"She also said she might go to see someone else in your building. By the way did you know she's also seeing a psychiatrist?"

"No. She never told me. That means she's on medication."

"Right."

"I'd like to talk with him too. Can you give me his name and number?"

"Sure." Jay jotted it down.

"Okay, thanks. Say, do you need a report for the court or anything?"

"No, we're okay. Let's just let the transition happen. I'll probably contact the other therapist later just to keep the continuity going."

"Alright then, thanks. You're great. I really appreciate your insight and help. Have a great day."

Jay leaned back in the chair, feeling greatly relieved. He pondered momentarily what was best to do next. He still felt the sting of the rebuke over his sign and was faintly apprehensive of a state launched investigation. It seemed the best thing to do was to call the psychiatrist and then place a call to Leroy for good measure. He called the psychiatrist and got some unexpectedly useful information before dialing Leroy.

"Leroy, it's Jay."

"Yes, how are you doing?"

"Well, I'm doing okay but there's a drama unfolding that has some turmoil for me and I felt the need to talk with you now rather than wait for our talk next week."

"It's probably best to call when there is more feeling of urgency."

"Okay. Well, this all stems from an incident that took place last year. There is a person, an older woman, I was seeing in counseling that was sent by the courts. She got drunk and got in a fight with some family members, slapped her child, an older daughter, and got put on probation for two years of counseling. She's an older woman, more of a grandmother type, an Alaskan native, an old Indian lady, a nice person really. I really liked her, but… well, anyway, and we had about four or five months of counseling, in which she seemed to be making some progress. And at first her husband was laid off and working irregular shifts and she doesn't drive so he was able to bring her, but then he started back up – he works for the railroad – and so she had no way to my office cause she lives far from the bus line, so I said I'd drive over and see her for a home visit. And I was really in the throes of working crazy busy for Bea's company and I didn't have many clients and so I wanted to keep seeing her somehow if possible and she was mandated to do it so I decided to go to her place on my lunch hour when the phone calls were least busy and all seemed well enough, at least so I thought."

"Mm-hm."

"And things have gone well enough since we first started counseling, so that sometimes we didn't always talk exclusively about counseling related topics. Once she brought me photos of her childhood and family. Anyway, we would sometimes get off on other topics, like food, and yesterday, which was the first time we started this home visit thing, we got off on Italian food, and I'm really not sure what I said, but I must have said something like there's this new Italian restaurant nearby and it's fantastic and I'd love to take you there or something like that. So then I left at the end of that session and everything seemed to be fine. But then later that night she called me and was upset and seemed to have been drinking. And she accused me of wanting to take her out on a date. And I was shocked. So I started to explain to her how I could understand how she might have taken my remarks and she just started screaming at me that I was a liar, etc. So I asked to talk with her husband and asked if he believed her and he said he didn't know what to think. So that's what happened but its all pretty crazy. And I mean I really did like her. I really liked them, but there's always been this quality that's kind of like lowlife people, for lack of a better word, but I just never thought this kind of thing could happen."

"Yes, in my view of it they are the kind of people that show up on these shows like Jenny Jones or Ricki Lake or Jerry Springer. Lowlife drama."

"It is like that. That's true."

"They are being lowlifes. It's not who they really are but it is how they are acting."

"Okay, but somehow I missed that or overlooked it and I did some good things with them, we did them together, for a long time."

"Sure, because you see what's there. You see the innocence and the intelligence and the goodness of people."

"That's what I'm supposed to see."

"But you are not their savior. You cannot save people from being how they want to be."

"Well I appreciate what you are saying but let me just tell you the further convolutions this has led to. I just called their lawyer, whom I'd spoken to once earlier, and told him what had happened and he offered to call her and then he called me back. He did that and told me that she got hysterical with him when he suggested she'd misinterpreted things. He also said he got the impression that it was really all about trying to make her husband jealous, which hadn't occurred to me. That does seem very plausible though because they have a long history of fighting and she is deeply resentful of his supposed many infidelities. So… who knows? Anyway I learned that she had a psychiatrist so I just talked with him and he believed me too and said he had refused to work with her anymore because she was too unreliable. I asked him what I should do and he said there is a sort of form letter I could write her that is used to jettison people. And so I'll follow his advice and write her a letter saying I'll no longer see her and suggest she seek help elsewhere. So that's that."

"Mm-Hm."

"But the bigger problem I'm facing right now is that she called the psychologist whom I'm subletting an office from. And she gave her an earful and I just found out about it earlier this morning through a phone call with that shrink, which is basically why I've called you. To make a long story short she's taken my sign off the door based on all this garbage, a sort of guilty until proven innocent stance, and I feel upset about it, especially since I know it's bullshit. So…"

"When is your next rent check due?"

"It's technically due yesterday."

"Did you pay it?"

"No."

"Good. Tell her you'll pay it when the sign gets back on the door."

"I was thinking of doing that but then she may say 'To hell with you – get out of here'."

"Well then, go."

"Well, that's what it may come too, but it feels so drastic. I mean I don't feel I can justify having an office of my own with such a light client load."

"The problem here is that you are momentarily distracted from your innocence. Are you familiar with the saying about being too concerned with the opinions of those who have better reputations than they deserve?"

"No, but it sounds good."

"Right, and this is an example of how that works. Everyone in this situation whose opinions you feel threatened by have better reputations in your mind than they deserve. It would be better for you to just think of them as a total waste of time."

"Well, I appreciate that and I find myself thinking 'I don't give a shit what you guys think, I just want my sign back up'. But I'm concerned that that's ego. I'd like to respond to this from a higher place."

"To an extent your reaction is ego. That is, your sense of having been offended and having been attacked is ego but the fact is that your demand to be treated appropriately is not ego. It's mixed in with your feeling of having been impacted by something, which we've talked about before. The truth is that if you felt good, if you felt clearly your innocence, you would say 'I want my sign up and I don't want any crap about it and that's that'. That is not ego. That is authority. It is that state of mind of not going to take no for an answer, which we've also talked about before. There is no feeling of being opposed that really counts for anything. You see, being awake is not always being nice. Do you see what I'm saying?"

"Yeah, I know. You mean like how Jesus drove the money changers from the temple."

"Exactly. It's like 'Stop it and get out of here and don't ever do it again'."

"I feel partly that way but it gets mixed in with taking offense and getting really hurt and pissed."

"Right, you are not centered. You are feeling off balance by the impact, which causes you to lose your innocence. And that arises from the conditioning of an 'us versus them' mentality. You are identifying with one of the poles of that polarity. That puts you at the mercy of whatever craziness is going on and causes you to fell impacted by the circumstance. So the first thing to remember is that the opposite of impact or density is solution. In other words you want to get into that place of loosening or ease. Then you will find yourself being brought back automatically to that place of balance or peace. And then having done that you can say with peace of mind, 'Well I really don't care what these people think but I am certainly not going to pay rent if my sign is not on the door'. That is, if you are being treated with less than appropriate respect then you will not pay to be there. And you can afford to leave too."

"Well, on one hand I'm afraid that I can't afford to move or I can't justify it. Actually I'm probably starting to make enough money at the other work to pay for a counseling office if I wanted to. On the other hand I'd like to identify enough with the movement of life, as we've been talking about it lately, to think that if I feel I need to leave, so be it."

"There is no problem in leaving there."

"You don't think so, huh? That's a wonderful thing to believe. If I thought I could justify having my own office I wouldn't have left for this deal in the first place. Also I'm thinking that wherever I go they are going to ask where I was last and she will bad mouth me."

"You can conduct your business wherever you want."

"Alright."

"It is not necessary for you to feel dependent upon a circumstance."

"Well, I know I'm not dependent upon other people's egos for my goodness."

"No, you're not."

"But still, (laughing) the circumstances do seem a bit challenging."

"Yes, but the issue here is ultimately forgiveness, because you want to recapture your experience of your innocence. Part of the problem is that people such as yourself find themselves in situations where on one hand you are trying to be in communion with God and other hand you are trying to deal with the world. So you end up serving two masters. And you tend to try to use God or connect with God in a way to help you deal with the other master. And the truth is that that stops at some point. There is no way that God answers that indefinitely. For a while there is movement in that direction that is fulfilling and supportive, but then it stops at some point because you cannot afford to allow all of these nemeses to appear to be independent from God in your mind while you are trying to be in communion. You cannot be privately in communion with God while believing that these other people or the problems they represent are independent of God."

"I see."

"At some point you must insist that all of the people, all of the elements of this problem, do not exist apart from God. And that's final. Then you can give it all to God. And then you have to be willing to forgive God, in effect, for what appears to be a big mess. You have to be willing to say 'I desire to forgive all this and I desire to feel forgiven'. You see, otherwise you are not fully willing to have innocence restored. Innocence does not know right from wrong. God only has one overriding interest and intent, and that is the expression of love, in innocence and grace. And in giving this all to God, you are no longer serving a second master, or the world, and you have forgiven it all and everyone in it. And once that reconciliation has been reached, it is no longer a personal thing."

"But that doesn't mean I will feel good about how they are being towards me, does it?"

"It will mean that you no longer will feel that you are a target or that you are at the end of something. You will feel in the middle, or centered. You will feel the unity of communion because you have forgiven it all. And then you express your desire that the form look different or the situation be more fulfilling and the movement of God will manifest the appropriate changes."

"So like, if I put this all in practical terms, if I call up Marianne and tell her to put up my sign or else – that is, I won't pay her or I may even leave – that'll be the appropriate thing to do?"

"If you do this process first, whatever you say will be relevant at the time. What you want to do first however is to feel fearless and to have your innocence restored. Through this process, which is restoring your covenant with God, you want to have your innocence restored and you want to feel nothing against anyone else. That is the atonement or the restoration of the covenant, and that will heal the moment. And that is what will make whatever is appropriate for you to say or do more apparent."

"Hm."

"And that will do a lot of other things as well. It will help shift these feelings of being stuck, of being in a rut, of not expanding enough. All of that can change. Practicing this kind of forgiveness will allow for significant change in your life."

"By not doing anything but aligning myself with God?"

"Right. And events will manifest in ways that are beyond your expectations."

"Hm. You sound so matter-of-fact about all this."

"I am."

"Hm. Well, you seem so clear, for example, that it's appropriate to refuse to pay rent with the sign down."

"Why would you want to pay rent?"

"So I wouldn't have to go looking for another building to be in. I've been in this one a long time and it's the nicest one in town."

"Well, do you want to be humiliated in that way? Is that what you think is appropriate? Your sign was up and now it's down."

"No, that's what I'm not liking. It seems like I could try not to be humiliated. I could perhaps attain that but it seems like a wrongdoing."

"It is a wrongdoing. It is unfair. It is not appropriate and it must change. And if you will go with this process it is likely to transform with a week or two."

"You know, this whole thing is unfair to me in a larger sense than is being discussed. I know things about her that she doesn't know that I know. I've seen her with her husband. They look really miserable together. Moreover I know that she's having a lesbian affair with one of her clients no less. Here she actually has the nerve to accuse me of something I didn't do when she's actually guilty of the false accusation she making towards me. I think she has some real issues going on and is acting them out in more ways than one. It's really a crazier scene than it seems."

"Just don't pay."

"That doesn't seem right. I do have a rental agreement with her."

"I don't care if you have a rental agreement or not."

"Well, I think the honorable thing to do would be to call her and say that I want the sign up or I'm going elsewhere."

"Good. I can endorse the clarity of what you just said. Again, you'll know for yourself as you begin to move into this exactly what steps to take at what time."

"So do you think I should call her right now?"

"I'm not saying that. I'm more interested in you feeling your own experience of reconciliation with God. When you know that what you are doing is a harmless act to harmless people, when you have no ill intent, when you feel that in your heart, that's when you do what you are moved to do."

"When I can make that statement to her in the right state of mind…"

"Right. It is a difficult point or a fine line to walk when you know there is unfairness, and you want to correct it, but you don't want to get hooked on seeking justice. That is something you must feel in your heart. You want to feel that you are not getting justice but simply radically allowing this situation to transform."

"Fairness with peace."

"Exactly."

"So I want to see them in a forgiving way while continuing to insist on my point."

"Yes, but you can only see them in a forgiving way if you stop seeing them as independent from God."

"So its like, as Jesus said, 'Father forgive them, they know not what they do'."

"Yes. Bring them to the Father. Do not let them have independence in your perception. Then you can say to God that this is a mess or a problem that you are giving to Him. So the basis for forgiving them is through forgiving their ignorance or unconsciousness rather than their egos or personalities."

"Okay. I got it. Now I've just got to do it. I am worried about finding or affording another office space though. I'm paying a fraction to her of what I was paying before."

"Be open to everything. See what you are moved to do after going through this process of forgiveness here of the whole thing."

"Okay."

"You see, when I say it is unfair, it is unfair. But I'm not interested in you having any justice here. I would like for you to have your name on the door. I would like for you to have a nice place to work. That has to be part of the asking too."

"Peace and harmony in the workplace?"

"A good place for you to do your work. That is not a separate issue from the events that are unfolding. I mentioned earlier that if you could allow for the reconciliation of all of this, then within a week or two you would be allowing for the unfoldment of something quite fun."

"You get that feeling? That message?"

"Yes."

"How?"

"It just comes to me. I know it."

"Well, that's interesting. But the rent is due right now and I don't know if I should call her right now and say -"

"The issue is not what to say to her right now. The issue is forgiving the whole situation, having your innocence restored, and being willing to have no separate master from God. That is the issue. Remember, it is everyone's unconsciousness or ignorance that needs to be healed. And when you go through this process of forgiving their apparent independence by giving it all back to God, you are restoring everyone's innocence. They no longer have a separate point of view that matters to you. They are blameless and you are too. Their points of view no longer have any relevance. They are not to be catered to. But everyone has to be forgiven so that there can be transformation or rebirth."

"Well, I understand that. But the thing I guess I am most hung up on at the moment is that I don't think I can experience forgiveness and withhold money from someone that is due her. I mean to me they are separate issues. I have an agreement in writing with her to pay rent. The agreement to have the sign on the door was simply a verbal one. And since one is not contingent on the other it seems dishonorable to me for me to be withholding the rent check. Even though I think she's being ruthless, underhanded, selfishly self-protective, unreasonable and unfair, it still doesn't seem right to not pay her. It's like two wrongs don't make a right."

"I understand that. But my point is that you need not come to a conclusion about these separate issues. Don't look at the details. What you need to do is seek the restoration of innocence everywhere you look so that separation from or independence of God is no longer tolerated. That is the central issue. Then you may or may not withhold rent. At that point you will then be guided internally whether or not to pay rent."

"Well maybe, but it just seems like the honorable thing to do is -"

"We're not talking honor here. Your attention is on paying the rent right now and I want you to not be concerned about it one way or another."

"And I wonder about giving notice, or not giving notice. I think our agreement calls for thirty days notice."

"Again, I don't want to focus much on these details for now, but if the service is unsatisfactory that is cause for termination on your part."

"Would that nullify a thirty day notice clause?"

"Maybe or maybe not but you can do it anyway. Let her pursue it. It is not relevant to the primary issue. And the primary issue is that you do not want to deal anymore with the crazy client, you do not want to deal with the gossip between her and the psychologist, and you do not want to deal with her disrespect. As long as you are willing to uphold the apparent independence or separation from God by these individuals you will have a difficult time. You have to say 'Enough'. You give the entire mess to God. They are now on the altar of your communion with God. You are giving up the insanity, the struggle, and that includes your part in wanting to be right. You give up wanting to be right. Not wanting to be forgiven because you are right is a mistake or in other words, a sin. Instead you allow yourself to feel forgiven as you give it to God. Then your innocence and everyone's is restored."

"Yeah, okay. I think I get the basic idea. It seems like then, in terms of practical implications, that it's best at the moment to do nothing."

"Until you feel that you are at the center again, and not at the position of one pole or another. You want no sense of the 'us versus them' polarity of the ego. That will always distract you from your innocence and give you instead the feeling that you have done something wrong or that something wrong is being done to you."

"Well, okay, it seems tricky to do this but I guess it's just so foreign to me. I'm thinking back now about how I had a client there last week and when I arrived to use the office Marianne was in it on the phone and didn't leave till about ten minutes after the hour, which seemed really rude to me since I had paid for that day to use the office, so...I guess these things aren't as cut and dried as I was trying to seem them in terms of what's honorable or appropriate. Still it doesn't feel right not to pay. I don't know."

"I can only reiterate that you need to be unconcerned about it in the management of that issue for the moment. You see, what you can anticipate from the forgiveness of the unconsciousness of everyone is that things will happen. Healing changes will occur. This is not all about being able to walk through shit and not minding it while expecting that it stays that way. Your reconciliation with the situation by giving it to God includes your understanding that it is supposed to be good. It is not supposed to be a mess. One way or another it will work out well for you if you will forgive it and then ask the Father that it be transformed."

"Okay. I understand. I'll try. I better go. I've got an appointment just a minute away. Thanks. Thanks a lot."

"You're welcome."

"Good-bye."

"Bye."

Jay sat in the chair pensively wondering what to do next. A glance at the clock said it was time to forgo his personal concerns for those of a client. He sat still for a moment, rolling over the recent events in his mind, then got up to fetch Howie from the lobby.

Chapter 63

"When the ego was made, God placed in the mind the call to joy. This call is so strong that the ego always dissolves at its sound. That is why you must choose to hear one of two voices within you. One you made yourself, and that one is not of God. But the other is given you by God, Who asks you only to listen to it. The Holy Spirit is in you in a very literal sense. His is the voice that calls you back to where you were before and will be again. (A Course in Miracles)

THE PINK FLOWERING CLUSTERS of the cherry trees bobbled in the breeze as Bea leisurely walked by the blossoms, observing the bustle of another daybreak. All around her birds were atwitter, gaily spinning in the bright blue sheen, as the new sun sent its golden streams to warm the cool green foliage. With the speed of light they spread across the earth, heating the asphalt lane ahead of her, and setting the wet grass bordering it alive with steam as from a hot teapot. She sauntered past the sunlit treetop shadows stretched across the street, knowing they were shrinking imperceptibly each second. It was too long a time since she had last taken an early morning jaunt and the latter part of May left little to be desired to her resonating senses. The sapphire sky was as clear and as deep as a crystalline sea in unwavering stillness. She felt the residual chilliness of evening slowly evaporating while being increasingly warmed by her walk.

The events of the preceding days had been brewing in her thoughts like an impending storm. She had awakened from sleep with a feeling of needing to get out in the morning, the sunshine, the fresh air, the beauty of nature and the promise of late spring. Had she more time a ride on Cheyenne would have been vastly preferable but the pressures of work would not permit such a prolonged leave. With two cups of coffee in her belly she was ready for a sunrise stroll while the boys were still snoozing, tightly tucked underneath covers. She was used to handling stress, multitasking, tolerating egos, but the increased burdens of this past year's events seemed definitely more serious than at any time earlier. Being swindled by Perry, pressured by Toshi, and outmaneuvered by Kazuo, all on the heels of losing a sister, had left her feeling worse than she ever remembered, except perhaps since the loss of her mother. Even that had been different, a clean cut, a hole, a hurt in her heart. This was a heaviness, a persistent brooding, a load on her mind that was wearing her down.

Knowing Mother Nature could be a strong tonic, she instinctively sought it's healing power on arising just before dawn. With each passing step through the glory of sunrise she had felt the weight gradually receding away and certain biblical verses began bubbling in her head...*consider the lilies of the field...how they grow...they neither toil nor spin...*She had been walking now for a good half hour at least, going up the street around the corner until it dead ended, then doubling back to her own driveway. She felt moved to mosey on and slipped past the side of the house, down the grassy pathway leading to the lake.

Walking out on the dock she surveyed the dwellings along the far and surrounding shoreline...*He leadeth me beside the still waters...*She watched a lone fisherman sitting in a rowboat in a distant corner of the lake. He cast with the effortless touch of a spider spinning a net, back and forth, a gossamer thread sailing through the air, making a small splash...*follow me and I will make thee fishers of men...*The willow trees next to her rustled in the gentle wind with the leaves dancing to the dangling chimes up on the deck. Sunlight sparkled on the surface of the water like a field of broken glass while the currents of air caressed her skin smoother than a soft sable brush...*He restoreth my soul...* Feeling lighter in spirit, just as she had hoped, she hiked back up to the house to have breakfast and embrace the day.

An hour later she was downstairs as usual busily engaged in the various activities that her work entailed. Today was one in which both Jay and Candy would be working together alongside her in the office. She was expecting them both to show up any moment and hoping to be relatively undistracted by whatever tensions they brought out in each other and into the workplace. Though things had improved slightly, she had given up hoping for an absence of any tension. It was simply a given when the two of them were together. Thankfully at least most of the time Jay was in a separate room. She was diligently piecing together a month long itinerary for a group of Japanese high school students when Candy came in through the sliding glass door on the lakeside.

"Good morning," chimed Bea glancing up from her task.

"Good morning," replied Candy in her typical sweetly forced tone. She headed for her desk and began rifling through some papers. As though on call the telephone rang and

Candy picked it up while Bea continued working. She had learned to trust Candy's handling of most of the office affairs and knew not to pay attention unless she was summoned. While Candy became immersed in the phone conversation Jay entered the room from the adjoining space inside, the laundry room down by the foot of the stairs. He had taken Phil to school and was back home to handle his particular programs. In the six months of his tenure with her company he'd firmly established some successful new ventures for which Bea was extremely grateful. The extra income was a welcome addition to their finances and also added prestige to her expanding enterprise.

"Good morning," called Bea, looking up again from her work.

"Good morning, boss," joked Jay as he swept past her desk to the small room in the back.

"How was Phil?"

"He's good. Except for his taste in music. Are you sure you don't have some African relatives in your family tree?"

"You never know."

Jay sat down at the desk in his office and looked over his long list of "To Do" items. He had insisted on a large desktop on which to organize his business and it took up a disproportionate amount of space in the little room. Nevertheless it served well to keep everything organized, for Jay was adamant about his materials being orderly. He had neat stacks in straight lines spaced appropriately apart. Bea on the other hand was inclined to have many piles and papers loosely if not randomly interspersed on her desk, but she always seemed to know exactly where everything was. The arrangement of documents and notes on Candy's desk was a combination somewhere in between the two extremes.

For most of the day the three of them worked well together, industrious and methodical, each with their own chores. At mid-afternoon a call came in on the third line, which normally meant a college call for Jay. Almost out of reflex Candy picked up the phone at the same time as Jay did, apparently forgetting his instruction to let him answer that line.

"I've got it," he called out, waiting for Candy to hang up. She hung on for a moment listening for the caller's voice. "I said I've got it," repeated Jay, on not hearing the disconnect click.

"Sorry," she yelled to him in an exasperated tone. "Just doing my job." She turned and looked at Bea as she hung up the receiver.

"It's her again," she muttered, just loud enough for Bea to hear.

"Who's that?" said Bea with a blank look on her face. She was deeply involved in penning a letter to Hundai and had hardly noticed the telephone ringing.

"Oh, I don't know. I don't think I'm supposed to." She looked at her computer screen and began typing again. "You know, that woman, the one that always calls. From the college."

Though she felt the tension creeping into her shoulders, she wanted to ignore it. She didn't have time for Candy's speculations, real or imagined, at least not right now. She was knee-deep in trying to negotiate a settlement with Hundai without having to resort to seeking legal counsel. The cost of that option would nullify what little money she made from keeping the deposits they wanted back.

"I'm sure it's okay," she said somewhat absently without taking her eyes off her work. She was hoping to diffuse the issue through disregarding it; a gentle course of benign neglect.

"I sure hope so," said Candy in her best singsong voice. "But I don't understand," she began to whine in a higher pitch, "why it's so all-fired important that I simply can't answer the phone like any other call."

Though Bea preferred not to reply to her complaint at all, the growing shrillness of her manner seemed to require some response...*not again...i thought this was done...*

"It's just the way he likes to conduct his business. It allows him to work efficiently. He has his own little operation in a sense going on in the middle of our bigger one."

"That's the truth," snorted Candy caustically. "His own operation."

Bea finally looked over at her secretary directly. She spoke in a flat tone intending to end the conversation.

"Just let it go, will you? Please. We've already discussed this. We've got enough problems to deal with without creating more."

Candy averted her eyes and resumed typing. "Oh, I know, believe me, I know." She typed with seemingly even greater intensity. "I'll just mind my own business," she added off-handedly while becoming very attentive to the task on her computer screen.

Bea returned to her letter, wishing to focus completely on the troubling matter of Hundai. She felt fretful enough about the debacle in Japan without the additional distraction posed by Candy's skepticism, however well meaning it was intended to be. The peace and inspiration she had found in the morning by the lake had been slipping away slowly as the day had worn on. She had never before been sued nor even faced the remote threat of it and was finding the experience extremely unnerving. It was especially galling that the entire fiasco had sinister overtones. She was certain that Kazuo, her ex-partner turned archenemy, was somehow engineering a sinister scheme. He was plotting underhandedly to undermine her careful efforts and single-handedly destroy the budding empire she was building. It was uniquely dispiriting to fall prey to the efforts of a madman who would stop at nothing to annihilate her. She knew that his vindictiveness recognized no ethical or legal bounds. Worse yet, she was fighting an unseen fiend; an opponent who was virtually invisible. No one would admit he was involved in any way and furthermore he was far away, in the country where the action was. Her position was weakened by having no presence in Japan; no representative, no witness, no support there of any kind.

Feeling frustrated and uncertain at how best to approach the topic, she stopped writing for a moment and looked outside the big window alongside her desk. The afternoon sun burned brightly at its apex; a distant dandelion in an otherwise vacant sky. Undulating waves in the wind from the south rode the surface of the lake, weaving gently to and fro like prairie grass on a plain. She lay down her pen and closed her eyes for a respite. She rubbed them, seeing subtle specks of light like the Milky Way infused behind her eyelids and took a deep breath. She sat up and folded her hands in her lap, then continued the motion into a stretch above her head. Again, as in the morning, verses trickled into her train of thought… *seek and ye shall find*…She brought her hands back down into her lap as though to pray… *ask and ye shall receive*…With another sigh she relaxed still further and focused intently on just feeling at peace, trying to recapture the mood of the morning. She felt one word simmering within, coming sincerely from the center of her heart. Letting it emerge as easily as a simple exhalation she gave it up to God…*help*…

Amidst the sounds of the office she felt momentarily undisturbed. Another phone call came through, interrupting Candy's typing. Somewhere outside, for the first time today, she heard the harsh caw of a crow and found it inviting. She got up from the chair and walked over to the slider. Through the glass she watched the willows leaning over the water's edge. Behind her the fax machine rang, then began ratcheting out a message. She opened the sliding glass door and stepped outside, then walked out a few feet, savoring sunlight, soft breeze and fresh air. The yellow and orange azaleas that lined the zigzag trail to the lake were brightly in bloom. She closed her eyes again to feel the warm air more intently, as Candy popped her head through the open door behind her.

"Bea," she interjected. "Sorry to spoil your break. But there's a fax here from Japan. It's a short message but it could be important. It's from Hundai…*now what*… Someone named Tomoko."

Chapter 64

"Time is kind, and if you use it on behalf of reality, it will keep gentle pace with you in your transition." (*A Course in Miracles*)

AT A CORNER TABLE in the courtyard, Jay sat opposite Bea, listening to the brassy hum of a muted trumpet wafting through the outdoor speakers at Jake's Place. With the warmer May weather outdoor seating was made available to patrons for the dinner portion of the show. Everyone moved indoors for the jazz performance following the meal. On the far end a bubbling fountain with a waterfall gushed into a lower pool, adding an enchanting element to the neatly landscaped lawn and colorful gardens between the terrace and the surrounding woods. A round brick fire pit in the center was ablaze with small logs occasionally crackling while warding off the advancing coolness of night. He poured their first glasses of plum-colored wine as they savored the sensations; lush sights and lilting sounds.

"To you, my dear," he said, lifting the glass in a toast. Bea widened her hazel eyes in acknowledgement of the gesture and simply smiled at him as she tentatively sipped her own wineglass. Given it was Friday night he felt momentarily relaxed but the recent developments of his practice were churning just under the surface of his mind. He had not yet contacted Marianne nor left a rent check in the office for her. Something would have to be done by next week. With his sign down and the rent unpaid neither of them could tolerate the situation as it was now for long. He decided to put his those concerns out of mind and focus on Bea instead. She'd been working long hours again and they'd had little time to talk during the week. He reached across the table and cupped her hand in his.

"You seem rather pensive this evening. Got things on your mind?"

"Oh, always," she sighed with a little laugh. "The activity in the office is heating up again for summer."

"How's your situation with Hundai going?"

"Well," she said carefully, drawing out the word. "That situation is still up in the air." She sighed again. "It's a longer story than I feel like getting into right now. I'd just rather relax tonight and forget about the Japanese for awhile."

"No problem," responded Jay. "I know the feeling, believe me." He thought for a moment before making his next remark. "Not to push a sore subject, but it seemed to me that Candy was acting a little testier than usual the other day. Is she getting harder to have around?"

"Actually she's only worse on the days that you are there. The rest the time she's better."

"I might have figured. She sure doesn't like me answering my own phone."

"Well, yeah. That has been her job for almost two years now."

"I don't see why she can't be content to let me run my own show. It's her own damn fault. She's always been so uptight ever since I started working there that I'd rather just exclude her from my affairs as much as possible. Why can't she just adapt? It's less work for her anyway."

Bea stared at him without replying, wondering if she should introduce what could be a hot button topic. The wine was relaxing her customary defenses.

"You know," she began hesitatingly, "it's more than just that."

"Yeah, I know. She doesn't like men. Tough toenails."

"She doesn't trust men," Bea corrected him with emphasis. "And so she doesn't trust you."

"What's that supposed to mean?"

"It means," Bea eyed him carefully, "that she still wonders if you may be having an affair."

"What crap. What complete and utter crap. Is that what she's saying?"

"No, not exactly. Let's just say its what she insinuates."

"An affair with who, another untrustworthy guy?"

"No, of course not, smarty. The woman who calls you so much."

"Oh God, that's so dumb. Those calls are for work. She works for Western, our very best customer." Jay felt himself getting irritated. "She is such a twit and also a troublemaker. I'd really like to say something to her."

"No don't, please." Bea put her hand on his forearm in gentle restraint. "Not now, at least, with summer coming. I probably shouldn't have brought it up. It's just another tension. I guess I hoped hearing you say that it's nonsense would allow me to let it go."

"It's nonsense."

"Thanks. I knew that. I guess." She laughed, then sighed. 'But thanks anyway for saying it. I'm just tired, and don't want any more tension in the office than necessary."

"God, I just hate to see that twit for brains spreading rumors behind my back."

"It's okay. She doesn't affect me. It's just the tension that affects me. I don't want it. Just let it go, please. I don't want to be sorry that I mentioned it." She met his eyes imploringly and squeezed his forearm slightly tighter.

"Okay," sniffed Jay, then he smiled. "Just for you. For now at least."

"Thank you." She smiled back and nodded, lifting her glass to his. "You know," she said cheerfully, happy to move along, "Faye will be here almost before we know it."

"That's right," answered Jay, feeling buoyed at the prospect. "I forgot all about it. Plus we'll get to meet her boyfriend."

"That's right. He seemed nice. I spoke on the phone with him when I was there in December." Jay instinctively sensed he wanted to avert any recollection of the plane crash.

"So how's she doing anyway? On the go as usual?"

"Well, I'm sure that's true. She's coming out her, isn't she?" Bea chuckled, feeling the wine's elevating effects. "Still," she mused reflectively, "she did make a comment about her health."

"What about it?"

"Oh nothing really. Just that she was getting some tests done or something. Said she was feeling a little less energetic lately."

"Hm. Could it be that old age is finally catching up with Auntie Mame?" teased Jay. "The dashing world traveler and sophisticated party queen." He took another swig, draining his glass.

"That's what I said." Bea laughed. "I don't know. Guess we'll find out."

"Well, anyway, it'll sure be great to see her. I love that gal."

"I know you do."

Jay reached for the bottle and filled both their glasses halfway up. He spun the wine around the inside of the glass and inhaled its fragrance. He had persuaded Jake to let his patrons bring their own wines for a hefty corking fee. The rich smell of a ripe Cabernet Sauvignon was heady perfume to his nostrils. As he looked around the setting, enjoying the beauty of the flowers, the fountain, the forest and the fireplace, he recognized a familiar face climbing the stairs from the parking lot.

It was his colleague, Will Ringer, whom he had not seen nor spoken with since last September when they'd talked of marriage counseling. He was leading Colette, his lovely diminutive and dark-haired wife, by the hand as they walked into the courtyard. He looked around the area as though waiting to be seated until he saw Jay motioning him over to the table. Jay got up to greet them as they neared.

"Will! How are you? I can't believe it."

"Jay! Good to see you. Wow. It has been a long time. We're good. How are you?"

They shook hands vigorously then gave each other a hug before making introductions with their wives. Jay and Colette had met once at Will's office years ago as the men were going out to lunch together. He wondered as he watched her how they'd fared in the aftermath of her husband's dalliance...*looks like they survived...*

"Please, sit down," urged Jay insistently, "and join us. Won't you?"

"Are you sure?" asked Will. "We don't want to intrude."

"No intrusion," said Jay. "Please. We'd be happy to have you, really." He looked at Bea. She nodded, looking pleased to see Will again. They sat down beside them, ordered more wine and eventually their meals, while conversing pleasantly with each other. As the conversation wore on, the women wound around to talking about their children and the men began discussing the vicissitudes of their careers.

"Frankly, Will, it's been a bitch for nearly a year now. Ever since the advent of managed care my practice has gradually dwindled to less than half of what it was."

"But why? Mine hasn't suffered at all really. I mean there's a lot more paperwork and all, and I don't like it much, but hey, what the hell. It pays the bills."

"Yeah, but you've a got that doctoral degree. The insurance companies prefer working with someone like that."

"That's not true. Where'd you get that idea?"

"A psychologist in my office told me last year when things were starting to change."

"That's bullshit. I don't know why someone would tell you that. The companies just have a different pay schedule for Masters degree therapists as opposed to doctoral ones."

"Yeah, I know that, but I thought they were phasing out people without a Ph.D."

"No, I don't think so. I've never heard that."

"Really? Well, I did, and I just assumed you were safe because of your degree."

"Oh no, that's not the case. I don't think there's any phase out. And my degree's not recognized by them as a doctoral one anyway. It's just a PsyD., which means a degree in educational psychology. I'm not a clinical psychologist at all. It's nice to have the doctor title but really it means nothing to the insurance companies. They only consider someone with a Ph.D. in psychology, clinical psychology, to be a real psychologist. I'm getting paid at the same rate as Masters degree therapists."

"No kidding?"

"Yeah, I thought you knew that."

"No. Sounds like there's a lot here I didn't know actually...*why the hell would marianne tell me that?*...Well, I don't know whether to feel good or bad about this news, because I haven't signed up for any of the managed care programs and I hear it's too late now to get into them anymore."

"That's not true either. Where'd you get that idea?"

"From the same person."

"Well, they're misinformed. It is not too late to get into most of these programs. I just joined a new one recently. You should apply to some of them. It will turn your whole practice around. You used to have such a good one. Sounds like you've been single-handedly letting it die without realizing you didn't need to."

"You're right. In a way I have. I just didn't know. Thanks a lot. I'll check it out next week."...*letting it die all right...but not single-handedly...that damn marianne...was she misinformed or misinforming...should have checked it out myself...*

They finished their dinner and moved inside for the show with the rest of the clientele. It was a three-piece jazz combo with a large overweight vocalist who could croon a soulful standard or belt out an upbeat tune with the same precision craftsmanship as a Broadway professional. She had the crowd in her hand from the start of the opening number. Though Jay was entertained with the rest of the audience his thoughts kept slipping to the news Will had given him and he was suddenly looking forward to next week with an eager curiosity. At the break between sets he excused himself to the bathroom. He was standing at the urinal when Jake came in to do the same. He nodded a greeting as they exchanged places.

"Nice show, Jake. I like these guys."

"Great. Glad to hear it. They've got some CD's on sale out there if you're interested."

"Maybe. I'll look 'em over." Jay finished washing his hands and was starting to leave when Jake spoke up again in a more serious tone.

"Hey, I really appreciate your ideas with the wine. I did what you suggested and most folks responded to us."

"Oh, you mean the survey?"

"Yeah, that and the corking fee. Thanks a lot."

"So what did you learn?"

"Well," he laughed, "you probably won't like it but most of them preferred Columbia Crest." Jay snorted and smiled.

"I'm not surprised. It is a good wine," he said, adding "for the money. Most folks don't really know that much about great wines, or want to spend too much anyway."

"They might if they were educated," said Jake thoughtfully. "This is an up and coming wine region, you know."

"Oh, believe me, I know. I know this region and I know wine. At least better than a lot of people," stated Jay confidently. "But I have no way to educate them, except at my house."

"That's just my point," Jake's voice rose a bit. "How'd you like to be in charge of the wines here?" Jay looked at him with surprise.

"Are you kidding?"

"Nope."

"What do you mean?"

"I mean I want someone to help me make this place a classy one for wine lovers. And wine lovers are a growing part of this community. It could all be good."

"Wow. That'd be wonderful. I mean, I'd be delighted. But what exactly have you got in mind. How would we go about it?" Jake winked and flashed a broad grin.

"I've got some ideas, about food too. Let's talk more after the show."

Chapter 65

"The miracle comes quietly into the mind that stops an instant and is still."
(A Course in Miracles)

As QUIETLY AS SHE could, Bea cracked open the white slats of the thick wooden shutters to the left of her bedside and peered out the large window at the shadowy lake. On her right lay Jay, asleep on his side, curled up like a ball bug with his bare back to her, his long pillow wrapped around his head as usual. She had awakened much earlier than needed today. It was Saturday, which afforded a slightly more leisurely pace than the hectic weekdays would allow. Even on weekends she was busy with work but at least had the luxurious option of sleeping in if desired. Today she was stirred in part by habit but more so in anticipation of an event this afternoon. Ever since receiving Tomoko's fax a few days ago she'd been eagerly awaiting the arrival of the weekend. 'Please call me this weekend' had been her terse note along with her home telephone number in Japan.

The v-shaped crevice in the tree-covered hills to the east began glowing, dimly at first but intensifying gradually, with the flush of a bright rosy red petal hue, heralding the inevitable ascent of the sun. It was an uncommon crimson, strikingly beautiful, and the occurrence was doubled by the perfect reflection of the inverted image in the lake beneath it. As she watched, absorbed in the unfolding splendor, the luminous ruby grew incandescent pink, shifting slowly into peach, then radiating orange so rich that it scorched the bright sky for a moment as intense as a fiery field of wild poppies, all the while flawlessly mirroring the procession parallel on the water. Silhouetted pine trees stood in the distance like Halloween candles, black against a huge pumpkin lit up and bulging between the dark hills. The orange became amber then turned a pale yellow as shafts of white sunlight streaked upward into grayness, broadening the spectrum of light into the sky and diffusing the intensity of dawn until slowly the sun emerged fully, beaming golden blessings and calling it a day...*God that was gorgeous*...

She glanced at the clock and confirmed it was early. It would be another six hours before midday her time and too early to call Tomoko until at least two o'clock. Though burning with curiosity she would just have to wait. She picked up a book from her beside table. It was the last in a trilogy she had started last fall. She'd become engrossed in the life of the heroine, a rigorous existence in prehistoric times. It was only through strength of character and timely twists of fate that the woman had survived against insufferable odds. Bea believed more in the hand of the Creator than fortune or fate, but she identified closely with the woman's strong need for a courageous spirit to counter adversarial conditions and cunning adversaries. Reading was a pleasure she rarely indulged in as spring became summer, and she did so now readily as the sunlight cut through the mists in the evergreens, skimming over water like a flat stone flung, brightening her bedspread through the slats of the shutters like soft melting butter spread over warm toast.

She enjoyed her novel for nearly an hour before yielding to the unending call of the office; the unfinished conflict beckoning below. While the boys were still sleeping she stole through the bedroom and into the kitchen to brew the stout beverage that served as reinforcements for entering the fray. Armed with a hot steaming cup in her hands she silently slipped down the carpeted staircase and softly stepped to the piles on her beleaguered desk. Although there were infinite projects to attend to an aura of grace permeated the air. It was a feeling exclusively reserved for the weekends, secure in the fact that no one but her would inhabit this space. This knowledge allowed her to function more easily without distractions from Candy or Jay. The absence of tension made work almost pleasurable and reminded her of how it once was at the start. The emphasis then had been novel and fresh, bridging two cultures, providing a meaningful service to students and families alike; both grateful parties.

It was delightedly different from her previous career for so long as a teacher, and yet kept her active in the field of education, her very first love and chosen profession. Even teaching was fun in the beginning and for a long while thereafter, but eventually the monotonous grind of routine and an unchanging curriculum grew stale over time. The worst of it though was the coarsening of the students, more rude and unruly with each passing year. As society shifted with the values of the sixties and seventies by liberating traditional mores, the children of these decades reflected the loss of those outworn constraints in their liberated behavior, primarily through rebellion and disrespect for authority. After two and half decades she was considering a change and on that early June day when a surly sixth-grader, the Mexican girl with the brother in prison, swore at her in the classroom with open contempt, she vowed that she would not be back in September. When her small BMW was keyed that same week, no doubt by the same girl, her resolve was cemented.

The move that soon followed from California to the Northwest had been a fresh breath of air in more ways than one. She had moved here with Jay without either of them having jobs, braced by the bucks from the sale of their house and the belief in their abilities to make something happen. Answering an ad that led to the position of regional coordinator for a student exchange firm served to apprentice her well in the field in which she shortly founded her own corporation. Yet as she grew more successful the pleasure of the work was slowly receding into the background. Once again tedium was creeping into the regimen due mostly to the sheer volume of business. The price of success was long hours growing longer with precise implementation of meticulous plans. The joy of her job had been working with people; the folks and the kids. But as her company continued to enlarge, her duties required greater delegation of that function, as fun as it was, to unfamiliar others in far away cities. She'd become an administrator, liked and respected, but engaged in supervising coast-to-coast work in impersonal ways. Like teaching, it was becoming less and less fulfilling.

From her picturesque office, casual and cozy, on a lake in the woods, she was managing affairs in the four corners of North America by phone and fax, mail and email. Toronto, Boston, San Diego and San Francisco were all now growing concerns that could eventually rival her successful Seattle endeavor in size. Aside from those cities were plans for expansion throughout the country and further into Canada. Florida, Arizona and Vancouver would soon be in play. Jay's efforts for the company were also expanding, as more and more universities wanted Homestay programs. Her work with Japan though perilous at times seemed potentially poised for unlimited growth. She just had to ride out the turbulence now. The possibilities for collaboration with European countries had also improved since going to Vienna. She was feeling caught up in a riptide of her own making, sweeping her out into an ocean of success. Every day was an effort to keep her head above water in a sea of paperwork and a swift current of calls.

She took another sip of coffee and surveyed her desk, emitting a sigh as she scanned the stacks. At least for today the pressure was less, the morning was bright and the office was quiet. The sunny quiescence reminded her of Saturday mornings in Ohio as a child in her old-fashioned home. Mom downstairs in the kitchen with the radio on, frying up breakfast to the big band tunes; sausage and eggs, pancakes and bacon, or maybe her favorite, heavenly French toast ladled with butter and pure maple syrup made at a local farm. Dad in the living room reading the paper waiting like the girls for the call to the table. She wondered what her father was doing right now.

It had been a couple of months since they'd spoken on the phone. He seemed of good spirits. The caretaker, Carrie, was working out well, but he also sounded tired, perhaps just of living. His customary zest for life had been truly remarkable when she was a child, but it had declined steadily as time wore on, and most notably after the death of her mother. Once a feminine foursome, a near family of girls, she now just had Faye as her only surviving female family member. As busy as she was, it would be good to see her. She thought of the difference between Faye and herself. Everyone had said that of all of the girls, Bea was obviously the most like her mother. It was clear to her now how distinct the woman had been; pleasant, unassuming, tireless in her tasks, nurturing to all, irreplaceably so. It had all been summed up, as many had noted, by her perfect name, Grace, assigned to her at birth. How could her parents have known it to be fitting?...*did the name make the woman like the clothes make the man*...Bea had met no other woman quite like her, with the lone exception possibly, now that she thought about it, being the one in Japan; Tomoko... *tomoko...tomoko...wonder what that name means*...Her thoughts drifted curiously with some trepidation to what her call to Japan would uncover...*what could she want*...

Stirrings upstairs could be heard as she sat there, drawing her back to the moment at hand. Probably Jay was finally awake. He wasn't too much of a late sleeper either. Phil on the other hand could still sleep until noon. She decided to work for an hour or two now, and then go upstairs to see if they might all have breakfast together. With everyone's schedule going all ways at once, it had been a long time since they'd shared a morning meal. She looked at the lake beaming broadly in the sun's high glare as ducks and geese cruised contentedly on its gently flowing surface. In the distance on her right a whitish gray seagull was approaching from the southern bank of the water by the marshes. Slowly flapping its wings as it steadily advanced it seemed to be floating through the air without effort. As it neared the large cedar tree outside her window it banked towards the lake along the curvature of the shoreline and sailed over the water with an elegant ease. It seemed to embody a message of peace, gentle persistence and infinite patience. She glanced at the clock...*just four more hours*...

Chapter 66

"Some of my pleasantest hours were during the long rain-storms in the spring or fall, which confined me to the house for the afternoon as well as the forenoon, soothed by their ceaseless roar and pelting; when an early twilight ushered in a long evening in which many thoughts had time to take root and unfold themselves."
(Walden, Henry David Thoreau)

IN THE SHADOWS OF the mid-week evening sat Jay on his covered deck, sipping red wine and watching the sudden summer shower on the lake. Sweeping gusts of misty rain blew in south to north, rattling the wind chimes and rocking the rowboats of the few fishermen unwilling to be driven ashore. A rolling peal of thunder boomed loudly across the darkening gray sky like successive blasts from a long row of cannons. He took another sip of the hearty Chianti letting it glide back slowly over his tongue. He was pensive, reflecting on the strife in each workplace. Phil was at soccer and had a ride home. Bea was at a meeting. He had finished his run and downed his Corona. Alone with his wine glass he mused over the recent stresses in his life as the raindrops began striking and sliding down the glass roof above him.

It had started on Monday when he went to the office to see his normal fare of clients. During his lunch break he'd called the major insurance companies in his area and learned that he could indeed still be admitted to their networks. Ringer was right. The doors were open and the sky was suddenly the limit. He wondered if Marianne had intentionally misled him or merely was misled herself. It really didn't matter anymore so much since the fact was he now had an avenue out of her office and back into one of his own. His previous office had been rented to another tenant, an insurance agent, and so was unavailable. He was all right with that. There were other office buildings around town with space to lease. He was actually angrier at the conspicuous absence of his sign on the door; a glaring reminder of Marianne's only too willing complicity in Naimee's fatuous farce. He had tried his best over the weekend to give it all to God as Leroy had suggested. That had brought him intermittent peaceful interludes but they went by the wayside when he saw the door again Monday morning. Later in the day, armed with the knowledge of new possibilities for financial freedom, he had called Marianne at her home.

"Hello," she had answered.

"Hi, it's Jay," he said curtly. "Can you talk for a moment?"

"Sure, what's up?" He thought she sounded tense. He knew he was.

"Well, a couple of things, actually," he started to explain.

"If you're wondering about the sign," she brusquely interrupted, " I can tell you right now that I haven't changed my mind."

"I didn't think that you would," responded Jay quickly, "but I thought I'd give you a last chance to anyway."

"What do you mean by that?"

"Because," he continued, "if you don't I'm moving out."

"Well, that's your prerogative," she sniffed. "I can't stop you. I remind you that you do owe me this month's rent though."

"Yeah, I know you might think that and I've given it some thought."

"What does that mean?"

"I've decided not to do it."

"But we had an agreement."

"We also had an agreement for my sign to be up."

"Well, I'm sorry but I told you I'm simply not comfortable with that being the case, given your client's accusations."

"What ever happened to innocent until proven guilty?"

"I'm sorry Jay, but this is not a court of law. This is my office and I simply do want the sign up, period."

"That's fine and I totally respect that it's your decision to make. I simply do not respect the decision you've made. It is unfair, unwarranted and ruthlessly selfish, and I won't tolerate it."

"Whatever you think is completely your business but I'm entitled to the money for this month."

"This month's just started and you can make do without me because I'll be practicing elsewhere before the week ends. Now that, by the way brings up another point that I wanted to share with you regarding compensation." He paused and caught his breath, savoring the moment as he drove his point home. "You told me last year that my days were numbered. You said the new managed care companies were phasing out working with all psychotherapists except those, like you, with a doctorate degree."

"I heard that they were," she stated warily.

"Yeah, maybe you did and maybe you didn't but either way I know now that was just a lie."

"What are you saying? Are you calling me a liar?" She was coming unhinged slightly, losing her customary cool professional facade.

"I'm saying I spent the noon hour talking with several insurance companies, all of them now with managed care programs, and all of them assured me I could join their networks. They're happy to work with masters-level therapists. They just pay a bit less. What do you say to that?"

"Well," she sputtered, slightly taken aback. "I say if that's true it is news to me."

"Yeah, maybe it is. Or may be it isn't. Maybe you wanted to be the only shrink in Forestville and thought getting rid of me was the best way to do it."

"Oh, that's ridiculous." She was clearly angry now and bit off each word. "I won't even dignify that with a response." He imagined her putting her nose in the air. "I might add however, that such an accusation is unseemly and suspect when coming from someone who's been accused by a client of inappropriate behavior!"

Jay was quiet for an instant, letting the suspense build, before delivering his verbal deathblow.

"Well at least I haven't been fucking my clients now, have I Marianne?" The silence was deafening. She was stopped in her tracks like a head-on car crash into a wall.

"What's that supposed to mean?" she said carefully, cautiously. Jay lingered momentarily as he let her hang in suspension…*dangle in the wind bitch*….

"I think you know," he stated slowly, in a measured tone, steeped in confidence, bordering on scorn. For another moment all was completely silent between them. "Well," he said cheerfully, "consider this your notice. I'll be leaving soon. It's certainly been real. Thanks for everything and…have a nice day."

He'd gotten off the phone feeling satisfied and focused, if not spiritually correct. Now he needed a new office soon. Several calls turned up one a few blocks away and he made arrangements to visit it by Friday, as the landlord was unavailable till then. With any luck he could move in the coming weekend. At this point he had to trust that Leroy was right. He could conduct his business anywhere he wanted to, because somehow there was a God, and somehow God was giving him his good, and somehow he just needed to trust it all worked. Still, at the moment, it was comforting to have the wine. He thought about the possibility of having a smoke and managed to resist it, at least for the time being. Sipping another draught he looked through the rainfall at the ducks on the lake…

just water off their backs...He tried to imagine the feeling of nonchalance he assumed they must have.

His mind drifted onto the other conflagration; one that had occurred yesterday with Candy. The day had started innocently enough; everyone busy with his or her separate tasks amid the incessant ringing of phones and faxes. Looking back on it now he wondered if the tension between them, always simmering just beneath the surface, had increased for her with each call he took on the third line. There had been an inordinate amount of them that morning. He knew Candy as always would resent his answering them, as if it were somehow usurping her duties and jeopardizing her job. He couldn't care less. He thought the real issue was one of control. If their man-hating secretary had lost control of her environment by having to endure a male in her vicinity she at least wanted to maintain the protocol of being the one to screen his incoming calls. It was arrogance and nosiness as far as he was concerned and with her hostile attitude toward him from the outset, she had paved the way to be excluded from his activities whenever he could do without her. To merely type what he gave her and mind her own business was all that he wanted. It seemed ironic to him that a woman who wanted to answer his telephone calls, while speculating derisively on the nature of those calls, would simultaneously accuse him of listening to hers...*that's called projection, num nuts...look it up...*

The fireworks started when Bea left for town to pick up some supplies and run a few other errands. As he'd noticed she'd done when Bea was out of state last year Candy made several personal calls to whom he knew not. It was only because that her tone was different that he was even aware her activities had shifted. She was talking in a louder and less formal voice than she normally used with business-related callers. Even that might have passed as inconsequential. He really didn't care whom she talked to as long as Bea was satisfied with her work. But when he left his office to sharpen his pencils she lowered her tone almost conspiratorially as he walked by her desk. It was odd and seemingly uncalled for. He looked at her as he passed by on the way back, watching her shoulders hunch up and her voice change to uttering tersely phrased monosyllables.

"No," she had said with finality to someone. "Not now. Maybe later. We'll see. Okay?" As he approached his desk in the far room beyond her he heard her say abruptly "Can't talk now. Gotta' go."

He turned and closed his door to emphasize the point that she could certainly have her privacy if she so pleased. But his curiosity was piqued and he wondered what exactly could prompt her to such exaggerated secrecy. A short while later as he went upstairs for lunch she took another call. He assumed it was another one unrelated to work since she lowered her voice as he passed by her....*as if i care*...Through the kitchen window while making his Swiss cheese, tomato and mayonnaise sandwich on whole wheat he saw Bea come rolling up the driveway. She hopped out and retrieved her supplies from the car then took the brick walkway halfway to the house before cutting over the lawn and down the concrete steps to the door leading downstairs. He found some baked barbeque potato chips and stepped out onto the deck to be in the sunlight while eating. Through the open window beneath him he could hear them talking without making out the words. Candy was doing most of the talking and the topic seemed serious. He thought he heard her say the word "phone" and wondered if she had complaints about it once again. He sighed and decided it really didn't matter. He truly didn't care who she talked to if that was it and would be glad to tell her so, right after lunch. If she was complaining again about not taking his phone calls then that didn't matter either because it wasn't going to change. At the moment he was just going to enjoy his lunch break…*let her burn off some steam…i'm choosing peace…*

He munched on his sandwich and looked at the lake, deliberately ignoring the voices below. A large puffy cloud drifted by like a dirigible, reflected in the water like a floating cauliflower. A duck sped across the water buzzing like a motorboat, leaving a narrow line of froth receding in its wake. He smelled the sweet honeysuckle wafting in the wind while listening to the crows cawing out to each other. Its bright red berries were starting to burst out. The weather was warming; as May became June…*soon we'll go swimming…maybe even sailing…*He took a slug of Pellegrino, his favorite mineral water, chilled and bracing as it bubbled down his throat. No matter his circumstances, nothing could dampen the resurgence of pleasure he felt every year with each returning summer; the glorious season. A gaggle of gray long-necked geese cruised calmly by his dock like a squadron of Viking ships, proud and forbearing, intent and unruffled. He finished the last tasty morsels of mealtime and returned to the kitchen to put his dishes in the washer.

Bea came upstairs just as he was finishing. The tense look on her face gave him pause as she approached.

"What's wrong?" he asked, before she could speak, knowing she usually wasn't easily upset.

"It's Candy," she stated flatly, but looking apprehensive. "She says that you've been listening in to her phone calls, doing the phone thing again, as she calls it."

"Oh God," he replied, feeling disgusted. "She is so out to lunch it's not even funny. Do you really think I give a damn about her personal phone calls? She's lying or she's nuts or both."

Bea shook her head slowly in consternation. "I don't know what's happening but I know I can't afford to lose her, especially now with summer coming on. She's the only one with the technical smarts to handle the computer and she also knows where everything is that we need."

"You've been through several secretaries in the past; all of them seemingly irreplaceable and all of them eventually successfully replaced."

"I know, but I don't want to have to take the time to train someone now and besides she's doing a perfectly good job."

"For a paranoiac."

"Whatever. I don't want this stress right now. Can't you two just get along?"

"I'm trying. I'm telling you I didn't do anything."

"Okay. All right. I don't want to deal with this now. Let's just say she's imaging things and let it go at that." Jay wondered if that was what she really thought or if she was just placating him.

"Is that what you're going to say to her?"

"Not exactly. I'm just going to tell her that you say she's mistaken and hope, at least for now, it will not become an issue. Okay?"

"It's okay with me, but it sure is crazy." Jay could see that she really would prefer to drop it. "I'll get back to work now," he said reassuringly. "You coming?"

"No. I'm going to have some lunch."

He nodded, then washed off his dishes, put them in the dishwasher and went downstairs without another word. As he entered the room he saw Candy hanging up the phone. She turned around and handed him a note as he approached her desk.

"This call came for you just a moment ago. I know you prefer I not answer your line but you weren't here and I just did it without thinking." She smiled smugly and batted her eyelids. "I hope you don't mind. Just doing my job."

Jay sighed and felt a growing irritation as he took the note. It was from the woman with Western…*bet she loved that…*

"Look," he started, intending to sound reasonable. "I really would appreciate it if you'd just leave my affairs to me."

"I'm just doing my job," she reiterated. "Sorry I forgot for a moment how you want it. It's just so unusual…but it's none of my business."

"You're right, I know, it is unusual. I just find it easier to take my own calls and not have to interface with you on who they are and what they want and if I want to talk with them. I can handle it faster myself while sitting in there doing ten things at once. I've given certain people the number for third line. That's all that it is."

"Mm-hm," she intoned in a saccharine manner as she turned her back to him to sort through some files. "I'm sure that's all it is." Jay felt his irritation turning to outrage at the insinuation.

"And what do you mean by that exactly?"

"Oh nothing," she replied, continuing to sort through the folders. "Nothing at all," she added with finality. "I'm sure you have your reasons for keeping your calls to yourself."

"I just told you my reasons!" he exploded. "Why are you so suspicious of my calls?" She turned to him suddenly and glared up at him. Her face was flushed and her eyes flashed in fury.

"Why are you so suspicious of mine?"

"I am not suspicious of yours, you…" He decided not to say it.

"You what?" she retorted. "Go ahead and say it. Call me names if it makes you feel better. I know what you've been doing no matter what you say." Jay could feel things spinning out of control just as Bea did not want.

"You are imagining things," he said more calmly. "That's all I was going to say," he lied. "I wasn't going to call you any names...*you paranoid schizo freak*...Look, Candy," he tried to say gently, "I don't know where you get the idea that I would listen to your phone calls. I don't know where you get the notion that there's anything wrong with the ones I take. But on both counts you are wrong. That's all I can tell you."

"Oh, of course," she sniffed while turning back to her work. "I'm wrong and you're right. The woman's always wrong and the man's always right. I know. I know. Believe me, I know."

Jay threw up his hands in a gesture of futility, searching for a way to bring the conversation to a better close. "Look, Candy," he began.

"What's going on here?" Bea appeared in the doorway. "I can hear you two upstairs. I can't afford to have this. Things are hard enough as it is. Can't the two of you just agree to disagree and let it go for now?"

Candy kept flipping through files without looking up. "I have nothing more to say," she said with adamant sweetness. Jay looked at Bea and saw her weariness.

"Me neither," he said, striding into his office. "We're done," he added, over his shoulder. But he didn't believe it. He knew that tomorrow while he was in counseling, Candy would be in the office with Bea and would likely have much more to say behind his back. And sooner or later something would have to give.

He sloshed back another astringent splash of wine and reached for the bottle to refill his glass. The rain showed no sign of letting up soon. The last remaining fishermen had given up and gone ashore. Several diehards were fishing in yellow slickers on the dock at the park. Dozens of geese were gathered on his neighbor's dock. It was larger than his and floated lower in the water, thus encouraging more feathered campers to park there, who in turn deposited greater globs of goose crap upon it than on any other dock on the lake. Oblivious to the drizzle they were picking at themselves and flapping their feathers as though taking a shower. Intermittent honks filled the air with the sounds of the self-satisfied creatures preening themselves. Feeling jaunty and bittersweet between the wine and his troubles he hoisted his glass and tipped it towards them in a toast...*into each life a little rain...*

Chapter 67

"A single gentle rain makes the grass many shades greener. We should be blessed if we lived in the present always, and took advantage of every accident that befell us, like the grass which confesses the influence of the slightest dew that falls on it; and did not spend our time in atoning for the neglect of past opportunities."
(Walden, Henry David Thoreau)

IN THE MUFFLED SILENCE of the rain-soaked summer night Bea sat at her desk deeply immersed in putting the finishing touches on the letter she was writing to the principal of Hundai High School. Alone in her office she could concentrate better on this paramount project than with employees around, especially as their tensions had so recently spiked.

Her own tensions had grown ever since she'd received the fax from Tomoko late last week. They'd peaked when she finally placed her call to Japan on Saturday afternoon as requested. Since then the revelations she had learned from that conversation had unleashed a myriad of thoughts and feelings. She finished the paragraph that she was writing and paused to read the letter so far.

A long bang of thunder cracked through the sky like a volley of gunfire echoing from a cavern deep in the clouds. She stopped reading to observe a sudden surge in the rain descending in sheets and contemplated the weather. The early June storm had caught everyone off guard, even the weathermen, whom everyone had learned to distrust anyway. Forecasting in the northwest was a risky proposition. Mistakes were common but acknowledgements were not. TV weather forecasters blithely moved on to the next day without apology if it had rained on your parade...*oh well, that's life...full of surprises*...

She was taking full advantage of her own surprise now; Tomoko's fax and the following phone call with the resultant opportunity to be rescued from the brink. Staring at the wind-swept shower on the lake, she mused for a moment on that transformational talk. She had placed the call at exactly two o'clock.

"Mushi, mushi," came the first words out of the orient, in a wan and weak voice, weary with age.

"Mushi, mushi to you," chuckled Bea in reply.

"Is it Bea?" gasped the woman.

"Yes it is. Is this Tomoko?"

"Oh, yes, and thank you. Thank you for calling." Tomoko sounded tired but pleased just the same. Bea was aware it was still early morning there.

"I'm sorry if I woke you."

"Oh no. It's okay. I hoping you would call. I hope you get my fax." She sounded so sweet and starting to perk up.

"Well, yes, I surely did and it was a great surprise. I've been waiting ever since then with bated breath for this call."

"Bad breath?"

"No, no. Bated breath."

"Oh," said Tomoko pensively. "What mean 'bated breath'?" Bea chuckled again at the child-like inquiry.

"I'm sorry," she said. "It means I've been dying to speak with you."

"Dying?" repeated Tomoko with some alarm.

"Oh no, not dying. Not really dying. That's just an expression like...well, it means I have been looking forward to, I am very interested in, talking with you."

"Oh," replied Tomoko. "I very glad. I very want to talk with you too."

"Yes, yes, I know, and I'm wondering why. What is it that you would like to say to me?"

Tomoko cleared her throat and sounded as though she were sipping a liquid...*green tea, no doubt*...

"Oh," she began, "I have some information." She stopped for a moment, as though afraid to continue, or perhaps have another sip. "I have very serious, very serious information."

"I see," said Bea, as patiently as she could. "Well, go ahead please, if you like, I'm very curious."

"Yes, I will. Of course I will tell you. I will because I must. I must tell you everything."

Bea felt her curiosity rising like a launched rocket. "Thank you," she said tactfully. "Please go ahead. I'm listening."

Tomoko cleared her throat again and took a deep sigh. After a pause she began talking slowly, earnestly, deliberately, sharing her secret, unloading her burden.

"Do you remember," she started, "when you visit last time?"

"Oh yes, I remember well. That's when we got to know each other."

"Yes," said Tomoko. "And you were very kind to me."

"Oh, that was easy. You were very kind to me."

"But you were my guest; the guest of the school. You were important person. How you say, VIP?"

Bea laughed out loud at the mention of that acronym. She didn't regard herself in such regal terms but knew the Japanese extended a dignified protocol to guests, especially prospective business partners from America.

"Yes, yes, we do say that, but I'm not so important."

"Oh yes. You very important to us. You are guest of whole high school. You have business with principal and come from America."

"Well, yes, I understand. It seems like VIP."

"Oh no," stated Tomoko. "You are VIP. And more," she continued, "you are a woman too."

Bea reflected on this, understanding its importance to Tomoko, and decided it was best to just continue listening.

"Yes," she confirmed. "That's true." There was a lapse in their dialogue as she waited for more...*loves that tea...*

"You see," said Tomoko with another soft sigh, "I work at school for almost thirty years."

"Oh my, that's a long time."

"Yes, a long time, a very long time."

"Yes."

"And all of that time I work very hard. I work very hard in principal's office. Same office as now."

"I see. That is a long time in one place."

"Yes," said Tomoko, sounding nostalgic. "And I see many principals come there and go."

"Oh, I bet. I'm sure you've seen many changes at the school."

"Yes, I do," she explained slowly. "And I see," she said with additional emphasis," many businessmen come and go too."

"Yes, I'm sure. You're at the center of the action."

"Yes," she said proudly. "I see many things. I see many people. But no one, no businessman, even no principal ever treat me as kindly as you."

"Oh," said Bea, flushing slightly and touched by the woman's humble admission of gratitude. "I'm glad you thought so. You were very kind to me also. Remember," she laughed gently, "you showed me how to find the ladies room."

"Hah!" laughed Tomoko. "That's true. I help you too. But you brought me flowering plant on last day, and no one ever bring me flower. Ever."

"Well, I 'm glad you appreciated them. It was a simple thing to do and I was happy to do it. I appreciated your kindness. You were always very helpful and friendly to me at the school."...*is this it?...just wanted to thank me...*

"But you see, I am wanting to help you again." She paused presumably to take another sip; a long one. Then she sighed once more and said quietly, "I'm retiring this year."

Bea listened intently....*that's it...a heartfelt thanks at the end of a long career...*

"And I must tell you, for my honor, for the honor of my school. I must tell you what is happened. I must tell you the truth."

Bea could almost hear the phone line crackle aloud with transcontinental curiosity as she waited on edge for the woman's next words. She could not contain herself.

"The truth about what?"

Tomoko cleared her throat again, made a sipping sound and then resumed talking in a very measured tone. "The principal, Mr. Takahara, my boss at the school, is not honest to you. He is not telling truth to you about Homestay program."

Bea's heart skipped a beat as she listened intently and just for a second she felt short of breath.

"What do you mean?"

"You see," said Tomoko, hesitatingly, "Mr. Takahara work with Mr. Kitagawa."

"Kazuo?" she queried sharply. "Kazuo Kitagawa?" There was a tightness in her chest like a fist enclosing...*i knew it...*

"Yes."

"I see." Bea exhaled. "Well, thank you for telling me. I thought so, but couldn't prove it."

"But you see, I have proof," declared Tomoko stoutly. "And I have proof he take bad money."

"He took bad money?" repeated Bea in amazement. "He took a bribe, you mean?"

"Yes." Her voice was flat with finality. "He did."

"How do you know?"

"I saw the faxes. I saw the faxes in Mr. Takahara's office. He has his own machine."

"Oh."

"One day I was looking for information on his desk. He was out. He does not mind. He knows I take care of his duties. I was looking for a list of student names for Homestay program. I must make sure parents have made deposit. The deadline was next day. After that it is too late for student to be in program."

"I see." Burning with inquisitiveness, Bea pressed her ear to the phone, unaware the receiver was getting warmer by the moment.

"I could not find list on his desk so I decide to look in his drawer. We have no time to wait."

"Yes, I understand. And what did you find?"

"I see the faxes from Mr. Kitagawa."

"Kazuo, yes, Mr. Kitagawa. And what did they say?"

"They say about program. Mr. Kitagawa, Kazuo, as you say, want to do program in Australia. He want to do program with his company."

"I see."

"Yes. And he offer, he give, Mr. Takahara much money to change program plan."

"How much money?"

"He offer Mr. Takahara five hundred thousand yen."

"Five hundred thousand yen!" Bea gasped. "That's fifty thousand dollars! That's an awful big bribe for just one summer program."

"He say he want to do program always, maybe for many years. Maybe pay him more later. I don't know how much. I just know Mr. Kitagawa offer him money and in other fax Mr. Takahara say yes. Then he cancel your program."

"That's right. He did."...*oh my God...that rat*...She felt both elated and alarmed simultaneously...*oh my God...i should have known...but still, what can i...*

"Tomoko?"

"Yes."

"Can you get copies of these faxes?"

"I have copies." Bea heaved a heavy sigh out and said nothing, feeling as though she were in the Twilight Zone. "I decide to make copies when I decide to tell you the truth. I see your letters to Mr. Takahara and I have to type his letters to you. I know he threaten to sue. I know what he is doing. And I know it is wrong. It is bad and unkind to you, a kind person. I cannot say nothing. I will help you."

"I see." Bea heaved another deep sigh. "Well, I thank you. I can't thank you enough really," she spoke slowly. "You have saved my life, or least my company. Thank you. Thank you. Thank you so much." She had another thought, somewhat unrelated to the matter at hand, but one that might prevent further such episodes. "Do you know of anyone in Japan who could represent my company as my employee?"

"I sorry, no." There was a a long pause. "But I will think about it."

"Well, thank you for that. It think it would help. But in any case, I can't tell you how grateful I am for your help with this problem now. I thank you again from the bottom of my heart."

Another loud peal of thunder broke loose like a snare drum solo on an elongated roll. Bea looked out the window at the swirling mist saturating the lake from shore to shore. The wind was whipping up the smallest lip of whitecaps curling and tossed in cross current lines. No birds to be seen but some hunkered down geese that had sequestered themselves in a tight knit group and were stoically waiting out the storm on the sidelines of the neighbor's wide dock. She glanced down at her letter and reflected again on the conversation that had inspired it.

"You are welcome," said Tomoko. "I glad to help you. I glad to do what is right."

"Yes, well that's certainly true. You are helping me and you are doing right." Bea paused, reflecting on how best to proceed from here. "I'm wondering what we should do next. I'm concerned that confronting the principal with the facts will get you into trouble."

"I cannot get in trouble. I am retiring next week. Next Friday is my last day at work."

"Next week is your last?"

"Yes. I leave after lunch."

"Perfect."

By the end of the conversation they had formulated a plan for Bea to contact the principal right after Tomoko's departure. She faxed Bea copies of the papers, which clearly detailed the two men's nefarious arrangements. Bea could hardly believe her sudden good fortune and was keenly awaiting the moment of reckoning. The letter she was writing now was to be faxed tonight, which was Friday in Japan, after the noon hour there. Tomoko would be long gone. She had said that the principal would be there in her absence.

A bright flash of lightning lit up the sky briefly like crooked white hot strands of electrical wire and a few seconds later thunder ripped through the air like a fresh deck of cards being shuffled fast and hard. It seemed to dramatize the moment she was facing.

She finished rereading the letter and decided it was worded well enough to accomplish the task. It was essentially straightforward and right to the point. She was informing him that she knew of the bribe and insisting that her program be reinstated. Otherwise she would inform the school's board of directors of his corrupt behavior. She had received from Tomoko a list of the names and addresses of each board member and warned that if necessary she'd send them copies of the incriminating documents.

Looking over to the Japanese clock on her shelf she noted that it now was well past mid-day there. She bowed her head asking God's blessing for her action then slipped the paper in the fax and sent it on its way...*that's that*...She sat back in her chair as it chugged through the machine, feeling relief that the deed had been done, plus some apprehension over what it would yield...*nothing to do but wait*...As she rested at her desk, just watching the rainstorm, her mind wandered back to other recent events.

Just when she thought things were going along well enough, strife had erupted again in the workplace. Thank God Jay was only there every other day. She pondered what could be done to prevent further outbreaks. They were both, Jay and Candy, little time bombs with a short fuse, just waiting to be lit, ready to blow. It seemed the only reason they had not had a major free for all was because of their respect for Bea; a slender silver thread holding the office fabric together.

She looked at the white plastic board on the wall on which was inscribed the summer group schedule. It was busy through early September with students, the first of which would be arriving very soon. She had not heard back from Faye yet with specific dates for her visit but at last mention it had seemed that early June was very likely...*wish she'd let me know* *for sure…*Though she wasn't panicked she was feeling growing pressure and considered calling Faye right now to see what was up. It was barely past ten in the evening on the east coast but her sister was often up late into the night. Suddenly she felt simply compelled to do it. After finding the number in her ornate address book, another elaborate gift from her Japanese hosts, she dialed it on the home phone without further thought and was heartened to hear it answered on the first ring.

"Hello."

"Faye, it's Bea."

"Bea! What a surprise. I was just going to call you."

"Why?"

"Because we've decided we're coming out in two weeks." Bea gasped softly.

"Wow! Okay. So you'll be here in mid-June."

"Right. I just bought the tickets today. They're cheaper if two weeks away."

"Sure. Okay. I was wondering. That's why I called."

"Well, now you can rest easy. Everything's all set."

"Well, I'm glad it's all set, but I won't be resting easy. I've got a ton to do."

"I know, I know, and we'll stay out of your way. I promise. Don't you worry. We'll rent a car and do our thing and see you when you're free."

"Well, sure, that's fine. But it's not so much that you'll be in my way. I'd just like to spend time with you and am somewhat concerned that will be hard to do."

"Don't worry. We'll spend time together when you can. That's the main reason I'm coming – to see you – don't forget."

"Oh that's good to hear. Okay, we'll make it work I guess, somehow. We'll do the best we can."

"That's the spirit."

"rrriiinnnggg"

The first line on the work telephone rang loud in the room like a woodpecker riveting a bell. Bea felt her stomach flip-flop in excitement…*could it be*…

"Faye," she interjected, "I'm sorry but I think I better take this call. I've got an extreme situation going on."

"Will you call back?"

"Maybe. It depends. Gotta' go. If not, we'll talk tomorrow. Bye for now."

She hung up the home phone with a hard clack and snatched the work phone up from its cradle.

"Homestay Connections. This is Bea. Can I help you?"

"Ahhh, yes," came the tentative reply from afar. "This is Mr. Takahara."

Chapter 68

"A Pew Research survey released yesterday stated that President Clinton 'stands out for his extraordinary low credibility'…The survey found that overall 46 percent of the respondents believe 'almost nothing' Mr. Clinton says."
(Inside Politics, Jennifer Hopper)

UNDER A SUNDAY NOONTIME sun lay Jay in his hemp-strung hammock, sagging and stretched between two twisted trunks of willow trees leaning by the lake. Beneath the shady boughs he watched the fresh leaves wiggle in the wind above him like a billion baby butterflies just freed from their cocoons. Their little green wings spread all around billowing aflutter and seemed to be as one big soft-breathing creature. The weather for the weekend had surprised him, as it had everyone, shifting swiftly past the spring with a short rainstorm and transforming without warning into brightness and warmth. Basking now in the sun he could not recall feeling such a depth of tranquility for a very long time.

It seemed to him perhaps, though done at best in fits and starts, that his willingness to approach life as a spiritual experience might finally be working. Whether or not it was he surely had some recent reasons to feel happier. Although Leroy had more than once instructed him simply to sit and do nothing he could never quite bring himself to find the time or place to do so. Suddenly today, with the new summer air, and so much having happened in the preceding week, he simply felt seized with the desire to be still and reflect on it all, while enjoying the beauty of a warm day by the water. He had brought with him a tape that arrived in the mail yesterday, bearing the contents of last week's conversation with his mentor. Slipping on the headphones he pushed in the button, crossed his legs at the ankles, put his arms behind his head and closed his eyes to listen while floating in the breeze.

"Hi Leroy. It's Jay"

"Hello Jay, what's up?"

"Well, there's some stuff going on here in relation to Bea's company and I didn't want to wait till our next scheduled meeting to talk about it."

"Sure. What's going on?"

"Bea is losing Candy, her secretary and computer hand, for several of stated reasons but probably because of me or the tension between us. I mean she says she wants to spend more time at her dance studio and try to be home more in the summer with her kids, but that latter reason was never an issue for the past two summers so I doubt it's true. I don't know if I ever mentioned she does dance, or teaches dance some evenings, with another woman at a studio and it's never done very well and she says she wants to spend more time trying to make a go of it. And maybe that's true but I really think she's just finding conditions in the office too intolerable ever since I started working there because as I've mentioned before she doesn't seem to like men, except maybe as sex toys. Anyway, I'm glad she's going but Bea is unhappy about it because she's worried about finding another computer person and so I'm wondering what you could say about what it all means and what we should do."

"Oh just do what is practical at the moment, whether you have to advertise or go to a temporary agency, and trust that it will work out."

"Well, of course I guess we will. We have before. Bea has been through other secretaries over the years that have worked out well but had to leave eventually and they always seemed irreplaceable at the time, but someone always shows up to replace them and do the job just fine as well. Her business is just bigger and busier now than ever before. But I guess I'm actually more concerned about Bea feeling not only worried but also mad at me for Candy's departure. I remember once we talked about this and you said that Candy really wasn't very happy here and would need to change her attitude or leave."

"Right. It's good. She's ready to go. I mean it was almost impossible for her to stay because she would have had to make a significant adjustment in her attitude in order to have done it."

"That's it exactly."

"All's well."

"Yeah, okay, but Bea feels mad at me because I was the one who had conflict with her. Candy was happy with no men around. We have friends who know Candy socially and essentially they see the same dynamic. She is friendly with the wife and is caustic with the husband for being a rabid baseball fan. My oldest son also worked one summer in the office with her when he was home from college and said he felt the same antagonism coming from her though he didn't know why. I know the guy she's been trying to make her boyfriend has felt it was difficult. It may be unconscious on Candy's part but to Bea the simple fact is they were getting along fine until I came along. So she's afraid it will hurt her business which in turn threatens her, and I feel for her."

"Look, I understand all that but the basic point here is that it was time for her to go. There's no point in recriminating here and there's no point in making Candy the villain either because it is simply time for her to move on."

"Great. I'm fine with that but the thing that makes it kind of villainous is that she is accusing me once again of listening to her phone calls, which is utterly false, and she's essentially insinuating that's the real reason why she's leaving. And if we didn't have a good friendship with her boyfriend, Randy, actually now her recent ex-boyfriend, who had a good talk with Bea just this week, I'm afraid she wouldn't know which one of us to believe. And it bugs me that she's trying to drive a wedge between us, especially with a lie or an imagined complaint."

"What did he say?"

"Well, he said he was discouraged about having a relationship with her because she was always so completely into herself. He said even in lovemaking she was totally selfish, always focusing only on what she wanted him to do to please her. He also thought she was way too hard on her young son. And she has a never-ending fix-it list of tasks around her house for him to do – he's s handy fix-it guy. And he's an easy-going, upbeat and warmhearted fellow, so it's pretty hard to have a bad relationship with him."

"I see."

"But the main thing he said that tipped the scales in my favor was that she was always fantasizing, making things up that she really believed or often had strong opinions about stuff based on inconclusive or misinterpreted data."

"I see. Was she saying you were listening on the line or overhearing her?"

"Oh she means listening in on the line, which is just pure…I mean, I assumed she was lying but now I'm starting to think she's just a bit more of a disturbed person than I realized. I mean it appears to me she is a genuine paranoiac."

"Just tell her she doesn't know what she is talking about and be clear about that and don't mind the accusation. Just shrug your shoulders and say 'Well, this didn't happen'."

"Well, that's pretty much what I have done except to make it especially clear to Bea, but I can't help wondering how Candy drew that conclusion or what's going on with her."

"Indeed, and what was she doing making personal phone calls?"

"Well, right, and what does she have to hide anyway? But beyond that, last year, when I first started working there and Bea went to Toronto fireworks first erupted between Candy and me over the same issue. Eventually things seemed to go along a little better though I always felt it was hard to be around her in a confined space. She always seemed moody or uptight. I found it hard to focus with someone beaming hostile vibes but I'm not sure really how much of it was my stuff. But anyway, I think that in regard to the Toronto situation that it started when I came in to the office one day and she was at Bea's desk with her feet up on it talking away to some friend and though she took her feet down it continued for a long time and it bothered me because it seemed so disrespectful and sneaky and just plain inappropriate. She never did that when Bea was around.

"So after a while that day I called her on another line from my cell phone just to see if she would interrupt her personal calls to take the business ones and she did, though I'm sure she resented my checking on her. So I felt a little better about it but still…Anyway, that's the only thing I did. And when I told Bea about her being different and she said to forget it and cut her some slack so I did and that was that. But even then it never even occurred to me to listen to her phone calls. Later I learned she had told Bea that I was and Bea didn't know for sure what to believe. Plus apparently she's been insinuating that I'm having some kind of an extra-curricular relationship with a woman from a college who calls me on the third line – the one I don't want Candy to answer. So anyway, then this week when she announces she's quitting she apparently starts out by saying 'Jay's doing the phone thing again', whatever that means."

"I see. Look, this is all connected to her basic resistance to joining in with the work and getting past her own assumptions of being special in the workplace, which is why she can't just do the job and get along. She's devoting alot of her mental energy to upholding a view of herself, which doesn't allow the kind of yielding it takes to be efficient, unobtrusive and agreeable in this kind of setting; a community of work. Do you see what I'm saying?"

"Yep. That's exactly as I see it, though I hadn't thought of it in those precise terms."

"Right. She could not get past the need to be special while working and that's a drag."

"Yeah. And being a dancer she's probably used to being a prima donna and unhappy that her dance school is the least successful of the four or five around here. There's probably a lot of little things going on in her life that contribute to her feeling unhappy and I used to feel compassion for, like being a single mom or not having a man in her life, but I don't feel it at the moment at all. I'm just glad she's gone. You know, I said to Bea the other night that if she had just been willing to be a little more mature and friendlier she'd still be here, which is my way of saying what you just said."

"Yes. There are just too many grievances and if she got rid of those grievances she'd be likely to get new ones. So it's good riddance here."

"That's the phrase that came to my mind but I'm trying to take pains not to act out my ego."

"Oh please. (laughter) Spare me the spiritually correct stuff here,"

"Well, I don't mean to be doing that, I hope. It's more I notice I feel bad if I get into vindictiveness. It's that quick of a boomerang. I don't want to keep having bad feelings about her. Good riddance has always seemed a hostile phrase to me."

"Sure, but it's not about justice. You should feel relief that she's gone. I mean that's what you say good riddance for; thank God she's gone."

"I think I'll feel bad if I get into any counter-hostility. Thank God you're gone and don't let the door hit you on the way out. If I said that I'd feel bad an hour or a day later."

"If you could say that without any sense of conflict though it becomes light-hearted. Almost anything that is serious could be turned into something comedic."

"Well, I understand that but when I first got the news from Bea she had this terribly sick look on her face and kind of bemoaned 'Candy's quitting' so it seemed pretty tragic and I think being funny would not have gone down well."

"I see. Yeah, well, she's quitting. Good. I mean it's been pending for a long time."

"Yeah, okay so we'll work on getting solutions. Life goes on. I just wanted to run that by you, because it really killed me that she said I was listening in to her phone calls and I honestly don't know if she's lying or crazy."

"Well it sounds like your friend has a good explanation for it. Just accept it at that and let it all go with relief."

"I understand that and could easily do so but I'm concerned that Bea seems so panicked over the loss. Neither of us knows the computer like she did and to some degree they had a decent friendship or at least a friendly relationship. Actually it is pretty hostile and hurtful of her to do this now because summer is Bea's busiest season and she knows that very well. That's part of the panic."

"I understand that and perhaps the friendship can still be maintained or perhaps she is really not such a good friend but in either case it was time for her to change or move on and she has made her choice and it's perfectly alright. It's all right for everyone and Bea has to trust that if it is fulfilling for her business to continue to prosper, and my sense is that it is, the appropriate person will emerge to take her place. That's all I'm saying."

"I knew you would say that. Sooner or later the right person will come along."

"Yes. It will happen that way, but you and Bea are going to need to have no problem with the status quo. This is not something that requires urgency."

"Good. Now if Bea would believe that."

"Well, she will see that it is true and in the meantime you can be helpful to her here. Let me clarify it this way. Always acknowledge your general good. Before you specify anything in your life that seems desirable or appropriate, always acknowledge your general good. Then you can ask for whatever it is or state your willingness to receive it without any urgency at all. You are recognizing the foundation for your fulfillment. This is another way of saying what Jesus meant by saying 'Seek ye the kingdom first'. Seek the general good first. What happens if you don't have that experience is that what you specifically desire starts to matter in a way that provokes urgency."

"In other words, to use your language from previous talks, it's like urgently seeking an advantage to rectify the general bad or the apparent lack of order in life, when the only real urgency is to get back to God, where no advantage is necessary because life is always unfolding or being created in a meaningful and fulfilling way, even if it's not readily apparent at the time."

"Right."

"See, I get this stuff. (laughter) Intellectually anyway."

"Yes, you are right on target. You see, if you do not acknowledge your general good then you fear the consequence of not having your specific desires met. But if you do acknowledge your general good you know there is no consequence. It does not matter. You don't know specifically how it will work out but you still experience feeling good. You know, you trust, that the general good will always yield specific good in a manner that meets your needs. And that line when you understand this process will define failure and success from now on. Being in that place where you feel the general good will always yield good, in one form or another. And if you find yourself desiring something and it doesn't happen, don't worry about it. Go with the next desire. It is like there is a recipe going on with respect to creation or the manifestation of your endless desires. You are desiring one thing and then desiring another and then seeing what actually manifests. It may be something quite beyond your foreknowledge. You see?"

"Mm. No."

"Okay, look. It is like you are baking a cake. Let's say you tried cake and you loved it but you had no idea about food preparation. And you were being guided or instructed to create a cake and the first guidance or instruction was to crack an egg into a bowl. You would think that was crazy. What does that have to do with cake? It would be shocking to be guided to do that when what you wanted was cake. But you accept the idea that the way to have cake is to break eggs and then rather than listening to new desires or further guidance you continue to crack eggs and you wonder why you are not getting cake. It's because you now have to abandon the first step or desire now that you have agreed with it and go on to the next one. But in doing so you continue to acknowledge or experience your general good while agreeing with the desires or guidance that you feel that keeps moving through you and eventually you end up with something like cake that essentially fulfills the need you were feeling, possibly in a way that is better than you imagined, but definitely in a way that is sufficient or satisfying."

"Okay, I see. It comes back to trust and the realization that we know nothing and are not in control."

"Exactly."

"That's' so hard."

"Yes, but you are learning it. You don't want to go back to conflict and the attempts to control life. You do it this way because it feels natural or free of conflict in the moment and yet it doesn't matter. And that is a very high road to be on. It does not allow you to deny the general good while waiting for a result. That's why, as I have said before, that you stay with the essence of your desire. The actual form of your desire as it manifests simply does not matter. And that keeps this process at the level of no effort. It makes it all actually sublime. Things keep working out, transforming endlessly, and you realize that having them work out in God's way is entirely fulfilling and can be trusted. So it's fine to be specific in your desires but not on a foundation or feeling of lack or on an insistence of the resulting form. In the mundane world, the world of the ego, that is how things work but you do not have peace of mind. You have fear and effort. In always acknowledging your general good you know your desires will manifest appropriately."

"Okay, I think I understand this and it almost makes me hesitate, but not quite, to ask you with some impatience, when am I going to be rich, or at least financially secure?"

"When are you going to feel your general good is my question to you in response to that, because there is no other rich other than that, because the bounty of that is no pressure of time. You see, when you feel your general good you are not going to feel any imposition of time. You are not going to be impatient."

"Hmm."

"So what you want to do is go innocently on your way with your recipe, which is whatever you are expressing at the moment. Recognize your desire and agree with it and continue living your life or dealing with other continuous desires as they arise."

"Hm."

"Now, it is interesting that the word recipe comes from the word receive, as in recipient. But the connotation of recipe has nothing to do with receiving. It has to do with creating, according to directions or a plan. So what recipes do is to give you a sequence of steps that allows you to receive. So when you are expressing a desire, whatever impulse you have in any moment, connect with that, express it, agree to have it, while feeling your general good, and you have taken that step in the recipe of your fulfillment. And who is to know why you are desiring one thing and then another. You don't have to make sense out of it. It doesn't have to be logical. It doesn't have to be rational. Please, don't get into that that. It's like I was saying about cracking an egg in baking a cake without any experience in the kitchen. The steps would seem absurd."

"Well…here we are then."

"Right. So this is a way of occupying yourself, of being entertained. You get to feel what you desire. You don't have to deny yourself anything. But you stay in the conscious awareness, the abiding experience, of your good in general, as you feel your specific desires, and be open or receptive to their transformation into being or creation."

"Got it. Now, if I do that with respect to my practice, it comes down at the present time to finding a new office and also contacting companies about joining their networks and desiring the result of having twenty or so clients a week to make enough money to quit working with Bea's company."

"Great. That's a desire. Just know what you desire and simply agree to have it while feeling at the same time that your life is good in general."

"It's good to be alive."

"Right. And along with that process allow yourself to feel that it doesn't really matter whether it happens or not. And if you can do that then you are at the level where there is perfect transmission of your desire and it doesn't come up against any of your grief or grievances."

"Anything can happen and that which is miraculously appropriate will."

"Exactly. You see, if you work on the other level, that of the ego urgently clamoring for what it thinks it needs, you are going to come in contact with that wall of grief."

"Oh, I'm familiar with it."

"Which has always blocked your heart's desire from coming to pass. So this overrides that. Even before you are awake completely, you know that you have the capacity to experience your good miraculously and this is the way to do it; by just feeling the general good. That doesn't trigger any feeling of grief. You see?"

"Yes, I do. I can get into it while we're talking and it's a wonderful feeling."

"Right. Good. And there you are."

"Hm. Thanks. Ah, listen, is our half hour almost done? Because if it is I'm happy to get off now and go with this."

"We have about five more minutes, if you care to talk longer."

"Well, sure, ah, let's see…You know for what it's worth I think I've given up Clinton-hating."

"How's that?"

"Well, I just don't seem to have the interest in it so much, especially as I continue to concentrate on what we're doing."

"Good."

"Yeah. I still don't think much of him. I have no doubt he cornered Paula Jones in a hotel room as Governor and pulled his pants down and asked her to 'Kiss it' as she says. He denies it of course so it's funny that he just gave her eight hundred and fifty thousand dollars to go away. If that were a republican like Bush the mainstream media would be hounding him day and night like they did Nixon until he left office. Also it seems likely to me he brutally raped Juanita Broaddrick in a hotel room while Attorney General. She seemed very credible on 60 Minutes. It's odd but it appears every liberal in America chose to watch Monday Night football the evening her interview was aired and none of them that I've ever spoken to have ever heard of her. And it's amazing the news blackout that followed that hourly expose. Nary a word on public-funded NPR. Not so if Bush.

"And it could be humorous if it weren't so shameful because the left likes to think they're these compassionate beings, though I've never meet any that were more so than any other person, nor any less either, but now that it's come out what vile things he has done and probably continues to do to women, they all say 'Hey, the economy's good – it's his private life' etc., as though that excused it.

"If he were a republican and that were offered as a rationale for ignoring it they would say 'Oh you greedy heartless republicans have no compassion for women and only think about money' – so their hypocrisy is so obvious. And so it's pathetic to me that anyone would stoop so low as to vote for him. I'm glad he got less than fifty percent of the vote each time, but he is a democrat so most of the media just gives him a pass. And it seems to me on political matters driven by the media most people are like sheep and usually buy what they hear on TV, and they hear 'Hey, he's making us money – we better not impeach him', which is such a shoddy principle to live by. So anyway, that's the human condition with respect to politics as I see it and it's been that way a long time."

"I see."

"And I've thought this for years, but am feeling it more now, thanks to our work together, how the entire field of politics is polarization and the illusory realm of the ego; insanity by definition. And in that sense the right's no better than the left. So while I think he's a rapist and his supporters are being shallow, they are still all my brothers and no one is perfect. I'm certainly not. And to the degree that we stay in our ego, feeling separate from God, everyone, including me is basically insane. So I'm trying to be forgiving when it comes to politics. It's like Jesus said, 'Let ye who is without sin cast the first stone'."

"Right."

"And frankly I'd rather disregard it altogether. I just want to focus on feeling my communion with God as much as possible, and not be concerned if someone else isn't. In effect, as you were saying earlier, the only sane thing to do is to feel my good and my guidance from God. It's the only way I can help myself or my fellow man, as opposed to being angry at apparent hypocrites. That just ultimately makes me one too. So finally I've arrived at this one conclusion: everyone's got their hands full with themselves. Hating Bush or Clinton is just a distraction from the only task at hand worth doing; loving yourself and everyone else through constant and continuous forgiveness."

"Yes. And also being indignant or self-righteously judgmental is really such a drain. Watch how you get angry at things just in general, at people in the news or at people around you who trigger your anger, and understand that you are projecting your own feeling of injustice at what you think is happening or has been done to you. It is your own demand for compensation and that has to be let go. You cannot fulfill yourself if what you want is justice or compensation. That's all in the realm of the ego and polarization, as you say, and how to manipulate everyone through guilt. Life is a gift and until people are feeling that fact of their existence they are going to be frightened and they are going to be manipulative and at times they are going to be vicious. That's why what we were talking about earlier is important. You want to feel your general good. You want to feel your connection with God. You want to know that you are being given to."

"Life is the gift that keeps on giving."

"Exactly."

"You know, another metaphor, though it's actually very real, comes to mind to me about that. I'm reminded of when I was a boy growing up in southern California, basically from first grade through graduate school, and I always had this feeling, though I wasn't as keenly aware of it until I moved to the northwest and lost it, that anything was possible and every day was good because the sun was always shining and it didn't matter what I did."

"Right, that's a great metaphor."

"It was actually a real feeling, and in astrology by the way the sun is often referred to as the life giver, but moreover I remember being with my friends or even by myself and just feeling 'Well, it's another good day – what do you want to do?'. In other words I felt my general good all the time and went with my desires at the moment or whatever it was I felt moved to do."

"Yes. You absorbed it and you reflected it."

"Yeah. So I'm wanting to get back to that feeling. Anyway hey, now I'm sure our time is up."

"Yes, it is."

"So thank you again and I'll talk with you later."

"Sounds good."

"Bye for now."

"Bye."

He took off the headphones and placed them in his lap. Opening his eyes he looked over at the lake eyeing the sunlight gleaming on the surface. The light breeze made it a watery carpet covered with a trillion sparkling twinkle lights. Given it was the first weekend in June there was a distant crowd of swimmers to the left by the park where the highway rolled by. He heard the clunk-clunk of an approaching paddleboat. If Leroy was right, and he believed that he was, the trick was simply conveying to Bea that his enlightenment work was starting to bear fruit. If it worked for him it could work for her. In essence they could only trust in God while taking the obvious practical steps, but without any panic. Somehow things would work out in good time, just as his practice was seemingly starting to...*seemingly... seemingly...seemingly she might say...*

Three teenage girls passed by in the blue paddleboat, soaking up the sunshine, giggling and chatting amongst themselves. Near the far shore a yellow sailboat with a bright orange sail billowing full with the south wind behind it cruised along silently. It reminded him of his own sailboat laid dormant under the deck a few yards away. The thought of resurrecting it seemed more work than it was worth...*someday maybe...*Still, the water was very appealing. On impulse he decided to go for a swim; his first since last year.

Since he was wearing trunks, which he often did as shorts, he rolled out of the hammock, leaving the tape player in it, and walked down to the dock. It was warm underfoot and creaked slightly with each step, wobbling a bit as he neared the far end. He had built it himself and felt pleased with its construction given that he knew next to nothing of such things. With no trace of hesitation he dove into the water preferring to adapt to the temperature quickly. He came up twenty feet from the dock and rolled over on his back to swim in the way he enjoyed most. Breathing deeply while stroking both arms back simultaneously in full sweeps of motion, he swam toward the center of the lake in a line straight and true, as one who had done this many times, which he had, by focusing on the top of the huge cedar by his house. Whipping his legs in the motion of a frog he looked up at the sky as he glided along. This had been his favorite position for years. His ears were submerged so as to drown out the sounds of whatever noises might be around him, but his nose and his eyes were free to breathe and see and he loved taking in the blue breadth of sky spreading wide overhead like a pastel ceiling; a heavenly dome.

The experience always felt like a wet meditation, alone and isolated in the middle of a crowd. Many times he had been the only one in the water but weekends were different with more folks around, especially in summer. Still he felt centered and cushioned by nature. It was easy to relax into the sensations of cool water and warm sun simultaneously while in motion. Scanning the canvas above him he noticed the various birds soaring in flight. A flurry of small ones raced off in the distant corner of his vision while an egret climbed slowly above him flapping its graceful wings deliberately. Higher than that a gray passenger plane bore towards the airport too high to be noticed by those on the ground. Soon as the summer wore on the big balloons would drift by, like huge colorful Christmas tree ornaments, dipping their passengers dangerously close to the water, thrilling them sometimes with a slight splashy scare. This was the season and reason he lived for.

Summer for him had truly arrived unexpectedly even if it was not unannounced. Perhaps a few TV weathermen had heralded it but he'd had little time for them or the news this year. They were not relevant to the activities that absorbed him and this most recent week was completely absorbing to the exclusion of all else. He thought of the shift in his practice or at least the promising turn of events in these last several days. Closing his eyes while continuing to swim he envisioned the scenarios, one after another, as they unfurled daily. First he had found a prospective new office nestled in a nearby new business park. Next he had managed to negotiate the rent for a smaller amount than the landlord was asking by signing a longer lease. Then he had contacted more insurance companies, other major players and payers in his line of work. Again, his colleague and friend, Will Ringer, was proven right. They were open to the possibility of adding him to their networks.

In both cases he had to justify by virtue of a letter why he should be considered, as their ranks were virtually full by now. Marianne was right that the networks were selective in whom they would allow to join their panels. But he had a strong rationale to offer them all; the only male psychotherapist in town. He had spoken to the provider representatives of each company and been advised they desired to have male and female practitioners available in each community. Marianne may have had a Ph.D. but she couldn't be a man, even if her gender preference was bi-sexual. He had decided to forego paying her rent and had not heard a word from her since their last chat.

He continued to swim smoothly through the lake, knowing he was nearing the center of it soon. His habit was typically to turn around at that point though today he felt good enough to go a bit further. A self-satisfied smile slipped over his face as he moved through the current like a fish on vacation. Feelings of gratitude mingled with hope crept into his heart and for a moment he considered singing aloud. The run of the water across his cheeks cautioned against such a move so he sang in his mind while keeping his mouth shut. It was a tune he had taught both his boys as they flew through the water in the sailboat seasons past. It used to make them laugh…*it's a sailor's life and the life for me and a sailor's life is a life that's free and i never ever ever give a damn about the weather cause the weather never ever gives a damn about me*…He chuckled inwardly and opened his eyes. Having careened off toward the park, he adjusted his course to keep going straight across the lake from his house.

A few swollen clouds had coasted in on the wings of the south wind, lingering above the lake. They seemed like a group of floating white whales, pausing to observe the water as they trailed listlessly northward. As he reached an approximate middle of the lake, he took several more strokes and then stopped swimming. It felt right to stop here. Floating, he drifted slowly closer toward the homes across from his own. While laying motionless he imagined the water as a wet metaphor for feeling supported by his general good. Lately he had been meditating more intensely, going deeper into the stillness each morning for a longer duration; at least half an hour. After a few minutes he felt a desire to move again… *guess this is how it works…*

He flipped backward underwater and emerged facing his own house on what was now the farther shore, as he stood upright while treading water. Turning around, he lay again on his back and commenced swimming towards it. It was tentative in so far as it was new, but he felt, if only faintly yet, a budding sense of optimism. Suddenly it seemed somehow appropriate to express his gratitude. He closed his eyes again and focused inward…*thank you Father…thank you Father…thank you Father… thank you…*He released the feelings upward, outward, away, wherever they were meant to be sent and received. The buoyancy of the gratefulness being expressed seemed to lighten his movements and lift his body even more easily through the water. He was heading toward home with a mission in mind. The next thing to do was to lighten if possible, through sharing his newfound fledgling optimism, the heavy-hearted matters that weighed on the mind of his luscious and lovely comforting creature, bountiful beautiful sweet baby Bea…*ahhh its good to feel some happiness again…*

Chapter 69

"In warm evenings I frequently sat in the boat playing the flute, and saw the perch, which I seemed to have charmed, hovering around me, and the moon traveling over the ribbed bottom, which was strewn with the wrecks of the forest."
(Walden, Henry David Thoreau)

RISING AND FALLING TO the continuous undulations of the effervescent ripples on the surface of the water Bea languished in the comfort of her floating rubber raft that was tethered to the dock beneath a late afternoon sun. It had been a week of changes marked by endings and beginnings not the least of which was summertime, which had caught her completely unawares. Not only had the temperature ascended rapidly as Saturday sunshine burst on the scene, but she had been so busy throughout the year, particularly this last week, consumed with harrying work concerns that she was virtually oblivious to the seasons altogether. They were defined for her by schedules not the climate anymore. Yet aside from a business that was all engrossing still the rhythms of the school year were imbedded in her psyche from her many years of teaching and the raising of her boys. It was just that they'd been relegated to a near subconscious status as the specter of an avalanche of Japanese school children loomed nearer each passing day...*thank God that jay has time to parent...else our child would flounder...*

She thought of Jay momentarily and the talk they'd had earlier in the day. He was hopeful and cautiously excited about his new prospects with counseling. It seemed to him a confirmation of all he had done with Leroy while grappling with her company and gamely keeping his practice alive. She was glad for him and shared his hopes while also feeling touched that he was concerned for her morale. His enthusiasm did affect her but her own spirits were even more buoyed by the calls she'd received today in response to her newspaper ad. She'd counted over twenty on the voice mail while he was swimming and more than half of them had also faxed her their resumes. It had been such a hard week starting with Candy suddenly quitting and especially with her giving only one week's notice. That had seemed downright hostile, almost, though her manner had been duly respectful. Replete with apologies she'd reluctantly concluded that the job was simply too time-consuming for her to manage her children and other affairs well.

Bea could have contacted temp agencies but knew they would take a hefty cut of the wage she would pay an employee. She preferred to take her chances first with hiring someone directly and so far the recent responses seemed to reaffirm that hunch. With her inner clamor ceasing, as job applicants appeared, her initial shock, anger and anxiousness gave way to a twinge of sadness and wistful questions about Candy...*why this...and why this way...what had we anyway...what's really the matter*...While the rolling waves of water bobbled by and gently rocked her raft she recalled her short conversation with Leroy this past week.

"How are you doing Bea?"

"Well, I'm not sure, as Jay has probably told you, given what has happened."

"Are you concerned about finding a replacement for Candy?"

"Well, yes, that's the first thing, though it's not the only one."

"Let me tell you right now that there is no cause for alarm."

"There isn't?" (laughter)

"No, absolutely not. Just take the steps you are moved to take and you will find the appropriate people forthcoming."

"Well, that's good to hear but part of me wants to say 'That's easy for you to say'." (laughter)

"Yes, it is. (laughter) Because I know it's true."

"I hope so."

"No worries. Just do what you need to do and trust it will work out."

"Okay. I would of course, anyway, but it's good to hear you speak with such reassurance in your voice."

"Sure. Now what else is on your mind?"

"Well, I must say I was a little devastated. I don't understand Candy's behavior. It's been a bit of a mystery to me, because we were so close and...uh...she's really shut it all down. And maybe it's because it was hard for her to leave, but...ahhh...it has been painful for me."

"Well, it was a question of not blending in enough; being obtrusive in some way as a personality and not getting the message that she couldn't continue to do that."

"Mm-hm."

"It was simply that. What was being asked for here was setting aside a little bit more ego. Just a little bit more. Not all of it. Just enough so there didn't have to be the conflicts in the office. Who needs that?"

"Yeah, and it was pretty much you could cut your way through it."

"Right, and it couldn't go on. It couldn't go on. And so, she didn't get the point that she didn't get to be right. Or she did get to be right but she had to leave in order to continue to do that."

"Uh-huh."

"So there you are."

"Hm. What about…you know… I want to say something to her about all of that but not at the expense of the friendship, so I wonder if it's possible."

"Not yet. Well, you can communicate. You can send a nice card or something like 'Thank you for your help all this time' or whatever but-"

"But not to unpeel the onion, huh?"

"No, not at this time, because she is still intent on being right and she has remorse also for the fact that her obstinacy led her to take that step. You see? So it's not entirely easy. She's angry. She feels the need to be compensated somehow for … God only knows what. You see?"

"Mm-hm."

"And that's how the ego operates. So she had to do that because she wasn't clearly willing to become connected to the work in an impersonal way and just enjoy doing it."

"Well, I don't think she really enjoyed doing it."

"Well…then bon voyage. (laughter) No problem with that."

"Okay. Well then, as I was saying, now I struggle with how to fill the hole that's here."

"Do you mean in terms of personnel?"

"Yes."

"Well, that's just part of the job of running a business. Don't mind that. Please."

"Well, (laughter) the panic is subsiding somewhat as we speak."

"Good. Good. Yeah, that always is the first thing, you know, when the boat tips a little bit or the plane hits a bump or something 'Oh no! – not now!'."

"Well, I sort of felt like my right arm was cut off but now as we talk I am feeling it's not necessarily so."

"No."

"And when Jay was typing at the computer yesterday it was totally amazing."

"Oh. He doesn't use it?"

"He doesn't want anything whatsoever to do with them."

"Oh."

"But that appears to be suddenly changing."

"I see."

"Actually he said that if Candy could do this then anybody can, but he has always avoided them until now and so I just had to take a picture of him." (laughter)

"Great." (laughter)

"So again, you're are saying to me that the right people will appear."

"Yes."

"To put my right arm back on."

"More than enough."

"Really?"

"Yes. There's an abundance of good people, who would rather work for you than work in a some big corporate hierarchy, which in of itself is very stressful."

"Mm-hm. Well, all right. I guess that's my immediate question here. Oh, also, I think I should go to Russia in the fall."

"Go to Russia in the fall."

"Yes, I have an opportunity. How about Japan? If I had to choose?"

"I'm feeling strongly that it would be much more inspiring to go to Russia."

"Me too. I've been to Japan several times and I have many friends and contacts there but I would really love to do something new."

"Do it."

"How about Spain? I seem to be getting some opportunities opening up there too?"

"That feels good. I encourage you to explore them both."

"Thank you, for everything."

"You are welcome."

"Here, I'll give you back to Jay. Oh, one more thing. How can I be a better partner to my husband at this time?"

"Just be patient."

"I'm trying." (laughter)

"And have fun."

"I'm trying." (laughter)

"And know that there is enough ease, grace, and freedom in the relationship where you can both be yourselves."

"Okay. That sounds good. Actually that sounds great. Thanks. Thanks alot."

"You're welcome."

Bea opened her eyes and blinked up at the sunlight. That had been a helpful conversation to have. She had rarely talked to Leroy at all since last year, letting it be Jay's thing, and too busy herself to even consider it. Ever since the fiasco with Perry in Toronto she had also been somewhat uncertain of his powers. Perhaps he had been right about that all along. He certainly had been clairvoyant about Vienna. Plus his recommendation to keep Perry was the same as her own instinct. And it was true that a seemingly suitable candidate had been found to replace him; someone with actual experience in the field. How this summer's Homestay programs fared in Toronto would soon tell that tale. And if it went poorly that could be good-bye to a portion of Japanese business, Toshi's anyway, and all the more reason to say hello to Russia.

Currently though Japan was looking better than ever. Her talk with Mr. Takahara had been incomparably rewarding both financially and psychologically beyond her greatest hopes. The glory of that turnaround triumph was overshadowed by the darkness of Candy's sudden departure but that cloud was lifting too. Only since the weekend as she began to feel secure with the office transitions was she starting to let herself feel the joy over Hundai. She stretched her arms leisurely out to the sides trying to keep from taking in cold water on the float as she savored the memory of their last conversation.

"Hello, Mr. Takahara. I am so glad you called."

"You give me no choice."

"Well, you do have a choice, and I hope you choose to work with me. I'm sorry it has to happen like this. It was not what I wanted. I think you know that."

"Mm. So you want I should reinstate your program."

"Well, yes. I think that you should. We have done a lot of work on your behalf, as you know. And I am sure we can give your students a very satisfactory program."

"I think Mr. Kitagawa will be very unhappy."

"I am sure that he will. But I think he will be much more unhappy if these documents are made known to the authorities."

"Mm. Yes, I see. I think that is true."

"Matter of fact I am going to contact him myself to make sure he understands."

"Mm. I see. I am not knowing what to say to school board and also parents why to change program again."

"I've thought about that."

"I think the best way to handle it is to say that Kazuo, that is Mr. Kitagawa, has decided he cannot do the program in Australia this year after all. The two of you can decide exactly what that reason might be."

"Mm. I see. Mmmm, you know, he has given me much money."

"Yes, I know. You might want to give it back. But I leave that up to you."

"Mm. Yes. So, if we, Hundai, now do your program, mmm...can I know ..."

"Can you trust me not to divulge your secret?"

"Mm. Yes"

"Yes, you can. I do not want to make trouble for you. I never wanted any trouble at all. It is not my fault that we have this problem."

"Mm."

"I don't ever want to have to use this information to make any trouble for you or him."

"Mm. What do you want?"

"I just want the chance to do a good Homestay program for your students. And if it is successful I would like to continue to do them as long as they are good and your school would like to do them with us."

"Mm. I see."

"So do we have a deal?"

"Yes. We have deal. There is no problem."

"Good. Thank you. I was hoping you would feel that way. And I really do not want any bad feelings. I am sure it was very tempting to you to be offered so much money."

"Mm."

"I know that school principals do not make nearly as much money as travel agents in Japan."

"Yes."

"So I would like to just say that a mistake was made. And now it has been corrected. And as we say in America, there are no hard feelings. Do you understand?"

"Mm. Yes. Yes, I do. We do not have that saying in Japan."

"No. I understand. And I know it very important in Japan not to lose face."

"Yes."

"And I can tell you that people in America don't like to lose face either."

"Mm."

"We have another saying in America called forgive and forget."

"Forgive and forget?"

"Yes. Do you understand?"

"Mm. Yes. I think so."

"Good. And even one more. Everyone makes mistakes. Understand?"

"Mm. Yes, I understand."

"Good. So I would like to put this behind us, and go on with a new relationship. Forgive and forget. Okay?"

"Mm. Yes. Okay. Very okay."

"Good. Thank you. Will you please contact me as soon as possible to confirm everything is set again for our original program as planned?"

"Mm. Yes. Of course."

"Thank you. Thank you ever so much. I look forward to working with you again and my company will work very hard to make your Homestay program a big success. Okay?"

"Yes. Okay."

"Okay then. Well, I will wait to hear from you. Good-bye now."

"Mm. Good-bye…and …thank you. Thank you very much. Thank you very much."

"Do itashimashite."…*hope i pronounced 'you're welcome' right…*

After she hung up with immeasurable satisfaction bordering on smugness except for her glee she faxed a copy of her letter to the principal to Kazuo. As expected she had not heard a word in reply. Her international nemesis, her perfidious foe, the naughty ninja lord of dark hearts, was apparently at a loss for words or possibly, just perhaps, busily consulting his Oxford. Even Toshi too had been easier to deal with as of late. Apparently his exchange with Jay had given him food for thought. Amazing how easy it was to get along with Japanese businessmen once you understood the delicate art of approaching them.

Her water raft wobbled as a small skiff slowly skimmed by, scouring the waters for any big bass lurking beneath the dock. It was powered by a shiny metal muffled electric motor. It held a father and his young son gripping a fishing pole with grim expectation on his angelic face. She waved and smiled as they puttered past her. A slew of ducks, maybe a dozen, slid by the other way, stoic yet stylish like soldiers on parade. The arc of the sun angled down towards the treetops hovering over the horizon as it made its way westward. She heard the commonplace clunk-clunk of a paddleboat just like her own approaching from behind her and turned to take a look. There were three girls sporting sunburns chugging along merrily. Two of them were very fair-skinned and they looked to be sisters…*they must have been out on the water all day…*

She instantly felt the connection to the other pressing matter on her mind. Her sister, crazy sister, beloved sister, capricious sister, sometimes cruel, sometimes kind, but often fun and the only one she'd ever see again, was coming to town and with her boy friend in tow. In the hectic wake of losing Candy she had given it little thought. But armed with Leroy's firm assurances and moreover the strong ad response, not to mention Jay's apparent turn in fortune and her own luck in Japan, she was feeling up to planning an itinerary fit for a queen; which was fortunate as she would soon have one in her home. There was enough time to interview, hire and train new personnel, maybe even more than one, to make sure that everything was well in hand for summer. If she planned ahead now for both work and play the pending week and weekend could possibly be wonderful. Without perfect planning they could easily be a pain.

Emitting a gentle sigh, more relaxed than tired, she tugged on the rope that tied her raft to the dock. On reaching it she swiveled gracefully around to stand in the shallow water and stepped up on the creaking cedar planks of the little pier. After tucking the float under the deck by the willow trees she walked unhurriedly up the grassy hillside, feeling the pleasure of a cool breeze brushing by her wet legs. With each advancing step up the zigzag path she felt the familiar heaviness of her wearisome workload descending on her shoulders. But her ears perked in wonder to the felicitous sound of a flute song faintly filtering down from her dwelling…*hasn't played that since last year…*and the lilting notes lent a light lift to her spirits and slipped a slight spring into her supple step.

Chapter 70

"I was never molested by any person but those who represented the state."
(Walden, Henry David Thoreau)

THE MERCEDES CIRCLED STEADILY up the hillside behind the cars of students and other parents driving their children to school. The warm air from the weekend had wrought a perceptible shift in the foliage of the woodsy areas through which the way wound upward. Spring flowers had given ground to summer ones, surrendering in the sun-drenched heat of the past few days. Tired tulips and faded daffodils were replaced on the roadside by lobelias of red, white and blue and the sapphire spires of stately delphiniums were rising triumphantly as roses erupted in every hue of the rainbow. Early morning rays had dried the dew on the unshaded sections of the gardens and yards that they had motored by. Slowing down as they approached the parking lot Jay cast a look at his youngest son bobbing deftly to the sounds from the stereo.

"Well, a few more days and you're out for the summer. Bet that feels good."

"I hadn't really thought about it much," replied Phil, while surveying the scene of students.

"Really?' said Jay, with some surprise. "Boy, when I was a kid summer was the best thing about school except for PE and recess. Not to mention girls. Think much about them?"

"Let me think about that and get back with you, dad," smirked Phil, as he picked up his backpack from the floor. A pencil case fell out of an unzipped side pocket and lodged in between the seat and the console. He dug his hand in to retrieve it. "It's stuck."

"How about trying it from the around the backside? I bet that'll work."

Phil slipped out the front door, opened the back one and peered under the passenger seat.

"There's an empty beer bottle under here? Jeez, do you drink and drive?"

"Oh no…*damn*… not usually anyway. That was a special situation, really. I can explain." Phil wedged his fingers further into the crevice then pulled out the pencil box and the bottle too.

"Not now, dad. I gotta' run. Man, I sure hope not. It would sure be a special situation if you ran into somebody."

"Here, let me have it. It's not what you think." Phil handed him the empty Corona container, put his pencils in his pack and eased back out of the auto.

"Okay, dad. I'll talk with you later. See you tonight." He slammed the door shut without waiting for an answer and disappeared into the motley pack of pupils.

Jay tossed the beer bottle onto the passenger side of the front seat floor and eased the vehicle out of the parking lot wheeling his way on to work…*that was not good*…He pondered how he would explain to Phil that this was an exception but not one that he should ever make.

He turned off the pulsating ghetto blast gratefully and opened his glove compartment to find a tape. The ones in the car were mostly a month or two old. Though the circumstances of his life were changing gradually for the better the recorded information was still helpful to hear, especially since he did not consider himself as of yet even semi-enlightened. He pushed in the tape and pressed the on button.

"Hello Jay. What's up?"

"Well, it's pretty much more of the same still, but I have the tapes and I listen to them a lot, and they are basically uplifting. Though I haven't seen much change in my life yet, they do make me feel better."

"Well, that is the main thing."

"Yeah, I understand. Anyhow, lately I find myself wondering about death. You know we've seen some people die recently, Perry, and Bea's sister, and I just wonder what you might say in general as to the nature of life and death."

"Well, I can say, and this will relate to you personally, that every creature on the planet is experiencing ego while having the opportunity to evolve to the clarity of their divinity. That is, everyone has the sense of themselves as one thing and everyone else out there as something else or other. So people have the opportunity to evolve out of that dichotomy."

"You mean go from feeling separate from everyone to feeling our unity?"

"Exactly."

"Hm. Well, maybe I'll get a better grasp on that after I pass on. Or maybe not."

"Well, maybe you won't pass on. Maybe that will be how you get your grasp on it."

"Okay, yeah, well…"

"You see, even that cycle of birth and death is stopping. The wheel is going to stop."

"Really?"

"Yes."

"What's God's going to do then?"

"Then everybody would be awake. It is unnecessary to experience that cycle and the only way you can experience it is by being unconscious. By virtue of becoming fully conscious you are experiencing eternity rather than the passage of time. Now there is still movement. Life is always being created anew but it doesn't require this grievous experience of birth and death because there is no corruption anymore. There is no dissipation of life that leads to what you call death. And then of course in between incarnations there is the opportunity for some renewal where an individual has a clearer sense that there is no death. And then they go back into the world because there is some compelling interest in that and so they find themselves in the world and once again entering it quite unconsciously, and having to go through the same thing, hoping that maybe they will start to remember enough that they will have the wonderful and splendid experience of waking up right where they are while incarnated, which is what Jesus did, which is what Buddha did. You see? There are others who have approached that but none to the full extent besides those two."

"Hmmmm. Do you think of yourself as Leroy going to die?"

"Oh never."

"But in this lifetime with the physical body you are in."

"Never."

"Well don't you think that people who see you now think you look older than you did ten years ago?"

"Maybe. Maybe not. Probably not."

"Well why don't you look the same then as when you were one or two or three?"

"Because of the fact that I have been on the wheel. But also I have been turning in towards the center. There is some evidence of rotation on the wheel of life but also I am not staying on the circumference, but spiraling in to the center. And at the point of being in the center then all of those phases that are experienced sequentially on the circumference are experienced right at once because they all radiate from the center. All of those segments for example between noon and three or six and nine on the clock are experienced on the perimeter sequentially, but they all radiate from the center of the wheel and as you spiral in off the circumference you come to that point where you are accessing all of whom you are simultaneously rather than in sequence."

"Hmmm."

"You see, as soon as your experience of independence, of being a personal consciousness, is gone, then you can't die."

"Got it. But it seems like, even if that is true, I mean Jesus was awake but he didn't look like a twelve year old when he died at thirty. He looked like his body had been aging."

"Right, but he looked like he was mature and young both. But the childlike or young quality was more expressed in a sense of freedom and unselfconsciousness, not in a sense of being immature physically."

"Timeless innocence."

"Right, but with a sense of maturity."

"Interesting."

"What you would call ageless."

"Well, I think I will only grasp this by intuiting it, living it, feeling it because the concepts don't seem to contain it very well; what you are trying to convey to me."

"Well, what would happen if you had no idea that you ever were going to die? What if you felt so renewed in each moment that you were not going to die?"

"Well, that would be interesting."

"That's the point. The reason there is the experience of death is because there is a denial, an on-going denial, of the experience of regeneration. The real issue here is that if you can feel yourself being renewed in each moment or even intellectually acknowledge that as a possibility you will begin to feel more and more open to the idea of experiencing your awakening, your perfection, right here and now. This is happening to the planet. The planet is going to have to give up its addiction to the perception that there is birth and death going on."

"When?"

"As soon as it will. The earliest we are looking at it happening will be over the next several decades. And this is why I say to you that you are a pioneer."

"Hm. Well, it all makes sense to me somewhat more intellectually, but better than that, if I really try to identify for a second now with what you are saying, I feel it right here in the moment. It's something like I recognize that I am awakening to the fact that I will always be awake."

"Yes, and the absence of grief in your life, the absence of any experience of displeasure, you see, is going to constitute the moment of truth for you, because grief is that wall between your heart, what's in your heart, and what's out there. The discrepancy between what's out there and what's in your heart seems to be justification for grieving or feeling aggrieved. You see? People grieve because they are not having what they desire and the fact of it is that it is really the wall of grief itself that is the block. In other words, do away with the grief and there will be an alignment between what's in your heart and what is out there automatically. That's what God wills."

"Hm. It reminds me of something you said once about people feeling unconnected but if I would allow myself to simply feel connected all the time then I wouldn't feel lonely, etc, and that really hit home. I have been able to play with it, to do it, in those rare times I've remembered to, when I am in a situation where I feel disconnected from the people around me, and I just think 'No, I'm not – it's just in my mind' and I shift automatically to feeling connected to everyone."

"Right. It is very simple. And what you want to do is to spend some time, perhaps a couple of times a day for twenty minutes, improving your reception."

"Hm. I see. So I guess that constitutes another step in this process."

*…another step…another step…*Jay stopped the tape as he pulled into the parking lot of his new office. He gazed at the two-story building, gray with white trim, in an office park setting with trees and shrubs around. It was more secluded than his other place had been on the main drag. This location was merely a few blocks from that one but the city was small enough that all roads off the major one were essentially side streets. He delighted in the windows overlooking the valley though the angle was such, more westward rather than south, that he could no longer see Mt. Rainier in the distance. It would however give him a pleasurable view of the sunset; an aesthetically much to be desired experience. He scampered up the indoor stairs to the second level and let himself in the office. Turning on the lamps and the fountain for just the right effect he sat at his desk and thumbed through his appointment book…*mmm…howie…country boy… seattle girl…and one new one…looks interesting…*A few minutes later as the clock ticked to the top of the hour he walked down the hallway to meet Howie in the lobby.

It was unexpectedly empty and he wondered if perhaps his client was having trouble finding the new office. He stood there for a moment in the stillness of the room when he heard his telephone ringing from his office up the way. Whisking through the hall he picked it up briskly.

"Forestville Counseling, Jay speaking."

"Jay, its Howie." He sounded frightened.

"Yes, Howie are you lost?"

"Worse than that. Sharon's lost her mind."

"What? What do you mean?"

"She's barricaded herself in the bathroom of our house and won't come out."

"Oh no. How did you find this out? We're you there?"

"I was coming out this morning to see you from my friend's house in Seattle and my neighbor called me on my cell phone and said she heard her screaming. She went into the house and found her locked inside the bathroom. Sharon yelled for her to leave and said she wanted to be alone."

"Maybe she should be for awhile."

"It's worse than that. She has a hammer or something and is banging the walls, breaking things like the mirror and making a horrible commotion. She told the neighbor she didn't want to talk to anyone and was going to tear the house apart. What should I do?"

"Call 911 and explain what's happening. Say you've talked with me and I say she needs to be taken to Harborview hospital. They'll probably sedate her and lock her up for observation and eventually treatment. I'll call Harborview right after we hang up."

"Should I call the cops?"

"Yeah, they should probably be there in case she's violent with the paramedics but really I want to see that she gets help instead of just being hauled off to jail."

"What about the kids?"

"Where are they now?"

"They're still in school till this afternoon."

"Well, probably they will hold Sharon in the psych ward for awhile, possibly weeks. Can you pick them up this afternoon and move back into the house with them for now?"

"Yeah, I can do that. I guess it's the best thing. But what about Sharon?"

"What she's doing is a cry for help, just like a suicide, and that's what we're getting her."

"You think they can help her there?"

"We'll have to see what happens, but getting her to a treatment center is the best thing for now. It's better than jail."

"Okay. Should I call them now?"

"Absolutely and then call me back."

"Alright. Thanks."

Jay hung up the phone and called the hospital admissions. They were willing to receive her on the basis of his referral and faxed him some documents regarding her background. Howie called back shortly after to report he'd called 911 and the police.

"Where are you now, Howie?"

"I'm outside my house waiting for the cops and paramedics to arrive."

"Can you hear Sharon inside?"

"Oh yeah. She's howling like a banshee and banging on the walls and door."

"Did you try to talk with her?"

"No way! She is nuts. She'd probably kill me. Believe me."

"I know you said she has a temper."

"This is way past any temper blow up she's ever had. And she's had some doozies."

"I see."

"I think she's lost it. She's whacked. A meltdown. She has crossed the line."

"Alright. Well, I'm sorry. I had hoped it wouldn't come to this."

"You and me both. And I feel like such a schmuck. It's all my fault."

"Not really. I know you feel guilty about your secret and your actions but not everyone goes quite this crazy in situations like this."

"Yeah, well, Sharon sure is."

"I know, and all we can do is let her have her explosion, try to keep her from hurting herself or anyone else, and get her some serious help as soon as possible. And we're doing that. We're doing all we can at the moment."

"I just feel so bad. What should I tell the kids?"

"Just tell them mommy got really upset because you've been arguing, and because you left, but that you are back now and you will be with them till mommy comes back from the hospital and then you and mommy will work everything out. Tell them the people at the hospital are going to help mommy feel better."

"That sounds good. What about the bathroom? I'm sure it's in shambles."

"Just close that door and have everyone use the other one. Get someone in there tomorrow or as soon as you can and have it repaired. Just try to keep everything matter-of-fact and simple now."

"It doesn't feel so simple."

"I know. That's why you want to try to make it that way; for the sake of the kids and for the sake of your own sanity. Call me later when the dust clears a bit."

"I will. Bye. And thanks."

"Sure. Bye-bye."

Jay sat down in his desk chair and leaned as far back as it would go...*holy shit... sometimes they snap*...He felt a certain sadness, almost a nausea, creeping in...*life can be such a lonely business*...Suddenly he felt an impulse to open up and ask for guidance...*Father help me help these people... help me help anyway i can*...He sat in silence for the rest of the hour and then went to retrieve his next client.

It was the young man, Ray, from the poorer section of the countryside. His mother had accompanied him to the office this time. She was a large woman in contrast to her son's slender physique and her stern countenance bore the look of a tired but persistent matron. Jay half-expected her to march the boy down the hallway by his ear. They settled in the soft chairs and began to talk.

"I'm Raymond's mother, Mrs. Karl."

"Pleased to meet you. Hello, Ray. I'm glad your mother was able to join us."

"I'm not."

"You shush," hissed Mrs. Karl as she grimly smiled and reached over to shake Jay's hand. "Pleased to meet you, sir."

"Just call me Jay, thanks, please, and tell me, what's on your mind ma'am with respect to Ray?"

"Well, I don't know what he's told you but he's in a pack of trouble."

"Am not," protested Ray.

"Boy, don't you back-sass me." Mrs. Karl glared at her progeny with a vengeance. "If you weren't we wouldn't be here. Now you let me do the talking."

Ray pursed his lips to pout in disagreement while lowering his head in acquiesance. "Aw ma."

"Well, since you are concerned I'm glad you've joined us," offered Jay politely. "Now please, tell me what's on your mind."

"Well," she began with a slight drawl, "I don't know if he told you but Raymond here has a girl friend."

"Yes, he mentioned that."

"And she is a cute little thing, but she's only sixteen years old." She stared at Jay meaningfully to make sure he was grasping the full import of this fact. "And he's eighteen."

"Yes, I understand there is a two year age difference."

"*And...*" she paused for effect, "her father caught them in the hayloft of his barn last weekend with their clothes off!"

"I had my socks and shirt on!" objected Ray.

"I see," said Jay.

"*And...*her father called the police, while he kept Raymond in the barn."

"Wouldn't gimme my pants back or I woulda' run off," Ray intoned in his behalf.

"*And...* the girl's father said he wanted to press charges and the policeman said it was statutory rape."

"Like I raped a statue or somethin'," Ray smirked.

"Boy, be quiet," shushed his mother. "This is not a laughing matter. You may be goin' to jail!"

"Is that what the policeman said?" Jay inquired.

"Yes, he did. Took him to the station and I had to make his bail. Now we got to go to court."

"Oh boy," sighed Jay.

"Now, I want to know," said the mother as she leaned forward toward Jay, "can you help us? Can you help my boy?"

Jay took his glasses off and leaned back in his chair. "Maybe," he nodded, rubbing his hands. "It depends on what Ray does in counseling with me and it depends on what the judge thinks of him and the whole situation."

"What do you mean?" asked Mrs. Karl.

"Well, if I think that Raymond wants to participate in counseling sincerely, with an eye towards bettering himself and his life circumstances – getting a job, getting an education, no more sexual relations with this girl, no more fights at parties, and no more drugs and alcohol – I can write him a strong letter of support to give the court."

"Do you think that would help?"

"It often seems to."

"I see."

"But moreover, aside from whatever happens in court, because that will pass in time, he could make some significant positive changes in his life that could be long-lasting and put him on a better path permanently than he seems to be on at present."

"Well, that would be nice." She turned to her son with an imperious stare. "Wouldn't it Raymond?"

"Yeah," he muttered weakly. "Guess it would."

"Look," declared Jay, "just for the record, for the sake of perspective, I just want to note that two years is not a great age difference between two sweethearts, though legally you're right – he's in trouble. For what it's worth, ma'am, though, the truth is that your son's behavior is no worse than the president of the United States."

"I want him to be better than that, for God's sake!" she exclaimed in outrage. "That varmint's just a lowlife and everybody knows it."

Jay smiled graciously in agreement. "True," he added deferentially. "Sorry to draw the comparison. I didn't mean to imply your son was a lowlife, just that certain moral standards vary in the public eye sometime. Hopefully Raymond will get a judge who views him leniently."

"I sure hope so," said Mrs. Karl wistfully. "Life's been hard enough for us as it is already."

"I don't doubt that," Jay concurred, as he looked over at Ray. "Raymond," he spoke with a gentle tone of firm authority. "Would you be willing to come here weekly for awhile and see if I can help you make some changes in your life?"

"Well," Ray hesitated. "I guess so. What choice do I have?"

"You can choose whatever you want, as far as I'm concerned," stated Jay. "But I think that's your best choice and I'd like to see you realize that too."

"Raymond," said his mother bluntly, "do you want to end up like your father?"

"He weren't so bad," said Ray in dissent.

"He was a drunk, in and out of jail, who couldn't never hold down a job for month. And it was the booze and the cigarettes that killed him, when you was just a young boy." She got tearful, paused a few seconds and reached her hand over to his knee. "I want you to have a better life than that, son."

Ray saw her hand, looked at the rug, and then turned his gaze to his mother.

"Alright," he said quietly, but decisively. "I'll do it. I'll give it a shot."

Jay saw them off with a commitment to meet regularly starting next week and glanced at his watch...*maybe take an early lunch...wonder how sharon and howie are doing*...He looked through the window of his new office at the view below. The vista swept across the valley that held the town and rolled up the hillsides on the western perimeter. Behind the sloping hills rose more rugged crests higher in the distance with evergreens like sharp furry thorns against the clear blue sky. A white sedan, nondescript but clean and polished, pulled into the parking lot beneath him and stopped behind his Mercedes momentarily. Then it swung into the stall next to his vehicle. A short ruddy-faced man got out of the car, wearing a rumpled inexpensive suit. He strode warily over to the window of the driver's side of Jay's Mercedes and peered into the car. His curiosity aroused, Jay walked down to the parking lot, as the man appeared to be trying to read the registration information on the visor above the steering wheel.

"May I help you?" ventured Jay. "Are you a Mercedes aficionado?"

The man smiled and shook his head. "Not really," he said curtly. "Just curious. Are you Jay?"

"Yes. Were you looking for me?"

"Yes," he said solemnly. "I'm Detective Clark."

"Oh," said Jay, extending his hand as he recoiled inwardly. "Nice to meet you."...*crap*... The grip was firm. "I was wondering when we might meet."

"Yes," said the detective. "I was wondering that myself."

Jay thought about inviting him into his office then thought better of it.

"What can I do for you?" he asked in a tone intended to sound more helpful than he felt.

"Well, it's about your client, Mr. Thomas."

"Oh, yes, of course, Barry. I was wondering when I would get those release papers from you."

"I see, mmhm, so you didn't receive anything in the mail?"

"Why no, did you send something?"

"Yes, I did," stated Detective Clark flatly as he searched Jay's face for clues. "Sometime ago."

"No kidding. Wow. I never received it. Did you send it to my old address?"...*as if you would have known my new one*...

"Yes, of course, I did. We were unaware that you had moved."

"Oh right, of course. How could you have known? How'd you find out?"

"Some folks at your old building told me. I was just there. I assume you're having your mail forwarded?"

"Of course, absolutely. But I'm not sure I'm getting it all. There seems to have been some problem with the Post Office getting it all to me."

"I see. Did you move recently?" inquired the detective, seemingly curious on this point.

"Oh yes," Jay assured him with a friendly smile. "Only a week or so ago."

"Hmm," said the detective, looking down as he spoke. He looked up quickly as though having reached a sudden conclusion. "I sent it several weeks back."

"Really?" said Jay compassionately. "Hmm. That's amazing. Funny anyway. Was it a big document? Sometimes the Post Office has kept mail for a while that they couldn't fit into my mailbox."

"Yes, it was in a larger sized envelope."

"Hm..." said Jay, seeming puzzled. "I don't know what to tell you. That could have prevented them from putting it in my box. Anyway, as much as I'd like to help, I really can't say anything about a client without a signed release from them."

"I know," nodded Detective Clark sympathetically with a slight smile. "That's why," he said, while lifting an folded envelope from his suit coat inner pocket, "I brought a copy of it with me." He pulled the document from the envelope, handed it to Jay and watched him inspect it. "I hope that satisfies your requirement," he added softly.

"Indeed it does, I do believe. This is great….*damn*…How can I help you?"

"Do you mind if we step into your office for a few minutes?"

"Actually I was just leaving for a luncheon meeting….*with taco bell*…Would you like to come back at another time? Or can we talk briefly here now?"

Detective Clark stared at him coldly, flinty steel gray in his eyes. He waited for a moment, holding the gaze steadily, then sighed inaudibly and shrugged in nonchalance.

"Sure."

"Please ask whatever you wish, sir.".…*here goes*…

"Did you know Mr. Thomas was using marijuana?"

"I don't believe he mentioned that, no."

"You don't believe?" Detective Clark sounded somewhat incredulous.

"I don't recall him ever mentioning it. He came to see me about marriage counseling you see, not drug use."

"I see."

"Did you know that he was growing marijuana in his garage?"

"Oh my, no."

"And did you happen to know that he was selling marijuana?"

"Oh, my goodness, no. Barry? Are you sure?"

"Yes sir, we are quite sure. One of his customers informed on him."

"I see."

"That gentleman's name was in his little black book, along with a number of other individuals, on a certain page with phone numbers.

"I see."

"Your name was on that page."

"Really?…*oh shit …what's barry told them?*…I wonder why?"

"So do we."

"Well, of course. I mean, that's your job. What did Barry say about the names on that list?"

"I'm not at liberty to disclose that at this time."

"I see…*aha …maybe nothing… maybe you're just fishing*…Well," Jay offered in what he hoped was a very reasonable tone, "perhaps those names were just friends or people that were somehow personally important to him."

"Like his therapist?"

"Yes, or his marriage counselor," said Jay with a smile. "You never know."

"No, we don't." Detective Clark's eyes narrowed as he grunted dismissively. "At least not yet anyway." He turned to go.

"Well, good luck," sallied Jay cheerfully. "Sorry I can't be of greater help to you.".…*heh heh heh*…

"That's okay," said the detective over his shoulder as he stepped away. "You may be hearing from me again." He paused again at the window of the Mercedes and looked inside, then tuned again to Jay. "Nice old car."

"Thanks."

"What year is it?"

"Seventy-six."

"Wow. That's nearly twenty years.'

"Yeah."

"And in such immaculate condition."

"Thanks."

"Is that your Corona beer bottle in there?"

Jay felt the nervousness he'd held down during their talk suddenly break full bore into his chest and neck. His mind wheeled rapidly, groping for an explanation.

"What? Oh that," he said lamely. "The bottle, yeah, the beer bottle. I picked it up this morning. Someone left it in the parking lot here overnight."

"Mmhm," murmured the detective, as he turned again to leave. "You take care," he said ominously, without looking back. He shot Jay a level glance as he slipped into his car and eased silently out of the parking lot into the street. Jay waved good-bye and waited, watching till he left then trotted back up the stairs to his office. Sitting down in the chair he stared out at the skyline feeling a residue of tingling anxiety mixed with a tentative rush of relief...*whew*...

He felt like doing something to steady his nerves and had lost his appetite for an early lunch. Picking up the car keys off of his desk he remembered the unfinished tape from Leroy he had been listening to on the way to work. At the moment it might be nice just to go for a drive. He backed the car out of its space and pushed in the tape as he headed for the soothing landscape of the Ste. Danielle Winery's grounds nearby. He headed for his favorite haunt in the corner of the dirt lot by the small creek. Its comforting sounds would give a background of solace to the wisdom of Leroy as he listened to their talk. As he drove down the road he rewound the tape a few sentences back to recall where they had left off in the morning.

"Right. It is very simple. And what you want to do is to spend some time, perhaps a couple of times a day for twenty minutes, improving your reception."

"Hm. I see. So I guess that constitutes another step in this process."

"Right. You see, it's like right now you are able to receive but you are also living in a world where, and some of it is because of your own consciousness, you have distractions or static, where you can't receive. Imagine if you were walking around with a transistor radio and in order to get the station you had to hold it a certain way. You've had that experience, I'm sure."

"Sure, as a kid."

"Right, and that is what reception is. And what you want is to go to where there is reception, and that feels like a sense of ease and relief in the heart. Because in the moment you get that you will find that something is being transmitted as well, and that transmission and that reception can carry anything. It allows you the experience of immediate manifestation. And the reason is that at that point of acceptance, that point of acknowledgement, that point of receptivity you are not requiring any justification for anything happening. When you are less receptive you can't have your good without justification, i.e., without a reason, without a cause, without a means, etc. The only time that you can have the miracle of it, which is with immediate fulfillment and without an intervening medium, is when you are absolutely receptive. So you come to that point and you want to practice reception. Now you don't know at each moment what that impulse of reception or transmission is about but it feels good. It always feels like love, you see. And so the more that these pulsations of love are transmitted and received, the more you are keeping that frequency, that channel, open, which is the channel of the miracle."

"Got it."

"And it feels better for one thing, so there is very little justification to do it. And if there is something beyond, which is the promise of God, 'Seek ye first the kingdom', then you'll have even that much more to be celebrating."

"Hm. Ah, I think a few months back I shared with you that I had a wonderful meditation one morning. It just pulled me in to a deep feeling and later it actually felt like pure sweetness for a while. And you said I was getting a taste of what it will be like, and so the last couple of days when I wake up early in the morning, I go out and sit in a chair and look at the lake. Then I meditate for a bit. I even gave up coffee. I'm drinking decaf herb tea. But I meditate first and although I've been casual about it, it feels like a step."

"That's the right approach. There's nothing to do about anything except to be in that place of clear reception where there is really no grief. And what happens is that you will find more and more that you are able to slough off the suggestion to be grievous that the world will still offer you; someone, for example, will take your parking place. Whenever there seems to be cause for grief, you might just have a little moment and be able to see yourself feeling aggrieved and just know 'Oh God, I am not going to do this again'. You see?"

"Yes."

"You find that little shift there and you are able to become receptive once again. And that is very nurturing."

"It's a good word; reception. It reminds me of peace."

"It's a little more than that. You have to get to the peace part first, because that is a point at which you are still more actively fighting the ego, where it has more sway. But it doesn't have as much sway anymore. I mean, you are pretty disillusioned with ego, and now you need something more than just being disillususioned with ego and being somewhat placid.

You need to have some experience of being nurtured at that point. Otherwise it is just poverty, with which you are coping well. Poverty is really just the out picturing of grief."

"Hm."

"There is no poverty unless there is grief. Poverty is not really a real state of affairs, a real state of being."

"It's just a manifestation of holding a grievance?"

"Yes, exactly."

"Yeah, I understand what you are saying but most people wouldn't get it. That's why it is so useless, counter-productive actually, for all these well-meaning left-wingers to be running around screaming tax the rich and making war on poverty. They just keep it going."

"It's a manifestation of pain, the pain of holding a judgment. The pain always insinuates that compensation is called for. And if you never had the idea that compensation was called for you could not conceive of something called poverty."

"You'd be balanced."

"Exactly. You would be balanced. And you see, what keeps you out of balance is that wall of grief, because in a natural world, what is in your heart, the desires of your heart, would resonate through creation. The will of God is felt as your heart's desire and as you have the clear reception of it, it becomes manifest. What happens instead is that wall of grief says in effect that you cannot have it because, and then because has to be worked out. And that is what the ego does. It insists on creation, manifestation, your fulfillment, being done on its terms."

"Hm."

"And so here you are. You're still not awake but you are getting there and you have the opportunity to experience miracles. You have the opportunity to have at least one channel open. You might have to be very still. You might have to take the time to hold the radio in the right way to receive, but that is a hell of a lot better than not knowing that you have that reception. When you are awake you will not have to do that because you will not have to be vigilant around your receptivity. But right now you do. You need to find a way to aim the antenna so that you can receive."

"Got it."

"Now, the thing about it is, you are moving to a point, to continue with this metaphor, where your reception is becoming digital rather than analog. In other words, when you receive, when you've got that impulse, when you feel it and your heart is moved, that's it. It's not as partial. It is not a near hit. It is the full experience of it."

"I'm not sure how that applies to digital and analog."

"Well, digital is that it is either one or zero. You can't have a partial digital transmission. With analog you can. You can tune it, you see. And you can get a little bit less clear of a signal. Maybe that's the best you can do. But what you are getting right now, these transmissions of love that occur when you are being clearly receptive, are digital. They are full. They don't have to be better than they are. They are the full expression of love and you are fully able to receive it."

"Hm."

"And what I am saying is that there is enough receptivity in you right now to be able to receive anything. Now the problem is that you don't want to get too caught up in having objectives here. You will know what you desire, quite casually and off-handedly, and what you are going to be more needful of paying attention to is the receptivity. The problem has never been not knowing what you desire. The problem has always been a lack of receptivity because of the wall of grief and the judgment or the ego's need to have a rationale for the desire to be fulfilled. So what you want to do here is to practice the receptivity, and just feel good, and believe that nothing is denied you. And that will provide the channel for all of your good happening just because it is supposed to happen."

"Hm."

"So I am going to recommend that you do that a couple of times a day and more if you have the inclination to do so. It is more important that you be in that place than focusing on your desires per se at this time. As you feel that love is being transmitted it will be greatly relieving. You will more and more have a sense of great relief."

"Alright, I'll try it, at least during the day. At night I still like my beer, wine, etc., but as I said earlier this seems like another step in the enlightenment process. I mean it seems like I've made some progress in understanding and doing what we've been talking about, but it has been in little steps or increments."

"Right. Well, you can only tolerate so much light at once and so the increment is always based on your ability to tolerate light. You see, the point is that you are desiring to become conscious, not to be rendered dumbfounded and stunned by an increased experience of light, so it has to go at the rate you can tolerate. Now what happens is that the absence of grief is going to bring this to fruition, because the only thing that causes you to resist light is grief; that reservoir of pain in your heart that goes back to the first moment of separation from God, in your mind, and basically has been used by the ego to maintain its existence. If it didn't have the emotion of grief, it wouldn't be able to create all the craziness and keep itself going."

"It's like grief and grievance having the same root that forgiveness is meant to undo."

"Yes, it is like two sides of the same coin, depending on whether you are the one complaining or regretting at that moment. But both, complaint or regret, have the common assertion that harm has been done; that the integrity of life has been violated."

"Hm. Well, I have to say this feels good to me as we talk about it."

"Yes, and you will feel a sense of expansion in your chest and in your heart. You will notice that you can walk down the street and find yourself repeatedly experiencing this feeling moment by moment. There will be an expansion and then perhaps a little withdrawal and then another expansion again as you are willing to do it, and that it is great fun, great practice."

"So in effect I'm increasing my tolerance to light until that's all there is."

"Right, and that is all there is anyway."

"That seems almost too abstract to contemplate, but it helps me understand how it was that Jesus walked on water."

"Exactly."

"I think our time is almost up for this session."

"Yes, it is, almost. Have you anything else to ask?"

"No, frankly, that is plenty for me to ponder. Thank you.'

"You're welcome."

"I'll just call you as I see fit."

"That's fine."

"And send you some money when I can."

"That's fine too." (laughter)

"Bye for now."

"Bye."

As the tape subsided the hoary chorus of the creek waters rushing by the open window on the passenger side served to lull Jay into an afternoon reverie. He practiced momentarily the exercise from the tape, feeling expansiveness in his chest, imagining them to be transmissions of love. Yet even in the midst of these few moments of enchantment, in this idyllic place, his mind wandered back to the events of morning...*detective clark... raymond...howie...sharon...phil...the beer bottle*...Realizing this process was what Leroy called withdrawal he tried once again to prolong the expansion in his heart. He felt the tussle back and forth of head and heart, head and heart, until the pull of thinking asserted its supremacy. Gliding away from the grounds of the winery his curiosity mounted as he neared his office, wondering what news Howie might have to share.

Chapter 71

"I have met with women whom I really think would like to be married to a Poem and given away by a Novel." (John Keats, in a letter)

THROUGH THE RISING STEAM from the hot cup of coffee couched in her lap as she sat outside on the upper deck, Bea intently observed the daybreak activity of the lakeside life forms slowly stirring into conscious commotion, under the wakeful and watchful eye of a June sun's lazy ascent. Creatures of water and air commingled in the welcoming warmth of another summer day. Approaching mists from the left and the right like advancing armies over the water met in the thickening middle and rose in encircling ethers to a steamy nothingness like the condensation of the coffee vapors as though the lake were a large slab of dry ice. A gaggle of geese were primping and pruning themselves on the neighbor's wide dock while a pair of brown ducks coasted cautiously by then accelerated their paddling to the lily pads clustered on the shore in search of a mud-splattered breakfast. Two swallowtail butterflies flickered about briskly, wavering and weaving in and out of the willows, flashing their yellow and black-trimmed wings in nervous delight like a duo of daisies dancing in the wind. She sipped the warm liquid and sighed with a mixture of contentment and concern as the blue sky leisurely brightened above.

It had been a wild week of anticipated ups and unexpected downs culminating in the day, this very afternoon, when Faye would arrive. Bea had been engrossed in hiring and training a new secretary as well as creating an itinerary for her sister, along with the normal bustle of her busy work schedule. Miraculously all of it seemed to be going well. The new secretary, Bernadette, was a wife and mother whose children had recently graduated from college while her husband was a successful insurance salesman. She brought none of the pressures from home that Candy had felt as a struggling single parent and prima donna diva, plus had worked part-time in other small offices and had the appropriate computer savvy required for the job. Her personality seemed harmoniously balanced and pleasant especially in comparison to her problematic predecessor. Bea had liked her from the outset of the interview and was impressed with her ability to absorb knowledge quickly and professional manner in responding to callers. It had given her pause to reconsider what exactly it was she had liked about Candy, but she had neither time nor much inclination to dote at present on the past.

With Bernadette learning the ropes so readily Bea had more opportunity to develop a tour of the area's scenic sites for her worldly-wise and well-traveled sister. She had covered the pastoral countryside's most spectacular site with a six-course breakfast reservation on Sunday in the stunning lodge at Snoqualmie Falls. She'd reserved a table by the window overlooking the cascading water in a posh private booth with a vast lookout spanning for miles toward Seattle across a rugged range of rumpled green mountains. Its majestic view was rivaled only in contrast by the sights of the city from atop the restaurant crowning the Space Needle, an architectural wonder spawned by the World's Fair of 1962. It spun in a circle in unhurried grace offering its occupants a panoramic vista of landscape and seascape as they munched contentedly on over-priced fare. The city itself contained other sites to see and since Faye was renting a car she would just need directions when Bea had to work. Simply being at the lake was a joy in its own right and Faye had always been especially partial to Jay's fine wine and culinary concoctions. Starting next week there would be concerts in the evening at the park across the water, which were easily heard from the deck down by the willows. Failing that, Bea and Jay were quite capable of making music themselves and the way things had been going lately they might even feel merry enough to do it. All in all it promised to be a most enjoyable time.

The one wrinkle in the week, the unexpected downturn, had come in relation to their sons, their beloved boys. Jess had hinted at times in the last few months that his marriage was not going well. The couple had differing ideas over many things but the most difficult one was that his newlywed wife had decided to go back to school. It had been agreed upon prior to the wedding that each of them would seek to find jobs, build careers and later a family after a measure of security had been established. Though Jess had found work relatively quickly as a Spanish teacher for a private high school, his wife had languished among the unemployed until ultimately taking a job with Boeing as a buyer, a position with little relevance to her biology degree and even less relevance to her interests in life. The work was uninspiring, the commute pure drudgery, and she felt out of place within a workforce of lifelong administrators, many well past twice her age. In her angst she had cast her imagination far and wide and decided that the medical profession was her true bent. Though she had applied to graduate school at neighboring colleges none had accepted her and she eventually felt forced to look afar in her search. Finally a university in Boise, Idaho was willing to accept her and after much consultation, primarily with her mother, she had decided to make the move, with her husband or alone.

As Jess was averse to leaving his job as well as his friends and family roots, they had disagreed, quarreled and withdrawn from each other to their own separate corners and divided bedsides. In the most recent weeks as her intentions had hardened he had felt increasingly disheartened and though he had initially kept the conflict to himself he was moved in this last week to finally visit his family, share his sorrow and unburden his load. His pathos was revealed in a most poignant moment that was almost pathetically painful to observe were it not for the sweetness that accompanied the revelation.

He entered the house of his parents in the evening by the front door quietly unannounced. In the darkness dog-bird had missed his approach. On the far shore windows were glowing with amber lights that streamed across the lake in the evening breeze. Bea, reading by lamplight in the living room, was the first to encounter him.

"Well, hello stranger. What a pleasant surprise." She stood up to hug him and felt the heaviness in his embrace. "It's so good to see you. What's brought you home tonight?"

"Oh," he said softly, "I just felt like seeing you guys. Do you mind? I mean I hope it's not too late since I didn't call or anything."

"Oh no. Glad you're here. We're always glad to see you. I just wasn't expecting…"

Jay entered the room coming from the den where he'd been playing music on the keyboards. He was glad to see Jess and in his joy did not notice that the lad seemed dispirited.

"Hey, how are you doing? Good to see you, my boy. Wanna' beer? Glass of wine? Give me hug." He wrapped his arms around Jess's big frame and gave him a squeeze and a slap on the back. "Have a seat. Sit down. How are ya', anyway? Boy, it's been awhile."

"Yeah, I guess it has," agreed Jess. "I get so busy." He shuffled over to the cushy recliner chair, sat down and heaved a sigh. He smiled weakly.

"Oh man, don't we know it. The days just fly by. Is your life going okay?"

"Well, actually, that's what -"

"Hey, bruz!" Phil's high-pitched voice filled the air. He'd come out from his room on hearing the racket. 'Bruz' had been his affectionate term for his brother since time immemorial. "I thought I heard voices like someone was here." He ran over and gave his bruz a warm hug, then climbed into his lap sitting sideways against him as though it were though most natural thing in he world. He laid his head against the broad chest as he hooked his right arm lovingly over his big brother's muscular neck. "I love my bruz!" he declared proudly, a sweet grin on his impish face. He sat there happily ensconced on a throne of thick thighs, then looked over at his parents to take in the scene.

Jess appeared to be touched by the display of devotion and wrapped his arms gently around his adoring young sibling. Both parents gazed fondly at the sight of their children locked in a grip of mutual esteem and sat themselves down on the couch facing the boys. No one spoke for a moment; all of them simply feeling the spontaneous presence of their precious wholeness filling the room with love. It was an uncommon occurrence for the native family members to gather as the foursome that they had once been for years. It was only when Jess had left for college in his junior year that the clan had been diminished by a quarter of its size. It brought back a flood of fleeting memories for Bea and the last one she happened on was the moment of his departure as he strode down the walkway with the family in his wake, with his little brother suddenly calling out in earnest, "Remember bruz, safe sex! Safe sex!" The advice had proved valuable as far as anyone knew.

Somehow a sound, a soft whimper, a repressed moan, perhaps an intuition sensed in innocence by a young mind, or possibly an awareness of muscular tension, unusual, unexplained but clearly felt as a different vibration caused Phil to look up into his older brother's face with pure curiosity tempered by concern.

"Are you alright, Bruz?" The question hung in the air.

Jess paused and seemed to crumple slowly like an imploding pyramid.

"No," he said sadly, choking back tears. "I'm not." And he circled his little brother with a stronger squeeze as though each were a blanket, a comforter to each other.

Instinctively Phil turned his cuddle into a clinch, pulling himself up as he pulled his brother down to him. Jess started to cry softly, letting the hurt seep out; droplets dribbling slowly down his cheeks.

"What's wrong?" Bea cried aloud, alarmed at his tears.

"It's Annie," he managed to stammer mournfully between suppressed sobs. "She wants to go away!" With that the dam burst and he wept openly for a minute in his brother's frail arms as his parents knelt by him on either side of the chair. Flanked by the comfort and caring of family he told the whole tale down to the bitter end.

Everyone was floored and unsure what to say. An animated analysis, occasionally heated, followed in the vacuum of a short stunned silence. Annie had always seemed so sweet in her wan way. She was especially devoted to animals, at least in theory, professing a profound and lasting love for any and all endangered species. Her treatment of her own little kitty cats, which she'd defanged and declawed, ostensibly for their own good, seemed to illustrate the sweet if not saccharine snuggly teddy bear nature of the quality of her lovingness. No matter they could no longer go outside the apartment for fear that they were now easy prey for any passing animal. The point was she desired to love them to death, even if it happened to kill them with kindness. No, it didn't make sense to see Annie as in any way deliberately heartless; incidentally mindless possibly, with regard to consequences, but to be fair her intentions were meant to be high-minded. Perhaps a bit of an impractical romantic with everything seemingly more appealing at a distance, but her mother, they suspected was the ultimate culprit. The fact she had been married (to the same guy!) three or four times (or was it five?), lent her a lingering air of marital instability. Yes, there was the problem. Separation had been modeled. Problems in your marriage? No problem. Break up. Mom and dad do it all the time. The discussion devolved quickly into an indictment of the mother-in-law, that proverbial pariah, that heartless home-wrecker, that profligate purveyor of post-modern promiscuity.

Nevertheless Annie's mind was made up. No point in skewering her elusive mom's fickle heart. She was going away to school in the fall and that was that. Jess was equally adamant that he was not. If fact if she went he wanted a divorce. To Annie her leaving did not necessitate that. She might change her mind and come back. Who knows? He might change his. Her mom and dad had managed to reconnect often, though actually they were now no longer together. To Jess her departure was disloyalty in the extreme and a severe violation of their autumn wedding vows. After an impassioned argument that night he had ripped off his wedding ring and buried it in the back yard as an expression of his hurt and disgust. Then he had tearfully headed for his family's home.

"What are you going to do?" asked Bea, when the clamor had subsided to a more rational point.

"I don't know for certain," said Jess thoughtfully. "But I think I want a break. I'd like to get away for a while. Maybe go back down to Mexico."

"Whoa," cautioned Jay. "Are you sure you want to do that?"

"Oh yeah," Jess affirmed. "I'll just go where it's safe. Where all the tourists always go, probably Puerto Vallarta."

"That's good," nodded Bea, having been there herself. "That's safe. Maybe you should take a little break. When would you go?"

"As soon as school's out," he said decisively.

"But that's next week," she countered. "Where would you stay?"

"I have friends down there, remember? Several guys that I worked with at Pablo's restaurant are living there now. I've stayed in communication with them for years by email. Their families are there and they live in nice houses. I could stay with them for free, no problem."

"I want to go too!" Phil piped up enthusiastically.

"Sure, buddy," said Jess. "Why not? I'd love to have you with me."

"Wow! Can I, mom? Can I? Can I, dad? Huh? It's okay with bruz!" He gave a big squeeze to his benefactor and jumped up on the floor. "Oh boy! Would I love it. I'm taking Spanish at school, you know."

"You're only fourteen," admonished his mother.

"But Jess is twenty-two and he speaks perfect Spanish. He's a black belt in Karate and he knows the people there. We'll be safe, mom. We'll be safe!" He turned to his big brother with widening eyes. "Right?"

Jess smiled and said only, "It's up to mom and dad."

Bea stared at Jay with a twinkle in her eye. He stood motionless and expressionless, contemplating the idea. She smiled and shrugged her shoulders.

"Maybe it would be alright," she said plausibly. "As long as you stay safe. Let your dad and me talk about it."

"I can practice my Spanish there!" chirped Phil. "It'll be educational."

"Yeah, yeah, yeah," said Jay in a tone of amused skepticism. "Let's talk about it a while."

The discussion evolved from there for an hour, matching pros to cons, and calculating expenses. It was finally agreed he could go there as long as Bea and Jay communicated first with the parents of the household where the boys would be staying. When Jess left he was noticeably happier than when he'd arrived and his torrid little brother, the family bambino, was heard speaking Spanish as he scurried off to bed.

A blue jay landed on the railing of the deck a few feet away from her. He jerked his head sharply in several directions then lit off when he saw her as fast as he had landed. She followed his flight till he was lost in the trees then looked to the geese by the neighbor's dock. They had wobbled to the water in search of a morning meal, their long necks looking like submarine periscopes until they dove into the deep, leaving only their bottoms up, staying submerged for quite a few seconds. Concentric circles rippled outward in the lake when fish poked through the surface snipping at bugs. Several pinecones landed on the roof with a pop as acrobatic squirrels clambered in a frenzy shaking the limbs of the huge cedar tree. Bea smiled at their antics, took another sip and found her coffee had grown lukewarm.

She decided it was time to get down to work. Not only was Faye arriving today but also she had unresolved business matters to face. There were questions to answer in preparation for Russia; a trip she had all but committed to in writing. She wanted a companion to accompany her there and knew of a colleague, a long-time business associate on the east coast, who might be persuaded. They could split Homestay programs between the two coasts. He was older and had some experience with the Russians and she knew from past dealings that he could be trusted; a key ingredient now in all business dealings. After Perry she was taking no more risky chances. With Leroy's encouragement she felt all the stronger in her decision to go abroad sometime in September. The only loose link left was Spain for new business. She was wondering just how she might handle them both. To do them in one trip would be an arduous task but she wanted with a passion to expand beyond the limits of her ties to Japan. She tossed her cold coffee over the railing, went inside for a refill and then downstairs to engage her compelling challenges.

For hours she worked nonstop with only a brief break for lunch at her desk. The atmosphere in the office was so much easier now with the new help aboard. Jay was only there two days a week, spending three now in his new office as his clientele had increased. They had talked about her hiring another person to take his place. Someone he could train in the running of his programs and eventually hand over the reins altogether. She had a good enough response to her ad to consider his replacement from that pool of applicants and hoped to interview some of them in the coming weeks for at least consideration on a part-time basis. This week was too eventful as it was already.

As the day wore on her plans for the Russian trip began to fall into place. Her east coast associate was more than willing to go along with her. He even knew of some Russian families they could stay with in Moscow. She could feel her excitement growing at the prospect of pioneering student exchanges with the fledgling free nation that Russia was becoming; so rich in history, so massive in girth, so exotically different in all aspects of the culture. She also felt with each passing hour the growing excitement at her sibling's imminent arrival and almost jumped out of her chair when Bernadette handed her the phone in the late afternoon saying, "It's your sister."

"Where are you?" she virtually shouted with glee. "I thought you were coming right here."

"I'm at the Safeway store!" Faye nearly shouted back. "We got a little lost. The question is where the hell are you?"

"I'm at my house, silly. You called me, remember?"

"Don't be funny. How far away are we?"

"You're close. Don't move!" Bea laughed. "I'll be there in a minute!"

Chapter 72

"The real world is a state of mind in which the only purpose of the world seems to be forgiveness." (A Course in Miracles)

As he bade farewell to his last client of the day Jay closed the door behind him and walked over to his desk. He called the answer service to check for messages. On finding his slate clear he sat down in the plush black leatherette desk chair and swiveled around to the window overlooking Forestville. It had been a satisfyingly full day for him filled with six hours of therapeutic encounters. In another hour he would pick up Phil at school and his sister-in-law was due at the house sometime soon. She might even be there when they got home. Listening to the bubbly fountain trickling unhurriedly behind him he watched a cluster of elongated clouds trail idly towards the western horizon. He felt unusually calm. Fridays had always had a special feel to him. He regarded the workdays as a long drum solo, with the pounding rhythms of the week bursting out Monday morning, throbbing to a full crescendo Wednesday at noon and pulsating down to soft palpitations by the time late Friday afternoon rolled to an end. It had been his favorite day for as long as he could remember.

He tried meditating and found that his mind was so packed with feelings and thoughts of the last several weeks it were as if he had reached a pinnacle of momentum. It was harder than usual to be in a state of not thinking and merely feeling at peace. He decided instead to have a quiet period for review and reflection. Even today events had been momentous or at least significant for some of his clients. It had begun with the young bi-sexual woman from Seattle, Lee, whom he'd also seen earlier in the week. After a session of revelations about her childhood she had wanted another meeting but this time with her father, Bruno, and was anxious to meet as a threesome as soon as possible. The bearded and burly man was agreeable to joining them, saying cryptically to Jay on the phone, "Frankly I've been waiting and hoping for this moment." When they met this morning there was tension in the air, a discomfort not dispelled by the comfortable chairs.

In essence she had discovered and released a deeply suppressed memory of being fondled by her father inappropriately during the period when they had lived alone together; her pre-teen years. It only happened once but it burned in her memory like an undying ember she could neither douse nor dislodge. Her father in turn had suffered from guilt, also long buried, and had yearned for the day when it could be released. He believed his actions were somehow responsible for her experimentation with bi-sexuality, his only concern being lesbianism and his dreadful fear that he had condemned his only daughter to a lifelong antipathy toward men. After their greetings and initial small talk Jay invited the young woman to disclose her concerns.

"Dad," she said hesitatingly, squirming in her seat, "I don't know how to say this to you so I'm just going to blurt out."

"Good," said Bruno. "That's what I'd like. I want to hear whatever you have to tell me."

"Do you remember that time," she continued plaintively, "after mom left, when I was about ten or twelve, and I was sitting on your lap and you were reading me a story?"

Bruno cleared his throat. "I remember many times reading you stories on my lap. We went through the entire Nancy Drew mystery series." He clasped his thick hairy hands in his lap and looked at her expectantly.

"Yeah, I think we did. And it took a few years. And at first it was fine. And it was fine for a long time. But as I got older, when I began to grow breasts and puberty and stuff, then somehow things started to change."

"Yes, that's true," he acknowledged, looking uncomfortable. "But you were always my little girl."

"Yeah, but Dad, I was becoming a big girl."

"I know."

"And Dad, do you remember that time that you brought your hands up…you brought your hands up and sort of cupped them around my breasts?"

The father looked aghast as his mouth dropped open slightly. His head inclined sadly to one side in resignation. "Yes, I do. I'm sorry to say it, but I do. I do remember. I could never forget."

Her voice rose in anguished protest. "What were you thinking?"

"I don't know," his voice intensified to match hers in its grief. "I don't know. I…I…I wasn't thinking, I guess. I wasn't thinking at all. I just reacted without thinking. Suddenly it hit me that I was losing my little girl."

But Dad," she said indignantly, "you had an erection. I could feel it. It was terrible. It was scary. It wasn't right for you to do that."

"I know," he confessed, looking sorrowful and bewildered. "I didn't want to have one. I didn't try to have one. It just happened. That one time! And then I never asked you ever to sit on my lap again."

"I didn't want to," wailed his daughter. "I was afraid to after that!"

"I know. I know. And it broke my heart." He put his palms to his face and started to weep. "And I'm so sorry," he choked out. "I'm so very sorry."

Lee was silent for a moment and then spoke in grave amazement.

"I've never seen you cry before, Dad."

At that he erupted into another explosion of sobs that shook his belly in their convulsions.

"I never...I never...felt this sad ever before!" He continued crying for several moments and then looked over at Jay. "Thank you."

"For what?" asked Jay.

"For helping us get this out. I always wanted it out but was afraid to touch it."

"Oh sure," Jay assured him. "That's my job. And you're welcome." He looked at Lee. "Have you more to say?"

She inhaled noticeably, as though screwing up her courage. "Dad," she said more softly, "I understand how you might have had an unexpected erection, though its weird, but why did you have to touch my breasts like you did?"

Her father stopped crying, wiped his eyes with the Kleenex Jay handed him and tried to regain some semblance of his composure. He shook his head wearily.

"I don't know," he finally said. "I've wondered that myself for years. It was all so fast and now so long ago, but it seems to me, and I know this may sound like an excuse, but it seems to me it was an unthinking gesture, almost automatic, that I was confirming to myself that indeed you were becoming a woman. That my erection had somehow signaled that fact to me and I needed confirmation – confirmation of what I hoped wasn't true; that I was losing my little girl for good."

With that he started to sniffle, then blew his nose forcefully instead. "I don't know. I think that was it." He heaved a deep sigh, blew his nose again and slumped in his chair looking utterly defeated. "I never touched you inappropriately again. In fact, I was overly careful any time I hugged you after that. And, like I said, never had you on my lap again."

"I know, Dad. That's true. But Dad, there were some times when I saw you looking at me naked. When I would come out of the bathroom or some other times that seemed accidental. Still, the way you looked at me."

"I know. You're right. But those were not looks of desire. I never felt that way. I promise you. I never felt that way at all. Those looks were filled wonderment that you were really changing in front of my eyes. And those looks were filled with sadness, sadness that I was losing you, and with guilt, that perhaps I'd harmed you. That's all." He started to cry again, but more softly this time. "That's all." He looked again at Jay.

"Do you think I've ruined her?" he exclaimed in anguish. "Do you think I've ruined my only child?"

"Because she may have homosexual inclinations?" inquired Jay gently.

"Yes!" he yelled in torment. "Exactly that."

"No," Jay answered firmly. "I don't think it matters whether someone is homosexual, heterosexual or bi-sexual."

"Then what does matter?"

Jay took a deep breath and blew it out to feel more centered before answering.

"That they are expressing the capacity to love. That they are loving persons, period. Let her explore her sexuality. The function of a parent is to love, and from that basic standpoint, you have done your job. I think you have loved your daughter, despite your mistakes, and tried to model and instill healthy values. And you have done some things that were traumatic for her. But that could probably be said of many if not most parents. And I also think that forgiveness can heal relationships. And that self-disclosure can restore trust. And just as she has done here, you are willing do that – to love your self and her enough to do that, disclose your mistakes, disclose your pain and regret, and thus healing is already underway as we speak."

It was silent in the room for several minutes as the clock ticked and the fountain gurgled. The young woman cleared her throat and spoke softly but in a clear strong voice.

"Dad, I love you."

That had been an especially moving session, heartrending, heartbreaking, heart mending, he hoped. The others had not been as intensely dramatic, though any of them could be on any given day. Sheila and Peter, the black and white couple, had been attempting to communicate in the manner he had taught them and were encouraged by their progress. They continued to come but on a twice monthly basis. They had built a new social device, date night, into their relationship, finding it valuable to get away periodically from their highly energetic boys. The dentist and his wife had returned from a week's vacation in Mexico feeling tentatively hopeful that their love could be renewed. He had confessed his transgressions and affirmed his desire to stay married. She was surprised, then saddened, but ultimately forgiving. They were coming to counseling every other week as a couple while the dentist came the alternate weeks on his own. They were also having lunch together once or twice a week and planning other getaways on a regular basis. They had joined a gym and she was working out frequently. They both were pleased that she was losing weight and he too was now going several times a week at lunchtime, a healthier pastime than his previous one.

The large heavy gentleman who had a passion for pornography was also doing marriage counseling with his wife. Jay had noticed him jogging on he road while driving home last week. He was huffing and puffing in a baggy gray sweat suit and looked doggedly determined as the sweat gleamed on his forehead and darkened his armpits. They were both reading suggested books on sexual intimacy. Skyler and Melanie had also returned to therapy as a couple, bent on mending their fractured marriage. They now went to church together each Sunday as well and seemed to find the combination of counseling and worship much to their liking. They were talking optimistically about having a baby as soon as Melanie's medical condition was treated. Lynette had forgiven Michael for his indiscretion with Eva, their alluring Swedish foreign exchange student, from whom gratefully nothing was heard since her return home. He had been so contrite and sincere in his misery that Lynette was recovering better than Jay had expected from her ground-shaking sense of devastation. They too, for now, came every two weeks but he foresaw a time in the near future when they need not at all.

Others not so fortunate flashed through his mind. Steve was adjusting to life without Amanda. Limping gamely along at first with his boys, he had started to regain his footing in life. She had relinquished all custody claims on the children, preferring to live with her newfound body beautiful beau from the gym. The young woman who had become hysterical in hypnosis had returned for a few months of sessions after the first of the year. Her boyfriend had been offered a job promotion that required moving to another state. They had recently gotten married and were happily immersed in relocation plans. At her last session she had announced she was pregnant. She did not foresee visiting her parents any longer on Thanksgiving or Christmas, stating that the young family would rather start up their own familial traditions. She regretted leaving her mother but was convinced she would probably always feel somewhat uncomfortable in the presence of her stepfather. At least now she knew why. Her mother would be more than welcome to visit. Howie and Sharon were still an open question. The hospital had accepted her for observation and Howie had moved back into their home that day to care for his daughters. It was too soon to say what would happen with them next.

Still others he had little to no awareness of at all. The flower lady had not been heard from for awhile which he took as a good sign…*no news is good news*…The Eskimo lady had also disappeared entirely from his radar…*good-bye…good-luck…good riddance*…The professionals that had played a key part in his life had their own fates to contend with. Judging from the appearance of Will and Colette at Jake's Place recently, they were doing fine. Marianne he might see occasionally around town but she was a fading and soon to be forgotten figure in his mind. It seemed likely to him she would need to make a hard choice sooner or later. Recently he had taken the time to follow Leroy's advice and done his best in meditation to give his grievances to God. He had gone through each individual in his mind, letting go of any bad feelings as best as he could. One by one he had held Candy, Marianne, Naimee, Perry, Toshi, Kazuo and Detective Clark in his focus while feeling peaceful and forgiving toward each one. Using a specific meditation technique from *A Course in Miracles* he separately envisioned each of their images in an aura of light while grounding himself in the fundamental fact that in essence each and every one of them were all just like him; a spiritual creature confounded by his ego. The experience had lasted well over an hour and he had emerged from it feeling noticeably lighter, happily relieved of some cumbersome baggage.

He had a new office now and a new lease on life, personally and professionally. Given his membership acceptance by the major insurance companies, his fortunes looked to be potentially as prosperous as they had been before; maybe even better. He had existing clients, such as Raymond to attend to and new ones on the horizon unfettered by his fees. Now it was wonderful if they had health insurance. If not, he cut his fee down by half. If they couldn't afford that, he was still open to barter. He had already accepted several new clients this week and was happy to be spending three days at counseling per week instead of two. He hoped to continue to extend that ratio until his practice was all that occupied him again. Also he had recently written on new topics for the newspaper – loss, parenting, and self-esteem for now – and intended to do more. His growing sense of tranquility was slowly becoming ever so sweeter.

Apart from the increasing fulfillment in his profession he had also been writing and playing more music. He desired to make another demo for record companies, this time playing all the instruments himself, using his four track recorder. Remembering this he opened the middle desk drawer and pulled out a tablet with his most recent composition on it; nearly completed....*maybe finish it now*...He read through what he'd written so far, pleased with the opening lines of the chorus which also served as the title for the song.

Life is beautiful, baby
Life is beautiful
Life is beautiful, baby
Life is beautiful

First you take it as it comes
Then you have to let it go
Make mistakes along the way
Nothing's unforgivable

Life is beautiful (Repeat Chorus)

Some days your heart is filled with pain
Your body aches, it's gonna rain
Some days your soul will soar with bliss
With songs to sing and lips to kiss

Life is beautiful (Repeat Chorus)

A shiver of satisfaction ran through his body. He loved the melody and regarded the tune as possibly his very best...*now what*...A instrumental bridge would follow the second verse and that would have to be worked out on the guitar...*finish the lyrics*...Closing his eyes he let the meaning of the song permeate his being, feeling the rhythm of it unfolding sequentially. The first verse was the opener, the second the middle and the third one the closer...*how's it end*... He took a deep breath, sensing the gist of it gathering momentum, articulating itself into translation.

It seems to start and then to end
But really it begins again
And all the times you have you see
Just moments in eternity

Life is beautiful, baby
Life is beautiful
Life is beautiful, baby
Life is beautiful

...*perfect*...Setting the tablet gently on the desk, he relaxed into a feeling of utter delight, that rare sensation that always followed the completion of a song. He put his fingertips together, fingers apart, and brought them to his chest as though to pray but merely sat motionless and unthinking, absorbing the joy of the moment. After a minute he noticed his guitar standing the corner and wondered if he had time to work out a bridge. A glance at the clock said it was time to get Phil.

He stood up and gazed through the window at the town below him. It was in motion. In the distance he heard the solemn dong of the church bell. The streets were crowding up quickly with frenzied commuters heeding the freedom call of Friday. For many children this was also the last day of school, making this weekend particularly liberating. He raised his gaze to the tree covered hills that framed Forestville on the western perimeter. The slopes were studded with proud evergreens pointing to the indolent clouds stretching westward from both north and south, apparently bent on a rendezvous at sunset. He grabbed his keys, locked his office and unlocked his car door; pausing only to retrieve and fling in the trash bin the empty beer bottle that had rolled out again from under the seat.

The trip to Phil's school was a tangled throng of drivers and he slipped in a tape from Leroy to pass the time.

"Hello, Jay. What's going on?"

"Well, I'm doing better. I think I just want to hear you say whatever you feel like saying."

"Very good. Well then, I want to talk a little more about transformation and circumstances. You've definitely gotten better at this, but specifically what you are going to have to persist in more and more is not minding your circumstances. Not because you are going to tolerate shit, but rather because not minding them allows you to give up your defense more easily which then is conducive to what I would call miraculous unfoldment; of things that are not being caused by you but nevertheless are yours to experience.

"You know, if you want to have alchemy, figuratively speaking, if you want to turn lead to gold, you have to love the lead. That's how it works. It isn't because you disapprove of the lead and it ought to be gold that you get anything. So a little bit more easiness around your circumstance, around where you are at any time, no matter how it may appear to be, will help it transform. We have talked about this before but I feel moved to expand on it because it is still a little bit of an issue for you. Now, this requires too that you give up thinking you know what is going on. You tend to react not only to the circumstances but also to something of your own spin on the circumstances and if you were not interpreting them and just simply experiencing them as they are you would see in any situation the potential for immediate transformation.

"So that's where you need to be clued in, every moment of your being, every moment of your consciousness. You need to be clued in to the imminent and full potential for transformation. That then lets you behave freely, wherever you are and you feel less constrained by the interpretation, by the mass mind agreement, as to what is going on. You see, you'll know that's what everybody thinks but you won't care. You'll just do what you feel moved to do and it will be heaven."

"Hm. That'd be nice."

"Right. It will be like being on vacation all the time. That's a good metaphor for what I'm talking about here. It's the freedom from responsibility that feels so wonderful, and that's what vacation is supposed to be. You give up thinking that you control your circumstances. Another good metaphor is the experience of entertainment. You used to spend too much time trying to solve your problems and not allowing yourself to be entertained. But entertainment, mind you, is really an experience of communion. Now reflect on that. People love to be entertained because they are absolutely present with what's going on. They are not judging it. They are not resisting it. That's communion. And so, everybody knows that it feels good. And so what you want, is to connect to the feeling of being entertained, no matter what the circumstances of your life. You want that feeling of communion; to be present, to be balanced, to be at ease, to be undefended. It feels like being entertained. Now I use the word communion. You see, to entertain is to hold, to hold the attention. To be entertained is to be held, to have your attention held. That is communion; the embrace. Do you see?"

"I do."

"What you call entertainment in the everyday sense of the word is great because that's as close to peace and freedom as most people feel. That's as close to their true nature as most people come to in the course of their day."

"I guess you're right. I never thought of it that way. People are often listening to the radio or music in their cars or staring at the TV in their homes to be entertained; to have their attention held, even if it's crap, at least by my standards."

"Right. So be entertained. It's vital."

"Yeah. I understand. I think you said something like that before but I'm glad you elaborated."

"Good. That's all I have to say about that at the moment. Is there anything on your mind now?"

"Well, I guess I am curious about something. You know how it says in *A Course in Miracles* how there are no coincidences?"

"Right."

"Well, to make a long story short, a client of mine told me about a local jazz club, so I went there just for the sake of curiosity and ended up getting to know the owner and now I'm going to be his chef and his wine guy too. Just appetizers on the weekend, but still…"

"That's marvelous."

"Yeah, I love cooking food and dealing with wine but the funny thing is that it's as though my desires were being manifested without me doing anything about it."

"Yes, of course. That can happen and will increasingly so as you continue in what you've been doing."

"But wait, it gets better. I was there the other night and an old friend, a colleague actually, came in and we started talking about our practices and, again, to make a long story short, now it appears that I was misinformed about how the game is being played for Master's level counselors. I'm thinking, hoping, that I can get in on that. I'm compiling a list of insurance companies to contact. It looks like it's being done on geographic necessity; wherever they need a counselor with my credentials. So I want to start to explore that. Do you have any sense about that?"

"Oh yes, absolutely. I certainly encourage you to do that. It is a good idea and you will benefit from it. It will happen. It will manifest. Now, I want to encourage you in your staying off the weed."

"Oh, don't worry. I'm pretty much past that. I just need something better to be doing."

"Right, but you are going to need to stay off it for the sake of clarity."

"Oh, it's obvious to me. Frankly I'm actually enjoying it."

"Good."

"I find it's a better high being natural."

"Good, because you can't really embrace communion until the reliance on the other stuff is gone. So, good. That's really what has always been needed."

On approaching the parking lot of the school he punched out the tape and put it back in the glove compartment, mulling over its message...*what's always been needed*...as he turned his attention to the schoolyard. He was feeling good enough to willingly suffer the excruciating exhortations and racial recriminations of the rabid black rappers for one more run because it was the last time he would endure their crap until September; a full season away. By then perhaps Phil's musical tastes may have changed again. Across a riotous sea of school children's faces and the chaos of cars coming and going he saw Phil leaning against a light pole, talking to a taller red-headed boy. He hated to do it but he honked his horn once lightly, in the hopes Phil would recognize the sound. He did, grabbed his bag, slung it over his shoulders, said good-bye to his friend and trod over to the car, slightly bent in that characteristic posture he'd acquired from bearing a heavy backpack for the last nine months.

"Happy graduation, my boy," beamed Jay. "It's finally over. Upward and onward."

"Yeah, I guess," said Phil with typical nonchalance. It wasn't cool to be seen being too friendly with your parents in the midst of the school grounds. He tossed his bag in the back. "Hey, did you get rid of that bottle?"

"Oh yeah. Long time ago. That was just an aberration."

"What's that?"

"An unusual occurrence. A freak incident. Something that very rarely, almost never ever happens."

"Oh."

"Anyway," continued Jay, happy to change the subject, "how was your last day?"

"Alright." He seemed uninterested in conversing and opened the console of the car for a familiar CD.

"You been waiting long?" Jay felt light-hearted enough to continue seeking common conversational ground. After all, it was Friday...*and soon no more rap crap...*

"Yeah, actually they let us out a little early."

"Just to be nice?"

"I think they were hoping if some kids left a little earlier it wouldn't be such a huge mess in the parking lot for once. A lot of parents let their kids drive today as a special thing just because it's the last day."

"Oh." Jay contemplated this new piece of information. "So I could have come to get you sooner?"

"Yeah, I guess so."

"Well, why didn't you tell me? I could have done that today and maybe saved us from this mess of people. I had a little time I was just sitting."

"That's cool. I don't know. I just forgot about it."

"A chance to leave school early and you forgot about it?" Jay spoke with mock incredulity.

"Yeah, sorry. I just forgot," said Phil, seeming slightly defensive.

"Oh, that's okay." Jay wanted to keep things feeling upbeat. "So what you been doing? Just talking with your friend?"

"What friend?"

"That tall red-headed guy that was next to you by the lamp post."

"Oh him. That's Ryan."

"Uh-huh. I've seen him with you before."

"Yeah."

"Is he someone you'd like to see during the summer?"

"Oh, probably not. He lives sorta' far away. I just see him at school. We're in band together."

"Uh-huh." Jay was absorbed in navigating through the thicket of vehicles as he crawled toward the road winding down to the boulevard. "So he's a musician too, huh?"

"Yeah."

"That's great." He finally made it to the pavement and joined the meandering mob of autos snaking their way down the coiled descent. The cars were close together and required his attention. "Anything else in common?" he said absentmindedly.

"Look, Dad, why all these questions?"

He was surprised by the strained query. "What? Hey, I'm just talking here. Just making conversation." He looked over at Phil. He looked tired. "Just curious about your new friend. I mean, if you want to be friends and you're not just because he lives far off we could probably hook you up in the summer sometime."

"Yeah, okay. I don't know. Thanks. I'll think about it. He likes to go for walks in the woods. We have that in common. We did that before you came just to pass the time."

"Good for you."

Phil yawned. "I'm tired. I just want to hear some music. Do you mind, Dad?"

"Not at all," he said. "You know I love rap music. I was just listening to it on the way here."

"Sure," smiled Phil.

"Really. I was dancing like they do with my hands and fingers all twisted up in weird positions. I chanted 'bitches and ho's and homies'. I even said the 'N' word. It felt groovy."

"No one says that anymore, Dad."

"Thank you for sharing that. That's the last time I'll ever say it."

"Sure. See how you like this song."

"Okay, but just one more thing. Don't forget that you're going to Mexico next week."

"Oh, yes!" Phil grinned broadly. "I almost forgot. Yes!"

"How could you forget?"

"I don't know. It's so new and I guess I've been so busy with school and stuff."

"And one other thing."

"What's that?"

"Soon we're going to see your Auntie Mame!"

"Who? Oh, you mean Aunt Faye."

"Yeah, that's just my nickname for her based on a movie character. The point is: she's a lot of fun."

"For you maybe."

"No. You're going to like her too. Don't you remember her?"

"A little. It's been a while."

"Well, she remembers you and you'll see, she can be a lot of fun."

"Okay, Dad. Sounds good. Now can I play this?"

"Sure."

Phil slipped in the CD and began to gyrate with the bass undulations. He turned up the volume. "How do you like this song?" he said loudly. "It's got a good beat and I think you'll like the lyrics."

"Yeah, maybe, if I could understand them."

"What?" yelled Phil louder, not wanting to sacrifice the listening pleasure of a high volume.

Jay glanced at him as he accelerated onto the main road into the traffic. He smiled benignly and nodded as he shouted back.

"Groovy!"

Chapter 73

"Every loving thought is true. Everything else is an appeal for healing and help, regardless of the form it takes." (A Course in Miracles)

I F VIEWED FROM THE air Bea's green SUV would have seemed to be a speeding turtle hurtling down the highway even faster than a hare. True to her word she was at the super market parking lot veritably within minutes of leaving home. Scanning the lot like radar screen she saw her sister standing near the entrance of the Safeway with a tall handsome balding man beside her...*must be david...*She felt a flood of joy expanding in her heart as she approached them, locking eyes and matching their smiles with hers. Parking the car along side them with a lurch she jumped out and flung her arms around Faye who embraced her with the same gusto.

"Well, it's about time!" teased Faye. "We've been waiting."

"If you could just follow directions," Bea quipped in mock exasperation. "But then you never could." She turned aside and gazed upward. "And this must be David."

"That's me," he replied as he bent down, warmly wrapping his long arms around her for a hug.

"Welcome to Forestville," declared Bea, beaming with delight. Her sister beamed radiantly back at her while David looked at them both.

"I understand you live on a lake," he stated politely.

"Cottage Lake, that's right, come on. Follow me and we'll be there in no time." The two-car caravan cruised the short distance quickly, coming to a halt at the end of the driveway.

Bags were unloaded and stored in the guest bedroom downstairs which until just a week ago had been Jay's separate office. He now worked at smaller desk in the bigger room with the rest of the crew. They met Bernadette just before she left, then marched up the stairs to the sound of the bird screeching.

"That probably means Jay is here," explained Bea. "That's our dog-bird. He's an ever ready alarm for anyone coming up the driveway." On reaching the top step she saw Jay and Phil through the window. "Yep. It's them," she said proudly, grinning like a child on an early Christmas morning.

The boys tumbled out of the car and advanced towards their guests with welcoming smiles. They hugged, exchanged greetings and took stock of each other. After a few minutes of sharing pleasantries they went into the house to sit down and relax. The adults gathered in the sunroom surveying the lake as Phil slipped into his bedroom to do teenage things.

"What's a girl got to do to get a drink around here?" demanded Faye with a devilish grin on her face.

"Just ask," said Bea. "What do you usually do?"

"Oh, you don't want to know," David quipped.

"Oh, shut up," retorted Faye. "As if I was a wild thing."

"As if," smirked Bea.

"I've got a great bottle of Montrachet chilling in the fridge," said Jay, as he went to retrieve it.

"Whoa," David said. "That's expensive stuff."

"Only the best for my sister-in-law."

"That's right," confirmed Faye. "But I'll share."

"Since when?" said Bea.

"How come," said Faye in mock exasperation, "everyone is giving me such a hard time?"

"Cause you deserve it!" Bea looked at her with amusement. "I suffered forever as your little sister."

"Now don't start that again; rewriting history." Faye glared back but with a twinkle in her eye.

"Girls, girls!" interjected Jay, reentering the room with a bottle in one hand and four wine glasses in the other. He set them on the coffee table, poured the wine and held his glass aloft.

"To us," he said simply. "May the past be forgotten and the present made memorable."

"Where'd you hear that?" queried Bea with a smile as she raised her glass high.

"I don't know. I just made it up. Sounded good at the time."

"Works for me," quipped David, sipping his drink. "Ahhh, that's nice."

"Yummy," nodded Faye. "Now where are those famous appetizers?"

"Are you hungry?" Jay asked.

"For your food, anytime."

"Coming right up," said Jay with a smile. "Bruschetta in ten minutes."

"Mmmmmm," intoned Faye. "And what's our plans for this evening?"

"You mean for dinner?" Bea asked.

"I just meant if you don't have plans we'll be glad to take you out."

"Oh no," responded Bea. "Jay's got something wonderful in mind I can assure you and we can pass the night away sitting leisurely by the lake. Maybe now's a good time to go over the great itinerary I've put together for your visit."

"Sounds good."

Bea started recounting the various planned activities as Jay stirred about fastidiously in the kitchen. She was just finishing up when he served the round platter of diced Roma tomatoes mixed with fresh basil on warm thick crusty slices of toasted and garlic rubbed whole-wheat bread.

"Mmmmmm," said Faye again. "One of my favorites."

"Ours too," added Bea as she took her first bite. "Welcome to Jay's kitchen."

They were almost done when the home phone rang. Bea let the machine take it and listened to the caller.

"Hello, Bea." The voice sounded old and distant. "This is Carrie, from Ohio."

"Who's that?" whispered Faye.

"Oh my," said Bea, her curiosity deepening. "It's the nurse I hired to look after dad."

"Bea," the voice continued. "I'm sorry to have to call you so late in the evening, but-"

Bea had jumped to her feet and plucked the phone from its base. "Hello, Carrie," she said. "It's not too late here." Her voice quavered slightly. "Is everything okay?"

With Bea on the line the speakerphone was inactivated and the others in the room listened intently to cues from her voice as the wind chimes on the deck dangled softly in the background.

"What?" said Bea, sounding startled. "When? I see. I see. Can you give me the name of the doctor and his number? Thanks." She wrote down the information and listened for few moments more. "I see. Okay. No, that's all right, I'm glad you did. Thank you for everything. Okay. Don't hesitate to call with anything at all to report. Thanks again. Good-bye."

She returned to the room with inquisitive faces looking up at her.

"Dad's been hospitalized with some chest pains."

"Oh no," gasped Faye. "Do they know if it's serious?"

"They don't know anything for sure right now. Actually he was having some chest pains but they stopped. Carrie took him there anyway. They're running tests and hope to know what's happening by tonight."

"What happened?" asked Jay. "Did he have to go by ambulance?"

"No, it wasn't that bad. Carrie drove him over. She said he complained about feeling some tightness in his chest when he woke up from his nap and she didn't want to take any chances."

"Good thing she did that," muttered Faye.

"That's for sure," affirmed Bea. "One reason I hired her was because she was an ex-nurse."

Everyone sat in silence, contemplating the possibilities, feeling surprised as well as concerned.

"Well," sighed Jay, "could be a number of things. He's in the right place."

"Right," said David, trying to sound reassuring. "And he got there quickly. That's always helpful. Maybe it's minor."

"Right," added Jay. "And whatever it is, they can hopefully diagnose and respond to it quickly."

"Exactly," said David. He looked anxiously at Jay, uncertain what to say or do. All of them sat uncomfortably in the quiet while the wind chimes clanged aimlessly outside the screen door. Bea looked worried and lost in thought while Faye appeared grave. Her face was ashen. Their eyes locked as Bea extended her hand to her sister, who grasped it firmly in her own.

"Let's say a prayer for dad," she said gently. "Father," she began, closing her eyes. "Please watch over our father in his time of need and protect him with your loving strength as he may need it. Thank you. Amen."

"Amen," the others murmured, then were quiet for a moment.

"Did she say anything about how he was doing now?" Faye asked finally. "I mean, what's the latest?"

"She said he was resting comfortably in a hospital bed and that his tightness had subsided and hadn't returned at the moment."

"Oh, that's good."

"Yeah," said Bea pensively. "That's probably a good sign."

"Does it make you think about flying back there?" David looked at Faye intently.

"Oh God," she heaved a sigh. "After such a long flight out here?" She paused to reflect. "No, but I was just wishing I was there. There's really nothing I can do at the moment. You said the pains have stopped, right?"

"Right."

"Might as well just relax here and stay connected by telephone."

"Well," said Bea, "I'll call the hospital in a little bit. Carrie had just left his side a few minutes earlier. She said they were just starting to do some tests and it would take awhile to get results. She said he was joking that it was gas."

"That sounds like dad, always the jokester. Might as well wait and enjoy ourselves as best we can," said Faye. "Maybe it will pass and turn out to be nothing serious."

"Maybe," seconded David. "Maybe."

Feeling the need to be a congenial host, Jay stood up. "I'll go ahead and start on dinner. Why don't you guys go down by the lake? I have a very nice red wine, an Amarone actually, I've been saving for just this occasion and I'll bring it down to you there."

"Can you join us soon?" inquired Bea. "I don't want you to be slaving away in a hot kitchen while were outside having fun."

"No worries, hon. The lasagna noodles are pre-cooked, the cheese pre-grated, the soy meat's pre-cooked and the sauce is in jar from Italy. I'll put it together in no time and let it bake while we socialize. Sound good?" A sense of celebration though muted was returning to the assembled multitude, which despite the ominous news from Ohio were still feeling pleased to be with one another.

"Yeah, great," nodded Bea. "Though I would rather stay up here with you until you are ready to go down to the water with us."

"All right, darling," said Jay pleasantly as he walked towards the stairway. "Just let me get that bottle of wine from the cellar and we'll keep this party going."

"Sounds good," she chirped *…oh God, please…take care of dad…*

When Jay rejoined the group they sauntered down to the lakeside deck and stretched out in the lounge chairs under the shady enclave of the willow trees. After a half hour of sipping, munching and chatting Bea slipped away upstairs to telephone the hospital. She returned to the gathering with a relieved look on her face.

"Carrie says the doctors say whatever it was appears to have passed and he's resting comfortably right now," she announced. "They're going to keep him there for a few days just to watch him."

"Did you talk with dad?" asked Faye loudly, her cheeks beginning to blush pink with wine.

"No, he was sleeping, actually. I just spoke with Carrie."

"Did you talk with his doctor?"

"No. Carrie said he was tending another patient. I've got his name and number and left word for him to call us."

"Well, I would have insisted that he speak with us," sniffed Faye. "It's a long distance call."

"Well," said Bea, bristling slightly at the implicit criticism. "I guess that's the difference between you and me."

"What's that supposed to mean?" said Faye, sounding piqued. She tipped her empty glass toward David and wiggled it impatiently, motioning for a refill.

"Oh, never mind," said Bea as she settled into her chair.

Faye took a long draught of her newly filled glass. "No, really," she insisted. "What did you mean?"

"Oh, just let it go," suggested David in a soft voice. "And have some more snacks." He offered her a tray of pesto stuffed mushrooms. "You're drinking on an empty stomach and after a long flight."

"I'm feeling fine, thank you," said Faye as she pushed the tray away. "And it was a simple question." She stared at Bea, tilting her head expectantly.

Bea sighed and returned her gaze steadily as she spoke. "I meant," she said in a measured tone, "that it is just like you, and not like me, to insist on interrupting a doctor in his work to get your questions answered."

"This could be a matter of life or death!" Faye snapped.

"Everything a doctor does could be a matter of life or death!" responded Bea. "It's just that your life or death matters always take precedence over anyone else's."

"How dare you speak to me like that? I'm just concerned about dad." She slugged the rest of her wine down and thrust her glass again to David while glaring at Bea.

"Well, you weren't so concerned to make time to hire his caregiver, were you?" shot back Bea. "You left that to me, and thank God I hired a nurse, though you bitched about her pay while you foo-fooed away at Spazios with the Mayor."

"I beg your pardon! Foo-fooed? I couldn't get away!"

"You never get away, except when you want to."

"My work is demanding!"

"And so are you, so get off my back." Bea leaned forward in her seat. "I'm doing the best I can to check on dad and I don't need you telling me how to do it, anymore than I needed your help in Pittsburgh."

"Well, I never -" started Faye, somewhat beside herself. She looked at David exasperatingly. "Will you fill this please?"

He hesitated then did so, very slowly and just halfway.

"Ladies, please," interjected Jay gently. "It's an emotional time. You're worried about your father. But he's okay at the moment. And we've all had perhaps a bit too much to drink and not enough to eat. Let's all settle down and enjoy being together. It's a beautiful moment in a beautiful spot. There's nothing else to be done for Gabe but wait for the results of his tests. He's in the best place for him to be." He cleared his throat. "I'm going to go check on the lasagna. It's probably ready."

He glanced at both women who seemed content at the moment to have a tentative truce, then walked up the path hurriedly to the kitchen. Bea sat back in her chair, gave a sigh and gazed at Faye.

"I'm sorry, Faye," she stated diplomatically. "I don't want to fight with you."

"Well, I just don't understand why you're being so touchy," said Faye with a strain in her voice as she twiddled the stem of her wine glass back and forth.

David cleared his throat and spoke in a gentle tone. "Let's just let it go."

"Will you stay out of this?" demanded Faye angrily. "I'm just trying to have a talk with my sister." She turned again to Bea. "Have I done something to upset you?"

"Oh, not more than usual," said Bea with a laugh, hoping to diffuse the issue with humor.

"This is not funny," said Faye in a slurred tone as she polished off the remaining dregs with a dash.

"I don't think now's a good time to get into it," spoke Bea evenly. "But as you know, at times, you can be a little bossy. And as I grow older, I'm less inclined to tolerate it."

"Less inclined to tolerate it!" barked Faye with a vengeance. "I'm someone to be tolerated? Do you realize what you're saying? As your older sister I deserve your respect!"

"Faye, please," cautioned David as he reached out to touch her.

"Don't placate me! I've had enough of this nonsense. I know what's going on here and I've had enough of it."

"You've had enough to drink," David said in an emboldened voice. "That's for sure. Now please. Don't start an argument."

"Don't tell me what to do! I'll say what I please. I had enough over the years of hearing what a bad sister, what a mean sister, what a bully I was when she was growing up. I won't have it anymore. It's simply not true. I did the best that I could. You are so ungrateful!"

"Yes, I know," said Bea in a pretense of resignation. "As you told me as a child, I'm just an ungrateful dog."

"Oh!" sputtered Faye. "How - how - how dare you say those things. I don't ever remember saying such a thing."

"I know you don't. At least I'll grant you may not. But that doesn't take the pain away from the memories. I'm sorry, Faye, but the truth is that I have a lot of bad memories of you as an older sister; haughty, mean, unkind, bossy. You hurt my feelings often, whether you meant to or not. And because of how you were I vowed not to be that way to Polly. I never wanted her to feel hurt like I did."

"Maybe," challenged Faye, "just maybe your feelings got hurt too easily. Ever think of that?"

"Maybe," said Bea in a tactful tone. "It doesn't really matter now."

"Well," stammered Faye indignantly. "It - it - it matters to me, because it hurts me now to hear it. And if you only knew," her voice rose in pain, strident, "how much I'm suffering now…"

She left off talking, covered her face with her hands and began to weep deep sobs.

"I was afraid this would happen," muttered David fearfully. He sprang from his chair and took her hand in his as he knelt beside her and wrapped his other arm around her shoulders.

"Oh, Faye," said Bea sympathetically. "It isn't that bad. The past is past. Our relationship is better. And besides, you're the only sister that I have left now. I want us to be good. Let's not fight about this. Dad wouldn't want us to fight, especially now."

"No," burbled Faye, as she looked up at Bea. Her tear-stained face was flushed with wine, despair and anguish. "You don't understand. I have cancer."

Chapter 74

*"The repugnance to animal food is not the effect of experience, but is an instinct...
I believe that every man who has ever been earnest enough to preserve his higher
or poetic faculties in the best condition has been particularly inclined to abstain
from animal food."* (Walden, Henry David Thoreau)

A S HE GATHERED THE mail from the big green mailbox on the street Jay noticed a letter had
arrived from Phil's school...*probably his report card...* Climbing back into the Mercedes
he whistled to the flute sounds of "Life's a Long Song" from Jethro Tull, his favorite group,
pulsating from the speakers as he rolled down the rest of the long driveway. He could hear
dog-bird screeching its familiar welcome warning as he strode up the brick walkway to the
front door. Against the evergreens that bordered his lot a mix of blooming hydrangeas and
rhododendrons encircled his front yard in broad colorful splashes of pink and purple. They
were interspersed with tall staked delphinium towers, grouped in contrasting royal and
pastel blues. Completing the mix of large blossoms around the lawn were feathered lupine
spikes in mauve and magenta curving upward and pointing to the cerulean sky. June was
festooned in fresh summer flowers under a dauntless mid-day sun and he was not due back
to the office for several hours.

He set the mail on the grand piano as the screen door closed behind him and decided to
slip into his bathing suit for a swim. He also took his portable tape player and a Leroy tape
for listening to afterwards while sunbathing. A morning of clients had gone well as usual

and though no one was home he was happy to be alone…*oh that's right, city tour today… bea must have gone too*…Grabbing the mail and a towel from the bathroom he moseyed down the trail to the water expectantly. He took off his glasses and set them in a pile with the mail and the tape player on his towel. The water sparkled a wet welcome greeting in the warmth of the light early afternoon wind. Noticing that nary a soul was in the lake he dove off the dock quickly with a splash, rolled onto his back as he broke through the surface and began to backstroke his way to the middle. Taking his typical deep and measured breaths he fell into the familiar rhythm of gliding through the water almost effortlessly while gazing overhead at the vast cloudless sky amidst occasional splatters and spray from his movements.

His mind raced through the myriad of people and events that peppered his life at the moment. The boys had left early in the week for Puerto Vallarta, more excited than two Mexican jumping beans. This was certainly a curative tonic for the older one and a cultural bonanza for the younger one too. They had agreed to converse only in Spanish for the last few days before departing to the south and their spirits were high for fun and adventure… *oh God i hope this eases jess's pain*…With the thought of pain his attention turned to Faye, his normally carefree in-law whose mind was now shackled with the threat of cancer. Her stunning admission had turned the dinner party into a profoundly sobering event that evening. Yet it also had seemingly served to bring the two sisters together past any lingering estrangements from their differing recollections of distant childhood memories…*thank God their old man is doing okay*…Gabe had fortuitously been discharged from the hospital with a clean bill of health for the time being. Although there were concerns, as he was getting up there, everyone breathed easier knowing he was doing better at the moment and in Carrie's competent hands.

Continuing to course through the water on his back, his thoughts shifted from Gabe to his own parents. He hadn't seen them since Jess's wedding, coming upon almost one year ago. Deeply ensconced in their lives in California, they were younger than Gabe, who was in his mid-nineties, by at least fifteen years and apparently enjoying good health…*maybe they'll come for a visit this fall*…While indiscriminately viewing the expanse of sky as he slid through the water an unusual sight caught his eye. Two planes, fighter jets judging by their supersonic speed, were climbing almost vertically to the higher reaches of the atmosphere. The planes themselves were barely visible, two soaring specks of silver in tandem, but left parallel streams of thin vaporous lines as they streaked farther upward soon beyond sight in a matter of seconds…*maybe its like that when you die…fading memories trailing in your wake…*

He stopped swimming to take stock of his progress toward the center. Another twenty strokes and he would be close enough. Diving as deep as he could he felt the temperature turn colder with each passing instant as he descended into the darkening gray blue depths. He swam underwater like a frog while his breath held, then kicked his way up through the warming waters till he popped through the surface, surrounded by ever widening circular ripples. Surveying the lake in all directions he noticed that no one was even visible on the shore…*everyone's away…working…shopping…eating…driving… leaving this little old lake all to me…*

He recalled how he used to go swimming naked in the water the first few years after moving to Washington. Diving off the dock he would then slip his suit off and hang it on a nail there while treading in the water, then swim to his heart's content. No one could tell as he moved through the lake what he might be wearing and assumed it was more than his birthday suit. In innocent fun Bea had shared his secret with a neighbor lady who in turn had loudly yelled out encouraging remarks from her deck one day as he was swimming au naturale. Ever since then he'd discontinued the practice out of self-conscious concern for his reputation. Forestville was a small town, especially then, and he preferred to be regarded as a sensible professional among its residents. He feared he might seem already eccentric enough with a guitar in his office, an astrology book and an old Mercedes, without having it shouted out from the neighborhood rooftops.

He bobbed up then dove straight down again into the deep, trying to swim as far down as possible. The depth of the lake was unknown, at least to him, but it had a muddy bottom according to local lore and it was definitely too dark to see very far. Scurrying to the surface one last time from the murky depths he flung over on his back and began paddling back to the shore, humming like a harp in celestial satisfaction, being strummed at the hands of an angel.

Although the mainstay of his happiness at present was the fact that his practice was growing and well poised to continue so, in the back of his mind was the pleasing sensation of a recent surprise. Jake of the jazz club had followed up his comments on seeking Jay's expertise in food and wine. Not only could he be a wine sommelier to patrons of the grape but was also being offered the fantastic opportunity to feed them as well. Jake had had trouble keeping a professional chef employed at his place. Most of his customers came for the music not for a meal and though it seemed there was a reasonable demand for appetizers, the catering services he'd attempted to engage had repeatedly declined due to not enough money for the work involved. He had taken to heart Bea's remark that Jay was a gourmet and wondered if he would be willing to try his hand at hors d'oeurves for the crowd. Jay was overwhelmed with happiness at the offer and promised to prepare a menu of minute feasts finely designed to please the palate of a prince. His only condition was that the dishes be vegetarian, as Jay's diet had been since his twenty-first year. At first Jake balked at what seemed to him an undesirable and unprofitable stipulation. But at Jay's invitation he joined them for dinner one night on the lake and discovered the delights of non-flesh cuisine.

A creative quartet of dishes was then crafted for quick preparation and a variety of customer tastes. They included Nachos covered with sharp cheddar cheese plus toppings of guacamole, frijoles, sour cream and salsa. A large portabella mushroom was broiled and set on a bed of warm spinach graced with a scoop of soft goat cheese and sun-dried tomatoes. Sautéed asparagus spears were wrapped in thinly sliced soy meat, drizzled with a lemon dill sauce and laced with fresh garlic toasts. Lastly, for those inclined toward sweets, there were thick fresh strips of papaya, lightly layered with diced cilantro and dribbled with hand-squeezed lime juice. The ingredients were affordably obtained from Costco and to be readily prepared in the upstairs kitchen over the space that housed the jazz club. It was scheduled to start the next weekend and continue every weekend after that, at least for the summer. It was a happening well beyond his fondest dreams and thinking of the menu now made Jay realize he was getting hungry...*listen to Leroy a bit and have some lunch...*

Turning on his side he swam the rest of the distance to the dock and hauled himself up with the curved metal ladder that dipped into the lake. After toweling dry he put on the headphones and stretched out on his back on the towel on the dock to relax in the hot sun.

"How are you today?"

"Well, okay, I guess. I don't really have any specific issue to talk about. I'd just rather hear whatever it is you feel like saying today."

"Well, I'd be happy to do that."

"Great."

"Well, you know, when you get hit with something, you experience impact. And it is appropriate for you now in your spiritual development to move past the normal human conditioning of being impacted or being attacked. And what I mean by impact is those moments when you have frustration, concern, distraction, anger; anything other than peace and pleasure. Impact is where density begins to take hold. Now, the only way that you can ever be impacted by anything is by being unconscious of who you are, by simply conceding to the illusion that you are a body in circumstances; some poor little guy walking around being subject to the slings and arrows of circumstance, as Shakespeare would say. Now, to the degree that you realize that you are not just a body in separate circumstances, but are in fact part of a unified body, a unified whole, the universe, the whole of God's creation, then you are less susceptible to being impacted. And as you become freer of being impacted the tendency to want to defend yourself also is diminished, because you feel integrated, safe and supported by this body called the universe of which you are not only part of but the whole thing in a certain regard."

"You're a drop in the ocean and also part of the whole ocean."

"Exactly. So anyway, let's say you are being impacted. Anytime you have a problem that seems more important or more pressing than just curiosity then you have an experience of impact."

"Got it."

"Now, I'm going to ask you to reflect for a moment, what is the opposite of impact?"

"Passing by?"

"Yes, you're right in a sense, but I mean that if there is contact made, and so the word that I am using is 'solution'. Solution is the opposite of impact, in that to impact something is to make it dense and the opposite of that is to blend or join, in a solution, to make it looser."

"Like water does with most things."

"Precisely. Now, the word 'solution' is used to mean answer and the word 'impact' is used to mean problem. The Latin word 'solvere' means to loosen. So solutions are about loosening, about loosening up. And so what I am going to suggest here as a practice, as a point of learning, is that solutions and answers are not the same thing. You can have the solution without having the answer. And what the ego demands is that you have the answer, meaning that you have the understanding, before you have the solution. And what I'm saying is, that that is mistaken. It's actually backwards. You want to have the solution, regardless of what you may or may not understand, and by doing that you will come to the answer."

"Hm."

"Do you remember the tale of my missing TV remote?"

"When you looked all over your place for an hour and couldn't find it anywhere."

"Right. That was a situation wherein I felt impacted by the problem of not finding it. But clearly I needed to have the solution, which was to be still and let go of the fear around locating the remote, while still maintaining my interest or desire in what I wanted, and then the very next thing was that I had the answer. It was at my feet in the potato chip bag. I had to be at peace to see what was literally under my nose."

"I see."

"So, without having to know more than you know right now, with respect to any issue, practicing being in the solution is really what is necessary. It is a further step in experiencing nothing but relevance. Because that which is relevant will never impact you. It will move you or uplift you, but it will not impact you. So if you are being impacted it is because something which actually is of no importance, but has claimed a certain degree of importance, has crossed your path and demanded you to respond."

"Hm."

"So that's the issue here. You are learning now to be not only at peace but also to feel more at ease or looser with things that seemingly impact you."

"So you respond to these demands, or the impact of apparent problems, by feeling loose or at ease?"

"Yes, and you may have to stop at the time and say to God or Jesus or the Holy Spirit or your Spirit Guide, 'Hey, I need some help', and understand that that ego would want you to react to being impacted. You see, being impacted is always going to feel like an offense. And if you start living in the realm of being offended, then you begin to be righteous, and you start to judge what is right and wrong. And what is wrong is feeling that way and whoever did that to you is a villain. Do you see?"

"Yes."

"And so that is how all of that starts; the ego reaction, the justification for attack."

"I get it. It reminds me how the PC crowd, the political correctness types, the thought police, whose big thing is to control how people talk, use the rationale of being offended – 'Oh, I'm so offended by your use of this or that word' – as if they had the right to judge and couldn't help but be offended, while the silly twits never realize they're choosing to take offense. I always want to say 'Oh, I'm so offended you're offended'."

"Exactly. And so the first step, when you feel yourself being impacted, is to remember to stay conscious. Because it is not being conscious, staying unconscious in your ego, which allows being impacted to continue on and on. Staying conscious and saying 'Take this from me – I don't want it', is the relevant step to take. And then the next step is to understand that the experience of solution, of being unimpacted, does not constitute becoming vulnerable. What constitutes becoming vulnerable is staying unconscious."

"I understand."

"So that's the practice there. And what this will do for you is to put you in a place where you feel like more and more you are leading a charmed life. It will be easier, more relevant, and more and more outside of the perception of time. Because as you don't experience time passing, or pressure, or impact, you don't really experience time at all. You can't experience time in the way that people experience it, unless you are being impacted."

"That's reminds me of times, so to speak, when I have been lost in creating music or writing poetry or essays, and I get so involved in it in such a way that could certainly be called easy and relevant, that I later find, usually at some point of completion, that many hours have past when it seemed like five minutes."

"Yes. That's it exactly. And that's how eternity begins to dawn in your life on earth."

"Hm."

"So that's the story on that. What's experienced as impact is what's left of your conditioning. It doesn't really mean anything. It's not to be taken with seriousness or gravity. It's not to be reacted to. That is, the circumstances are not to be reacted to that apparently caused the impact. And just remember to stay conscious and ask to experience solution. You see, the word solution is great, because it means answer. It means joining or blending. It is the root word of absolution, which is to be forgiven or relieved, and resolution, which is to see clearly or to have a distinct answer, or finality around something."

"And the word 'sol' means sun, or the source of life, in some languages."

"Right. And so solution is great. And impact is not. And I'm saying that impact is an appropriate area of work on yourself right now. It truly means nothing, and you want to learn to recognize it for what it is. And it is always something other than a feeling of pleasure or ease. It always creates density. It always tightens you up."

"I got it."

"Good. Do you remember Paul Tuttle's book 'You Are the Answer'?"

"Yeah. I read it."

"Well, it could have been called 'You Are the Solution'. And when you are in that place, that state of mind, you become lucid. And lucid is a word used in common speech to mean clear, intelligent, and so on, but it actually means to be infused with light. And so if you are lucid, you are infused with light. And so what happens in that place, if you are lucid, is that you are able to know the obvious. You are able to know what is intelligent, without having to reason it or having arrived at it by thinking. You see?"

"Yep."

"Good. Now, just for the sake of illustration, let's take an example. Let's say that you got a notice from a collection agency that you owe them money, and you're impacted by the experience. You want to have more money and you're mad at not having enough money and you're also a little angry at the creditor just because they sent the letter. Now that's impact. And it is useless to be in the space of being impacted by that. So you want to get a little movement inside, that is, you want to ask to let go of that and to feel the solution. And when you arrive at the point of feeling the solution, that is, feeling at peace again, then you can say 'Of course I want to pay this bill' – 'Of course I want to honor this debt'. But there is no fearful reaction in that. It is merely being intelligent. You see that?"

"Yes."

"And so the further point I want to make is that you don't have to tolerate irrelevant things continuing to exist. Just because you are awake, just because you are fully conscious, doesn't mean that you become tolerant of everything. But intolerance does not have to be felt as conflict. Intolerance is expressed as authority and wisdom. And so when you feel yourself in your peace, in the solution and past the impact, then you can say 'I want out of this debt and I want to have more money'. But there is no edge to it. You are just expressing the honest truth and wisdom. And it is a good idea to allow yourself to do that, so that more and more what the world begins to look like is complete relevance. So, in your peace, in the solution, always say what you want and what you don't want. Be very clear about it.

"But don't go into the experience of peace and solution with the intent to say what you want specifically, as though you could arrive at it by thinking ahead of time. Get into your peace first and feel the solution completely, then say what comes to you as the obvious and intelligent answer you desire. Then express that desire unequivocally. That's when there is power. There's no power in the experience of being impacted; quite the opposite. But there is power in the experience of solution. Even though you don't have control, there's still power. And so you can speak your word, 'I want the remote control' or 'I want the debt paid'. Do you see that?"

"Yes."

"That's power. That's freedom. That is your saving grace, at that point; to be able to be in your peace and say what is true beyond dispute. Isn't is better to be able to pay the debt, to have it handled, rather than not? Is that a question open to debate? No. But in the moment of being lucid, where you are free of the impact, that's when you have power. That's when you can express God's will."

"Got it."

"And that's what you want. So every time an irritation or an experience of some kind of impact occurs, you want to get free of it as easily as you can. You really can't do anything until you are free of it, except ask to be free of it, and then when you are lucid again, you can look at the situation without an ego reaction and simply declare that you want what is relevant. Always ask for what is relevant and ask that anything irrelevant be taken from you."

"Forgive us our debts."

"Right."

"Deliver us from evil."

"Exactly. And there are a lot of things that people accept, like debts or bad relationships, for example, that can actually be dismissed. And they need to be dismissed as often as they come up, because you don't want it. You simply don't want it."

"Hm."

"And there is another point I want to make along these lines. You are doing a lot of work here learning to be at peace and to be undefended, and it is helpful to ask that you live in a world of hospitality, where people are hospitable, so that you being undefended is not just this inner activity that you are attempting to achieve in the face of people being unconscious and hostile as a rule. I always pray for hospitality, because it makes it much easier. Aren't you naturally more yourself and more undefended when people are gracious and friendly? Of course. And that is not generally the case, but it is something that I recommend praying for, because it makes waking up easier."

"Asking for hospitality?"

"Right. It's absolutely great to have hospitality, because otherwise you feel the inherent alienation in the world as though it were an immutable fact that could never be changed until everybody wakes up. But actually everyone has the capacity for hospitality and so to pray for it would be completely intelligent; lucid."

"I see."

"You see, it could be said that about ninety per cent of waking up is about you being in your peace regardless of circumstances, and ten percent, let's say, on circumstances reflecting the truth. There is a certain point of view that teaches you to have no regard for circumstances whatsoever and just try to maintain your peace, but that's not the full picture. There is a need for relevance, and the Lord's Prayer, which we've gone over before, is all about relevance. It's all about the world being relevant. And so when you come to a certain point where you say 'This has got to change', well Hallelujah, because that is powerful and that is appropriate."

"Once again, like Jesus tossing the money lenders out."

"Exactly. It's just that you can't declare the truth in that way if you are being impacted. So Jesus was at peace, was in the solution, when given the answer to that circumstance. And he was able to do it with an appropriate sense of power while being in that peace."

"I understand what you are saying."

"Good. So the most important thing now is to stay the course, but to let the road widen. For a long time you have been on the straight and narrow, the very narrow, feeling extremely confined. And as I have said before it is like walking on a tightrope without realizing the rope is on the ground."

"Yes."

"And the nature of God or life is to be generous. And so the more you can disregard impact, and allow yourself to move past it, or into solution, into greater expansion, the more you will experience having more right now, without any greater effort, thinking or willfulness required. You'll be able to feel more free without needing to have a reasoned understanding to find an answer. You'll feel your life expanding, the broadening of horizons, by means of doing nothing but being in the solution and desiring, asking for that which is relevant and the release or elimination of that which is irrelevant."

"Okay. I get it. Well, that has been an interesting half hour's food for thought. Essentially a different slant on the same information."

"Yes."

"But I like having different ways of thinking and feeling about it all."

"Right. It keeps you looser." (laughter)

"Right. (laughter) Has it been a half hour?"

"Yes, almost exactly."

"Okay then. Well, I'll call you in two weeks."

"That's fine."

"And probably send you a check before then."

"Thank you. I appreciate it."

"But I don't know how much."

"Just do what you can."

"Thanks."

"You're welcome."

"Bye."

"Take care."

As the tape ended Jay rolled over onto his stomach and slowly stood up. He threw his towel over his shoulder, put on his glasses and picked up the mail, feeling too hungry to go through it now. As he wound his way up the grassy trail to the house he saw that the letter from Phil's school was on top...*wonder how he did*...Mounting the short stairway to the upper deck he tore open the top of the envelope and pulled the report out. As he paused at the foot of the next flight of stairs, a longer one that connected to the house, he scanned the scores of his son's academic status. Like ice in a desert his merriment melted as he stopped, stood and was stunned by the column of C and D marks. He read the instructors' remarks unbelieving, wondering how this could possibly be. Teacher after teacher commented at the sudden and significant downward shift in grades from a boy who typically made A's and B's. It seemed as inexplicable to them as it was incredible to his father.

Several instructors noted that he had seemed sleepy in class. One wondered if he had too many extra-curricular activities for the second half of the year. Some others mentioned the quality of his handwriting had deteriorated along with a paucity of homework turned in. Shocked and disgruntled, more amazed than angry, Jay entered the house and called the school from the nearest telephone. He felt intensely impacted and in desperate need for some immediate answers. When the secretary answered he asked to speak to Phil's school counselor. Their conversation went instantly to the point, as Jay was much too alarmed for niceties, and his concern increased as they continued to converse.

"Hello, sir. I'm so glad you called. I had you on my list of parents to contact."

"Well, I wished you'd done so earlier, I must say. I just opened my son's report card and am utterly flabbergasted."

"Yes, I understand, and I'm sorry for not trying to reach you sooner. It's been hectic here with graduation and all. There was some hope he might do well on his finals."

"I see. Well, I hope you understand my concern. These grades are not reflective of Phil's abilities or his past achievement. These are just terrible. Something is wrong. I've got to find out what the hell's going on. Do you have any idea?"

"I know. It's disturbing. I know you're upset."

"Of course I'm upset, and I'm sorry I swore – I don't mean to imply it's your fault – but can you give me any insight at all into what's happening?"

"Well, first of all, the transition from a small elementary school to a much larger junior high can be difficult for many students."

"Sure. I know that. Everyone knows that. But he was doing okay the first two trimesters. What's different now? Is the third one that much harder?"

"Actually you're right. He was doing rather well. It's been a bit of a mystery to all of us and frankly we hoped it was a temporary slump."

"A temporary slump? Well, that may be, but it's not just the grades. These comments are disturbing. 'Sleeps in class?' This is crazy."

"Has he been busier this last semester with activities?"

"No, not really. He's always been busy and bore his academic load well too."

"Mm-hm, I see."

"Do students sometimes have an end of the year breakdown? I mean, I just don't know how to account for this."

"Have you been going on-line, sir, to check his grades? You do know that service is available, don't you?"

"No, I haven't. I guess I should have. I will from now on. If I had I would have been contacting his teachers. It never occurred to me there was a problem."

"Mmmm, yes. That's so often the case."

"What do you mean by that exactly?"

"Well, sir, I hate to say this without any actual proof or concrete evidence of any sort, but there's been...ahhh...some concern recently that perhaps he has been experimenting with drugs."

Chapter 75

"Men come tamely home at night only from the next field or street, where their household echoes haunt, and their life pines because it breathes its own breath over again; their shadows, morning and evening, reach farther than their daily steps. We should come home from far, from adventures, and perils, and discoveries every day, with new experience and character." (Walden, Henry David Thoreau)

FROM THEIR TABLE ON the third story balcony of the restaurant Jess and Phil viewed the vast expanse of shimmering blue sea in the late afternoon. Periodically passersby were observed as they strolled the white sidewalk of the wide malecón stretching below in the bright sunlight.

"Look at that babe in the blue bikini, bruz," said Phil as he sucked on the straw of his second lemonade. "That's a hot mama."

"Little brother," replied Jess, as he reached for another Corona from his bucket of ice, "you've got good taste in women. But she's a bit old for you. Better leave those for me."

"Hey, you're married. At least I'm available."

"Yeah, right," Jess intoned sarcastically. "At least I was." He popped open the beer and took a long slow draught.

"Jeez, you almost finished that in one swallow."

"I'm thirsty, amigo. Nothing like a beer on a hot summer day."

"Well, I'm glad you said that because I'm getting awful tired of lemonade. All this sugar's not good for you." Phil paused, then looked at his older brother wistfully. "You mind if I try one of your beers?"

"What?" said Jess, feeling slightly surprised. "Are you nuts? You're too young."

"I'm fourteen. That's not so young. In some countries people are getting married at that age."

"Yeah, well, I wouldn't advise it, at any age."

"In some countries people join militias and fight wars."

"Well, I wouldn't advise that either." He nearly polished off the bottle with a second swig, set it down still held in his hand with his arm outstretched and stared at his little brother curiously. "I don't think you'd like the taste."

"How do you know? You like it don't you?"

"Yeah, well, kinda'. It's what they call an acquired taste. It grows on you."

"Well, it could grow on me."

"Plenty of time for that."

Phil thought for a moment then tried another tack.

"How old were you when you started drinking?"

"Oh," reflected Jess, "sometime in high school."

"See? I'm almost in high school now."

"That's a big almost. You're still in junior high."

"Kids start doing things a lot earlier now. Sex, drugs, you know, everything."

Jess laughed. "Well, I hope you're not doing any of those things yet." As Phil didn't respond Jess eyed him seriously, angling his head as though to see into him more deeply.

"You're not are you?"

"Well, um…"

"Oh, no. You haven't really, have you?"

"Well," said Phil hesitantly, "I've been to parties where other kids were."

"Were what?"

"Smoking marijuana."

"And did you?"

"Uhhh…just a little," he said meekly.

"Oh no. That is not a good idea. You are way too young."

"I know. Don't worry. I just tried it once. Once or twice, you know, like the president, and I didn't like it."

"Yeah, and like the president said, ha ha, you didn't inhale either, I suppose. Right?"

"Just a little."

"And? Did you like it?"

"Nah. It made me cough."

"Good. You know that stuff is not good for you."

"You've done it, I bet."

"Well sure, but I'm older."

"Yeah, that's what everybody says about everything. Wait till you're older. It's not fair. I bet mom and dad did it."

"Yeah, but they grew up in the sixties. Most of their generation did it. Besides, it's illegal. Stick to alcohol. When you're older."

"Yeah, okay, you're right. So can I have just a little to see what it's like?" Jess pondered his request and answered in a decisive voice.

"If you'll promise me you'll stay away from smoking that stuff I'll let you try a sip." Phil looked pensive as he considered the proposition.

"Sure," he said. "At least till I'm older anyway."

"Good. All right then, here, just this once. There's a taste left. Have the rest of it. I think you'll see you don't care for it much." He slid the near empty bottle to Phil, whose countenance lit up in gratitude and expectant pleasure.

"Really? Thanks."

"Just this one time now."

Phil grasped the wet bottle and brought it to his lips. He gave his brother a mischievous smile.

"Here goes!" He swallowed the remainder of the bottle in one quick gulp then started to cough in dismay. "Yuck!" he exclaimed. He spat on the floor and wiped his mouth on his sleeve. "That sucks! How can you stand it?"

"Like I said," replied Jess with a big grin. "It takes awhile to like the taste."

"I don't think I'm ever going to like it. Puke!" He spat again on the floor and grabbed his lemonade glass. Bypassing the straw he had a big swallow. "Whew."

"Hey, what about all that sugar?"

"Who cares? Hey, maybe I could try a sweet drink?"

"You already got one."

"No I mean like a Margarita or something."

"That will, believe me, knock you on your ass. You're too young. What's the rush? Grow up a little more."

"Hey, maybe I'd like to get knocked on my ass. You do it. Grown-ups do it. Mom and Dad do it. Dad drinks wine every night. He even had an empty beer bottle in the car once."

"Yeah, well, they're grown up. You're not." Jess looked at Phil and shook his head. "You know," he said loftily, imparting a bit of arcane brotherly wisdom, "you may not believe this, but sometimes people, of legal drinking age mind you, will drink what's called hard liquor, like whiskey or vodka, and then drink a beer with it to help wash it down. They call it a chaser."

"A chaser?"

"Yep."

"Well, they can call it crap as far as I'm concerned."

"Told ya'," mused Jess. "You're too young to drink."

"A lot of kids at my school drink. They do all kinds of stuff."

"Well, sure. Look, I know kids mess around, experiment with these things, and all that, just like sex, but it's really not a good idea at your age."

"Inquiring minds want to know," stated Phil in pretend seriousness.

"Yeah, yeah," nodded Jess, reaching for another beer. "Someday they will. Now enjoy your lemonade. Or switch to a coke. Or some water." He pulled another one from the bucket. "And by the way, when you do drink, someday, remember to drink in moderation, and never on an empty stomach."

"Why?"

"No hangovers, no car wrecks, etc." Jess popped opened his Corona, drank half of it, and then slid his chair back. "I gotta' go to the bathroom," he said. "Why don't you get us some more chips?" he suggested, standing up. "Hey," he called back at the top of the stairs. "I'm gonna' get a little more cash at the machine down here too. May take a few minutes."

"Okay."

Phil watched Jess head down the stairs to the bathroom. In the back of the restaurant, in a far corner in a booth, was a pretty young Mexican girl, maybe eighteen, looking somewhat uncomfortable under the arm of a swarthy young Mexican man, slightly older than her. There was a half-filled pitcher of Margaritas at their table. He could not hear their conversation above the loud Mexican music on the jukebox but he could tell she was resisting his attempts to kiss her neck. A waiter, a grizzled old man with a gray mustache, entered the room, saw Phil glancing back and approached his table.

"May I get you something, señor?"

"Yeah," said Phil, meeting his gaze. "Some more tortilla chips, por favor."

"Anything else?" asked the waiter. There was pause in the conversation.

"Uh, yeah," Phil responded. He nodded toward the couple in the back. "I'll take one of those." The waiter raised his eyebrows.

"Are you eighteen, senor?"

"Yep, just turned it last week."

"You have your identification?" Phil reached for his wallet in his back pocket and produced an empty hand.

"Not on me, damn. It's back at our friend's house, here in town. Hey, don't worry. I am old enough. Just turned it." The waiter hesitated, staring at Phil through eyes that had seen many an underage gringo having illegal fun in Mexico. "And," Phil added with emphasis, "my brother will leave you a big tip too. We're celebrating my birthday." He pointed to the beers. "I just don't like the taste."

"I see," said the man.

"I'd like something sweeter."

"You want a pitcher or just a glass?"

"Oh, just a glass. You know, moderation." He smiled knowingly at the waiter. "No hangovers."

"Sí. You done with your lemonade?"

"Almost. That was just a warm up. I'm ready for a real drink now. And please don't forget the chips too. I hate to drink on an empty stomach."

"Do you want to order some food?"

"Maybe when my brother returns, thanks." The waiter nodded, picked up the empty chip basket and spun around towards the kitchen, leaving Phil to contemplate his newfound adventure. He felt giddy and was wondering how to explain the situation to his brother should the timing prove awkward. Casting a glimpse back to the stairway to see who might return first he noticed the girl in the booth squirming uncomfortably as she pushed the man's hand away from her breast. As he watched the unlikely couple in their dance of advance and resistance, she glanced over at him with fear in her eyes. He felt for her predicament but hesitated to respond...*shit...i'm just a kid...that guy's twice my size...*

The waiter reemerged with a platter in hand, sporting a frosty margarita glass along with a fresh basket of chips. He set the drink and chips on the table and reached for the near empty glass of lemonade.

"Hey, I'll keep that," said Phil as he waved him off. "For a chaser, you know?"

"A chaser, señor?" The waiter seemed nonplussed.

"You know, a chaser, like to wash it down," he said earnestly, searching for signs of recognition in the waiter's face. "They do it in America," he added. "A lot."

"Ahhh, I see. A chaser. Of course, amigo." The man creased his lips in a tight smile and nodded as he backed up a step. "Okay, señor. Happy Birthday."

"Thanks. I mean, gracias. Gracias a lot."

"De nada, señor," he called over his shoulder as he left. Phil watched him retreat down the stairs and then turned his attention to the concoctions before him on the table. Picking up his glass of lemonade he swiftly tossed the remnants of it into a potted palm tree in a corner of the balcony. He then poured the contents of the margarita drink into it, licked off an inch of the salt on the rim and set the empty glass on a tabletop several tables away. Studying his secret potion with anticipation, desire, curiosity and fear he jumped when his brother pulled back the chair next to him.

"Got a new drink, huh?"

"Yeah. Yeah. These chips make me thirsty."

"I thought you were sick of sweet stuff."

"Oh well, what are you gonna' do?" He took a small sip and licked his lips. "Mmmm. Did you get some more money?"

"Not yet, the line's too long. I'll go back in a bit. I got tired of waiting. It's awfully hot on that sidewalk and there's no shade out there." Jess finished the half bottle of beer he had left. "Ahhhh."

"We ought to give this guy a good tip," remarked Phil. "He's given us a lot of chips."

"Don't worry. I always tip them well. They don't make that much money, especially compared to us."

"Right." Phil took a larger sip of his drink and emitted a muted groan of surprise and satisfaction.

"Pretty good, huh?"

"Yeah," agreed Phil. "Pretty good, pretty good." There was a squeal from the back and both boys turned around in response to the sudden noise. The young woman was wrestling half-heartedly with the hands of the persistent man in the booth. Phil looked at Jess.

"Maybe we ought to go back there and help her."

"I don't know." Jess shook his head slowly while watching them. "I don't think someone who lives here would take kindly to a gringo getting involved in his business."

"He's just one guy."

"Yeah, but you can bet he has friends. This is his city. We're tourists. We're foreigners. If there's a hassle the police will probably take his side. The last thing we want to do is end up in a Mexican jail, believe me." As if overhearing their conversation the man suddenly glared at them. For a moment the couple stopped struggling. The boys turned back around. Jess shrugged. "I don't know what she expects to happen when she comes into a bar with a guy and lets him buy her drinks."

"Yeah, I guess you're right." Phil took another sip.

"I tell you what, little brother, if he actually starts to push things to the point where she's really freaking out I will get the waiter. Right now it looks like they are just struggling over some kisses and hugs. For all I know it could be she's his girl friend."

"That sounds good," said Phil, reassured. As though on cue, perhaps self-conscious from the unwanted attention, the noise from the booth behind them subsided and the brothers focused outward on the sights from the balcony. A large white cruise ship was chugging towards the harbor, like a gigantic glacier, dwarfing the assorted other crafts in the ocean.

"God, that boat is huge," Phil remarked.

"Yep," returned Jess, "and huge for the economy here too. They'll unload at least several hundred passengers in the harbor for a few hours and all the Mexicans will get rich quick off of them."

"Mm." Phil nodded as he sucked hard on his straw. "Good for them."

"Yep," agreed Jess, polishing off another lager. "And that reminds me, we still need some cash. I'm going to run back down there and see if the line's any better. Once that cruise ship docks the cash machine lines will be impossible. Be right back."

"Okay. Take your time," Phil advised, as Jess dashed down the stairs. He considered the possibilities of another secret drink. Hearing a chair screech across the floor and bang against a table he turned wondering if it were the waiter...*perfect timing*...and was surprised to see the man from the booth lurching hurriedly toward the stairs headlong...*bet he has to pee*... As he disappeared down the stairway Phil peered back at the woman. She met his gaze with beseeching eyes. Feeling flush from his margarita he downed the last of it and wheeled around to face her fully. She was a young Latin beauty with long black hair, flashing eyelashes and a turquoise necklace above her white blouse that was opened to the button just below her breasts, revealing a buxom cleavage in a racy silken black bra. Her face was lightly sweat-stained from the alcohol, the heat and the struggle against the amorous assaults on her virtue. When she gave him a sweet but sad smile he overcame his resistance to remain uninvolved and stood up.

Wobbling slightly with alcohol, he walked directly toward her. As her face brightened, beckoning him forth, he forged onward buoyed by a growing sense of confidence, entranced by the luminous call of her eyes, a clear homing beacon, until he tripped on a chair in the middle of the room and sent it crashing violently to the tile floor. He bent over as gracefully as he could manage, feeling foolish and woozy, and set it upright before reaffixing his gaze on her limpid pools of light. Her smile broadened sweetly with unmistakable compassion at his understandable difficulty in navigating a challenging obstacle course of ill-positioned furniture and he approached her booth feeling as gallant as Sir Lancelot victoriously fending off dragons for a damsel in duress. Placing both hands on her table for support he leaned over slightly a foot from her face.

"Are you okay?" he blurted out.

"No," she answered starkly. Her eyelids flashed as though to hold back tears. "But I don't know what to do."

"Just leave," he urged. "Now, while he's gone."

"I don't know where to go," she whispered fervently. "My girl friends are probably still with his friends at the bar down the street. We left them to come here for some food. I can't go back to them."

"Just go home."

"I can't. My friend drove here, not me. She's probably having fun and won't want to leave."

"Take a taxi. There's plenty of them."

"I can't do that. We're from a town several hours from here."

"Oh. Why'd you come here?"

"Just to have some fun. Maybe meet some nice boys. Only he is not so nice now."

"Oh. I see." Phil wavered gently back and forth, comprehending her dilemma. "Well, can you just - "

The girl screamed as two large hands gripped his shoulders tightly, abruptly spun him around and whammed him against the wall.

"You looking for trouble, hombre?" yelled the woman's companion hoarsely. "You want some beeg trouble, cabrón?" He glared into Phil's eyes menacingly. "Keep away from my girl! Comprende?"

Phil faced the ugly scowl on the unshaven face of the burly man, as he stayed pinned upright. He noticed his teeth were stained brownish yellow and his breath reeked of liquor. The scene felt surreal and a remembrance of the game Pin the Tail on the Donkey flashed through his mind. He gave a futile try to wriggle out of the man's grasp and protested.

"She's not your girl, man. And let me go." The man threw his head back and laughed derisively, then tightened his grip.

"You going to tell me whose girl she is?" he sneered. "I could keel you. I could break you in two. I could -"

Suddenly the man's head was jerked back in a chokehold as the girl screamed again.

"Let go," said Jess grimly, like the calm before a storm. The man did and was pulled backward then thrown to the ground. "Now leave," Jess ordered, quivering unmistakably with deadly determination. "While you can still walk out of here."

The man lay like a cornered beast, his haunted eyes filled with hate, staring up at Jess, weighing his options. He was larger but distinctly at a decided disadvantage and his willingness to fight seemed to be ebbing.

"Yeah, do you feel lucky, you big piece of shit?" Phil had regained his composure.

The Mexican's eyes narrowed angrily as he shifted his gaze from one brother to another.

"Stay out of this!" snapped Jess to Phil. He looked back down to the man on the floor. The fellow's muscles relaxed visibly as he rolled over to regain his feet and then grabbed a chair to help pull himself up. For a moment he paused, both hands clenching the back of the chair, as though considering swinging it as a weapon. Jess stiffened when he noticed the dirty yellow stains on the man's fingertips as he watched his hands curl around the wooden backing. His own fists clenched as the memory of a former moment, another Mexican standoff, shivered through him like high voltage current...*that night on the bus...* Only this time he was ready. This time he was willing to risk aggressive action...*don't mess with my brother...*

"Don't even think about it," Jess warned him flatly. "Leave while you can walk." He nodded toward the stairway. "Now."

The man gave him a sideways glance while starting to move to the stairs. "I'll be back," he growled threateningly, then slouched down the stairway with heavy plodding steps.

Jess turned to Phil. "Are you okay?"

"Yeah, I'm fine." He wiggled his head around to loosen up his neck. "I was just thinking about kneeing him in the balls when you showed up."

"Yeah, right. Well, I'm glad you didn't. I'm telling you a fight here could be dangerous for us. What the heck happened anyway? What are you doing here at their table?"

Phil shrugged. "I don't know. It just seemed like the right thing to do. She was crying. He had left to go to the bathroom or something. I was just trying to help her."

"Don't stick your nose into other people's business here. We're in a foreign country."

"No, señor," pleaded the girl. "Please don't be mad at him. He was just trying to help. He saved me."

"Well, actually my brother saved you," corrected Phil. "And he saved me too." He rubbed his left shoulder to ease the muscle ache away. "Thanks, bruz. Sorry I got you into this."

"Well," said Jess forgivingly. "I know it's hard to resist helping a sad señorita, especially a pretty one." He smiled at the girl. "But the stakes are much different when you're in someone else's backyard."

"I know," responded Phil. "I'm sorry. I drank that margarita so fast that-"

"What! You had a margarita?" Phil looked sheepishly at the ground...*uh-oh*...

"Just one."

"Just one. And how did that happen?"

"Well...I asked the waiter for one while you were gone before."

"And he gave it to you."

"Uh, right. I guess he thought I was old enough."

"Uh-huh. I bet. Jesus Christ. What were you thinking?"

"I just wanted to try it," said Phil feebly. "Everyone at my school does it."

"Uh-huh. Oh man," Jess spoke in disgust. "I can't even trust you for a minute."

"Sure you can. I'm sorry. I won't do it again. I didn't even like it, much."

"Oh, señor," wailed the girl, blinking back tears. "Please forgive him. He saved me. Your leetle brother is very brave. Just like you. Please forgive him that he help me."

"It's not that," started Jess. He stopped, looked at them both and then over the balcony out to the ocean. "Oh, never mind." He turned back and stared at Phil. "Just don't do it again."

"I won't," he said contritely. "I won't."

Suddenly the waiter bounded up the steps into the room. "What happened, señores?" he said worriedly, looking around the area.

"Oh, nothing," Jess reassured him. "Just a little misunderstanding."

The waiter frowned suspiciously. He scanned their faces searchingly. "I heard some loud noises." He looked at the girl and at the empty space next to her where the man had been sitting. "I think it is best if you leave now, señor. We don't want any trouble here."

"Yes," agreed Jess. "We're just about to leave." He pulled out a wad of pesos and handed them to the waiter. "That should take of our bill. Keep the change."

"The waiter smiled through tight lips and nodded. "Si, señor. Gracias."

"I told you he'd tip you big," said Phil, grinning at the man.

"And here, señor." The young woman thrust some currency toward the waiter. "For the drinks."

"Gracias," said the waiter, seeming mollified by the sudden emergence of funds. He cupped the bills in a roll in his hand. "Muchas gracias."

"De nada," Jess answered. "Let's go." The boys turned toward the steps.

"Wait!" called the señorita. Smiling sweetly she rose from the booth, walked up to Phil and cupped his face in her hands. "Muchas gracias, muchacho," she said kindly. He smiled back as she bent forward to kiss his lips, which parted into a large grin as she let him go. "Adios. Vaya con Díos." Phil swayed back slightly, reeling from the poignant but unexpected affection. His eyelids fluttered, intoxicated with a heady mix of romance and tequila. He looked at Jess.

"Maybe we should stay."

"No," urged the señorita. "Your brother is right. Vámanos."

"Right," said Jess. "Let's go, lover boy." He started down the top steps and looked back at Phil still lost in the eyes of the dark-haired young woman. "Now, buddy, now!" Phil jumped as though reentering a new gravitational field. He smiled and wiggled his eyebrows flirtatiously at her, then spun around and followed his brother's lead. They scrambled down the stairs like firefighters off to a five-star alarm, burst out on the sidewalk and peered both ways up and down the boulevard.

"So far so good," declared Jess. "Let's duck down the alley over here near the river and make our way out to another part of town." He moved with the determined speed of a racehorse leading the pack as he whizzed past the pedestrians thronging the walkway. A half block away from the restaurant he slipped into a narrow alleyway off the main drag and waited a few moments as his younger brother caught up.

"Whoa, you were hauling," said Phil, catching his breath. "Think we're safe?"

"I don't know," Jess replied, as he looked around cautiously. "Let's keep moving." They began walking briskly past backdoors, trash bins and the litter that lined the long slender lane. As they neared the first cross street four men emerged suddenly, rounding the corner and standing in the alley twenty feet in front of them. The one from the bar was there with his friends, grimacing darkly, his eyes filled with vengeance. Jess twirled in his tracks to face the far end of the alley as two more of their companions appeared at that end. They began walking slowly towards the two brothers, stalking their prey. He wheeled around again and glared at the four hombres. His anger flared up as he stared down his antagonist, recalling the scene he'd beheld in the bar. He whipped off his shirt, threw it to the ground and jumped into a threatening karate fight pose.

"C'mon motherfuckers!" he bellowed ominously, bristling with rage. "Let's go! Right now!" His tense stance and tone stopped the four men abruptly. Phil took the same position beside him, looking as mean as he could possibly muster, a fuming mad midget of a bantam rooster. "Yeah," he yelped in a high-pitch holler even louder than Jess. "C'mon!"

The man from the bar took a hesitant step forward then looked back to see his associates still rooted to their spots. They were blinking with doubt and wavering resolve while assessing the unexpected upsurge in threat. The fire in their belly appeared to be faltering. Jess leaped a step towards them like a killer kangaroo, maintaining his fight stance, hands held up like knives. Phil glanced back at the other end of the alley. The two men behind them had stopped in their tracks and were watching the spectacle from a safe distance. Jess suddenly let loose a deafening cannonade of ferocious expletives in a fiery Spanish tongue and leapt a yard closer to his would-be attackers. The blood drained from their faces and one of them mumbled something to their leader as they took a few steps back. The man turned to see their waning enthusiasm then looked back at the brothers. He swallowed perceptibly, pride with saliva, looking angry but defeated.

"Ahhh," he muttered disgustedly. "Gringos". He spat on the ground then turned away with a dismissive wave of his hand and retreated with his group as they shuffled around the corner. Jess breathed a noticeable sigh of relief. Phil pivoted back to the two men still watching at the far end of the alley while holding his karate stance and glared at them.

"Wanna' piece of me?" he yelled. "C'mon! Make my day!"

"Will you stop it?" said Jess quietly, concealing his amusement. With the wounded hubris of their friend no longer at issue the two men warily turned around and departed.

"Nice work, bruz," exclaimed Phil with heartfelt admiration. "You scared the hell out of them."

"Yeah, well, it seemed like a good idea at the time," he said, in a matter-of-fact tone of voice. "And it's a good thing you were with me."

"You mean that?" Phil asked, as he looked up at his brother in wide-eyed astonishment.

"Well, yeah, of course. You yelled louder than me."

"Yeah," Phil giggled. The boys began walking slowly back to the main street. "Do you think we're safe now?" Jess shook his head.

"Hard to say really. After dark when they're drunk they may find some more courage at the bottom of their bottles."

"Mm, yeah, I guess that could happen." He pondered that possibility. "Well, we'll be with our friends tonight and just hang with them, right?"

"Sounds good," said Jess as he slipped on his t-shirt. "Let's go get some food. I'm really hungry now."

"Me too," chirped Phil, keeping stride with his hero. "Hey, I was wondering. What'd you say to those guys when you were yelling in Spanish?"

"I told them," he said, "they couldn't mess with my little brother. I said I'd kill them for messing with my family. That sort of thing."

"Ahhh, I was wondering."

"The Mexican culture has a strong respect for family. I figured that plus acting like a madman with nothing to lose might do the trick."

"You were right."

"I guess so."

As the boys ambled back toward the embarcadero, contemplating the potential perils of the night, Phil wrapped his thin arm around the waist of his brother, towering above him, and leaned his head gently into his side. Jess laid his sinewy arm across Phil's shoulders, draping the smaller build like a Mexican serape. They walked together in silence, tired but exhilarated, letting the adrenaline drain from their system. As they proceeded, after a moment, Phil spoke softly from his upturned face.

"I love you, bruz," he said, with quiet conviction, squeezing the muscled girth in a hug. "I love you a lot."

Chapter 76

"Each one is responsible for his growth. Each one is responsible for his enlightenment. Each one is responsible for any suffering that he seems to experience."
(You Are The Answer, Paul Tuttle)

FROM HIGH ATOP THE outdoor observation deck of Seattle's Space Needle Bea leaned against the metal railing and gazed south to Mt. Rainier. The cool wind whipping through the circular terrace was a refreshing counterpoint as it brushed by her face in the warm summer sun. The mountain was a huge pointed pile of vanilla ice cream beaming against the backdrop of a cosmic blue horizon. Beneath her spread the city like a wacky patchwork quilt of lakes, trees and fields interspersed with streets and buildings. She glanced at her sister holding hands with David and was glad to see her enjoying the view. Now she knew why the woman was thinner. They'd had a good sisterly talk last night stretching late into the evening as Faye had unraveled the secret of her suffering. She had intended to confide in her sisters at the reunion but decided against it when the plane crash occurred. She didn't want to burden Bea with another possible tragedy then.

She had a form of lymphatic cancer, leukemia, which if it continued to advance as it was, would soon get to the point where hospitalization was mandatory. That had been suggested to her several months back but Faye had disavowed treatment at the time in favor of continuing her high-spirited lifestyle: she wanted to visit her sister in Seattle. Despite the adamant dictates of her doctor and over the heated protests of David, she insisted on making the trip in the summertime. She knew that the region was at its best then weather wise, with the least likelihood of the downpours and drizzles that drenched and dogged its waterlogged denizens. With growing progressively wan and weaker in the past few months she had come to accept the inevitability of succumbing to the last-ditch hope of carcinogenic care; chemotherapy. With the loss of one sister so fresh in both their minds any time spent together now was especially precious. She had promised Bea and David last night that she would check into the hospital upon returning to Pittsburgh. For this week she just wanted to have some fun times.

Leaving Faye and David to look through a large telescope, Bea turned and strolled westward, tracing the stark uneven outline of the Olympics beyond the islands that dotted the sparkling waters of Puget Sound. Ferryboats, cargo and cruise ships chugged back and forth below her leaving vanishing white lines through the choppy sea-lanes of busy Elliot Bay. As she continued around to the north side she noted the curvature of the hills in the distance along with Lake Union slightly off to the right where seaplanes were taking off and landing in graceful succession, as precise and delicate as dragonflies on a pond. Completing her walking tour she took in the rugged range of the chiseled-tooth Cascades far to the east and came upon her guests as she rounded the bend still entranced in their telescopic view of the area.

"What are you guys looking at?" she asked. "Did you find a nude beach?"

Faye pulled back from the scope and leaned into the encircling arms of her boyfriend. She smiled mischievously. "Nude beach? No. Where is it? We were wondering."

"About two states southward in Southern California."

"Ah-hah. I don't think this scope is that powerful." She laughed and gave her head a little toss as she ran her hand through her hair. "This whole area is just so beautiful. This view reminds of the one from the veranda at my condo in Pittsburgh."

"Yes, I remember that," agreed Bea. "Though it was covered in snow when I was there last."

"That's right," chimed in David. "I remember that time. We talked on the phone. You were visiting then, back for a -" He suddenly stopped talking; backing off from the subject he had been warming to. "I'm sorry. I didn't mean to…uh…"

"It's okay," Bea assured him, sensing his embarrassment. She patted his arm and looked at Faye. A twinge of pain passed between them as they locked eyes. No one spoke for a long still moment. "Life goes on," she finally said. "And I'm so glad you're here."

"Me too," said Faye, as she reached for Bea's hand and gave it a squeeze. "I'm starving," she announced, changing gears quickly. "Let's see what your fancy restaurant here has to eat."

"Sounds good to me," concurred Bea. "Let's go." She led them through the gift shop inside the deck level and down the stairs to the round restaurant. They were given seats at a window table and studied their menus as they leisurely spun around in a circle five hundred feet above the Emerald City. Sampling the region's fresh King Salmon provided an appetizing lunch for the two visitors while Bea made do with the vegetarian tart, taking a portion of it home for her culinary critic, who was always curious what was cooking elsewhere. After the meal, just as they were entering the elevator Bea's cell phone rang out in her purse. She fumbled through the jumble of various items in her bag and managed to retrieve the phone mid-ring as the elevator closed and began its descent.

"Hello," she answered. "Yes, it's me." Her face grew serious as she listened intently to the caller's voice. "Oh, my God. When? How?" Water welled in her eyes as she looked at Faye gravely. "Dad died," she said solemnly, tears running down her face.

"What?" gasped Faye, turning pale as a sheet.

"In his sleep, peacefully," she murmured.

"Oh, no."

"He was taking a nap, at home in his favorite chair, and never woke up." Faye's knees buckled as she collapsed in David's arms.

"Oh God," Bea said. "I've got to call you back. My sister just fainted." She clicked off her phone and dropped it in her purse. "Faye!" She looked up at David, who was straining to hold her up. "Can you hold her?"

"For a while," he said anxiously, looking fear-stricken. "She's not so heavy, just limp."

"I'm calling 911," said the elevator attendant, a serious-looking young woman. "Always better safe than sorry." As the elevator came to a stop and opened to the lobby David half carried, half-dragged a lifeless Faye through the doors and onto a couch where he sat down beside her.

"The ambulance will be right here," said another uniformed attendant. He was young, Bea noticed, like the elevator girl...*probably both college kids in new summer jobs*..."Please don't panic." He looked at Bea. "What happened anyway?"

"Oh," she said, staring down at Faye, while feeling numb with grief and shock. "She fainted. We got some bad news on my cell phone just as we were coming down."

"Must have been pretty serious."

"Yes," she replied, choking back tears. "Our father just died."

"Oh, I'm sorry." The young man looked uncomfortable. "I'll go outside to make sure the paramedics get right in."

Though it seemed a longer time the paramedics arrived in minutes. When they could not quickly rouse her they became more concerned. David was informing them of her recent medical history when she started to regain consciousness. She immediately began crying inconsolably as Bea and David sat by her, each holding a hand. Concerned that her present trauma might adversely impact her generally weakened condition, the paramedics were politely resolute that she be taken to a medical center. At Faye's request they permitted David to ride along in the back of the ambulance while Bea trailed behind in her car shedding her own tears. She was taken to the emergency room of the nearest hospital where the physician in charge suggested she be admitted for an overnight stay there for observation. Bea and David stayed in the waiting room for several hours before being advised that Faye was resting comfortably under sedation and would not be awake nor receiving visitors until the next morning. They drove home in silence, each feeling stunned from the distressing ordeal of events that had suddenly transpired. They went to bed early, exhausted from it all. Bea spent several hours lying next to Jay, grieving for her father and fearful for her sister, until she eventually fell asleep, nestled in his arms on a wet tear-stained pillow.

In the morning she and David were both at her bedside attentively as the breakfast meal was being served. The color had returned somewhat to Faye's cheeks but her face was drawn in somber sorrow with the corners of her mouth turned down and the characteristic sparkle erased from her eyes. Bea pushed aside her own grief gently and tried her hand at humor.

"What some people won't do for attention," she teased, taking her sister's hand in her own. "Now you're getting your breakfast in bed." Faye smiled wanly and looked at the tray of food beside her on the stand.

"Not my favorite foods," she said feebly. "I think I'm still too tired to eat."

"Maybe the sedative hasn't worn off," offered David from the foot of her bed as he massaged her feet.

"Mmmm…that feels good," Faye murmured. The stood in silent contemplation as he continued rubbing and Bea stroked her forearm. "Maybe," she mumbled wearily. "Maybe." She sighed. "I just can't believe he's gone."

"I know," agreed Bea. "It's a shock. I feel the same way. And yet, I'm glad he passed away peacefully while sleeping at home. There's probably no better way to pass on."

"That's for sure," said David soothingly, continuing to rub. "No better way at all."

"And now he's with mom, at last, like he wanted," Bea added.

"What about the funeral?" Faye inquired listlessly. "What should we do?"

"It's all being taken care of," said Bea. "Don't worry. Your daughter is handling all of the details."

"Oh….she's so good and grown-up."

"That she is," nodded Bea…*she had to be*…"So don't you worry about it. Just focus on getting well yourself. We'll do what needs to be done when the time comes."

"Okay," she whispered, closing her eyes.

"How about some food?" David asked eagerly. "It'd be good if you could eat something."

"I'm not too hungry." She cast a glance at the tray. "Maybe in a bit. Do you know when I get out of here?"

"They're going to do some tests today," said Bea, in measured tone of good cheer. "And then, depending on what they find, we'll know when you're getting released."

"I see," said Faye in resignation. "Okay." She opened her eyes and looked at David. "Why don't you get you and Bea some coffee? You can pull up some chairs and stay awhile, can't you?"

"Sure," he replied, happy to do something helpful. "I'll go find some. It's probably in the cafeteria. Be back as soon as I can." The women watched as he left the room then Bea turned back to Faye.

"He's a nice fellow."

"Yes," breathed Faye wearily. "He is."

"Do you guys ever talk about getting married?"

"Oh, I don't think I'll ever get married again.

"Really?"

"Why bother? We've got a good relationship. The only difference is that then we would live together. We can do that now as much as we want. When we want a break or want to be in our own space we've got that option. I like that."

"I see."

"Actually he would like to get married. I don't know. Maybe I just like feeling independent."

"Yes, maybe you do."

"And of course then our finances would be pooled. I'd have to think twice about certain purchases. I don't have to do that now."

"Mm-hm."

"This works okay the way it is."

"Sure. Just curious." She bent forward to Faye a few inches. "Are you just feeling tired or sad about dad?" Tears welled in Faye's eyes, which brought them in turn to Bea's.

"Both, I guess." Bea nodded and squeezed her hand tighter.

"I know." Their eyes engaged with a depth of understanding beyond the ability of words to express. "We're all we've got now of the old guard, the Ohio clan," she said tenderly. Faye nodded as a tear rolled down her cheek. Bea pulled a tissue from a nearby box and dabbed it away.

Suddenly a nurse, a large black woman, breezed into the room, gave the sisters a big smile and proceeded to open the curtains on the window by Faye's bed. Bea was struck by her brisk and jaunty confident manner and also how beautifully white her teeth looked in contrast to her dark skin when she smiled. The sunlight suddenly pouring through the window seemed to equate with the radiance of her presence. She threw the tissue in the wastebasket and regarded her expectantly.

"Good morning," she said airily, turning to Faye at her bedside by the breakfast tray. "My name is Delilah. How are we doing today?"

"Okay, I guess," responded Faye, sensing a change in the room. The woman's energy felt slightly uplifting to both sisters.

"I see you haven't touched your food yet," the nurse observed. "Is there something wrong with it?"

"No," Faye replied. "I just don't feel very hungry."

"Well, it looks to me like you could stand to get some meat on those bones. How about starting with some juice?" The woman tore open the tin foil lid on a small cup of orange juice and handed it to her patient. "Would you like a little sip? Just to see how it goes down?"

"Oh, I guess I could." She propped herself up higher on the bed into a sitting position and took a small sip. "Thanks."

"That's my job, honey. To help you get well." She looked at Bea. "This must be your sister."

Bea chuckled. "How could you tell?"

"That's easy," Delilah answered. "You look like two peas from the same pod."

"Yeah," Bea countered, "but who looks older?" Delilah grinned broadly.

"I'm not going to answer that question, darlin', no way." The women laughed. Delilah tucked at the corner of the bedspread near the foot of the bed, straightening out some wrinkles in it. "You keep eatin' now, you hear? The doctor will be in to see you soon and it would be best to have you with some nourishment in you and this tray out of the way when he does." Faye sighed and smiled faintly.

"Okay," she said. "I'll try."

"That's a good girl." She stared a Faye inquisitively. "Are you comfortable enough? Do you want an extra pillow?"

"No, I'm all right."

"Are you too cold or too warm?"

"No. I'm okay."

"All right then. Let me take your temperature then and I'll be on my way." She whipped out a thermometer from her pocket and placed it in Faye's mouth with the gentle precision of someone who had done it many times. She crossed her arms and looked out the window while waiting for the temperature to register. "Looks like it's going to be another bright sunny day in Seattle." Everyone quietly took in that fact appreciably.

Bea broke the short silence by extending her hand to the nurse. "I'm Bea," she said pleasantly.

"Glad to meet you honey. You both live here in Seattle?"

"Actually I'm from Forestville and she's from Pittsburgh." Faye watched the two women talk as the thermometer did its work, looking like a kid sucking on a lollipop.

"Pittsburgh! My, my, my. That's a long ways away." She glanced a Faye, who merely nodded. "Just visiting?" she asked. "Don't answer," she cautioned and looked back at Bea.

"Right," replied Bea. She took a deep breath. "Actually we were up in the Space Needle, the elevator really, when we got word that our father passed away."

"Oh, I'm so sorry." Delilah's visage transformed from heartiness to heartfelt compassion. "I'm sorry to hear that. Was it completely unexpected?"

"Well, not exactly. He had been in the hospital recently and he was very old, in his nineties." She looked at Faye, still lying with her lips tightly sealed around the glass instrument. "He had a good long life."

"Oh, well, that's good." Delilah nodded knowingly. "And is your mother still alive?"

"No," Bea said. "She died years ago."

"I see." She turned to Faye and extracted the thermometer. "My parents passed away years ago too," she said absent-mindedly as she read the temperature gage. "Looks like you have a mild fever, honey. I'm going to get you some Tylenol." She looked back to Bea and smiled sweetly. "It's good to have sisters, isn't it?" Bea smiled back at her then turned to look at Faye.

"That's what we always say," she said quietly, then turned back to the nurse. "The problem now is that she fainted in the elevator and was rushed here by ambulance. So we're waiting to see what happens next."

"I see. Okay," she said in a professional yet genuinely sympathetic manner. "Well, I'm going to get that Tylenol and I'll be right back." She turned on her heels moved swiftly toward the hallway, stopping halfway out the door. "You know," she said, with a conspiratorial air of sharing, "I have a sister too, and she means the world to me. Don't you worry," she added with a note of kind finality. "We're going to take good care of you here."

Both women smiled as she left the room, feeling somewhat relieved and in a lighter mood. Moments later David reappeared with coffee and bagels. They all chatted amiably as Faye consumed her food unhurriedly, eating bit by bit like a bird pecking at a lawn. Shortly after she finished a doctor came in, introduced himself and announced Faye was being carted away to a lab on a different floor of the hospital for some routine blood work and other customary tests. He asked Bea and David to leave until the afternoon, at which time they expected to determine her prospects for further observation and treatment or release.

David offered to buy an early lunch at any restaurant Bea had in mind and she took him to their favorite Thai place in the city. Over Phad Thai for him and Bea's favorite, Angel Rama, they discussed their hopes and concerns for Faye's health.

"I'm really worried," disclosed David, "that she's not taking good care of herself."

"How do you mean? Too much drinking or what?"

"Not that so much," he demurred, "though it wouldn't hurt her to cut back a bit. More that she's always on the go. Parties, formal social gatherings, you know, auctions, balls, late night meetings at restaurants."

"Ah, yes, Spazio's," joked Bea as she pushed a chunk of tofu through the peanut sauce. "How'd you know that?"

"In the short time I visited there it seemed we, and especially she, went often."

"Okay, well, then you know. She likes to have a good time. All the time."

"Maybe too good a time?"

"Right. You know, her doctor advised her not to make this trip. But she wouldn't have any of that. No, siree." He exhaled in frustration and lifted his eyebrows for emphasis. "She always wants to do just what she wants to do."

"That's how she's always been."

"And I can't control her."

"No one ever could."

"I don't know what to do."

Bea reached over and patted his wrist. "Just love her," she urged warmly. "That's all anyone can do and it's really all she wants."

"I'm trying to," he responded. "I'm trying."

"I think you're doing fine," she asserted, letting her touch linger a moment more. She checked her watch for the time. "I'll take you for a walk after this and show you Seattle's waterfront. Then it'll be about time to head back to the hospital."

After finishing lunch they drove to the harbor and casually walked about the area soaking up sunlight, the seaside and the sights. Perusing the shops for souvenirs and keepsakes they subsequently left the sidewalk and strolled across old wooden planks that comprised the pier. They leaned on the railing at the water's edge to watch a small white cruise ship dock and disembark a full boatload of passengers, predominantly tourists, clearly from out of town if judging by their dress. Seattleites more typically wore the requisite khaki, Birkenstocks, and casual grunge wear of the citified bohemian, rather than Hawaiian shirts, polyester pants or the stiff straw hats of curious sightseers. A loudspeaker blared a welcome to the next group as they were herded up the stairway planks to board the three-tiered vessel. They seemed eager to navigate the bay and be titillated from the open-air decks by the topical points of interest circumventing the city shore.

"Ever done one of those?" asked David to his hostess, as they watched the people walking up the stairway to board the craft.

"Yes, both this one and the one in Kirkland."

"Did you like it?"

"Well," replied Bea, "they were like night and day. The one on the Eastside is great. It's relaxing. Less crowded. It's also a good historical tour of the area and how it developed. Both tours offer drinks and snacks so you can really have a leisurely time for a few hours. The one in Seattle though, this one right here, gave us a headache. Their loudspeakers were too loud and it felt a little like being treated like cattle. Herd 'em on, herd 'em off, blare away at 'em in between. It seemed like hucksters doing a hustle. I can't even remember anything that was said. Frankly, we thought it was a bit nerve wracking and were glad when it was over. If we have guests we do the Eastside one."

"Hm. I wonder why the two tours are so different. Are they run by the same company?"

"Yes, they are. I think that's just the difference between a big city and a small one. They're used to getting tons of tourists here. It's like anywhere. The bigger it gets the less personal it becomes. That's why I try to keep my company from getting too large. I want to keep the personal touch alive."

"Looks like you've been pretty successful," David said approvingly

"So far, so good," Bea laughed. "Actually it's been a really good year. I got some serious problems worked out with Japan that were plaguing me. And Jay was a big help this year in getting some new programs off the ground."

"And he's still involved, right, while doing his counseling practice too?"

"Well, he's pretty much back to his counseling now, but still works with me two days a week. He'll probably stop being involved altogether pretty soon."

"I see." He looked up to watch some seagulls encircling the water, screeching intermittently as they dipped down and back up. "So you've been through some staffing changes this year, Faye said."

"Yep, I had a secretary quit who had worked with me for a long time." She paused thoughtfully. "People have to follow their own paths, I guess. Anyway, I've got a great replacement, so…" She smiled and shrugged. "Life goes on."

"Is your business still expanding then?"

"Oh yes, that's what I was saying. It could easily grow much bigger than I really want it to."

"So how do you keep it working? I mean, if you don't grow with your competitors, won't you get crowded out of the field?"

"Well, I try to stay philosophical about it. Maybe a better word for it would be spiritual. There seems to be, as someone once said to me – a friend of Jay's actually who's something of a psychic, his therapist you could say – enough business for everyone to meet their needs."

"Hm," he reflected, looking at the dirty harbor water beneath him. "That's a good way to think."

"Yes, it is, if you can remember to do it. In the meantime I try to pick and choose what programs I want. As a case in point," she added with pride, "I think I'll be going to Russia this year. And Spain if I have the time."

"Wow! Russia. That should be wild." Bea lifted her arm to shield the sun from her eyes and looked at her watch. "Speaking of wild, meaning Faye that is, it's just about time for us to go back to the hospital."

"Let's do it. I'm anxious to see what the doctor has to say."

Chapter 77

"I believe that water is the only drink for a wise man; wine is not so noble a liquor."
(Henry David Thoreau)

As he sat in the rocking chair in a black silk robe sipping his decaffeinated herbal blueberry tea, Jay watched the gray morning sky merge into a soft fuzzy amethyst glow above the tall pines across the water. The clouds that had converged overhead last evening were beginning to burn off with the arrival of the sun. With his family still sleeping the household was as quiet as the lake; a vacant playground amidst the velvet green landscape. A long-legged egret was standing on his dock surveying the scenery with motionless focus. With a sip of his drink Jay contemplated the concerns that were weighing on him as he watched the shifting colors of the sunrise turning lighter into pink. In the back of his mind were uneasy feelings around the medical condition of Faye, who was still hospitalized with a questionable prognosis. He feared for Bea's sanity if she lost another sister. It was bad enough losing Gabe, though easier to accept, given his age and the gentle manner in which he had departed. Fortunately at least the women were here together amidst some family support. Faye's treatment needs had taken precedence over any immediate plans to attend their father's funeral, so the cremation had been scheduled to take place without them. They were hoping to attend the memorial service as soon as her health permitted.

The egret leapt deftly into the air as gracefully as an acrobat, flapping its heavy wings in a slow and steady sweeping motion. He flew as on a tightrope, in a straight and narrow line, toward the eastern shore while keeping roughly a yard above the water without the slightest variance in any direction. Clutching his warm cup in both hands Jay watched intently as the bird came to a soft landing in the distance, alighting gently on the end of a cedar dock stretching out to greet him. He folded his wings as though putting them in his pockets, swiveled leisurely around and stared at the lake once more. As the rising sun slowly molted into gleaming yellow tints of blue sky the lake began to sparkle like a field of dancing candles, a big birthday cake of aquamarine icing lit up to make a wish. Jay inhaled the fragrant vapors of the blueberry brew, took a sip and sighed, feeling the pressing matter in the forefront of his mind.

The boys had arrived from Mexico last night and as Jess had elected to stay there, both were still fast asleep in Phil's bedroom. A friend of Jess had met them at the airport to drive them home, saving their parents a very late night trip. Jay pondered what exactly to say about school to Phil and how best to say it. Bea had been as equally dismayed as Jay with the report and more so with the remarks of the counselor. As she had plenty on her hands with her father and sister Jay had gently insisted he be the one to speak with Phil first. Though he had not admitted it to Bea the one thought that was bothering him greatly, aside from the mess that Phil was in, was the inescapable thought that he had been the one to bring this curse upon his child.

He was the one as a schoolboy hippy, a college liberal, a guitar-playing surfer dude, who had introduced Bea to pleasures of marijuana. Spouting the platitudes, the fatuous sophistry, hip to the times from rock stars to college profs, that drugs were cool. Getting high was not only fun but also deep. From the high priest of academia, Timothy Leary, whose advice to turn on, tune in and drop out was heeded by a whole generation to a long list of musicians now dead – Hendrix, Morrison, Joplin – to name a few, the message was clear; lose your mind and come to your senses. Of course years later it was even evidently more clear that no one had reached a state of higher consciousness through drugs; at least not one that lasted when they wore off. The hippies had started a revolution that had ended with the Manson gang and recycled itself with yuppies. They in turn had transmuted the growing political power of their generation through the eighties and into the hands of a man who swore he didn't inhale nor have sex with that woman and lied like it was his native tongue. He felt as disgusted with himself as he used to be with Clinton.

How was he going to tell Phil to lay off pot when he himself had been doing it? Knowing the best teaching was done by example, what could he do but quit. He had quit, sort of, but was it too late? It had been months since partaking of the herb but he still had smoking paraphernalia in the house. Even his drinking had continued. The message was the same; find peace of mind through an external substance, legal or not. Struggling with feelings of self-contempt and fear for his young son's future, he felt moved to make a defining gesture. Now was the time, if he was ever going to do it, to make a break with everything that impeded the growth of his spiritual consciousness and threatened the well-being of his child. He had for a year now been employing the services of a spiritual teacher to give him the goods on God. He had guiltily dodged and defied a narcotics detective for the same period of time because of his affiliation with a dope dealer. He had nothing to show for his fine wine collection but fewer funds in the bank, cloudy nights on the keyboard, some groggy mornings the next day and probably a worsening condition in his liver. And now he had a son starting down the same slippery slope, the gilded trail of illusions, the golden path to nowhere, the fast track to oblivion.

Finishing the tea he decided to meditate and sat the cup down on the rug next to him. In the brilliance of the dawn the lake life was awakening. A procession of ducks swam by in silence. There was a large one, obviously a parent in the front, leading the way with a column of babies trailing behind in linear succession, seven in all with a another parent bringing up the back like a rear guard...*that's how its done... lead and protect...* Closing his eyes he folded his hands in the lap of the silk robe and took several deep breaths until feeling more relaxed...*Father, Jesus, Guide, whoever...give me the guidance, the knowledge, the strength, the courage to do what is right here...* He stayed focused on that request for a few minutes more until he felt he had held it long enough to communicate the sincerity of his desire. When he opened his eyes he felt suddenly decisive about what to do. There had to be changes, big changes, in their lives, starting at the top.

He got up and went into the bedroom, taking care not to disturb his sleeping wife. Slowly, quietly he opened the drawer where he kept his pipe and lighter hidden in an eye glasses case. He walked back to the living room, noticing the day was even brighter yet now with birds fluttering in the trees and flying over the lake. Passing through the area he headed down the stairs. Opening the back door by the big green plastic trash bin he lifted its lid and threw in his articles of artificial pleasure. Letting the lid drop with an air of satisfaction he proceeded toward the little closet serving as his wine cellar. He slid open the door and contemplated the contents; almost three cases of handpicked aging bottles. Squatting down he lifted up the nearest one and carried the heavy box outside the back door; following suit with the two remaining ones...*jess can have 'em...*

He stood outside on the small cement stoop by the trash bin and the cases. Listening to the birds as they began to chirp and twitter served to stir his senses into the mix of morning air. A few feet away a gentle wind wafted through the evergreens that lined the southern side of his lot. The fresh scent of earthly delights, the pines and the moisture in the air from the dewy grass and foliage, gave him a sense of a new start on a new day. There was one more step he felt compelled to take. Returning inside he bounded lightly up the stairs, went into the kitchen and pulled out the last of the Corona beers in the refrigerator. He popped them open one by one, a half six-pack, and poured them all down the sink methodically. With a feeling of satisfaction he dropped the empty bottles in the trashcan under the sink, glanced at the clock over the stove and returned to his place in the cushy rocking chair. He knew the boys would probably sleep for another few hours. By then he would have worked out exactly what it was that he wanted to say to his wayward son.

Chapter 78

"The holiest of all the spots on earth is where an ancient hatred has become a present love." (A Course in Miracles)

A S THE HOSPITAL ELEVATOR climbed steadily higher Bea tightened her grip on the bouquet of red roses she had purchased from the floral shop when entering the building. She had never been to the cancer center before and the modern facility seemed brighter and cleaner than the one from which Faye had just been transferred. David coughed nervously at her side clutching a small portable CD player in one hand and a plastic bag of discs in the other. He had been ill at ease ever since the doctor at the first hospital had pronounced Faye's condition serious. Bea herself was well beyond nervous. She had been grounded in a sense of dread since that day, hoping for the best, but fearing the worst. Since then her sister had already received one round of chemotherapy at her new treatment center. It had seemingly worsened her condition with fatigue, though that was to be expected as a short-term effect. When the elevator stopped at the sixth floor they emerged from the metal cube unsure of where to go next.

"Let's ask the nurses station for her room," said Bea, striding toward the counter. They were directed to the right room and walked down the corridor, each of them holding a heavy heart with every step. Peeking in first from the doorway to ensure they were not interrupting a doctor's consultation or a treatment by the nursing staff, they were heartened to see her awake in the quiet room looking out the window.

"Good morning," called Bea, as gaily as she could. "We brought you some things." She held out the flowers while moving to Faye's bedside and gave her a soft kiss on the cheek.

"Oh, thank you," responded Faye, with an air of gentle surprise. "Red roses, my favorite."

"That's what he said," offered Bea as she nodded at David. She held the flowers close to her sister's face for a fragrant whiff as David stood silently on the other side of the bed.

"Ahhhh," intoned Faye. "Smells good."

Bea set the bouquet in a vase on the windowsill and opened the slats on the blinds a little wider.

"Enjoying the view?" she asked. David leaned over and kissed Faye lightly on the other cheek.

"Hi sweetie, how are you?" he inquired in a sensitive voice. He held up the CD player and the discs. "We brought you some music."

"Oh, that's nice, thank you," Faye murmured wearily. She stared at him thoughtfully as he reached down to a wall socket and pushed in the plug.

"Can I set it on your little table here?" asked David.

"Perfect," she said.

"Would you like to hear something now?" he asked.

"Okay, that might be nice."

"What would you like?"

"Oh, just pick anything you like." David pulled a handful of discs from the bag and stacked them on the table. He read the headings on each label and selected one from the pile.

"Here's one with flute and harp. Jay said he thought you'd find it very pleasant and peaceful."

"Sounds like something he'd say," she said. As he slipped it into the machine and hit the play button, the room was instantly filled with a melodic run of airy strings vibrating in harmonic progression while the temperate trill of a sweet flute softly accompanied them in counterpoint. "That's pretty," she remarked. She smiled at David, then turned to Bea. "Well, how are you?"

"Well, between sad about dad and worried about you, I'm okay I guess," said Bea matter-of-factly. "How are you?"

"I'm tired," sighed Faye. "Those treatments are exhausting." The room was silent for a moment but for the music as neither Bea nor David was quite sure what to say to in reply.

"Well," finally offered Bea, "it's probably best to be glad you can get the treatment, as tiring as it is. May be the best thing for you."

"Maybe," Faye replied. "Didn't do mom much good though."

"Well," countered Bea, taken aback at the pessimism in her voice. "Mom was a lot older than you, you know."

"Yeah, I guess so." Faye cleared her throat. "I'll tell ya', the best thing about this place is that Delilah works here too."

"You're kidding!" exclaimed Bea.

"Nope. She works here part-time, actually on-call, she said."

"That's great," Bea affirmed. "I really liked her spirit."

"Yeah, me too." Faye extended a hand to each of them and gave their hands a little squeeze. "I'm glad you're here."

"So are we," they both said at once.

"So what have you been doing since we saw you last night?"

"Oh watching TV, looking out the window, sleeping." She smiled weakly. "Thinking."

"Oh that's different," mused Bea, searching for some humor. "What were you thinking about?" she teased. "You're usually so busy you don't have much time to think, do you?" David chuckled.

"Funny girl," retorted Faye, managing a bigger smile this time. "I get plenty of time to think when I'm flying somewhere important."

"Like vacations."

"Right."

"Ha!" Bea laughed, glad to see the humor taking. "Well, now you can just rest awhile. Just pretend you're between flights."

"Yes," Faye agreed." She looked over at David. "And how are you?"

"All right," he said unconvincingly. He took her hand, bent over and kissed her lips lightly. "Just thinking about you a lot."

"I know," she reassured him, patting his hand as it held hers. "I'm okay. I'm okay." She breathed a big sigh through her nose and looked him and down. "Would you mind getting Bea and yourself some coffee?"

"Oh, that's okay," interjected Bea. "I've had my two cups for the day." David stood still, unsure of what to do.

"David likes to drink it," stated Faye. "Go get some, hon, will you? I would like a few minutes with my sister alone."

"Okay," he demurred, nodding his assent. He squeezed her hand affectionately, looked at her with tender concern, then turned and left the room.

"He's so sweet to you," Bea said flatly. "You're lucky to have him."

"Yes," said Faye, with a certain resignation. "And I love him, but it's you I want to talk with right now for a moment."

"Yes," said Bea, searching her eyes with deepening interest. "What is it you want to say?"

She reached for and cupped Bea's right hand in both of hers and as she pulled her nearer, Bea sat down on the edge of her bedside.

"I've been thinking," she started slowly. "About a lot of things. About Ohio. About our family. About our childhood."

"Yes?" Tears welled in Faye's eyes and she squeezed Bea's hand slightly tighter.

"Well, I've been thinking...about what a...what a rotten sister...what a mean big sister...I was to you at times...and-"

"Oh, Faye," Bea interrupted, tears welling in her own eyes. "Forget it, please. Just forget it. It doesn't matter now. I don't care about that anymore. Really, I don't. I really don't care now."

"No," she said determinedly, forging onward with her point. "It does matter. It's always mattered. And I don't want to pretend or ignore it anymore."

"Oh, Faye," gushed Bea sympathetically, tears streaming down her smiling face. "It's okay. Really it is. It's okay now." She wiped her arm across her wet cheek. "Just get well. That's all I want."

"But you see, my darling sister, the most angelic one of us all...I may not get well...and I don't want to...I don't want to take this to my grave." She started to cry, whimpering softly, as the tears flowed freely downward.

"Oh stop," Bea urged compassionately. She tried again for humor. "You'll get your pillow all wet."

"Hand me a Kleenex, would you?" Bea reached across the bed for the Kleenex on the table by the CD player and dabbed her sister's cheeks with a tissue. "Thank you."

"What's past is past," said Bea. "Let's let it go and move on."

"I can't," Faye countered. "I can't let it go if I ignore it. I can't move on without acknowledging it." She looked up at Bea plaintively. "Just hear me out, please."

"Okay, but you don't have to -"

"Yes, I do," she insisted. "I really do, please just listen."

"I will," she assured her. "Go ahead. Get it off your chest if it'll help."

"Thank you." She cleared her throat. "Would you give me a glass of water?"

"Sure." Bea poured some icy water from a wet pitcher into a star foam cup and handed it to her. "Got it?"

Faye brought the cup to her lips and swallowed a small amount, then breathed a sigh. With a meager motion of her arm muscles she lifted it back on the table at her side.

"I just want to say," she began again, "that I am so sorry for all the things I ever did to you, for all the ways I ever hurt you, for all the unkind words and deeds."

"It's okay. It really is. Forget about it. It's over."

"Don't say it like that," protested Faye, as she continued. "I know I hurt you. I know I did. I didn't really realize that then, when we were kids, but I do know, looking back. And..." she hesitated, seeming to falter for the right words or reasoning, "and I'm not exactly sure why I did it but, looking back on it, I think ...I think I was jealous."

"Jealous?" Bea said incredulously. "How could you be jealous? You were the older sister. You had all those privileges. You had everything."

"I had everything until you came along." Her voice was firm now though noticeably hoarser. "Then all of a sudden I was no longer the one and only child."

"I see."

"All of a sudden you were the baby, the darling of the family, the apple of their eye."

"Oh no, it's not true. Mom and Dad were so proud of you. Going to the big universities. Studying abroad. Snagging the big job in DC."

"I know, I know. You're right. They were proud of me. But they loved you best." She began to cry again, softly. "They loved you best."

"Oh no." Bea moved to stop the pain. "I don't think so at all. They just loved us differently." She reached for another tissue and wiped Faye's cheeks caringly. "And I'm sorry that you thought that."

"Well, it wasn't your fault," said Faye in gentle defiance. "So you don't have to apologize. Don't be so damn angelic. It's just how it was. And it was because you were so damn angelic. It's just how you are. It's why you were voted most popular in high school. It's why everyone loves you. And I know that's why I was so mean to you. And I'm sorry. I'm really really sorry." With that she burst into tears again and sobbed aloud. "Please forgive me."

"I do," Bea cried, "I do." She leaned down and hugged Faye to her breast. "I completely do."

They cried together in each other's arms for several minutes. They were crying for everything; the loss of their father, their sister, their mother, their childhood, their heritage, their past, and the present. Bea rose up slightly, a few inches from her sibling's face and smiled mournfully through the tears as she gripped her shoulders firmly.

"You're all of my family, my original family, that I have left. I don't want any more tears or sadness or arguments between us. Thank you for saying that. It helps me understand you. It makes it easier for me to forgive you. And all I want to do now is to love you." She bent near and lightly pressed her cheek against Faye's. "And I do love you, so much. So much, my big sister."

"Thank you," whispered Faye. "I love you so much too." Bea kissed her cheek as Faye kissed hers also and pulled back, straightening up. They smiled at each other, looking drained but restful at the same time.

"Besides," taunted Bea with a twinkle in her eye. "You taught me how not to be to my little sister."

"Oh, shut up," said Faye, amused. "You brat."

"Knock, knock!" said David pleasantly with a wary look on his face. He was holding a star foam cup of steaming coffee in one hand. "Have I come back too soon?"

"No," chimed both of the girls simultaneously. "Please come in," uttered Faye. She slid an outstretched hand toward him. "Come here."

He moved to her side, set down his coffee and took her hand in his, looking expectantly into her eyes. Bea took her sister's other hand and reached across the bed to clasp the free hand of David. They all held hands in silence for a moment. Finally Faye spoke.

"You guys better go. I really feel like I could fall asleep."

"Really?" said David, sounding disappointed.

"Yes," she said sleepily. "I'm sorry hon, that we didn't get to visit more. But I had a good talk with my sister. Thank you for letting us do that. You can come back in the morning. I'll be more rested then."

Bea heard his disappointment as clearly as she read it on his face and felt a compassionate pang for his conundrum. If he loved her, then he must leave her be for now. Faye saw it too.

"Actually," she relented, "I think I would like a few minutes with you alone too." Bea was pleased to have the perfect cue for her exit.

"I'm leaving now," she stated with finality. "I've got to go to the bathroom anyway. You guys have some alone time together for a bit. I'll be waiting for you in the downstairs lobby, David."

"Thank you," he said with feeling. She turned to Faye and bent to embrace her again.

"I'll see you in the morning," she said brightly, snuggling up to her ear. "And don't forget," she whispered warmly, "that I love you very much."

"I won't," Faye whispered back. " I love you too, my angel."

Bea stood up, smiled at Faye, nodded at David then walked to the door. She stopped halfway through it then turned around, her face beaming bright with love. "Thank you," she said gratefully. "See you in the morning, sister."

Faye smiled wanly but with evident happiness and nodded. "See you later," she murmured. "Bea!" she called, raising her voice a notch in afterthought.

"What?" asked Bea, grinning broadly as she leaned backwards in the doorway.

"I have a little gift for you. You'll get it in the morning."

Chapter 79

"Creation is something that is most holy. That's the most sacred thing in life, and if you've made a mess of your life, change it...This is the last talk. Do you want to sit together quietly for awhile? Alright, sirs, sit quietly for awhile."
(Last words of Krishnamurti's last talk, 1/4/86)

AS THE SAILBOAT TILTED, gaining speed across the lake, Jay slackened his grip a few inches on the rope that held the sail taut to avoid taking on water. The Sunfish was a small craft, designed to hold two adults comfortably at best, perfect for a body of water like Cottage Lake. With it all to himself he lay back on the stern while holding the rope in one hand and manning the rudder behind him with the other. The wind was often up in the late afternoon and he was making the most of it under a bright glaring sun. This was the first time in almost two years he had taken the boat out for a run. He loved flying through the lake with the wind whipping by and the spray of the water flung high on both sides. As he neared the far shore he readied himself for one of the sharp turnarounds he liked to take when crisscrossing back and forth. Pulling the rudder sharply to one side, he loosened the sail, letting it go slack. The craft spun around smoothly on its momentum like a skater at a standstill encircling the ice till it faced the direction from which it had come. In an instant the billowing wind blew a bulge in the sail that sent the boat racing back towards his dock. He stretched out again with the rope and the rudder, while the breeze swept him over the lake like a snow skier shooting the slopes.

As he lay back in his swimsuit, feeling the warmth of the sun and the wind whipping by, he reflected on the most recent momentous events thronging his consciousness. Bea was with David now visiting Faye at the hospital. It had been quite a scare to discover her condition warranted immediate treatment. He shuddered inwardly to think of the impact on Bea if things didn't go well...*they must go well*...Shifting from that topic to a more positive one he was pleased with the talk he'd had earlier with Phil. Jess was still sleeping when they sat down together. It was difficult at first to get him to shift gears from the holiday high he'd returned with from Mexico. It was bad enough that his grandfather had died and his aunt was suddenly seriously ill in a hospital, but to face the facts of his academic demise laced with the provocative comments of his counselor was almost more than he could handle. Jay had deliberately tried to go slowly to move through each issue as kindly as possible despite his own underlying tensions and concerns. Their talk about Grandpa was simple and direct. He had died in his sleep. He had lead a good life and lived a long time. Now he was with grandma. They weren't sure about attending the memorial service until they knew what was happening with Faye. Both boys had only met their grandparents a few times, with the last meeting being years ago at their grandmother's funeral.

Though they respected and felt a certain fondness for the man their emotional tie, especially Phil's, was not particularly strong and his concern, on hearing the news, had been primarily for his mother. Their talk about Faye was as simple and direct but more laden with feeling as she was alive now and very much with them while fear was in the air that she might soon not be. Sadly the inescapable fact was she had cancer. It appeared to have become very advanced in a short time catching them all unawares and pushing them close to panic. His parents would like both boys to visit her soon, when they felt it was advisable. The nursing staff had cautioned against wearing her out with too many visitors at this critical juncture. They could hope, they would pray, they would do whatever they possibly could to help her in any way. That was it for the moment.

But Jay's greatest focus of concern was on his son and what must be done now to get him back on track. Moreover he wanted to know how he had gotten so severely off track. At first Phil was closed mouthed and evasive, complaining his grades were only representative of the fact that transitioning to junior high from grade school was harder than expected. When Jay informed him of the counselor's speculation that drugs were involved he vehemently denied it, sputtering with outrage over unproven rumors. It was only when Jess emerged from the bedroom where he had been listening to the father-son talk that things began to change. He emerged in the doorway holding a blanket, sleepy-eyed and yawning, but with a serious frown of brotherly concern fixed on his face.

"C'mon, buddy, tell him the truth," he admonished his younger sibling warily. "Dad won't get mad. He's just worried about you, and I am too."

Taking a cue from the older boy, and feeling cautious at his admonition to his little brother, Jay leveled his gaze at the younger one and spoke in a tone of precisely measured kindness. He reached over and touched Phil lightly on the knee.

"I promise you, whatever's going on, I will not get mad. I just want to help you. Now what is the problem?" Phil's lower lip trembled as he paused before speaking. He glanced up at his older brother for a second then looked back at his dad.

"Okay," he said reluctantly, sadly. "It's true. There are drugs involved."

"Which ones?" asked Jay, feeling himself becoming tense.

"Just marijuana," Phil mumbled begrudgingly.

"Honest?" queried Jay. Jess leaned against the wall, feeling glad for the admission but concerned as well.

"Yeah," he said flatly. "And I tried some booze at a party once."

"What kind of booze?"

"A wine cooler. I didn't like it much. I'd rather smoke pot."

"So you're smoking pot at school?"

"Yeah….most everybody does."

"Not everybody, son."

"Okay, you're right. But a lot of people do. That's why they call it Bakeside."

"What?"

"The school – Lakeside Prep. That's why they call it Bakeside."

"Who calls it Bakeside?"

"The kids – the students. A lot of them anyway."

"I see." The school was a haven for well-off boys and girls. They had money for recreational activities of all sorts, including apparently illicit intoxicants. Jay sighed aloud and looked askance for a moment.

"How'd you get into this?" he asked.

"There was a guy at school."

"Which one?"

"I'd rather not say. There's lotsa' guys at school doing it, dad. It's not his fault."

"Hm. I see." Jay paused reflectively, looked up to the older boy then back to Phil. "Do you like going to school there?"

"Not really."

"Why?"

"Oh, there are a lot of rich kids there. People who think they're cool. A lot of them are stuck-up. They don't talk to you or act like they're better. You've seen the kinds of cars the seniors drive. I don't know. I just don't feel like I fit in."

"Does pot make you feel like you fit in and or just make you feel better, more relaxed?"

"A little of both I guess."

"I see. Well, this has got to stop."

"I know."

"It's not healthy for your mind or your body. It's messing up your academic future too."

"Yeah."

"What do you think we should do that would help you?"

"I don't know."

"Let's throw out some ideas."

They talked for good half hour after that, discussing options; counseling, changing friends, changing schools. As they spoke Phil warmed to the prospect of leaving the ranks of Lakeside. His older brother had gone through the public education system and was making his way in the world just fine. He was willing, even eager, to try public school. He knew a lot of the kids from his sports activities. The only thing he'd miss when it came right down to it was the jazz band class and its performances at school. He had learned to read music and play the bass guitar as the former was a requirement and the latter his only opportunity to play. The school already had a senior playing regular guitar. Jay suggested that if Phil really wanted to play music he could form his own band; an idea that was met with enthusiasm. By the end of their discussion there was hope in the air. Plans had been made. Schemes were being devised. In September Phil would not be going back to Lakeside. He'd be going to Forestville Junior high school. During the rest of the summer he could concentrate on putting together a music group with some friends. He already knew of several boys from his soccer team who played the guitar.

Jay leaned with the boat as it tacked sharply to the right with a strong burst of wind. A little water spilled over the edge of the side and flowed to the center of the hull, wetting his feet then dampening his bathing suit. He found the cool effect refreshing as he loosened the rope to let the sail out a bit and right the tilting craft. Leaning back in the boat again he felt relieved and lighthearted as he savored the conversation with the younger boy. He hoped that encouraging his musical interests in the form of a rock band would provide the sort of thrill, excitement and pleasure that weed had promised for the impressionable lad, without the down side. That plus going to a new school for a new start with new friends just might be the right combination of moves to put him back on track to success and happiness.

Feeling pleased with himself for his early morning choice to give up his own drugs, legal and illegal, he felt strong in his resolve, secure, and at peace...*like leroy said, this was what was always needed*...And Jess had been delighted to be the recipient of some newly jettisoned fine wine. He too had seemed more at ease with his domestic scene since returning from the south. Although they had only talked for a brief while it was clear Jess was taking a more philosophical approach to the matter at hand; a sort of wait and see attitude. Let her leave if she wished and see what that brought. He seemed to have reached the sobering realization that living entailed reckoning with unexpected departures, which in turn paved the way for unforeseen arrivals. Suddenly it seemed to be a period of new starts for each of the sons, and for their father as well.

Streaming back towards his dock for one of the countless times that day he sensed the wind seemingly subsiding. It had been good sailing for almost an hour. Feeling satisfied with his cruise and the day's events also he decided to return to the land for now. Perhaps tomorrow he would do it again and take someone with him. He wondered how Faye was doing at the moment. He realized now that he loved her like a sister. When she was released from the hospital he would take her out for a tour of the lake in the sun if she wished. Initially he had planned with Bea to take their guests out to Jake's place. Hopefully she would soon feel strong enough for a night out. He could show off his new office to her and David. The thought of his new office and a resurgent practice rekindled a depth of contentment he had not felt in years. He mulled over the prospects of his apparent good fortune in work and play.

His practice was recovering its former glory. Two of his own private interests at present, music and the culinary arts, were being served by the delightful chance Jake had given him. He could still advise the man and his patrons on the pleasures of the grape without actually imbibing himself. It was a joy to contemplate the roster of upcoming artists he would see and hear there, when not in the kitchen. Jake normally presented two performances each weekend night and had arranged with Jay that he would cook during the first and attend the second show as a member of the audience. He had actually been scheduled to start this very weekend but that had been postponed with the advent of Faye's health crisis. He felt relaxed in the knowledge that it would happen soon enough, along with a different sort of hope and pervasive optimism than ever before. Now that he was willing to function with a clear head, a cleaner consciousness devoid of stimulants and soporifics, he felt quietly excited at the unlimited possibilities of what meditation might do for all aspects of his life.

The boat slowed down as he slid it around in a wide sweeping circle to approach the dock. He let the sail go completely slack and it flapped gently in the dying breeze as he coasted toward the cedar planks, maneuvering the rudder to bring the craft alongside the landing. It glided as smoothly as a child down a slide as it gently grazed along the wood. He picked up the rope coiled near his feet and grabbed the metal steps attached to the dock. Slipping the cord around the hollow metal tubing he lashed the line to the ladder with a knot he'd learned years ago in boy scouts. The craft eased to a stop as gracefully as a swan and left him with a feeling that mirrored his mood; at peace in the stillness. Wondering what to do next with the rest of his day as he climbed out of the boat and onto the dock he realized he'd really like to meditate right now. The thought of it drew him like a magnetic current, a burgeoning feeling of newly found freedom. It seemed long overdue, an ancient call from afar, unanswered until now; time to go home.

Chapter 80

"Learn to be quiet in the midst of turmoil, for quietness is the end of strife and this is the journey to peace." (A Course in Miracles)

"*RRIIINNNGGG*" THE PHONE BY the bedside table rang out sharply in the abiding dark silence of the pre-dawn hour. As Bea was suddenly jolted from a deep dreaming sleep she reached blindly for the phone while a whirlwind of scary thoughts ran through her brain and came to rest on one word: Faye…*oh no…*

"Hello."

"Is this Bea?"

"Yes."

"I'm sorry if I woke you, darlin'," came the vaguely familiar voice. The words poured out as thick and sweet as molasses from a pitcher. "This is Delilah."

"Who?"…*delilah…delilah…*"Oh! The nurse?"

"That's right, dearie. Your sister's nurse, at the cancer center." Bea gasped for a second as her mind raced ahead. From under the rumpled folds of the thick nylon comforter she turned over on her elbow to get more situated then uttered the question she was dreading to ask.

"Oh yes, she said you worked there too. I was really glad to hear that. Is there something wrong?"

"Well, I don't know exactly," she replied in a cautious and considered tone. "I mean yes, I guess, she's had a turn for the worse, but she may be okay. I'm actually just calling because she asked me to do it."

"What's happened?" asked Bea with increased apprehension.

"Well, she had a rough time last night, couldn't sleep well and had a high fever. It looked to me like she might have an infection. We gave her a Tylenol but that didn't do much. We finally took a blood test and sent it to the lab. We'll be getting a report back from them later today. In the meantime the doctor has put her in ICU."

"ICU? That's serious."

"Well, it is. You know, your sister came here in a serious condition. And sometimes people contract infections while they are here that complicates matters and her doctor just doesn't want to take any chances."

"I see." Bea paused to gather her thoughts. "So is she going to be okay?"

"Well, darlin'," said Delilah hesitatingly, "I can't really say. It's up to the Lord. I'm really jus' callin' you cause she asked me to. I don't want to be the bearer of bad tidings or false hopes but I couldn't say no to her. She half-pleaded half-insisted I do it."

"Yes, I know how she can be insistent."

"I bet you do. Anyway, I guess she didn't want you to hear it from someone else. She also said to tell you not to worry, though I know you probably will, of course."

"I'm worried all right." She squinted at the blurred red numbers of the digital clock on the dresser across the room. "What time is it anyway?"

"About five-thirty in the morning, honey. I apologize again for such an early call but was afraid if I didn't do it now I mightn't have time. I've got a lot to do here before my shift ends. Then we have a staff meeting for the changeover and we don't take or make calls during that hour, so I thought it would probably be best to just call you now."

"Oh, thank you. I really appreciate the call, truly." Bea yawned aloud. "Excuse me," she said, "but is there anything else you say about her condition?"

"Well, her spirits are good. She is a spunky gal." Delilah's tone sounded more tentative than her words.

"That she is," agreed Bea, feeling more worried by the moment. "Listening to you, I'm starting to get scared."

"I'm sorry. I really don't know what to tell you. I really hate having to call you at all."

"Well, I'm glad you did, but I don't know what to do."

"The best thing for you to do is go back to sleep and wait for the report to come back from the lab," advised Delilah. "And of course pray," she added firmly.

"Oh, don't worry," said Bea with another loud yawn. "I've been doing plenty of that."

"I bet you have, darlin'. I do bet you have." There was a moment of quiet before Delilah spoke again. "She'll be sleeping for awhile and that report won't be in till later in the morning, so there's no use you coming out here this morning."

"I see. Well, can we visit her later today?"

"Oh sure, but she really could use a good sleep now. She had strong sedative early today and has been sound asleep ever since then. It's probably the best thing for her to be doing so why don't you call back later in the morning? When she wakes up the doctor will probably spend some time with her and then she'll likely have lunch. You can probably see her sometime after that."

"I see. Okay."...*if she's alive...*

"Again, I'm sorry to wake you but I could see she really did want me to call you and I just couldn't look her in the eyes and say no."

"Oh, no, don't mention it. I'm really glad you called. Thank you. I mean it. I really do mean it."

"Well, thank you. I appreciate you understand. Now you try to get back to sleep if you can."

"I'll try."

"It's the best thing to do."

"You're right. Okay, thanks again. Bye-bye."

"Good-bye, and you have a blessed day now."

"Thank you. You too. Bye now. Bye bye."

Bea placed the telephone back in its cradle and layback down on her pillow feeling tired but wide-awake and filled with foreboding. She stared through the skylight over the bed at the vast sea of distant stars sparkling brightly in the depths of the darkness, anonymous points of light like the unknown caregivers attending to her sister...*nothing to do but trust in God...* That thought brought her to the realization that she wanted to pray and she closed her weary eyes in precious reverence as she made the sentient shift into the stillness of communion...*please Father protect my sister...sustain her with the gift of life...if it be thy will i humbly ask thee...in the name of Jesus Christ...amen...*

Opening her eyes again she saw a star speeding across the heavens for a second before it disappeared into darkness...*that's what its like...a mere moment then nothing...what's left to hold onto...*She felt the resurgent sense of dread that had hit her when the phone first rang...*what if she dies...*Tears sprung to her eyes at the thought of the unthinkable. With so many losses in such a short time she was starting to feel undermined and overwhelmed. Just when it seemed like her business world was working smoothly her personal one was falling apart. She'd lost a sister, a father, perhaps a new daughter-in-law to divorce and now possibly another sister to death. She'd lost her connection with her youngest son as well while trying her best to provide for everybody. That was something she was determined to get back. Thank God they had discovered he was losing his way before he'd become even more deeply lost in the depths of drug hell.

The changes Jay wanted in Phil's life for the summer and next fall were just fine with her but she wanted to make some changes herself. For the rest of the summer she wanted to spend more quality time with Phil and be also more available during the school year. She had decided to go to Russia in late August rather than September in order to be home when he started his new curriculum. That trip would only be for ten days. Until then she would attempt to be more in touch with him through the rest of the summer break. She and Jay had agreed to have more family time together with their young son through various activities in the summer to ensure he was not neglected in any way.

They wanted to see more of Jess as well and had agreed to start a new tradition: Family Night; where the four of them would spend every Sunday evening at home together with pizza and a movie. This year of personal losses and professional overload had vividly underscored the realization that success in the world of work was meaningless if it left little time for the people you loved.

Thinking of work reminded her that even Candy's departure had been a big loss. She mused for a moment on the latest bit of information she had heard from another parent, a Host Family mom and a mutual friend of theirs, whose daughter took dance lessons from Candy. Candy had taken money from the parents for the graduation pictures of her students at the dance studio. But several days later the studio was found to be vacant with its doors locked and no explanation given anyone as to why. Her business phone was disconnected while repeated calls to Candy's home went unanswered and unreturned. Several parents had ventured out to her house only to find that no one would answer the door. At present it was a mystery to a group of disgruntled parents as to what had happened to the studio, the graduation photos, and even Candy herself...*maybe jay's right...everybody's crazy...well maybe candy anyway more than i knew......*

She sighed and looked out once more at the stars. The distant dots were still distinct but fading into the twinkling tapestry of the morning sky as it slowly shifted into to a lighter hue. It felt too late to return to sleep. She looked over at Jay, who was wrapped in a long pillowcase around his head. That stuffed wrapping plus the earplugs he wore had probably kept the telephone call from disturbing his sleep. He'd always been a light sleeper. She considered her options: get up and put on the coffee, lie there and think, or read the book on her bed stand. Her body felt as though it were immovable; only her mind was activated and that realization led her to the next thought: meditate. She rarely made time for meditation, feeling alternately too busy or too tired, but now was actually as good a time as any. She had not tried since that time in her office when the phones and faxes kept interrupting.

Closing her eyes again she took a deep breath, exhaled slowly and then took several more. Her body was as relaxed as it could possibly be and but her mind was tugging away with worry. Although she had spent little time meditating her confidence had grown in the sensation that she was accompanied by a presence, a felt spiritual presence of a being or an entity, which she regarded as her Spirit Guide. She had read of such phenomena in the sixties and seventies, and even later in the eighties when new age literature had abounded and peaked. But it was only recently, encouraged in part by the talks with Leroy, that she had actually discovered that she could seemingly connect with an internal voice of a spiritual nature. She had felt a presence once and had asked for a name, then received the response through the airwaves of her mind; Alahee.

It wasn't exactly a voice but a clear communication unlike anything she had ever experienced. It was like being spoken to in terms of intuiting a meaning, which someone else might call a conscience. But yet it felt different than a message from one's conscience, which came from within. This had a sense of coming from without. She thought of it as her heavenly angel. She couldn't clarify or explain it any better than that, and since she'd told no one but Jay and Leroy, who both accepted it without doubt or judgment, she felt no need to explain anything to others. She knew anyway that such matters could never actually be proved nor disproved. Faith was the belief in things unseen. The experience was truly the only evidence, and it was evident to her that she was having this experience.

She continued deep breathing, as Jay said he did with hypnosis, to allay her worries for the moment at least....*nothing better to do than this*...After feeling sufficiently focused in a more tranquil state she shifted her awareness into the intention to connect with her guide... *Alahee...are you there*...The response was as swift and gentle as a stream...*I'm here*...The words in reply to her question were reassuring and carried with them a feeling she could best describe as being loved. She reveled in the feeling of communion for a moment or longer perhaps; it was all timeless now. And then the question came...*what can you tell me of my sister*...The response was immediate and as sure as her breathing...*fear not...your sister is in the hands of God*...As reassuring as it was she sought for something more definitive...*but will she live*...Again the swift response...*no one ever dies*...Now she wanted more. It was eluding her grasp...*but will she live or die in the hospital*...She felt a sense of anticipation rising, a desire for certainty that throbbed amidst her peace...*it is not for me to say...I tell you in perfect certainty and assurance to trust in the way and the will of God...wish your sister peace within the will of God and rest in peace knowing you have done that which is sufficient...she feels your love...*

She felt the dual strains of a desire to know more mixed with a willingness to be at peace with what she was hearing...*is there nothing more i can do*...This seemed to her the final question that she had to ask...*to love your sister fully and trust in the will of God is sufficient unto the moment and indeed unto eternity...now rest and rest in peace in knowing all is well and as it is meant to be*... She could think of nothing to say to this and felt a sense of reassurance growing that she had done all that she possibly could. A wave of peace and relaxation swept over her mind and body like a cloud drifting by and she slipped back into sleep in the thick folds of her comforter like an infant snugly nestled in the warm fullness of its loving mother's arms.

Two hours of sleep later she was up and in the kitchen making the morning coffee when David walked up the stairs from the guest bedroom.

"Good morning, Bea," he said pleasantly. "How are you today?"

"I'm okay," she announced, trying to sound better than she felt. "But I have some news that I need to share with you."

"Some news about what?" he asked anxiously while approaching her. She handed him a cup full of steaming coffee.

"No cream or sugar, right?"

"That's right, just black," he replied. "What news?" he repeated. "About Faye?"

"Yes," she sighed, filling her own cup. "Let's sit down at the table and I'll tell you all about it." He followed her to the table by the corner windows that looked past the tall cedar tree to the lake.

"Anything serious?" he ventured cautiously.

"Well..." she started. And she told him the tale of the early morning call. At the end of her story he nodded, looking glum, then asked her a question.

"So there's nothing to do but wait for awhile?"

"That's right," affirmed Bea. "We can call mid-morning but the likelihood seems we won't see her till after lunch or so. In the meantime, as the nurse said, we can always pray." David interlaced his fingers around his cup and closed his eyes as though in prayer. After about half a minute he opened them.

"I think I have something I'd like to give you," he said mysteriously, rising from his chair.

"What's that?"

"You'll see. I'll be right back." He bounded downstairs quickly and returned in a few minutes with a wrapped package about the size of a shoebox.

"Oh no, a gift? You needn't have done that."

"It's not from me. It's from Faye," he stated, handing it to her. "She asked me yesterday to give it to you this morning. Originally she intended to give it to you herself."

"Did you guys buy this here?"

"No. She brought it all the way out from Pittsburgh. She wanted you to have it today because today is the summer solstice; the longest and sunniest day of the year. She said you were the sunniest hearted person she knew so today was the best day to give you this present."

"Oh my," said Bea, tears welling in her eyes as she smiled. "How sweet." She looked at the gift and back up at David. "I hope she doesn't mind not giving it herself."

"No, it's okay," he replied, then paused and resumed with a wan smile. "She said she wanted you to have it first thing in the morning so you could feel her love all through the long day."

"Wow, that's so touching and so different than she used to be."

"That's what I thought," he said quietly. He cleared his throat, looked down at the floor then back to Bea's gaze. "I don't know what's going to happen to her. I hope she lives. I hope she recovers. I hope we'll be seeing her this afternoon, but she wanted you to have this now, this morning. So please, open it, and know it's from her."

Bea's eyes sparkled with pleasant anticipation and growing curiosity as she untied the bow of the ribbon around the gift. Pulling away the powder blue tissue paper revealed a shoebox."

"Shoes?" she asked, incredulously.

"Keep going," was all that David would offer.

She lifted the box lid and looked at its contents; a small pillow covered in black velvet laced with gold trim.

"A pillow?"

"It's about the message embroidered on the other side. That's just the back."

She took the pillow out of the box and turned it over, feeling the soft dimpled braid of the weave. As she read the black flowing letters stitched in stylish long hand across the pleaded fabric of the gold colored cushion, tears reemerged in her eyes. She held it in her hands on her lap endearingly, rereading the words, absorbing and appreciating their fond sisterly sentiment; *I Believe in Angels.*

"I want you to know," he related with gentleness, "that she told me the only reason that she believes in them is because she knows that she has one for a sister."

"Ahhhh," Bea intoned. "So sweet."

Bea brought the pillow up next to her cheek and brushed its soft texture against her moist eyelids to stem the budding saline streams. She smiled through glistening eyes and laughed softly.

"It takes one to know one," she chuckled sympathetically.

The confession that Faye had made in the hospital had smoothed away all the coarse spots in her childhood memories from the faraway days of Ohio. She felt finally at peace in their long rough relationship and the pillow was as perfect a symbol for it all as she could possibly imagine. She too had her angels and though one was in heaven there was still one on earth, and they both were her sisters.

"Thank you," she stated sincerely to David, feeling a lump arise in her throat. "Now I really cannot wait to see her."

David stared down at the floor to conceal the quickening tears in his own troubled eyes and whispered quietly, "Me too" and then added, after a pause, almost inaudibly, "I just hope we can."

Chapter 81

"Acting out from mind will make you appear to be quite successful from the three-dimensional frame of reference, but the reason you will appear to be successful is because nothing is happening from that frame of reference."
(*You Are The Answer, Paul Tuttle*)

THE SLEEK WHITE INFINITI rolled down the driveway away from the house in the bright summer morning with the luxurious feeling of floating on air. Jay had thought that the Mecedes was a comfortable ride but he had to admit that the current crop of automakers had learned a few things in the last twenty years. As part of his resurgence back into a life that felt once again like one worth the living he had traded his German antique of a car in for a brand new Japanese model. Congruent with his feeling of a new lease on life and lacking the funds for a down payment he had chosen to lease the new car as well. It was cheaper than buying one and he wasn't yet rich but he did feel inspired with the strength of renewal. The fat tires melodiously ground down the gravel as he gripped the clean wheel with a strong sense of purpose and turned onto the asphalt lane leading up the half-mile to the highway. He'd decided that now was the right time to redeem a wrong he'd regretted ever since last winter.

On entering the kitchen that morning he'd encountered two worrisome faces over coffee at the table. His heart grew heavy as he heard the grave news between pensive sips of hot raspberry tea. Through the course of breakfast he shared whatever words of comfort and hope that came to him, but felt increasingly uncomfortable as the morning moved along in sluggish slow motion. Though they tried to present a brave face to each other he could see that both David and Bea were very worried. Not wanting to sit idly by with the strain of faint premonitions and dire helplessness he decided instead to make a quick trip to town to tend to a unfinished task. Perhaps he could find some respite, however brief, from the household heaviness on the uplifting wings of his new fun machine. More than that, however, there was a particular mission to accomplish that felt way long overdue.

Aside from the lift that his latest car lent he was buoyed by the fact that he was going to the music store to reclaim the flute he had sold there last year. It was a second hand flute, not as fine as his best one, which he kept in a case just for parties or gigs. But it was one he used to play, practicing daily, that he'd kept on a shelf near the stereo system. He had often grabbed it on a whim whenever walking by, from one room to another, tootling whatever notes fed his fancy. At other times he played with the music on the stereo or with Bea who could play any piece on the piano. It symbolized gayety, harmonious good times, and he was more than ready to recapture that mood. Steering onto the highway he gave it the gas, enjoying the first burst of power and speed, as it surged ahead swiftly then held the pace smoothly like a small ocean liner.

Contentedly feeling the quiet grace of the auto he mused to himself how it had all come about; driving by a car lot on a mere whim a few days ago. The unabashed beauty of it sitting outside amidst all the other shiny hunks, the only one white, glossy as a pearl, in a sea of many colored new and used vehicles. It stood out like a new bride-to-be among maidens, chaste, pure, and beckoning to him. He recalled with an inward smile how briskly he had acted; a quick test drive and he was completely sold. After signing the agreement with the car dealership he had driven it home to surprised family members, who nonetheless happily accepted his choice. They knew he had driven the Mercedes for many years. It was only his own self-doubt that had plagued him when he had awakened the next morning with a mild case of buyer's blues. He had decided right then to give Leroy a call to see if he could provide an enlightened perspective. They had not spoken for nearly two months now as things had finally been progressing more satisfactorily. As he drove toward the freeway he reflected on their conversation.

"So how are you doing?"

"Well, actually rather well. It seems like everything you said is actually coming true. I'm becoming successful again in my practice and still do a little bit of work with Bea's company too, which generates good revenue. So I'm finally able to pay my rent on time and I'm also gaining on some large credit card debts."

"Good."

"But I got a little carried away the other day and wonder if perhaps I didn't blow it, in the sense that the side of me that's extravagant just went out and leased a new Infiniti and-"

"Which model?"

"The J-30. It's very nice. Of course, that's the allure. But I'm just a little worried that maybe I'm getting carried away too soon."

"Do you enjoy the car?"

"Oh yeah. Definitely."

"Well then, that's the answer. I mean, the worst thing that can happen is that you can't pay the lease and they take the car from you and then you ask for another car and you get it. There's not a standard here that you are really being held to. That's the thought that gets you uptight. The world indeed seems to have a standard and you know that you are expected to perform. You've had a period of time here in which there has been a lot of movement and you have felt very supported and then you start to think 'Oh my God, it could go back to how it was'. Now, your best bet is to stay grateful and also to not feel as though you are personally responsible for maintaining the order or integrity of things. You did pretty well at that while it was dry. You see, you were able to go through that dry period with more consciousness than the average guy. The average guy would have gone through it and thought it was terrible and not tried to let go. But you were willing to let go sufficiently to become clearer, then the movement started again. Now, as you wake up you are going to find that whether the movement is apparent or not, your good is always provided for because you are inseparable from it in your own experience and it is not likely to look like misfortune. It's not likely to look like anything that you wouldn't desire."

"Hm."

"So stay with the moment. Be grateful for the car. Understand that it is a gift and that you are free to enjoy it. I'm glad you got it."

"Okay. I wonder if it is intelligent to ask if you see me being with this car for a long time."

"Well, the answer comes differently. I see no problem around the car. You must understand that the car itself is a creation and has its fulfillment, its sense of purpose. Let's say the car desires to be with you and your mutual desires create an alliance between you and the car. That car doesn't have a desire in the same sense that you do but the creator of the car and the creator of you brought the two of you together. So let the car be a gift for as long as it's appropriate, for as long as you want it to be."

"Hm. Well, that's funny you put it that way because it reminds me of an incident once that happened with Jess, my oldest son. He'd been driving a very reliable Volvo, his very first car, for several years, and he'd reached the point where he was going to sell it and buy something nicer. And he said he was on his way somewhere in it, driving alone, the last day before he sold it, and he was feeling very grateful towards the car for all it had meant to him, all it had been through with him, all the good and bad and wild and crazy times a teenager can have with or in a car and how it had never let him down, had always performed well and held up well in the winter or whatever. So he expresses this thought, this feeling, out loud to the car as he's driving along and lo and behold but the car blinks its internal lights on and off at that very moment and he felt so blown away. It seemed so obvious to him that the car was responding to his expression of gratitude with a sort of salute or gesture back, and so of course no one thinks that sort of thing is possible and will come up with all sorts of explanations how it happened or insist that it was just his imagination but Jess was very clear and very definite about the experience and the felt meaning of it. He found it delightfully amazing, and now when you're saying what you did about the mutual desire of the car to be with me…well, it just hits home more in a way I can appreciate, though I don't normally think of things that way at all."

"Sure."

"So just keep doing what I have been doing. It's like another opportunity to see things spiritually."

"Right. Simply pay attention in the moment and try not to feel alone. You can't be in the world and be in your peace if you feel alone, if you feel unsupported. If you feel connected, if you feel there's a guardian angel or a guide supporting you, or if you feel it's the Holy Spirit that is supporting you and that you are with it all the time, then it is much easier to be in your peace. Not only that, but recognize that you cannot be in your peace and be active in the world unless you are supported in every way necessary."

"This is just what we talked about in our very first conversation last year; support, feeling supported."

"Yes, exactly. It is fundamental. I always tell people to find their peace, but I recognize too that for someone who's life is a mess, for someone who's life is in shambles, that they may not be able to find their peace except in the most restrictive way, like for example by hiding under their bed. They are finding it just too hard to be in the world and find their peace at the same time. They may have the intent but they can't seem to will it to be. And that is because you cannot have your peace and be actively involved in the world unless you can feel your support, see it and touch it, for that involvement. So it is important, when you have found your peace, when you have found that moment of connection, that you ask to be supported to be in the world. You see, that affords you freedom of movement then and allows you the wonderful comfort of being at peace and still able to be active in the world. It allows you to be in or look at circumstances in the world that may seem daunting or upsetting to others but you are still able to maintain your peace because you recognize that there is support for your existence, because you are asking for it. You are consciously asking for it because you value it because it allows you to stay in your peace while you are actively involved in the world."

"It reminds me of Jesus saying "I am in the world but not of the world.""

"Right."

"You find your peace through feeling support. That's where we started."

"Yes. It is impossible for someone who doesn't feel their support and see it to be in their peace and be active in the world. Anyone can find their peace while being in a sanctuary.

And if that is the only place you can find it then you have to do it there. Maybe they have to go under their bed. But to be in the world requires support; divine support that manifests as whatever meets the need."

"I think I understand that but it is good to be reminded. Thank you."

"You are welcome."

As always, he felt better after talking with Leroy. Already the dread that he'd felt regarding Faye had diminished somewhat just from that recollection. But now as he thought about her condition once again the heaviness returned. Between the two he was on an emotional seesaw. Realizing the beneficial effect of the words of his mentor made him to want to hear more, especially given the foreboding alternative. As he stopped at the light before entering the freeway he reached over and pushed in the bright metal button on the smooth leather finish of the roomy glove compartment and pulled out a cassette. Accelerating his pace as he placed the tape into the mouth of the polished wood dash he raced down the entrance lane onto the freeway, gathering momentum like a fast-braking wave as he merged with the oncoming tide of traffic.

"So how are you?"

"Well, I'm okay I guess. Life has its problems but I'm trying to stay more peaceful."

"What problems are you having?"

"Well, I recently lost my temper with Toshi, whom I've renamed 'ohshit', when he called Bea the other night, though that seems to have smoothed over."

"What happened exactly?"

"Well, the Japanese are of course just like everyone else in the world. They are good at heart, but, like everyone else, they do have their egos. And those egos are influenced or shaped a bit by their culture in respect to other cultures. And just like the French seem to have an egotistical or arrogant attitude that they make the best wines, which may have been true once, or the Germans are arrogant that they make the best cars, it seems the Japanese are arrogant in dealing with foreigners in general. And actually every nationality does this to some extent. It's ethnocentrism. And you can even see it in regions of different countries. The northerners think they are more sophisticated than the hicks in the south and so on. And that's provincialism. I know people can be very provincial in their attitude that their city, their religion, their race is the best one. I get all that. I'm probably the same way about certain things.

"But it's really hard for me to accept it when dealing with the Japanese because it translates into they are right and you are wrong in any business dealing. And Toshi wants us to start a Homestay program in Los Angeles and so I went down there and checked it out and decided it was not a good place to do that. Well, they say, he says, we have to do it anyway. And I hate having my perspective neglected. I hate being bossed around. And moreover, I really hate the arrogant way that Japanese businessmen treat women as lesser beings, especially if it is my wife. To me he is always being arrogantly demanding with her. So, to make a long story short, he called on the home phone the other night, which he has not done before, to essentially demand we do this program and I happened to take the call, and had had a little wine, and gave him holy hell about it, which Bea did not appreciate. And, as I reflect on it later, I wish I had handled it differently. So I don't know if that's a question or if you can help me with it but its bothering me that I didn't handle it better."

"Well, yeah, there's a sense of self-importance there that is hard to take. And indeed what you are going to come to is learning how to not take shit without feeling any conflict about it."

"Oh, that's good."

"And to be able to express yourself freely and spontaneously, without it coming from prejudice or having an opinion. You just say, 'This has got to stop, right now', because it is inappropriate. In other words, you can learn to express intolerance without conflict. Jesus, for example, was intolerant of the moneychangers in the temple without being angry with them. He felt the power of rejection, of pushing away. They simply had to leave. And you can yield to this experience of negative energy without conflict. It is part of the energy of change. You look at everything that you do not like, everything that is not appropriate, and say it has to go. It is a way of facilitating what God will have be there. People often do not get this because they personalize everything. They take personally what is happening that they do not like. They fear it as a problem and so they get angry. You see, it could be that the energy of rejection, or saying no to something that is not appropriate in your life, is coming through you unconflicted but you are taking it personally. It would be good for you to spend time in a peaceful state rejecting that which you want to go out of your life. It is then a prayer, and that is a very powerful moment. You can say no in communion as well as yes. It simply means that you desire things to be better or different. You are setting in motion then the clear intent for there to be transformation."

"Hm."

"So do that with anything in your life that you don't like; debt, arrogant people, whatever problematic circumstances that arise. Simply sit down, get into your peace and then say to God 'I don't like this any of this stuff. I don't want to have to cope with it anymore. I want it to be different. I want it to change. So I am going to give it my whole-hearted rejection to this'. That's all you do."

"Rather than trying to change things on your own?"

"Yes. You see, there is a subtle belief here, operating in the ego, that you have to deal or cope with adverse circumstances. You want to change them and are searching for a means to change them. But understand that only in the third dimensional perception is there the experience of you as a separate body being in circumstances; an ego. But in the fourth dimensional perspective, there is the experience of you as part of and connected to the universe. Now, as I have said before, the nature of the universe or creation is constant regeneration or movement. So if you will seek to align your self with the movement of creation by choosing to be at peace, with the realization that you are then aligned with the movement of God, and in that peace have the desire and intent for change, things will change."

"Are you saying that when we choose peace we align with the will of God and thus can say 'I want this because it sustains peace and I don't want that because it doesn't' and the peaceful thing will happen?"

"Yes, because God's will is for you to be at peace."

"Or I might come to a different way of looking at a circumstance if I get into a peaceful place, a spiritual place, with it and it may not have to change."

"That's true too. But the experience that I want you to understand at the moment is that you can say no to something without hate, without conflict, without taking offense, by entering a fourth-dimensional perspective on it and it will change. You can do it as easily as pushing away junk mail. It just does not interest you and you will not have it. And your experience will be different or better, as you have desired."

"Hm. Well, that's interesting. I guess I will have to try it."

"Right. And with the Japanese, for example, if you were to do this, you might find that the arrogant attitude of someone did not bother you as you were to assert what you would or would not do."

"But the fear would be that we would lose their business."

"Yes, but if you are feeling your peace as well as your support, you know your needs will continue to be met in a fulfilling manner. You do not know exactly what form the transformation may take. You may find that if you were not taking offence, were not in conflict, that the peace you were experiencing may have a transformational effect on the other person. Or that other business came into play. So you do this with trust. And that can be hard. But you have already trusted your support to some extent when it was extremely hard for you to do so and have experienced transformation of your desires into manifestation."

"That's true. Hm. Well, I guess practice makes perfect, and I'm not there yet, but along those lines, I was thinking last night, as I wondered what to ask you about, that the only thing I really need to do to make my life any different is to meditate. Period. And by that I mean slow down, feel connected to God. But then it all goes on in the mind after that, right?"

"Right. And you need to be willing to do things, like I suggested here – just rejecting something outright – that may seem not spiritually correct. There are often a lot of rules that you don't realize that you are following that you will want to break. You may find at times that you are tired of waiting. You are tired of the silliness of the world and the apparent inertia of spiritual growth. You want to see a miracle, you want it to be relevant and you want it now. Sometimes it comes to that point."

"Hm. I had two things occur very recently that seem to be driving home that point in a way. One is I wanted to buy something and I needed cash and it was going to be one hundred and sixty-five dollars exactly and I needed cash and I didn't know if I had enough money so I called my bank account and I had one hundred and sixty-five dollars and one cent."

"Hah."

"That just seemed so …"

"Relevant."

"Right."

"And then the other day, I was going to the Mariner baseball game with my youngest son and a friend of his and his dad, and his dad had set up a deal with one of the cashiers he was friends with at the stadium who was going to hold onto some tickets for us that were especially good seats but she could only hold them for so long for some reason and we hit a big crowd of traffic outside the stadium and the guy was getting uptight and worried that we'd miss these tickets and have to settle for some poorer seats and so, just because I've been thinking this way more lately, without telling anyone in the car or letting on what I was doing, I meditated or communicated with God. And in the old days when I was trying to be more spiritually correct I would have said well just give me any old crummy seats God and I'll feel grateful for them, blah, blah, blah but this time, for some reason, I just said I really want some good seats.

"The excitement for this game was really high because they had just set a club record of twenty hits the night before and that was done on the night after voters had passed the bill to fund the stadium so the team wouldn't go to another city and the team was doing really well and so all this fanfare was even higher than usual and so I really did want some good seats. So I said to God basically this is what I want and I don't know what's going to happen but I feel very clear in this desire and so I'm giving it over to you and if we don't get these good seats, well whatever, I want good seats, so see you at the ball game God, thanks a lot. So I jumped out of the car, which was going to take awhile to park and time was running out on these tickets, and I sprinted through a bunch of cars over to the line at the specific ticket booth we were supposed to meet the dad's friend and the line was very long and so I was concerned but had to wait and I finally got there and I addressed the woman as the one we were supposed to meet but it was the wrong lady because she'd been transferred to another booth unexpectedly and then it all seemed totally insane and I thought we were sunk and would have to buy some crummy seats and then within a few seconds she looked up at her information sheet and exclaimed 'but these four tickets just opened up!'."

"Ha, ha, ha, hah."

"And they were really great seats. And somehow I had this feeling the whole time that this was going to work. I guess that's trust. So this seems to speak to what you are talking about."

"Right. That was relevant. There is a question here about getting to flex your muscles a little bit."

"Seeing that they work?"

"Right, and to ask for things, to extend yourself. You see, you have yielded here a great deal. You have given up a lot of personal preferences. And now you get to ask for what you want because you are doing it without attachment or an agenda or the insistence that it be done according to the dictates of your ego. I mean, you can always have a beautiful home or a luxury car by desiring it from the right state of mind but you have always had other issues that got in the way."

"Like what?"

"Your relationship to the world, status, responsibility, the insistence on things having to come according to understandable means. It is all of this other stuff that has to go away and basically what waking up involves on one level is to be free of the dependency upon anything other than consciousness; consciousness of God as a resource. And then you are stripped of all other intermediary resources. So you've come this far and you say 'Well, I still want to have these things' and God says 'Fine'."

"So, as always, 'Seek ye the kingdom first and all things shall be added unto you'."

"Exactly."

On that note Jay popped out the tape as he pulled into the parking lot of the music store...*and now Father, if it's all the same to you, i'd really like to have my flute added unto me...*

Chapter 82

"When his Aunt Louisa asked him in his last weeks if he had made his peace with God, Thoreau replied quite simply: "I did not know we had ever quarreled."
(Wikipedia)

THE RAYS OF THE afternoon sun through the open sunroof filled the luxury car with a light and warmth that gave scant comfort to its cheerless occupants as they soared down the freeway hospital bound. Their hearts were held in precarious balance between hopes for the best and fears for the worst. A call to the nursing staff earlier in the day had revealed that Faye had indeed an infection, a highly resistant form of staphylococcus. The appropriate antibiotics were duly administered and now it was simply a matter of time to see if the medicine would meet the task. The nurse had advised Bea to come after lunch and forewarned her that visits to the ICU were generally shorter than those on other wards. She mentioned as well that Faye still might be drowsy so no one was clear on how long or meaningful a visit it would be. Jess had agreed to stay home with his brother in case the visitation became a long vigil.

As they reached the last hilltop before the descent onto the Evergreen Point Bridge leading into Seattle, the pensive trio took in the broad vista of the immense waterfront that stretched before them to the west. The sweeping hillsides from the north and the south tapered down to the point where the bridge ran through. Just off to the right the cantilevered metal roofs of the university's football stadium jutted out sharply. On the immediate left of the bridge was a cluster of high-rise condominiums overlooking the water. Behind and around the stadium and condos were big city structures sculpted and cobbled into a motley menagerie of manicured parks and old neighborhoods amidst tall trees. It was nearly breath-taking on a good summer day, when drenched in bright sunlight the city was profiled against the vast backdrop of the Olympic Mountains, jagged and snow-tiered, with the width of Lake Washington flooding the foreground and flanking the floating gray bridge on both sides. Blue sky above and blue waters below served to stagger the senses as they sandwiched the glorious mix of natural evergreen beauty and man-made formations in a striking first glimpse from the concrete crest on the knoll of the freeway. Though Bea had always regarded the view as the best cityscape to behold in the area, its magnificent splendor was all but lost on her now.

Deep in contemplative concern for her sister she pondered what else she might do besides pray. As a recently designated angel of light, a sister of mercy, she hoped that her presence would be a powerful healing one. She hadn't the chance to help her late sister, the younger one, foil the clutches of death but here was an opportune time, however slender, to now make a difference between life and loss. Since according to the nurse Faye still could be sleeping, her influence might be confined to sitting at bedside and holding her hand. Bea was prepared to do that if needed for as long as the medical staff would allow her to be there. She had even decided to stay the night at the hospital if the situation was serious enough. At the moment it seemed that it might be indeed.

As they traversed the long narrow bridge in the fast lane the rollicking waves on her right went unnoticed. Rapt in reflection she was also oblivious to the cornucopia of sailboats and other crafts crowding the lake. A beautiful day, with the rarefied spectacle of sun in Seattle, went completely unheeded while they sped on their way. Passing all cars in his haste to the medical center her husband was making good time. For once in her life she stifled the impulse to make the suggestion he ought to slow down. In mere minutes from exiting the bridge they had deftly maneuvered through the turmoil of city sprawl traffic and wound their way into a parking lot space safely sequestered for ICU visitors. Climbing out of the car Bea sighed with relief for having survived the fast trek to the unit along with a heaviness that hung on her heart like a weight; a leaden-chained locket, a lodestone of love. She eyed the double doors with a profound sense of purpose and strode with the men toward their mission of light.

On reaching the unit they were met by a locked door with a sign on it saying to buzz the intercom for permission to enter. When they identified themselves to the staff through the intercom they were informed that Faye was still sleeping and instructed to come back in an hour. Bea pressed for an update on her condition and the attendant nurse came out to speak with them. With a serious tone and look on her face she stated that Faye's condition was critical, emphasizing rest was vital to her health. Later in the day or possibly next morning they would have their first indication if the medicines were significantly arresting the course of the infection. Until then there was nothing to do but wait and another hour's slumber at this juncture was better than whatever benefits a visit might bring. Disappointed but begrudgingly accepting the verdict they retired to the hospital cafeteria to regroup. Over glasses of lemonade they discussed their predicament.

"That nurse didn't seem overly optimistic," said Bea, absently stirring the ice in her drink with a straw. "I'm not sure what to make of that."

"I know," agreed David, looking worried and wearied as he hunched over the table, staring at his glass.

"Oh, I wouldn't read too much into it," Jay cautioned. "She's probably just trying to keep expectations low."

"Well," Bea countered, "maybe that's a good thing, but it doesn't feel too good at the moment."

"If she gave us false cheer we'd only be all the more crushed if…if…" Jay stammered for the right words, "thing didn't work out as well as we'd like." He took a long sip through his straw in the silence that followed his comment, inwardly reproaching himself for his words.

"You mean if she dies?" David finally said.

"Don't say that!" Bea snapped, without actually raising her voice.

"Sorry," he uttered. "I just meant…"and trailed off looking vacantly out the cafeteria windows at the smokers hovering nervously in the little cement square of an outdoor patio.

"I know," she acknowledged apologetically. "I'm sorry. I know you're feeling the same way as me."

"You know," he responded, his eyes moistening, "I'm sorry that I've never asked her to marry me." Bea's eyes widened slightly with surprise at this remark.

"Do you mean you feel guilty?" asked Jay. David paused as he sipped, considering his answer.

"Actually, no," he said with conviction. "It's more like remorse."

"Just a feeling of regret?" asked Jay, feeling as though he were being a therapist.

"Yeah," answered David. "I just wished now that I'd asked her."

"You think that she would?" queried Jay intensely. "I mean, don't get me wrong, you're a wonderful guy and you seem to love each other, but I don't know that she really wants to be married."

David clasped his hands over his drink and leaned forward slightly on his elbows toward his companions. "Maybe you're right," he said earnestly, and then wistfully added, "I'd just like her to know that we could if she wanted to. I want her to know that I love her that much." He took a long swallow of lemonade and set it down. "And if I get the chance to see her today, I'm going to tell her."

"You mean you're going to ask her," Jay clarified slowly, "to marry you today?"

"Yep," David said.

"Do you really want to propose to a woman under these circumstances?" Jay eyed him intently.

"I think it's a wonderful idea," interjected Bea, with a reassuring smile back at David. "It's very touching and romantic too," she noted tenderly. Her eyes seem to sparkle with an unspoken afterthought as she gazed at him pensively.

"What?" said David, sensing there was more.

"As long as you mean it," she posited gently with a decisive nod, as her smile slowly widened, " because she just might say yes."

Everyone laughed, feeling short-lived but welcome relief from the tension that hovered threateningly about. They finished their drinks then went for a walk outside in the sun around the perimeter of the hospital to whittle away the remaining minutes until they would be permitted to visit.

Upon their return to the ICU unit they learned that she was finally awake but were cautioned that due to medical considerations only one person could be in her room at a time. Furthermore each visit would be restricted to no longer than ten minutes per person. They were lastly also informed that visitation privileges were exclusively extended to family members only, with no exceptions. To circumvent the emergence of this unexpected challenge they confidently affirmed to the dutiful staff their respect and appreciation for all regulations, guaranteeing to honor them, while adding that David of course was her husband. The nurse accepted their words without question and suggested in turn, ironically to Bea, that he be the first one admitted to the patient's room. She had mixed emotions over having to wait longer as she watched his backside disappear beyond the carefully secured door.

When he returned within the mandated timeline she searchingly scanned his countenance for a sign or a clue. He shrugged with a sad smile as they passed through the doorway, exiting as she entered, giving her no hint. Not knowing what to make of his impassive visage she entered Faye's room with guarded hopes and apprehension. She was taken aback at first sight of her sister's frail features in the bed, which was inclined slightly. Her face, with eyes closed, was much paler than it had been at their most recent visit a day earlier and she appeared overall in a more weakened condition. Bea felt herself blanch inwardly as she struggled to appear less concerned than she actually felt. Affecting an expression of happiness to cover the fear she felt creeping into her chest, she moved to Faye's bedside and gently took her hand. She was hesitant to speak, not wanting to wake her, if she had drifted back into the safe harbor of sleep. Faye blinked as though startled at the touch of her fingers and gave a wan smile with a feeble squeeze of her hand.

"Hello, my angel," she murmured to Bea drowsily.

"Hello," she replied as cheerily as she could. They held hands in silence to the efficient sounds of the apparatus near her bed that monitored her vital signs. "Thank you for the pillow."

"Oh, you're welcome," she said, looking up at Bea before her eyelids fluttered closed once again.

"Would you rather sleep than talk with me now?"

"Oh no, I'm glad you're here. I'm just feeling so sleepy. Forgive me."

"Oh I do. We already had that conversation. Remember?" Faye gave a slight smile at the attempt of humor.

"Oh yeah," she said.

"So how are you feeling?"

"Well, better than last night. Boy, that was a bad night. Couldn't sleep, felt feverish, weak."

"I guess you have an infection," Bea offered tentatively.

"I have," said Faye in authoritative tone, "staph, the demon that haunts all hospitals." Bea wasn't sure what to say to that declaration and instead just squeezed her hand. "That silly boy," Faye continued, "wants to marry me."

"I know," admitted Bea. "He just told us too."

"I don't want someone to marry me because I'm sick."

"I don't think that's it. I don't think that's it at all. I think it's cause he loves you."

"Well he sure picked a funny time to pop the question." She looked over to her side at the table next to her. "Would you give me a little water please?"

"Sure." Bea poured a stream of ice water into a plastic cup and handed it to her. Faye tried to take it but was too weak to grip it tightly.

"Just hold it to my mouth," she said, and took a series of small sips. "That's good." She tried to clear her throat, seeming hard-pressed to find the strength.

"So what did you tell him?" Bea tingled with curiosity.

"I told him," Faye answered hoarsely, "that I would tell him when I got out of here. I don't want to say yes or no in this circumstance. It's not fair to him."

"And what did he say to that?"

"Well, he said he understood. But he didn't look too happy about it. That made me think he's afraid I won't get out of here."

"Oh no, no. Don't say that. I doubt he thinks that." She was trying to sound as reassuring as she could. "He's probably just disappointed that you didn't say yes."

"Maybe so," demurred Faye. She paused and then softly said, "By the way, my angel, did you like your present?"

"Oh my, yes. It was touching. Thank you so much. David gave it to me bright and early in the morning, as you apparently instructed him."

"Yes, at least someone does what I tell them." She forced a weak smile. Bea merely smiled back as Faye continued with a sigh. "He's such a darling really."

Bea stood silently by her bedside for a moment as Faye stared at the ceiling. "Listen, angel," she finally uttered softly, " I really appreciate your being here, but I think I could sleep a bit for a while. Do you mind?"

"Oh no, absolutely not. Sleep is probably the best thing for you. I'll stay here at the hospital. I'll see you later when you feel more rested."

"Oh, don't do that," Faye protested weakly. "You go home now and be with your family. You don't have to stay here all the time."

"But I want to. Are you crazy? I want to stay near you." Faye smiled again wanly.

"I may be sick, but I ain't crazy," she teased. "I'll feel better if you do. I don't want to cause you more stress than I already have. And I know you'll be a lot more comfortable at your home."

"If it would really make you feel better," said Bea, placating her sibling. "Then I will, though I'll be checking on you constantly."

"It really would make me rest easier, knowing I wasn't inconveniencing everyone."

"Okay," Bea affirmed. "Consider it done. Now you get some sleep. I'll see you later." She patted her arm.

"Thank you, dear. Yes, I'll see you later." Bea bent over and kissed her on the cheek, feeling the slackness of her skin. Tears came to her eyes as she straightened up beside her and felt the lifelessness flowing from her hand's grip.

"Good night," she whispered, letting go completely. But Faye was already peacefully sleeping. On leaving the room she approached the nurses station and spoke to the head nurse. "I'm spending the night here," she said decisively. "Have you a cot or do I sleep on the couch in the waiting room?"

She departed the unit and rejoined the men whom she strongly encouraged to return home. There was nothing any of them could do besides wait and it was, after all, her sister. There was no way that she would be leaving the hospital until things took a definitive turn. They both were willing to accede to her wishes, sensing that she really preferred that they do so. David was willing to abide with her desire on the stipulation that he could take everyone out for dinner. They went to a popular Italian eatery nearby and feasted in relative silence. Although their spirits were somewhat restrained, held in the tentative grasp of uncertainty, the meal was a refreshing break for them all and a time to rekindle their spirits in the glow of the growing camaraderie they felt in their cause. When later in the evening they revisited the hospital only to find that Faye still was asleep, the men bade their farewells to Bea and left her there, promising to stay in touch by phone and willing to return by early morning or even sooner at her slightest beckoning.

Bea gratefully accepted some pillows and a blanket to stake out her temporary sleeping quarters in the lobby. She had the room to herself, as no one else was waiting, and after reading several magazines cover to cover she fell asleep to the banal broadcast of late night television. Shortly after the shadowy light of a faint pre-dawn radiance began to materialize she was awakened from a stiff and groggy snooze by a plaintive familiar voice at her side.

"Darlin', wake up." She blinked several times, brushed the hair from her face and arched up from the couch that had served as her bed. "Yes?" she said, holding her breath. "Delilah! It's you."

"I'm so sorry, darlin'," she said in a tone clearly meant to be comforting.....*oh no...no...no...no...no...no...no...* "to be the one always waking you up."

"It's okay. Just tell me. How's my sister?"

"It looks like she's going to make it alright."

Chapter 83

"So we saunter toward the Holy Land, till one day the sun shall shine more brightly than he has ever done, shall perchance shine into our whole lives with a great awakening light, as warm and as serene and as golden as on a bankside in autumn."
(Walking, *Henry David Thoreau*)

As Jay opened his eyes from a morning meditation on the back deck outdoors his gaze was drawn, as it so frequently was, to the splendor of the lake and surrounding scenery. It was nearing nine o'clock and the sun was promising another hot one as the last few days of August dwindled down. With cooler September strolling in shortly he knew the green tree leaves would be soon turning yellow. He wondered if they'd have another Indian summer. Two in a row seemed an unlikely occurrence. He glanced at his watch and saw he must leave for the office in a few minutes. Saturday was a day in which he normally did not counsel but last evening a young man had called, sounding weary with despair and wondering if Jay did weekend appointments. After a few minutes of conversation, Jay had agreed to see him today. With nearly a half hour of sitting in silence, he was feeling as relaxed as the lone white seagull soaring over the lake, gliding blissfully against the thick backdrop of evergreen pinnacles on the far shore.

He felt a calmness that was becoming more customary ever since he had exchanged his prior means of relaxation for simple meditation twice a day, morning and evening. Taking in the wide array of colors clustered in his backyard, vivid chrysanthemums, purple, pink and yellow, alongside bright red and orange dahlias, he scanned the lake from side to side looking over the twin willow trees bent down to the water's edge. Their dangling branches twisted gently like knotted lengths of leafy twine in the same breeze that blew through the tingling wind chimes behind him. Both ducks and geese floated about under the watchful eye of the eagle he could barely see perched in its favorite tree high above the coastline on the left by the park. Beyond that lay the highway in the distance where occasionally the rumbling of large trucks could be heard above the hum of the caravan of cars streaming to and fro. It was his vista and it was good.

In the back bedroom swathed in sleep was Phil who typically slept till almost noon. Jay had left him a note on the refrigerator in case the boy awoke before his dad returned from the appointment, although that was not likely to happen. The lad stayed up late now practicing in the garage with his band almost every night and letting him sleep in late was a small price his parents were happy to pay. A commercial aircraft emerged in the blue expanse to the right, heading for the airport miles south of Seattle. It was hardly audible but reminded Jay of Bea's recent flight to Russia just over a week ago. She was due back in two days and the reports she had given him by telephone indicated that things were going very well for her.

It appeared she would no longer be exclusively dependent upon business from Japan. Moreover she had succeeded in landing a lucrative contract with Spain for next summer just before her departure. As this year's activity had wound down in late August new business was taking shape for the future. The crowning glory of the Spanish Homestay program was that Jess, their oldest son, had agreed to supervise it. Since he spoke fluent Spanish, learned in high school and in college, his willingness to run it was a boon for all concerned. He had also indicated an interest in shouldering more of the work left in the wake of Jay's exodus from Bea's company. With Annie soon leaving for school out of state he would have both the need and plenty of free time to work a second job. He and Bea would work together on the Christmas programs for Toshi and the colleges. Then Jess would run the Spring Break program and the summer ones. It appeared to be a perfect solution for them all. What would come of his marriage remained to be seen, but Jess had decided to let it ride for awhile. He was content to embark on the venture with Spain, with an eye on the broadening of his career, while his wife was doing the same with hers.

Thinking of Bea's work reminded him of how this summer had eventually gone well for her. Tomoko had unexpectedly referred a Japanese man, a recently retired teacher, to serve as Bea's representative in Japan. While providing a stronger local presence for her company, work could be delegated, expanded and generally handled more smoothly. Bea had been ecstatic. Not only had her world of work taken a huge turn for the better but also her sister had sufficiently recovered to be discharged from the hospital by the end of June. The cancer was still present in her body but she was cooperating with the doctors in Pittsburgh and was showing marked improvement through chemotherapy treatments there. Bea had accompanied her on the flight back east where in turn they had attended the funeral service for their father. In July Faye and David had announced a wedding date for late September and both Bea and Jay were intending to be there for the occasion.

The only other significant change that summer that Bea had to make was getting used to drinking wine without Jay. She had pointedly made it clear to him that she had always consumed her wine in moderation and preferred continuing to do so at dinnertime. Jay paved the way for that small adjustment by buying a case of her favorite wines to replace those which had been given away and the situation had proceeded smoothly after that. It was amazing to Jay how easy it was to live without his customary forms of relaxants after so many years of relying upon them. Without meditation it would have been more difficult but the fortunate fact was that he was not without it. In actuality, he enjoyed it immensely, and had also incorporated into his practice, offering it to anyone who wanted peace of mind, which one way or another was what everyone wanted. He glanced again at his watch, rose from his chair, walked out to his car and drove off to the office. On route he plugged in a tape from Leroy. It had become his habitual practice now when driving alone to listen to a tape irrespective of its date. This particular one was just over a week old.

"Okay. We're going now. The tape is on. Bea get off to Russia all right?"

"Yeah, she got off just fine."

"Is she there yet?"

"Yeah, I figure she arrived around midnight there last night."

"Good. So how are you feeling?"

"Well, I'm doing okay. I lately seem to get a big juicy volt of independent energy whenever she leaves, which I'm feeling right now."

"Well, it's good to be apart. It really is. Sometimes if you are defined as being a part of a couple you have to have a bottom line experience of yourself as an individual without any attachment to anyone. I mean it is just very important."

"That's right. That's what it is. Because the way I tend to operate in my mind is to be somewhat adaptive, like a chameleon, to being part of a couple and it does seem like losing some individuality. It's not anyone's fault but my own. She's not domineering. But I notice that I feel more free, kind of like I'm just bursting out, when she's gone. I mean, I miss her, and I'll be glad when she comes back, but still…something about being alone for awhile is good."

"Well, that's great. That's delightful."

"Yeah, good."

"So what's on your mind?"

"Well, a couple of things. First I want you to know that I've been meditating a lot; daily in the morning, and also at night, sometimes for an hour."

"Good."

"And some interesting things have happened."

"Go ahead."

"Well, for one thing, the method I'm using is one of going through different feeling states. First, I get grounded in peace, and that may take a little time – usually at least five or ten minutes. I just hone in on feeling peaceful to the exclusion of everything else, which means primarily thinking, by just gently pulling myself back to the sensation of peacefulness whenever I realize I've started thinking about something and eventually that works, and I get deeper and deeper into the feeling."

"Good."

"Then next, I focus on feeling supported using some concrete imagery; actually realizing that life is beating my heart and giving me infinite oxygen, for example. And I stay with that for a few minutes or more until I have a real sense of it; essentially that I'm being continuously given to by God or the Source of life."

"Yes."

"And then I move into the feeling of gratitude for the support, for my life, for everything just as it is."

"Right. Great."

"And then eventually I move into feeling my desire, whatever it may be, if I have any at that time. And I do just exactly as you taught me. I stay grounded in peace while simultaneously feeling the burning intensity of whatever my desire may be, whether it is for something mundane, like a new dishwasher, or something grander or more abstract, like more clients in my practice. Mainly I've just been focusing on that."

"Sure."

"So I sit there and I reflect, after having gone through the feeling states sincerely and thoroughly, 'Well, do I want more clients or not?'. And I realize that I do. And so I essentially agree with that desire, as you said. I agree with or allow for or simply feel the burning intensity of that desire while remaining at peace at the same time. And eventually – and it may take awhile – I reach a point where I simply feel I've sufficiently expressed and felt or agreed with that desire and I let it go, as though giving it up to God and say 'Thy will be done', and I'm done. Then I just feel curious and receptive as to when and how the desire will manifest."

"Perfect."

"And I've been getting quite a resurgence of phone calls from new clients."

"Of course.'

"And the funny thing is, I don't feel that I'm doing anything to make that happen at all."

"Right, and that's the beauty of it. And it will continue to happen that way if you stay with this."

"Great. And another thing."

"Yes?"

"Two other things actually, two incidents."

"Go ahead."

"When I was younger, as a child, my nickname was Sparky. I don't know why. I guess because I had a lot of energy. But anyway, it was a name I went by all the way up to the point where I got married. And then, when I did that, I felt like I had donned a real heavy cloak of responsibility like I had to be a man, whatever that means. I had to get tougher and be stronger to deal with the world and earn a living. And I remember the very day I decided to no longer be Sparky and just go by Jay. It was like I reached up to an imaginary cap on my head and pulled it down tightly, as though I were going outside on a cold windy day and had to brace myself for it."

"I see."

"And you know we've talked about Spirit Guides before."

"Yes."

"And I don't know what exactly to make of this, but the other night I woke up about three in the morning, to go pee I guess. Anyway that's what I did. And I was walking back to the bed and all of a sudden, quite out of the blue, the darkness actually, a voice spoke in my head, and it was really rather loud in a way. It was quite clear and strong though gentle at the same time, forceful in a kind way, and it just said 'Sparky!'. And that's all it said and the rest was silence. And I must have the strongest ego or the thickest conditioning in the world, I don't know, but I just kept walking back to bed and went back to sleep without really pausing or doing anything. In a way it was that natural too. I don't know how else to account for my reaction or nonreaction really. I've since decided the best description of the nature of that tone would be 'soft lightening'."

"I understand."

"It was like how I was when the entity once said 'Yeshua' to me when I said 'What's your name?' that time, where I then seemed to have quickly tuned out or turned off the interaction without even realizing it. I guess they just seem too otherworldly to comprehend or sustain – just too incredible, meaning almost unbelievable."

"Right."

"But the thing is, the felt meaning that was clear to me upon waking that morning and reflecting on the experience, is that when I was Sparky, I was like a boy, an innocent child. Sparky was a nice guy, basically kind and friendly and good. But when I became Jay, and felt saddled with new adult responsibilities, I felt like he wasn't such a nice guy; kind of a tougher guy. And it reminded me of Jesus saying 'You must be like little children to enter the kingdom of heaven', which now I know is just a state of mind."

"Right."

"And so it felt like I was very clearly being told, being reminded, that I needed to identify with that good person I used to feel like when I was young. And being told it in a way that was very personal, very meaningful and very instructive to me – like something being communicated with extraordinary effectiveness in just one word instead of volumes of explanation.”

“Right.”

“So anyway, that’s that. It feels both wonderful and full of wonder too.”

“Yes, exactly. And what was the other incident?”

“Oh, it was something. Again, I don’t really know what to make of this, or if I imagined it, though it doesn’t seem so, but I can’t seem to sustain these moments of connection.”

“What actually happened?”

“Well, I was meditating at night. Everyone had gone to bed and I wasn’t tired yet. I’ve so much more energy now that I’m not drinking and stuff.”

“Right. Sure.”

“So anyway, I decided to meditate, just felt drawn to it, and got into a really deep sort of blissful sweet feeling, and said rather spontaneously, to whom exactly I don’t even know, it just sort of happened, but I said ‘I feel so good I don’t know what to do’, as though I were supposed to do something with feeling so great I guess – just habit I suppose – and anyway this voice or it seemed like a voice – it was more distant or faint than the Sparky episode – just said right back to me ‘So you see, there is nothing to do but handle every task at hand lovingly’.”

“Ah-hah.”

“And again, I don’t know why or how, but I just sort of took it in stride like it was the most natural thing in the world and yet somehow I also lost the connection. I mean it seemed to fade and I can’t get it back on command so to speak, but yet it feels good. It seems real. I don’t know. It’s encouraging to get it and a little discouraging to lose it without exactly realizing how I’m getting it in the first place.”

“I understand.”

“So I wondered if you have anything to say about either of those incidents.”

“I think for now the best thing is for you to keep doing what you are doing and simply see what happens. Continuing the process of curiosity or wonder and discovery or revelation will simply allow you to get further grounded in it. And that will prove more valuable than anything I have to say about it at the moment.”

“Okay. I though you might say something like that.”

“Yes. You’re doing fine. Keep meditating. Now do you have any questions?”

“Yeah, I do. I have several questions, and the first one was something along the lines of how does it feel to be awake all of the time?”

“Oh, good. It feels as though there is always room. You feel as though you are never on the margin. You’re never in a corner. You always feel like life can move in any direction to be whatever it has to be. The thought of impossibility never crosses your mind.”

“Total freedom?”

"Yes, and freedom from fear. And as a result you don't have any need to defend yourself. What you experience is that there is a thing called relevance and all creation will strike you as being completely relevant.

"Now, I want to speak to the word relevance. I have used it before without elaborating on it. When a ballet dancer goes up on her toes, that's called relevate. It means to rise up. It is a word rarely used anymore but is a real term. Now, if the movement of life is an on-going forward flow of current, it also has other movements that happen on that forward movement; little movements that raise up. Those movements are relevancies. They rise up as responses to curiosity, questions, and needs; essentially experiences of desire. The movement of life becomes relevant. It uplifts at those points. So life continues to have this flow of forward movement with the experience of relevance here and there as creation occurs and as desires are expressed.

"So what you have to do when wanting to be awake is to want relevance. You have to first want your peace and to be still and to feel the basic current of life. And then, you'll find that your essential Being also desires this other experience of relevance. You will have desires and if they are from your Being rather than your ego you will find life rising up to meet them. And you will feel the integrity of life, the perfection of life, as it moves forward while rising up at points to fulfill your desires or answer your questions. You are always eternally experiencing new aspects of the perfection of creation being revealed to you as a response to your desires or curiosity about it. So relevance is a good word. It means more than just pertain to. It is a movement, not an understanding."

"If it's relevant it's related."

"It's more than related though. It means raised up. To relevate is an uplifting movement. It's the forward movement of life having the capacity to move up and down. It raises something up to show you something, as a response to your interest. And there's a feeling of being uplifted in that movement. And so when you are awake you have the experience of relevance in your day, in your life. It will feel as though God is there. It will feel as though your inner life has connection to the world. And how you identify that is through the natural movement of creation called relevate; to raise up. Okay. So stay with that and make relevance more important than any of your particular concepts of fulfillment that you might hold. It is okay to have a concept of fulfillment around your desires, but it is more important to experience relevance, because that's the movement that will bring you your good."

"I'm not sure I get this. Being raised up?"

"It's as though you were riding in a train, enjoying the scenery, desiring to see it, and as you pass by the landscape a mechanical tree just pops up. As you are being conveyed on the movement of life you want fulfillment to pop up out of the flow of movement. If you understand that relevance is a movement before it is a concept or an idea that you have about your fulfillment, then you simply desire to experience relevance. You desire to be uplifted. And that is what a miracle is; an experience of relevance, as a derivation of the word relevate."

"That reminds me that one of the stated principles in *A Course in Miracles* – I think its the first one of fifty or so that start out the book – Jesus says something like 'Miracles are happening all of time and if they are not, something is wrong'."

"That's right. Perfect. So my advice to you is to ask to experience this moment by moment, because then your life will be easy.

"Now, in the process of doing this, you're going to have to understand that there is a lot of crap in the world that claims to be relevant and isn't. All the creations of the ego have not come about through upliftment. They have been fabricated, manipulated, manufactured, engineered, in other words falsely created; man's creations from the viewpoint of the ego. And how you know they are not relevant is that they demand responsibility from you and you feel the pressure from that. Real relevance never feels like pressure. It feels like 'Aha', the solution. It never feels like responsibility. It never feels like you have to make it or force it to happen. So you are going to have to pay attention to the fact that the ego's world has usurped this idea of relevance and has applied it to its own creations. And so you are going to have to say 'Wait a minute – this is irrelevant – I don't want to get anywhere near it'. And you can always tell because it will be something that feels like pressure, tension, obligation or responsibility. That feeling means it is not a relevant experience and God does not intend for you to have that experience.

"So if you find yourself in that kind of a situation, feeling tense, feeling afraid, pressured or responsible for making something happen, then you have to stop and allow yourself to be centered again in the feeling of peace. Be still. And in the stillness you allow yourself to feel the movement of life moving through you and then you ask for relevance. You desire to feel connected and the movement of life will carry you forward as you realign with it, with relevant moments of being uplifted as the need arises.

"So that's what it feels like to be awake all the time, to answer your question. There is nothing irrelevant going on. You don't know irrelevancy anymore. There is only what God is creating through the means of relevance. Your good is going to come to you through upliftment or relevance and that is all you need to know."

"So it's like if I suddenly realize I'm hungry some means to satisfy the hunger will appear without a lot of contrivance on my part."

"Yes, if you understand that's what creation is all about. If you ask for relevance that which is relevant will occur. You can't have the experience of relevance with something if it doesn't truly apply to your interest, if it doesn't truly reflect the will of God for you. It would be irrelevant, you see? Relevance is a divine movement that is specific to your interests as defined by God."

"So this is like when you spoke once about desiring your general good, desiring the essence of what you want without insisting on the form that you think is should take."

"Yes, but it is a different take on it. This is more about actually connecting with the feeling of the movement and desiring to feel the movement rather than focusing on the desire. You have your desires or questions about something but you trust that by feeling connected to the movement of life and asking only for relevance that the desire will be met or the question will be answered, and in a way that is totally specific to your interest."

"Could it be like…ahhh…let's say what I really need is transportation somewhere. And my car is not working. I may think I need a new car. I may desire a new car, but I instead focus on asking for relevance and discover that the bus runs right by my house and near the destination I wanted to go to and at a convenient time. Would that be a good example of what you are talking about?"

"Exactly. And you might well discover that the means to get a new car is also readily apparent or rises up. Or that the means to repair your car becomes easily accessible as well. However the need for transportation plays out, it simply appears or rises up and you feel it as an uplifting experience with no irrelevancies involved. As you ask for relevance, life simply responds naturally to the relevant need or desire at hand. It is another way of saying, as we've done so often, seek the kingdom of God first and all things shall be added unto you. And so, again, that's what it feels like to be awake all the time. Now what are your other questions?"

"Actually that gives me enough to chew on for awhile. I'd just as soon stop for now, if you don't mind."

"Not at all. It'll be good for you to spend some time with that."

"So upward and onward is actually a perfect metaphor for the movement of life."

"Absolutely."

"Well, thank you very much. Thanks for everything."

"You're welcome."

On that note he punched out the tape as he finished the short ride from home to office and turned into a marked space in the asphalt parking lot. He noticed a young man, maybe in his early twenties, peering at him from a small sports car parked two spaces away… *that's probably him*…Darkened circles under the eyes of his observer fueled his intuitive speculation and a quick exchange of names as they got out of their cars served to confirm it. Jay led him into his office and they sat in chairs across from one another. He was tall, of medium build, and handsome with dark curly hair, well trimmed, that splayed over his forehead. His eyes, aside from the dark lines, gave an appearance of sensitivity and he spoke in a soft voice that underscored that impression. He said his name was Paul and he slumped into the cushioned chair with an air of depression.

"Well, Paul," said Jay casually, trying to put his guest at ease, "what seems to be the problem?"

"Well," he replied hesitantly, "I'm not sure where to start."

"Well, then, when people say that to me I often ask them what hurts the most."

"Mm. I guess that would be my girl friend."

"Your relationship with her?"

"Right."

"What's the trouble with it?"

"We fight a lot."

"I see. About what?"

"Everything. She has a temper."

"I see. And you don't?"

"Not really. But I get mad too, sooner or later."

"What sorts of things cause the arguments?"

"Well, she's got two younger kids from a previous marriage and she's going to school to finish her degree, and she doesn't have a lot of time for me and I end up loaning her money or paying for stuff and, I don't know…she just gets uptight easy."

"Sounds a bit complicated."

"Feels like it," Paul agreed with a shy grin.

"Un-huh. So on the phone you said you called because of a recent fight with her."

"Yeah, that's right, partly." Paul twisted a little in his seat, unwinding to sit taller. "But I've been feeling a little down about everything lately; my work, my relationships." He laughed derisively. "About my life in general I guess." He glanced at Jay's guitar in the corner. "You play guitar?"

"Yeah, do you?"

"Yeah, well, I used to. I haven't played in a while lately."

"Hm. Well, perhaps this is a good time to take a look at your life in general."

"Yeah, I think I'd like that."

"What do you do for a living?"

"I work for a telemarketing company."

"Do you like it?"

"Not really. It's okay. It pays the bills."

"How'd you get into that?"

"Oh, a friend of mine worked there and got me in."

"I see. Well, is there anything else you'd rather be doing?"

"Probably, but I don't know what."

"Did you go to college?"

"Yeah."

"You graduate?"

"Yeah."

"What was your major?"

"Communications."

"Hm. I see. Well, I guess you could get into a lot of things with that."

"Maybe." Paul cleared his throat and spoke with greater confidence. "Actually I'd like to be a writer."

"An author?"

"Maybe. Maybe a journalist."

"I see. Well, would you have to go back to school for that?"

"I'm not sure."

"I see." Jay paused, sizing up his new client. He decided it felt like a good time to give him the spiel that he'd been giving everyone since moving to his new office and changing his ways. It always came on the heels of the next question.

"Do you have any kind of spiritual beliefs?"

"Yeah, well sort of. I don't go to church or anything but I do believe in God."

"Good. I'm not into church. I'm not talking about religion. I don't care if people are. I'm not against it. I'm just not into it. I'm just talking about God, or a belief in a spiritual power."

"I understand."

"I've found, as I've gotten older, that I've come to see life more as a spiritual experience. So it's affected how I live, and think, and moreover, as far as you're concerned, it affects what I do in counseling with people." Paul nodded and observed him noncommittally, awaiting more.

"So," continued Jay, "what I'd like to do is give you an understanding of what I think is true, with respect to psychology, and thus what I have to offer you as a psychotherapist. And if you're comfortable with it, if how I see life makes sense to you, then we're off to a good start and you will probably find our time together helpful." He looked at Paul intently, to let the point sink in, and then smiled. "If not, you're probably better off with another therapist."

"Okay," said Paul tentatively. "Sounds good so far. Go ahead."

"Alright," responded Jay. He sighed gently and began. "Basically people have two states of mind. One is who we really are and the other is who we think we are. Most of us are caught up most of the time in who we think we are, our self-concept, or as they say in psychology, our ego. It is essentially born of our conditioning, that is, information that was given us about ourselves, primarily by our significant others, virtually from the moment we emerged from the womb. How our parents saw us, how they treated us, and the expectations they gave us about who we were and how we were to be, constitutes what is known as our conditioning. The ways they identified us through their words and actions created the sense of identity, or self-image, with which we grew up. Through our early childhood and adolescent conditioning we formed beliefs about ourselves, other people, good and bad behavior and in general what life was all about. You understand?" Paul nodded.

"So we take that sense of self, that cluster of ideas about who we are and how we're supposed to be, into adulthood and we usually don't question it until we reach a time when we are not happy. People don't come here when they're feeling good. They don't do preventative maintenance. They come in when the shit hits the fan. You understand?" Paul nodded again, seemingly interested. "And at that point people are willing to take a look at themselves. They are usually moved by the suffering in their lives to be introspective. They desire to know themselves better and make changes in their lives.

"So, the fundamental process of therapy, in a sense, is to help people be aware of their conditioning. To help people transcend or rise above their conditioned ways of thinking and being, so that they may make new and enlightened choices about who they are and how they want to be, in order to be happier or in some way more fulfilled. And I do that by trying to help them get in touch with who they really are, which is a unique spiritual being, or the self that God created, as opposed to who they think they are. So there is the true self, a creation of God, a child of God, or who you really are, and there is the ego, or who you think you are, a product of the God-given ability to think and the conditioning that has shaped or influenced it. Okay? Are you with me?"

"Yeah, you're making sense. Go ahead."

"Okay. So my job is to help people be their true self. Now, because God is the creator of all life, being at one with our true selves also means to be at one with the nature of life. Life is a movement. It is the unceasing movement of creation and it is a felt movement. You feel alive. You may feel bad or good but you feel alive. The energy of life emanates from the source of life, God, and moves through us. Life is moving through everything and everyone simultaneously all the time. If you took a little piece of the wood of this chair and put it under an electron microscope you would see life moving on a molecular or atomic level just like it is on the level of the planets and the seasons. Life is a movement or flow of constant change or transformation emanating from God. Life is on a roll. Life is a gift from God that keeps on giving. And, life is also a creative movement that is meant to be experienced as supporting our fulfillment. If we are in tune with ourselves, being true to ourselves, at peace with ourselves, not our ego, our life unfolds in a manner that is fulfilling which includes sufficiently meeting our needs. The problem for most of us is that since we are not in tune with our true selves, but are instead operating from our ego, we are not in tune with that flow; the movement of life.

"Because people do not feel connected with and given to by the source of life they feel alone and fear they must fend for themselves. They don't feel supported. So they are out looking for resources all the time. Instead of feeling that we are being given to, we think we have to go out and get it. And there is never enough. Because we think or imagine that the infinite and unlimited source of life, God, is not giving us what we need, we assume we must get it from a state of limited or finite resources through rational means. God is infinite or beyond rational; irrational. He doesn't have to ration out resources. And just as the true self operates on the principle of abundance, or actually infinite resources from the source, the ego operates on the principle of scarcity. There's not enough money, there's not enough love, there's not enough food, etc. It's all part of being or actually of thinking we are apart from God or that there is no God. So we feel scared about the scarcity and responsible for meeting our needs. Do you understand?"

"Yeah, I get what you are saying."

"Good. Okay, then. So being at one with your true self also means being in alignment with the unceasing movement of creation or life or God's will. They are all the same thing. And the way to get aligned with the movement of life is to be at peace. If you are into your ego you are not at peace by definition. You are in a state of mind that thinks itself apart from God. This is called the separation in theology. It is called existential anxiety in philosophy. I'm alive and I'm alone and I'm afraid. It is not true because you can never be separate from God except in your imagination but most of us are in that state of mind most of the time. It is called normal. It is not natural but it is very normal, which is why the world is in such a mess all the time. Just flipping on the news shows you the constant array of conflict, or fearful behavior, that is going on everywhere. So being at peace, actually choosing to be in a peaceful state of mind irrespective of how your circumstances are or appear, is the way to align yourself with the movement of God called life. It is the way to align your self with God's will. And specifically it is the way to align yourself with God's will for you.

"Each of us is unique, like a snowflake or a fingerprint. No two are alike. Everyone has some unique God-given talents or attributes that distinguishes us from others. And everyone has some unique God-given purpose or function in their lifetime. And being in tune with that function constitutes fulfillment. If you are being true to yourself, you are at peace with yourself. And if you are at peace, then you can feel in alignment with the movement of creation. And if you are in alignment with the movement of creation, or God's will, then you do that which you feel moved to do. And as you feel moved to do it, you are moving with the movement of creation known as you. And it will be fulfilling, both physically and psychologically. Your needs will be met and you will feel fulfilled. Am I making sense to you?"

"I think so."

"Well, stop me anytime if you have questions."

"I will."

"So, to continue, being moved to do something does not originate in thought. It is a felt experience. It is felt in a way we often refer to as our intuition, or our conscience, or our heart. So, for example, I learned to play the guitar because I felt moved to do so. That probably applies to you as well. I have a certain God-given gift for music and I experience that gift as a desire, or feeling moved, to make music. I also have a certain knack, for example, for understanding the thoughts and feelings of others. I always did, even as a child, and would often intercede in arguments or misunderstandings between friends or other people in such a way as to help them understand what the other person was saying. It's just something I have talent or gift for and feel moved to use. I am not much good at mechanical things or computers. But lots of other people have those gifts. In an ideal world, which is what we are desirous of, everyone is moved to utilize their talents in such a way as to form a mutual support system. I can help the person who fixes my car or computer with his marriage and vice versa. Some people are good at business, some at sports, some at managing others. It's endless. There are as many gifts as there are people. You with me so far?"

"Yes, I think so."

"Okay then. So life is meant to be experienced as fulfilling in the two main areas; self and other. Or, your individuality, self-expression, which is work, hobbies, interests, whatever activities are found to be fulfilling, and relationships. God intends for us to experience fulfillment in our selves and in our relationships with others. Now how you feel about yourself is what you have to offer others so the two are inextricably linked. Or as Jesus said, love your neighbor as thyself, which means you've got to love yourself one hundred percent in order to love your neighbor fully. Okay?"

"I understand what you're saying."

"Okay. So we need to know what is appropriate or fulfilling for you as an individual before we can sort out your relationships. Do you see that?"

"Of course."

"Okay, good. So this brings us back to the point of being at peace. Everyone who comes to see me is seeking peace of mind. They may not present it that way. They may not realize it. They may think they simply want their circumstances changed, but whether they do or not, they want to feel at peace and they do not. One way or another they are in conflict, whether sad, depressed, anxious, angry or whatever. They are experiencing negative emotions and they want to have positive ones instead. They want to feel happy. As I said earlier, the basic state of mind known as the ego is a fearful state of mind. I exist and am required to meet my needs in a hostile or impersonal world and I'm afraid. There appears to be no God. Or if there is, I do not feel a loving connection with one. I may worship him on Sunday, pray to him nightly, give money to institutions founded in his name, but I do not feel in constant communion with him. Whether he's uncaring or indifferent or angry or nonexistent or whatever, I don't feel the connection and so I do not feel supported. I do not feel divine support in my life.

"Now, the way out of this apparent problem is to simply choose to be at peace so you can feel the support. Again, life by nature is supportive and fulfilling. You want to be aligned with the movement of life moving through you, moving you to experience what is appropriate or relevant for you, whatever that may be. So whatever problem someone brings me, I try to teach them that a solution is available through aligning themselves with the movement of life or the will of God, which really means being true to themselves. And so I try to help people learn how to do that, initially by learning how to choose to feel at peace.

"But first, as we're doing now, I try to help them understand why that is the intelligent thing to be doing. And then, aside from educating people that peace of mind is actually a choice, and the best one they have, I also teach them how to cultivate it. That is, I help people practice choosing peace and staying in that state, primarily by teaching them how to meditate. You can simply choose to be at peace if you desire without meditation, but it is often difficult, especially at first, for people to do. They are so used to running around in fear all the time feeling pressure and deadlines and obligations as their normal way of being."

"Boy, that's the truth."

"Right. Now you can find activities that bring you peace, such as exercising or going for a walk, or going fishing, or listening to music, or some form of art or gardening or whatever. The options are unlimited, but it usually takes a concentrated effort of practicing being at peace to sustain that state until it starts to become a new way of being, a new reference point of existence. And I find meditation the best way to do that. So I teach it to people. And the more you become accustomed to operating from a peaceful place in consciousness the more you find that you know what to say or do in any given situation. The more you realize you can choose peace in any given situation, no matter how problematic it looks, in order to know the appropriate response or solution, the more you find you want to do it. It feels good and it works. It's self-reinforcing. And that becomes how you operate in life. Feeling at peace, which allows you to do what you feel moved to do when you feel moved to do it, becomes a preferable way to live. If you have a problem you pick the solution that brings you peace. If you have choices, not even problems, you make the choice that brings you the most peace. And you are operating then in congruence with God's will. So there you are. Does all that make sense?"

"Well, yeah, I understand what you are saying. But it seems at lot easier said than done."

"You are so right. But, on the other hand, nobody comes here unless they are ready for a change. They already have conflict of some sort or they wouldn't be here and I offer them a new way of being. It is not only to resolve their current conflict, but a profoundly comprehensive way of living as well and thus dealing with all issues as they arise in the course of their lives."

"Well, that sounds good. How do we start?"

"Well, the first thing is to get you squared away with yourself. That is, to help you get used to feeling at peace, simply by making the choice to be at peace, starting today. I have a meditative exercise we can go through right now, to help you with that task. And also, when you leave, I'll give you a fifteen minute meditation tape I've recently made for my clients, using music and nature sounds from my keyboard synthesizer. I used a four track recorder. I basically take people through a guided imagery tour, using my hypnosis training, to relate spiritual concepts and hopefully create a feeling of deep peace, relaxation, and overall a heightened sense of general well-being."

"Alright, thanks."

"Sure. And the second thing is, let's look at whatever issues are of greatest concern to you at the present. If your relationship is the most problematic matter on your mind at the moment, we'll move into that next. Sound good?"

"Yeah, I think so. What exactly do I need to do?"

"Well, if you're ready, let's see if we can help you simply feel at peace right now."

"Okay, let's do it."

"Good. So actually what I am going to do is to lead you through a series of feelings. Just allow yourself to feel them as best you can. These are not emotions, which are more often than not just a product of the ego. These will be simply feelings, or felt states of mind, that are a part of being alive, part of feeling the connection to or communion with God, with life, with the movement of creation that we want. You understand?"

"I think so."

"Okay, good enough. So the first thing is to sit up straight, uncross your legs and plant your feet firmly on the ground. Good. I usually place my hands on my thighs, near my knees, and touch my forefinger to my thumb in a circle in each hand, reminding myself of the wholeness of life. That's it, good. Now close your eyes…and take several deep breaths… and just let yourself relax. Good. Feel yourself letting go of any tensions you are aware of, and just focus on your breathing for a minute. Inhaling deeply, exhaling fully. That's it. Just relax. A peaceful mind and a relaxed body. Simply allow yourself to feel peaceful. Sink into the cushions. Give over to gravity. And if it seems like feeling peaceful is too hard, as though you were unable to do it, then simply imagine what it would feel like to be at peace, and slip in through that door. Are you feeling more peaceful?"

"Yes. Somewhat. It's funny just to try to be at peace. I mean, it's different. I'm not used to it."

"Right. Like most of us, you're used to thinking all the time instead. So that's okay. We want different. Now, along with feeling at peace, as much as you can, as much as you will, a little more with each and every breath you take, add unto it a feeling of being at one with God. At one with your creator, however you envision that, however it feels. And it feels like a sense of being connected…which of course you can never not be…though you can be unaware of it. And that is what we are correcting. That's right. Just let it sink in…a feeling of being at peace and a feeling of being at one with God. In religion this is called atonement and usually implies atoning for some sin, some transgression. What we are doing is understood as the at-one-ment; a feeling of being at one with God, which is actually your natural and fundamental state. Just steep yourself in those feelings for a minute and continue to relax. Your heart is breathing effortlessly. You're not doing it. You need do nothing but be.

"Okay, now…along with those feelings, try your best to allow yourself a feeling of being supported…as though you were floating on a cloud…or resting gently in the arms of God… whatever image helps you to feel that feeling. Like a blade of grass, which is supported by the earth, the sun, the rain. It does nothing but be, and receives what is given, in being supported by whatever is needed. So…feeling peaceful… feeling connected…feeling support.

"Now, along with those feelings, as much as you can, as much as you will, allow yourself to feel the feeling of love that you truly are, in the depth of your heart. Love emanating from God unto you, through you, and radiating out into the world in all directions at once as though from the spokes of the hub of a wheel. Love in, love out. Feeling loved, feeling loving…transmissions streaming from God to and through you.

"Now, along with feeling at peace, at one, supported, loved and loving, allow yourself to feel grateful for it all…just grateful for your life, for your consciousness itself. It feels good to be alive. Life is a gift and you feel grateful for it. Grateful for all you are, all you have, all you love, simply grateful for the beautiful mystery of life itself. Life is a gift that keeps on giving. Just breathe it in…and let it out…effortlessly, endlessly.

"And now lastly, along with all of these other states of experience, feeling at peace… communion…support…love…and gratitude…let yourself feel trusting. Imagine how you would feel if you knew that by simply being yourself, being true to yourself, somehow life would work…somehow you could trust life to continuously unfold in a fulfilling manner. And you do that, you reach that feeling of trust, by choosing to be at peace. So we go full circle. Feeling peaceful, feeling at one, feeling supported, feeling love, feeling grateful and feeling trusting. So your task is always, first and foremost, to be simply at peace, balanced, centered, riding tall in the saddle of fate, enjoying the journey. Trusting the horse knows the way. Just allow yourself to be steeped in feeling all of those feeling for a few moments."

Jay paused for half a minute while watching his client be seemingly absorbed in the cumulative state of the exercise. There were no sounds in the room above the soothing trickle of the fountain in the background.

"Now, I'm going to assist you in coming back from this state, back into the state of visual awareness, by counting to three. But I want you to be aware that you have experienced these felt states of mind simply because you chose to do so. And you can choose them anytime, any place, simply by closing your eyes, touching your thumbs and forefingers in a circle, taking a deep breath or two, and feeling at peace, and then moving through the other feelings if you wish. Sometimes just choosing peace is a sufficient prerequisite for knowing what, if anything, to do in whatever situation arises. And the more you practice feeling this way, the more easily it becomes your normal, which is actually your natural, state of being. And as much as you can, as much as you will, I encourage you to leave here today with these feelings and with the awareness they are always available, because they reside within you. They are your feelings.

"So, one…feeling good….which means 'of God'…two…glad to be you…feeling peaceful, at one, support, love, grateful, and trusting…three…back to the world of you and me." It was silent for several seconds as Jay observed Paul shifting back into a more normal state of being. Paul opened his eyes slowly and blinked a few times before looking at Jay. "Well," said Jay, "how do you feel?"

"Peaceful…good. I'm just not used to feeling this relaxed."

"Well, yeah, that's the point. Most of us aren't. But it can be your new way of being in the world if you want."

"I think I do."

"Good. Now let's see if we can relate it to your most pressing problem; your girl friend."

"Okay. How do we do that?"

"Well, what's going on currently between you? You just had an argument, right?"

"Yeah, that was yesterday."

"And you argue a lot, more than you would like."

"Yeah. She says I'm too demanding of her time. I wanted to get together last night and she had to study."

"And that's a typical hot button, right?"

"Yeah, she's always so busy."

"Well, she probably is pressed for time with school and two kids."

"Yeah, that's true, and it seems like if I want to see her at all I need to do it when she wants to. Period. And when she wants to, then she's pretty insistent about it. I mean, when she has time for me, she expects me to be there. But sometimes I've got other things to do and she seems to think I should schedule my time around her."

"Well, it's an option. Do you want to do that?"

"Not really. It seems too one-sided."

"I guess it comes down to how badly you want a relationship with her."

"I guess you're right."

"When are you supposed to see her again?"

"She wants me to come over there tonight."

"Do you want to do that?"

"Not really. It's a long drive. That's another thing. If I want to see her I have to go over there, Seattle, which sometimes feels like too much after a hard day's work, especially with all the traffic."

"I see. She won't come to your place?"

"Never."

"Well, it's probably harder with two kids."

"Right. That's what she says. But still…"

"Have you thought about living together?"

"Yeah, she's mentioned it but then I'd have a horrendous commute, which I don't want. I don't even think I want to live with her and her kids, with everything so uptight all the time."

"Okay. Look, let's try this here. Do you want to go over there tonight?"

"Not really."

"Why not? The drive, the tension, what?"

"All those things, I guess. Actually it's also because we fought yesterday. She tends to stay angry for awhile after we fight."

"What would you rather do? Stay at home?"

"Yeah, I think so."

"Have you told her that yet?"

"No, she'll just get mad and start yelling at me."

"Okay. Look, let's do this, just for practice. Take moment and close your eyes. That's good. Now, try this on. First consider going to see her tonight. See how that feels." Jay let a few moments pass before continuing. "Alright, now consider staying home." He waited another half minute in silence. "Now, which decision brings you the most peace?"

"Mmmm, staying at home, definitely." Paul opened his eyes and blinked.

"Good, what's the downside? She'll be angry, right?"

"Exactly."

"Well, feel that through. Close your eyes again. What brings you the most peace? Going over there thinking she'll be angry from yesterday or staying at home and having her be angry with you for that?"

"Mmmm, it feels slightly better still to stay at home."

"Okay, good. You're getting this, I think. Now, which bothers you more: that she will feel angry or that you will have to endure it? There's a difference."

"I see what you mean. Actually, I've gotten used to thinking that if she was angry I was just going to have to put up with it. Or have a fight."

"Right. I understand. But our work here is predicated on the idea that everyone is responsible for their own consciousness, their own state of mind, and not anyone else's. It's not your fault if she decides to get angry. That's her choice. You are just desiring to do that which brings you peace, that which is fulfilling to you. You are intending no harm to her at all. Correct?"

"Right. I see what you mean."

"So let's say you decide not to go there this evening and she starts to give you hell about it. What do you do?"

"Well, not fight back I guess if I want to keep the peace."

"Well, I agree. But you're not responsible for keeping the peace. You're just responsible for keeping your peace."

"So I just listen to her without arguing?"

"No, not necessarily. You can listen to her if you want to, if you can stay at peace with it."

"I don't know that I can. She's pretty intense."

"So don't listen to her."

"Just hang up?"

"Well, yes, in effect. But you can say before doing so, if that's what you decide to do, that you do not want to fight about it, and that you do not want to listen to her yell at you. Tell her, while staying at peace yourself, that you would like to talk to her about it without fighting and if that is not possible then you want to discuss it when she feels she can do so without fighting."

"That could be forever."

"Well, then the questions arises, do you want to spend the rest of your life with someone who will treat you in that manner?"

"Hm. I never really thought of it in that way."

"Well, think about it now. Do you really want to be with someone who is willing to constantly jeopardize your peace of mind by being antagonistic with you?"

"No. Not really."

"Okay. And it's good to realize that it doesn't have to be that way. It doesn't have to be that way for her either. But that's up to her. You are just serving notice that it is unacceptable to you. It may come down to would you rather be in a relationship where you felt tense and harried a lot or would you rather be alone and at peace?"

"Well, I'd prefer to be at peace and be with her, I think."

"Yes, I understand. But that may not be an option if she prefers to be angry. Have you ever entertained the notion of life without her?"

"Not really. At least not until now. I mean, I think I do love her. And I know I want to have a loving relationship with someone."

"I understand. But you may need to be willing to be alone, rather than settle for a unhappy relationship, in order to ensure that you can have a happy one, with someone, at this point preferably her. You see, what you are feeling too often now is not love. It's fear. It's stressful. It's a more negative experience than you want to tolerate. That's why you're here."

"You're right."

"I'm not saying you have to be alone or that you will be. I'm just saying it's essential to realize, if you want to feel good, that you would rather have peace of mind and be alone than have a relationship without peace of mind. That decision may even influence her to consider being more peaceful herself, which is really what she wants."

"I see." Paul paused and looked away reflectively.

"It's not really fun for her to be upset."

"True. It sure would feel funny to stand up to her like that though."

"Well, I know, but you don't have to think of it as standing up to her. You are simply standing up for yourself, gently insisting on your peace of mind, and are unwilling to be bullied out of it. And it might feel good. Any relationship that you must sacrifice your peace of mind to maintain is not worth having, because, as I said before, how you feel about yourself is what you have to offer others, and if you don't feel that your peace of mind is more important than her demands, then your self-esteem or self love isn't very high. So you don't really have a very loving self to offer her. Do you understand what I am saying?"

"Yeah, I do. I just hadn't thought of it in these terms before. Thanks."

"Well, you're welcome. But that's my job." Paul chuckled, stroked his chin thoughtfully and then mused aloud.

"But I don't know how I'd feel telling her that I'm not coming over and that I don't want to fight about it."

"Well, you'd feel at peace, I imagine, as that is the point of it. Unless her approval means more to you than your own. You'll find out. Secondly, you might find you feel moved to do something else, like play the guitar." Paul smiled at that remark and nodded.

"Could be," he said wistfully.

"Look, let's see how it goes. You deal with this situation tonight as best you can. You practice being at peace more often, as much as you can, between now and our next session. And we'll see where you are next week. Possibly we'll deal with other aspects of your life, perhaps your career if you wish. We can decide that then."

"Okay. Sounds good. Thanks again." They set an appointment for the following week and Paul departed, feeling better than when he'd arrived and carrying the meditation tape given him. As Jay left his office and got into his car he started to reach, almost reflexively, for a cassette from Leroy, then decided instead to ride home in silence, musing contentedly. He felt infused with gratitude for what he'd learned from his mentor, his patient persistent teacher on tape, and for how he could further strengthen and deepen that learning by sharing those teachings with others. So much from their talks was now woven into his work. Immersed in a light-hearted reverie he flew past the green trees and fields in the sunlight like a white bird in flight over the highway and onto his street.

The gravel crackled crisply as he rolled down the length of the driveway to his home. He could hear the shrill shrieks of the ever-alert cockatiel sounding its alarm as he walked up the curved brick pathway to the house. A shaft of bright sunlight piercing a gap in the pine trees momentarily blinded him as he crossed the cement patio to the front door...*mmmmm sun*...The house was quiet as he entered which probably meant that Phil was still sleeping. Otherwise the likelihood was that loud music would be heard pulsating from his bedroom door. He stared at the lake in its mid-day stillness, scanning for signs of aquatic or avian life, especially an eagle; the most inspiring and dramatic one to observe. It was nowhere to be seen in the tranquil moment, as scattered groups of ducks and geese floated gently by on the glistening water.

He slipped off his shoes and strode into the sunroom for a closer view of the scene. As always when he took the time to really look at it, the floor to ceiling splendor of the panoramic view filled him with a deep sense of serenity and pleasure. Feeling no compunction to do anything in particular he sat down on the thick cushion of the rattan chair and looked about the landscape for greater detail. To his right in the corner of the room near the lake, a few short yards outside the wall of glass, a squirrel scrambled part way down the gnarled trunk of the great cedar tree, stopping to survey the site. He gave the bare bird feeder next to him a quick searching look, then glancing briskly side-to-side, darted down to the ground and off into the shrubbery lining the southern hillside...*need to put some bird seed in that*...

As he turned his gaze east again to the fullness of the lake a red-winged blackbird flew in from his right and lit on a long branch of the leafy willow tree. It bobbed gently up and down under the weight of its feathered occupant. The bird's bright orange shoulders beamed like fluorescent patches in brilliant contrast to the subdued field of green. It was a common sight throughout the spring and summer months...*wonder if it's always the same bird*...A subtle breeze rippled through the willow leaves and set the wind chimes tingling in motion on the deck to his left...*sounds like music*...In the distant sky a huge balloon carrying a cargo of sight-seers drifted by overhead on higher gusts. Its red and yellow colors brightly sailing through the blue lent an air of pageantry in celebration of the day. He considered getting his guitar and then wondered if he'd rather meditate. Suddenly he felt moved to make an entry in his journal while being in a reflective mood.

He walked into the bedroom, sat down at his roll-top oaken desk in the corner and pulled out his leather-covered notebook from the middle panel. Thumbing through the pages he came to rest at his latest entry, made nearly half a year ago. Unsheathing the black pen attached to the book, he contemplated exactly what it was he wanted to write. As he gazed absentmindedly out the window towards the lake he felt a movement of expression welling up inside him like a sudden flow of water spilling onto the page.

8/30 In the last six months there has been consolidation of the work I've been doing on myself this past year. The fruit of my labors has finally shown forth in my personal and professional lives in a manner exceeding my fondest aspirations. More than anything I have learned that nothing is more important than having the peace of God, and that once having that I can truly have any thing else worth having. I know not where this will lead but trust it will lead there peacefully, which in turn will engender happiness along the way. I know I will lose my peace on occasion but I've learned that I can always find it again and that in fact there is nothing else better or necessary for me to do when those occasions arise. I feel so grateful to be so fortunate as to have had such a wonderful teacher as Leroy and also for the continuous opportunity as well to be a teacher for others, while continuing to learn, through my counseling practice and personal relationships. I have found, as I was told, that fulfillment is indeed God's will for us all and available for the asking as long as we ask from the inner stillness of our being; the level of the heart. Great changes have been wrought in this last year for not only myself but for all members of my family and I believe we are all emerging the better for it. My next entry in this book will most likely serve to chronicle that course. Until then I hope to be doing my best at learning to live in the present moment, moving with the momentum of the eternal movement of life, at one with the flow of God's creation.

He paused and let the feel of what he'd written sink in…*lofty thoughts…hope i can live up to them*…There was so much more that could be said and yet somehow this seemed to say it all well enough. As he had noted in the next to last sentence, his subsequent entry, from somewhere down the road, would tell the tale from here. With a sense of satisfaction he sheathed the pen, closed the notebook, snapped its strap and placed it back into the slot on the desk. He turned his focus to the lake again as though, which he had often felt, his attention was being pulled by a powerful magnet; the captivating allure of water in the woods under sun in the sky – heaven on earth.…*be nice to see the eagle*…The wavering willow trees in the soft wind suggested the possibility of sailing, perhaps with the boys, when the telephone rang. He picked it up after the first ring.

"Hello, this is Jay."

"Jay, this is Barry." His mind reeled back to a voice from the past and he wondered if it would bring him pleasure or pain…*whatever happened to detective clark*…

"Yes, Barry. How are you? It's been a long time."

"I'm fine. Actually, I'm great to tell you the truth. I was just sitting here finishing breakfast when suddenly I thought of you. I just got a feeling to give you a call."

"Well, it's good to hear from you, man. I've often wondered how you were doing. Whatever happened to your legal troubles? Frankly I was a little nervous to call you. That guy, the detective, was on my case for a while and I feared he might be bugging your phone."

"Detective Clark?"

"Yeah. Haven't heard from him lately."

"And I'm sure you never will ever again."

"Really? How's that?"

"Well, eventually, like your friend said, I got me a lawyer and plea bargained my way with the judge to a sentence of community service."

"Oh, well that's good. Glad you didn't have to go to jail."

"Yeah, me too, but that's not the half of it."

"What do you mean?"

"They gave me a choice of several options and one of them was to coach a basketball team of underprivileged kids though the YMCA."

"You're kidding. That sounds like fun."

"It was, but get this. This is the best part. We came in first place. I had a ball."

"Well, congratulations. That sounds great."

"It was. In fact it was so much fun that I'm doing it again this year just for fun."

"Ah, that's wonderful. Good for you."

"Yeah, thanks. So how you doing?" Jay smiled inwardly as he reflected on the question. How could he answer the question truly without spending most of the rest of the day on it?

"I'm doing good, pal. Thanks for asking."

"Still counseling?"

"Oh yeah, you bet, still the same old stuff.".…*but with a brand new twist…*

"Glad to hear it, man." Barry paused for moment and then added in slightly more serious tone: "Jay, I just want you to know that that cop kept after me over and over, 'Why's your therapist in your little black book?' They told me if I would turn you in for getting pot from me they'd be easier on me, and I never ever did. I just want you to know that."

"Well, I don't know what to say. I had no idea you were under such pressure. I'm sorry to hear it."

"Oh, that's okay. It's all cool now. And I could never have hurt the man who saved my marriage." Jay laughed heartily.

"Well, that's good to know. I'm glad you feel that way."

"I do." They savored several seconds of silence between them, feeling the mutual gratitude, before Barry spoke again.

"Well, I better get going. Got a lot of chores to do today. Just wanted to check in and say hi."

"Well, I'm glad you did. Thanks for calling."

"Sure. Well, you take care."

"You too."

"Hey, maybe you'd like to watch my team play sometime."

"Yeah, you never know. Give me a call when a game comes up."

"Okay, will do. Good-bye, Jay."

"Good-bye, Barry. Thanks for calling."

Pleased with the news he'd just received, he replaced the phone on the desk while uttering a deeply felt sigh of satisfaction. He leaned back in the chair and raised his arms high overhead in a long slow stretch of his muscles. Turning his attention once more to the sparkling surface of the undulating current that flowed downstream through the middle of the lake, he caught sight of the eagle circling towards him as it left a tall treetop wavering on the far bank. It dipped toward the middle of the lake as it crossed, then swept up again continuing towards him. Just before reaching the willow trees below, it swerved to the right, gracefully completing its arc as it turned, then flapped its wings twice and continued to climb, rising directly in front of Jay's field of vision; white head and feathered tail with contrasting black body. Feeling uplifted, he watched it ascend, angling in the distance slightly toward the sun while it elegantly streamed over the long sloping curve of fading shoreline…*upward and onward*…as though gently bearing his heart on its back.